JOURNAL FOR STAR WISDOM 2016

JOURNAL FOR STAR WISDOM

2016

EDITED BY ROBERT POWELL

EDITORIAL BOARD

Brian Gray
Claudia McLaren Lainson
Lacquanna Paul
Robert Schiappacasse

Lindisfarne Books

Lindisfarne Books

an imprint of Steinerbooks/Anthroposophic Press, Inc.

610 Main Street, Suite 1

Gr. Barrington, MA, 01230

www.steinerbooks.org

With grateful acknowledgment to Peter Treadgold (1943–2005), who wrote the Astrofire program (available from the Sophia Foundation), with which the ephemeris pages in the *Journal for Star Wisdom* are computed each year.

Disclaimer: The views expressed in the articles published in the *Journal for Star Wisdom* are the sole responsibility of the authors of these articles and do not necessarily reflect those of the editorial board of the *Journal for Star Wisdom*.

Design: William Jens Jensen

ISBN: 978-1-58420-196-0 (paperback)

ISBN: 978-1-58420-197-7 (eBook)

CONTENTS

Preface   9

The Rose of the World (*Rosa Mira*)
  by Daniel Andreev   14

Editorial Foreword
  by Robert Powell   20

Working with the *Journal for Star Wisdom*   23

The Healing of the Man-Born-Blind and the Central Sun:
  Foundations of Star Wisdom (Astrosophy)
  by Robert Powell   24

Celidonius: The Man-Born-Blind
  by Estelle Isaacson   41

The Star of Lazarus: A Reading of the Starry Script
  by Estelle Isaacson   43

The Towers We Build: The Uranian Double Bind
  by Claudia McLaren Lainson   47

In Memoriam William Bento
  by Claudia McLaren Lainson   69

The Fall of the Spirits of Darkness and the Rise of Rudolf Steiner
  David Tresemer, with Robert Schiappacasse and William Bento   72

Shepherds, Kings, and the Birth of Jesus: A Stellar Imagination
  by Brian Gray   87

Position of the Ancient Star-Zodiac
  by Nicholas Kollerstrom   110

The Fall of the Spirits of Darkness: A Spectral Reflection
  by Kevin Dann   119

How the Grail Sites Were Found: A Review
  by Robert Kelder   130

Working with the Star Calendar
  by Robert Powell   134

Symbols Used in Charts / Time   136

Commentaries and Ephemerides for 2016
  by Claudia Mclaren Lainson
  with Monthly Astronomical Sky Watch *by Sally Nurney*   140

Glossary   229

Bibliography and References   236

About the Contributors   239

Book Announcements   242

ASTROSOPHY

The Sophia Foundation was founded and exists to help usher in the new Age of Sophia and the corresponding Sophianic culture, the Rose of the World, prophesied by Daniel Andreev and other spiritual teachers. Part of the work of the Sophia Foundation is the cultivation of a new star wisdom, *Astro-Sophia* (Astrosophy), now arising in our time in response to the descent of Sophia, who is the bearer of Divine Wisdom, just as Christ (the Logos, or the Lamb) is the bearer of Divine Love. Like the star wisdom of antiquity, Astrosophy is sidereal, which means "of the stars." Astrosophy, inspired by Divine Sophia, descending from stellar heights, directs our consciousness toward the glory and majesty of the starry heavens, to encompass the entire celestial sphere of our cosmos and, beyond this, to the galactic realm—the realm that Daniel Andreev referred to as "the heights of our universe"—from which Sophia is descending on her path of approach into our cosmos. Sophia draws our attention not only to the star mysteries of the heights, but also to the cosmic mysteries connected with Christ's deeds of redemption wrought two thousand years ago. To penetrate these mysteries is the purpose of the yearly *Journal for Star Wisdom*.

For information about Astrosophy / Choreocosmos / Cosmic Dance workshops
Contact the Sophia Foundation:
4500 19th Street, #369, Boulder, CO 80304
Phone: (303) 242-5388; sophia@sophiafoundation.org;
www.sophiafoundation.org

PREFACE

Robert Powell, PhD

This is the seventh edition of the *Journal for Star Wisdom,* which is intended as a help to all people interested in the new star wisdom of astrosophy and in the cosmic dimension of Christianity, which began with the star of the magi. The calendar comprises an ephemeris page for each month of the year computed with the help of Peter Treadgold's Astrofire computer program, and a monthly commentary by Claudia McLaren Lainson (with Sally Nurney). The monthly commentary relates the geocentric and heliocentric planetary movements to events in the life of Jesus Christ.

Jesus Christ united the levels of the earthly personality (geocentric = Earth-centered) and the higher self (heliocentric = Sun-centered) in so far as he was the most highly evolved earthly personality (Jesus) embodying the Higher Self (Christ) of all existence, the Divine "I AM." To see the life of Jesus Christ in relation to the world of stars opens the door to a profound experience of the cosmos, giving rise to a new star wisdom (astrosophy) that is the Spiritual Science of Cosmic Christianity.

The *Journal for Star Wisdom* is scientific, resting upon a solid mathematical-astronomical foundation and also upon a secure chronology of the life of Jesus Christ, and at the same time it is spiritual, aspiring to the higher dimension of existence that is expressed outwardly in the world of stars. The scientific and the spiritual come together in the sidereal zodiac that originated with the Babylonians and was used by the three magi who beheld the star of Bethlehem and came to pay homage to Jesus a few months after his birth. In continuity of spirit with the origins of Cosmic Christianity with the three magi, the sidereal zodiac is the frame of reference used for the computation of the geocentric and heliocentric planetary movements that are commented upon in the light of the life of Jesus Christ in the *Journal for Star Wisdom.*

Thus, all zodiacal longitudes indicated in the text and presented in the following calendar are in terms of the sidereal zodiac, which has to be distinguished from the tropical zodiac in widespread use in contemporary astrology in the West. The tropical zodiac was introduced into astrology in the middle of the second century AD by the Greek astronomer Claudius Ptolemy. Prior to this the sidereal zodiac was in use. Such was the influence of Ptolemy upon the Western astrological tradition that the tropical zodiac became substituted for the sidereal zodiac used by the Babylonians, Egyptians, and early Greek astrologers. Yet the astrological tradition in India was not influenced by Ptolemy, and so the sidereal zodiac is still used to this day by Hindu astrologers.

The sidereal zodiac originated with the Babylonians in the sixth to fifth centuries BC and was defined by them in relation to certain bright stars. For example, Aldebaran ("the Bull's Eye") is located in the middle of the sidereal sign/constellation of the Bull at 15° Taurus, and Antares ("the Scorpion's heart") is in the middle of the sidereal sign/constellation of the Scorpion at 15° Scorpio. The sidereal signs, each 30° long, coincide closely with the twelve astronomical zodiacal constellations of the same name, whereas the signs of the tropical zodiac, since they are defined in relation to the vernal point, now have little or no relationship to the corresponding zodiacal constellations. This is because the vernal point, the zodiacal location of the sun on March 20/21, shifts slowly backward through the sidereal zodiac at a rate of 1° in seventy-two years ("the precession of the equinoxes"). When Ptolemy introduced the tropical zodiac into astrology, there was an almost exact coincidence between the tropical and the sidereal zodiac, as the vernal point, which is defined to be 0° Aries in the tropical zodiac, was at 1° Aries in the sidereal zodiac in the middle of the second century AD. Thus, there was only 1° difference between the two zodiacs. So, it made hardly any difference to Ptolemy or his contemporaries to use the tropical zodiac instead of the sidereal zodiac. But now—the vernal point, on account of precession, having shifted back from 1° Aries to 5° Pisces—there is a 25° difference and so there is virtually no correspondence between the two. Without going into further detail concerning the complex issue of the zodiac, as shown in the *Hermetic Astrology* trilogy, the sidereal zodiac is the zodiac used by the three magi, who were the last representatives of the true star wisdom of antiquity. For this reason the sidereal zodiac is used throughout the *Journal for Star Wisdom*.

Readers interested in exploring the scientific (astronomical and chronological) foundations of Cosmic Christianity are referred to the works listed below under "Literature." The *Chronicle of the Living Christ: Foundations of Cosmic Christianity,* listed on the next page, is an indispensable source of reference (abbreviated *Chron.*) for the *Journal for Star Wisdom,* as, too, are the four Gospels (Matthew = Mt.; Mark = Mk.; Luke = Lk.; John = Jn.). The chronology of the life of Jesus Christ rests upon the description of his daily life by Anne Catherine Emmerich in her four-volume work *The Life of Jesus Christ* (abbreviated *LJC*). Further details concerning the *Journal for Star Wisdom* and how to work with it on a daily basis may be found in the general introduction to the *Christian Star Calendar*. The general introduction explains all the features of the *Journal for Star Wisdom*. The new edition, published 2003, includes sections on the megastars (stars of great luminosity) and on the 36 decans (10° subdivisions of the twelve signs of the zodiac) in relation to their planetary rulers and to the extra-zodiacal constellations, those constellations above or below

the circle of the twelve constellations/signs of the zodiac. Further material on the decans, including examples of historical personalities born in the various decans, and also a wealth of other material on the signs of the sidereal zodiac, is to be found in *Cosmic Dances of the Zodiac,* listed below. Also foundational is *History of the Zodiac,* published by Sophia Academic Press, listed below under "Works by Robert Powell."

Literature

(See also "References" section)

General Introduction to the Christian Star Calendar: A Key to Understanding, 2nd ed. Palo Alto, CA: Sophia Foundation, 2003.

Bento, William, Robert Schiappacasse, and David Tresemer, *Signs in the Heavens: A Message for our Time.* Boulder: StarHouse, 2000.

Emmerich, Anne Catherine, *Visions of the Life of Jesus Christ* (new edition, with material by Robert Powell). San Rafael, CA: LogoSophia, 2014.

Paul, Lacquanna, and Robert Powell, *Cosmic Dances of the Planets.* San Rafael, CA: Sophia Foundation Press, 2007.

————, *Cosmic Dances of the Zodiac.* San Rafael, CA: Sophia Foundation Press, 2007.

Smith, Edward, *The Burning Bush: An Anthroposophical Commentary on the Bible.* Gr. Barrington, MA: SteinerBooks, 1997.

Steiner, Rudolf, *Astronomy and Astrology. Finding a Relationship to the Cosmos.* London: Rudolf Steiner Press, 2009.

Sucher, Willi, *Cosmic Christianity and the Changing Countenance of Cosmology.* Gr. Barrington, MA: SteinerBooks, 1993. *Isis Sophia* and other works by Willi Sucher are available from the Astrosophy Research Center, PO Box 13, Meadow Vista, CA 95722.

Tidball, Charles S., and Robert Powell, *Jesus, Lazarus, and the Messiah: Unveiling Three Christian Mysteries.* Gr. Barrington, MA: SteinerBooks, 2005. This book offers a penetrating study of the Christ mysteries against the background of *Chronicle of the Living Christ* and contains two chapters by Robert Powell on the Apostle John and John the Evangelist (Lazarus).

Tresemer, David (with Robert Schiappacasse), *Star Wisdom & Rudolf Steiner: A Life Seen Through the Oracle of the Solar Cross.* Gr. Barrington, MA: SteinerBooks, 2007.

ASTROSOPHICAL WORKS
BY ROBERT POWELL, PhD

Starcrafts (formerly Astro Communication Services, or ACS):
> *History of the Houses* (1997)
> *History of the Planets* (1989)
> *The Zodiac: A Historical Survey* (1984)
> www.acspublications.com
> www.astrocom.com
> Business Address:
> Starcrafts Publishing
> 334 Calef Hwy.
> Epping, NH 03042
> Phone: 603-734-4300
> Fax: 603-734-4311
> Contact maria@starcraftseast.com

SteinerBooks:

> Orders: (703) 661-1594; www.steinerbooks.org
> PO Box 960, Herndon, VA 20172

The Astrological Revolution: Unveiling the Science of the Stars as a Science of Reincarnation and Karma, coauthor Kevin Dann (Gr. Barrington, MA: SteinerBooks, 2010). After reestablishing the sidereal zodiac as a basis for astrology that penetrates the mystery of the stars' relationship to human destiny, the reader is invited to discover the astrological significance of the totality of the vast sphere of stars surrounding the Earth. This book points to the astrological significance of the entire celestial sphere, including all the stars and constellations beyond the twelve zodiacal signs. This discovery is revealed by the study of megastars, illustrating how they show up in an extraordinary way in Christ's healing miracles by aligning with the Sun at the time of those events. This book offers a spiritual, yet scientific, path toward a new relationship to the stars.

Christian Hermetic Astrology: The Star of the Magi and the Life of Christ (Gr. Barrington, MA: SteinerBooks, 1998). Twenty-five discourses set in the "Temple of the Sun," where Hermes and his pupils gather to meditate on the Birth, the Miracles, and the Passion of Jesus Christ. The discourses offer a series of meditative contemplations on the deeds of Christ in relation to the mysteries of the cosmos. They are an expression of the age-old hermetic mystery wisdom of the ancient Egyptian sage, Hermes Trismegistus. This book offers a meditative approach to the cosmic correspondences between major events in the life of Christ and the heavenly configurations at that time 2,000 years ago.

Chronicle of the Living Christ: Foundations of Cosmic Christianity (Gr. Barrington, MA: SteinerBooks, 1996). An account of the life of Christ, day by day, throughout most of the 3½ years of his ministry, including the horoscopes of conception, birth, and death of Jesus, Mary, and John the Baptist, together with a wealth of material relating to a new star wisdom focused on the life of Christ. This work provides the chronological basis for *Christian Hermetic Astrology* and the *Journal for Star Wisdom*.

Elijah Come Again: A Prophet for our Time: A Scientific Approach to Reincarnation (Gr. Barrington, MA: SteinerBooks, 2009). By way of horoscope comparisons from conception–birth–death in one incarnation to conception–birth–death in the next, this work establishes scientifically two basic astrosophical research findings. These are: the importance 1) of the sidereal zodiac and 2) of the heliocentric positions of the planets. Also, for the first time, the identity of the "saintly nun" is revealed, of whom Rudolf Steiner spoke in a conversation with Marie von Sivers about tracing Novalis's karmic background. The focus throughout the book is on the Elijah individuality in his various incarnations, and is based solidly on Rudolf Steiner's indications. It also can be read as a karmic biography by anyone who chooses to omit the astrosophical material.

Journal for Star Wisdom (Gr. Barrington, MA: SteinerBooks, annual). Edited by Robert Powell and others in the StarFire research group. A guide to the correspondences of Christ in the stellar and etheric world. Includes articles of interest, a complete sidereal ephemeris and aspectarian, geocentric and heliocentric. Published yearly in November for the coming year. According to Rudolf Steiner, every step taken by Christ during his ministry between the baptism in the Jordan and the resurrection was in harmony with, and an expression of, the cosmos. The journal is concerned with these heavenly correspondences during the life of Christ. It is intended to help provide a foundation for Cosmic Christianity, the cosmic dimension of Christianity. It is this dimension that has been missing from Christianity in its 2,000-year history. A starting point is to contemplate the movements of the Sun, Moon, and planets against the background of the zodiacal constellations (sidereal signs) today in relation to corresponding stellar events during the life of Christ. This opens the possibility of attuning to the life of Christ in the etheric cosmos in a living way.

Sophia Foundation Press and Sophia Academic Press Publications

Books available from Amazon.com

JamesWetmore@mac.com

www.logosophia.com

History of the Zodiac (San Rafael, CA: Sophia Academic Press, 2007). Book version of Robert Powell's PhD thesis on the *History of the Zodiac*. This penetrating study of the *History of the Zodiac* restores the sidereal zodiac to its rightful place as the original zodiac, tracing it back to fifth-century-BC Babylonians. Available in paperback and hard cover.

Hermetic Astrology: Volume 1, Astrology and Reincarnation (San Rafael, CA: Sophia Foundation Press, 2007). This book seeks to give the ancient science of the stars a scientific basis. This new foundation for astrology based on research into reincarnation and karma (destiny) is the primary focus. It includes numerous reincarnation examples, the study of which reveals the existence of certain astrological "laws" of reincarnation, on the basis of which it is evident that the ancient sidereal zodiac is the authentic astrological zodiac, and that the heliocentric movements of the planets are of great significance. Foundational for the new star wisdom of astrosophy.

Hermetic Astrology: Volume 2, Astrological Biography (San Rafael, CA: Sophia Foundation Press, 2007). Concerned with karmic relationships and the unfolding of destiny in seven-year periods through one's life. The seven-year rhythm underlies the human being's astrological biography, which can be studied in relation to the movements of the Sun, Moon, and planets around the sidereal zodiac between conception and birth. The "rule of Hermes" is used to determine the moment of conception.

Sign of the Son of Man in the Heavens: Sophia and the New Star Wisdom (San Rafael, CA: Sophia Foundation Press, 2008). Revised and expanded with new material, this edition deals with a new wisdom of stars in the light of Divine Sophia. It is intended as a help in our time, when we are called on to be extremely wakeful during the period leading up to the end of the Mayan calendar in 2012.

Cosmic Dances of the Zodiac (San Rafael, CA: Sophia Foundation Press, 2007), coauthor Lacquanna Paul. Study material describing the twelve signs of the zodiac and their forms and gestures in cosmic dance, with diagrams, including a wealth of information on the twelve signs and the 36 decans (the subdivision of the signs into decans, or 10° sectors, corresponding to constellations above and below the zodiac).

Cosmic Dances of the Planets (San Rafael, CA: Sophia Foundation Press, 2007), coauthor Lacquanna Paul. Study material describing the seven classical planets and their forms and gestures in cosmic dance, with diagrams, including much information on the planets.

American Federation of Astrologers (AFA) Publications (currently not in print)

www.astrologers.com

The Sidereal Zodiac, coauthor Peter Treadgold (Tempe, AZ: AFA, 1985). A *History of the Zodiac* (sidereal, tropical, Hindu, astronomical) and a formal definition of the sidereal zodiac with the star Aldebaran ("the Bull's Eye") at 15° Taurus. This is an abbreviated version of *History of the Zodiac.*

Rudolf Steiner College Press Publications

9200 Fair Oaks Blvd., Fair Oaks, CA 95628

The Christ Mystery: Reflections on the Second Coming (Fair Oaks, CA: Rudolf Steiner College Press, 1999). The fruit of many years of reflecting on the Second Coming and its cosmological aspects. Looks at the approaching trial of humanity and the challenges of living in apocalyptic times, against the background of "great signs in the heavens."

The Sophia Foundation

4500 19th Street, #369, Boulder, CO 80304; distributes many of the books listed here and other works by Robert Powell.

Tel: (303) 242-5388

sophia@sophiafoundation.org

www.sophiafoundation.org

Computer Program for Charts and Ephemerides, with grateful acknowledgment to Peter Treadgold, who wrote the computer program *Astrofire* (with research module, star catalog of over 4,000 stars, and database of birth and death charts of historical personalities), capable of printing geocentric and heliocentric/hermetic sidereal charts and ephemerides throughout history. The hermetic charts, based on the astronomical system of the Danish astronomer Tycho Brahe, are called "Tychonic" charts in the program. This program can:

- compute birth charts in a large variety of systems (tropical, sidereal, geocentric, heliocentric, hermetic);

- calculate conception charts using the hermetic rule, in turn applying it for correction of the birth time;

- produce charts for the period between conception and birth;

- print out an "astrological biography" for the whole of lifework with the geocentric, heliocentric (and even lemniscatory) planetary system;

- work with the sidereal zodiac according to the definition of your choice (Babylonian sidereal, Indian sidereal, unequal-division astronomical, etc.);

- work with planetary aspects with orbs of your choice.

The program includes eight house systems and a variety of chart formats. The program also includes an ephemeris program with a search facility. The geocentric/heliocentric sidereal ephemeris pages in the yearly *Journal for Star Wisdom* are produced by *Astrofire*. This program runs under Microsoft Windows. Those interested in *Astrofire* may contact:

The Sophia Foundation
4500 19th Street, #369, Boulder, CO 80304
Tel: (303) 242-5388
sophia@sophiafoundation.org
www.sophiafoundation.org

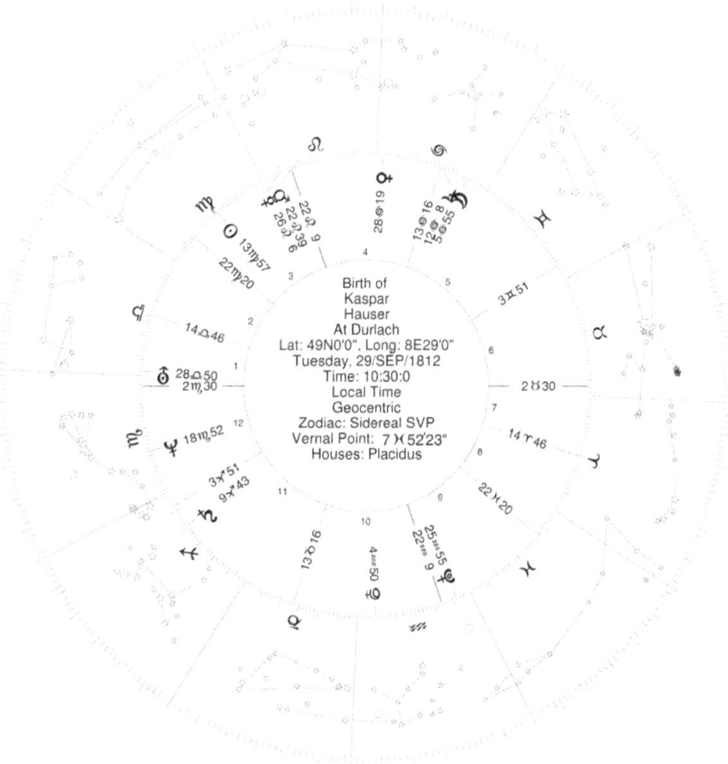

A horoscope generated by the Astrofire program

THE ROSE OF THE WORLD (*ROSA MIRA*)
Daniel Andreev

By warning about the coming Antichrist and pointing him out and unmasking him when he appears, by cultivating unshakable faith within human hearts and a grasp of the meta-historical perspectives and global spiritual prospects within human minds...[we help Sophia bring to birth the new culture of love and wisdom called by Daniel Andreev the "Rose of the World."]...[Sophia's] birth in one of the *zatomis* will be mirrored not only by the Rose of the World; feminine power and its role in contemporary life are increasing everywhere. It is that circumstance, above all, that is giving rise to worldwide peace movements, an abhorrence of bloodshed, disillusion over coercive methods of change, an increase in woman's role in society proper, an ever-growing tenderness and concern for children, and a burning hunger for beauty and love. We are entering an age when the female soul will become ever purer and broader, when an ever-greater number of women will become profound inspirers, sensitive mothers, wise counselors, and far-sighted leaders. It will be an age when the feminine in humanity will manifest with unprecedented strength, striking a perfect balance with masculine impulses. See, you who have eyes.[1]

[These words are those of Daniel Andreev (1906–1959), the great prophet of the coming Age of Sophia and the corresponding Sophianic culture he called the "Rose of the World" (*Roza Mira,* or Роза мира, in Russian). In this quote, *zatomis* refers to a heavenly realm within the Earth's etheric aura. Andreev refers to Sophia as *Zventa-Sventana,* "Holiest of the Holy."]

A mysterious event is taking place in the meta-history of contemporary times: new divine-creative energy is emanating into our cosmos. Since ancient times the loftiest hearts and most subtle minds have anticipated this event that is now taking place. The first link in the chain of events— events so important that they can be compared only to the incarnation of the Logos—occurred at the turn of the nineteenth century. This was an emanation of the energy of the Virgin Mother, an emanation that was not amorphous, as it had been before in human history [at Pentecost, when there was an emanation of Sophia into the Virgin Mary], but incomparably intensified by the personal aspect it assumed. A great God-born monad descended from the heights of the universe into our cosmos (ibid., p. 356).

[The words of the great Russian seer, Daniel Andreev, are prophetic. As indicated in *The Most Holy Trinosophia,*[2] he points to the descent of Sophia and the resulting Sophianic world culture, the Rose of the World, in a most inspiring way.]

She is to be born in a body of enlightened ether.... There She is, our hope and joy, Light and Divine Beauty! For Her birth will be mirrored in our history as something that our grandchildren and great-grandchildren will witness: the founding of the Rose of the World, its spread throughout the world, and...the assumption by the Rose of the World of supreme authority over the entire Earth (ibid., p. 357).

[The Sophia Foundation was founded and exists to help usher in the new Age of Sophia and the corresponding Sophianic culture, the Rose of the World, prophesied by Daniel Andreev and other spiritual teachers.]

---

1 Daniel Andreev, *The Rose of the World*, p. 358. Words in brackets [] here and in the following text are added by Robert Powell.

2 Robert Powell, *The Most Holy Trinosophia: The New Revelation of the Divine Feminine.*

As quoted at the beginning, "warning about the coming Antichrist and pointing him out and unmasking him when he appears" is important, as discussed in the article "In Memory of Willi Sucher" (*Journal for Star Wisdom 2010*).

Humanity's encounter with the Antichrist is part of the initiation trial of humanity as a whole crossing the threshold. The external aspect of this initiation trial is the meeting with the Antichrist as the embodiment of the sum-total of humanity's negative karma, *the double of humankind as a whole.* The inner aspect is the encounter with Christ or the Archangel Michael as the Guardian of the Threshold. The result of successfully passing through this initiation trial is the opening up of conscious awareness of the angelic realm. This is one aspect of the great event at the culmination of the process of humankind as a whole crossing the threshold. Another aspect of this culmination is depicted in the article on World Pentecost.[3]

More than anyone else, Daniel Andreev, as prophet of the coming Sophia culture, the Rose of the World, had a visionary experience of the coming of the Antichrist. His words concerning this are not in the English edition of the *Rose of the World*. Because of the importance of Daniel Andreev's vision of the coming of the Antichrist, his words about this appeared for the first time in English in this journal.

The German translation of Daniel Andreev's book *Rosa Mira: Rose of the World*, in three volumes, comprises a translation of the *whole* original Russian text, whereas the English edition corresponds to volume 1 of the three German volumes.[4]]

THE PREPARATION OF HUMAN BEINGS FOR THE COMING ANTILOGOS

Certainly, humanity has not lacked warnings. Not only the *New Testament* but also the *Qur'an* and even the *Mahabharata* have warned us in the distant past. Have spiritual seers in the East and in the West not proclaimed the Antichrist as an unavoidable evil? All leaders of the Rose of the World will concentrate their forces upon the work of warning about this monster.... This bearer of a dark mission will probably not truly grasp whom he serves and for whom he prepares the way. With all his intellectual genius, his mind will be completely closed to anything of a mystical nature.... He will be greeted enthusiastically: "There he is! The one for whom we have been waiting!" He will show his true force only much later, when the "savior" holds the entire power in his hands....

Is it a matter of a human being? Yes and no. On several occasions [in *Rosa Mira*] I have indicated that this individual was incarnated as a Roman emperor and how, over the centuries and from life to life, he became enveloped in demonic substance. Concerning this monad, whom Gagtungr [Ahriman, or Satan] himself has kidnapped...enough has been said about his previous incarnation [as Stalin] in Russia.... [In that incarnation,] the forces of providence hindered [Satan's attempt] to make of him a dark, universal genius.

[Now, in 1958, he is being prepared] for the successful fulfillment of the historic role of the Antichrist. Stalin's tyrannical genius and his ability to control hypnotically the will of others is well known.... [When he reincarnates as the Antichrist,] he will have at his disposal an enormous capacity for work and a multitude of talents.... He will be uniquely and terribly beautiful. From his facial characteristics, it will be difficult to place him in any particular race or nation. Rather, he will be seen as a representative of the collective of humanity.... [At a certain point in his life, he will undergo a transformation.] His transformation will be noticed by people immediately, yet they will be unable to recognize the meaning or the "how" [of this transformation]. The external appearance of the transformed one will remain virtually unchanged. However, a terrible and frightening energy will proceed from him.... Anyone who touches him will receive an electric shock. An invincible hypnotic force [will proceed from him].... The disturbing influence [on spiritually striving human beings] and upon the entire population set in motion by the transformation of the Antilogos will be extraordinary....

---

3   See Robert Powell, *Prophecy–Phenomena–Hope.*

4   The following translation from German into English is by RP.

After a rigged vote, he—the miracle worker—will crown himself.…Humanity will be divided [into those who accept him as world ruler] and those who refuse to acknowledge the usurper.… Of course, force will be used against anyone who refuses to follow the Antichrist. Dark miracles will increasingly occur, shattering the consciousness of people to the very roots of their being. For many, Christ's miracles will pale into insignificance. Crazy enthusiasm will roll in waves across the world.… Eventually, the Antilogos will hold the sole rulership of the planet in his hands. Yet, the true and highest leaders will not subject themselves to this usurper. This will also be the case for millions, perhaps hundreds of millions, of people in every country of the world.

The age of persecution commences. From year to year, they become increasingly extensive, methodical, [and] cruel. Here, the cunning Gagtungr [Ahriman/Satan] even makes use of the heroic protest of the masses. The candidate for the Antichrist who had failed…who had taken his life at the end of World War II,[5] advances now to become the self-appointed leader of the rebels in the struggle against the world ruler.… His thoroughly dark movement will draw the hearts of many into a spiral of raging wickedness and senseless hatred.… Christ's significance will continually be weakened. Then his name will be denied—and finally enveloped in silence.…

Shock and terror will take hold of many. Millions of those who had previously distanced themselves from religious matters, who occupied themselves primarily with concerns in their own little world or with artistic pursuits or scientific research, will sense that an irrevocable and very dangerous choice confronts them. In the face of this, even torture and execution pale.…Countless people will turn away from this offspring of hell…from the dark miracles and the charm of the superman, as well as from his immeasurable intelligence and frighteningly cynical wickedness.…The majority of people will fall away from God and allow themselves to be led astray by Gagtungr's protégée.…

Stalin wanted not only to be feared; he also wanted to be loved. The Antichrist, however, has need of only one thing: the conviction that everyone [should hold] without exception, [to] believe in his superiority and [to] subject themselves to him without hesitation.…

When [during the reign of the Antichrist] the machine civilization begins its total assault on Nature, the entire landscape of the Earth's surface will be transformed into a complete Anti-Nature.…Nature, having become inwardly empty and outwardly crippled, will no longer awaken aesthetic or pantheistic feelings.…

Certainly, too, during the complete rule of the tyrant, there will be many whose innermost life will rebel against the senseless existence under the Antichrist. However, psychic control will stifle such thoughts as they arise, and only a few will succeed in acquiring a system of psychic self-defense to protect them from being physically destroyed.…

All written or other testimonies that could be dangerous for the Antichrist will be destroyed.…

[The suffering of human beings gives nourishment (*gavvach*) to the demons.]… No world wars, revolutions, or repressions, no mass spilling of blood, could have produced *gavvach* in such amounts.…In fact, even humanity in its demonized aspect will not satisfy the Antichrist. He needs humanity as his source of *gavvach*.…[However,] even in the most sinful soul, an inextinguishable spark of conscience gleams. However, despair, increasing ignorance, and sheer boredom with life will also take hold of many people, and this will lead to their rejection by the Antichrist. Of what use to him is the intellectual paralysis that sets in after such excesses of despair? Such people are hardly suited to the further development of demonic science and technology or to the conquest of the cosmos or the satanizing of the world.…

---

5 Daniel Andreev depicts the two main candidates for the Antichrist in their twentieth-century incarnations: Adolf Hitler and Joseph Stalin. In those incarnations, they competed with each other to become the most evil. In the following incarnation, the most evil one would become the vessel for the incarnation of the Antichrist. According to Daniel Andreev, Joseph Stalin outdid Adolf Hitler to become the chosen one, the Prince of Darkness.—R. Powell

[After the Antichrist's death] the world state will rapidly collapse, and only drastic measures will hinder anarchy in various parts of the world.... "And there appears a great sign in heaven: a woman clothed with the Sun" [Revelation 12:1]. Who is the *woman clothed with the Sun?* It is *Sventa-Sventana* [Sophia], embraced by the planetary Logos and chosen to give birth to the Great Spirit of the Second Aeon. The reflection of this event in world history is the Rose of the World, whose utmost striving before, during, and after the time of the Antichrist prepares humanity to become a vessel for the Great Spirit.... An unimaginable jubilation will take hold of this and other worlds as humanity passes through a great, light-filled transformation.

The prince of darkness will terrify human beings.... Christ, however, will take on as many forms as there are conscious beings on Earth to behold him. He will adapt himself to everyone and will converse with all. His forms will simultaneously yield an image in an unimaginable way: *One who appears in heaven surrounded by unspeakable glory.* There will not be a single being on Earth who will not see the Son of God and hear his Word.[6]

✦

[In her vision of April 30, 2014, Estelle Isaacson describes the connection between Christ's Resurrection and his Second Coming. On the day of April 30, the Sun was at exactly the same location in the sidereal zodiac—$15\frac{1}{2}°$ Aries—as where it was located on Sunday, April 5 AD 33, at Christ's resurrection. That day—April 30, 2014—was the cosmic commemoration of the greatest event in the history of the Earth: the Resurrection. At the present point in time the cosmic commemoration of the Resurrection happens each year around April 30.]

As this vision began, I experienced the resurrection body streaming out through the Sun and filling my entire being. The sunlight rays bearing the resurrection body touched every cell. Every cell was awakening. By the power of the Sun, and due to its position in the cosmos (for it was positioned exactly where it was on Resurrection morning), I merged with the resurrection body. I was in awe to behold this body in its present form; I beheld how it had evolved over time to become the body of the Second Coming. All the various forms—everything that I witnessed in the resurrection body when I saw it being formed two thousand years ago[7]—have evolved in the course of time to become what they are now, at this time of the Second Coming. The mystery of his resurrection body, and how it has evolved over time to become the body of the Second Coming, is something truly vast and unfathomable. I beheld that on this very day the resurrection body was streaming from the Sun to the Earth as the body of Christ in the Second Coming. This was beautiful! Everything in his resurrection body is incomparably beautiful—so wondrous was it that my spirit soared to meet him as he was descending toward me.

This is something new, the onset of which is now, at this time of the Second Coming. For there is something very special happening with the Earth at this time. Indeed the Earth is being enveloped and embraced *in* the resurrection body.

After beholding these things, I was able to then experience many dimensions at once—past, present, and future were all before my inner gaze. In my lifted state I was able to perceive in the eternal round, and did not need to make sense of things in linear time.

I found myself in the garden of the holy sepulcher, where I saw Mary Magdalene on the morning of the Resurrection, and I witnessed the Resurrection as it happened for her. I was at the point in time when, with her whole soul, she went toward the Risen One and he said, "Touch me not, for I have not yet ascended to the Father." There is a profound mystery in these words. Within these words lies the key to the soul's journey from the point in time of the Resurrection through the Ascension and culminating *for each and every soul* at this present point in time, during the unfolding of the Second Coming. These words were given to

---

6 Daniil Andrejew, *Rosa Mira: Die Weltrose*, vol. 3, pp. 202–226.

7 Isaacson, *Through the Eyes of Mary Magdalene*, vol. 2, pp. 232–236.

Mary Magdalene first. She was the first soul who received this instruction.

Near to the end of Christ Jesus's life, he had taken Mary Magdalene through certain initiations, which made it possible for her to experience mystical union with Christ. In mystical union one experiences spiritual touch, which is the ability to discern another being, by giving that being the space to dwell within one's own heart. From her initiations, Mary Magdalene was able to inwardly come into communion with—to "touch"—the Christ being, to know him in a deeply spiritual way. After his death on the cross, she lost touch with him. He descended into the heart of the earthly realm, and she was severed from this inner relationship. On the morning of the Resurrection, he appeared to her just after he had acquired his resurrection body. At that moment of their meeting there in the garden, he had not yet ascended with this new body to present it to the Father. He needed to take all that he was—everything that was his body—and present it to the Father—and could not be in a state of union with a human being until a later time. Thus, Mary Magdalene could not experience spiritual touch with him. The resurrection body had yet to be presented to the Father.

The culmination, the fulfillment of these words: "Touch me not, for I have not yet ascended to my Father" comes now, at this time of the Second Coming. For this particular soul the fulfillment is *today* [on this day of the cosmic commemoration of the Resurrection—1,981 years after the Resurrection on Sunday, April 5 AD 33].[8] In the Second Coming the fulfillment of those words is, "Touch me now, for I have descended unto you."

Part of the soul's journey is to follow the path of Christ, to do the things he did and to bear one's cross, and then to spiritually encounter him at the Resurrection. And having spiritually witnessed Christ's earthly path culminating with the Resurrection, one then follows the path of the Risen One that takes one from the Resurrection through the Ascension[9] to the Second Coming, where this spiritual touch happens.[10] It is happening today for the Earth and Nature. I bear witness to this. *And it can happen in those individual hearts that are prepared.* Prior to today it already began happening for certain souls. *Today, however, is the new day for the spiritual touch of the body of the Second Coming that is manifesting on the Earth.*

For most people this day will pass unknown and unrecognized—this day on which the resurrection body of the Second Coming has now touched down upon the Earth. To this point in its unfolding, I have been experiencing the resurrection body through the course of time in its progression from the day of the Resurrection. And today is the first time that this fulfillment of the spiritual touch of the body of the Second Coming to the Earth is truly fulfilled. The experience of the Second Coming will be, for most people, a process that unfolds and deepens over the course of time. It happens in a way that the person can experience him without being overwhelmed by the utter majesty and radiance of his presence.

On this day—never before had I seen him like this!—it is in red robes that he appeared to me. The body of the Second Coming is thus clothed in glorious red, and he is pouring out his love and mercy in radiant streams of light from his

---

8   It is noteworthy that 1,981 years equates with 167 orbits of Jupiter around the sidereal zodiac. That is, on this day it was not only the Sun that was where it was at the Resurrection. Also Jupiter was at almost exactly the same location in the sidereal sign of Gemini as where it was at the Resurrection, closely aligned with the star Sirius at 19½° Gemini. Interestingly, 1,981 years is seven periods of 283 years. From the baptism in the River Jordan in AD 29 to the year 312 is a period of 283 years. It was in AD 312 that the Emperor Constantine the Great (after having had a suprasensory experience expressive of Christ—or rather, of Christ's name) converted to Christianity. Constantine's conversion, 283 years after the baptism of Jesus, completely changed the destiny of Christianity.

9   Powell, *Cultivating Inner Radiance and the Body of Immortality*, maps out a path of daily spiritual practice leading one through the stages of the Transfiguration, the Crucifixion, the Resurrection, and the Ascension—toward the next step, which is the Second Coming. The *inner radiance* sequence is thus a daily practice, a schooling, to align one with the Second Coming.

10 What is meant here is the spiritual touch indicated in the words: "Touch me now, for I have descended unto you."

wounds. He showed me the wound in his side from which—as with all his wounds, but especially from the wound in his side—unfathomable mercy and compassion is streaming. His love and mercy is for the world—for the entire Earth: for all human beings and for the whole of Nature. These mysteries are unfathomable.

All human souls must find their own "I" and claim it for themselves in the light of the Resurrection. This is an experience of the Resurrection anew, which is happening now, at this time during the unfolding process of the Second Coming.

I was able to witness these things while being *inside* the body of the Second Coming, which is nothing other than the resurrection body that has evolved to a very high level beyond its initial manifestation to Mary Magdalene. The only way I could gaze upon all of these things *outside of time* is through this body. Now I understand the cosmic history of the resurrection body: from the Resurrection through the Ascension to the Second Coming, to the present point in time—to this special day of fulfillment when from now onward the Earth is being enveloped and embraced in the resurrection body, with the resurrection body streaming from the Sun to the Earth. *Today is the new day for the spiritual touch of the body of the Second Coming that has now touched down upon the Earth, and this event signifies the inauguration of a new era for humanity and the Earth.*[11]

---

11 [Footnote added by RP]: The profound meaning of this vision of Estelle Isaacson from April 30, 2014, on the day of the cosmic commemoration of the Resurrection, can be deepened in light of the significance of the year 2014 described in my article "2014 and the Coming of the Kalki Avatar" in *Journal for Star Wisdom 2014*. See also Powell and Isaacson, *Gautama Buddha's Successor,* which focuses on *the cultural wave that began in 2014* in connection with the Maitreya individuality awaited by Buddhists as the next Buddha, who is the same as the Kalki individuality awaited by Hindus as the next Avatar. The mission of the Maitreya individuality, according to Rudolf Steiner, is to proclaim Christ in his Second Coming and to transmit the power of morality, the power of the Good, through the word—the Good, now, for humanity and the Earth, being Christ in his Second Coming, who is bestowing the power of the Good upon those who align themselves with him.

In the twentieth century, there began for humanity the vision of Christ in the etheric realm.... Now the Etheric Christ walks among human beings the whole world over. This event must not pass by unnoticed by humanity. Humankind must awaken to Christ, so that a sufficient number of people may behold him in the etheric realm. He is already present.... It is possible today, if we do but seek him, to be very near to Christ, to find him in a quite different way than has been possible hitherto.

Christ spoke some words, which should be deeply engraved in the human soul: "I am with you always, until the end of time." This is a truth, a reality. He is here. He is now making his presence felt in a new way.

Christ is not a ruler of human beings, but our brother. He wishes to be consulted on all the details of life. In everything we undertake we ought to ask of Christ: "Should we do this or not?" Then human souls may have the experience of Christ standing by them as the beloved companion, and they will then not only obtain consolation and strength from Christ, but will also receive instruction from him as to what is to be done. The figure of Christ Jesus is now able to draw near to us and give us the strength and force in which we can live more fully here on Earth. If we seek him, Christ is able to guide us, to stand beside us as a brother, so that our hearts and souls may be strong enough to grow in our further development.—RUDOLF STEINER, February 6, 1917

EDITORIAL FOREWORD

Robert Powell, PhD

The *Journal for Star Wisdom* (formerly *Christian Star Calendar*) has appeared every year since 1991. From the beginning, the central feature has been the calendar comprising the monthly ephemeris pages together with commentaries drawing attention to the Christ events remembered by the ongoing cosmic events. The significance of following the Christ events in relation to daily astronomical events is an important foundation for the new star wisdom of astrosophy.[1] This new star wisdom is arising in our time in response to the Second Coming of Christ—known as his return in the etheric realm of life forces—as a path of communing with Christ in his life body (ether body). It should also be mentioned that, with the onset of the Second Coming of Christ during the course of the twentieth century, Christ is now the Lord of Karma, and this is important to take into consideration in the development of a new relationship of humanity to the stars in our time, particularly with respect to the horoscope as an expression of human karma or destiny.

The events of Christ's life lived two thousand years ago are inscribed into his ether body, and to meditate upon these events at times when they are cosmically remembered is a way of drawing near to Christ. The recently updated version of my article "Subnature and the Second Coming" (in *The Inner Life of the Earth*[2]) outlines the background to contemporary events as a confrontation between good and evil in relation to Christ's descent at this time through the sub-earthly realms and also gives an overview of the various cosmic rhythms unfolding in relation to his Second Coming, including the thirty-three-and-one-third-year rhythm of his ether body.

The *Journal for Star Wisdom* encourages the reader to engage in the practice of stargazing, which is fundamental to the development of the new star wisdom of astrosophy. One of the foundations of astrosophy lies in the science of astronomy, providing the new star wisdom with a secure scientific foundation, which can, moreover, be brought into the realm of experience through the practice of stargazing. In astrosophy there is no longer a separation between astronomy and astrology. For example, when in the *Journal for Star Wisdom* it is indicated that currently Mars in the heavens is at 15° Taurus then, assuming that Mars is visible, the red planet can be seen in conjunction with Aldebaran marking the Bull's eye at the center of the constellation of Taurus, whose longitude, as the central star in this constellation, is 15° Taurus. In astrosophy, the astrological fact of Mars at 15° Taurus is identical with the astronomical reality of Mars' location at the center of the constellation of

---

1   There are many different approaches to astrosophy and not all use the equal-division sidereal zodiac that forms the basis of the approach followed in the *Journal for Star Wisdom*. All references to the zodiac and to planetary positions in the zodiac in the *Journal for Star Wisdom* are in terms of the sidereal zodiac as defined in my book *History of the Zodiac*. Moreover, in astrosophy there are different chronologies of the life of Christ, and the chronology that forms the basis of the approach followed in the *Journal for Star Wisdom* is set forth in my book *Chronicle of the Living Christ*. Thus, all references to planetary positions at the Christ events in the *Journal for Star Wisdom* are in terms of the scientifically established chronology of the life of Christ set forth in my book *Chronicle of the Living Christ*.

2   O'Leary (ed.), *The Inner Life of the Earth*, pp. 69–141.

Taurus. Astrosophy thus relates to sense-perceptible reality and to the Divine "background of existence" (the spiritual hierarchies)[3] underlying this reality, whereas astrology is generally practiced in such a way that there is a split between astrology and astronomy (in this example, modern astrology, which uses the tropical zodiac rather than the equal-division sidereal zodiac used in astrosophy, would say that Mars is "in Gemini"). The historical background as to how this separation between astronomy and astrology arose is described in my book *History of the Zodiac*.[4]

The present issue of the *Journal for Star Wisdom* is the twenty-fifth, and the seventh published under the new title; the first eighteen issues were published under the title *Christian Star Calendar*. By way of explanation concerning the new title, this publication is intended as an outreach from the StarFire research group (an astrosophy group) that meets yearly in Boulder, Colorado (sometimes in Fair Oaks, California); see the website www.StarWisdom.org.[5] The *Journal for Star Wisdom* is intended as an organ for the development of the new star wisdom of astrosophy. This was also the purpose of the *Christian Star Calendar*. However, there the focus was, at least initially, primarily on the calendar—the monthly ephemeris and commentaries. In the course of time, more and more research articles on the new star wisdom of astrosophy came to be published in the *Christian Star Calendar*. A point was reached where

it became clear that the publication is more of a journal than a calendar, although the calendar continues to play an important role. It is therefore a natural transition from the *Christian Star Calendar* to the *Journal for Star Wisdom*.

Perhaps the greatest prophecy of our time—one that is little known, but that is the reason for the existence of this journal, and is a source of tremendous spiritual light—is Rudolf Steiner's prophecy from the year 1910, just over one hundred years ago. On January 12, 1910, he prophesied that the Second Coming of Christ would begin in 1933, an event called "Christ's appearance in the etheric realm"—not a return in a physical body but in an etheric (life) body, the realm of life forces. Here with my translation of Marie Steiner's notes from this important, hitherto unpublished lecture:

> 3000 BC: Kali Yuga commenced and lasted until 1899—a time of great transition.
>
> 1933: human beings will appear with clairvoyant faculties, which they will develop naturally. At this time, which we are approaching, the newly beginning clairvoyant faculties have to be satisfied, to experience what they [human beings] should do with them.
>
> I am with you always, even unto the end of the world.
>
> Christ will appear in an etheric form. The physical Christ became the Spirit of the Earth—this was the midpoint, the balance, of Earth evolution.
>
> 5th Letter of the Ap(ocalypse): I will come again; however, take heed that you do not fail to recognize me.
>
> 2,500 years is the time that humanity has to develop again the gifts of clairvoyance. Around 1933 the Gospels must be recognized in their spiritual meaning such that they have worked preparing for Christ. Otherwise untold confusion of the soul will be caused.
>
> Around 1933 there will be some representatives of black magical schools, who will falsely proclaim a physical Christ.
>
> Each time that he becomes perceptible, Christ is perceptible for other faculties.[6]

---

3   According to Rudolf Steiner, the constellations are the abode of the first hierarchy, called Seraphim, Cherubim, and Thrones. The movement of the planets takes place against the background of the zodiacal constellations, which—considered as the abode of the first hierarchy—form the Divine "background of existence" in the heavens. "Suppose you wanted to point to some particular [group of] Thrones, Cherubim, and Seraphim, one denotes them by a particular constellation. It is like a signpost. In that direction over there are the [group of] Thrones, Cherubim, and Seraphim known as the Twins, over there [the group of Thrones, Cherubim, and Seraphim known as] the Lion, etc." (Steiner, *The Spiritual Hierarchies*, p. 99; words in brackets added by RP).

4   Robert Powell, *History of the Zodiac*.

5   Other astrosophy websites: www.sophiafoundation.org and www.astrogeographia.org.

6   Translated from the first page of Marie Steiner's notes, published in German for the first time in *Der Europäer*, vol. 14, Dec./Jan. 2009/2010, p. 3.

This was Rudolf Steiner's greatest prophecy: the Second Coming of Christ, which he called the appearance of Christ in the etheric realm, beginning in 1933. It is this event, the presence of the etheric Christ, lasting from 1933 for 2,500 years (until 4433), that is pivotal for the approach to astrosophy (star wisdom) outlined in the *Journal for Star Wisdom*.

In conclusion I would like to express gratitude to our publisher, Gene Gollogly of SteinerBooks, and to the able assistance of Jens Jensen of SteinerBooks, for making this seventh issue of the *Journal for Star Wisdom* available, and to all those who have contributed to make this issue possible, in particular to our authors for presenting their research articles as contributions to the foundations of the new star wisdom of astrosophy, and to all our readers who ultimately are the reason for the existence of the *Journal for Star Wisdom*.

To starry realms,
To the dwelling places of Gods,
Turns the Spirit gaze of my soul.

From starry realms,
From the dwelling places of Gods,
Streams Spirit power into my soul.

For starry realms,
For the dwelling places of Gods,
Lives my Spirit heart through my soul.
—Rudolf Steiner

WORKING WITH THE
JOURNAL FOR STAR WISDOM

The listing of major planetary events each month is intended as a stimulus toward attunement with the Universal Christ, the Logos, whose being encompasses the entire galaxy. The deeds of the historical Christ wrought two thousand years ago are of eternal significance—inscribed into the cosmos—and they resonate with the movements of the heavenly bodies, especially when certain alignments or planetary configurations occur bearing a resemblance with those prevailing at the time of events in the life of Jesus Christ. With the rare astronomical event of the transit of Venus across the face of the Sun that took place June 8, 2004, at exactly the zodiacal degree (23° Taurus), where the Sun stood at Christ's Ascension, a new impulse was given from divine-spiritual realms for the further unfolding of star wisdom, *Astro-Sophia*.

The calendar may be found beginning on page 101. It comprises ephemeris pages for the twelve months of the year with accompanying monthly commentaries on the astronomical events listed on the ephemeris pages. Indications regarding the similarity of contemporary planetary configurations with those at events in the life of Christ are given in the lower part of the monthly commentaries, and the upper part gives a commentary on the notable astronomical occurrences each month. Unless otherwise stated, all astronomical indications regarding visibility mean "visible to the naked eye." See the note concerning time on the page preceding the monthly commentaries.

With this calendar, astronomy and astrology, which were a unity in the ancient star wisdom of the Egyptians and Babylonians, are reunited and provide a foundation for astrosophy, the all-encompassing star wisdom, *Astro-Sophia*, an expression of Sophia and referred to in the Revelation of John as the "Bride of the Lamb."

THE HEALING OF THE MAN-BORN-BLIND AND THE CENTRAL SUN
FOUNDATIONS OF STAR WISDOM (ASTROSOPHY)

Robert Powell

NEW ASTROSOPHICAL RESEARCH SHEDS LIGHT ON CHRIST'S WORDS "I AM THE LIGHT OF THE WORLD" SPOKEN AT THE HEALING OF THE MAN-BORN-BLIND.

As indicated in the book *Chronicle of the Living Christ*, with the event of Christ's healing of the man-born-blind—in contrast to other Christ events discussed in the *Chronicle*—it was not possible to determine the date of this Christ event with 100% certainty.[1] For the healing of the man-born-blind belongs to the ten-month period (313 days) missing from Anne Catherine Emmerich's account. Some information is provided by the description of the healing of the man-born-blind in the Gospel of St John, but not enough to enable an accurate dating. The Gospel of St John mentions that this healing took place on the Sabbath, i.e., from sunset/dusk on Friday to sunset/dusk on Saturday. From the John Gospel account it can also be inferred that the healing of the man-born-blind took place *after* the Feast of Tabernacles and *prior to* the Feast of the Dedication of the Temple in Jerusalem. Thus, within the framework offered by the *Chronicle*, the healing of the man-born-blind must have taken place on one of the following dates (Friday sunset/dusk to Saturday sunset/dusk) in AD 31: October 5/6, October 12/13, October 19/20, October 26/27, November 2/3, November 9/10, November 16/17, November 23/24. Again based on the Gospel account, it is evident that Jesus attended the Feast of the Dedication of the Temple in Jerusalem (November 28-December 5), where the Pharisees tried to arrest him (John 10:22-39). Given this fact, that Jesus was present in Jerusalem at that time (November 28-December 5), and since the healing of the man-born-blind took place in Jerusalem, it is also possible that this healing took place around that time—for example, on the Sabbath day November 23/24.

Hitherto some students of astrosophy believed that the healing of the man-born-blind could have taken place on October 6 AD 31, exactly one year after the healing of the blind youth Manahem on October 6 AD 30—*exactly one year* signifying that the Sun returned to the *same location in the zodiac*. The miraculous healing of Manahem is described in great detail by Anne Catherine Emmerich.[2] The author of this article also accepted the date October 6 AD 31 as a likely date of the healing of the man-born-blind, given the return of the Sun to the same zodiacal location as at the healing of the blind youth Manahem. Recently (2015), however, based on inner certainty of experience the author has come to a new, revised perspective. For spiritual research indicates that this Christ event of the healing of the man-born-blind took place at the pool of Siloam in Jerusalem early on Friday evening, November 23 AD 31. Having received this specific indication by way of spiritual research, I computed the horoscope for six o'clock that evening (see geocentric horoscope opposite). To my astonishment, in this horoscope for the healing

---

1 *Chronicle of the Living Christ*, p. 455, refers to the near 100% certainty offered by way of scientific proof of the accuracy of the dating of the Christ events based on the visions of Anne Catherine Emmerich as determined in relation to the Hebrew calendar reconstructed for that time of the life of Christ.

2 Emmerich, *Visions of the Life of Christ*. Regarding the near 100% certainty offered by scientific proof referred to in the previous footnote, see the lengthy discussion in volume 3 of this new edition of Anne Catherine Emmerich's visions.

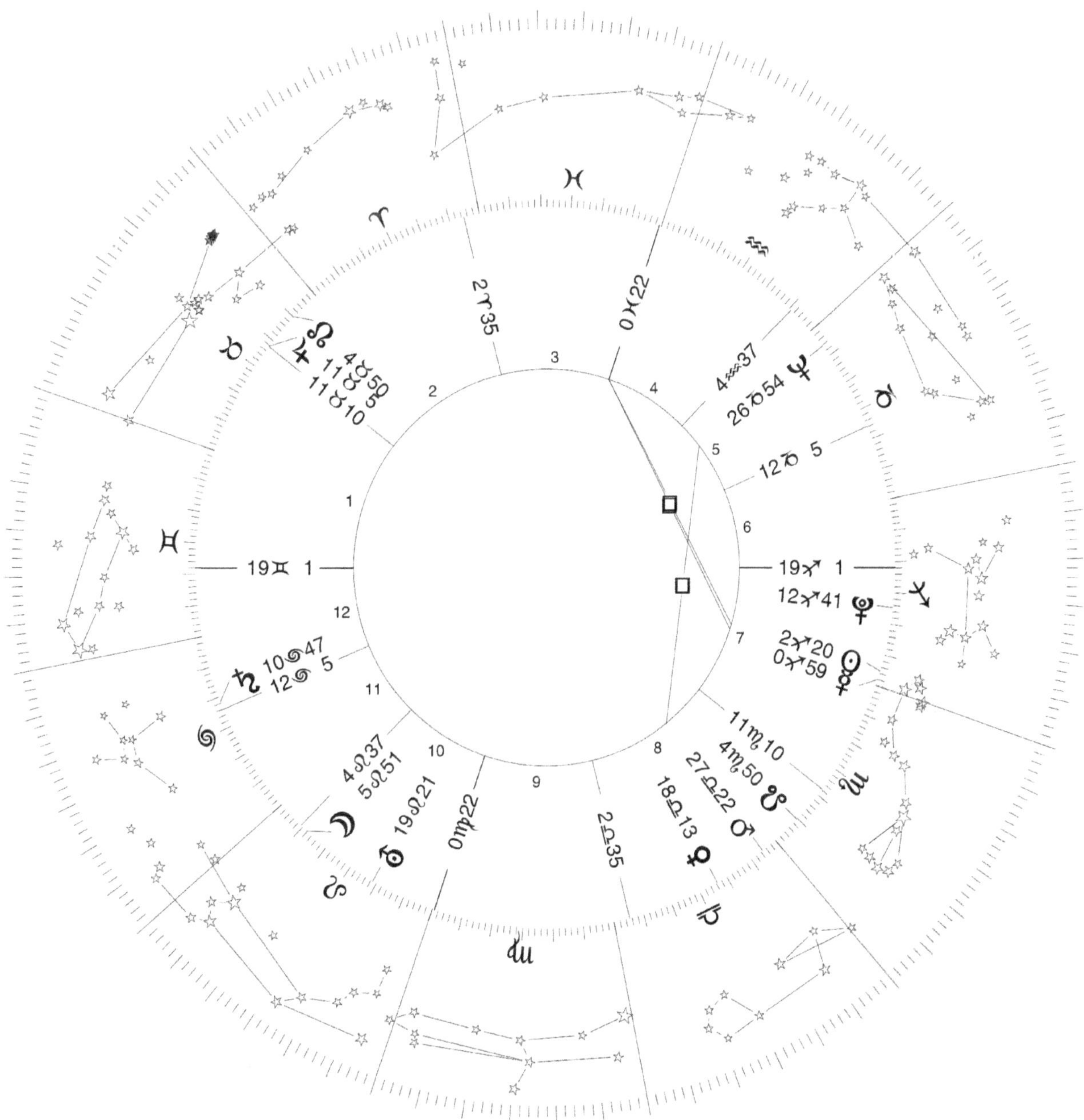

of the man-born-blind the Sun is located at 2°20' Sagittarius—that is: the Sun is almost exactly *in conjunction with the galactic center at 2°06' Sagittarius*! Moreover, the Moon at 5°51' Leo is conjunct the star Regulus at 5°12' Leo, as was the case at Christ's greatest miracle, the raising of Lazarus from the dead.[3] In fact, in the heliocentric/hermetic (Tychonic) horoscope of the healing

---

3 *Chronicle of the Living Christ*, p. 173, shows the horoscope of the raising of Lazarus, indicating that it was New Moon, with the Sun and Moon in conjunction, both close to the star Regulus: Sun at 3°04' Leo and Moon at 4°30' Leo.

of the man-born-blind (see Tychonic horoscope opposite[4]) it can be seen that the Moon (5°51' Leo) and heliocentric Venus (5°36' Leo) are in conjunction in close proximity to Regulus, i.e., this is a "hermetic conjunction" of the Moon and Venus, as also took place on Holy Saturday at Christ's descent after the crucifixion and immediately preceding his resurrection.[5]

Given that Christ's words "I AM the light of the world" (John 9:5) were spoken in connection with the healing of the man-born-blind, it is possible to begin to sense the great significance of this healing having taken place at that point in time in the year AD 31 when the Sun was in conjunction with the galactic center, also known as the *Central Sun* at the heart of our galaxy. Before deepening further into this, let us first consider the import of research into the planetary configurations at events in the life of Christ.

Megastars

Those readers who are familiar with my book *The Astrological Revolution*, written together with Kevin Dann, will know of the research presented

in chapter 5 of that book.[6] The essence of this research is the discovery that at Christ's miracles described in the Gospel of St John and elsewhere, our Sun was always aligned with one or other so-called *megastar* (Greek: "great star"), i.e., stars with a luminosity at least 10,000 stronger than our Sun.[7] The term "great stars" is used by Rudolf Steiner in a meditation he gave: *"Christ's Light from great stars streams into my heart."*[8] The point of departure for this research was Rudolf Steiner's statement made in 1911:

> In Palestine during the time that Jesus of Nazareth walked on Earth as Christ Jesus—during the three years of his life, from his thirtieth to his thirty-third year—the entire being of the Cosmic Christ was acting uninterruptedly upon him, and was working into him. The Christ stood always under the influence of the entire cosmos; he made no step without this working of the cosmic forces into and in him…. It was always in accordance with the collective being of the whole universe with whom the Earth is in harmony, that all which Christ Jesus did took place.[9]

These words of Rudolf Steiner do not indicate anything specific in relation to the "working of the cosmic forces into" Christ in connection with all that he did. Our research finding, however, is very

---

4   *Geocentric horoscopes* are computed on the basis of the Earth at the center (Earth-centered = geocentric). *Tychonic horoscopes*, also referred to as *hermetic horoscopes*, are computed according to the astronomical system put forward by the Danish astronomer Tycho Brahe (1546-1601), in which the Earth is located at the center, the Moon and the Sun (viewed from the perspective of their apparent movement) are considered to orbit around the Earth, and the planets are considered to revolve around the Sun, i.e., heliocentrically (Sun-centered = heliocentric). As discussed in the two volumes of *Hermetic Astrology*, the helio/hermetic (Tychonic) horoscopes are of great significance in terms of revealing the *spiritual level* of the human being's destiny—Robert Powell, *Hermetic Astrology*, volume 1 (1987) & volume 2 (1989), reprinted in 2006, are available through Amazon.

5   Estelle Isaacson (*Through the Eyes of Mary Magdalene, vol. 2: From Initiation to the Passion*, pp. 99, 212–214) describes the significance of Christ's descent to the center of the Earth, planting his seed of love into the Earth, beautifully expressed by the hermetic conjunction of the Moon and Venus, which, however, at that time on Holy Saturday was in *Libra*—rather than in *Leo* as at the time of the healing of the man-born-blind.

6   Powell and Dann, *The Astrological Revolution*.

7   *Luminosity* measures a star's intrinsic brightness. The luminosity of our Sun is set at the value one (L=1). By way of comparison, then, the luminosity of Sirius is 24 (L=24). In other words Sirius, if it were to be placed alongside our Sun, would appear twenty-four times brighter. From our perspective, our Sun is an extremely bright star, because, as our local star, it is so close to us. Other stars are much further away and thus, even if they are intrinsically very luminous stars, their apparent radiance does not in any way match up to that of our Sun. However, if the Earth were revolving around Sirius—in other words, if Sirius were our Sun—it would be seen by us as twenty-four times brighter than our Sun, i.e., L=24 (or L=25) is the intrinsic brightness (luminosity) of Sirius. The term *megastars* is applied to those very powerful stars whose luminosity is 10,000 or more.

8   Steiner, *Soul Exercises: Word and Symbol Meditations, 1903–1924*, p. XXX.

9   Steiner, *Spiritual Guidance of the Individual and Humanity*, p. 28.

Healing of the man born blind of by Jesus Christ (V. GC) - Tychonic

At Jerusalem, Latitude 31N46', Longitude 35E14'
Date: Friday, 23/NOV/31, Julian
Time: 18: 0, Local Time
Sidereal Time 21:59:55, Vernal Point 2♈36'54", House System: Placidus
Zodiac: Sidereal SVP, Aspect set: Conjunction/Square/Opposition

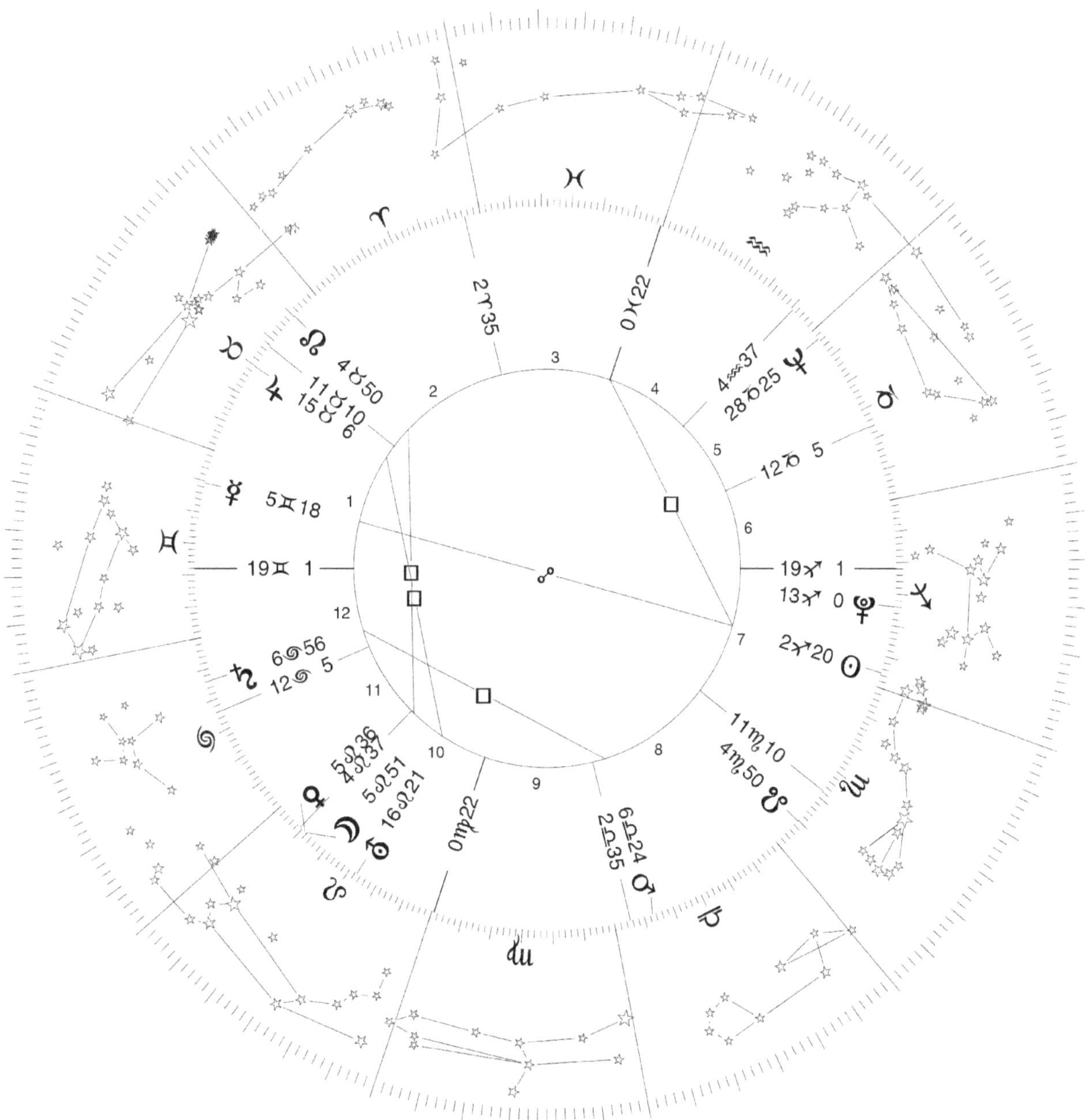

specific. By way of an example which clearly illustrates the specific research finding, let us consider the central miracles of Christ reported in the John Gospel: the feeding of the five thousand immediately followed (that night) by the walking on the water. These two miracles occurred in rapid succession: the feeding of the five thousand on January 29 AD 31 between four and six o'clock in the afternoon, and the walking on the water took place later during the hours of darkness some time later, after nightfall. At that time of the feeding of the five thousand the Sun was located almost exactly at 10½° Aquarius, which is the sidereal longitude of the megastar Deneb marking the tail

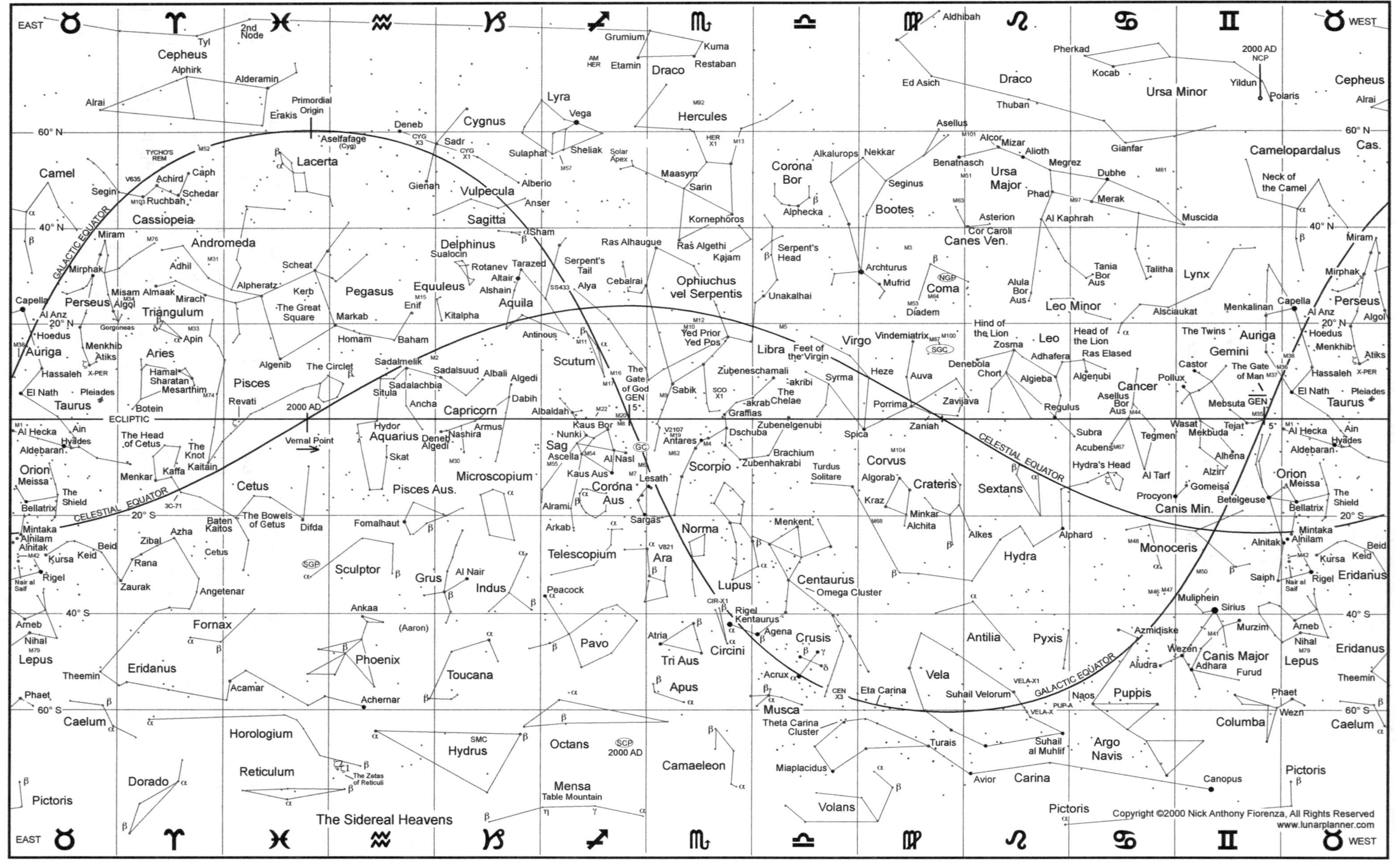

The Sidereal Heavens
Copyright ©2000 Nick Anthony Fiorenza, All Rights Reserved
www.lunarplanner.com
EAST
WEST
2nd Node
Primordial Erakis Origin
Vernal Point
2000 AD
2000 AD NCP
SCP 2000 AD
GALACTIC EQUATOR
CELESTIAL EQUATOR
ECLIPTIC
60° N
40° N
20° N
20° S
40° S
60° S
Cepheus
Tyl
Alphirk
Alderamin
Alrai
Camel
Cassiopeia
Achird
Caph
Schedar
Ruchbah
Segin
Miram
Mirphak
Perseus
Algol
Misam
Almaak
Mirach
Menkhib
Atiks
Hassaleh
X-PER
El Nath
Pleiades
Botein
Taurus
Hamal
Sharatan
Mesarthim
Aries
Andromeda
Alpheratz
Triangulum
Apin
Al Anz
Auriga
Capella
Hoedus
Lacerta
Aselfafage (Cyg)
Cygnus
Deneb
Sadr
Gienah
Scheat
Kerb
The Great Square
Markab
Homam
Baham
Pegasus
Algenib
The Circlet
Pisces
Revati
Cetus
Menkar
The Head of Cetus
The Knot
Kaffa
Kaitain
Baten Kaitos
The Bowels of Getus
Difda
3C-71
Mintaka
Alnilam
Alnitak
Nair al Saif
Rigel
Bellatrix
Orion
Meissa
The Shield
Kursa
Keid
Beid
Zibal
Rana
Zaurak
Azha
Cetus
Angetenar
Eridanus
Ameb
Nihal
Lepus
Theemin
Phaet
Caelum
Pictoris
Dorado
Reticulum
The Zetas of Reticuli
Horologium
Hydrus
SMC
Fornax
Acamar
Achernar
Phoenix
Ankaa
Sculptor
Fomalhaut
Grus
Al Nair
Indus
Pavo
Peacock
Toucana
Apus
Octans
Mensa
Table Mountain
Camaeleon
Volans
The Sidereal Heavens
Lyra
Vega
Sulaphat
Sheliak
Solar Apex
Cygnus
Deneb
Vulpecula
Anser
Sagitta
Delphinus
Sualocin
Rotanev
Tarazed
Altair
Alshain
Aquila
Antinous
Equuleus
Enif
Kitalpha
Aquarius
Sadalmelik
Sadalsuud
Sadalachbia
Situla
Ancha
Albali
Albali
Capricorn
Dabih
Albaldah
Algedi
Armus
Nashira
Deneb Algedi
Skat
Microscopium
Pisces Aus.
Telescopium
Scutum
M16
M17
The Gate of God GEN 5'
Sabik
Kaus Bor
Nunki
Sag
Ascella
Kaus Aus
Alrami
Corona Aus
Sargas
Ara
Norma
Lupus
Rigel Kentaurus
Agena
Crusis
Acrux
Musca
Circini
Tri Aus
Atria
Centaurus
Omega Cluster
Eta Carina
Theta Carina Cluster
Miaplacidus
Turais
Avior
Carina
Vela
Suhail Velorum
Suhail al Muhlif
Naos
Argo Navis
Puppis
Canopus
Pictoris
Grumium
Kuma
Restaban
Etamin
AM HER
Draco
Hercules
Maasym
Sarin
Kornephoros
Ras Alhague
Raś Algethi
Kajam
Serpent's Tail
Cebalrai
Alya
SS433
Serpent's Head
Ophiuchus vel Serpentis
Yed Prior
Yed Pos
Unakalhai
Sabik
The Chelae
akrab
akribi
Graffias
Antares
Dschuba
Zubenelgenubi
Zubeneschamali
Zubenhakrabi
Brachium
Scorpio
Lesath
Norma
Menkent
Lupus
Libra
Feet of the Virgin
Virgo
Vindemiatrix
SGC
Heze
Auva
Porrima
Syrma
Zaniah
Zavijava
Spica
Corvus
Algorab
Kraz
Minkar
Alchita
Crateris
Alkes
Hydra
Antilia
Vela
Pyxis
Aldhibah
Draco
Ed Asich
Thuban
NGP
Coma
Diadem
Denebola
Chort
Zosma
Leo
Algieba
Adhafera
Regulus
Ras Elased
Hind of the Lion
Head of the Lion
Leo Minor
Sextans
Hydra's Head
Al Tarf
Procyon
Gomeisa
Canis Min.
Monoceris
Alphard
Pherkad
Kocab
Yildun
Polaris
Ursa Minor
2000 AD NCP
Thuban
Gianfar
Alcor
Mizar
Alioth
Megrez
Dubhe
Phad
Merak
Benatnasch
Seginus
Asterion
Al Kaphrah
Ursa Major
Bootes
Alkalurops
Nekkar
Archturus
Mufrid
Alphecca
Corona Bor
Cor Caroli
Canes Ven.
Camelopardalus
Cas.
Neck of the Camel
Muscida
Tania Bor Aus
Alula Bor Aus
Talitha
Lynx
Alsciaukat
Menkalinan
Capella
Al Anz
Perseus
Algol
Mirphak
Miram
Hoedus
Menkhib
Atiks
Hassaleh
X-PER
El Nath
Pleiades
Taurus
Auriga
The Twins
Castor
Pollux
Gemini
The Gate of Man
Mebsuta
GEN
Cancer
Asellus Bor Aus
Subra
Acubens
Tegmen
Al Tarf
Hydra's Head
Alhena
Wasat
Mekbuda
Tejat
Alzirr
Orion
Meissa
Mintaka
Alnilam
Alnitak
Bellatrix
The Shield
Kursa
Keid
Beid
Saiph
Nair al Saif
Rigel
Muliphein
Sirius
Azmidiske
Wezen
Adhara
Aludra
Furud
Canis Major
Murzim
Ameb
Nihal
Lepus
Theemin
Phaet
Wezn
Caelum
Columba
Argo Navis
Canopus
Pictoris
Eridanus
Ain
Hyades
Aldebaran
Al Hecka
Orion
Cepheus
Alrai

of the Swan—or the head of the Northern Cross—depending on how one looks at this constellation (with "Greek" or with "Christian" eyes).

In contrast to Sirius (luminosity of 24, i.e., twenty-four times that of our Sun), Deneb is a megastar—that is, a star whose luminosity is 10,000 or more. Sirius *appears* much brighter than Deneb, because Sirius, at a distance of 8.6 light years, is relatively close to our Sun. Deneb, on the other hand, is estimated to be about 2,600 light years distant from our solar system. However, like Sirius, Deneb is—according to its apparent brightness—a 1st magnitude star. Still appearing so bright (1st magnitude star) to our naked eye vision, and yet being at such a vast distance, it is clear that Deneb's *intrinsic brightness* (luminosity) must be enormous. Indeed, Deneb is estimated to have a luminosity of about 200,000. In other words, Deneb is shining with a light some 200,000 times more powerful than our Sun and is twenty times the luminosity of the "least" luminous megastar (L=10,000 being the minimum luminosity for a star to qualify as a megastar). Deneb well illustrates the significance of megastars and is, after Alnilam (L=275,000, the central star in the belt of Orion), the next most luminous first magnitude star in our local part of the galaxy, known as the *Orion Arm*. Looking up at Deneb, we see that it is 60° north of the zodiac—this is its latitude. If we trace an arc down from the *north ecliptic pole* through Deneb and continue the arc down to the *south ecliptic pole*, it intersects the sidereal zodiac at 10½° Aquarius—this is Deneb's longitude in the sidereal zodiac.[10] At the feeding of the

five thousand the Sun was at 10½° Aquarius, longitudinally in conjunction with Deneb (see sidereal heavens star map opposite.

From extensive research it is clear that it was not mere coincidence that there was a *conjunction* between the Sun and the megastar Deneb at the feeding of the five thousand. In line with the foregoing statement by Rudolf Steiner, quoted above, it is evident that the cosmic forces streaming from Deneb were transmitted via our Sun and were received and transmitted further by Christ at the time of the miracle of the multiplication of bread and fish underlying the feeding of the five thousand. Here the word "conjunction" means a conjunction in *longitude*, with both the Sun and Deneb at 10½° Aquarius. Even though the Sun and Deneb were 60° apart in terms of latitude, there was still a conjunction in longitude, with the Sun crossing the *Deneb meridian* at the time of the miracle. How may this be understood?

MERIDIANS OF THE STARS

Just as there are meridians—lines of energy flow—in the human being, these meridians exist also in the greater cosmos of the macrocosm. As may be understood from the law of correspondences—*"as above, so below"* attributed to Hermes, the great teacher of the ancient Egyptians—if there are meridians in the human being, it follows that they also exist "above" in the cosmos, and that the meridians in human beings mirror the heavenly meridians of the stars. We can picture an energy flow streaming from each star and intersecting the zodiac, the place of intersection indicating the point of influx where energy flows from the greater cosmos of stars into our solar system.[11] For Deneb, this point of influx is 10½° Aquarius. Thus, whenever the Sun or any planet in our solar system crosses the Deneb meridian at 10½° Aquarius, the Deneb energy flows in to unite with that planet

---

10 The sidereal longitude of a star is determined by tracing an arc down from the *north ecliptic pole* through the star and continuing the arc down to the *south ecliptic pole*, determining where this arc intersects the *ecliptic*—the ecliptic being the apparent path of the Sun along the central axis through the the sidereal zodiac. This stellar arc is also called the *meridian*. The point of intersection of the star's meridian with the ecliptic specifies the sidereal longitude of the star. The latitude of the star is found by examining how far the star—in terms of angular distance along its meridian—is located above (north) or below (south) of the ecliptic. As referred to later in this article, the significance of the meridian is that it indicates the "energy flow" emitted by a star, and its sidereal

longitude shows where the energy of the star, streaming along its meridian, flows into our solar system. This understanding is important in order to grasp the research finding that at Christ's miracles the sidereal longitude of the Sun always coincided with the meridian of one or other megastar.

11 See preceding footnote.

or with our Sun. (Here, the word *energy* refers to the energy of Divine Light radiating from the stars described earlier in this article—quoting from Rudolf Steiner: "Christ's Light from great stars streams into my heart.")

The fact that at the feeding of the five thousand Deneb was 60° *north* of the Sun is not so relevant. Why? The key concept here, as mentioned above, is the *meridian* indicating the energy flow running through the star and then intersecting the ecliptic. The ecliptic (the apparent path of the Sun through the zodiac) can be regarded as the *heart meridian* of the cosmos—the point of entry of stellar influences streaming in from outside our solar system. The important point at the feeding of the five thousand was that the Sun was crossing the Deneb meridian, since the Sun and Deneb were in conjunction at 10½° Aquarius in terms of sidereal longitude. Focusing upon the meridians as *energy lines* flowing through every star, the *entire celestial sphere* becomes astrologically significant. The figure of the Sidereal Heavens on page 28 shows the entire celestial sphere with each star in its position (sidereal longitude and latitude), giving an overview. Thus, for example, Deneb can be seen at 10½° Aquarius, 60° north—and similarly with every other star shown on this map of the sidereal heavens.

Research into the planetary configurations during the life of Christ—inspired by the words from Rudolf Steiner quoted earlier that, *"It was always in accordance with the collective being of the whole universe with whom the Earth is in harmony, that all which Christ Jesus did took place"*—reveals that the most important stellar meridians in the life of Christ are those running through certain megastars. We have already seen the example of the Sun at 10½° Aquarius on the Deneb meridian at the miracle of the feeding of the five thousand. It should also be noted that, since the miracle of the walking on the water occurred that same night, the Sun at this miracle (at 11° Aquarius) was still very close to the Deneb meridian also at this miracle. In fact, taking account of Deneb's *proper motion*, at the time of Christ the longitude of Deneb was—as shown in the table

near the end of this article—actually 11° Aquarius, whereas at the present time it is 10½° Aquarius.[12]

Ten days prior to the miracles of the feeding of the five thousand and the walking on the water—the fourth and fifth of the seven miracles described in the Gospel of St John—Christ had healed a paralyzed man at the pool of Bethesda in Jerusalem. At this miracle—the third described in the John Gospel—which took place on January 19 in the year AD 31, the Sun was at 0½° Aquarius on the meridian of the star Sadr which, at the time of Christ, was located at 0½° Aquarius (owing to Sadr's proper motion it is now closer to 0° Aquarius).[13] Like Deneb, Sadr is in the constellation of Cygnus the Swan, also known as the Northern Cross. *Sadr* means "breast," and this star, which marks the breast of the Swan (the central star of the Northern Cross), is also a megastar, since its luminosity is estimated to be about 33,000 and that it is located at a distance of approximately 1800 light years.

From these two examples of megastars in the constellation of Cygnus the Swan, the Northern Cross, a picture emerges, as indicated by Rudolf Steiner, of Christ Jesus working "in accordance with the collective being of the whole universe" that (for humanity and the Earth) comes to expression in the starry heavens. As with Deneb, which is 60° north of the ecliptic, Sadr is also far to the north, being located 57° north of the ecliptic. This discovery shows that true astrology—the word *astrology* meaning "the science of the stars"—is a science that takes into account *the entire celestial*

---

12 *Chronicle of the Living Christ*, p. 276; see p. 171 for the horoscope of this event. The miracle of the walking on the water is described in Matthew 14:25–33. The *proper motion* of a star is the motion of that star which, over long periods of time, leads to a small shift in the star's sidereal longitude and latitude. In the case of Deneb, for example, its proper motion amounted to almost ½° from the time of Christ to the present time—having shifted from 11° Aquarius to 10°35' Aquarius (see table near the end of this article).

13 Ibid., p. 273; see p. 169 for the horoscope of this event. The healing of the paralyzed man at the pool of Bethesda is described in John 5:1–15. Also, see note in the preceding footnote regarding a star's *proper motion*.

sphere and not just the stars composing the signs of the zodiac. As we shall see, this is one aspect of a step for humankind from solar to galactic consciousness. Copernicus pioneered the step from geocentric (Earth-centered) to heliocentric (Sun-centered) astronomy, and now a next step would be from Sun-centered (heliocentric) to *Central Sun*-centered (galactic) astronomy.

Deneb, seen by the Greeks as marking the tail of the Swan, is at the head of the Northern Cross. It is remarkable to consider that the cross is the symbol of Christ, and that—in the sense of "as above, so below"—his central miracles in the John Gospel (the feeding of the five thousand and the walking on the water) were aligned via the Sun with Deneb at the head of the cross, and the miracle he performed shortly before these two (the healing of the paralyzed man at the pool of Bethesda) was aligned via the Sun with Sadr—the star marking the breast of the Swan, located at the center of the Northern Cross. Here we gain a glimpse into the mysteries of Cosmic Christianity and we can begin to understand that Christ truly was a *cosmic being* who had a relationship with the stars in the heavens—not just the stars in our cosmos, our local part of the galaxy known as the *Orion Arm*, but also with the stars beyond, in the greater galaxy, as shown in the further discussion of this research in chapter 5 of the book *The Astrological Revolution*.

Now, we are in a position to begin to evaluate the discovery discussed in this article that at the *following miracle* in the John Gospel (the sixth miracle, following the third, fourth, and fifth miracles referred to in the foregoing)—that is, at the miracle of the healing of the man-born-blind—the Sun was evidently aligned with the galactic center (*Central Sun*) itself. In order to grasp the significance of this, it is helpful at this juncture for us to devote some consideration to the *Central Sun*.

THE CENTRAL SUN: THE DIVINE HEART AT THE CENTER OF OUR GALAXY

Our Sun, and the vast number of different Suns/stars in our galaxy, have ultimately all come into existence from the galactic center at the heart of

the Milky Way galaxy.[14] In the Platonic tradition reference is made to the *Transmundane* or *Supra-Celestial Sun*[15] and our Sun is conceived of as a miniature copy of this *Transmundane* or *Supra-Celestial Sun*—here we could also say *Central Sun*, if we identify Plato's *Supra-Celestial Sun* with the galactic center.[16] Could it be that Plato, in referring to the *Transmundane Sun*, had an inkling of

---

14 New stars are born in different parts of the galaxy, yet they are offspring of stellar regions which originally were born from the galactic center, and in this sense the center of our galaxy is the ultimate source for the existence of all stars in the Milky Way galaxy. Nevertheless, it is appropriate to speak of *first generation stars* born directly from the galactic center and *second generation stars* that are born elsewhere in the Milky Way galaxy—for example, the Orion nebula is a "stellar nursery" where new stars are being born, and the four brightest "newborn" stars in this nebula, known as *The Trapezium*, each only a million or so years of age, are visible with amateur astronomers' telescopes in the "stellar nursery" of the Orion nebula. However, the birth of new stars from the galactic center does not seem to be taking place currently.

15 Reference to the *Intelligible Sun*, i.e., not the visible Sun but the Sun belonging to the intelligible world, as the source of Divine Goodness, is found in Book VI of Plato's *Republic* (509b). Immediately after, at the start of Book VII, in the famous allegory of the cave, the *Supra-Celestial Sun* is indicated to be the source of truth and intelligence, and the visible Sun, together with its light, is said to be an offspring thereof: "In the visible realm it gave birth to light and its sovereign; in the intelligible realm, itself sovereign, it provided truth and intelligence" (517b-c). Subsequently this reference recurs often in the Platonic tradition. For example, the Neoplatonist Proclus refers to the *Supermundane Sun* in his Commentary on Plato's *Timaeus*: "There is the true Solar World and the Totality of Light [where] the Sun, also being *Supermundane*, sends forth the Fountains of Light" (*The Chaldean Oracles*, p. 45).

16 The term *Central Sun* is a simplification of Plato's *Transmundane Sun* or *Supra-Celestial Sun*. The term *Central Sun*—conceptually identical with Plato's *Supra-Celestial Sun*—brings to expression its central location, i.e., its location at the center of the Milky Way galaxy. Note that Plato himself did not explicitly use the expressions *Intelligible Sun, Transmundane Sun, Supermundane Sun,* or *Supra-Celestial Sun*, but these expressions, which were used in the Platonic tradition, are implicit in Plato's work and are employed by later commentators on Plato's works when referring to the *Sun in the intelligible world* spoken of by Plato.

the heart of our galaxy, conceived of as a *Central Sun* from which, ultimately, everything in our Milky Way galaxy has proceeded?

Let us consider—along the lines of Platonic cosmology—that there is a *Central Sun* at the heart of our galaxy. However we designate what is at the galactic center, it is of immense power, as may be grasped by way of the following analogy. If one imagines the force exerted by our Sun in holding the nine planets[17] and countless asteroids and other cosmic objects in their orbits, one will get a sense of the power and majesty of our Sun. Now, if we think along the lines of Platonic cosmology of a *Central Sun* at the galactic center, the scope of its power is such as to hold more than one hundred billion Suns (not planets!), in their orbits around it, including our Sun!

To explain this immense power, modern astronomy postulates the existence of a "supermassive black hole" at the center of our galaxy. We have to bear in mind that this is a theoretical construction of modern astronomy. Moreover, from my perspective it is an inadequate theoretical explanation of what takes place at the transition point from the realm of material creation to the realm of pure spirit. The alternative perspective that is offered here is that at the galactic center there is a *Central Sun* (the *Supra-Celestial Sun* referred to in the Platonic tradition) and that all the Suns/stars in the heavens, including our Sun, are—ultimately—offspring of the *Central Sun*.

By way of analogy and in support of this alternative perspective, let us consider Rudolf Steiner's description of our Sun, and then apply this on a galactic level to the *Central Sun* at the heart of our galaxy. This is actually how one can arrive at a true concept of what is at the galactic center (rather than the current inadequate concept of a "supermassive black hole"). This true concept is offered by Steiner in at least three different lecture cycles.[18] In one of them, the *Astronomy Course*, he gives indications concerning the interior of the Sun: moving from the outside toward its center, it declines more and more in its physical-material composition to eventually become what he calls "negative, sucking matter." Hence, he says, our Sun exerts a tremendous sucking force and "then you do not need any other explanation of gravity than this, as this is already the explanation of gravity."[19] (Here he means, of course, what is conceived of as the gravity exerted by our Sun to hold all the planets and other heavenly bodies—asteroids, etc.—in their orbits around the Sun). And elsewhere he says: "I have often said that the physicist would be greatly astonished if he could travel to the Sun and find there nothing of what he now imagines, but simply a hollow space; nay, even a hollow space of suction which annihilates everything within it. A space indeed that is less than hollow. A hollow space merely receives what is put into it; but the Sun is a hollow space of such a nature that anything brought to it is immediately absorbed and disappears."[20] Here, in these words, Rudolf Steiner gives a true concept in place of that of a "black hole." This concept given by Rudolf Steiner to explain the gravitational pull exerted by our Sun can, by way of analogy, also be applied on a much vaster scale to describe the working of the *Central Sun* at the heart of our galaxy, which has been inadequately described as a "supermassive black hole." It is the "tremendous sucking force" of the *Central Sun* that holds all the billions of Suns/stars in their orbits in our Milky Way galaxy. The *Central Sun* at rest at the galactic center, around which—looking down from the north galactic pole—all the Suns/stars are moving in a clockwise direction, is evidently what Aristotle called the *Prime Mover*.[21] Everything in our galaxy is moving around this great center.

Now we are in a better position to understand what the galactic center is. When we look up to the constellation of Sagittarius, we behold—traced out

---

17 Nine planets, including Pluto, or eight planets, if Pluto is no longer considered to be a planet—see my article "Pluto and the Galactic Center": www.sophiafoundation.org/articles/.

18 See, for example, Rudolf Steiner's lecture of January 18, 1921 as part of the *Astronomy Course* (Complete Works vol. 323—not yet [2015] published in English translation).

19 Ibid.

20 Steiner, *Man: Hieroglyph of the Universe*, p. 47.

21 In his work *Metaphysics*, Book Lambda, Aristotle calls the source of all movement the *Prime Mover*, which is at rest at the center of all movement around it.

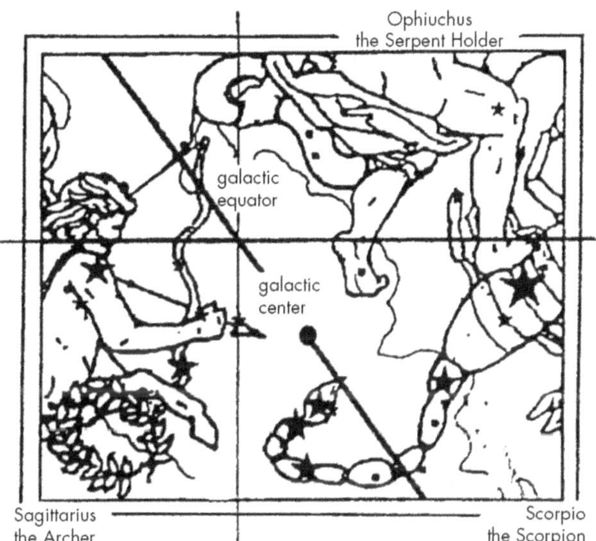

Image by, and courtesy of, Raymond Mardyks

by the pattern of the stars—the figure of an Archer who is aiming his arrow. It is an extraordinary fact—see figure—that his arrow is aimed directly at the galactic center (located at 2° Sagittarius), where an extraordinarily intensive point of infra-red light has been discovered.[22] This energy source, approximately 50 light years in diameter—called Sagittarius A*—has been identified as the actual center of our Milky Way galaxy. Located some 25,000 light years from our solar system, it is estimated that this energy source is about 500 million times more powerful than our Sun. From here emanates the power that holds our galaxy of more than 100 billion stars together. This is the *Central Sun*, if we adhere to the conception of Platonic cosmology, i.e., the *Transmundane* or *Supra-Celestial Sun* described in the Platonic tradition as the source or origin of all the Suns/stars in the cosmos.

All the stars that we see in the heavens are Suns, like our Sun. All of them, if they could be viewed looking down from the north galactic pole, would be seen to rotate slowly in a clockwise direction

Dante and Beatrice viewing the Empyrean in the form of a snow-white rose; the word Empyrean *derives from the Ancient Greek* pyr, *meaning fire, which reminds us of Daniel Andreev's expression "Astrofire" for the galactic center (illustration by Gustave Doré for Dante's* Divine Comedy: Paradiso)

around the *Central Sun*, "*Like a wheel that is evenly moved by the love that moves the Sun and the other stars.*"[23] In light of these words of Dante from his great work *The Divine Comedy*: Could it be the fire of Divine Love emanating from the *Central Sun* that supports and sustains all the Suns/stars in the heavens such that it is literally "*Love that makes the world go round*"?

To gain an idea of the immensity of the *Central Sun* at the heart of our galaxy, let us imagine a second Sun alongside our Sun. And then in our imagination let us add a third Sun, and a fourth Sun, and a fifth Sun… and so on, until there are 500 million suns there. This imaginative exercise can offer us a glimpse of the power, majesty, and glory of the *Central Sun* at the galactic center, which holds more than one hundred billion Suns/stars in their orbits around it.

---

22 The two-dimensional image of the Archer aiming his arrow at the galactic center has to be thought of in three dimensions in order to grasp that the two-dimensional perspective is really an optical illusion, since the visible stars making up the constellation of Sagittarius are relatively close to our solar system (the most distant bright stars—with some exceptions—being not more than a few thousand light years away), whereas the galactic center is located at an enormous distance of about 25,000 light years.

23 Dante, *The Divine Comedy: Paradise* 33:144–145.

*A rendering of the Milky Way Galaxy
(NASA/JPL-Caltech)*

Daniel Andreev once had a vision of the galactic center, which he called *Astrofire*, and which he describes in *The Rose of the World*, his *magnum opus*:

> I remember seeing a glowing mist of stunning majesty, as though the creative heart of our universe had revealed itself to me in visible form for the first time. It was *Astrofire*, the great center of our galaxy.[24]

Let us look back to someone who had a deep relationship with Sophia: the Italian poet Dante. In Dante's vision, which he had at Easter in the year 1300 and which he spent the rest of his life writing down as *The Divine Comedy*, he beheld the highest realm. In Dante's vision of the highest heaven he calls this highest realm the *Empyrean*, signifying a realm of fire—the fire of Divine Love. Let us now contemplate the depiction by the French graphic artist Gustav Doré of Dante's vision of the *Empyrean* (see page 33), and let us then compare this with an image of our Milky Way galaxy (see page 34). One can immediately see the similarity. It appears that what Dante beheld in mystical (inner) vision has now been found outwardly by modern astronomy—in the shape of our galaxy—seven hundred years later. Dante describes in his vision the throne of God at the center and countless beings around

the throne of God. According to Dante, the whole is fashioned in the form of "a snow-white rose."

CHRIST AND SOPHIA: THE LAMB AND HIS BRIDE

Those who know the mystical tradition will recognize that this image invoked by Dante relates on a deeper level to Sophia. In the *Litany of Loreto*, for example, the Virgin Mary is referred to as the *Mystical Rose* and this appellation clearly applies also to Sophia, by way of her association with the Virgin Mary.[25] Further, often the Virgin Mary and the Christ child are found in the central rosette of the glorious rose windows in French Gothic cathedrals, thus associating the Virgin—and, again by way of association, Sophia—with the image of the rose. It is as if the creators of the rose windows were inspired by the same archetype spoken of by Dante as the "snow-white rose." Moreover, in the mystical tradition the creation itself is seen as a rose that is unfolding or blossoming over the six days of creation— this rose being Sophia, who is the plan of the creation and is thus called *Rosa Mundi*, meaning *the Rose of the World*. In contemplating an image of our galaxy, what are we actually beholding? Are we on some level beholding an image of Sophia in the form of a snow-white rose? Is Sophia, as the wisdom or plan of creation, one and the same with what we see revealed in the structure of our galaxy? Considering that Sophia—according to her own words from chapter 8 of the *Book of Proverbs*—has always had a relationship with our evolution "from the beginning of creation," is it reasonable to conclude that Sophia is a being connected with the heart of our galaxy, the galactic center being the source or origin of the entire creation of our Milky Way galaxy?

One of the important things that Rudolf Steiner indicated was that the being whom we call Sophia is the same as the goddess whom the Egyptians called Isis.[26] We know of the great significance of Isis for the Egyptian culture and also of the sig-

---

24 Andreev, *The Rose of the World*, p. 198.

25 Schipflinger, *Sophia–Maria : A Holistic Vision of Creation*.

26 Steiner, *Isis–Mary–Sophia: Her Mission and Ours*.

nificance of Osiris. Isis and Osiris were regarded as sister and brother and also as bride and groom. If we take this idea of Rudolf Steiner and work with it, that Sophia is the same as Isis, then whom were the Egyptians referring to as Osiris? In various lectures Steiner describes that Osiris was how the Egyptian people saw Christ before his incarnation on the Earth. We could think of this as a pre-incarnatory revelation of Christ to the Egyptian people in the form of Osiris, before Christ incarnated upon the Earth. Against this background we can understand the words of St. Augustine, who indicated that there was a "Christianity before Christ."[27] And this applies not only to the Egyptians, but to other cultures as well.

> Although Christ appeared only later, he was always present in the spiritual sphere of the earth. Already in the ancient Oracles of Atlantis, the priests of those Oracles spoke of the "Spirit of the Sun," of Christ. In the old Indian epoch of civilization the Holy Rishis spoke of "Vishva Karman"; Zarathustra in ancient Persia spoke of "Ahura Mazda," Hermes [in Egypt spoke] of "Osiris"; and Moses as the harbinger of Christ spoke of the Power which, being eternal, brings about the harmonization of the temporal and natural, the Power living in the *Ehyeh asher Ehyeh* ["I AM the I AM"]. All spoke of the Christ.[28]

If we grasp this background concerning the ancient Egyptian mystery religion of Isis and Osiris, we can begin to understand that the Egyptians were indeed "Christians before Christ." Before Christ came into incarnation on the earth, they worshipped him in his pre-incarnatory form as Osiris. The Egyptians recognized that Osiris and Isis have a deep relationship to one other; they are the same beings whom we know now, in the post-Christian era, as Christ and Sophia. This is addressed in the revelation to John, the last book in the Bible, which is the revelation of the Ascended Christ to John the beloved disciple on the island of Patmos. It is clear that the one who is called the "Lamb" in *Revelations* is Christ. That is also the name that John the Baptist gave to Christ, as indicated in John's words: "Behold the Lamb of God" (*John* 1:29). In Chapter 21 of *Revelations* reference is made to the "Bride of the Lamb" who is Sophia. We may conclude that if Sophia is associated with the *Central Sun* at the heart of our galaxy, then so also is Christ, and thus the *Central Sun* is the provenance, originally, of both the Lamb and his Bride, who is called the Mystical Rose (*Rosa Mundi*), the Rose of the World. That Christ came originally from the Central Sun explains his relationship "with the collective being of the whole universe" (Rudolf Steiner), bearing in mind that at that time (1911), when Steiner spoke these words, the Milky Way galaxy was conceived of in the astronomy of that time as "the whole universe." It was only on December 30, 1924 that Hubble announced his discovery that the Andromeda nebula is in fact a vast conglomeration of distant stars, which he recognized as another galaxy at a great distance from the Milky Way galaxy.[29] Previously, nebulae, such as the Andromeda nebula, were thought to lie *within* the Milky Way galaxy. All of a sudden Hubble opened the door to a quite different astronomical view of the universe, one comprised of a number of galaxies, the Milky Way being just one of them, and thus not comprising "the whole universe."

THE *CENTRAL SUN*, PENTECOST, AND THE HEALING OF THE MAN-BORN-BLIND

The *Central Sun* is not only the provenance of the Lamb (the Son) and his Bride (Sophia), but is also the ultimate abode of the Holy Spirit—this being a discovery of astrosophy, a finding that is supported by the following astrosophical considerations. The archetypal historical manifestation of the Holy Spirit was at Pentecost, descending upon the disciples in the form of tongues of fire (*Acts* 2: 3). At the event of Pentecost the Sun was

---

27 St. Augustine: "What is known as the Christian religion existed among the ancients" (*Retractiones* I, xiii).

28 Steiner, "The Deed of Christ and the Opposing Spiritual Powers: Lucifer, Ahriman, Asuras" (Complete Works, vol. 107), lecture of March 22, 1909—words in brackets [ ] inserted by RP.

29 See www.cosmictimes.gsfc.nasa.gov/online_edition /1929Cosmic/andromeda.html.

located at 2½° Gemini.[30] The fact that at Pentecost at sunrise on May 24, AD 33 the Sun was located at 2½° Gemini signifies that the Earth—as seen from the Sun (thus diametrically *opposite* the Sun in the zodiac)—was at 2½° Sagittarius, in conjunction with the galactic center (2° Sagittarius). There was thus an alignment at Pentecost: Sun—Earth—*Central Sun*. Divine Love proceeded from the *Central Sun* in the shape of the Holy Spirit seen as tongues of fire above the heads of the disciples.[31] This emanation of Divine Love from the *Central Sun* was transmitted *directly* to the Earth at the cosmically effective moment in time of the Earth's conjunction with the galactic center on this day of the original, historical event of Pentecost.[32] This astronomical fact confirms that the ultimate abode of the Holy Spirit is indeed the *Central Sun*.[33]

The theme of fire symbolizing the Divine Love emanating from the *Central Sun* is a recurrent one. As indicated above (see Gustav Doré's illustration), Dante refers to this highest world (the galactic plane at whose center is the *Central Sun*) as the *Empyrean*, and *pyr* comes from the Greek, meaning *fire*. The *Empyrean* is thus a world of fire, the fire of Divine Love that pours forth from the *Central Sun* and sustains all existence. The source

or heart ("hearth") of this fire is the *Central Sun*, which Daniel Andreev refers to by the name *Astro-fire*, meaning *Star Fire*—the fire of Divine Love emanating from the *Central Sun* which is received, and then transmitted further, by every star in the heavens, including our "local star," the Sun. "The stars are the expression of love in the cosmic ether.... To see a star means to feel a caress that has been prompted by love.... To gaze at the stars is to become aware of the love proceeding from divine spiritual beings."[34]

Against this background concerning the *Central Sun* at the heart of our galaxy, we can begin to grasp the significance of Christ's words, "I AM the light of the world" spoken at the healing of the man-born-blind, when our Sun was aligned in conjunction with the *Central Sun*. The *Central Sun* is the "SUN behind the Sun"—not just behind *our* Sun, but behind *every Sun/star* in the Milky Way galaxy. The "light of the world" has to be understood in the sense of the Divine Light of the Godhead shining from the "SUN behind the Sun": "In purest outpoured Light shimmers the Godhead of the world"—this being the first line of Rudolf Steiner's morning meditation.[35] The *Central Sun* is the manifestation of the Divine Heart of the Creator ("Godhead") in our galaxy, and as Christ said: "I and the Father are one" (John 10:30)—*Father* being Christ's name for the Creator ("Godhead"). In other words, Christ the Lamb, as also Sophia, the Bride of the Lamb, are eternally born directly from the Divine Heart, the *Central Sun*, and it is in this sense that Christ is truly "the light of the world." Further, it is in this sense that we can grasp what is meant by speaking of the *Central Sun* as the *provenance*—source of origin—of both Christ and Sophia. The extraordinary significance of the healing of the man-born-blind—assuming that this Christ event truly did take place on the date (November 23 AD 31) indicated earlier in this article—is that the *Central Sun*, the "SUN behind the Sun," was actually physically placed behind our Sun, when Christ performed this miracle and spoke the words: "I

---

30 Powell, *Chronicle of the Living Christ*, p. 178.

31 At the same time an emanation from Sophia, who at that time was still united with the *Central Sun*, passed into the Virgin Mary, who was present at Pentecost amidst the twelve disciples who became the twelve apostles at this event; see Tomberg, *Christ and Sophia*, chapter 12 ("Pentecost") of the *Studies on the New Testament* in this volume.

32 Normally what streams out from the *Central Sun* is received by our Sun and is "stepped down" in the process of being transmitted to the Earth. Christ, having descended from the *Central Sun*, prepared the disciples to receive *directly* from the *Central Sun* at Pentecost. The alignment: Sun—Earth—*Central Sun* is repeated each year in our time on June 17 or June 18, when the Sun returns to 2° Gemini in the sidereal zodiac. The cosmic memory of the Pentecost event takes place some twelve hours after this exact alignment, when the Sun reaches 2½° Gemini.

33 This localization of the ultimate abode of the Holy Spirit to the *Central Sun* in no ways limits the omnipresence of the Holy Spirit but simply points to the ultimate source from which the Holy Spirit proceeds.

34 Steiner, *Karmic Relationships: Esoteric Studies*, vol. 7, lecture of June 8, 1924.

35 Steiner, *Guidance in Esoteric Training*.

AM the light of the world." The alignment at this miracle was: Earth—Sun—*Central Sun*, whereas at Pentecost it was: Sun—Earth—*Central Sun*. At the first alignment (healing of the man-born-blind) it was more the Divine Light aspect of the Godhead that came to the fore, and at the second (Pentecost) it was more the outpouring of Divine Love from the Godhead, manifesting as the tongues of fire upon the heads of the disciples, that was emphasized.

In our time, each year the Sun returns to align with the Central Sun (2° Sagittarius) on December 18 or December 19. This is perhaps the most important alignment of our Sun in the whole cycle of the year, aligning not simply with one or the other megastar, but with the Divine Heart at the center of the Milky Way galaxy that continually pours out Divine Light, Divine Love, Divine Life—sustaining every star (i.e., every Sun, including our Sun) in the galaxy. In the life of Christ, according to the new research presented here in this article, it was at the alignment of our Sun with the *Central Sun* that the sixth miracle in the John Gospel, the healing of the man-born-blind, was fulfilled, when Christ spoke the words: "I AM the light of the world." This miracle, although performed for one human being, serves as an archetype for every human being, in the sense that anyone who is not a true clairvoyant (such as Rudolf Steiner was) is "born blind" and is in need of healing in order to be able to behold the fullness of spiritual reality, as Rudolf Steiner did. As indicated in my book *Cultivating Inner Radiance and the Body of Immortality*, which describes a path to experience of Christ in supersensible form in his body of life forces (etheric body), the words "I AM the light of the world" are the Christ mantra for opening the "third eye" in the region of the brow, this being the organ of true seership or clairvoyance.[36]

Thus, what better time of year than on the day of the Sun's alignment with the Central Sun, recalling the healing of the man-born-blind and Christ's speaking of the words, "I AM the light of the world," to live into this Christ mantra, with the intention that with the help of Christ we may no longer be "born blind" but may truly see.

Similarly, the most appropriate day of the year for living into the healing significance—that is, communion with Christ—of the feeding of the five thousand for the heart chakra and Christ's speaking of the mantra "I AM the bread of life" for the heart chakra is February 23 or February 24, when the Sun is transiting the Deneb meridian at 10½° Aquarius. And so it is, also, with the other healing miracles and I AM sayings of Christ as indicated in the table on page 38.

APPENDIX REGARDING THE MAN-BORN-BLIND

The name of the man-born-blind was Celidonius or Chelitonius, sometimes referred to as Cedonius or Sidonius, although there are at least two later saints who bore the name Sidonius. In this connection, here with an important reference stemming from the thirteenth century collection *The Golden Legend*:

> Now that the disciples were scattered, it took place that Saint Maximin, Mary Magdalene, her brother Lazarus, her sister Martha together with her true maidservant Marcella, and the blessed Cedonius, who was born blind but healed by the Lord...were put on board a boat without a rudder and were pushed out to sea, so that they would all sink. However, through the providence of God it transpired that they came to the region of Massilia [present-day Marseille].[37]

---

36 Powell, *Cultivating Inner Radiance and the Body of Immortality*, pp. 44–47. Here the seven I AM sayings of the Gospel of St John are described as the seven Christ mantras for bringing Christ's Light into the seven chakras—in this case "I AM the light of the world" as the sixth I AM saying being the Christ mantra for the sixth chakra, the "third eye." Also the relationship of Christ's seven healing miracles to the seven chakras is described—in this case the healing of the man-born-blind, as the sixth healing miracle of the John Gospel, being the archetypal healing, applying to every human being, of the "third eye" chakra.

37 *Legenda aurea* ("The Golden Legend"), compiled in the thirteenth century by the bishop of Genoa, Jacobus de Voragine, tr. William Caxton, ed. F. S. Ellis (London: Temple Classics, 1900). Reproduced in Medieval Sourcebook, Fordham University: www.fordham.edu/halsall/basis/goldenlegend—vol. 4, p. 40.

Chakra and I AM saying	Miracle of Christ	Historical date and time of miracle	Sun's sidereal longitude at miracle	Sun at miracle conjunct megastar	Current sidereal longitude of star	Current date when sun is conjunct megastar
Root — I AM the true vine	Changing water into wine at the wedding at Cana	Dec. 28 AD 29, approx. noon	8°19' Capricorn	8°18' Capricorn HIP 99457 in Capricorn L= 2,700,000*	8°17' Capricorn	Jan. 23/24
Sacral — I AM the way, the truth, and the life	Healing of the noble-man's son	Aug. 3 AD 30, 1 p.m.	10°37' Leo	11°38' Leo Rho Leonis in Leo L=295,000	11°39' Leo	Aug. 29/30
Solar Plexus — I AM the door, the entrance and the exit	Healing of the paralyzed man at the pool of Bethesda	Jan. 19 AD 31, approx. 6 p.m.	0°36' Aquarius	0°26' Aquarius Sadr in Cygnus L=33,000	0°06' Aquarius	Feb. 13/14
Heart — I AM the bread of life	Feeding of the five thousand	29 January AD 31, 4 p.m. to 6 p.m.	10°37' Aquarius	11°00' Aquarius Deneb in Cygnus L=200,000	10°35' Aquarius	Feb. 23/24
Throat — I AM the good shepherd	Walking on the water	Jan. 29/30 AD 31, evening	10°55' Aquarius	11°00' Aquarius Deneb in Cygnus L=200,000	10°35' Aquarius	Feb. 23/24
Third Eye — I AM the light of the world	Healing of the man-born-blind	Nov. 23 AD 31, approx. 6 p.m.	2°20' Sagittarius	2°06' Sagittarius Central Sun in Sagittarius L=500 million**	2°06' Sagittarius	Dec. 18/19
Crown — I AM the resurrection and the life	Raising of Lazarus	Jul. 26 AD 32, approx. 6 a.m.	3°04' Leo	3°08' Leo Eta Leonis in Leo L=19,000	3°10' Leo	Aug. 20/21

* The extremely high luminosity of this star (L=2,700,000) is given in the Hipparchos catalog. It has not been possible to confirm the high luminosity of this blue giant variable star in any other source, since no other source consulted gives this star's luminosity. Apart from this star and the *Central Sun*, all stellar luminosity indications are given by the Wikipedia articles on each of these stars. In general, however, the luminosity indications are very approximate, since they depend upon parameters that are sometimes difficult to determine reliably.

** This estimated luminosity of the Central Sun is of a speculative nature.

Here, now, with an account based on Anne Catherine Emmerich's description:

After the events of the Resurrection and the Ascension Mary Magdalene withdrew to live the life of a hermit in the desert, rather like John the Baptist had done before he began to baptize people in the River Jordan. However, when she was visiting her brother and sister in Bethany, about three years after Pentecost, because a persecution of Christians by the Jews had started, she was arrested. On this occasion Lazarus, Martha, and Mary Magdalene were all taken into custody, as well as the sisters' maidservants, Marcella and Sara, and two other people who were visiting Lazarus at the time: one of the seventy-two disciples, named Maximin, and the man who had been born blind and was healed by Jesus, Chelitonius, also sometimes known as Sidonius. These seven were taken to the Mediterranean coast, somewhere close to present-day Tel Aviv. They were put into a little boat, towed out far into the sea, and cut loose. The idea was that they would perish, but that did not happen. Through divine providence, this little boat made it across the Mediterranean so that the family with the servants and companions came ashore at a place in the South of France now called St Maries-de-la-Mer.[38]

Finally, let us consider the description offered by a modern highly-gifted seeress in the tradition of Anne Catherine Emmerich, Estelle Isaacson, from her three-volume work *Through the Eyes of Mary Magdalene*:

Magdalene and her fellow prisoners in Jerusalem—Lazarus, Martha, Sarah, Marcella, Maximin, and Celidonius—were standing together on the shore of the Mediterranean Sea. Their hands were bound and they were blindfolded. Soldiers and other officials surrounded them as ominous clouds and boisterous winds gave notice of an oncoming storm.... Next to a pier a small rudderless boat was anchored. No oars were to be seen, no tools, no provisions of any kind. Still blindfolded and bound, the group

was pressed by soldiers into the boat, which was then set loose into the bay. The small craft was lashed to a larger boat, similar to a fishing boat, which carried many oars and sails. Two soldiers had boarded the small boat with the captives, and many others were to be seen on the larger one. For several hours those in the larger vessel rowed with great vigor out to sea, until they were far enough from shore to suite their purpose. At this point the two soldiers in the small boat heaved themselves over the side and swam to the ship. After this the rope binding the boats was cut. Thus were the bound captives abandoned to the sea in a precarious vessel lacking any means of navigation, as the ship that had consigned them to this fate came about and made for land....

Sarah, emaciated and weak, lay her head in Magdalene's lap and listened to the soothing tones of her consoling words. All were still bound, but now that they were on their own, each was struggling to work free. Celidonius was first to do so, and then unbound the others.... Upon their journey the seven suffered all manner of afflictions from the winds and the Sun: their skin erupted in sores, and their lips cracked for want of water. But throughout they were graced to transcend their mortal bodies, to dwell in profound accord with one another, living together a higher life in a place of pure light. The "matter" of their souls became more refined. They came to know the Silence in a more elevated way, and the Word was with them....

Their passage was by no means what might be expected in such circumstances, rudderless and without oars, lacking provisions of any kind! This journey had a *purpose*, and the winds knew it. The waves knew it. The creatures of the sea knew it. They traveled by the light of the angels and arrived at the very place God desired them to go. And so were they delivered to the southern shores of Gaul (now known as France) in a miraculous way, sustained by Christ, who was ever in spiritual communion with them—and also by the power of the communion of fishes.

When at last the small company disembarked upon the Gallic shore, they fell to the ground rejoicing. Their oneness in Christ, joined to the light of their transcendent journey,

---

38 Powell, *The Mystery, Biography, and Destiny of Mary Magdalene* (Gr. Barrington, MA: Lindisfarne Books, 2008), p. 12.

would in time bless the people who lived there. They prayed together and consecrated this foreign land, that it might be for them a Promised Land—a land of milk and honey, in like manner as their forefathers had found their Promised Land through angelic guidance. At that time, they did not know that they would indeed *be* milk and honey to the people of Gaul.[39]

As can be seen, Estelle Isaacson's account is much more comprehensive than that of Anne Catherine Emmerich or that found in *The Golden Legend*—bearing in mind that several pages of description have been omitted from the above quote. What Estelle Isaacson offers is a detailed description of the dramatic journey across the Mediterranean Sea of the seven and how they survived with the help of the communion with fishes. It is to be noted that she refers to the name of the man-born-blind as Celidonius, whereas Anne Catherine Emmerich speaks of Chelitonius. Estelle Isaacson describes, further, that shortly after the group of seven landed in Gaul, they managed to come by bread and wine—or, rather, grape juice—so that the Holy Eucharist could be celebrated by the group, with Lazarus officiating. After this sacred celebration, Celidonius was the first to speak. He spoke in the language of poetry:

> First to break the silence was Celidonius, who spoke poetry as the spirit touched his heart:
>
> *The Lord hath opened mine eyes.*
> *Yea, not the outer only,*
> *But those within—even my heart:*
> *Horizoned miracle of sight;*
> *Deep-breasted wonder of love!*
>
> *I was blind in eye and heart,*
> *For, eye-dark and heart-veiled,*
> *How could I love?*
> *Then He touched my eyes and gave them light.*
> *But more—He gave His very sight!*

> *In vision, through His own eyes,*
> *Did all His Love I see!*
> *Myriad love-drenched wonders*
> *Clear-glowing all for me.*
>
> *But see! What miracle!*
> *As saw He through human eyes,*
> *So also did I see.*
> *And seeing thus, did gently feel*
> *How 'twas Christ to be,*
> *Who all life's forms full-true beheld*
> *In like wise as do we.*
>
> *This Love-Gift so my soul did fill,*
> *I prayed the Lord help bear it,*
> *That the wine-skin of my soul burst not,*
> *And in this Love I perish!*
>
> *When I was blind, in shadows lost,*
> *Doomed never more to see,*
> *Love I could not offer, nor take it unto me.*
> *Now, knowing Love, I see through Love,*
> *Full clear and bright as day.*
>
> *For if we in truth Christ's Body be*
> *Of His eyes am I not a ray?*
> *Schooled by His loving gaze?*
> *And by it close embraced?*

With these words, Celidonius looked into the eyes of each of his companions, and it was as if Christ himself were beholding them.[40]

In conclusion, Rudolf Steiner indicated a great mystery connected with the healing of the man-born-blind:

> When the writer of the Gospel of St. John speaks of the healing of the man born blind, he is then speaking out of the depths of the Mysteries, he is demonstrating, by means of an example, that the force of the Christ is a healing force when it appears in full power. It may be asked: Where is this force? It is in the body of the Christ, in the Earth! But this Earth must, in truth, be fully permeated by the being of the Christ Spirit or of the Logos.[41]

---

39 Isaacson, *Through the Eyes of Mary Magdalene, vol. 3: From the Ascension to Journeys in Gaul,* pp. 127–130. For an excellent overview of and introduction to the visionary Estelle Isaacson, see the Foreword to this work by publisher James Richard Wetmore.

40 Ibid., pp. 134–135.
41 Steiner, *The Gospel of St. John,* lecture 7.

CELIDONIUS: THE MAN-BORN-BLIND

Estelle Isaacson

Before he had been healed, Celidonius—the man who was born blind [John 9]—had strongly developed his other senses. As is often the case with the blind, his hearing, touch, and taste were much more acute than in those with sight.

Yes, Jesus had given Celidonius the gift of sight, but along with this miracle had given him also the power of a new, inner sight.

Over the past three years, Celidonius's gift of spiritual vision had been increasing. Initially he had been aware only of faint images—flashes of knowing that seemed to come without rhyme or reason—but the gift had now awakened to such a degree that he could "see" at will.

On the night of Jesus's death, Celidonius had been forced to go into hiding, and so was unable to be physically present with the Master—yet was he able now to witness the Crucifixion in spirit.

Celidonius was much sought after by the authorities because he was living proof of Jesus's miraculous powers. And more than this, he had become quite vocal, proclaiming to all who would listen, "the Son of God touched my eyes and restored my sight!"

Some who heard his story, however, were not disciples of Jesus. And later, when Jesus was condemned to death, the "man born blind" would be betrayed by both family and friends.

This is why he had gone into hiding.

On the evening of Jesus's death, in a small cave hidden from the authorities, Celidonius had wept in devastation, for he knew the Son of God was hanging on the cross. In his anguish he rent his clothes and threw dust and ashes over himself, wishing he were again blind—both inwardly and outwardly—so that he might not know such horrors!

In the agony of feeling the Lord's suffering in his own heart, he cried out to God.

Just when he felt he must die of grief, Celidonius was taken into vision and beheld Jerusalem stricken with a terrible plague. Swarms of black hornets descended upon the streets, dividing the city in two—evil to one side, good on the other.

The plague attacked the evil ones, and cries of anguish pierced the gloom.

Then he saw the good rise up triumphant, encircled with light.

These were the disciples of Christ. Each held a small book all of light. These disciples, or emissaries, walked out through the gates of Jerusalem and on to other cities and towns, spreading further the Word they held in their hands.

He knew he himself was one of the emissaries of light, and so it was with horror that he watched as many of the disciples were imprisoned, tortured, and killed.

In vision he was shown a cave where he could hide when the danger became too great, and he found and entered the cave.

It was as if he were with Jesus's body in the tomb, mourning his death, when suddenly an angel appeared to him, saying: This is the body of Christ, who suffered all things for the children of men. Behold him in death and know that even as he has died, so shall he rise again!

And he kept the angel's words close in his heart.

When finally the vision ended, Celidonius slept, and next morning awoke to the first shafts of sunlight stealing into the cave. Again Celidonius entered into vision, but this time not so much a seeing vision as a knowing vision.

Abundant rays of rainbow-colored light poured into his heart with such intensity that it opened like a rose, drinking in the light and expanding in the love, taken into the ecstasy of knowing the Divine.

He recognized the Risen One, for he was already familiar with his special light—the same light that had healed his eyes.

As the vision drew to a close, he was given a book of light, which was as though living in his heart. Upon its pages he could make out a spiritual text: Christ's words, beautiful redeeming words, words that would lead others out of spiritual blindness and into the light.

Filled with joy immeasurable and elation most profound, he rose from his bed vowing to seek out any who might give him audience. Many did come to hear him read from the book of light, and their eyes were opened; and these in turn brought others to hear him.[1]

------

1 Isaacson, *Through the Eyes of Mary Magdalene, Vol 3: From the Ascension to Journeys in Gaul,* pp. 117–119 and 134–135.

O Spirit of God…
Fill the hearts that seek Thee,
Seek Thee in deep longing,
Deep longing for health
For health and strong courage,
Strong courage that flows
within our limbs,
Flows as a precious divine gift,
Divine gift from Thee,
O Spirit of God.

—RUDOLF STEINER

THE STAR OF LAZARUS:
A READING OF THE STARRY SCRIPT

Estelle Isaacson

 This article focuses upon the star Eta Leonis (3° Leo), with which the Sun was exactly aligned at the raising of Lazarus from the dead. Looking up at the constellation of Leo, Eta Leonis can be easily overlooked, as it is so close to the much brighter (apparently brighter) star Regulus (5° Leo) marking the heart of the Lion. The apparent magnitude of the Regulus star system is 1.35—i.e., Regulus is a first-magnitude star, only 79 light years away, 140 times more luminous than our Sun, whereas the apparent magnitude of Eta Leonis, also known as Al Jabhah, is 3.51 (fourth magnitude), and is at a distance of some 2,000 light years. In terms of intrinsic brightness (luminosity), however, Al Jabhah has a luminosity of more than 13,000, and is thus a megastar (luminosity greater than 10,000) as defined by Robert Powell and Kevin Dann, *The Astrological Revolution*, chapter 5. There, it is shown that at all the great miracles of Christ reported in the Gospel of John, the Sun was aligned with a megastar. At the raising of Lazarus the Sun was aligned with the megastar Al Jabhah (Eta Leonis), and the Moon (it was New Moon, with the Sun and the Moon close together) was aligned with Regulus. (Robert Powell)

*O*ut of the womb of silence shall the Word be born: a reading from the starry script pertaining to the Moon's recent position of *alignment with Eta Leonis*, the star with which the Sun was aligned at the raising of Lazarus from the dead. The February Full Moon in the year 2015 took place on February 3 and on the following day, February 4, the almost-Full Moon was aligned with Eta Leonis—the star *directly above Regulus* in the depiction below of the constellation of Leo.

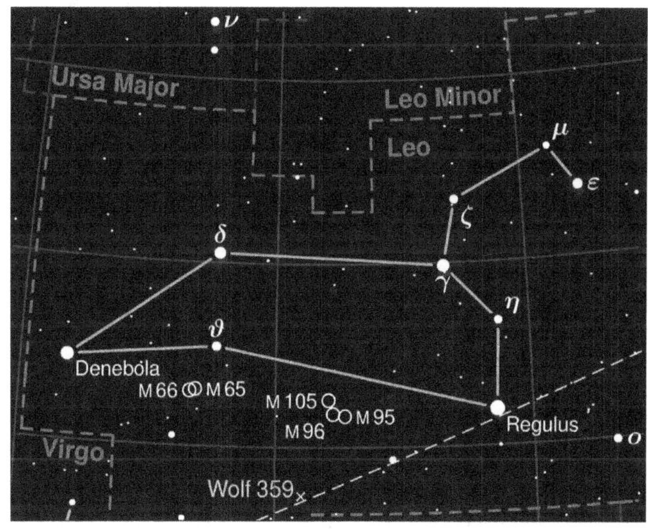

The alignment of the almost-Full Moon on February 4, 2015, with the star Eta Leonis remembers the death and raising of Lazarus, as do also those other planets and heavenly bodies which were in aspect to the Moon at this position. The Moon in conjunction with the star Eta Leonis recalls the Sun's position at the death and raising of Lazarus. Truly, by contemplating this cosmic configuration one is able to receive the light of Lazarus's being. At the historical event of the raising of Lazarus on

July 26 AD 32, it was almost exactly New Moon, since the Sun was in conjunction with Eta Leonis at 3° Leo and the Moon was just two degrees from the Sun in conjunction with Regulus at 5° Leo. In contrast to the New Moon at the historical event of the raising of Lazarus, on this occasion in February 2015 the Moon was almost full. This means that the light of the Sun was streaming to the Moon, which was illuminating this most important event as the greatest miracle Christ Jesus performed during his life.

Reading the starry script of this configuration of the almost-Full Moon in conjunction with Eta Leonis (the "Lazarus star") on February 4, 2015, what is the message Lazarus has for us in our time?

What has been written in the stars shall never pass away, just as the Word shall never pass away—the Word that is the Logos, Christ, who is our brother. What he has spoken and will speak in the future—what he has created and will create by the power of the Word—shall not pass away. *Therefore is the starry script eternal.* It cannot be read in a linear way, for it is the Word in an eternal round. But for the sake of bringing a portion of this script forth for human understanding it is spoken in a linear way. Yet to be fully received it must be taken in through meditation, so that its fullness may come to rest within as angelically-inspired thought.

As one contemplates the Moon's journey through the zodiacal constellations, one experiences the waxing and waning of the light of the Moon. There are times and seasons as the Moon waxes and wanes. When the Moon waxes to its fullness in a constellation, something powerful can issue from the beings radiating through the stars of that constellation, and this can have a great effect on human life, especially for those who are able to meet what the Moon is illuminating—just as the almost-Full Moon illuminated for us in February 2015 the death and raising of Lazarus. This gives us the opportunity to work upon the concern of death in our lives and the question of resurrection.

The Moon is connected with the human feeling life, with the shadow aspect of the soul, and with the will.

When we consider death, we are confronted with the power of Ahriman. Originally the "evil force" was simply darkness. There was darkness and there was light. And at the very beginning of the darkness, the light—and all beings who were of the light, who *were* light—knew to surround the darkness, to merge with it, to return it to light. But the darkness became more and more separated and took on a will of its own. Throughout time and through the process of evolution this darkness showed in various forms; one form that emerged was *death.* Thereafter, certain high beings were sent from time to time to our world to turn the tide of evolution, working upon consciousness in such a way as to protect human beings from succumbing forever to death. They taught us also how to approach the darkness. Such was the work of these high beings—whom we call Manus—who were not human beings.

The Manus oversee cycles of evolution. Thus, there was a Manu who oversaw the Lemurian Age, who was followed by a Manu who oversaw the Atlantean Age, who in turn was followed by another Manu—the one who oversees the present post-Atlantean Age comprising seven cultural epochs. The present Manu will be succeeded by yet another Manu—for the first time in the evolution of the Earth this next Manu will be a human being—who will oversee the subsequent cycle of seven cultural epochs.

This very high being, the next Manu, incarnated as a human being at the time of Christ. He was a high and noble one, whose central mission and purpose was to *enter into the realm of death* and be then raised therefrom by Christ. Not much is known of him in the world, but he is one of the most important figures appearing in the life of Christ, for he works in the mystery of death and resurrection. To be raised from death and restored to the body, the soul must face the angel of death and win itself from the darkness, *willing* itself back to the light of life.

Upon his death, the one of whom I speak—the son of the widow of Nain (Luke 7:11-17)—found himself engaged in the conflict between darkness and light. The great miracle that followed was accomplished, not through the power of Christ's will *only*, nor through the grief and yearning of his mother and others who knew him—no, this great miracle had to be accomplished by the power of *his own will* in union with Christ's will. Having won for himself his own soul, *he stood in absolute freedom*, and so was himself able to make the decision to take up his body again. Thus it was that he came to be restored by the breath of the Holy Spirit, which in its fullness can breathe only into those who are truly free. And freedom is only gained through love. Because *his love for the darkness was equal to his love for the light,* the youth of Nain was truly free.

Having passed through this profound experience—the experience of death and of returning to life after being raised from the dead—this individual later reincarnated in the third century as the great prophet Mani, the founder of Manichaeism. His life as Mani is emblematic of the life of all souls. He was the slave of a benevolent woman who was inspired to purchase for him his freedom, after which he went on to found a spiritual stream having as its goal the transformation of evil. Like Mani, we are all striving to be truly free so that we can live out our life's purpose. Although this stream that Mani founded is scarcely known to our world today, it has flowed on and evolved through the centuries. It is through this stream (and through the work of those who serve it) that the means whereby darkness is to be transformed shall be made known—and that in due course darkness shall be overcome.

Think of the beautiful almost-Full Moon illuminating us in February 2015 as it stood in alignment with Eta Leonis, the star of the raising of Lazarus. This light was of the Sun, reflected to us. But let us consider also that the side of the Moon facing Eta Leonis was its dark side, so that in truth the light of the star Eta Leonis was shining toward the dark side of the Moon. Our shadow side—the part of us that is "dead," or suffering death in some way or other—was symbolically turned to receive the light of Lazarus. As we contemplate our own shadowy depths, we also may receive the inspiration and guidance of Lazarus, who understands the descent of the soul. If you would be truly free

of the death-bringing constriction of Ahriman's chains, you must first win from him your soul—and this you can do only through the power of love.

The Son promises resurrection. Since his resurrection two thousand years ago, now—from the standpoint of divine-spiritual evolution—there exists the promise for every human being eventually to be resurrected. All have the gift of free agency, a gift won for all human beings by the Son himself when he prevailed over the dark forces that would otherwise have forever bound humanity to the earthly realm. The Son of the Father won for all human beings the power to choose between darkness and light, so that all might take charge of their own mortal probation. This is the glory of God: that through the power of free will human beings may participate in the work of creation and fulfill the goal of evolution, which is to follow in the footsteps of the Son and one day attain resurrection.

All that is indicated here, drawn from this present-day reading of the starry script, belongs to the domain of what could be called *sacred magic*. Let us continue to read the starry script further.

Opposite the almost-Full Moon was Venus, the planet of love, in Aquarius. Venus was holding the space of love for this particular time, for spiritual community. But as this time points further to the *future* of humanity, Venus was saying also: "Yes, even as did Lazarus and the widow's son, the youth of Nain, so also may you face the darkness, and through love rise anew!" As you allow your gaze to rest upon this configuration, the hierarchical beings present and radiating through it become aware of your own God-authored destiny. And they will assist you, so that out of free will you may choose to transform darkness by the power of love.

Mani was filled with the Holy Spirit. So filled was he with the Holy Spirit, that he could work in a light-filled way, in the sense of sacred magic. *He was indwelled by the Holy Spirit,* and it is the Holy Spirit that enlightens human beings and dispels darkness. Seek then for the Holy Spirit to guide and direct you, to enlighten you. Breathe with the breath of the Holy Spirit. Breathe the seven breaths that brought Lazarus forth from the grave, restored his body, and dispelled the seven evils. To be truly free, one must overcome the seven evils within. And by the Holy Spirit one may do this, breathe the holy breath of the Spirit in each of the chakras, invoking the Holy Spirit to cleanse them.

At the close of this vision relating to the starry heavens, this reading of the starry script, which took place on February 7, 2015, I experienced the presence of Lazarus. I felt his gratitude and heard him speak these words: "Be therefore like little children, who are innocent. Love all, and forgive all. The little children shall bless the world. They shall carry the spirit of love and quicken it for the world. Be as little children, who do not judge, but behold all with loving gaze. Make room in your heart, such that the Holy Spirit may abide there. Then will the Christ child be born within innocence, childlike faith, and compassion, which are three gifts of the Christ child."

Those who find the star of the raising of Lazarus may have a relationship with this star in the constellation of Leo.[1] Know this star, and you shall know Lazarus on a deeper level. This may come to pass through Christ and Sophia, the Lamb and his Bride. In this way shall your destiny come to meet the destiny of Lazarus. For what is written of the destiny of this great individuality in the starry script then becomes imprinted within your own starry script also.

∾

---

1 The star Eta Leonis, a white supergiant, with which the Sun was in conjunction at 3° Leo at the time of the raising of Lazarus from the dead on July 26 AD 32, is estimated by the Hipparcos satellite to be some two thousand light years away and to be about 15,000 times more luminous than our Sun. In the Arab astronomical tradition Eta Leonis in the constellation of the Lion is called Al Jabhah, meaning "the Forehead."

"If you lift your arm and point upward, you have up there the realm of particular Thrones, Cherubim, and Seraphim. If you move and again point upward, you would find other Thrones, Cherubim, and Seraphim above you.... Suppose you wanted to point to some particular Thrones, Cherubim, and Seraphim. They are by no means identical, like a group of twelve similar soldiers, for instance. They differ considerably from one another. Each bears its individual stamp, so that as one looks upward from various points, one sees quite separate beings. In order to locate particular Thrones, Cherubim, and Seraphim, one denotes them by a particular constellation. It is like a signpost. In that direction over there are the Thrones, Cherubim, and Seraphim known as the Twins, over there, the Lion, and so on. The constellations of the zodiac are more than mere signposts.... It is important to realize that, when we refer to the zodiac, we are speaking of spiritual beings."

—**Rudolf Steiner**, *Spiritual Hierarchies and the Physical World*, April 17, 1909

THE TOWERS WE BUILD:
THE URANIAN DOUBLE BIND

Claudia McLaren Lainson

What are towers? We may see them as the scaffolding the ego must build in order to survive in the material world. What happens to the towers we build? They fall. History is filled with the tragedy of fallen empires.

We have to build towers. If the towers have enough windows, the light can still find us. Towers without windows, or with too few windows, are the buildings of vampires. Vampires are our new heroes and heroines. They feed on us, but only with apparent remorse; and so we sympathize with them; we even admire them. Our teens are ravenously filling their souls with their stories. They are our beloved new protagonists. There are other vampires—some of whom live on Wall Street. There are also the Google vampires, the social media vampires, the Hollywood vampires, and so on. They're everywhere. These vampires of the 21st century are very appealing. We take them everywhere we go. There are also the vampires we bring from our previous incarnations. These affect our lives mightily. In Buddhism they constitute what is called the *linga sharira*. The linga sharira is a vehicle of consciousness that is propelled by past-life tendencies. Linga can be translated as "characteristic mark" or "impermanence"—and the term sharira as "form" or "mold." These are the ghosts we drag from one incarnation into the next. Some are very aged, others quite young, and still others are only now forming. They feed on us, but this is not a problem. Not wanting to wake up to them is the problem.

There are times when, despite the comfort of our illusory realities, a lightning bolt strikes out of nowhere—and what we thought could not fail…fails. Our towers fall. Sometimes the lightning bolt is an illness, or an accident. But there are times when the lightning bolt is a collective event, coming out of nowhere, destroying the indestructible. A lightning bolt occurred on September 11, 2001. The towers literally fell. The lightning bolt is not always destructive; it can be a strike as sharp as a razor's edge that can illumine us immediately. Such was the case with St. Paul at the gates of Damascus, to cite a momentous example, and also for Brunetto Latini.

Brunetto Latini (1210–1294) from Italy was the friend and teacher of Dante (author of *The Divine Comedy*). He was sent as ambassador to the ruler of Castile (Spain). It is reported that Latini was struck by a kind of "sunstroke" while returning to Italy. Steiner noted that this was actually caused on a spiritual level by the mighty spiritual emanations issuing from the magnificent Cathedral of Chartres, where a schooling was taking place where a number of great Platonic teachers of that time were then instructing—the School of Chartres. These teachers were remarkably adept in their ability to receive higher revelation.

Brunetto Latini's initiation began through his encounter with Natura, an actual being sometimes referred to as the Goddess Mother. Natura became his guide. He perceived Her through his Imaginative cognition. Latini's "sunstroke" can be imagined as the temporary annihilation of ordinary intelligence by the brilliance of wisdom—a lightning bolt. Upon recovering, Latini knew certain aspects of esoteric wisdom, such as that concerning the seven planetary intelligences (the "spiritual hierarchies"), and he then instructed Dante on all he had experienced. Dante received this inspiration concerning the planetary intelligences and infused this into his great work, *The Divine Comedy: La Divina Commedia.* What we read in La Divina Commedia offers a true expression of what Bruno Latini experienced through his initiation ("sunstroke"). Latini was led through his inner striving to soul realms lying ever deeper within human nature. Initially, he attained access to his energy body of life forces; from there he consciously entered into the physical nature of the senses, and thence progressed into the outer world of the four elements: Fire, Air, Water, Earth. He then arose into the spheres of the seven planetary realms. Lastly, beyond the highest of the planetary realms, he entered the ocean of forces at rest—and stood before the highest beings: those who dwell within the twelve constellations of the Zodiac, through whom he encountered what Dante called the Empyrean— at the center of which is the "Throne of God," referred to also in the Book of Revelation. Latini, Dante, and St. Paul are wonderful examples of the Uranian lightning bolt that can propel the striving person into initiatory experiences.[1] We shall return to the significance of the lightning bolt of Uranus later.

During the thirteenth century, scientific abstractions had not yet completely tethered the human spirit to the rock of materialism. The Imaginal woman who appeared to Latini may sound like nonsense to us, for we have long been locked out of higher realms of cognition. It is Uranus that can awaken Imaginations as living form—realities that lie beyond the normal world of sense existence. Such worlds may nowadays seem impossible—but this will change. We will in the future remember these higher planes and the beings that live within them. We too will

become able to delve into our inner soul nature and explore all in us that, for now, lives in our unconscious; this was the path of the Buddha. And we will also learn how to rise into planetary and zodiacal spheres; this was the path of Zarathustra.

The shadow force of ignorance that we drag through our various incarnations, the linga sharira, is like unto original sin. It would be helpful to rephrase "sin" into "error"—as sin means "to miss the mark" and error is a "missing of the mark of truth." Freedom brought us the independence that gave us choice. We were free to miss the mark. We are indeed grateful for the gift of freedom and must now learn how to use it more wisely. The development of freedom began at the time of the event that is referred to in the Bible as "the Fall," which also brought the three primal curses: toil, suffering, and death. When we fell from our etheric Paradise, we lost our vertical connection with God, thereby becoming ever more familiar with the horizontal world in which the serpent who tempted Eve continues to reign— "Eve" denoting the human soul. Like Cain we became wanderers and fugitives upon the Earth.

It was at the time of the Fall when for human beings the cycle of incarnations upon the Earth in a physical body began. In the course of these incarnations, freedom has developed gradually and is now taken for granted. Freedom allows us freedom of choice and thus permits also the possibility of error—that is, we can make decisions that have negative consequences for our lives. A further aspect of the development of freedom is that there are spiritual beings who are actively seeking to lead us astray and do so through the principle of temptation. We are thus confronted with trials of temptation—the archetype being the three temptations in the wilderness with which Christ Jesus was confronted near the start of his ministry on Earth. We gain strength for the overcoming of all temptation from Christ's example of his overcoming of the three temptations in the wilderness. Nevertheless, at the present point in time, owing to a variety of circumstances, humanity has reached a crossroads where the

---

1 Brunetto Latini was aligned with the Guelphs, and it is interesting to note that in 1260, when the Florentine Guelphs were defeated by the Ghibellines, Uranus was transiting its position at the birth of the Nathan Jesus for the fifteenth time. This was the time when Brunetto Latini had his spiritual awakening. On the other hand, Dante, writer of *The Divine Comedy,* whose friend and mentor was Brunetto Latini was aligned with the Ghibelline party.

intensity of the trials we are now encountering are almost overwhelming in scope.[2]

Everywhere we look we see the tyranny of propaganda, the disintegration of the human psyche, and experience the almost perceptible stench of "slinking" underworld forces stealthily winning over ever more souls to negative—even destructive—paths of destiny. We are facing the ultimate trial: the survival of our species, and of the living breathing Earth upon which we stand. The wondrous creatures of this world belonging to the various kingdoms of Nature, beholding and experiencing the tragic plight of Mother Earth, in desperation look to us as their "saviors" at this time of destruction and disintegration in Nature. Seeing and experiencing that they await in vain true shepherding on the part of humanity, it is as if they are appealing to humankind along the lines of Christ's words from the cross, "My God, my God, why have you forsaken us?"

Money is too often the evil twin to the good. Spreadsheets determine moral behavior, and moral relativism allows indecency to permeate our cultures. Our world thus hangs in a precarious balance between redemption and destruction. Can we remember even a glimmer of the peace that was ours when we lived in unity with God in ages past? Our vertical attitude then was God-soul, rather than the horizontal attitude of soul-world. The horizontal attitude may have been comforting when we were just custodians of the natural world, but that time has passed. If we cannot regain the attitude of God-soul, we will become vagrants in a violent and destitute world of evil. There is good news on the horizon, however, and it is Promethean in character.

Prometheus and his brother Epimetheus were two sons of Ouranos (Uranus/heaven) and Gaia (Earth). Prometheus means "thinking in advance." Epimetheus means "thinking afterward, reflecting." These can be seen as two key activities of human thought life. Like the two fish of the constellation of Pisces, the activities of Prometheus and Epimetheus pull in different directions. One looks back, the other forward. Because of his forward thinking, Prometheus is a representative of the planet Uranus. He is also the representative of our entire 2160-year Piscean Age (215–2375).[3] Promethean thinking is manas-thinking,[4] which has a spiritual connection with the human heart and blood. The heart can be regarded as a kind of "fifth brain;" for when brain-bound thinking becomes heart-thinking, we become manas-thinkers capable of encountering the living beings in the Imaginal worlds. This capacity will gradually become more widespread as we free ourselves from the ever-tightening grip of materialism. Indeed, we will need a great many Promethean thinkers to turn the ship of humanity away from the iceberg sitting directly off our starboard bow.

Uranus has been in the constellation of the fishes (Pisces) since February of 2010. It takes Uranus approximately 84 years to orbit the Sun; therefore it stays in each constellation for about seven years. In 2016 Uranus will transit its position at the birth of the Nathan Jesus (24°59 Pisces); and it will continue to sojourn the entire year close to this degree. Those more Promethean in character will take advantage of this by very consciously opening to new—and even radical—possibilities. The more Epimethean among us will wait, and only later reflect on what may have been the results of this transit.

Promethean thinkers can be either magi or shepherds; both receive revelation—the shepherds

---

2 For an overview of the trials and temptations of our time and the assistance being offered to human beings for overcoming those trials and temptations, see Robert Powell, *Christ and the Maya Calendar* (with Kevin Dann); *Prophecy–Phenomena–Hope;* and *Gautama Buddha's Successor: A Force for Good in Our Time* (with Estelle Isaacson).

3 Astronomical ages are determined by the precession of the equinoxes. Every time the Sun, at the time of the spring equinox, rises in a new constellation, we enter a new astronomical age. In 2375 the spring equinox Sun will rise in Aquarius, thus marking the beginning of the Age of Aquarius. We now live in the final period, the last one-sixth, of the Piscean Age.

4 "Manas-thinking" refers to emanations from higher worlds that descend to fructify—and even to become—human thoughts.

through profound clairvoyant beholding, and the magi through the precision of exact and conscious higher knowledge. The magi are known to be astute in worldly ways, capable of conscientiously seeing the future, and daring enough to speak of what they see. The shepherds are quieter of soul; they have strong intuitive forces guiding them. They have a keen inner sense of direct-knowing that informs them of when the wolves are drawing near, and so they are able to keep their flocks safe. Promethean magi and shepherds will be called upon in 2016. There is no time for Epimetheus. It is time to act. Uranus is marking a significant memory in the Akashic record. There is a future to see, and a flock to protect.

⁂

Uranus/Ouranos is ripe with the unpredictable. It brings about sudden and often radical change; it rebels against restraint; it pulses in surging waves, pushing toward freedom, into sudden awakenings that open one to higher realms of cognition, to cosmic Imaginations streaming from this transcendental planetary sphere. Uranus is also known as an archive for our deepest memories; and when released into consciousness, the startling reality of long-forgotten remembrances suddenly coming into consciousness can cause one's soul to quake. On the other hand, Uranus can stun us with presentiments of future events. With Uranus quickening the memory of the birth of the priestly Jesus, Jesus of Nazareth, a virginal portal will open between the father of Prometheus in the heavens above (Ouranos), and his mother here below on earth (Gaia). A hermetic correspondence will be set in motion. When aspects to the position of the planets at the birth of Jesus of Nazareth occur, they deserve special attention, for with this individuality we are dealing with the most significant incarnation in the history of Earth's evolution. It is not a question of whether forces will be released, or stirred up. It is, however, a question as to whether enough Titans will be called to serve the event. Prometheus was a Titan (initiate) and his parents birthed eleven others of this rank. We need these Titans now—for Uranus is entangling us in a double bind.

A double bind is an emotionally distressing dilemma in communication, whereby groups, or individuals, receive two or more conflicting messages. An example of this is a phrase out of Harry Potter: "savage pleasure."[5] This is irreconcilable to the heart-mind. One message negates the other. The soul cannot confront the inherent dilemma, and therefore can neither resolve it nor opt out of the situation. A terminal confusion is stored in the soul, giving rise to vortices of endless disruption that threaten to undermine the psyche.

Double binds are often used as a form of control, without open coercion; the use of confusion makes both elements of the bind difficult to respond to—or even to resist. Propaganda uses this method of control. The declaration "war on terror," for example, proposes actions of violence to confront violence. For decades we have been using "war" as an illusory quick fix. What if, instead, we called for the solution to terror? Using the word "war" emphasizes the need for conquest; the word "solution" emphasizes the need for resolution wherein victory could mean that no one is defeated. Most importantly, invoking a solutions-based approach lays bare a nation's responsibility in co-authoring the situations it must face. "War on terror" presupposes that a nation or a people has no accountability for the rise of terror. It sets up a victim-perpetrator dynamic seeking the "patsy" other—state(s) or person(s) that may serve to justify its means.[6] War provides a lucrative enterprise

---

5   This is just one example of a great many double binds presented in the seven-volume Harry Potter series—see M. J. "An Exploration of the Harry Potter Series," *Starlight,* vol. 13, no. 2 (Advent 2013), pp. 54–72: www.sophiafoundation.org > Activities > Starlight Journal (Newsletter/Journal of the Sophia Foundation).

6   Patsy is a term used to designate a person or group of people who are deliberately "set up" by Mr. X or Group X (generally a criminal person or criminal group)—set up by some means or other—to be at a certain place at a certain time when some (usually major) criminal event is going to take place. The patsy is then accused by Mr. X or Group X (or some other colluding party) to be the perpetrator of the event, whereby incriminating evidence of some kind is usually produced to support the accusation. The classic example of a patsy is Lee Harvey Oswald, who was accused of assassinating

for the *corporatocracy* and the weapons industry. War discounts the reality that what we send into the world comes back to us from the world. What a nation has done, what it has sent forth, returns; and, in the case of war, the violence against others returns in the form of hideous conglomerations of insurgents spawned from those disenfranchised victims of previous conflicts.

When war is the first response, the assumption that war is a necessary and positive action for the benefit of good insinuates itself into cultural life. But war and "the good" present a double bind. War does not betoken anything good in the twenty-first century, since at this stage of human evolution we should have left war behind us—having learned the lessons of the senselessness and utter destruction and misery of war—particular after the examples offered in the twentieth century. Most thinking people in the twenty-first century do not want war; rather, they would prefer peace through diplomacy and means other than war, which has not in any way been proven to be an effective method of establishing peace.

However, through the constant propaganda of the double bind of "war in pursuit of peace," the weary human psyche in the case of a great many people in this country and elsewhere has been programmed to accept war as the answer to world dilemmas. Through relentless propaganda on the part of politicians and the mass media in cahoots with these political leaders, many silently become accepting of what was previously inacceptable for so many—in order to resolve the irresolvable dilemma of the use of violence in pursuit of non-violence. Double binds exhaust the soul, whereby often it finally gives up—allowing apathy to ensue. Madness uses very subtle weapons—in this case the double bind of the "war on terror" exemplifying the madness of those who launched this war and those who continue to pursue the senseless killing entailed by this war. And let us not forget that over three thousand years ago Moses proclaimed

---

President John F. Kennedy. However, as now indicated by various different studies, Oswald was "set up" in the role of Kennedy's assassin, but was not his assassin—see, for example, Douglass, *JFK and the Unthinkable.*

ten commandments, one of which states as divine law: "Thou shalt not kill." The proponents of the war on terror seem to have completely forgotten this divine commandment.

The great wave that crested with the thunderous proclamation of "Yes we can" has since fallen back upon itself, engendering intensified national egoism. As America continues its insidiously tyrannical path of destruction, waging war on all who oppose her, this great wave has instead dissolved into "Yes I will!" Having been programmed for war—war on drugs, war on poverty, war on terror—many have come to regard war as acceptable. The "worm" of war lives in the collective and national psyche, infiltrating ultimately—via the mass media—into the global psyche. This worm wreaks havoc as an in-seeded mass thought form that allows fear and ignorance to rule over conscience.

The Uranian double bind can be looked upon archetypally as springing from a dual nature—on the one hand reaching up to a sphere of illumined cosmic revelation and on the other hand, equal and opposite, as opening down to the sphere of electrical, and also electromagnetic, technological forces. In the latter case, the lower aspect of this duality can be seen as potentially carrying messages behind which the agendas of dark powers seek to sculpt public opinion. Thus, archetypically, Uranus can send wondrous cosmic Imaginations from higher realms, illumining suprasensory truth. On the other hand, however, mirror images that are caricatures of truth from subearthly realms may be stirred up through the influence of Uranus. From these lower spheres, adversarial beings can be observed at work against the good and the moral.

The Uranian double bind may appear on the surface to be Promethean in its heavenly strength. At the same time there is the possibility of the influence of Uranus being scintillatingly brilliant in its promotion of subearthly illusion. This contradictory nature makes it ever more difficult to separate truth from deceptive lies—and this at a time when it has never been more necessary that we do just that. As already stated in the Gospels, we cannot serve both God and mammon. So, how do we live in our world of towering delusion and still maintain our ability to perceive divine Imaginations? One direction of influence negates the other. We are on a precipice and we will not find safety as long as a select few are allowed to establish their One World Order using propaganda and indoctrination via the mainstream media as their subtle (and not-so-subtle) means of control of the population. The scariest part of the Uranian double bind is that by and large humanity is thoughtlessly choosing the lower aspects of Uranus and the disintegrating controversy it breeds, thereby making pacts with the devil (Lucifer). The consequence of this is that "giants" of the imagination are loosed into the world—luciferic imaginations that now control us, and are literally reshaping our cultures and even our souls. Parsifal struggled to find his way back to the Grail Castle. Inversely, we have an epic struggle before us if we are to free ourselves from the anti-Grail Castle (Klingsor's Castle) whose towers cover the Earth, incessantly broadcasting.

It is challenging to grasp the guidance of the star beings at the same time as their formative influences are streaming to us. Most often, it is only with the aid of historic reflection that we can look back and comprehend what was happening during any given period. With the dawn of new capacities now arising—capacities that will increasingly grow and flourish during the current millennium and into the distant future—this will change. The understanding of stellar effects will increasingly be comprehensible as they occur. Humanity is learning how to "speak to the stars."[7] This means turning our attention to current star events and humbly seeking to become actively aware of their wisdom. In these events the wisdom of Sophia—Queen of Heaven—speaks to us. It is She who decides what revelation will be released from eternity into time.[8]

The stars speak a complex language, one that does not usually descend into consciousness in such a way that an immediate, or complete, awakening is the result—though this too can happen, as was the case with both St. Paul and Brunetto Latini, the teacher of Dante. It is more common that we may gather a single beam (a part) radiating from the majesty of their cosmic discourse, and then take up responsibility for manifesting what has thus been received. This applies to entire generations when we are speaking of the transcendental planets—Uranus, Neptune, and Pluto. Therefore, although planetary aspects and their relationships to the zodiacal constellations, occurring at specific times, may be recognized, the deeper nature of their influences may often not be understood until much later. Thus they contribute in an ongoing way to the assimilation of patterns of stellar influences that later may become the subjects of Epimethean historians looking back into the past with discernment.

THE BUDDHISTIC JESUS

The Tower of Destruction is the Arcanum that portrays the negative side of the working of Uranus: the positive side is Ouranos, the regent of the starry heavens, whose light is the sum-total of the radiation of millions of stars, representing the Divine Mind, bestowing the faculty of Illumination.[9]

Have we ever needed radiance from the Divine Mind more than we do now? We stand juxtaposed between scintillating (but deceptive) brilliance

---

7   In ancient times, when clairvoyance was innate, the stars once spoke to human beings. Steiner speaks of how they are now silent and that our task now is that we must learn how to speak to them. One way to do this is by naked-eye observation of the stars combined with meditation on the starry vistas thus beheld. Steiner gave this verse: "The stars once spoke to human beings. It is world destiny that they are silent now. To become aware of this silence can cause pain for earthly humanity. But in the deepening silence, there grows and ripens what human beings speak to the stars. To become aware of this speaking, can become strength for the striving human spirit."

8   Sophia is the guardian of the far-side of the threshold, as Michael is the guardian between human beings and the near-side of the threshold to spiritual worlds—see Tomberg, *Inner Development,* lect. 1.

9   Powell, *Hermetic Astrology,* vol. 2, p. 325.

and the illumination of true spiritual Imagination. These represent two completely different activities of thinking—or, rather, of thinking-led-astray on the one hand and transformed higher thinking on the other hand—and we would be wise to know the difference:

> There is a world of difference between an illumined person and a brilliant thinker. The brilliant thinker is able to combine thoughts to his own pleasing, to make everything conform to the way he wants to see things, while an illumined person is interested solely in divine truth, for which he sacrifices his personal viewpoints. The brilliant thinker is in danger that his thinking becomes "electrified," while the illumined person has overcome this "earthly charged" thinking, so that his thought life is membered into the Cosmic Intelligence, which is beyond all electrical, polemical thinking.[10]

Not only are brilliant thinkers combining thoughts to suit their agendas, but through electrified cyber-reality they are sucking the willing masses into their ever-so-enticing Klingsorian towers. "It may be—indeed it often is so—that the entry to the spiritual world takes place by degrees. Then we grow slowly into the spiritual world. Nevertheless, very frequently it happens that the world is opened to us by a kind of shock that breaks in upon our life—by a sudden and unexpected event."[11]

Let us return to the good news of Uranus transiting its position at the birth of the Nathan Jesus—Steiner's expression for Jesus of Nazareth. Steiner has given us ample resources for understanding that there were two Jesus children, both descended from King David. One descended from the kingly line of Solomon described in the Gospel of Matthew; the other from the priestly line of Nathan described in the Gospel of Luke. It is the priestly Jesus, the Nathan Jesus, who is the subject of this Uranus transit. Steiner has also given us the knowledge that the other Jesus, the Solomon Jesus, united with the Nathan Jesus when the

latter attained the age of twelve. This took place at the event referred to as the Union in the Temple.[12] This occurred shortly after the Nathan Jesus had reached the age of twelve, and it marked the confluence of two initiation streams: that of Zoroastrianism from ancient Persia, stemming from Zarathustra, the founder of that ancient culture, and that of Hinduism (also its offspring, Buddhism) from ancient India, whereby Zarathustra reincarnated as the Solomon Jesus (Jesus of the Matthew Gospel), and Krishna, who had overlighted Arjuna, then incarnated upon the Earth for the first time—as the Nathan Jesus (Jesus of the Luke Gospel). The union of these two streams endured throughout the life of Jesus of Nazareth, following the Union in the Temple, although a great transition took place when Christ incarnated into Jesus at the Baptism in the River Jordan. From the Union in the Temple until the Baptism in the Jordan the Solomon Jesus was spiritually united with the Nathan Jesus; at the Baptism in the Jordan, Christ then united spiritually with the Nathan Jesus, whereby the Solomon Jesus "withdrew"—at least partially—to make way for Christ.

The Nathan Jesus is described in the Gospel of St. Luke. He was born on December 6, 2 BC, with Uranus geocentrically at 24°59 Pisces.[13] With Uranus at this same degree in 2016, the entire year will have the theme of a renewal of the teachings of the Luke Gospel—the teachings of love and compassion. Love is the virtue specifically associated with the constellation of Pisces.

---

10 Ibid. p. 312.

11 "Brunetto Latini"—lecture by Rudolf Steiner, Dornach, Jan. 30, 1915 (CW 161).

12 The Union in the Temple between the two Jesus children is a complex mystery. In order for a being as high as Christ to be able to incarnate upon the Earth, a perfect body had to be prepared. It required both the strength gained through the hereditary generations, stemming from Abraham, and the immaculate descent through spheres of pure consciousness. Thus was prepared a physical body, an energy body (etheric), a consciousness body (astral), and an "I" (individuality) that could unite in preparation for becoming a vessel for Christ.

13 Apr. 1, 2016, will see an exact geocentric return of Uranus to this degree, and 2016 will end with Uranus (25°35 Pisces) just 0°36' from its position at the birth of Jesus. The horoscope of the Nathan Jesus is given by Robert Powell in *Chronicle of the Living Christ*, p. 149.

The Nathan Jesus is intimately connected with Buddhism. It was Gautama Buddha who overlighted Jesus's astral sheath around the time of his birth. The radiance of Gautama's enlightened astral body, referred to by Steiner as Gautama Buddha's Nirmanakaya, was seen by the shepherds in their fields. The Nathan Jesus child, not having passed through the Fall, descended directly from spiritual worlds, without any hereditary influences affecting his incarnation. This is what is meant by his "immaculate conception." Trailing clouds of glory (representative of each of our pure, virginal natures), he incarnated into the womb of Mary as a pure and chaste being, having experienced nothing of the Fall. His virginal forces had never before been present on the Earth. Previous to this birth, these forces were protectively held in a "mystery lodge," guarded over by spiritual beings, including the great lodge of initiates known in the East as Bodhisattvas, who, when they are not incarnated, surround Christ in cosmic realms, just as the twelve disciples surrounded Christ Jesus during his earthly incarnation. In the Bible we read that the Tree of Life, in the east of the Garden of Eden, was protected by Cherubim wielding flaming swords. Similarly, we can imagine the Nathan Jesus soul protected by the lodge of great teachers surrounding Christ in spiritual realms. We can also imagine the descent of this pure soul by way of an immaculate channel through the spiritual realm through which Uranus sends "the light that is the sum-total of the radiation of millions of stars, representing the Divine Mind, bestowing the faculty of Illumination."

As Jesus brought these immaculate forces to the Earth, all things in Nature—including all human beings (initially primarily those in earthly incarnation at that time)—were seeded with the virginal qualities of original creation. From this time onward, souls on Earth had an avenue through which their redemption from the effects of the Fall became possible. The separation between individual human souls and their primal origins in spirit worlds was thus restored—through the divine grace transmitted to humanity by Christ—as a potential that could be attained through conscious

human effort over long millennia. At this time of the Second Coming, in the twentieth and twenty-first centuries, what Christ seeded at his First Coming two thousand years ago is now (through his Second Coming) being quickened, forming in more spiritually awakened human beings a new ether—the fifth ether, also called the moral ether—which can be lovingly directed by aware and compassionate humans into the world of Nature on behalf of all the creatures of Nature, as a contribution, together with the new activity of Christ in the etheric realm, toward the healing and regeneration of Mother Earth. The moral ether—over and above the life ether, tone ether, light ether and warmth ether—is the substance through which the virginal purity of original creation is now beginning to sound again into time.

The great Buddha[14] (that is, Gautama, the Bodhisattva who became Buddha in the fifth century BC) united from spiritual heights with the soul of the Nathan Jesus. It was the purified astral sheath (the manas body) of the Buddha that the shepherds witnessed over their fields, instructing them to go to the city of David—where the Nathan Jesus had just been born. Buddha taught the way of compassion and love. To this stream we can apply the powers of the more feminine capacities. Exemplifying this fact is the knowledge that the birth of the Nathan Jesus was announced to his mother, Mary. In his lectures on the Luke Gospel, Steiner depicts the Nirmanakaya[15] of the Buddha flowing down

____

14 Buddha's astral sheath was bought into connection with the Nathan Jesus by Rudolf Steiner as the Nirmanakaya of Buddha that shone upon the shepherds in their fields, announcing the birth of the Nathan Jesus. See also next footnote regarding the Nirmanakaya.

15 Robert McDermott, in his descriptive outline of Steiner's ten lectures on the Gospel of St. Luke, writes: "In these lectures, Steiner uses the term Nirmanakaya to refer to Buddha in his nonphysical body (presumable etheric and astral). In this respect, it would seem that he should have used the term Sambhogakaya. Since Steiner's references to Buddha in these lectures are very specifically to the Buddha of the sixth century BC, he might have understood the terms correctly and chosen Nirmanakaya to give this historical emphasis. It should nevertheless be acknowledged that a Buddhist reading this text would find

and enveloping the Nathan Jesus. Hence the Luke Gospel is regarded as the renewal of the teachings of Gautama, filled as they are with teachings of love and compassion, and with the inwardness of soul that was the signature of both the Buddha and the Nathan Jesus.

The uniting of the two Jesus individualities brought together Buddhism (via the Nathan Jesus and Zoroastrianism (via the Solomon Jesus). Thus the Luke and Matthew Gospels describe how, at the beginning of the Christian era, the currents of Buddhism and Zoroastrianism manifested in actual individualities. These currents came together to form a new stream, the Hermetic stream. Christ is the greatest Hermeticist of all time—through him the Father in the heights and the Mother in the depths were reunited. Thus did the Hermetic axiom ("as above so below") come to expression as the way of the cross, through Christ's deed on Golgotha.[16] Thus was the union between the two Jesus children in the temple, when the Nathan Jesus was twelve years old, essential for the impending birth of Christ in Jesus seventeen years later at the Baptism in the Jordan River, when Christ would take on human form—uniting the macrocosmic and the microcosmic mystery traditions.

In the story of the temptations of Christ, we are told of the dangers and trials that one encounters

when one descends into one's inner nature. In the legends of the Buddha we hear of similar encounters at the time when he met the demons who came to tempt him as he sat under the Bodhi tree and reached his enlightenment. In the story of the Transfiguration on Mt. Tabor, on the other hand, we are told the story of the radiance that united Christ with his macrocosmic self. There are great dangers on this macrocosmic path as well, for it takes specific preparation to hold the "I" together as it immerses itself into the vastness of the cosmos. If one goes unprepared, there may be grave consequences—even psychosis could result from this immersion.

In the fourth and fifth miracles of Jesus Christ, both the macrocosmic initiation associated with the bread and the microcosmic initiation connected with the fish were exemplified through the feeding of the five thousand and the walking on water. In the case of the latter miracle, herein lay the prophecy of his future descent into Hell (fish initiation) and his resurrection (bread initiation).

Through Christ Jesus, both the inward path of initiation and the outward path of initiation have been re-established—but without the suppression of the "I" (as was necessary in the ancient mystery traditions). The "I" remains completely aware, in a condition of total wakefulness when, through Christ, these initiations are undergone by individuals so prepared. Christ seeded the possibility for new manifestations of the mysteries, resulting in the potential for new human capacities. Steiner said that already in the twentieth century there would be some who would awaken into these new mystery streams. With Uranus transiting the birth of the Nathan Jesus, we can thus expect a potentization of illumining forces.

THE MANDALA AND THE ROSE

Now, with his Second Coming, Christ is manifesting in the etheric realm, in the vast aura of the Earth's light forces surrounding the Earth. Never again will he physically incarnate. The time of his renewed presence began in the early 1930s, and has quickened since then. To understand the concept of the Second Coming, we must approach it

---

the application of Nirmanakaya (ordinarily the physical incarnation of Buddha) for a spiritual appearance of Buddha (for example, as a choir at the Nativity) at least confusing and probably incorrect. Steiner says it was the Nirmanakaya Buddha that revealed itself to the shepherds so that they would attend the Nativity of Jesus. At the event in the Temple, when the twelve-year-old Jesus (as described in the Luke Gospel) was teaching the learned rabbis, the astral sheath (covering) of the Jesus described in Matthew united with, and so vitalized, the Nirmanakaya Buddha (or, perhaps more correctly, Sambhogakaya) that when it entered the Luke-Jesus he was able to speak with a power which would previously have been impossible" (*According to Luke*, pp. 231–231).

16 The two beams of the cross have a crossing point, where the horizontal and vertical are tied to one another. At this crossing point, two mystery schools become one. Christian Hermeticism is the path that works from this "heart" of the cross. None pass through the initiation into Christian Hermeticism but through Christ.

as distinct from any and all doctrines of denominational Christianity. In the sense this term is here being used, it is not connected to any particular religious convention; instead it is the focal point of all religions. Love is the center of the mandala. If the mandala is a rose, we could say that love is the heart of the rose and the different religions are petals on the rose. Christ is a cosmic being, much too large to be contained in any religious dogma. He is a universal spirit of Love. He is the center of every heart. He is the force that holds the world together, and also the force of peace that weaves among all who know him—by whatever name, by whatever religion or spiritual calling. To begin to grasp the mighty forces that hold sway in the highest realms of being, which are reflected in the lower worlds of matter, we can bring to consciousness the concept of respiration. We breathe in and out approximately 18 times a minute; the measure of seasonal respiration is once a year: from the autumn equinox to the spring equinox is one inhalation, and from spring equinox to autumn equinox is one exhalation.[17] Magnifying this to cosmic dimensions, we can imagine Christ incarnating on the Earth (inhalation); and, after his Ascension, he returns (exhalation) to the divine heart of our Galaxy, whence begins the reciprocal inhalation whereby he again draws near the Earth as a spiritual presence.

This return was prophesied at his Ascension when the Angels spoke to those there assembled on the Mount of Olives, and said: "Why do you stand there looking into heaven? This Jesus, who was taken up from you into heaven, will come back in the same way you have seen him go into heaven" (Acts of the Apostles 1:11). As Christ disappeared from the summit of the Mount of Olives into the clouds, so too would he return into the etheric realm surrounding the Earth—where clouds form. In Revelation 1:7 it is written: "Behold, he cometh with the clouds; and every eye shall see him." We are developing the eye that sees, referred to as the "third eye." The ebb and flow of spiritual

respiration can actually be traced through the remnants preserved of the most ancient mythologies. For there were times when the gods—the beings of the spiritual hierarchies—were near, when clairvoyance was commonplace, and times when clairvoyance was lost as the gods withdrew. It is thus not a far-fetched idea that Christ was once here, with us upon the Earth, after which he subsequently ascended into "heaven," and has now descended again near to us—in the realm directly bordering the sense world. This reflects the measure of cosmic respiration.

Adding to the concept of a divine presence intervening on behalf of all humanity, we can add the fact that we are now in the third millennium AD, referred to as the Abraham millennium.[18] But we can add yet another dimension to current meta-historical rhythms. We are also in the early beginnings of what is called a 600-year cultural rhythm.[19] In this light, the 2016 Uranus transit to the birth of the Nathan Jesus is especially signifi-

---

17 Steiner, *The Cycle of the Year as Breathing Process of the Earth* (CW 223), lecture of May 31, 1923.

18 Rudolf Steiner clairvoyantly perceived a millennial progression from Abraham, to Moses, to Solomon in the last three millennia BC (i.e., just prior to Christ's incarnation into Jesus of Nazareth). He saw the inversion of this in the AD progression: first the Solomon millennium, then the Moses millennium, followed by the Abraham millennium beginning in the year AD 2000. Abraham is known as the father of thinking—meaning he was the leader of a people who were the first to lose the ancient (universal) clairvoyance and begin the rudiments of thinking that is normal for human beings today. In the Abraham millennium AD, he foresaw a dawning into a new clairvoyance, one conducted in clear day-waking consciousness, not at all like the atavistic clairvoyance of old. For a penetrating description of the significance of the fact that we have now entered the post-Christian Abraham millennium, see the article "The Transition" by Robert Powell and Keith Harris in the Sophia Foundation newsletter (now journal)—*Starlight*, vol. 14, no. 1 (2014), pp. 11–39 (www .sophiafoundation.org/images/stories /Documents/starlight%202014%20easter _final_s.pdf.

19 This rhythm is based on the astronomical cycle of Venus, which has a great influence on cultural development. The new 600-year cultural rhythm began in 2014. See Powell and Isaacson, *Gautama Buddha's Successor: A Force for Good in Our Time*, ch. 1.

cant, as new mystery traditions are emblematic at the inception of these 600-year cultural rhythms. We can trace the history of this rhythm and notice seminal shifts that accompany them.[20] One signature of the last cultural rhythm (from 1414 to 2014) was humanity's shift from a faith in God, to faith in humankind. And justly so, for human beings still contemplated the presence of God and conducted their affairs accordingly. As this rhythm came to a close at the end of 2013, faith in God as well as in human beings was becoming scarce. Doubt, skepticism, and cynicism had eclipsed all but the last remnants of faith; and thus faith in the new god of technology is becoming more and more prevalent.

With the beginning of this new rhythm, we are wise to collectively restore a wisdom-based understanding of our true origins and our true mission. For we are ultimately spirit beings seeking a human experience. The alternative to ongoing ignorance will be a complete merger between the human being and the machine. This looms darkly on the horizon, through various laboratory experiments being conducted in relation to the Transhumanism[21] movement. Transhumanists advocate improving human capacities through advanced technologies. They seek to gain control over the atomic structure of matter, resulting in a "posthuman" species that is a merging of technology and biology. The human being itself may, in the future, become a kind of "tower," built from the self-will of humankind in obtuse forgetfulness that we have descended from higher worlds in accordance with Divine Law. Transhumanism is a perfect example of brilliant thinking as caricature of cosmic wisdom.

Tomberg prophesied—not in specific detail, but in broad outline—the Transhumanism movement as the sign of the presence of the third level of evil, which is an attack against the highest principle of life. He wrote his Old Testament Studies in the 1930s, before we had invited the third level of evil beings into the world through corrupt practices:

It is impossible for a being to oppose the Father in the cosmos unless the current of cosmic evil has been so developed that a karmic region is established, giving that being a foothold. Such a region does not yet exist, but it is being formed. It is made up of the physical results of ahrimanic activity [second level of evil]. Not physical in the sense of diseases, which indicate the karmic balance, but in the sense of ahrimanic health, producing a physical body no longer dependent for its existence on the inflow of forces from the region of the first hierarchy [the Father's kingdom], but able to draw them from another source. When the physical body has been brought into this condition—as the result of its having become ahrimanized—the moment of time will have been reached at which the Asura being can make his attack [third level of evil].[22]

Opposite the electrified Uranian brilliance (which collaborates with evil), the revelatory aspect of Uranus now, this year, 2016, is manifesting, in that Uranus is transiting (for the 24th time) its position at the birth of the Nathan Jesus,. To fully appreciate the potential of the Uranus transit to this birth, it will be helpful to distinguish the intrinsic connectivity working between the magi status of the Solomon Jesus and the shepherd-like quality of the Nathan Jesus.

---

20 For example, 215 AD marked the birth of the great teacher Mani, the founder of Manicheism and was the beginning of the astronomical age of Pisces, as outlined in Robert Powell's article "Zodiacal Ages and Cultural Epochs" in the previous issue of this journal (2015). The year AD 814 was that of the death of Charlemagne and the time of the activities of the Grail family, from which arose the various legends of the Holy Grail. The year 1414 was the dawn of the European Renaissance and the opening of Christian Rosenkreutz's mystery school, that of the original Rosicrucians. Christian Rosenkreutz, like Mani, is one of the great teachers of humanity. New mystery teachings accompanied each new 600-year rhythm. Therefore, we can expect new mystery traditions to be blossoming now, although these may not become transparent until later in time.

21 "Transhumanist thinkers study the potential benefits and dangers of emerging technologies that could overcome fundamental human limitations, as well as the ethics of developing and using such technologies. They speculate that human beings may eventually be able to transform themselves into beings with such greatly expanded abilities as to merit the label 'posthuman.'" (From the Wikipedia entry on Transhumanism.)

22 Tomberg, *Christ and Sophia*, p. 59.

The Nathan Jesus and the Solomon Jesus

The physical and etheric bodies were prepared in the individual initially described by Matthew, whereas the astral body and "I" were prepared in Luke's Nathanic Jesus, who was a different personality for the first few years of his life. Matthew's Jesus received the appropriate physical and etheric bodies, while Luke's [Solomon] Jesus received the necessary astral body and vehicle for the "I."[23]

There were initiation rites conducted in the northern mysteries (Persia) and others conducted in the southern mysteries (India). The meeting place between these two streams was where the Hebrew race developed (Palestine). In the Hebrew stream both of these initiatory paths were present. The prophetic stream inaugurated through Abraham is described in the Gospel of St. Matthew, wherein the birth of the Solomon Jesus is depicted. This Gospel traces the lineage of the Solomon Jesus back to Abraham. The Solomon Jesus was the reincarnated Zarathustra, through whom the macrocosmic path of initiation[24] was undergone by the initiates of ancient Persia. In his life as the Solomon Jesus, his physical and etheric bodies were prepared in such a way that he was able to receive the full light of the Yahweh principle directly into his physical and etheric bodies—through the blood of generations.

On the other hand, the Gospel of St. Luke depicts the birth of the Nathan Jesus, whose birth is traced further back, all the way to Adam—to the time of the Fall from Paradise. Unlike the Solomon Jesus, who had many incarnations behind him, the Nathan Jesus had never before incarnated upon the Earth. His astral body and Ego were perfect reflections of the unfallen human being. These forces had been preserved in a mystery lodge since the time of the Fall, protected by mighty spiritual beings.

Thus were the two Jesus beings perfect manifestations of on the one hand the horizontal forces working into the physical and etheric bodies through generations in time (Solomon Jesus); and on the other hand the perfect manifestation of the vertical forces working from spiritual worlds directly into the soul and spirit of individualities in space (Nathan Jesus). Through the union of the two, a cross formed. At the crossing point between time and space, a new place emerged: the heart of the cross, into which the Divine Heart of God—Christ—would later incarnate.

The Solomon Jesus could commune with spiritual worlds through the Yahweh influences in the blood of generations.[25] As Zarathustra, he had beheld Christ indwelling the Sun; as the Solomon Jesus, he would actually make way for the physical incarnation of Christ. Shortly before the Baptism, the Nathan Jesus had a profound conversation with his stepmother, the Solomon Mary, wherein the very selfhood of the Solomon Jesus poured out of the Jesus being. This marked his second sacrifice. (The first was when he departed from his physical, etheric, and astral bodies and united on the level of his "I" with the Nathan Jesus at the event called the Union in the Temple.)

It was the Nathan Jesus who thereafter would walk in his original purity to meet John the Baptist at the River Jordan. Just as the Solomon Jesus was known for seeing into cosmic realms, the Nathan Jesus was known for his inwardness—his ability to behold all consequences of the Fall in the inner life of humanity (the microcosmic path of initiation).

A cross thus formed between Yahweh's activity in the blood of generations, and the descending forces of original and immaculate purity. This cross would later be raised on the hill of Golgotha, upon which Christ would unite all mystery

---

23 Steiner, *According to Matthew*, p. 89.

24 This path leads the initiate into the vastness of the starry realm.

25 "He [Jeshu ben Pandira] also taught [the Essenes] that at a certain time in the future, completion of these stages would become natural because the bloodline would extend far enough for Yahweh, the spirit of the Hebrew people, to manifest fully in the Hebrew bloodline. Jeshu ben Pandira taught that, for Zarathustra, the bearer of Ahura Mazda, to incarnate in a human body, this body had to be produced over forty-two generations [the number of generations in Jesus' lineage depicted in the Gospel of Matthew] by the descent of the divine spirit living within" (Steiner, *According to Matthew*, pp. 93–94).

streams for all time—for the mystery of Golgotha marked the very turning point in time. After his death upon the cross, Christ descended into the depths of the Underworld, i.e., Hell, making his way through the evil layers of the inner Earth until he reached the golden realm of Shambhala in the heart of the Earth. This marked the end point of his path of descent. After having communed with the Mother in the lost paradise at the Earth's center—he turned, and this was the "turning point in time." From there Christ rose in an ascending direction, clothed with the Resurrection body. This is the body of the Risen One that Mary Magdalene bore witness to on the first Easter Sunday.

⁂

The Solomon Jesus enabled the Yahweh principle to fulfill its mission. For Yahweh was the cosmic preparer of the incarnation of the Sun God into a physical and etheric body. Yahweh is one of the seven Elohim comprising the seven-fold rays of the Christ Sun, and it was he who sacrificed himself. Instead of remaining in the Sun sphere of the Exusiai ("Elohim" in Hebrew), Yahweh Elohim left the Sun to become the ruler of the lunar sphere, which holds sway over the mysteries of procreation and the continuation of the species through successive generations. Moreover, Yahweh is the cosmic cross-bearer, who carries the Earth's rigidified corpse (the Moon) so as to prevent the Earth herself from death. Yahweh long ago infused the blood of humanity with the faculty of love. Without this sacrifice, egoism would have torn the human soul asunder—disintegrating humanity. Through the power Yahweh wields from his cosmic abode associated with the Moon, he offers resistance against the onslaught of dark beings who could otherwise unleash untold destruction through increasingly activating the lunar forces upon the Earth and in human beings. These dark beings live in a sphere that lies between the Earth and the Moon. Through the power of Yahweh, these forces are held back from causing excessive harm to either the lunar sphere itself or humanity and the Earth.

After the culmination of the incarnation of Christ, the six other Elohim present in the Sun sphere, working from there inspiringly into the being of the Nathan Jesus, were able to merge their solar impulses with Yahweh's lunar impulse that was borne in the blood of the Israelites down through the generations. Thus did the stream of light that Yahweh wove through the bloodlines of ancient Israel become "expanded" to become the power in the blood that represents the fullness of the Pleroma—Pleroma being a gnostic term referring to the totality or "fullness" of the seven Elohim (including Yahweh) serving Christ. As the bearer of the united entity of the seven Elohim, Christ was the "fullness" of the Pleroma. In this fullness the Christ impulse was complete—for when the impulse of Christ proceeding from his sacrifice on the cross came spiritually into connection with the collective blood of humanity, the seven-fold fullness of the Pleroma entered the evolutionary stream of humankind.

In the depths of our being, in the blood organism, we harbor the most sacred principles of existence, which long to emerge as the promise of resurrection for each and every one of us. When Christ sweated in agony in the little cave on the Mount of Olives arching above the Garden of Gethsemane, he sweated the blood of human error. In his blood-sweat, each individual's sins fell into the Earth's depths. After his death on the cross, Christ on his path of descent to Shambhala, the golden realm at the heart of the Earth, could then spiritually follow each bloody teardrop into the Earth's interior so that humanity could eventually live into its future redemption.

The eternal yearning of the higher "I"—which shines always above us—is to assist us as we descend into our inner abyss, so that we may each raise our individual cross in glorious celebration of our prodigal return. The Redeemer lives eternally as the one source through whom each of us will transform our lower, separate selves. Until this time, Christ carries the sins of the world.

TO BE BORN OF WATER AND THE SPIRIT

The incarnation of the Logos made possible for human beings to be born of water and the spirit (John 3:5). To be born of water leads us to cognition in spiritual worlds. To be born of spirit leads us to cognition of our own inner depths. One path opens the other, for Christ united the above and the below. In the Bible we are told of two kinds of disciples; disciples of the day, and disciples of the night. Nicodemus communed in the night with Christ; Lazarus communed with the inner depths of the Earth from which he was raised by Christ—in the light of day. From the turning point of time onward, Nicodemus serves our remembrance of the mysteries of the starry heavens; and Lazarus is the individuality through whom we overcome the vagrancy of our endless wandering—in that we receive the apocalyptic revelation sounding from the stream of time moving toward us from the future, healing all in us that has separated us from union with our divine selfhood.

Every birth unites the two streams representative of the Solomon Jesus and the Nathan Jesus (the hereditary and the immaculate). Our physical and etheric bodies are, for the most part, formed through lines of heredity; into these, our astral body and ego descend, bringing new capacities. The stronger the individuality, the greater is it a reflection of its divine image (and thereby the less is it influenced by hereditary forces). Individualities, who are not so highly evolved, draw more from hereditary influences, as they have not yet developed the higher stages of consciousness through inner efforts of past incarnations that make possible the shaping of the physical body to become truly a "temple of the spirit" or "I."

Consequent to the Second Coming of Christ, what was seeded through the Solomon and Nathan Jesus—at the turning point in time—is now to be realized through the new initiation mysteries that are calling us to awaken from the sleep of materialism. The Etheric Christ has opened these new mysteries, working in oneness with his Bride, Sophia. Together they are shining a light that we are to follow in order to turn away from the ravaging powers of the dragon—who preys upon purity, especially that of our children.

The lost Paradise of Shambhala is activated through Christ at this time, and the moral ether now forming is literally creating a new kingdom, one that radiates truth, morality, and apocalyptic revelation. Turning to this new state of affairs, however, necessitates a new orientation. In the same way that Christ in his first coming was recognized only by those who could free themselves from the mosaic laws—which had led Israel to exactly the event before which they stood—so too must we now free ourselves from sense-bound intelligence, lest instead of recognizing the Etheric Christ we too would crucify the one for whom Moses prepared.

THE VIRGINAL FORCES CARRIED IN THE DESCENT OF THE NATHAN JESUS

Steiner describes exactly what the nature of the virginal force was that entered evolution through the incarnation of Jesus Christ:

> Each human being contains a virginal element, as it were, which is not stimulated by the fusion of [hereditary forces from mother and father] but originates in completely different domains of existence. This element, which unites with a human embryo at conception, does not come from either of the parents, yet it belongs to and is destined for that specific individual. It pours into the "I" and can be ennobled by receiving the Christ principle, and its birth is virginal.[26]

Birth is an archetype that applies not only to an incarnation but also to an idea. This virginal aspect, which became active after it was first embodied as a human capacity by Jesus Christ, is now the archetype for all processes through which something new enters into the stream of time. By analogy, this virginal quality can be likened to a star-seed that Christ implanted in all things and is waiting to be born—through the free activity of human will striving toward spiritual truth. The Uranian Imaginations constitute a birthing force

---

26 Steiner, *According to Luke,* p. 203.

that, if received, can literally release a soul from its bondage to past habits (ghosts that the soul brings with it into incarnation). Gautama called these habits the desires that are the origin of all suffering. Through the virginal qualities inherent in the descending spiritual space traversed by the Nathan Jesus, the human soul can be lifted in consciousness to a causal plane that exists behind the maya of sense existence. If we can lift our thinking to these planes, we will discover new dimensions of causality that are the source of healing for all effects of the Fall. The eightfold path is a practice of immense importance, through which are revealed to us the aspects of our soul that have been led astray. The suprasensory realms of virginal causality, on the other hand, constitute the source of forces that can actually heal what the eightfold path reveals.

The Nathan Jesus, who brought these virginal forces to Earth, worked collaboratively with Gautama Buddha. In our time, as the birth of Jesus of Nazareth is remembered and Uranus quickens revelatory Imagination, we can rightly assume that it is not Gautama who is overlighting the new revelation; instead, it is Gautama Buddha's successor—known in the Buddhist world as the Maitreya Bodhisattva, who fulfills this role.[27] This

Bodhisattva is in the process of becoming the next Buddha. A Buddha cycle is 5000 years. Therefore it will not be until approximately AD 4500 that the Maitreya Bodhisattva will attain Buddhahood. Nonetheless, this Bodhisattva individuality who will become the Maitreya Buddha incarnates frequently as the guiding initiate of the stream of Christian Buddhism.

The Buddha taught the law of karma. The teachings of Christ were not simply teachings on the "wheel of the law"; Christ actually brought the living force of the "wheel of love." Christ's contribution is not a doctrine, but it is rather this living force. He brought to Earth the substantial and living content of Love, not merely its wise content. This is the essential difference between Buddha's teachings of compassion and the teachings of Christ—who through his incarnation actually infused the Earth with new life.

The phantoms we carry from one incarnation to another contain the influences we have let enter from luciferic and ahrimanic tendencies. At death we discard our etheric bodies like a second corpse; but we leave behind an extract, and carry this extract with us into kamaloka. We bring this back with us as we again come into incarnation. Previously we have named this (in Buddhist terminology) as the linga sharira. The effects of this negative influence, which is ours to bear, are borne through life as unconscious habits and desires that disturb our soul's harmony. In a sense we can say that we drag the burden of unconscious aspects of our soul through the world—and this burden seeks to dismember the soul by the very forces of the temporal world. If we do not receive the healing forces that directly descend when the "I" seeks spiritual light—forces that alone can mend the soul—then it will be the evil ones who will reconstruct, i.e., build, the soul according to mechanical laws.[28] Buddha called these forces those that are hidden behind the darkness of ignorance. These forces entangle us in covetous enjoyment of the material world.

---

27 "When a bodhisattva becomes a buddha, a successor takes his place. Ancient Indian legend tells us that when the bodhisattva who was to achieve buddhahood as King Suddhodana's son descended to Earth, he handed the bodhisattva's crown to his successor in the spiritual realm. This new bodhisattva, who is still active and will become the Maitreya Buddha, had a specific task with regard to human evolution. He was the spiritual guide for the movement that manifested in the Therapeutae and Essenes" (Steiner, *According to Matthew,* p. 78). Steiner goes on to write of Jeshu ben Pandira, the leader of the Essene community one hundred years before Christ, into whom the Buddha's successor worked. He is known in Talmudist literature as Jesus, son of Pandira. "We must recognize Jeshu ben Pandira as a protégé of the bodhisattva who succeeded the earlier bodhisattva who had become Gautama Buddha. This much is clear: A side stream in the development of Christianity depended on this bodhisattva and was played out in the activity of one of the messengers he sent into the Essene communities. This missionary was Jeshu ben Pandira" (p. 79).

---

28 Steiner, *Ancient Myths and the New Isis Mystery,* ch. 3.

The Buddha's pupils called it *samskara*.[29] The Buddha told his closest disciples that people of the present are typically unaware of this important element within themselves. Ignorance transforms this element, which we would otherwise recognize as coming from luciferic and ahrimanic beings, into the thirst for existence and all the dark, dormant forces persisting from earlier incarnations.[30]

Thinking influenced by the forces of the linga sharira are bound to a "thought organ"—whereby they are unconsciously driven to form personal opinions and personal likes and dislikes, thereby leaving one unfree in the domain of objective thought. The virginal forces from suprasensory realms are the balm of Gilead[31] that heals the soul, thus freeing it from these dark powers of attraction.

It is not an easy task to lift oneself out of the confines of old doctrines and lingering habits that occupy our souls as ghosts from previous (or current) incarnations. In this context there are two kinds of ghosts: those that the individual harbors and those that are carried by entire groups of people. Ghosts of this second category are called egregores; and they can successfully entomb a community, a body of thought, a political structure, or even a nation. It takes discipline and courage to open oneself into the vastness of spiritual potential. Not only are we living in a time when cosmic respiration has drawn the Christ close to us; we are also in a new Abraham millennium, during yet another 600-year cultural rhythm. We are living during a time when Uranus, the planet of higher Imagination, has returned to its position at the birth of the Nathan Jesus—he who brought the virginal substance of creation to Earth. This Jesus, who once walked the Earth, is now an angelic being who serves an archangelic being, in devotion to the progress of each one of

us. One aspect of a specific sacrifice he is making—on behalf of the initiation of humanity in our time—is that he is quickening our potential to gain illumination through the presence of the moral ether.

URANUS AND THE TOWER OF DESTRUCTION

Both the Hermetic treatises and the Bible state that the original sin was committed in heaven (Hermeticism) or paradise (the Bible) before the original Fall. Both pre-Christian Hermeticism and the Bible describe this original sin as an act of disobedience toward God, i.e., a separation of the human will from that of God, and a discordance between these two wills, caused by the desire for another type of knowledge than that of revelation and for another subject of knowledge than God and his revelation through the world.[32]

Through the Fall we entered into incarnation on Earth. Through redeeming the Fall, we will enter into the virginal revelation stream instituted by the Nathan Jesus as described in the previous subchapter. Uranus, the planet of revelation, acts like a thunderbolt, crushing what has been built out of egoism, and illumining what grows through the collaboration of human will with the will of God.

The Arcanum The Tower of Destruction teaches a general and universal law that it presents in the comprehensive form of the tower of Babel. A general and universal law—this means to say a law that operates both on a small scale and on a grand scale, in individual biography as well as in that of humankind, and in the past, present and future equally. According to this law, he who rebels against his "Higher Self" will no longer live under the law of the vertical but rather under that of the horizontal, i.e., he will be "a fugitive and a wanderer on the Earth." (Genesis 4:12)[33]

How wonderfully this passage reflects the Buddhist teachings of desire as the origin of all

---

29 *Samskara* is a blockage, an impression from the past.

30 Steiner, *According to Luke*, p. 61.

31 The name *Gilead* first appears in the biblical account of the last meeting of Jacob and Laban (Genesis 31:21–22). In this account Jacob takes his two wives, Leah and Rachel, his sons, his livestock and all his possessions, and heads for the hill country of Gilead. This is where his uncle caught up with him and where peace was made between them.

32 Anonymous, *Meditations on the Tarot*, pp. 436–437.

33 Ibid., p. 443.

suffering. It is also a wonderful accompaniment to the teachings of the virginal supra-revelation that issues forth from the Archangel Jesus at this very time in our history—for this is the archangel through whom Christ is now manifesting.[34] Our higher "I" is not born of hereditary forces; through ignorance, however, we bind ourselves to these ghosts. In actuality we descend from spiritual worlds of light, carrying with us the hope and aspiration that we will be able to separate our lower self further from its attachments to the temporal world, thereby being nourished from realms of light. All that we have built from revolt, possession, or desire are substitutions of self-will in the place of God's will; and all such structures will, in time, be struck with lightning and crumble into the dust from which the temporal revolt once rose.

The lightning strike is characteristic of the planet Uranus, which evidently has a close relationship to the sixteenth Arcanum of the Tarot, The Tower of Destruction. Is 2016 the year we will begin to choose more conscientiously against the revolt of the lower self in order to turn to the mighty revelation Uranus is bestowing in memory of the teachings and healing miracles fulfilled during the earthly life of the Nathan Jesus? This lies in the realm of possibility, although not necessarily as a once-and-for-all achievement. The thought that humanity will ascend without inner effort is the falsehood underlying the expectation of a collective rapture. It is usually a gradual process by which the Higher Self overcomes the forces lying hidden in the lower self. It is a matter of beginning a journey, not a matter of reaching a goal.

Through the brilliance of electrified thinking we are led into realms of trapped light (electricity), that have spawned the illusions that now encase us in scintillating towers, making puppets of our thinking. This results in a thinking that serves only the lower world of egoism. Uranus's higher aspect, that of Ouranos, on the other hand, bears the power of truth that overcomes all illusion. Truth is a hymn, a canticle to heaven.

---

34 Tomberg, *Christ and Sophia*, pp. 357–401.

THE COSMIC CANTICLE OF THE NEW ASTROLOGY

As we are considering the effects of the Archangel Jesus in relation to the Nathan Jesus—now manifesting in angelic form as the "Angel Jesus"—it would be appropriate to mention the Magnificat ("my soul magnifies"). The Magnificat, taken from the Gospel of St. Luke, is the Nathan Mary's hymn of praise to the Lord. It is also known as the Canticle of Mary. This is the law that puts down the mighty from their thrones and exalts those of low degree. It is the essence of the law of the tower blasted by a thunderbolt, and of the humble heart raised by the same thunderbolt to divine illumination. This is a theme for 2016:

> He has scattered those who are proud in their inmost thoughts. He has brought down rulers from their thrones but has lifted up the humble. He has filled the hungry with good things but has sent the rich away empty. (Luke 1:51–53)

Tomberg describes exalting oneself as developing in the sense of specialization, which gives temporary advantages. In contrast, "to humble oneself" means general growth, i.e., a balanced evolution of the physical and psychic faculties of beings. There is no desire of egoism that drives the soul in general growth. It allows the being of Time itself to collaborate in human affairs through one's humble attitude, God-soul. In the face of revelation, one must avoid knowing for "personal gain," and instead hunger and thirst for truth in order to win blessing for the betterment of the world. The lightning bolt that destroys our arbitrary towers will eventually strike those who think they can build something of endurance through egoism; whereas those who seek to serve the world attract the vertical attitude—God-soul—wherein the hungry are filled with good things.

In his ending contemplations on the sixteenth Tarot Arcanum that is evidently associated with Uranus, Tomberg speaks of astrology. His thoughts on this theme are profound, especially considering the opening to the divine "I" that we are here contemplating as the force of Uranus issuing forth from the remembrance of the Nathan Jesus's birth:

Thus, Christian Hermeticism of today has not remained behind in the great spiritual events that have changed factors of the first order in the domain of astrology—which events now play the role of "the thunderbolt that blasts the tower of astrology." What I have in mind here is that the planetary influences and the days and hours of these influences have given way to a power of a higher order. It is true that the day Sunday is the day of the Sun with respect to the human psychophysical organism, but nowadays it is the day of resurrection, with respect to humanity's psycho-spiritual life. Saturday is still the day of Saturn, but it is so only with regard to the natural, lower part of the human being. For the soul that turns toward the spirit and or the human spirit itself, Saturday is the day of the Holy Virgin. And the influence of Venus has given way to Calvary, to Christ crucified—Friday. Tuesday is no longer the day of Mars—for the soul that aspires to the spirit, or for spiritual personages—it is the day of the Archistrategist Michael. Similarly, with respect to the soul turned toward the spirit and with respect to the lives of spiritual personages, Monday is the day of the Holy Trinity, instead of being that of the Moon.... Wednesday is the day of the human pastors of humanity, instead of Mercury...and Thursday is the day of the Holy Spirit,[35] instead of Jupiter.[36]

The above passage, from the spiritual exercise of the sixteenth Arcanum that is so closely related to Uranus, depicts the descent of the wondrous Cosmic Fire that continuously makes all things new. Such revelation is not something that can easily be grasped by the ordinary intelligence of human beings living on Earth; for it streams from the World of Reason, directing Divine evolution in accordance with universal law. The highest hope of the mighty powers that dwell in these regions is that their revelation be reflected in human minds below:

It is from a world lying beyond both the World of Spirit and the Elementary World that forces stream down through these two worlds to build our brain. Spiritual Science has also called it the World of Reason (*Vernunftwelt*). It is the world in which there are spiritual Beings who are able to send down their power into the physical world in order that a shadow image of the Spiritual may be produced in the physical world in human beings' intellectual activity. "Reason" would have been spoken of when those who were initiates had risen into a world even higher than the World of Spirit and had direct perception there.[37]

Faint images of this world must illumine the shadowy human intellect if we are to find our way through the labyrinth of intellectual materialism that has resulted in our having lost our way. The "organ" of our true intellect is not constructed here below; rather, it has been created in lofty realms wherein we find the Beings working from the World of Reason—a world from whence great initiates draw forth their perceptions.

Tomberg's depiction of the supernatural power of the day (which reflects the day's planetary influences) represents what he calls "sacred magic." The revelations descending from realms of Divine Reason, received by human souls, become deeds through human will. He accords a certain applicability to the natural power of planetary influences, but notes these as relevant only in a restricted domain. He seems to be asking us not only to "cast the knowing glance"[38] to the natural domain, as a source of information, but also to set our sights on increasing our receptivity to the supernatural influences that are coming ever more to the fore. This will continue to be true as a renewal of astrology continues to dawn, breaking through the limitations imposed by the shadowy intellect—for the towers of old astrological superstructures threaten to sever us from the ever-evolving world of star beings.

---

35 Steiner, *According to Matthew*: "We must consider the fact that *Ruach-Elohim*—called the 'Spirit of God' in our Bible—is feminine in the Hebrew language" (p. 74).

36 Anonymous, *Meditations on the Tarot*, p. 458.

37 Steiner, *Macrocosm and Microcosm*, p. 114.

38 The knowing glance refers to one's willingness to acknowledge the temporal conditions but not place our attention on them. We are to place our attention on what we want to grow. In this case it is the higher octave of a situation, a person, or an event that is most worthy of our attention.

A priority is given to the supernatural power of planetary influences, over and above the influences rising from seeing merely the astral influences of the planetary spheres. Our tendency to impose merely these astral influences—of days, hours, and years—excludes the constancy of powers that descend into, and continuously transform, these realms. For the beings indwelling these spheres are also in a process of evolution, and their influences change accordingly. It is not an accident that sidereal astrology is rebirthing a new star wisdom. No, for the time has come! And if one thing changes, all things change. Hermetic astrology sees equally from God's eye, and from the earthly eye. But it is God's eye that shows us what is "first born" and is continuously birthing—wherein planetary and zodiacal forces are not separated from the Word:

> The priority of supernatural power with regard to the astral influences of days, hours and years—this is the "thunderbolt" that has "blasted" the tower of astrology and specialized astrological magic.
>
> Here is an example of this "thunderbolt" in action: a horoscope indicates a baleful configuration, a conjunction of Saturn and Mars in the eight house (that of death), predicting a violent death—however, it happens that it is not Saturn and Mars that act, but rather the Holy Virgin and the Archangel Michael; and instead of the predicted death, a spiritual illumination takes place.[39]

In this example, we witness the primacy of the divine worlds. Out of love and concern they will blast our towers. Astrological specialization has a tendency to crystallize—i.e., it contracts what is eternal into definition, thus imprisoning the human intellect, whereby it no longer perceives divine source. Specialization leads to impasse, and impasse calls forth the thunderbolt that saves us from hauling around corpses when we could otherwise remain open to a living relationship with star beings. The thunderbolt removes obstacles to our further progress. We are to keep pace with spiritual evolution, which requires taking the "leap" when the time has come. The

entire sixteenth Arcanum of the Tarot is a warning to all those whom Tomberg calls "authors of 'systems,' where an important role is assigned to a mechanical ingredient—intellectual, practical, occult, political, social, and other systems." He asks us to become "cultivators and guardians of the garden," instead of "builders of towers." These thoughts can send chills down the spine, for we are all sympathetic to building towers. This is what the ego is driven to do. Yet, it is just this that obscures our receptivity to revelation as illumination.

When we fill our minds with imaginations that spring from our own intellect, we obscure the truth.[40] Cosmic Imaginations approach only those who are empty—i.e., poor in spirit. Once one receives these Michaelic Cosmic thoughts, one patiently waits for such treasures to grow as divinely instructed. Ambition is the lure that sets the egoistic builders to work, and the fettered ego knows only how to build towers—edifices projecting self-will that become visible in the outer world. If we were to learn instead the silent art of opening to illumination, we would see a new way forward: a way filled with harmlessness, compassion, and love. We would be in communion with the Nathan Jesus being (now an Angel); and undreamt possibilities could unfold before us.

In our time the potential for the union of the human will with the will of God is growing. It waits as long as necessary for the revelation that then impels it to act. It knows the way of obedience, chastity, and poverty. It asks: "What is needed?" It seeks to serve. Like an oak tree growing from a tiny seed, it allows the seasons of time to determine its growth. One who tirelessly works to gather souls together, and then cultivates spiritual knowledge with them, is a gardener. Abraham, Moses, and Jacob were gardeners. Steiner, Tomberg, and the Elijah-John being are gardeners. And the new astrology is like

---

39 Anonymous, *Meditations on the Tarot,* p. 458.

40 "Whenever truth is in any way obscured, the path leading to Christ Jesus is also obscured and cannot be found" (Steiner, *Building Stones for an Understanding of the Mystery of Golgotha,* lect., Apr. 24, 1917).

unto an oak, planted by Steiner, cultivated by the foundational star work of Willi Sucher, and taken further by Robert Powell, together with his colleagues and others. It is watered by those who dismantle the towers and await the new. The pure and virginal forces are beginning to pour their heavenly light into all things. In light of this, Valentin Tomberg has depicted a new understanding of planetary influences.

Like St. Paul and Brunetto Latini we are standing in the presence of great mysteries. Messages are now issuing forth from the far side of the threshold. Sophia is speaking. She is calling her children to the light as she releases new dispensations. To receive her new teachings, we must enter the wilderness of silence as did John the Baptist, and from there cry out for the redeeming Imaginations—those that fill us with the Holy Spirit as was John filled with the Holy Spirit. The new Platonic teachings are to be sought in emptiness of soul, in the quietude of inner reverence. Just as the emanations from the great Cathedral at Chartres sent light throughout Europe, so now is the Etheric Christ forming a substance through which a new spiritual Cathedral is forming, radiating the new Platonic teachings; but first we must understand that something virginal is awakening, sculpting a place that is a seed form of our promised future.

Christ Jesus said: "Behold, I make all things new." The virginal forces of the "I" are to penetrate all space, ennobling our understanding of the planets and all aspects of life. Just as the "I" purifies the astral, so too is the world "I" revealing the higher aspect—the manas purity—of planetary potencies. The planets tend to behave in the manner we assign to them, in the way that we see them. If we become ever more aware of the virginal qualities that, through Sophia, are streaming into all things—planets, stars, human beings, animals, plants and even the stones—then will we cultivate them through the dictates of God's will, and thereby gain new capabilities.

This can happen one step at a time; but first we must recognize "specialization," dismantle our intellectual edifices, and then respond as if the

virginal purity of truth could still enter our fallen world. Our obsession with building towers will then wane; and instead of calling in the masons, we will call the gardeners. We will till the soil so light can find us. We will cultivate truth as the "force" that destroys all that eclipses our return to the attitude of God-soul. The scaffolding that imprisons us will become the garden that enlightens. The wheel of karma, which binds us, will thereby become the spiral of grace—and a new world of dharma will open before us.

Re-envisioning the Planets

The true horoscope will not be reached by a path of calculation but through a path of interaction with suprasensory beings. What Angels have imparted to humankind, that is the "horoscope" in the true sense.[41]

A closer look at Tomberg's re-imagining of planetary influences encourages us to re-imagine what we think we know about them in order for what we don't know about them to refresh our understanding.

Astrologers have a great deal of influence when giving their readings. The linga sharira in each client is hungry for information that feeds its further existence. The higher self of the client is, however, simultaneously hoping for the lower self to receive inspirations that help turn the temporal self toward its inherent longing for the Divine.

Each planetary sphere relates to realms of existence in which dwell beings of higher consciousness. Of the classical planets, the further away the orbit of the planet is (Moon, Mercury, Venus, Sun, Mars, Jupiter, Saturn), the greater the consciousness of the beings there dwelling. Similarly, with the transcendental planets, Uranus, Neptune and Pluto, the same principle applies—potentially, at least. I say "potentially" because, as Robert Powell explains in chapter 8 of his book Hermetic Astrology Volume 2, the opposite is the case with respect to the negative potential of Uranus, Neptune, and Pluto. Therefore, just as all new revelation seeks to guide us further in the evolution of

---

41 Tomberg, *Christ and Sophia,* p. 47.

our consciousness, so too are the cosmic spheres filled with beings who are also evolving.

> Hermetic astrology may be taken up as a seed impulse toward the development of a new wisdom of the stars (Astro-Sophia = "star wisdom"), in which case it can be regarded as being placed in the service of Sophia, who comes to meet inwardly…each human being's striving to bring Christ to birth within themselves. Christ and Sophia are central to the arising of a new star wisdom, and the New Age [of Christ's Second Coming] provides a unique opportunity for each human being to find a new relationship with these Divine Beings.[42]

Steiner noted that Isis-Sophia was long ago silenced, but that the veil to Her starry realms can be lifted by each mortal daring to gaze into Her holy spheres. Loyally aligning ourselves with Her wisdom opens us to cognize the virginal aspects of creation over which She reigns. The Comforter (Paraclete) is the bearer of Her wisdom; and from the vast reaches of world-wide space, Her wisdom is resurrecting. She is in the process of being wrested from the fallen luciferic powers and She is being called to life in those souls who seek Her. This is indicated in the following verse written by Steiner:

> Isis–Sophia,
> Wisdom of God:
> Lucifer has slain Her,
> And on the wings of world-wide forces
> Carried Her forth into cosmic space.
> Christ-will
> Working in the human being
> Shall wrest from Lucifer
> Isis-Sophia,
> Wisdom of God—
> And on the sails of Spirit knowledge
> Shall call Her to new life in human souls.

In seeking to understand what lies beyond the threshold of the sense-perceptible realm, our practice of ardently beholding the starry worlds can lead us into cognition of what streams into time from the womb of Sophia. The first seven Arcana of the Tarot are meditations that represent the seven classical planets; the subsequent Arcana represent the twelve constellations and the three transcendental planets (Uranus, Neptune, and Pluto). These spiritual exercises illumine the path that leads into higher realms of existence, and in these realms the virginal nature of the heavens weave in a living process of eternal transformation. In his re-envisioning, Tomberg gives us imaginations for pondering the virginal forces of the seven planets—which manifest in a truly hermetic way through those who speak to the stars. The hermetic astrologer finds that ever-deepening inspirations come to birth through meditation on the sacred truths contained in the Tarot. This is alchemical work.

If we concentrate solely on the astral signatures of the soul, in isolation from its higher manas nature, we increase the lower nature—we construct false idols, graven images. If, instead, we call in the higher octaves, we cast light upon the path our souls have pledged to walk. Astrosophy (the term Steiner used for the new astrology) means "becoming one with the wisdom of the stars."

> The calling of the hermetic astrologer can be likened to that of a priest who looks to the world of stars as a revelation of the glory of God. Like Moses, his task is to ascend to the top of the mountain, i.e., to attain the utmost peak of consciousness, there to receive the divine revelation of the cosmic law as to how human destiny is woven into the world of stars.[43]

In his meditation on the sixteenth Arcanum, Tomberg writes of the way of the cross as the law of growth, "that of perpetual dying and becoming. It is the way that does not lead to impasses of specialization, but rather to 'throughways' of purification—which lead to illumination and end in union."

Thus we are encouraged to remember the Hermetic axiom, "as above, so below," to avoid being paralyzed in the impasse created by a one-sidedness that inevitably tears the soul asunder.

The cosmic beings in the three Hierarchies interweave among themselves, forever passing from the

---

42 Powell, *Hermetic Astrology,* vol. 2, p. 351.

43 Powell, *Hermetic Astrology,* vol 1, p. 419.

Central Sun to Earth and back again. The three Hierarchies contain the following beings:

First Hierarchy:
　　Seraphim, Cherubim, Thrones
Second Hierarchy:
　　Kyriotetes, Dynameis, Exusiai
Third Hierarchy:
　　Archai, Archangels, Angels

Within each Hierarchy are beings devoted eternally to predominately one aspect of the Trinity:

The Thrones, Kyriotetes, and Archai directly serve the Father / Mother.
The Seraphim, Exusiai, and Archangels directly serve the Son / Daughter.
The Cherubim, Dynameis, and Angels directly serve the Holy Spirit / Holy Soul.

New portals open when we assimilate Tomberg's suprasensory planetary influences with the Hierarchies. We can thereby further enliven our perspectives:

Sunday / Sun: Resurrection—
　　Exusiai / Dynamis / Kyriotetes
Monday / Moon: The Holy Trinity—
　　messages from Angels
Tuesday / Mars: Archangel Michael—
　　messages from Thrones
Wednesday / Mercury: Pastors/Healers—
　　messages from Archangels
Thursday / Jupiter: Holy Spirit—
　　messages from Kyriotetes
Friday / Venus: The Passion—
　　messages from Archai
Saturday / Saturn: The Holy Virgin—
　　messages from Seraphim

There is a world of unknown things, and we are to journey there. The time is now upon us to begin a quest, for Uranus is again transiting (for the twenty-fourth time) the zodiacal degree marking its position at the birth of the immaculate soul of the Nathan Jesus in the constellation (Pisces)

whose virtue is Love.[44] We are encouraged to turn our Promethean gaze to the way of compassion. We can ask: "How can I participate with the creative substance of revelation?"

The reality of Paradise—as the foundation of our inner being and, concurrently, as the mighty surrounding cosmic sphere—exemplifies the inherent beauty of the Above, which ever reflects into the Below. Through the Fall, we left our vertical communion with God and became ever more entrapped in the delusions of the serpent's horizontal world. This marked our transition from obedience to disobedience, from poverty to greed, and from chastity to unchastity. Through the spiritual unity of the working together of the religious streams of Zoroastrianism and Buddhism in antiquity—continuing through the union of the Solomon Jesus and the Nathan Jesus—the path of initiates in the Western world has changed. For, if we are to regain the paradise we lost, it will be necessary to plumb both the heights and the depths.

The proclamation to the shepherds in their fields, spoken from the Star over Bethlehem, can be our guiding star for the year 2016 onward: "Be not afraid; for behold, I bring you good news of a great joy that will come to all the people; for to you is born this day in the city of David a Savior, who is Christ the Lord. And this will be a sign for you: you will find a babe wrapped in swaddling clothes and lying in a manger" (Luke 2:8-12).

The manger is the heart, the center of the mandala of Love. In the deepest recesses of our most inward being, a child waits. We journey upon sacred ground. For, if we become like this child, we can enter the kingdom of heaven, the starry mantle of Sophia—whence She is calling us. Behold, She makes all things new!

The commentaries in this Journal, inspired by Divine Sophia and the great teachers whom She inspires, are dedicated to the virgin nature of the planets and stars as they move through the starry signs during the coming year.

---

44 As the virtue for Pisces is expressed by Rudolf Steiner: "Magnanimity becomes love."

IN MEMORIAM WILLIAM BENTO

Claudia Mclaren Lainson

William Bento (June 8, 1951—June 5, 2015) suffered a stroke on the morning of May 22, 2015. Our dear friend and colleague crossed the threshold in Sacramento, California, at 9:41 p.m. on June 5, 2015. This was three days prior to his sixty-fourth birthday on June 8. The Sun on June 8 was at 23° Taurus, its position at the Ascension of Christ. The promise of the Angels at the event of the Ascension—the prophecy of the Second Coming—was Christ's etheric return ("in the clouds"). Thus did our friend die into the presence of Christ's loving embrace, which surrounds and imbues our earthly sphere. Rudolf Steiner prepared us to receive this cosmic event, and William Bento was a devoted student, throughout his adult life, of Steiner's teachings.

William's mantra was "interest creates warmth, and warmth is the womb of love." He loved wholeheartedly! He was driven by passion, enlivened by ideas, and enthusiastic in his interest toward others. His single purpose was to understand creation. He earnestly sought to part the veil to the spiritual world to behold the wisdom of Sophia. He faithfully persevered in all the wondrous teachings Steiner gave, through which his gaze was ever directed toward higher worlds and beings. William never stopped striving.

William died in the year Pluto was remembering Paul's illumination outside the Gates of Damascus. I rest with the thought that at the moment of his stroke, he encountered otherworldly illumination—as the kind of sunstroke that befell both St. Paul and Dante's teacher, Brunetto Latini. William's devotion to the mysteries of Grail Christianity occupied much of his attention during his life. Having sought Christ on the Earth, he most surely encountered Christ upon his death. The illumination that St. Paul survived became, for William, a bridge he would cross into spiritual worlds—for his time had come! The suddenness of his passing, however, remains a riddle to those of us from whom he departed.

At his death, William's heliocentric Mercury was rising, conjunct the Galactic Center (2° Sagittarius), and heliocentric Venus was conjunct the midheaven—which rested at 29° Virgo (Spica). From Spica the teachings of the feminine mysteries resound. The great Goddess who is the protector of the feminine mysteries was enthroned on high as William crossed the threshold, calling this man of genius into the mysteries she alone reveals—mysteries he sought endlessly to understand. Venus standing nearby tells us how dearly William loved his pursuit of the Sophianic stream. The Moon at his passing was conjunct Robert Powell's birth Sun. Surely the karmic connection between these two inspired students of Willi Sucher will continue into the future. Heliocentric Jupiter rested very close to the position of the Sun at the raising of Lazarus. William was no stranger to the karmic necessity of facing the darkness of the inner unconscious. These are some of the signatures of how William's Tychonic (heliocentric) death chart illumines his life work.

My friend and priest Diethart Jaehnig spoke of two wills that abide in the heart of each of us: the will to live, and the will to be. In William's heart dwelled the latter. If he could not be, he did not care to live. Such was the heart of many warriors for the spirit who came before him. William's health was not his primary concern—rather was his mission his guiding star, and he followed this until his body cried out for rest.

Now he rests in spheres where Angels dwell. They have opened his Book of Life; they are reading what he has there inscribed. He is now engaged in the mighty privilege of experiencing how his "will to be" affected all whom he encountered. We can imagine him standing stalwart before this chronicle, shying not away from errors he may now be facing, but rather jumping headlong into the center of each heart that will be presented to him. I am sure he is learning in these realms with the same relish with which he sought learning in his earthly life.

None of us can know the judgment William will place upon himself. What we do know is that the Angels judge not—they simply show us the content of our lives. Only to the extent we are willing to bear witness to their panorama of truth do we find their ready comfort. We pray William is embraced in this loving support as he makes his way through his life review. The courage he exhibited—as William—will most surely armor him with steadfastness on his new journey.

The winding road of William's biography is now seen from a new vantage. While on Earth he chose to learn the lesson of humility, and this he did through the travail of tears. It is so often the case that we assume our earthly vantage will render the same story as will the angelic vantage. Yet this is not so. Our mistakes are not brought down upon our heads like a sentencing gavel in a courtroom; rather do these "missings of the mark of truth" open portals through which we may enter, in order to find deeper understanding of both ourselves and others.

The foundational forces of creation sound through the sphere in which William now dwells. The symphony that performs the notes and cords representative of his eternal individuality surrounds him. This sounding of his innate selfhood is in harmony with the Christ he served. In this orchestration he is remembering the moral tones of his highest ideals. The discordant notes, born of any Self-betrayal, will sound as well; these jarring tones will penetrate into his bones, realigning his will, so that he may even better serve the Star that is intrinsically his when he again finds his way to Earth.

We remember William's Star in faithful devotion toward the light of his being that we here beheld on Earth—the William Star—and we will never relinquish this image. This we saw. William is our beloved friend to whom we remain loyal. And as loyalty is the constancy that never betrays what one has once glimpsed as the highest in the other, we carry this to him in prayer, in meditation, in remembrance.

William is not gone. He will continue to find us in our dreams and in our waking meditations. He now knows things that have long been veiled. He is our new messenger, who can offer us enlightened understandings of what really matters in earthly life. It is not the preservation of our temporal reputations, nor is it the will to be great. Rather, as he will he gently remind us, something truly noble—our spark of Christ's divine "I"—is striving to become one with us.

The priest in William learned the majesty that is born of humility. He is also most likely even more deeply aware of the sublimity which marks the path of service, knowing that both humility and service are the hallmarks of a true spiritual seeker. William learned how to suffer his individual passion, and in him the Rose Cross shone as his constant reminder that there are yet miles to go on our path of redemption.

William came to me in the night, showing me his recognition of a new octave in the revelation stream—it seemed he did not appreciate this as fully as he would have wished. Yet, along with his brothers and sisters in spirit, he now may serve the new revelation in ways not possible while he was on this side of the threshold.

As a brother of Christ and his Bride, William fervently followed his star, rarely asking for directions from the Herods he met along the way. He spent much of his life learning how to speak to the stars. Now the stars speak to him.

What would he possibly pray for on our behalf, but that we find our way to the Holy Grail—the center of Christ's heart? We send this prayer to him as well.

May we be at peace with his peace, and may the Light of the World, which surpasses all understanding, surround him and keep him. We celebrate his life, and we will endlessly carry our devotion for the Star that is his eternally. In times to come we will abide together in the Sun Sphere, and we will again make plans that soar above material concerns— so that we may continue the work of seeding the future that leads humanity ever forward toward the Omega Point of evolution's end.

We have much work to do! With his transition, William can now be thought of as a new inspiring "Angel" for the star wisdom of Astrosophy. The sweetness of his heart may be carried in our hearts. We may stand vigil for his presence, that we may hear his whisperings and glean knowledge from the many gifts he may now long to share with us. He will be missed!

⚶

William left behind a poem that elegantly expresses his experience of standing at the threshold, before life's greatest miracles and challenges. It seems his illustrious spirit touched into the mysterious depths he so ardently yearned to enter:

Notes To Self Taken in the Night... 9/9/2007

I am standing at the edge...
That threshold between the convention
   and the mystical.
Standing there, I feel my Self being seen
By the gazing presence of a waiting Angel.
Seeds within me have ripened.
The power of their awakening burst
Has my soul feeling the quenching
Of an intensive lifelong thirst.
 I am arriving in the midst of
A time that pivots on the
Faith and Hope of miracles.

I am opening to this collective
   sacred mission.
My Spirit Self is gradually
   and assuredly emerging,
As my Shadow is warmed, illumined,
   and melting like clay.
My trust in the light has been given to me
By Trials of Fire,
And by the tender touches of love
That have come my way.
I am ready to embrace it all,
And if it is too big to wrap
   my arms around it
I will just stretch this heart of mine.
Surely that glow of courage in my breast
Will shine like the Sun does,
Radiating light from East to West.

—William Bento

⚶

Publications:

In addition to the many articles that William Bento wrote year after year for the *Journal for Star Wisdom* (previously *Christian Star Calendar*) he was the author or coauthor of the following books:

Lifting the Veil of Mental Illness: An Approach to Anthroposophical Psychology (SteinerBooks, 2004).

A Somatic Psycho-diagnostic Approach to Personality Disorders, an Understanding of Personality through Spatial Orientation (Lambert Academic Publishing, 2009).

The Counselor... as if Soul and Spirit Matter: Inspirations from Anthroposophy (with Edmund Knighton, Roberta Nelson, David Tresemer, SteinerBooks, 2015).

Signs in the Heavens; a Message for Our Time (with Robert Schiapacasse and David Tresemer, SunShine Press, 2000).

THE FALL OF THE SPIRITS OF DARKNESS
AND THE RISE OF RUDOLF STEINER

David Tresemer

with Robert Schiappacasse and William Bento

In 1917, Rudolf Steiner gave a series of lectures in which he laid out a mythos for our time— a battle in heaven, ending in a victory for the principles of light, love, and order. The archangel Michael led the victory, and cast the enemy out of the heavenly spheres which the spirits of darkness had sought to control. Instead of a fairy tale "long long ago and far far away," Steiner gave dates for this event: The war markedly intensified in the early 1840s and ended in November 1879, suggesting a gradual beginning and a dramatic final conflict. We can celebrate with relief that Michael was triumphant...until we learn the outcome: The defeated spirits of darkness were thrust to earth and into the midst of humanity![1]

Given a recent time and a place right here amongst us, we cannot relegate this conflict to a fairy-tale realm. Yet how does this relate to our own experience? Can we notice any world phenomena that pertain to a war in heaven in those years? Do we perceive demons and zombies and other such enemies of humanity falling from the sky, disappearing in the dark, infiltrating politics, religion, art, science.... ? We can ask further: What kind of a friend is Michael to send such terrible beings into our midst? Or was there a plan in place to protect humanity? And finally: Does Rudolf Steiner have a special role to play in this drama? If so, what can we learn from him that might guide our own response to the spirits of darkness in our midst?

Context

In the Middle Ages, the heavens were seen to be alive with angels of all ranks and hierarchies, innumerable conscious beings. "Our Father who art in heaven" summarized this view. And so it was on earth, too. Here from the thirteenth-century "doctor of the church," Thomas Aquinas: "The entire corporeal world is governed by God through the angels."[2] In Anthroposophy, we look at nine hierarchies of angels, from Angeloi to Seraphim; to summarize all of these as angels is acceptable for this paper.

Devils and demons have long been perceived in the world, certainly before 1879. Emanuel Swedenborg described these in the eighteenth century:

> Lower-order hallucinations act against the patient's will, and are extremely verbal, persistent, attacking, and malevolent. They use trickery to deceive the patient as to their powers, and threaten, cajole, entreat, and undermine in every conceivable way. These are all characteristics of possession by evil spirits.[3]

Demons arise from a misuse of will and imagination, or rather find a home in a human being who has misused the powers of will (as in attraction to temptations coming from willing and feeling) and imagination (unsound use of thinking).[4] They thrive on denial of the truth—as in Mephistopheles' announcement to Faust: "I am the spirit that always denies."[5] They are typified by (and can be

---

1. Steiner, *The Fall of the Spirits of Darkness*, from original lectures of Sept. 29, 1917, to Oct. 28, 1917.

2. Thomas Aquinas, *Summa Theologica*, 1a, 63, 7. See also Sheldrake and Fox, *The Physics of Angels*.

3. A summary of Swedenborg by Wilson Van Dusen, *The Presence Of Spirits In Madness: A Confirmation of Swedenborg in Recent Empirical Findings* (at www.zianet.com/web/presence_spirits .htm). Though these might seem to typify Luciferic demons, one can understand Ahrimanic demons working also through these methods.

4. From Anonymous, *Meditations on the Tarot*, p. 408.

5. Richard Smoley, "Made in Our Image," *Parabola*,

identified by) a refusal to praise.[6] As praise comes from the natural response to awe, joy, and wonder, spirits of darkness can be identified by the absence of those capacities.

We won't here go into greater depth concerning angels and demons, a grand study in itself, but rather look at the issue of an extraordinary "fall" of spirits of darkness.

1840–1879

Since we ascribe to "as above, so below," do we notice in some way events on earth that reflect the war in heaven with its final greatest battle occurring in November 1879? Can we find phenomena on earth that reflect an uprising of activities in other spiritual realms? We tend to assume every event into a time line of what occurred before and what came after. It becomes difficult to say, "That particular point of development is more important than the others." We don't have in this period something radically unusual and dramatic such as the explosion of an atom bomb. However, let us note a few important occurrences during this time in different fields of human endeavor.

- August 27, 1859. The discovery of oil in Titusville, Pennsylvania, led to an oil rush, first in Pennsylvania, then in Texas and California. The oil economy has revolutionized the lives of everyone on earth, including vastly expanded possibilities as well as apparently irremediable pollution of air, water, and earth.

- November 24, 1859. The publication of *The Origin of Species* by Charles Darwin changed the way we think about ourselves. It rejected the dominant fixed belief at the time that the earth was six thousand years old and that nothing had changed since creation. However, the sentiment went much too far in the other direction toward materialism, finding in mechanism the source of life, and basing change on survival through violence.[7] Darwin's first

writing about his ideas occurred in 1844. The debate that brought Darwinian evolution to prominence occurred between Huxley and Wilberforce on June 30, 1860. All of these occurred in the period of agitation defined by Steiner.

- October 22, 1850. Gustav Fechner had a dream from which he formulated Fechner's Law (rise in sensation varies with the logarithm of increase of stimulus), attributed by Ken Wilber as the severing of soul and spirit from the brain.[8]

Kevin Dann has also probed history to give some hints about these years.[9]

November 1879

The importance of 1879 had been forecast by Johannes Trithemius, abbot of Sponheim, in the sixteenth century, here in the language of old: "The twentieth time in order, *Gabriel* Angell of the Moon received the moderation of the World, in the year of the World 6732. the fourth moneth, and fourth day of *Iune*: in the year of Christ 1525. and he shall regulate the world 354. years, and four moneths, untill the year of the world 7086. eighth moneth, but of our Lord Christ 1879. and 11. moneth."[10] This prophecy was affirmed and extended by Eliphas Levi.[11]

Natural Selection, or the Preservation of Favoured Races in the Struggle for Life, is important to note because the book did not actually deal with origins, and soon became confused as a treatise on the origin of life, rather than "how different forms come about." Had it been titled, *A Theory on How Forms of Related Flora and Fauna Diverge Due to Adaptations to Environmental Conditions*, it would not have had the impact that it did.

8 Wilber, *Integral Psychology*, early pages.

9 Kevin Dann, "Spectres," *Journal for Star Wisdom 2016.*

10 From Johannes Trithemius (1462-1516), *De Septem Secundeis* (Seven Secondary Intelligences), original 1508, translated to English by William Lilly, published London 1647. Accessed at www .esotericarchives.com/tritheim/tritem.htm. Ernst Katz, in "The Mission of Rudolf Steiner," refers to Trithemius, giving the places also where Steiner referred to Trithemius. See Katz's powerful address at: www.rsarchive.org/RelAuthors/KatzErnst/AGM _Address.php.

11 Eliphas Levi (1810-1875), "The Magical Ritual of

---

summer 2015 (issue on "Angels and Demons"), pp. 22–31, especially p. 26.

6 Matthew Fox in Fox and Sheldrake, "Return of the Angels," *Parabola*, summer 2015, p. 72, citing Hildegard of Bingen and Thomas Aquinas.

7 The full title, *On the Origin of Species by Means of*

Steiner referred to the prophecy of Trithemius in other lectures, though not in *The Fall of the Spirits of Darkness*. He does not footnote when he has undertaken to verify another's observation and thus report it as truth from his point of view.[12] Following Trithemius for the date, yet expanding upon this prophecy with greater detail, Steiner indicated that the great battle took place in the month of November, a time that we shall call the "Fall." Such a dramatic occurrence likely did not all happen in a day. It may have happened before, as we find the event spoken of in Revelation 12:7-9:

> Then war broke out in heaven. Michael and his angels fought against the dragon, and the dragon and his angels fought back. But he [the dragon] was not strong enough, and they lost their place in heaven. The great dragon was hurled down— that ancient serpent called the devil, or Satan, who leads the whole world astray. He was hurled to the earth, and his angels with him.

But that may have been a prophecy for this event of 1879—in November. The term of a month gives an astrologer a degree of specificity much more useful than, say, the cultural shifts of an entire age. What occurred in the celestial patterns of the heavens at this time?

What do we see when we examine the main astrological phenomena of November 30, 1879, the culmination of the month of November 1879.[13]

First observations:

- Pluto at Algol. In our book together, we identified the importance of the star Algol, the "Eye of Medusa," known since ancient times as the most malefic of the stars, at 2½ degrees of the Bull.[14] When two comets made a cross in the sky over that point on April 11, 1996 and 1997, we hypothesized that there had been a message given to the world, a message that cultural phenomena were working toward the hardening—the effect of the gaze of Medusa's eye—of the bodies and consciousness of humanity, in other words, a mythic picture of the work of Ahrimanic beings. At the event of the "Fall" in November 1879, Pluto (3 Taurus 9) lay very close to this point, suggesting that influences from afar were working to harden humanity.[15] When we set the Sun as exactly conjunct Antares,[16] on the final day of November, this put Pluto conjunct the ascendant. Pluto has the double nature of extremes of both the underworld and overworld. From our research, we have seen its potent effects in the world and on individuals. Here it gives its signature to a time-marker of a transition of an age. As we described in our book, *Signs of the Times*, we are in danger of turning to stone, becoming hardened, the continued work of what was unleashed during the time of the "Fall."

---

the Sanctum Regnum" (Ibis, 2004), version from www.selfdefinition.org. Also from a booklet *How the World Came to an End in 1881* (from www.anna-kingsford.com): "Pursuing his researches through the ages, Trithemius was brought by rigid calculations to the month of November, 1879, as the epoch of the reign of Michael, and the foundation of a new universal kingdom. This kingdom, he foresaw, would be prepared by three and a half centuries of anguishes, and three and a half centuries of hope.... 'We see then,' says Eliphas Levi, writing in 1855, 'that in twenty-four years, or 1879, there will be founded an universal empire, which will give peace to the world. This empire will be at once political and religious, and will give solution to all the problems which agitate our days, and will last 354 1/3 years.'"

12 In many other places, Steiner refers to Trithemius, however, not in this one.

13 As in the year 1508 Trithemius would have been

referring to the Julian calendar, the Gregorian calendar dates for "the eleventh month" would have been Nov. 13 to Dec. 12. Thus the choice of Nov. 30 in the Gregorian calendar sets us in the middle of the Julian month.

14 William Bento, Robert Schiappacasse, and David Tresemer, *Signs in the Heavens: A Message for Our Times*, op. cit., in which we attempt to translate the message of the seraphim in their placement of the comets in this particular way.

15 "The Signature of Pluto in the Events of Christ Jesus's Life, Historical Personalities, and Modern World Events," by David Tresemer and Robert Schiappacasse, *Christian Star Calendar 2008* (at www.StarWisdom.org, Research section).

16 As we explained, there are thirty choices in the month of November. Either the sun would be close to Antares (15 Scorpio), or directly conjunct. We chose the latter to investigate.

Event of 1879 - Fall with Sun at Antares - Geocentric
At London, Middlesex, United Kingdom, Latitude 51N30', Longitude 0W10'
Date: Sunday, 30/NOV/1879, Gregorian
Time: 15:16, Time Zone GMT
Sidereal Time 19:51:48, Vernal Point 6 ♓56'10", House System: Equal
Zodiac: Sidereal SVP, Aspect set: Conj/Sq/Opp WIDE

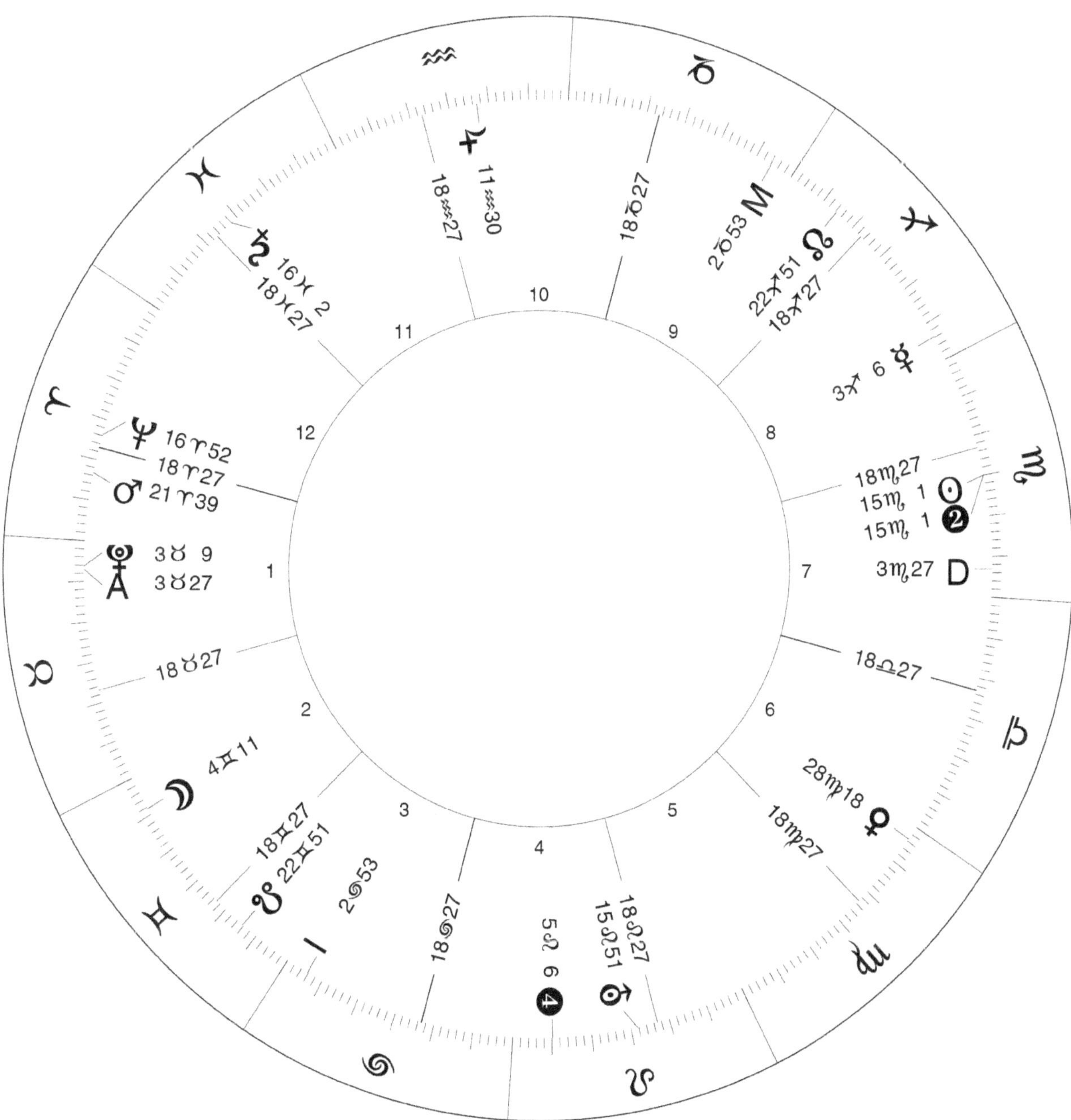

Dawn of the Michael Age, and Fall of the Spirits of Darkness

- Sun at Antares. In *Star Wisdom and Rudolf Steiner* and in other writings, we delve into the meaning of the Royal Stars of Persia.[17] We have come to call Antares the "Star of Death and Resurrection," finding there themes of destruction as well as self-sacrifice, a kind of destruction that has within it a great gift to others. At the "Fall" on the culmination day of the month of November 1879, the Sun lay exactly conjunct Antares (15 Scorpio 1, the number 2 in the chart above). From this signature, one might presume that we were entering an age when there might be destruction in service of a higher purpose.

- Sun position revisited. In *Astrogeographia*, Robert Powell links the city of Vienna with the star Aldebaran, what we have called "The Star of Life," life abundant, a sense of gifts overflowing.[18] Aldebaran is exactly opposite the star Antares. Watch for Vienna in the remainder of this study.

- Neptune at the place where the Sun lay at the Resurrection. Our reading of this has to do with an ideology that emphasizes rising up from life's pains and suffering. Without the preparation of living life fully, and enjoying its highs and its lows, and learning from the suffering of self and other, an ascension can become an empty distancing from the school. Neptune rules ideologies, and can lay these blankets of concepts upon any surface. To do so with the Resurrection can (and has) obscured its true teaching from many. The –isms in our lives seem to conceal more than they focus new thought. The intention of adversarial beings is to disguise, obfuscate, and confuse, in this instance, the true meaning of the future destiny of the physical body. As the main –ism of our time is materialism, repeatedly reinforced by technological

ubiquity (see sections below), the obscuration seems to be succeeding.[19]

- Mars conjunct Neptune, though wide for historical research (over four degrees), nonetheless empowers the Neptune dynamics spoken of above, by adding in what can become a tendency to violence as well as, in its positive guise, an ability to speak powerfully (Mars) something related to our ideas/ideology/ideals (Neptune).

- T-square amongst the Royal Persian Stars. Sun conjunct Antares (which means, by definition, opposed to Aldebaran), square to Uranus (15 Leo 51). Jupiter (11 Aquarius 30) lay conjunct Fomalhaut (10 Aquarius). These three form a T-square, with the empty corner of the box at Aldebaran (mid-Taurus).

- Other Royal Persian Stars: Pluto square Regulus (5 Leo 6, the number 4 in the chart above). The engagement of all of the four grand watchers of the skies suggests a plan by Michael to give celestial support to a "download" (to use the modern term) of difficult characters into the human sphere. We will speak about Antares/Aldebaran and the squares to that axis later.

- Other Royal Persian Stars: Venus exactly conjunct Spica at 29 Virgo. Concerning Venus on Spica, the Goddess Star, source of effulgent effervescence, we could say that the 1879 event was related to empowerment (Spica) of karmic groups (Venus), which we might see active in the world after the "Fall." Positive engagement in one's karmic groups involves identification of those of like mind, and working alongside them for the common good. Negative engagement in one's karmic groups involves regression to gangs that work against the common good. One could also see the timing of Michael to protect the "woman clothed with the sun, with the moon under her feet and a crown of twelve stars on her head" (Rev. 12:1).

---

17 David Tresemer with Robert Schiappacasse, *Star Wisdom and Rudolf Steiner: A Life Seen Through the Oracle of the Solar Cross* (Gr. Barrington, MA: SteinerBooks, 2007), and papers published in the *Journal for Star Wisdom*.

18 Powell and Bowden, *Astrogeographia*.

19 See reference papers, "The Signature of Neptune in World Events," and "Corporate Personhood: The Touch of Neptune," by David Tresemer, both from *Journal for Star Wisdom*, and at www .StarWisdom.org (research section).

World Events

Given that we're looking for evidence of a strong influx of beings who harden human life-energy and human consciousness, who insinuate themselves into relationships through deception, who desire to undermine human progress, and who manipulate belief and perception so that their presence and work shall not be noticed—what in Anthroposophy are called Ahrimanic beings— what then can we find in world events during this month of November 1879?

We have found a few themes in our cultural life that passed milestones in their development in November of 1879. Can we point to "impacts from recently defeated demonic beings"? No. These must remain as hypotheses. Yet, just as the comets crossing in the heavens atop a particular star does not "prove" a message was sent, such an observation can lead to questions that we can ponder. (As I write this, the fire alarm has gone off in the hotel where I am staying. Does this prove that a fire is in the building? No; we know that "false positives" in alarms are all too frequent. However, the alarm does constructively cause me to query about my readiness should there be a fire.)[20]

Photography

Of primary importance were developments in the field of photography, especially the essential precursors of motion pictures—a strong electric light and a way of arranging still pictures in sequence to simulate movement.

In 1879, Karl Klic in Vienna—a city we shall revisit in this study—perfected a new process for photogravure. This made the taking of photographs more mobile than before.

On November 4, 1879, Thomas Edison patented the electric light bulb.[21] Note that he had been experimenting with hundreds of materials. One of these, a filament of carbonized bamboo, still

flickers twelve hours a day in the Edison museum in Fort Myers, Florida, though the light is very weak. The 1879 patent was for the light bulb that became the world standard with a filament of tungsten. Thomas Edison once said, "My body is a bucket for my brains." His birth chart has many relationships to the November 1879 event, including Sun and Antares on November 30, directly opposed to Edison's Birth-Jupiter.

Also in November 1879, Eadweard Muybridge perfected the zoetrope (or zoopraxiscope). He had already mastered fast-repeating photographs—of horses running, of cats licking water, of people walking. Now he connected a sequence of stills in a circle, with small slits to view them.[22]

You could view only one still picture through a slit as it flashed by, then a new slightly different image through the next slit, then the next. As the circle twirls, the human mind tries to integrate the discrete images into a sense of a unified whole. Because you only see any of the images a brief percentage of the time, you need a much stronger

---

20 There had been a fire in the kitchen, which was put out swiftly but not before the whole hotel was alerted to a fire.

21 Thomas Edison was born on Feb. 11, 1847, thus a child of the 1840–1879 period. Note that Neptune was discovered at the same time as electromagnetism, thus the relation of the light bulb to 1879 Neptune atop the Resurrection Sun.

22 See www.filmsite.org/pre20sintro.html.

source of light to make a motion picture. That's what Edison brought, in November of 1879.

Muybridge called his invention by different names that all began with "zoe," meaning "life." It got the title "The Wheel of Life." Something fixed—a hardness consequent from Medusa's gaze—had come to life. We know that these images are not living, yet they show movement so surely there must be a kind of life here?

Now we have thousands of films that have been made, over six thousand new feature-length films per year.[23] Each one tells a story made of a series of stills made to appear living as in the zoetrope. We are overwhelmed by many twirling Wheels of Life, to the detriment of the life that we are actually living.

An Unexpected Impact on Life Processes— Refrigeration

On November 4, 1879, Thomas Elkins patented the refrigerator, relieving the necessity for harvesting blocks of ice from frozen ponds in the winter, packing in sawdust, and hoping the warehouses of ice for iceboxes would last until the next winter.[24] Cold slows the breakdown of foods through the activity of microbes. Elkins made this available to anyone who could power a compressor pump with electricity; he also made freezing possible. Though the convenience of refrigeration has now become commonplace and unremarkable, we have to understand its role in separating us from life processes, from the prior necessity to keep living things in the ground or on the hoof and thus requiring an ongoing relation to our food sources. Refrigeration has been granted the power of a

miracle in averting what Thomas Malthus predicted would be mass starvation.[25]

Psychology

Building on the work of Fechner whom we mentioned before, Wilhelm Wundt built the first experimental psychology laboratory in 1879. He has become known as the founder of experimental psychology. His approach came to be known as Voluntarism. As Steiner links voluntarism with the sphere of Mars, we are most interested in the Mars-Neptune conjunction in 1879. Wundt's work laid the groundwork for the experiments and philosophy of the behaviorist and cognitive psychologists—the dominant forms of psychology today.

The Bureau of Chemistry was formed in 1879, becoming later the Food and Drug Administration (FDA). We see this theme also in modern psychology: the emphasis on psychopharmacology, which began in earnest in 1879.

Darwinian evolution, which swiftly became social-psychological in its explanations of all behavior of animals, plants, and humans, got a boost from the founding of the magazine *Science* in early 1880, dedicated to promoting the case for Darwinian evolutionary theory.[26]

Independence

One of the great contributions of Anthroposophy is to assert and demonstrate that certain cultural changes are not wrong per se but rather premature. The advancement cannot be faulted as it "feels right"; however, adversarial beings bring on these advances too swiftly, before humankind is ready to take responsibility for them. The technological changes that we have noted here are not "wrong," but perhaps wrongly used. Here's

---

23 This number from www.chartsbin.com/view/pu4. Of course, this does not cover the many short films, commercials, TV shows, etc. that are produced.

24 Other inventors worked on refrigerators as well. Note that these machines brought people into close contact with ammonia, methyl chloride, and sulfur dioxide in the pipes. When those pipes leaked, accidents could and did occur. People responded by leaving their refrigerators outdoors. "Freon," a mixture of chlorofluorocarbons, came into use only in 1929. Back to Elkins and 1879: His refrigerator was also used to chill human corpses, thus slowing the after-death process. You can find his patent at U.S.#221222.

25 Malthus and Gilbert, *An Essay on the Principle of Population* (1798). At Malthus's death on Dec. 29, 1834, Saturn (29 Virgo 22), his mission of warning to the world, lay exactly on Spica, the Goddess star, where we find Venus on Nov. 30, 1879. Spica, as one of the Royal Stars of Persia, and from our research the renewing source of love and blessing, is challenged by Malthus, and has the connection with Venus, about which we have talked.

26 Charles Bleckmann, "Evolution and Creationism in *Science*: 1880–2000," *BioScience*, 2006, 56:2, 151–158.

another example: Henrik Ibsen's play *A Doll's House* was published at the end of November 1879, and produced in December 1879. Though termed a women's liberation play, Ibsen's biographer Michael Meyer argued that the play is not about women's rights, but rather "the need of every individual to find out the kind of person he or she really is and to strive to become that person."[27] We would call this "individuation," with which we would agree. However, the play depicting an intelligent woman's breaking apart her family because she felt imprisoned by the cultural norms for the female gender caused an uproar. In that sense, it was ahead of its time; in another sense, it gave a necessary push toward recognition of the rights of women.

Aquinas

In August 1879, Pope Leo XIII stated that the theology of Thomas Aquinas was a definitive exposition of Catholic doctrine; he directed clergy to take the teachings of Aquinas as the foundation of their theological positions; he referred to the "precious fountainhead of the Angelic Doctor" which will become a weapon to wage war against "false wisdom."[28]

Plasma

The fourth state of matter, later called plasma, different from solid, liquid, and gas, was "discovered" in late 1879 by an English physicist, Sir William Crookes. As this makes up 99% of the visible universe ("and perhaps most of what is not visible"[29]), its importance for 1879 should be explored. In plasma, particles are much less dense, not bound, intensely energized, highly electrical and magnetic, and extremely hot. These highly charged entities can be experienced in lightning, auroras, coronas, nebulas! We suggest that the

naming of these phenomena brought a materialistic interpretation of the wonders of the universe. What was once the realm of divine beings demonstrating the wonders of existence was now corralled into industrial uses.[30] What was once felt to be filled with spirits—"our Father who art in heaven"—is now seen as deaf and dumb particles, each of which can be labeled and predicted…and ignored. As Sheldrake has summarized: "The heavens have been handed over to science."[31]

The Atom Bomb

We said that there were no events in 1879 as clearly pivotal as the explosion of the atom bomb, a release of immense amounts of plasma into the other three states of matter. However, at the first explosion on July 16, 1945, we find Mars in its warlike aspect conjunct to the combination of Algol, Pluto, and the Ascendant at November 30, 1879.[32] Humanity was taken that day into another realm through the bellicosity of Mars, then into an underworld of physical matter become unstable. We also note that the time when the atom bomb was used most destructively, 1945, was 66 years after 1879…and that 66 years after 1945 came the terrible nuclear release at Fukushima, Japan.[33]

---

27 Michael Meyer, *Ibsen*, p. 478.

28 Par. 26 and 27 in the encyclical *Aeterni patris*.

29 From plasmas.org. Higher states of plasma became the basis for explanation of a further mystery, namely "dark matter" and "dark energy," which are considered to account for 95% of the universe. The relation of plasma to dark matter and dark energy is still controversial, as are any arguments about a force or a thing that cannot be measured or seen.

30 Note the etymology: *plasma,* from *plassein,* means something formed or molded—in other words, a "thing" rather than a wonder. Crookes initially called what he observed "radiant matter."

31 From Matthew Fox and Rupert Sheldrake, "Return of the Angels," *Parabola,* summer 2015, p. 73.

32 Of course, the ascendant for Nov. 1879 is hypothesized. The location of Pluto on Algol would be true throughout Nov. 1879. The position of Saturn at the first bomb blast (on July 16, 1945) is exactly on the South Node of the Nov. 30, 1879, "Fall," suggesting that the first explosion of an atom bomb relates to the destiny line of the 1879 event.

33 These observations from www.rileybrad.wordpress .com/2011/04/26/fukushima-dai-ichi-and-the-karma-of-japan-by-bradford-riley/. It's actually not quite 66 years between Nov. 30, 1879, and July 16, 1945, the first atom bomb, or Aug. 6, 1945, the dropping of the bomb on Hiroshima. At the initial meltdown at Fukushima in March 2011, the Moon lay near Algol (5 Taurus 14). Bradford Riley's long article links the 66 years to the Christ rhythm of 33 years, which is actually 33 1/3 years, making twice that 66 2/3 years, so this timing is close but not exact. Terry Boardman, quoted by Riley, has

Also, as for the relation of the atom bomb to the date of the "Fall," Albert Einstein was born in 1879.[34]

Enter Rudolf Steiner

Most pictures of Michael victorious over the demons of sub-matter would show him banishing them into oblivion. "The huge dragon, the ancient serpent, who is called the Devil and Satan, who deceived the whole world, was thrown down to earth, and its angels were thrown down with it" (Rev. 12:7). This prophecy was usually taken to mean somewhere else, not among us—not within us. Was this the right place to send the defeated? Or has there been a mistake of some kind?

We thought we had discovered the notion that Rudolf Steiner was sent here by Michael in order to help humanity counteract the demons among us. From a law of spiritual teachings, Steiner would not have been able to claim this himself.

However, others have noted Steiner's birth at this particular time, Ernst Katz being the most clear and articulate, and there have been hints in the biographies by Emil Bock and Peter Selg.[35] We are not aware of an analysis of Steiner's astrological chart in relation to this event.

Let's begin with a brief rendering of what happened in 1879 in Rudolf Steiner's life. As a young man, he moved to Vienna in August 1879 to continue his schooling. At that time, he was immersed in the writings and lectures of Johann Gottlieb Fichte on finding the spiritual stream

in the world and in one's personal life.[36] On the commuting train in the mornings, he met a herb-gatherer, Felix Koguzki. From Steiner's reports, Koguzki introduced him to another man, "The Master," from whom Steiner received at least powerful advice, and perhaps a blessing, indeed perhaps a form of initiation into higher knowledge. These facts did not become known until the end of Steiner's life. Once they were known, various investigators went to the places where Steiner lived in 1879, to find traces of the mysterious men who had such a profound effect on him. Even recently, Peter Selg visited these towns, their churches, archives, and cemeteries, to learn the facts and to feel the presences that he described are still there. For they have been convinced that Steiner was carrying out a mission from Michael, and that an important part of this mission was revealed to Steiner in November of 1879, just in time to take on the infusion and intrusion of subtle forces into the lives of many. This was the rise of Rudolf Steiner.

From an entry in the diary of Walter Johannes Stein, "Rittelm[eyer] says, when he was asked to write a short biography of Rudolf Steiner, Steiner told him in the presence of Mrs. Steiner that he had two initiators: Christian Rosenkreutz and Master Jesus (Zarathustra). The latter referred him to Fichte. The former worked through Felix Balde."[37] Felix Balde was the name that Steiner gave to Felix Koguzki in the "mystery" plays that he wrote later in his life. Though in a public lecture, Peter Selg wondered aloud if Felix Koguzki was the "master," in that Christian Rosenkreutz worked *through* him.[38] In any case, we see the encounter

---

also pointed to the 1879–1945–2011 sequence. The latter two events can be understood as making-visible the invisible downpouring—the "Fall"—of the Spirits of Darkness.

34 Born March 14, 1879, Pluto is naturally at the same place as it was in November of that year, on Algol. Neptune is slightly changed, conjunct the Crucifixion Sun rather than the location at Resurrection. Venus in Einstein's birth chart closely opposes the Venus of the Nov. 30, 1879, chart.

35 Ernst Katz, op. cit.; Bock, *The Life and Times of Rudolf Steiner,* vol. 1; Selg, *Rudolf Steiner: Life and Work: 1861–1890, Childhood, Youth, and Study Years.* In a public talk sponsored by SteinerBooks in New York City on Mar. 20, 2015, Peter Selg affirmed that Steiner's birth had been timed in relation to 1879, as an invitation from Michael and Christian Rosenkreutz.

36 With a mentor such as this, one can look at the legacy of the mentor in relation to the birth configuration of the mentee. J. G. Fichte died on Jan. 29, 1814. At his death, Jupiter—the realm of wisdom and philosophy—lay at 18 Leo 11, within Rudolf Steiner's birth T-square (Feb. 25, 1861), which involved the centers of the fixed signs of Leo (Saturn), Taurus (Uranus), and Aquarius (Sun). This immersion in Fichte (emphasized in Selg, *Rudolf Steiner,* ibid. 61-73) has to be seen as the milieu in which the events of late 1879 took place.

37 Selg, *Rudolf Steiner and Christian Rosenkreutz,* p. 4.

38 That lecture at a seminar sponsored by SteinerBooks in New York City, spring equinox 2015.

Comparison Chart

Outer - Geocentric
Event of 1879 - Fall with Sun at Antares

Date: Sunday, 30/NOV/1879, Gregorian
Time: 15:16, Time Zone GMT
Sidereal Time 19:51:48, Vernal Point 6 ♓ 56'10"

Inner - Geocentric
Birth of Rudolf Steiner (V. ^)
At Kraljavec/Yugoslavia, Latitude 46N22', Longitude 16E39'
Date: Monday, 25/FEB/1861, Gregorian
Time: 23:25, Local Time
Sidereal Time 9:47:41, Vernal Point 7 ♓ 11'52"

House System: Equal, Zodiac: Sidereal SVP
Aspect set: Coni/Sq/Opp WIDE

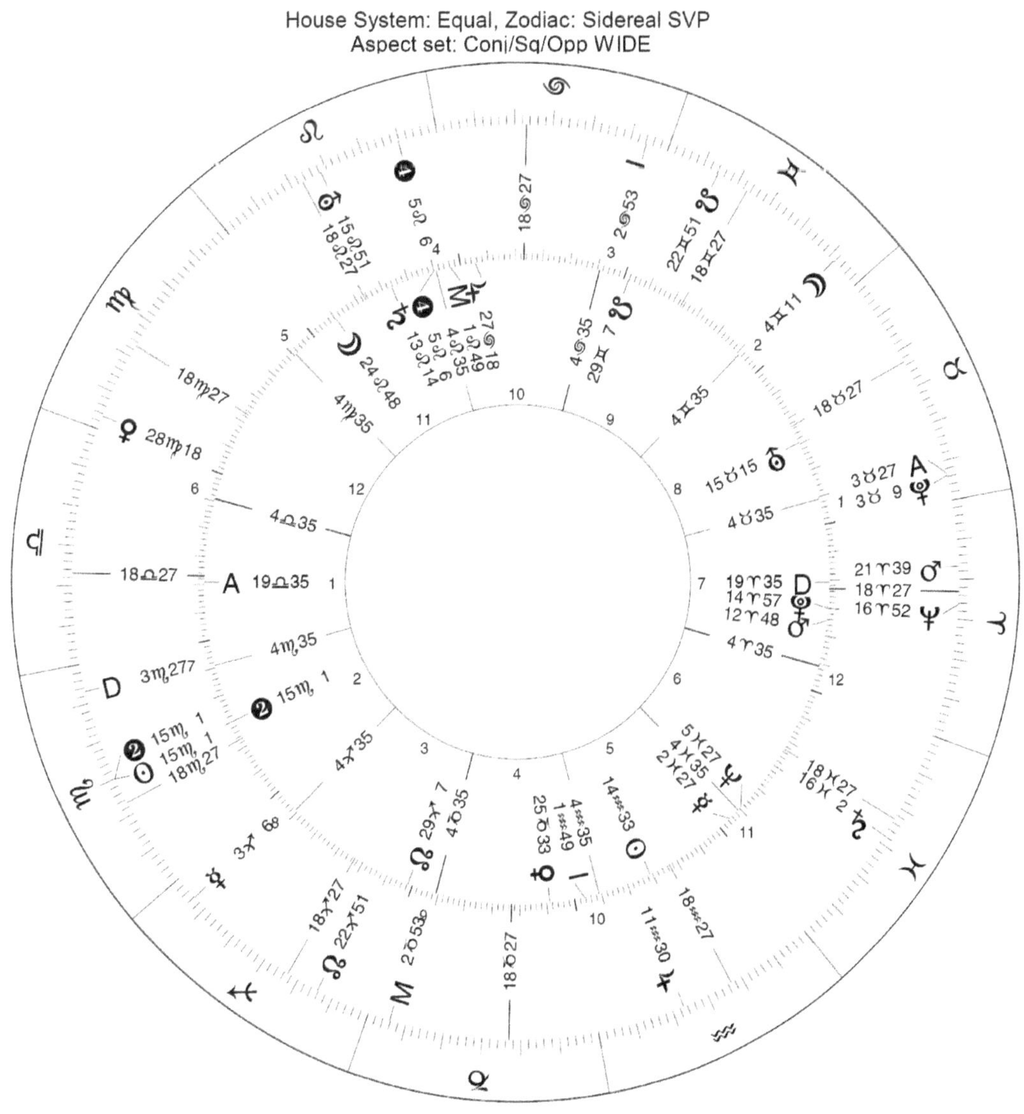

with Koguzki, Rosenkreutz, and perhaps other spiritual beings when Steiner came to Vienna in the autumn of 1879.

The encounter with "the master," which was not fulfilled until 1882 when Rudolf Steiner turned 21 years of age, began with his meeting the herb-gatherer Felix Koguzki that may have occurred on or near November 30, 1879. To "the master," Steiner expressed his deep concerns, here summarized by Bock: "How was he to tame the dragon of modern science and harness him to the vehicle of Spiritual Science?... How was he to overcome the wild bull of public opinion?"[39]

The master responded: "You will not conquer the dragon until you get inside his skin. As for the monster, you must take him by the horns. I have shown you who you are. Now go and be yourself."[40]

What do we find when we examine Steiner's birth chart compared with November 30, 1879? Steiner's birth chart lies in the center of this wheel.[41]

1. The Royal Stars of Persia. For the picture of the "Fall," we have shown the T-square with the Royal Stars of Persia—in Scorpio, Leo, and Aquarius. The birth chart for Rudolf Steiner shows the reverse T-square, with Uranus at Aldebaran in the center (15 Taurus 15), with one wing Saturn (13 Leo 14) conjunct the "Fall" Uranus (15 Leo 51), and in the other wing Steiner's Birth-Saturn (14 Aquarius 33) conjunct the "Fall" Jupiter (11 Aquarius 30). The open place for Steiner's birth lay in Scorpio, which is the center for the "Fall" T-square, featuring the Sun. These are very interconnected. Above is a picture of how these fit together.

The Sun and Uranus are important in both configurations, drawing on the higher functions of Uranus, the ability to bring forward new ways of thinking and being in the world. Jupiter and

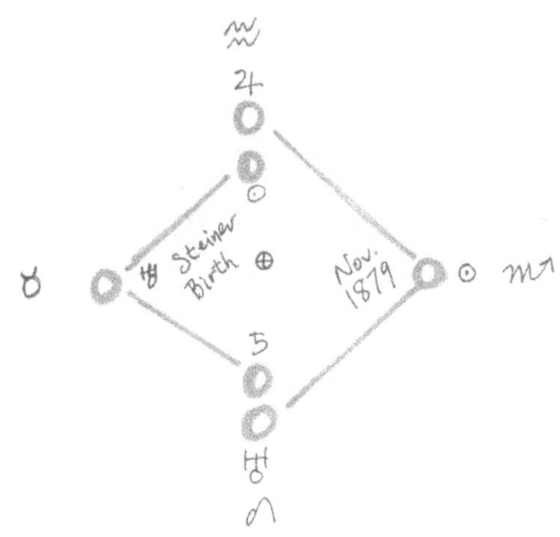

Saturn are also involved, bringing in the possibility of cosmic thought and cosmic memory. Steiner becomes the bearer of the signature of Michael's deed of November 1879. This is the way we can see the hand-in-glove configuration here.

At a young age, Steiner identified a bull of public opinion and a dragon of modern materialistic science. When we see the scorpion as a dragon, we have exactly pictured the encounter between Steiner's birth-Uranus at Aldebaran—in the center of the Bull—and the November 30, 1879, Sun at the center of the dragon-scorpion, at Antares.

Transiting Jupiter crossing Steiner's birth-Sun-Saturn opposition: This is a picture of guidance from an extraordinary personality who appears to assist Steiner to become the initiate to carry a new thinking into the world.

2. At the age 18.6, everyone experiences the return of the Moon's Node to its position at one's birth (29 Sagittarius 7). We usually interpret his as a facing of destiny in one's life, as the Moon Node line indicates something about what streams from the past as incentive in this life, and where the life is going into the future. For Steiner, the Moon Node had just passed the position of his birth. He was under the influence of this meeting with a destiny chosen before incarnation. One might think 18.6 too young to take on such a role in relation to the Spirits of Darkness. However, from this Moon Node return, Steiner was empowered by the forces active at this birth.

3. Where the "Fall" chart depicted Neptune at the same place where the Sun lay at the

---

39 Quoted in Bock, op. cit., 39.

40 Ibid., Steiner here quoting what the master said to him at that time.

41 We follow the research by Robert Powell showing Steiner's birth was on February 25, not February 27 when he was baptized. The documentation of this conclusion is summarized in Appendix C of *Star Wisdom and Rudolf Steiner*, op. cit., with references to the Powell works in which the facts are laid out.

Resurrection, Steiner's birth chart depicts Pluto and Mars nearby, but on the Crucifixion side, that is, earlier in the sign of the Ram. Steiner's task was to take on the suffering of humanity, not to jump to the solution of rising happy-faced into heaven without preparation, but rather to experience the daily grind and the challenges of grief and loss—as preparation for such as ascension.

Confronting the Spirits of Darkness

Questions: If Rudolf Steiner has come specifically to assist humanity in its confrontation with the spirits of darkness, are we meant to learn from him? From his teachings? From his example?

One thing that Steiner recommended was to identify the workings of adversarial spirits in oneself, in others, and in culture in general. This must always be delicate, as diagnosing others with "possession" is fraught with error as well as being very unpopular. Indeed, one of the techniques of Ahrimanic beings is to undermine our ability to see these beings, and indeed to name their presence as impossible. If human beings are relegated to the product of "natural selection," meaning survival through violence, then we cannot see the grandeur in each and every soul, an intrinsic power that deserves respect. Without respect, the worst of human behavior can be labeled "natural." We relieve each other of responsibility when we demean the nature of human-beingness. Steiner worked against that, promoting a remembrance of the true magnificence of every body, soul, and spirit.

For this Steiner recommended personal inner work on a regular basis. Instructions for this can be had through many classes and books. We should never take for granted the existence of these resources, for which we can be grateful.

Steiner can thus be a guide for our journey through the valleys of the shadows. The final task of an encounter with the spirits of darkness is to learn from them, and become better human beings.

The following further questions from Robert Schiappacasse are intended as leading thoughts, and must be pondered to have their full effect.

Think of a moment when you observed with awe and wonder the magnificence of another human being. How did this experience make you feel?

What spiritual or religious practices are central to your life? What is it that helps you?

Take a moment to review recent experiences in your life. Can you identify a moment when you were challenged to respond to an incident, involving yourself or others, that was dark, immoral, or thoughtless? Steiner emphasized awareness of self and self-knowledge as central to the path of individual development in our time. Making a mistake or doing something wrongly, and becoming aware of it, forms the foundation for becoming conscious—and doing it the right way the next time.

What helps you better understand/perceive the challenge to awaken and respond to evil in our age? Can you imagine that your increasing ability to recognize and encounter evil, in yourself and in the world, has been Michael's goal from the beginning?

Can you identify one instance in your life where you made a choice that you would not have been able to make unless you had become acquainted with Rudolf Steiner? That's the core of this study—in a dark time, with the help of Steiner as a mentor, finding the freedom to choose a path relating to your mission and destiny.

A Note from William Bento

(William Bento wrote some comments that he sent in response to early versions of this paper. Though he intended to add more, the following notes are possibly the last words that he wrote. Edits to his notes, as well as the footnotes, are by David Tresemer.)

The fall of the Spirits of Darkness can be evaluated firstly through the lens of a loss of human culture. We could group all the historical events of scientific innovation that, even while the 20th century became heralded as an "Age of Progress," have led to a mesmerizing of the senses.[42] We could then point to the outcome of

---

42 Kevin Dann has given an expanded version of this catalogue in his article in this Journal. "Mesmerizing" comes from the work of Franz Anton Mesmer (1734–1815) who developed a form

this "progress" for twenty-first-century humanity. Such a list would include, as you have done, the light bulb, refrigeration, photography, the film industry, and a plethora of technological distractions.[43] Second, we could focus on the emergence of a psychology under the ruse of a pseudo-science wedded with the psychopharmacology industry resulting in a materialization of the human soul.[44] For example, the challenge of *We've Had a Hundred Years of Psychotherapy—and the World's Getting Worse.*[45] Thirdly,

we could focus on the parallel development of a global economy of inequity—and inequity of economy—and the related disturbing demise of balance in our ecology.[46] The spirits of darkness *lead* us down a threefold abyss.[47]

One could imagine that this attack by fallen spirits of darkness is strategically aimed at

---

of hypnosis, which in Anthroposophy is understood as an unhealthy dominance of the willpower of another.

43 Pope Francis expressed similar concerns in the encyclical released just after William's passing over the threshold—in "Laudato Si'" (pub. June 18, 2015), especially in chapter 3, part I, numbers 106ff. For example, Francis wrote, and spoke, "The basic problem goes even deeper: it is the way that humanity has taken up technology and its development according to an undifferentiated and one-dimensional paradigm.... We have to accept that technological products are not neutral, for they create a framework which ends up conditioning lifestyles and shaping social possibilities along the lines dictated by the interests of certain powerful groups" (#106, 107). These sentences were among many others that reflect the subject of this paper and the tone of Bento's comments. "Laudato Si'" is a phrase from St. Francis's "Canticle to the Sun"; Bento had a particularly strong connection with the life, writing, and mission of St. Francis.

44 "Pseudo-science" is here not used in its usual way to typify those who evaluate phenomena via feeling and intuition, but rather to characterize so-called "scientists" who, through manipulation of so-called objective methods, come to conclusions that serve those who hire them rather than the human beings who are affected. One example that the three co-authors recently discussed involved the studies of effects of GMO seeds. When separated into two groups, the results were strikingly different. The group of studies performed by independent researchers found serious problems with GMO crops consumed by animals. The group of studies funded by the GMO industry found no such effects. This is an example of what Bento terms "pseudo-science."

45 *We've Had a Hundred Years of Psychotherapy,* by the transpersonal Jungian psychologist James Hillman and Michael Ventura (New York: Harper 1993), challenges the assumption in traditional psychotherapy that healthy individuals

make a healthy world, instead pointing out that the emphasis on individuals makes for a preoccupation with oneself, with nothing left over for the world—for relationships or the needs of the social fabric. The modern emphasis on the "inner child" leaves people feeling powerless; the modern emphasis on getting your thoughts more positively oriented (cognitive behavioral therapy) substitutes formulaic thoughts for one's ability to penetrate to the truth of the situation. These trends focus attention on personal needs, leaving the clients of psychology prey to the "plethora of technological distractions" to which Bento refers.

46 In Tresemer, *The Counselor...as if Soul and Spirit Matter,* and elsewhere, Bento often wrote about the threesome of the realm of economy (will in action, destined to become cooperation or fraternity), the realm of the social-political (the territory of feeling, in its best as equality, here undermined by a psychology that undermines community), and the realm of culture (the territory of thinking, at its best liberty, here attacked by mesmerizing technology). Pope Francis, "Laudato Si'," op. cit., #2: "This sister [Mother Earth] now cries out to us because of the harm we have inflicted on her by our irresponsible use and abuse of the goods with which God has endowed her. We have come to see ourselves as her lords and masters, entitled to plunder her at will. The violence present in our hearts, wounded by sin, is also reflected in the symptoms of sickness evident in the soil, in the water, in the air and in all forms of life. This is why the earth herself, burdened and laid waste, is among the most abandoned and maltreated of our poor; she 'groans in travail' (Rom 8:22)." Bento and the Pope here are thinking in parallel.

47 William Bento here suggests that the first abyss is that of fallen thinking, the second a fallen feeling, and the third a fallen will. The threefold social order—one which balances freedom (in the thinking sphere), equality (in the feeling sphere), and fraternity (in the economic sphere)—is something Bento has written about repeatedly and extensively, including in his chapters for the book *The Counselor...As If Soul and Spirit Matter*, op. cit. (See previous note.)

destroying the life of the senses,[48] the sensibility of soul,[49] and the life processes.[50]

Steiner has given remedies for each of these attacks on human beings and humanity.[51] But do we have sufficient sensibility of what comprises humanity—sufficient to know how to use the remedies?[52] We need a rise of the Spirits of Light. May we, as suffering and striving human beings, be the Rise of the Spirits of Light? If our answer is yes,[53] then how do we illumine the keys to our salvation that Steiner gave his entire life disseminating?[54] May the first task be in recogniz-

ing where the Spirits of Darkness are at work?[55] It is not so much that we wield a Michaelic Sword to vanquish them,[56] for that is Michael's calling.[57] Rather should we first with discernment weigh the consequences of the fall of the Spirits of Darkness.[58] What is needed is a type of thinking free

---

48 Anthroposophy identifies twelve basic senses, greater than the usual five, and proposes that each sense is a gift of the cosmos to the consciousness of the awakening human being.

49 Here "sensibility" is used in multiple ways, referring to the twelve senses that connect us with the physical realities, the senses' ability to expand to relate us to cosmic realities, and to the "good sense" or "common sense" of the existence and functioning of the soul that, while accepted by every normal person as real, has been attacked and rejected by materialistic science.

50 The "life processes" refers specifically to a teaching by Rudolf Steiner of seven life processes in the healthy human being (and community) that operate in every situation. These are detailed in Roberta Nelson's chapter 4 of *The Counselor...as if Soul and Spirit Matter*, op. cit.

51 Bento has written and spoken extensively about these "remedies," and founded the initiative of the Anthroposophic Psychology Associates of North America (APANA) in order to teach these remedies (www.APANA-services.org).

52 His point is that the present mainstream demeaning view of humanity as a violence-selection of random mutations of lesser animals cannot support the remedies suggested. Each person must ask the question from this sentence: "What is a human being?"

53 Do not miss here the opportunity to answer "no," and to assess the consequences of that action. And then to ask how often one has answered "no" in one's life.

54 The implication is that we have received those keys, and they presently lie in shadows, as yet un-illumined. "Salvation" never meant to Bento an attitude of bad-me-drowning-in-sorrow, but rather a revelation of the work of each individual in service of the transformation of the whole. Steiner has given a lead to this freeing from the chains of materialism. Karl Popper agrees: "Through modern physics materialism has transcended itself" (cited in Sheldrake and Fox,

The Physics of Angels, op. cit., p. 12). In other words, the investigation of matter has gone so far as to undermine materialism, though many materialists have not yet noticed.

55 This is not an easy task, as the spirits of darkness have insinuated themselves into every aspect of our lives and via the transhumanism movement which seeks to insert technological machines into our bodies as well. As Steiner said repeatedly, it is not a recommendation that we reject the culture in which we live but rather that we learn to balance the "plethora of technological distractions" with a healthy recognition and nourishment of soul. By citing James Hillman earlier, Bento implies a reference to Hillman's *The Soul's Code,* a study that Bento admired.

56 Michael was the archangel featured at several key points in the Bible. We have noted in this paper Michael's taking on the mantle of an archai, a "spirit of time," as the regent of the age, in Nov. 1879, without going into what this means; Steiner's lectures on the mission of Michael can assist that understanding. Although the account from Revelation 12:7-9 (cited earlier) does not show Michael with a sword, many artworks showing Michael, or his representative St. George, encountering the dragon (that summarizes the Spirits of Darkness) shows him with a sword. What is the sword? The sword is the power of discrimination between what serves truth, beauty, and goodness, and what does not serve those greater powers. In response to the query, "What is the sharpest sword?" the Buddha responded, "A word spoken in wrath is the sharpest sword" (from Paul Carus, translator and editor of *The Gospel of Buddha,* originally 1894, chapter 58). Though misspoken words can wield destruction, words used consciously become swords also to distinguish truth from falsehood, to distinguish beauty from vanity, to distinguish deeds of goodness from deeds of selfishness.

57 Bento, Schiappacasse, and Tresemer had many conversations about what is the task of humans to do, and what is the task of archangels, archai, the other hierarchies, and especially the spirit of our time, Michael, whose regency began in November 1879. When we confuse our role with that of more developed beings, and try to transform all of creation, we tire from lifting Michael's sword.

58 In other words, we should determine with a

from the illusions and magical powers of today's technological dominance. Naming the truth in distinction to appearances can set the mind free. Was that not the first lesson that Steiner taught us in his *Philosophy of Freedom*—his *Intuitive Thinking as a Spiritual Path?*[59]

Michaelic sword what have been the intrusions into our truest inner nature of layers of illusion, temptation, and misdeeds. Bento's journals show that he was deeply concerned with this introspection in the later years of his life.

59 When once asked what of his works would survive best the test of time, Steiner answered, *"The Philosophy of Freedom!"* (also published as *The Philosophy of Spiritual Activity* ; the newest translation is titled *Intuitive Thinking as a Spiritual Path: A Philosophy of Freedom*). Eduard von Hartmann wrote Steiner to suggest that the book should be titled *Ethical Individualism*, which Steiner liked (as reported in his lecture of Oct. 10, 1919). Originally written in 1894, before the major personal event in 1899 that pointed Steiner to the way of being that he came to call Anthroposophy, and before the outpouring of his five thousand lectures, this book tackles the predominant mechanistic pessimism of the

May this clarion call from William Bento continue to sound forth into our time.

≫

Note: The ideas in this paper arose from conversations among David Tresemer, Robert Schiappacasse, and William Bento. The three of us have written together in the past—*Signs in the Heavens* (see bibliography). For this paper, David Tresemer did the research and writing to demonstrate the ideas. Robert Schiappacasse has added questions after the main content. William Bento's comments given in preliminary form are at the very end.

time (then as well as now). *The Philosophy of Freedom* advocates an "ethical individualism" that overcomes the isolating barriers that Kant had set up to the limitations of human thinking. As Steiner later summarized his book: "When a person really experiences thinking [backed by healthy feeling and willing], he or she no longer feels as if outside the divine essence but within it."

"The stars are the expression of love in the cosmic ether...To see a star means to feel a caress that has been prompted by love.... To gaze at the stars is to become aware of the love proceeding from divine spiritual beings.... The stars are signs and tokens of the presence of gods in the universe." (*Karmic Relationships,* vol. 7, June 8, 1924)

"They looked up above all to what is represented by the zodiac. And they regarded what the human being bears within as the spirit in connection with the constellations, the glory of the fixed stars, the spiritual powers whom they knew to be there in the stars." (*Karmic Relationships,* vol. 4, Sept. 12, 1924)

"All the stars are colonies of spiritual beings in cosmic space, colonies which we can learn to know when, having passed through the gate of death, our own soul lives and moves among these starry colonies...with the beings of the hierarchies.... To understand karma, therefore, we must return once more to a wisdom of the stars. We must discover spiritually the paths of human beings between death and a new birth in connection with the beings of the stars.... There has come forth a certain stream of spiritual life which makes it very difficult to approach with an open mind the science of the stars, and the science of karma.... We can nevertheless go forward with assurance and approach the wisdom of the stars and the real shaping of karma." (*Karmic Relationships,* vol. 4, Sept. 18, 1924)

SHEPHERDS, KINGS, AND THE BIRTH OF JESUS
A STELLAR IMAGINATION

Brian Gray

THE FOUNDATION STONE MEDITATION

(fourth panel)

At the turning-point of time   Divine Light
The Spirit-Light of the World   Christ-Sun
Entered the earthly stream of being.   Warm
Night-darkness   Our hearts;
Had held its sway;   Enlighten
Day-radiant Light   Our heads;
Shone forth in human souls:
Light   That good may become
That warms   What we
The poor shepherds' hearts;   From our hearts will to found
Light   What we
That enlightens   From our heads will to guide
The wise kings' heads.   Purposefully.

—Rudolf Steiner, Christmas 1923

In the fourth panel of the Foundation Stone Meditation, Rudolf Steiner refers to two kinds of revelations concerning the birth of Jesus. One revelation warmed the hearts of poor shepherds; the other enlightened the heads of wise kings. The content of these two revelations differed considerably, yet each announced the birth of a child who would serve to bless, heal, and spiritually redeem the course of Earth evolution. These revelations were not given to single individuals, but rather to groups of individuals—a feeling of spiritual community awakened within the clusters of shepherds and kings who witnessed these revelations. With the birth of Jesus, the Spirit-Light of the World entered the earthly stream of being—a turning point of time for the Earth was at hand. Angelic proclamations and signs in the heavens stirred shepherds and kings to seek the child, pay him homage, and discover the deeper meaning of his birth.[1]

In his thirtieth year of life, when Jesus was baptized by John in the Jordan, the Cosmic Christ began to incarnate into his carefully prepared soul and body. As the Spirit descended from heaven like a dove and remained on Jesus, the Father in the heavens announced to John, "This is my well beloved Son, this day have I begotten Him."[2] Jesus

---

1   See Steiner, *According to Luke* (1909) and *According to Matthew* (1910), from which major portions of this paper are derived.

2   Steiner, *The Esoteric Significance of the Bhagavad Gita*, Lecture 7 (June 3, 1913). Rudolf Steiner's words express his spiritual perception of what is reported in Matthew 3:17; Mark 1:11; Luke 3:22.

was the human Grail prepared to receive the Cosmic Christ and serve Christ's intention to unite with humanity and to heal the Earth. As the Cosmic Christ united with the body of Jesus at the Baptism, the human Grail became the Holy Grail: Christ Jesus. Over the next three and a third years, the Spirit of Christ lovingly incarnated ever more deeply into the body of Jesus to experience and participate in the full range of joys and sorrows, sufferings and feelings of solitude that human beings go through on Earth; and even to go through the human experience of death to lessen our fear of its sting.[3]

This Divine Cosmic Being united fully with the human experience in a continuous deed of sacrificing love and compassion for humanity. Christ spiritualized the body of Jesus to prepare our future tasks and kindled the "I AM" within the soul of every human being, making it possible for individuals to unite and become membered into the human spiritual hierarchy as "Spirits of Freedom and Love." Christ united with the suffering of all existence, taking up the karma of the Earth so that the mission of humanity might be accomplished. In uniting with the Earth, all its kingdoms—elemental beings, minerals, plants, animals, human beings, angelic hierarchies—have become part of the Kingdom of Christ. Yet we are left in freedom to discover this for ourselves, right now or over the course of many lifetimes, and to become creative participants in this Kingdom. All this and much more were accomplished by Christ during his three-and-a-third-year ministry. As the closing words of the Gospel of St. John proclaim, "Jesus also did many other things, but if they were all written down one after another, I do not think that the world itself could contain the books that would have to be written."[4]

Shepherds, Kings and the Mystery of Two Jesus Children

The descent of Christ into the body of Jesus at the Baptism was the fulfillment of the revelations given to the shepherds and kings. Rudolf Steiner introduces this topic in 1920:

> The coming of Christ, of Jesus, is proclaimed to two types of human beings at the Christmas festival, though of course these two embody the same, single humanity: the poor, untutored shepherds in the field, who possess only simple common sense and a simple sensibility; and the wise kings from the Orient, that is, from the land of wisdom. To these latter the coming of Christ is proclaimed through their highest grasp of wisdom, their reading in the script of the stars. Thus Christ Jesus' coming is proclaimed both to simple shepherd souls, and in the loftiest wisdom of the three magi from the Orient. The profoundest meaning lies in this contrast of a proclamation to simple shepherds on the one hand, and to the wisest of the wise on the other.[5]

The shepherds and kings represent two kinds of human cognition. The angelic revelation warmed the feeling-will of the shepherds' hearts from within, nurturing seeds of love and hope and creative goodwill for future deeds. The stellar revelation appearing to the wise kings from the heavens awakened cognitive feeling–thinking in their hearts and heads. Memories of experiences from their previous lives on Earth were transformed through reflective thinking into wisdom and love inherited from the past.

While the shepherds' active willing bears seeds of strength for the future, the kings' reflective thinking bears wisdom as the fruit of past experiences. Both the shepherds and the kings experienced deep feelings of love in their hearts; in the presence of the child, they were deeply moved with the feeling that Jesus would indeed fulfill the promise of redemption for humanity and for the Earth (see figure 1).

Yet the child Jesus that the shepherds experienced and the child Jesus that the kings experienced were, in fact, two different children. Rudolf Steiner's spiritual research led him to declare for the first time in September 1909[6] that two different

---

3 Steiner, *The Sun Mystery and the Mystery of Death and Resurrection* (Apr. 2, 1922).

4 John 21:25 (Madsen, *The New Testament: A Rendering*).

5 Steiner, *Universal Spirituality and Human Physicality*, lect. 13 (Dec. 23, 1920).

6 Steiner, *According to Luke: The Gospel of Compassion and Love Revealed* (Sept. 15–26, 1911).

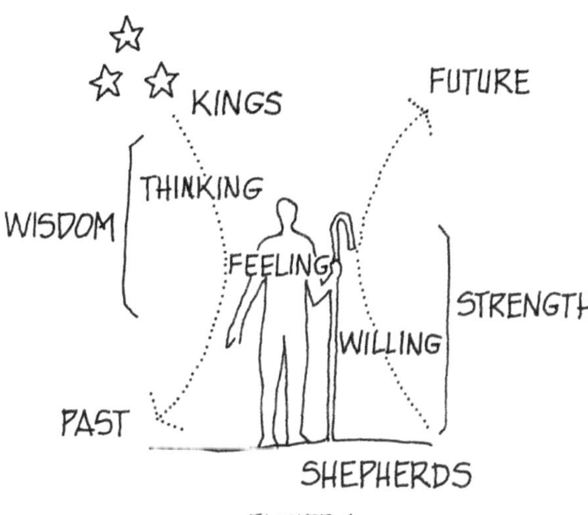

FIGURE 1

children named Jesus were born in Bethlehem within a short period of time. Both children were descended from the lineage of Abraham and David, but as stated in the Gospels of St. Luke and St. Matthew, the child Jesus described in Luke was a descendant of David's son Nathan of the priestly line (Luke 3:31), while the child Jesus described in Matthew was a descendant of David's son Solomon of the kingly line (Matt. 1:6–7). Each child bore unique gifts and qualities to the extraordinary degree needed for Christ's human mission to succeed. Christ could only dwell in the human body of Jesus for about three years before that human body would be shattered by the power of the spirit and waste away.[7] Hence the body and soul of Jesus had to bear the harvest of the fullest range of human potential and experiences possible, for Christ to transform these and unite with humankind—all within the narrow time frame of three and a third years.

It was not possible for one human being to be born fresh from Paradise, innocent of all earthly experiences and filled with virginal divine potential, and yet for that same human being to also bear the full experience of the effects of the Fall of Adam and Eve on human existence resulting from repeatedly incarnating on Earth.[8] The child Jesus to whom the shepherds came in Luke's account

was open, innocent, pure of heart and deeply loving toward all; this child bore aspects of the divine primordial human Being that had never before fully incarnated. The child Jesus to whom kings came in Matthew's account was the mature bodhisattva Zarathustra, who had harvested all humanity's experiences since the Fall. Zarathustra contributed to human evolution by repeatedly incarnating in different cultures over millennia to prepare humankind for the coming of the Christ.

A union of the attributes and experiences of both children was divinely arranged to provide the full range of human experiences needed for Christ to unite fruitfully with humankind. Thus when the Luke Jesus was twelve years old, the spirit of Zarathustra dwelling within the body of the somewhat-older Matthew Jesus voluntarily left that body and united with the twelve-year old Luke Jesus in the Temple, as described in Luke 2:41–52. In this way, the innocence of the Luke Jesus and experiences of the Matthew Jesus could be interwoven and brought to ripeness in stages of the biography of "Jesus of Nazareth" between the ages of 12 to 30 years. According to Rudolf Steiner, the technical name of the two Jesus beings united as one vessel between ages twelve to thirty was "Jesus of Nazareth." The uniting of the two Jesus children prepared Jesus of Nazareth to become the human Grail into which Christ began to incarnate at the Baptism, when Jesus was in his thirtieth year.[9] Just prior to the Baptism, Zarathustra voluntarily withdrew from the body of Jesus to make way for the Christ to enter in as "Christ Jesus." The experiences of the shepherds and the kings prior to the uniting of these two beings reflect the nature and bearing of the two different Jesus children (see figure 2 on page 90).

To understand the significance of Christ's incarnation at the turning point of time, let us explore the experiences each child contributed to the forming of Jesus of Nazareth, the human Grail prepared for Christ's appearance.[10] From 1909 until his death in 1925, Rudolf Steiner continued

---

7   Steiner, *The Esoteric Significance of the Bhagavad Gita*, lect. 7 (June 3, 1913); and The Spiritual Guidance of the Individual and Humanity, lect. 1..

8   Steiner, *The Concepts of Original Sin and Grace* (May 3, 1911).

9   Steiner, *From Jesus to Christ*, Lecture 8 (October 12, 1911).

10 Steiner, *The Mysteries of the Holy Grail*, lect. 2 (June 24, 1909).

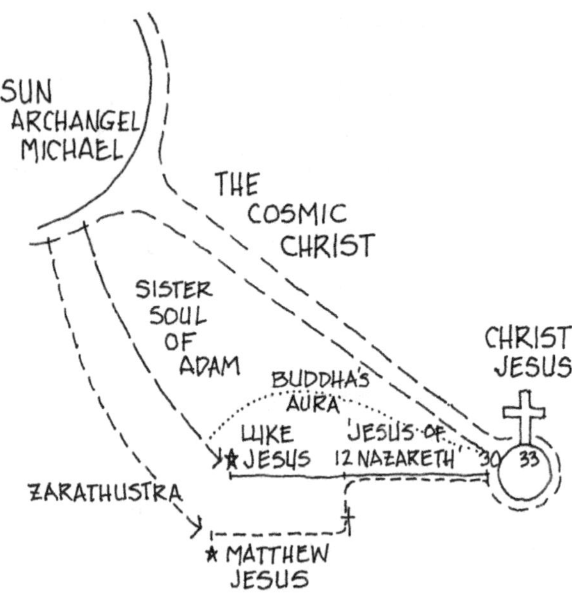

FIGURE 2

spiritual research on this and related themes. His insights became more and more expansive and complete, and a pupil of mystery wisdom can find no richer insights to study and contemplate. Since 1925, several authors have written exemplary works concerning the two Jesus children.[11] It is not the intention of this paper to repeat that research, but rather to extend those aspects that can help us form stellar imaginations of these profound spiritual realities.

Experiences of the Shepherds Concerning the Luke Jesus

The poor shepherds had common sense and little formal schooling; they bore deep piety of heart and goodwill. As they strode across the rolling arid Judean landscape near Bethlehem, they protected and guided their sheep in search of fertile pastures to feed them properly.[12] Through humble

attunement to nature and depth of heart, as the shepherds walked the land they sensed through their limbs the up-streaming expectancy from Mother Earth that Christ was approaching. The Gospel of St. Luke beautifully depicts the moment their inner clairvoyance and inspiration opened. One evening the shepherds saw and heard an angel announce to them the birth of a wondrous child who could be found nearby, lying in a manger. Then an entire heavenly choir of spiritual beings appeared, singing joyous praises about the goodness of this child. Finding the child, the shepherds' hearts were warmed with love and hope. St. Luke conveys the tenderness of love, compassion, forgiveness, and hope Christ brings to humankind and the Earth through this innocent child Jesus, who would grow to maturity and receive the Christ at the Baptism.

A mood of Paradise prior to the Fall permeates St. Luke's account of the birth of Jesus. Joseph and Mary had traveled south to Bethlehem from the verdant landscape of Galilee, leaving behind their Essene community of Nazareth. The Luke Joseph was descended from David through Nathan, the priestly branch of David's lineage.[13] Luke describes the birth of the child Jesus who along with his mother bore the pure, primeval part of all human beings "held back" in the sublime state of human existence that existed prior to the time of the Fall from Paradise. The Luke Jesus and Mary embodied the finest virginal qualities of divine potential within human nature because neither of these human spirits had fully incarnated since the time of the Fall.[14] They remained connected to abundant etheric forces of the "Tree of Life" that spiritually permeated all humanity in Paradise before the Fall. Their counterparts, the incarnated

---

11 See, for example, Bock, *The Childhood of Jesus;* Powell, *Christian Hermetic Astrology* and *Chronicle of the Living Christ;* Smith, *The Burning Bush;* and *The Incredible Births of Jesus;* Nesfield-Cookson, *The Mystery of the Two Jesus Children;* Childs, *Secrets of Esoteric Christianity;* Ovason, *The Two Children.*

12 "Pastor" is derived from the Latin *pastor* (shepherd), from *pas* (fed, or grazed), from the verb *pascere.* A shepherd feeds, or grazes, sheep in the pasture, just as a pastor, or priest, feeds the souls of a Christian congregation. Here we find a

link between the priestly lineage of Nathan and the shepherds. When Christ united with the Luke Jesus from age 30 to 33, Christ became known as "The Good Shepherd," who feeds the "I AM" to all human beings, his flock.

13 Steiner, *According to Luke,* p. 78.

14 Ibid. Indeed, with the incarnation of the Luke Mary and Luke Jesus, every created human spirit had now incarnated at least once. Adam and Eve were the first human beings to incarnate, and the Luke Jesus was the last to incarnate.

Adam and Eve, had been led by Lucifer's temptation to partake of the "Tree of Knowledge of Good and Evil" and to descend into human bodies prematurely, incarnating before the human form had been fully prepared.[15]

Jesus and Mary as presented in Luke had remained completely innocent of the experiences of the Fall, and the brief events described in Luke depict aspects of their first full incarnation. The aura of Paradise and purity radiating from Mary and Jesus had a remarkable effect, not only on the shepherds, but also upon Simeon and Anna, two elders who were deeply moved when they beheld the infant Jesus with his mother in the Temple (Luke 2:25–38). The Luke Jesus child was filled with inwardness, devotion, and love for all creation; having not previously incarnated, he lacked personal human "I" experiences that develop through living on Earth. Rudolf Steiner spoke of the Luke Jesus child as bearing a "provisional 'I.'" The higher spirit of this innocent child had been completely at home in the spiritual world and had served the evolution of humanity since ancient Lemuria, but in its first incarnation this innocent spirit needed the protection provided by his mother and father within the Essene community of Nazareth.

The peacefulness and loving compassion of Buddha also surrounded and permeated the aura of the Luke Jesus child. Rudolf Steiner identified the heavenly choir singing praises to the shepherds with these words:

> The image that appeared to the shepherds was the transfigured Buddha, the spiritual figure of the bodhisattva of ancient times, the being who had brought the message of love and compassion to human beings for millennia. Now that this being had completed his final earthly incarnation, he hovered in spiritual heights and appeared to the shepherds beside the angel who proclaimed what was to happen in Palestine....
>
> I must emphasize that this child had been chosen to be illumined and imbued from birth with the strength that had radiated from the Buddha ever since his ascent to spiritual heights [in the 5th century BC]. With the shepherds, we gaze at the manger where Jesus of Nazareth, as he is usually called, was born; we see the aura that hung over the child from birth and know that the image of the halo expresses the power of the bodhisattva who became the Buddha, the power that formerly streamed toward human beings and now influences humanity from the spiritual heights. This power worked toward the greatest event of all time as it shone above the child of Bethlehem and prepared him to take his rightful place in the evolution of humanity.[16]

Buddha had achieved Enlightenment and bestowed his teachings to humanity in the fifth century BC, during the archangelic Age of Michael (600–246 BC). The archangel Michael, ruler of Cosmic Intelligence, works from the realm of the Sun in service to the Christ. The circle of twelve bodhisattvas all serve Christ, and when a bodhisattva ripens new gifts and capacities that human beings can begin to generate out of themselves, a bodhisattva can become a Buddha, radiate that new capacity into humankind, and need no longer incarnate. Since the fifth century BC, Gautama Buddha assists in healing humanity from the spiritual world. His teaching of love and compassion completely permeated the aura of the Luke Jesus child. Christ would further deepen and extend Buddha's teaching of love and compassion by entering the body and soul of Jesus in his thirtieth year at the Baptism, in order to perform active deeds of love and compassion for all humankind.

Having completed his service to Christ as the Sun ruler of the period from 600 to 246 BC, Michael witnessed the Cosmic Intelligence descending into humanity as the Christ approached incarnation at the Baptism. Michael coordinated the efforts and spiritual gifts of Zarathustra, Buddha, and the pure soul of Jesus in preparing for Christ's descent. As the shepherds' hearts bear forces of goodwill to perform future deeds, the youthful will forces of the Luke Jesus child will shape the future evolution of humankind when kindled by the Christ.

---

15 Ibid.

16 Steiner, *According to Luke*, pp. 55–56.

What Resulted from the "Fall" of Adam and Eve?

To grasp the innocent nature of the Nathan Mary and the Nathan Jesus (who did not directly experience the Fall), we must inquire about the nature of "the Fall" of Adam and Eve into incarnation. In January of 1909 Rudolf Steiner gave an overview of "the Fall" and its significance for humanity today. After describing higher Beings who gave us our life of feeling, will, intelligence and form during previous stages of Old Saturn, Old Sun, and Old Moon, he tells us about the Spirits of Form (Elohim or Exusiai), the spiritual leaders of Earth evolution:

> On the Earth, the Spirits of Form endowed the human being with the "I" in order that by realizing oneself as distinct from one's environment the human might become an independent being. But even if through the deed of the Spirits of Form the human being had become independent relative to the surrounding external world on Earth, the human being would never have become independent of the Spirits of Form themselves; the human being would have remained dependent on them, the human being would have been directed by them (Spirits of Form) as on leading strings.
>
> That this did not happen was due to something that had, in a certain sense, a beneficial effect, namely the fact that in the Lemurian epoch the Luciferic Spirits set themselves in opposition to the Spirits of Form. It was these Luciferic beings who gave humanity the prospect of freedom—but also the possibility of evil doing, of succumbing to passion and desire in the world of sense.[17]

Luciferic beings took hold of the human astral body and possessed it, injecting into it seeds of self-interest and self-seeking. Self-interest does not stem from the true "I" of the human being, but from the results of Luciferic influence within the astral body. Without the intervention of Luciferic beings, the Spirits of Form would have remained solely in control of the astral body. The Spirits of Form would have instilled into the human astral body all that gives us our human countenance, all that makes us in the image of the gods—that is, all that makes us in the image of the Spirits of Form.[18] However, that would mean that for all eternity the human being would be completely dependent upon the Spirits of Form and would never achieve freedom:

> The Luciferic beings had crept, as it were, into the human astral body, so that beings of two kinds were now working in it: the beings who bring the human being forward (Spirits of Form) and the beings who, while obstructing this constant impulse, had at the same time established the foundations of human independence (Luciferic spirits). Had the Luciferic beings not approached, the human being would have remained in a state of innocence and purity in the astral body. No passions inciting one to crave for what is to be found only on Earth would have arisen in the human being. The passions, urges and desires of human beings were densified, debased, as it were, by the Luciferic beings. Had they not approached us, humans would have retained a perpetual longing for their heavenly home, for the realms of spirit whence the human being has descended. The human being would have taken no delight in earthly surroundings; earthly impressions would have aroused no interest. It was through the Luciferic Spirits that we came to have this interest, to crave for the impressions of the Earth. These Spirits impelled us into the earthly sphere by pervading our innermost member, our astral body. Why, then, was it that the human being did not fall away entirely at that time from the Spirits of Form or from the higher spiritual realms as a whole? Why was it that in our interests and desires we did not succumb wholly to the world of sense?[19]

---

17 Steiner, *The Deed of Christ and the Opposing Spiritual Powers*, lect. 1 (Mar. 22, 1909).

18 Gen. 1:1: "In the beginning, Elohim created the heavens and the earth." Gen. 1:26: "And Elohim said, 'Let Us make man in Our image, after Our likeness." *Elohim* in the Hebrew Old Testament is often translated as "God" when included with the Christian New Testament. References to the Elohim appear in the Hebrew Bible (Tanakh, or Old Testament) 2,602 times in eight primary forms or patterns.

19 Steiner, *The Deed of Christ and the Opposing Spiritual Powers*, op. cit.

Here we are given a remarkable insight: the Luciferic spirits who stimulated our astral body awakened in it cravings and desires for earthly pleasures, which remained in the aftereffects that reconnect with us whenever we reincarnate in succeeding lifetimes. Buddha later identified memory remnants of earthly enjoyments from previous lives as the factor that leads to human suffering: Buddha called it our "thirst for existence." But why did human suffering arise? Why do sense-enjoyments stimulated by Luciferic beings lead to human suffering?

It was because the Spirits who lead humanity forward (the Spirits of Form) took counter-measures; they inculcated into the human being what would otherwise not have been our lot, namely, illness, suffering and pain. That was the necessary counterweight to the deeds of the Luciferic spirits.

The Luciferic spirits gave human beings material desires; as their countermeasures the higher Beings (Spirits of Form) introduced illness and suffering as the consequences of material desires and interests, to the end that human beings should not utterly succumb to this world of sense. And so there is exactly as much suffering and pain in the world as there is interest only in the physical and the material. The scales are held in perfect balance; the one does not outweigh the other—so many passions and desires on the one side, so much illness and pain on the other. This was the effect of the mutual activities of the Luciferic spirits and the Spirits of Form in the Lemurian epoch.[20]

The Fall from Paradise took place in the middle of the ancient Lemurian epoch, during the age of The Twins (see figure 3).

Previously, during the beginning of the Hyperborean epoch—the age of The Ram—six Elohim separated the Sun from the Earth, while a seventh—the Spirit of Form known as Yahweh (Jehovah or Yahweh)—remained united with the Earth. During the middle of the Lemurian epoch, Yahweh separated the Moon from the Earth as "Adam's rib" to help offset Lucifer's influences upon the astral body of human beings. Simultaneously, Yahweh's

---

20 Ibid.

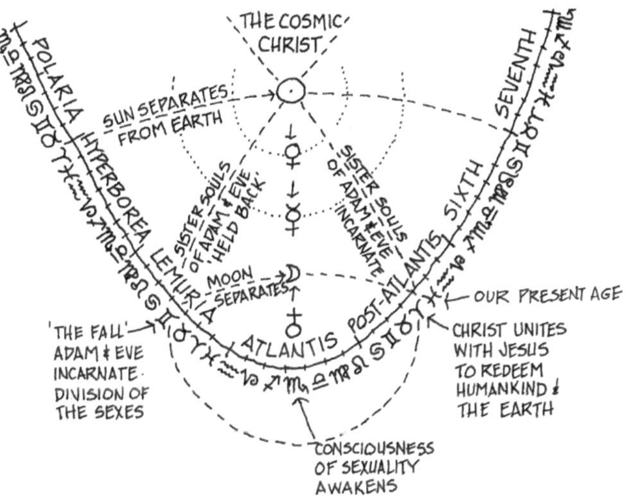

FIGURE 3

six companion Spirits of Form dwelling in the Sun separated out Venus and Mercury from the Sun and cast them toward the Earth. The Fall was of great significance both to the destiny of humanity and to the formation of our solar system.

As a result of the Fall, the formerly united procreative power present equally in Adam and Eve (male-female) was divided into etheric bodies of either male or female gender. Prior to the Fall, human spirits had remained outside human bodies and used the senses to mirror their activities; now sexual procreation became necessary to provide bodies for human spirits to incarnate. As human spirits began to work from "within" the human astral body and gaze out through the human senses, perception of the spiritual world changed dramatically for human beings; spiritual perception gradually receded as interest in the sense world increased.

Sexual procreation began during mid-Lemuria, in the age of The Twins, as a divinely guided process that did not enter human consciousness. Initially, no human desire or awareness of sexuality yet existed, any more than today human beings are conscious of their metabolic forces and the powerful processes of digestion. Only much later in evolution—during the middle of the Atlantean epoch, in the age of The Eagle/Scorpion—did certain initiates gradually become aware of the power of the etheric body and its relationship to sexual activity. Experimentation with, and selfish misuse of, the etheric forces (known as "black magic" and stimulated by Ahriman) unleashed chaotic counterforces within the etheric realms that led to the Flood and to the destruction of the Atlantean civilizations.

Since the Luke Jesus and Mary were not influenced by the Luciferic beings through the Fall of Adam and Eve, their astral bodies remained in a state of innocence and divine purity. Held back in the spiritual world in their virginal state while the rest of humanity experienced the ongoing results of the Fall, they retained the divine nature of the unfallen human being. They served spiritual beings and the Cosmic Christ in the gradual healing of humanity from the effects of the Fall. Since one can only develop an earthly "I" through incarnation, neither the Luke Mary nor Jesus bore normal personality traits typical of human beings. They were openhearted and filled with infinite love and innocent purity, and could cooperate with archangelic and angelic beings. Here Rudolf Steiner addresses the nature of the Luke Jesus:

> To discover who this individuality was, we must go back to a time that predates Lucifer's influence on the human astral body. Luciferic beings began to influence humanity when the Earth was populated by the single couple who were the forebears of all subsequently incarnating human beings. These two individuals were strong enough to conquer human substance so that they could incarnate, but they were not strong enough to resist Lucifer's influence, which entered their astral bodies. As a result of this influence, it was not possible for all of Adam and Eve's forces to be transmitted to their blood descendants. Physical bodies had to reproduce down through the generations, but the guiding powers of humankind sequestered an aspect of the ether body. The Bible expresses this by saying that human beings, having eaten of the tree of the knowledge of good and evil— that is, having tasted the consequence of the Luciferic influence—had to be prevented from eating the fruit of the tree of life. This means that a certain portion of the ether body's forces were retained and not transmitted to Adam and Eve's descendants.

Some of Adam's forces were taken from him after the Fall, and this innocent part of Adam was preserved in the great mother lodge of humanity, where care and attention were lavished upon it. This aspect of Adam's soul had not been involved in events leading up to the Fall and was therefore untouched by human guilt. In it, the original forces of the Adam individuality were preserved. They were later guided into the child who was born to Joseph and Mary. During the first years of Jesus' life, the forces of the original ancestral father of humanity served as his "provisional I." ...

How, then, does the Luke Gospel describe Jesus of Nazareth? It first describes a human being whose blood ancestry, the line of descent of the physical body, reaches back to Adam, to the time when human life on the depopulated Earth was saved by a single ancestral couple. It goes on to describe, from the perspective of reincarnation, the re-embodiment of the human soul that waited the longest to reincarnate. The Adam soul that existed before the Fall appears again in the boy Jesus. As fantastical as it may sound to modern humanity, we know that the individuality guided by the great mother lodge of humanity into the infant Jesus was not only descended from the physically oldest generation of humans but was also the re-embodiment of the first human being.... When Luke called this being the "son of God," he was not speaking about the present human body. He was testifying that this being was the reincarnation of the oldest ancestor of the human race.[21]

With the first incarnation on Earth since the Fall of the virginal parts of Adam (the Luke Jesus) and Eve (the Luke Mary) depicted in the Gospel of St. Luke, the turning point of time had arrived.[22] The songs of praise that the angelic hosts sang to the shepherds were in fact the radiance of Buddha shining and reflecting love and compassion that permeated this child and his mother.

---

21 Steiner, *According to Luke*, pp. 93–95.

22 The passage just quoted illuminates the "first Adam" / "last Adam" mystery articulated by the Apostle Paul (1 Cor. 15:45–49). See also Steiner, *From Jesus to Christ*, lect. 6 (Oct. 10, 1911).

Further insights from Rudolf Steiner about the Luke Jesus Being

Following Rudolf Steiner's initial discoveries about the Luke Jesus in 1909, his spiritual research added further insights about this first incarnation of the held-back part of Adam, whose aura was permeated with the purified astral body of Buddha. In lectures from 1912 to 1913 published in English in 2009 as *The Bhagavad Gita and the West*, Rudolf Steiner revealed that the being of the Luke Jesus child is deeply connected with the regeneration and renewal every human being undergoes during sleep, as well as with changes that take place with the onset of sexual maturity. The Luke Jesus had appeared as Krishna, the inspirer of Arjuna in *The Bhagavad Gita*. Rudolf Steiner shared this on June 3, 1913:

I wanted to call your attention to forces at work in human nature that we find at first in the regeneration of the sleeping organism. Now, these forces are closely related to other forces that also develop in humans with a certain unconsciousness: the forces having to do with reproduction. We know that up to a certain age this consciousness awakens. From that time onward the human organism is permeated by an awareness of the forces henceforth known as sexual love.

What lives as a sleeping force in earlier life and only awakens at puberty, seen in its original and essential form, is the very same as the forces that in sleep regenerate the outworn forces in the human being. It, however, is hidden by the other parts of human nature in which it is mingled. These invisible forces at work in the human being become capable of either good or evil only when they awaken, but they sleep, or at most dream, until the time of puberty. Since the forces that manifest themselves later must first be prepared, they are intermingled, though not yet awake, with the remaining forces in the organism from birth onward. During this time, human nature is permeated by these sleeping forces.

This is what meets us in the child as such a wonderful mystery. It is the sleeping generative forces that only awaken later on. Those who are sensitive to these things feel something like a gentle divine breath when they find, behind the naughtiness, obstinacy, and other more or less unpleasant characteristics a child may have, the same forces that awaken later, at puberty, but are held back in childhood. The child's innocent qualities are those of the grown-up person, but in childlike form. One who recognizes them as generative forces feels the breath of divine powers. While in later life they appear in a person's lower nature, they are so wonderful because they really breathe the pure breath of God so long as they work in unconscious innocence. We must feel these things and be sensitive to them, and then we shall perceive how wonderfully human nature is composed. The generative forces, sleeping during the tender age of childhood, awaken around the time of puberty, and from then on are still innocently active when at night we sink back into sleep.

Thus human nature falls into two parts. In every human being, two persons confront us— the one that we are from the time we awaken until we go to sleep, the other, from going to sleep to waking again. In our waking state we are continually at pains to wear and worry our nature down to the animal level with all that is not pure knowledge, pure spiritual activity. What raises us above humanity holds sway like a pure, sublime force within the generative powers as they were during innocent childhood, and then in sleep it is awakened in the regeneration of what was worn away in the daytime. So we have in ourselves one person who is related to the creative forces in humanity, and another who destroys them.

The deeply significant thing in the double nature of the human being is that behind all that the senses perceive we have to surmise another person in whom creative forces dwell. This second person is really never there in a pure, unmixed form during waking life, or even in sleep, because in sleep the physical and etheric bodies still remain permeated by the aftereffects of waking life, by the disturbing and destructive forces. When at last the latter have been removed altogether, we wake up again.[23]

---

23 Steiner, *The Bhagavad Gita and the West*, pp. 177–178 (emphasis added).

Rudolf Steiner links the source of the regenerative powers that work on each of us in sleep (connected with The Tree of Life) with the changes that took place when Adam and Eve partook of the fruit of "The Tree of Knowledge of Good and Evil" that led to the Fall during the middle of the Lemurian period:

So it has been since what we call the Lemurian age, the beginning, strictly speaking, of present day humankind's evolution. At that time, as I describe in greater detail in my *Outline of Esoteric Science*, the Luciferic influence in human nature set in. From this influence there came, among other things, what today compels humans continually to wear and tear themselves down to the animal nature. *The other element in human nature, which humans as now constituted do not yet know about—the creative forces in them—came into play in the early Lemurian time before the Luciferic impulses entered.* We rise in thought from human "completion" to human "becoming"; from human created to human being re-created. In so doing, we have to look back to that distant Lemurian time when the human being was as yet wholly permeated by the creating forces. At that time humans came into being as they are today, and entered a kind of lower nature. If we follow the human race from that epoch onward, we have this double nature continually before us in all that has happened since. Humanity then entered a kind of lower nature.

At the same time, as we can see clairvoyantly by looking back into the akashic record, *there appeared beside ordinary people, who themselves were permeated by the human creative forces, something like a brother or sister soul, a definite soul. It was as though this sister soul (in that ancient time there was no difference)—Adam's brother soul—remained behind.* It could not enter the physical process of human evolution. It lived on, invisible to the physical world. It was not born the way human beings are born, in the flowing stream of this life, because if it had gone through birth and death it would have been part of the physical human process. It could only be perceived by those who rose to the heights of clairvoyance, who developed those forces that awaken in the

state we otherwise know as "sleep." In that state, human beings are near the pure forces that live and work in the sister soul.

The human being entered evolution, but holding sway above this life there lived, in sacrifice, a soul that through all the process of human life never came down in bodily form. It did not strive like ordinary human souls for birth and death in successive incarnations, and it could only show itself to them when in their sleep they attained clairvoyant vision. Yet it worked on humankind wherever they could meet it with special clairvoyant gifts. There were humans who either by nature or special training in schools of initiation had this power and were able to recognize the creative forces. Wherever such schools are mentioned in history we can always find evidence that *they were aware of a soul accompanying humankind.* In most instances, it was only recognizable in those special conditions of clairvoyance that expand human spiritual vision into sleep consciousness.[24]

Rudolf Steiner describes how this "sister soul" of Adam remaining behind in the spiritual world later revealed itself to one living on Earth. This Being who had held back as the source of regenerating forces, appeared to Arjuna—the troubled warrior faced with the challenge to battle with his own kinsmen as proclaimed in *The Bhagavad Gita.* This "sister soul" of Adam, who spoke to Arjuna through his charioteer, referred to itself as *Krishna:*

When Arjuna stood on the battlefield with the Kurus and Pandavas arrayed against each other, when he felt all that was going on around him and deeply realized the unique situation in which he was placed, it came about *that this sister soul spoke to him through the soul of his charioteer. The manifestation of this special soul, speaking through a human soul, is none other than Krishna. For what soul was it that could instill into humanity the impulse to consciousness of self? It was the soul that had remained behind in the old Lemurian age when humans entered actual earthly evolution.*

This soul had often been visible in manifestations before, but in a far more spiritual form.

______

24 Ibid., pp. 178–179 (emphasis added).

At the moment of which the Bhagavad Gita tells us, we have to imagine a kind of embodiment of this soul of Krishna, though much concealed in maya.

Later on in history a definite incarnation takes place. This soul actually incarnated in the body of a child. Those of our friends to whom I have spoken of this before know that at the time when Christianity was founded two children were born in different families, both from the house of David. The one child is mentioned in Matthew's Gospel, the other in Luke's. This is the true reason for the external discrepancies between the two gospels. *Now this Jesus child of Luke's Gospel is an incarnation of the soul that had never before lived in a human body but is nevertheless a human soul, having been one in the ancient Lemurian age. This is the soul that revealed itself as Krishna.*

We touch here upon a wonderful mystery. We see how the human soul, as it was before humans descended into the course of earthly incarnations, enters the body of the Luke Jesus child. We understand that this soul could hold sway in the human body only until the twelfth year of its life. After that, another soul must take possession, the Zarathustra soul that had gone through all the transformations of humankind. This wonderful mystery is enacted that the innermost essence and self of humanity, which we have seen hailed as Krishna, permeates the Jesus child of the Luke Gospel. In this child are the innermost forces of humanity, the Krishna forces, for indeed we know their origin.

This Krishna root takes us back into the Lemurian time, the very primeval age of humankind. At that time it was one with humanity, before the physical evolution of humankind began. *In later time this root, these Krishna forces, flowing together and uniting in the unknown and unseen, worked to bring about the unfolding of each human's inner being from within. Concretely embodied, this root is present within a single being, the Luke Jesus child and as the child grows up, it remains active beneath the surface of life in this special body after the Zarathustra soul has entered it. Thus, all that the Krishna impulse signifies is incarnated in the body of Luke's Jesus child.* What was embodied is related to the forces that

are asleep in every child in their sublime purity and innocence, until they awaken as the sexual forces. In this child they can manifest themselves and be active until the age of puberty, when one ordinarily becomes sexually mature. But the *body* of this child that had been taken from common humanity would no longer have been adapted to the forces related to the innocent sexual forces in the child.

Thus the soul in the other Jesus child, which was the soul of Zarathustra, that had passed through many incarnations and reached its eminence by hard work and special striving, passed over into the body of the Luke Jesus child, and from then on dwelt in that body.

In the thirtieth year, at the time the Bible describes as the Baptism in the Jordan, there comes toward this special human body what now belongs to all humankind. This is the moment indicated in the words "This is my well beloved Son, this day have I begotten Him." Christ now comes toward the physical body from the other side. In the body that stands before us here, we have in concrete form what yesterday we thought of abstractly. What belongs to all of humankind comes to the body that contains what, through another impulse, has brought the inner human being to the highest ideal of individual strength and will carry it to yet greater heights.[25]

Pre-earthly Deeds of Christ in Relation to the Luke Jesus

Following the revelation that Krishna had been a previous appearance of the Luke Jesus, at the end of 1913 and in 1914 Rudolf Steiner discovered other significant deeds the "sister soul" of Adam performed in service to Christ and human evolution prior to his appearance as Krishna. Though the being who became the Luke Jesus had not formerly incarnated on Earth, this being was spiritually active in the archangelic and angelic realms during the intervening millennia between the Fall and the coming of Christ to Earth.

In 1911, in *The Spiritual Guidance of Individual and Humanity,* Rudolf Steiner revealed that Christ works in every child during the first three

---

25 Ibid., pp. 179–181 (emphasis added).

years of life, first lifting the child into uprightness to gain the ability *to walk,* then in the second year giving the child the ability *to speak* the content of its inner soul to others, and in the third year awakening within the child the ability *to think* and address conditions of life. Finally, during the fourth year of life the Christ kindles the sense of self within the child: the "I"-concept intuitively dawns and the child begins to refer to itself as *"I."* He correlated the first three of these with the fourth beautifully by quoting John 14:6: "I am the way, the truth, and the life." Rudolf Steiner:

> It is as if Christ had said: "Human beings, I want to be an ideal for you that presents to you on a higher, spiritual level what is fulfilled in the body." In the early years of life we learn out of the spirit, first, to walk—that is, we learn, under the guidance of the spirit, to find our *way* in earthly life. Then we learn to speak— to formulate the *truth*—out of the spirit. In other words, we develop the essence of truth out of speech sounds. Finally, we also develop the organ for our *life* as earthly "I"-beings. Thus, in the first three years of life, we learn three things. We learn to find the "way," that is, to walk; we learn to represent the "truth" with our organism, and we learn to express "life" in our body through the spirit. There is no more meaningful paraphrase imaginable of the words "Unless you turn and become like children, you will never enter the kingdom of heaven" [Matt. 18:3].
>
> Most meaningfully, therefore, the "I"-being of Christ is expressed in the words: *"I am the Way, the Truth, and the Life!"* [John 14:6]. The higher spiritual forces form our organism in childhood—though we are not conscious of this—so that our body becomes the expression of the way, the truth, and the life. Similarly, the human spirit gradually becomes the *conscious* bearer of the way, the truth, and the life by permeating itself with Christ. Thereby we transform ourselves in the course of our earthly life into the power at work in us in childhood.[26]

Rudolf Steiner did not reveal in 1911 the spiritual means by which Christ kindled these three

faculties in the first years of every child's life. That further understanding emerges at the end of 1913 and into 1914.

From at least two different lectures[27] we learn that the "sister soul" of Adam was held back at the stage of an archangelic Being in order to serve as the vessel through which earthly humanity could be healed by the Christ. These archangelic interventions occurred during the middle of Lemuria, although Rudolf Steiner also states that the "sister soul" took on the form of an angelic Being. Adam and Eve entered incarnation during the cosmic age of The Twins, Gemini. Not only was there a polar (vertical) separation between the heavenly nature of Adam and Eve and their incarnating counterparts, but also there was a (horizontal) division of sexes into male and female with the introduction of sexual reproduction. At this same point in Earth evolution, the Moon was separated from the Earth. Thus we can begin to appreciate the profundity of the glyph for Gemini, the Twins (see figure 4).

Because Lucifer coaxed Adam and Eve to incarnate into bodies not yet fully developed as human forms, they still bore an animal nature—the spinal column was parallel to the Earth's surface rather than upright. The sense organs of Adam and Eve, like most animals today, were initially focused primarily downward upon the Earth through their horizontal orientation. The horizontal orientation of the human spine would prevent the human being from becoming independent of the Earth. As stated, the Fall took place during the age of The Twins, Gemini, in the middle of the Lemurian epoch.

The archangelic sister soul of Adam (whom we may also refer to as the archangelic Adam Being) selflessly petitioned the Cosmic Christ dwelling in

---

26 Steiner, *The Spiritual Guidance of the Individual and Humanity,* lect. 1.

27 Steiner, "Pre-earthly Deeds of Christ" (Mar. 7, 1914); "The Four Sacrifices of Christ" (June 1, 1914). See also Steiner, *Christ in the Spiritual World and the Search for the Holy Grail,* lect. 2 (Dec. 30, 1913). Like all of Steiner's works referred to here, these lectures deserve to be read in full to bask in their warmth and depth of understanding. Here only the barest outline will have to suffice on our journey to develop a stellar imagination of these events.

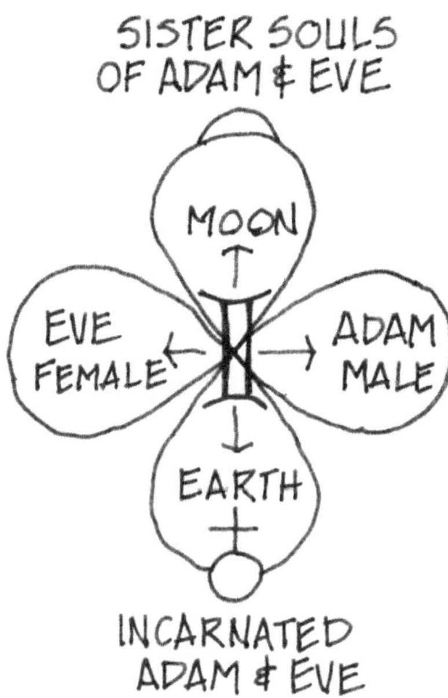

FIGURE 4

the Sun sphere to work through its being in order to lift the bodies of Adam and Eve and their off-spring into uprightness, and also to protect the senses from becoming self-aware so that they would report sensations without calling attention to themselves. The physical bodies of human beings were thus spiritually transformed. Neither the Christ nor the sister soul of Adam incarnated to achieve this result. They lifted human beings into uprightness, giving us the capacity to walk, freeing our arms and hands for creative activity, ennobling the human form and making it possible to later be able to receive the gift of self-consciousness. This first healing involvement of Christ through the sister soul of Adam is now repeated in the first year of the child's life: the child learns to stand upright and *to walk*.

During the first age of Atlantis—the cosmic age of The Waterman, Aquarius—the archangelic Adam Being once again entreated the Christ dwelling in the Sun sphere to give human beings the ability to speak through vowel sounds and to communicate mutually the content of their inner souls to one another. Christ also healed the vital organs, protecting them from becoming self-aware and helping them work together for the overall balanced health of the human being. In this way the etheric bodies of human beings were transformed

and ennobled. This second intervention of Christ through the archangelic Adam to heal humanity is repeated in the second year of the child's life: the child learns *to speak* and communicate.

During a later period of Atlantis—the cosmic age of The Scales, Libra—the archangelic Adam Being for the third time offered itself as vessel through which Christ from the Sun sphere could bring the faculty to more fully articulate speech by adding consonantal sounds. Christ also implanted the beginning of pictorial thinking within the human astral body—the ability to weigh and compare one situation with another in order to consider and judge potential outcomes of actions before performing them. In addition, Christ also balanced and unified the harmonious working of the soul faculties of thinking, feeling, and willing. This was accomplished by the Christ ensouling the archangelic Adam Being and overcoming the forces of the Dragon (combined attacks from Lucifer and Ahriman) that threatened the human soul. This third intervention of Christ to heal humanity within the astral body is repeated in the third year of the child's life: the child begins *to think* and form pictorial ideas. Rudolf Steiner noted that it was particularly this third deed of Christ from the Sun sphere that later became perceptible to Zarathustra during the period of Ancient Persia, the age of The Twins (Gemini) in Post-Atlantis.

Finally, during the Greco-Roman age, the age of The Ram (Aries)—the middle of Post-Atlantis—the archangelic Adam Being (the sister soul of Adam) incarnated as the Luke Jesus, to serve as Grail vessel for the Christ to incarnate and kindle the "I AM" in the human being (See figure 5 on page 100).

On December 30, 1913,[28] Steiner added further details describing how the loving sacrificial role the archangelic Adam performed was perceived in different mystery centers on Earth. During the first pre-earthly deed in Lemuria, the archangelic Adam Being was dwelling in the Sun sphere and permeated by Christ. This event was echoed in the Sun-initiation of Zarathustra during the age

---

28 Steiner, *Christ in the Spiritual World and the Search for the Holy Grail*, lect. 3 (Dec. 30, 1913).

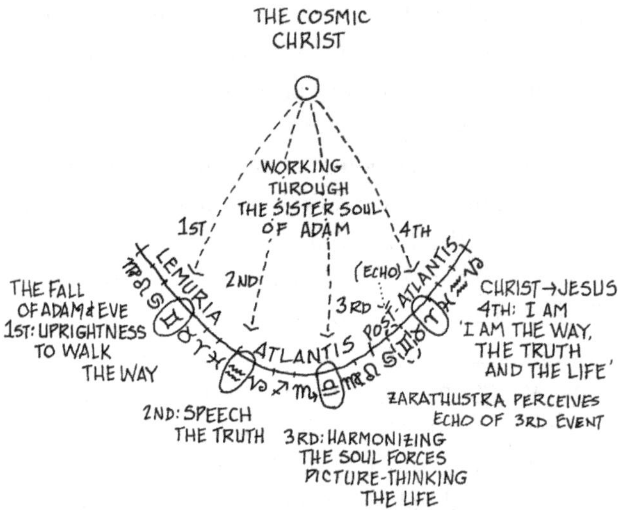

FIGURE 5

of The Twins, the ancient Persian period in post-Atlantean times.

Then, during the second pre-earthly deed at the beginning of Atlantis, the archangelic Adam Being moved among the seven visible planets, taking on a kind of human form through which Christ healed the seven vital organs. An echo of this activity arose later in the science of planetary activity cultivated in Chaldean astrology and Egyptian sun and star worship. It also was reflected in Greek mythology as their planetary gods:

> It is remarkable how for the Greek mind one particular divine figure emerged from the others. The Greeks, we know, reverenced a variety of gods. These gods were the reflections or projections of the Beings who originated from the journey round the planets of the Being, permeated by the Christ, who later became the Nathan Jesus child [the Luke Jesus]. (ibid.)

Hence the planetary gods of Greek mythology (Kronos, Zeus, Ares, Pallas Athene, Artemis, Hermes, and Aphrodite), as well as the gods of many other cultures, arose as reflections of the archangelic Being who became the Luke Jesus child. In particular, Apollo, the healer who worked through the etheric forces of the Sun harmonizing the human soul through the power of song and string music, is a poignant reflection of the Christ-filled archangelic Being who confronted the Dragon and worked from within the Dragon

to ennoble it and bring about a kind of harmony. The legend of St. George conquering the dragon is also a reflection of the third pre-earthly deed, performed during the cosmic age of The Scales, Libra. When this archangelic Being incarnated as the Luke child, he was given the name "Jesus":

> We see how the Greeks revered in the god they called Apollo the Being of whom we have spoken; and we might say that in the Being who truly corresponded to Apollo at the end of the Atlantean time, the Christ was ensouled. Who then was Apollo—not the reflection revered by the Greeks, but Apollo himself? A celestial being who from the higher worlds poured out healing forces for the soul, paralyzing the Luciferic and Ahrimanic powers. These forces brought about in the human body a harmonious cooperation of brain, breath, and lungs with the larynx and the heart, and it was this that came to expression in song. For the right cooperation of brain and breathing with the speech-organ and the heart is the bodily expression of harmony in thinking, feeling, and willing. We have seen this Being pass through three stages of evolution, and then the Healer, whom Apollo reflected, was born on Earth and men called him Jesus, which in our language means "He who heals through God." He is the Nathan Jesus-child, the one who heals through God, Jehoschua–Jesus.

> Now, at this fourth stage, this being made himself ripe to be filled with the Christ-being, with the "I." This came to pass through the Mystery of Golgotha. For if this Mystery had not been enacted—if the Being whom we have followed through cosmic ages had not given embodiment to the Christ—then in the course of later time human souls would not have found bodies in which the "I"-force could come to necessary expression on Earth. The "I" had been brought to its highest stage in Zarathustra. The souls who had taken part in the evolution of the "I" would never have found earthly bodies suitable for its further development if the Mystery of Golgotha had not come to pass. (ibid.)

In addition to Apollo, Rudolf Steiner tells us that the cult of Adonis celebrated festivals in ancient mystery centers near Bethlehem that are also devoted to the angelic being who later incarnated in Bethlehem as the Luke Jesus child.

Having explored something of the cosmic nature of the Being who incarnated as the Luke Jesus child, we recognize that the idea of Jesus as "the simple carpenter from Nazareth" is not only a complete misnomer but also fails to take into consideration the sublimity of the nature of the Luke Jesus and the healing role this Being has played throughout Earth evolution. This sublime Being was visited by the humble shepherds at his birth into a human physical body for the first time. Let us now turn to Zarathustra, the bodhisattva who became the Matthew Jesus, to whom the kings come.

Experiences of the Three Kings Concerning the Matthew Jesus

The Gospel of St. Matthew presents the visit of the kings to the child Jesus who, along with his father Joseph, descended from David through Solomon (Matt. 1:6–7). The three wise kings or Magi from the East bore remnants of ancient Persian and Chaldean star wisdom, the ability to read the stars and to solve mysteries of the widths of space and the evolution of time.[29] They realized that the fulfillment of a prophecy made by the bodhisattva Zarathas (who had lived and taught in Babylon in the sixth century BC) was now at hand with this child's birth. The kings remembered their solemn vow to follow the Golden Star and seek the child in whom it appears. They beheld the Light streaming from the Star in the East—the spiritual light of Zoroaster, the Golden Star. Zarathas, Nazarathos, Zoroaster, and Zarathustra are all names given to this same bodhisattva. For the child Jesus born in the royal house of David in the city of Bethlehem bore the spirit of their great teacher, Zarathustra.[30] The spirit of Zarathustra guided the three kings to the house in Bethlehem where he was dwelling.

Serpents and adversaries had threatened Zarathustra's childhood in several of his previous incarnations,[31] and Herod likewise intended to kill the Matthew Jesus child, the reincarnated

Zarathustra. Matthew dramatically conveys the opposition confronting Jesus in the brief description of the flight to Egypt to escape death threats from Herod, the massacre of innocent children in Judea, and Joseph's decision not to return to the family home in Bethlehem after Herod's death but to move his family to Nazareth in Galilee.

Zarathustra had faithfully served humanity as a bodhisattva since the ancient Lemurian epoch. He played major roles in preparing the way for the coming of Christ to the Earth during Atlantis and Post Atlantis, working in concert with the archangel Michael and Manu, the great Sun initiate. Around 6000 BC, Zarathustra was the first initiate to recognize that the Great Cosmic Spirit formerly identified by the Seven Holy Rishis as "Vishva Karman" (a highly revered being who dwelt beyond their perception) was beginning to enter the Sun realm. Rudolf Steiner tells us that Zarathustra named this revered Cosmic Being "Ahura Mazda," the Great Spirit dwelling in the etheric aura of the Sun. He also confirmed that Zarathustra had perceived the results of Christ's third pre-earthly deed around this period of time, as mentioned in the previous section.

Zarathustra became the spiritual guide for the Ancient Persian culture during the Age of the Twins, Gemini (5067–2907 BC). He encouraged humanity to cultivate the Earth and open it to receive the light and warmth of Ahura Mazda dwelling in the Sun. Agriculture was thus inaugurated by Zarathustra as a sacred ritual to invoke Ahura Mazda from the Sun to bless and spiritually redeem the Earth and heal the human body from the effects of the Fall, and to reclaim them from the clutches of Ahriman, the dark spirit who took deep hold during the middle of Atlantis. Zarathustra realized that Ahura Mazda would descend from the Sun sphere and enter Earth via a human body to redeem humanity. He dedicated his next fourteen incarnations to prepare a proper human body for the descent of this great Cosmic Being, and journeyed as teacher through various cultures to prepare humanity to receive Ahura Mazda.[32]

---

29 Steiner, *Universal Spirituality and Human Physicality*, lect. 13 (Dec. 23, 1920).

30 Steiner, *According to Luke.*

31 See Welburn, *The Book With Fourteen Seals.*

32 See Steiner, *According to Luke,* and Welburn.

As Zarathustra traveled he taught that the Sun was once part of the Earth, but that when the Sun withdrew from the Earth, a solemn promise was made that the Spirit of the Sun would return to walk the Earth. These legends of the Sun Spirit who would one day return were passed down for millennia, and helped awaken human beings to the reality that a Cosmic Being would become a human being.

Gradually, Zarathustra so completely purified his astral body and etheric body that he was able to bestow his purified astral body to his pupil who later became Hermes, the spiritual guide for the Egyptian culture during the Age of the Bull (2907–747 BC). Zarathustra bestowed his purified etheric body to his pupil who later became Moses, the great teacher, historian and lawgiver of the Hebrew culture, born in Egypt and lived around 1250 BC.

The Hebrew people had been led into the land of Egypt through Joseph, one of the 12 sons of Jacob/ Israel, where they absorbed the fruits of Egyptian mystery wisdom (initiated by Zarathustra through Hermes) without themselves becoming clairvoyant. Part of the mission of the Hebrew people was to forego clairvoyance and cultivate instead clairaudience and a full appreciation of the sense world created by Yahweh, and to develop the human brain to become the organ capable of logical thinking.[33] Once the Hebrews absorbed the mystery teachings needed from Egypt, Moses led them out of Egypt into the desert for forty years to integrate helpful influences and to purify hindering influences resulting from their sojourn in Egypt. Zarathustra had an influence in the shaping of the Hebrew people through their contact with Egypt.

But the Hebrews also needed to connect with aspects of star wisdom from the Babylonian and Chaldean mystery schools that Zarathustra had initiated in Ancient Persia. Abraham, the patriarch of the Hebrew people who bore the first human brain capable of logical thinking, had come from Ur in Chaldea. The unique qualities of Abraham's brain were slowly refined through hereditary forces as passed down through the three times fourteen generations outlined in the genealogy of the Gospel of St. Matthew. In order for the descendants of Abraham to be fully prepared by Zarathustra's teachings, the Hebrew people were led into captivity in Babylon for about seventy years. In Babylon, Hebrew teachers could be initiated and taught by Zarathustra, called Zarathas at that time. Thus the Hebrew people came under direct guidance of Zarathas in the sixth and fifth centuries BC in Babylon. Pupils of Zarathas during this period include Daniel the Hebrew prophet, Pythagoras the Greek sage, and Cyrus the Great, the Persian king. Rudolf Steiner noted in 1909 that the king who brought gold to the Matthew Jesus was the reincarnated Pythagoras, who bore the gold of wisdom from ancient Greece:

> What had Zarathustra once promised the high Sun Being? What was it that he sacrificed to Him? His body, senses, life, and speech. Zarathustra was born again as a contemporary of the great Buddha. He could then build up himself the etheric and astral bodies that he had sacrificed. He was reborn as Zarathas or Nazarathos and he became the teacher of Pythagoras. Pythagoras was reborn as one of the Three Wise Men of the East and he became one of the disciples of Jesus of Nazareth.[34]

One of Steiner's students, Hans Gsanger, wrote an article[35] proposing that, in addition to Pythagoras, the other two kings were the reincarnated Daniel and Cyrus the Great, all of whom had been pupils of Zarathas. Zarathustra taught his Magi pupils to witness carefully conjunctions of Jupiter and Saturn, which occur roughly every twenty years in different constellations of the zodiac. Zarathustra told his pupils that a Great King would be born when Jupiter and Saturn aligned in The Fishes. Robert Powell documents this beautifully in his book, *Christian Hermetic Astrology.*

Andrew Welburn quotes a Syrian text dating from the eighth century AD about a prophetic treatise given by Zarathustra to three of his disciples.

---

33 Steiner, *Deeper Secrets of Human History in the Light of the Gospel of St. Matthew,* Lecture 2 (November 9, 1909).

34 Steiner, *From Buddha to Christ* (May 31, 1909).

35 Gsanger, "Zaratas," *Mercury Star Journal,* Michaelmas 1979.

Zarathustra told them that a Great King will come into the world at The End of Times who will be a Child Begotten of the Word that creates all things. When asked who the Great King will be, Zarathustra stated, "He is I, and I am He. I am in him, and he is in me."[36] Welburn's research in his *Book with Fourteen Seals* traces the fourteen incarnations of Zarathustra as he planted seeds of Sun mysteries in different cultures, so that later generations would be prepared for the later descent of Ahura Mazda (the Cosmic Christ dwelling in the ether-aura of the Sun) into the body of Jesus at the Baptism. As mentioned previously, Zarathustra's final task was to bring the "I" to its highest stage and the "I"-force to full development in its earthly expression.

Since the Matthew Jesus (who was slightly older than the Luke Jesus) died in youth before his eighteenth year, Zarathustra had only a few youthful years to use that perfected brain to bring the human "I" to its highest stage. Zarathustra then withdrew his "I" from the body of the Matthew Jesus and united with the twelve-year-old Luke Jesus, bringing the harvested fruits of his "I"-force and wisdom from the Matthew Jesus experience to enrich and further guide the pure innocent soul and body of the Luke Jesus beyond the age of twelve. Zarathustra worked that "I"-force and wisdom into the soul and body of the Luke Jesus between the ages of twelve to thirty as Jesus of Nazareth, then withdrew from that body just before the Baptism so that Christ could enter the human Grail that had been so carefully prepared. Zarathustra thus offered the full fruits of his human experiences, "I" development and wisdom up to Christ, while the Luke Jesus served as the pure Grail vessel that could receive Christ and become the Holy Grail.

When Zarathustra withdrew from the youthful body of the Matthew Jesus, the sublimely cultivated body that bore the fully ripened fruits of the brain of Abraham died. However, the mother of the Matthew Jesus (the mother who had birthed Zarathustra) received within herself his cast-off etheric body and kept it intact until Zarathustra left the body of Jesus of Nazareth just prior to the Baptism. Zarathustra then reunited with his cast-off etheric body at the time of the Baptism. Christ became the "I" of Jesus and gradually ennobled and spiritualized the astral body, etheric body, and physical body between the Baptism and the Crucifixion. After the death of Jesus, Zarathustra gathered up and became the custodian of these human sheaths spiritualized by Christ; Zarathustra has since become known as the Master Jesus.[37]

Mysteries Concerning the "Star in the East"

The term *star in the east* appears twice in the Gospel of St. Matthew connected with the birth of Jesus,[38] and references to this "star" appear two additional times in the text.[39] The kings told Herod in Jerusalem that they had seen the *star* in the realms of the East and came seeking the child to pay homage. Herod asked the kings what time the *star* appeared. Once the kings left Herod in Jerusalem, the *star* they had seen in the realms of the East stood over the house in Bethlehem. When the kings saw the *star* they were filled with great joy, and they entered the house and beheld the child Jesus with Mary his mother, offering reverent homage to the child and bestowing gifts of gold, frankincense, and myrrh.

The Matthew Jesus was the Great King, Zoroaster (Zarathustra), whose star in the east had guided the Magi to his birthplace. The Matthew Jesus at a very young age reconnected with karmic intentions he made during the sixth and fifth centuries BC, when he was a teacher of Persian star wisdom and initiation mysteries in Babylon. The Magi's gifts helped reawaken Zarathustra's earlier connection with his spiritual mission from ancient Persia and Babylon.

It was also crucial for the young Matthew Jesus to reconnect with the fruits that grew from the seeds of mystery wisdom he had planted in Egypt through Hermes and Moses. After the three kings brought their gifts from Babylon, India, and Persia, Jesus was taken by his father Joseph into the land of Egypt. Their sojourn in Egypt during Jesus' early childhood was very important; while there, Zarathustra's seminal contributions to ancient

---

36 Welburn, *The Book with Fourteen Seals*, ch. 13.

37 Steiner, *According to Luke*, lect. 7.

38 Matt. 2:2 and 2:9.

39 Matt. 2:7 and 2:10.

Egyptian mystery wisdom were revitalized within him. The Matthew Jesus bore a destiny with mystery wisdom concerning Ahura Mazda—Christ, and even as a young child his task was to reconnect with the fruits of the mystery gifts he, as Zarathustra, had bestowed upon the Persian, Egyptian, Babylonian, and Hebrew cultures.

Now, gathering a few brief glimpses from the tremendous insights given by Rudolf Steiner's research and the work of some of his pupils, we can address the question many have asked: What (or who) is the "Star in the East" referred to in St. Matthew's Gospel? There are four possible explanations to consider.

1. The Star in the East was the radiant spirit of "Zoroaster," whose name translates as "Golden Star." The spirit of Zoroaster was not perceptible to the normal sense of sight but was visible as a "star" to the clairvoyant perception of the kings, according to Rudolf Steiner's insights.[40] The spirit of Zoroaster was the "star" guiding the three kings to the royal house of Joseph in Bethlehem where Jesus was living.

2. The Star in the East was a triple conjunction of Jupiter and Saturn in the Fishes in 5 BC. In the School of the Magi in the sixth century BC, Zarathas (Zoroaster) instructed his pupils to be attentive to the conjunctions of Jupiter and Saturn that occur roughly every twenty years in different parts of the zodiac. When Jupiter and Saturn aligned three times in The Fishes in 5 BC, the Magi were alerted to the imminent reincarnation of their great king Zarathas or Zoroaster.[41] This stirred them to strike out on their journey to find the child.

3. The Star in the East may have been a comet or the explosion of a supernova that appeared at the time of the birth of Jesus. An astronomical rarity may have stimulated the kings to go search for the child.

4. The Star in the East is the bright star Sirius, known in Egyptian mythology as the star of Isis. The three stars in the belt of Orion, known in Egyptian mythology as Osiris, represent the three kings seeking Zoroaster, the Golden Star in the East—that is, the star Sirius, the brightest star in the night sky.

Of these four possible explanations for the "Star in the East," the first (1) points to a spiritual reality. Rudolf Steiner confirmed that *the spirit of Zoroaster* guided the wise kings to the house in Bethlehem where Jesus was born. His insight expands our question: *Who* was the Star in the East described in Matthew?

The second explanation (2) has been considered by many astronomers, including Johannes Kepler. The triple Jupiter-Saturn conjunctions in the Fishes in 5 BC alerted the wise kings or Magi that Zoroaster was approaching incarnation and set them on their journey to seek the child and bring him gifts. Robert Powell's research deepens and confirms this understanding.

Explanation three (3) has led to great speculation, but there is little or no evidence that a comet or supernova explosion brightened the night sky when the Matthew Jesus was born.

Explanation four (4) surpasses mythology; Rudolf Steiner confirmed it as a spiritual reality. When in 1924 the Countess Johanna Keyserlingk asked Rudolf Steiner about Sirius, he replied:

"Sirius is the heart of Jesus–Zarathustra and is in the depths of the Earth." ... Where is the center in which all human suffering and all human joy in heaven and in the cosmos can be perceived? Then the answer sounded in my soul: it is His heart—the heart of Jesus–Zarathustra in the earth-depths of midnight. I asked Rudolf Steiner about this and he said: "Sirius is the heart of Jesus–Zarathustra and is in the depths of the earth.... Sirius is the world-thought that Christ produces out of His Heart—therefore it is to be found within the Earth." He drew a curve to represent the Earth and wrote on it "Metabolism and fulfilment," as though the thoughts issuing from the Heart of Christ—that is from the Sun—are sent through Sirius to the center of the Earth, where they obtain their fulfilment by means of metabolism.[42]

---

40 Steiner, *According to Luke.*
41 See Powell, *Christian Hermetic Astrology.*

42 Keyserlingk, *The Birth of a New Agriculture,* pp. 89–90.

Explanation four (4) is a spiritual reality, and it also yields an enduring sense-perceptible stellar configuration in the night sky that continues to stimulate in human beings the imagination of three wise kings (the three stars of Orion's belt) aligned with and following the star Sirius, the brightest star in our night sky—the Golden Star of Zoroaster, "the heart of Jesus-Zarathustra."

The first three explanations involve ephemeral conditions that left no physical trace as observable phenomena for us to consider today.[43] The fourth, however, refers us to a spiritual reality revealed in an enduring configuration of fixed stars in the night sky that we can see and think about. Given our present dependence on the sense world and brain-bound intellect, Rudolf Steiner's confirmation of its spiritual reality has an appeal. We may consider this star pattern as a stellar imagination of the three kings searching for the bright Star in the East, Zoroaster (Jesus-Zarathustra, the Matthew Jesus). The "tradition" that the three stars of Orion's belt are an imagination of the three kings can be traced back exoterically only a few centuries with certainty, although it could well have been held in esoteric circles. The ancient Egyptians considered the three stars in Orion's belt to be Osiris, and the star we call Sirius they perceived as Isis. There is an historical precedent for a stellar imagination connecting these particular star groups called up from ancient Egyptian mythology.

Skeptics today could claim that Christians merely borrowed the ancient Egyptian myth of Osiris, Isis, and Horus to derive an association of these stars with the three kings searching for Jesus. Such skeptics would miss the fact (discovered by Rudolf Steiner's research) that Zarathustra inspired Hermes to cultivate the myth of Osiris, Isis, and Horus around these stars during ancient Egyptian times. Zarathustra may well have inspired that star myth in anticipation of it later depicting the three kings searching for the child who is the "Star in

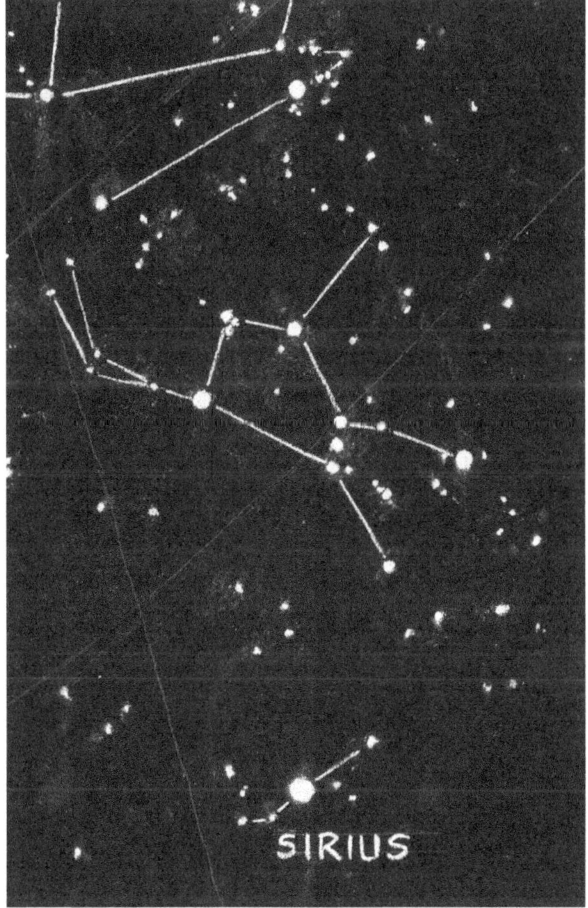

Figure 6

the East." Comparing the constellations with the visit of the three kings as described by Matthew, the star patterns of Orion's belt stars and the star Sirius form an enduring stellar imagination for us to consider. This stellar imagination becomes particularly vivid for stargazers in our time during the Thirteen Holy Nights between Christmas and Epiphany (see figure 6).

Orion's belt stars and bright Sirius bear worthy consideration as a stellar imagination of the three kings in search of the Star in the East, as depicted in the Gospel of St. Matthew. Sirius could be considered imaginatively as *Zoro-Aster,* the Golden Star in the East.

Might Another Star Depict the Luke Jesus Child?

Unlike St. Matthew's account, the Gospel of St. Luke does not describe a star connected to the birth of the Luke Jesus child. The shepherds'

---

43 See Steiner, *Death as a Metamorphosis of Life*: "Christ's existence must be grasped spiritually. This is the essence of the matter. Humanity will have to receive in the Mystery of Golgotha something for which there are no physical proofs but which must be grasped in a spiritual way."

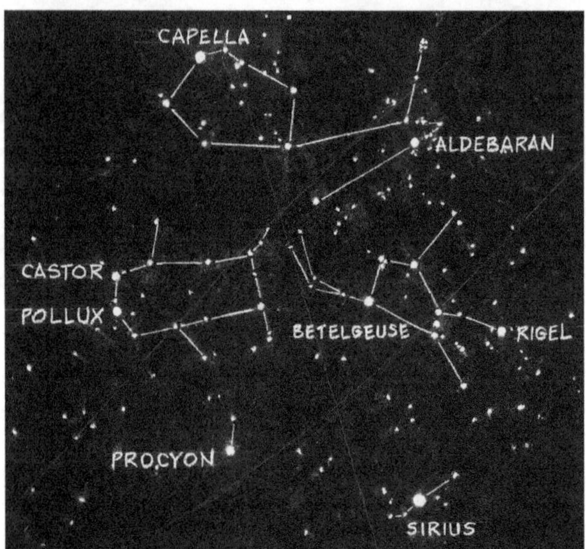

Figure 7

revelations are spoken by angels, and there is no mention of a star in Luke at all. The "Star in the East" clearly refers to the birth of the Matthew Jesus child, the reincarnation of Zoroaster/ Zarathustra (Golden Star) previously described. Considering the proximity of births of the Luke Jesus and Matthew Jesus[44] and their mutual missions to serve the coming of Christ to Earth, might we hope that the spiritual world would bless us with a stellar imagination that can help remind us of the birth of both children?

Let us contemplate the other bright stars of the Winter Hexagon, in which Sirius and Orion appear (see figure 7).

A few years ago I stood outside the Commons at Rudolf Steiner College in Fair Oaks, California on the night of Epiphany (Jan. 6), gazing eastward and contemplating how best to address a gathering of friends at the conclusion of the Thirteen Holy Nights.[45] Rising in the East were the three stars in Orion's belt pointing down toward the brilliant Sirius lower on the eastern horizon. At previous gatherings I had spoken about the three kings searching for the Star in the East—Zoroaster, the Golden Star. January 6, Three Kings Day, in part

commemorates the Visit of the Three Magi to the Matthew Jesus child, so pointing out this vivid stellar imagination in the night sky is a timely Epiphany theme.

However, January 6 (Epiphany) in the Eastern Church also commemorates the Baptism of the Luke Jesus in the Jordan, the moment when Christ begins to incarnate into the body of the Luke Jesus. "Epiphany" comes from the Greek *epi + phainein*, and depending upon context, means "to appear before (one's eyes)" or "to appear over or upon" or "to manifest" or "a manifestation" or "a glorious display." The epiphany experienced by some of those present at the Baptism of Jesus of Nazareth was the Christ Spirit beginning to manifest in relation to the body of Jesus, "descending in appearance like a dove upon Him"; the spirit began to manifest in the flesh.[46] Thus Epiphany commemorates the beginning of the fourth time the Christ united with the archangelic sister soul of Adam— this time, so that the Christ can incarnate into the body of the thirty-year-old Luke Jesus and kindle the "I" in humanity at the Baptism.

As on previous occasions while stargazing, a deep question arose within my soul: Is there a star in the heavens that represents the archangelic sister soul of Adam who incarnated as the Luke Jesus? It is clear that the constellation of The Twins, Gemini, represents the union of the two Jesus-beings. But what star represents the archangelic sister soul of Adam as a Cosmic Being? Contemplating the asterism known as the Winter Hexagon as it rises in the Northeast, a stellar imagination of the spiritual background leading to the birth stories of the two Jesus children suddenly appeared with vivid clarity.

Sirius, the lowest star in the Winter Hexagon as it ascends out of the East, appears closest to the Earth's horizon. It is easy to imagine Sirius as Zoroaster/ Zarathustra, the brilliant Teacher of humanity who repeatedly incarnated on Earth to awaken human beings to the coming of Ahura Mazda/ Christ and who brought the "I" to full development. Sirius very well represents the earthly twin—the Matthew Jesus. The three stars

---

44 Rudolf Steiner confirms that the Matthew Jesus was born earlier than the Luke Jesus child.

45 See Steiner, "The Birth of the Sun-Spirit as the Spirit of the Earth: The Thirteen Holy Nights" (Dec. 26, 1911).

46 Matt. 3:16, Mark 1:10, Luke 3:22, John 1:32.

of Orion's belt certainly provide a vivid imagination of the three kings of the East approaching the reincarnated teacher of star wisdom, Zarathas/ Zarathustra as described above.

In contrast, the Being of the sister soul of Adam long remained in the spiritual world in service to humanity, and was ennobled by Christ on three occasions prior to incarnating as the Luke Jesus child. What star might represent this Being?

With this question in mind, my gaze was drawn upward to the beautiful yellow-golden star **Capella**, towering high above Sirius at the opposite corner of the Winter Hexagon. This glorious star Capella, ascending high above the horizon— could this be the star of the archangelic sister soul of Adam who incarnated as the Luke Jesus? My heart leapt for joy!

To test the validity of this imaginative association, let us ask: how is Capella related to other stars of the Winter Hexagon? The Winter Hexagon[47] encompasses eight bright stars from six distinct constellations:

- Golden *Capella* (right shoulder of the charioteer, or a small goat being carried) in Auriga the Charioteer;
- Reddish *Aldebaran* (the Bull's Eye) in Taurus, the Bull;
- Blue-white *Rigel* (left knee) along with reddish *Betelgeuse* (right shoulder) of Orion the Hunter;
- Blue-white *Sirius* (the head of the greater Dog) in Canis Major;
- Whitish *Procyon* (the head of the lesser Dog) in Canis Minor; and
- White *Castor* and *Pollux* (the heads) of Gemini, The Twins.

Within the Winter Hexagon are very bright stars. **Sirius** is the brightest fixed star in the night sky, followed by *Capella* (sixth brightest), *Rigel* (seventh), *Procyon* (eighth), *Betelgeuse* (ninth), *Aldebaran* (fourteenth), *Pollux* (seventeenth), and *Castor* (twenty-third).

Only slightly dimmer, the three almost equally bright stars in Orion's belt are unique in the heavens: *Mintaka, Alnilam,* and *Alnitak* appear to form a straight line and are spaced nearly equally apart. Their alignment with bright Sirius and position midway between and at right angles to Betelgeuse and Rigel is distinctive. It is easy to picture the three stars in Orion's belt as three kings searching for the Star in the East, Sirius.

But what is the nature of the star *Capella?* It appears with a rich yellowish-white color, the sixth brightest star in the night sky, third brightest star in the northern celestial hemisphere (after Arcturus and Vega), and the fourth brightest star visible to the naked eye from latitude 40° N. Capella is closer to the north celestial pole than any other first magnitude star. Its northern declination results in its being invisible south of latitude 44°S, but it is circumpolar north of 44°N: for the whole of the United Kingdom and Scandinavia, most of France, Canada, and the northernmost United States, Capella never sets. Capella and Vega are on opposite sides of the pole star, at about the same distance from it; an imaginary line between the two stars will nearly pass through Polaris.

Capella traditionally marks the left shoulder of Auriga the Charioteer, or, according to Ptolemy's *Almagest*, the goat the Charioteer carries. In Greek Mythology, the star Capella represented the goat Amalthea that suckled Zeus. It was this goat whose horn, after accidentally being broken off by Zeus, was transformed into the Cornucopia, the "horn of plenty."

The crook of Auriga stood for a goatherd or shepherd. It was formed from most of the stars of the modern constellation; all of the bright stars were included except for Elnath, traditionally assigned to both Taurus and Auriga. *Capella* is sometimes called the *Shepherd's Star* in English literature. In Hindu mythology, Capella was seen as the heart of Brahma, *Brahma Hridaya*.

Capella—the shepherd's star in the crook of Auriga! The heart of Brahma! Capella could well be related to the pure, innocent, loving, and courageous Luke Jesus child descending with pure heart into incarnation and being visited by shepherds.

---

47 The name given this stunning array of bright stars reveals the seasonal bias of viewers in the northern hemisphere.

Capella's position high in the northern heavens, while Sirius rises further to the east, distinguishes Capella's role in the heavens as "complementary" to and opposite that of Sirius, just as the Luke Jesus and the Matthew Jesus played complementary roles in preparing for the incarnation of Christ.

But why does bright Capella—the "Shepherd's Star"—appear within the constellation of Auriga the Charioteer? How could a "charioteer" be related to shepherds or the innocent Luke Jesus child born and laid in a manger?

Rudolf Steiner's discovery that the Luke Jesus had formerly been Krishna awakens new understandings of the connections between Capella, the star of the Luke Jesus, and the constellation Auriga the Charioteer. Krishna did not incarnate into human form, but rather Krishna spoke to Arjuna through Arjuna's *charioteer*! Hence we find further connections between the Luke Jesus and the star Capella and their legitimate association with Krishna through Auriga, the Charioteer.

Wonderful legends in India describe Krishna playing the role of cowherd. It is remarkable that Auriga the Charioteer appears just above Taurus, The Bull—in fact, Auriga and Taurus share a star in common at the tip of the left horn of The Bull. Here is a further link between the Luke Jesus/Krishna and Taurus, the Bull. Many other imaginative connections can be found, and the reader is encouraged to observe the night sky, contemplate, and seek them.

The significance of the stars of the Winter Hexagon deepens when we behold their key position on the celestial sphere, located in close association with the Galactic AntiCenter at 2 degrees Gemini 6 minutes. The Galactic AntiCenter—the point opposite the Galactic Center at 2 degrees Sagittarius 6 minutes—is positioned in the midst between Gemini (The Twins), Taurus (The Bull), and Auriga (The Charioteer). (See figure 8.)

Capella is the closest of the bright stars of the Winter Hexagon to the Galactic AntiCenter, and Figure 8 opens up further considerations of Capella's significance for the reader to contemplate. If The Father forces work into our solar system from the heart of the Galactic Center near the tip of

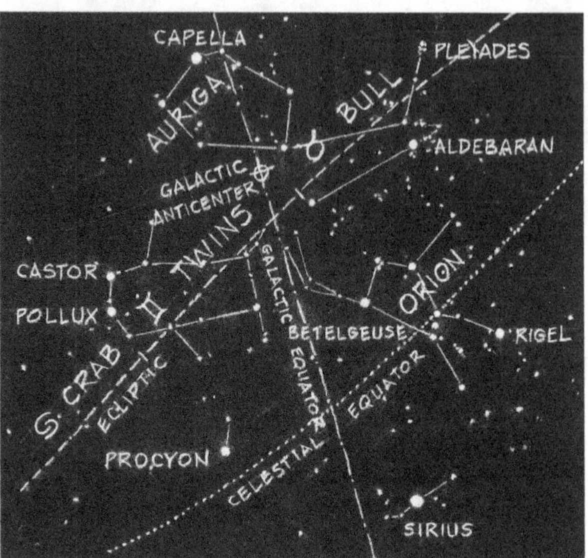

Figure 8

the Archer's arrow in Sagittarius—an imagination supported by Robert Powell and developed in his opening article in this issue of JSW 2016, "The Healing of the Man-Born-Blind and the Central Sun"—then The Son forces could very well be streaming into our solar system from the opposite direction through the Galactic AntiCenter, balancing, complementing and serving the Will of the Father through the realm of the Winter Hexagon, which bears the mysteries of the two Jesus Beings—two Beings who prepared the human Grail for the Christ's incarnation. If Sirius serves as the imagination of the Matthew Jesus child being approached by the Three Kings, Capella could serve as the imagination of the pure and innocent Luke Jesus child. The union of these two Beings during the 12th year of the Luke Jesus is depicted in the imagination of Gemini, The Twins.

Closing Considerations about Capella, Sirius, and the Two Jesus-beings

We have explored some aspects of the spiritual nature of the Matthew Jesus—the bodhisattva Zarathustra who incarnated repeatedly to prepare humanity for the descent of Ahura Mazda, who we know as Christ, into human incarnation. Zarathustra brought the human "I" to its fullest development, and offered the fruits of his labor to the incarnating Christ. Kings or Magi from the Orient came to pay homage to this child.

We have also explored some aspects of the spiritual nature of the Luke Jesus—the archangelic sister soul of Adam who remained connected to the Tree of Life after the Fall of his Twin counterpart, and who repeatedly served as a vessel through which Christ could ennoble humanity through the gifts of walking upright, speaking, and thinking. The sister soul of Adam served as Krishna, as well as informing mythologies of many cultures with images of divine gods, including that of Apollo. Finally, this archangelic being incarnated as the pure Luke Jesus child, overlit by Buddha and visited by shepherds who had seen the light of angels and heard the joyful news of his birth. This child was joined in his twelfth year by Zarathustra, under the guidance of the Archangel Michael, to become the Grail vessel into which the Christ entered at the Baptism. For three and a third years, the Luke Jesus became the Holy Grail in service to Christ's redemption of humanity and the Earth.

When you go outside into the evening's dark canopy filled with bright stars, behold these mysterious constellations of light with wonder, reverence, and an expectant mood of soul. Remember that spiritual beings dwell in these starry worlds, bearing mysteries that await our interest, inquiry, and exploration. Consider the cosmic roles that the archangelic Adam Being played in service to human evolution; ponder the meaning that humble shepherds in the fields were told by brilliant angelic beings of his birth as the Luke Jesus child. Awaken further appreciation for the star wisdom bestowed by Zarathustra/ Zoroaster, who incarnated as the Matthew Jesus. The Magi or kings faithfully kept star wisdom alive; the star science of astrology and star wisdom emerged from their seeking the reincarnation of Zoroaster, the Star in the East.

Filled with wonder and veneration, bring forth questions from the depths of your soul, and ask them of the Beings who dwell in starry realms. If we ask, seek, and knock, it will be revealed: "Ask, and it will be given to you. Seek and you will find. Knock, and the door will be opened to you" (Matt. 7:7).[48]

In the first three panels of the Foundation Stone Meditation we entreat our souls to practice spirit-remembering (to ask questions of the past), to practice spirit-sensing (to attentively ask questions in the present moment), and to practice spirit-beholding (to ask questions that can form and guide our future creative intentions as Spirits of Freedom and Love). This sequence is followed in the fourth panel of the Foundation Stone verse found at the beginning of this article. Observing the stars with questions concerning past, present, and future human deeds can become a fruitful spiritual practice.

Rudolf Steiner proposes that human beings today need to metamorphose the paths of the kings and shepherds in order to come to new universal understanding of what it means to be a human being:

> We must rediscover the secret of Jesus and Christmas, by cultivating within us everything that must nowadays come to expression. We must discover within ourselves the light of Christmas as the shepherds in the fields witnessed the light of the angels. And, like the Magi from the Orient, we must find the star through a true science of the spirit. Then the single, unified path to what the secret of Christmas contains will open to us, reminding us of our rebirth as human beings.[49]

As you gaze with wonder into the starry heavens and behold the stars of the Winter Hexagon, consider beautiful golden Capella as a stellar imagination of the unfallen sister soul of Adam, the Luke Jesus Being to whom the shepherds come. Consider brilliant Sirius and the three aligned stars of Orion's belt as a stellar imagination of Zoroaster being sought for by the three kings or Magi. Reflect, contemplate; ask, seek, and knock. Share your questions, insights, and discoveries with others. May your considerations of these stellar imaginations become ever richer and more meaningful! *

⁊

The author gratefully acknowledges the expert editorial assistance of Lelan Harris in preparing this paper for publication. Many thanks, as well, to Robert Powell and William Jens Jensen for their excellent work.

---

48 Matt. 7:7 (Madsen, *The New Testament*).

49 Steiner, *Universal Spirituality and Human Physicality*, lect. 13.

POSITION OF THE ANCIENT STAR-ZODIAC

Nicholas Kollerstrom

The ancient Babylonians recorded celestial longitudes, of stars and then of planets, with no hint that they needed to tell anyone what was their celestial reference: their zodiac had no arrow marked, "start here." Centuries later, in the Hellenistic world, we hear philosophers averring that the Babylonians had taken the Antares-Aldebaran axis as bisecting the thirty-degree signs of the Bull and the Scorpion. It is remarkable that two bright, first-magnitude stars both reddish in color should have been exactly opposite each other, within an arcminute, and it would have been reasonable for them to have taken that as their prime reference—but, we don't have any ancient Babylonian text saying that.

It's as if the ancient Babylonian stargazers on their ziggurats just "saw" the longitudes and somehow did not need to explain them.

If a single star-zodiac was used in antiquity, we should then see a consistent and simple relation between it and the modern sidereal zodiac used for investigating it. For this investigation we will mainly use the "Lahiri" star-zodiac (i.e., the Indian version of the sidereal zodiac) as given by the Solar Fire program. Thus our reference-zodiac is positioned with reference to the fixed star Spica.

In a couple of earlier articles, horoscopes of antiquity were analyzed by the author to try and ascertain what celestial reference system they had used.[1] A tropical-zodiac reference was used for this, and

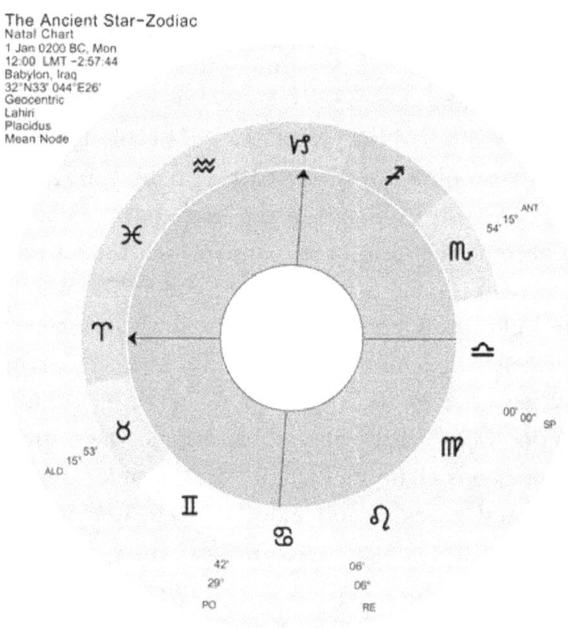

Stellar longitudes (200 BC) using Lahiri zodiac, of ANT–Anteres, ALD–Aldebaran, SP–Spica, RE–Regulus and PO Pollux.

that involved using the concept of an *ayanasmsa*—i.e., phase-difference between the tropical reference and whatever sidereal zodiac might have been in use in antiquity. Such an *ayanamsa* will vary with time because one of these systems is precessing and the other is not. However the whole analysis would be in many ways simpler if one just used a sidereal reference system, and forget entirely about the tropical reference.

A century of academic work has been done on this question, always using the tropical zodiac and laboriously converting from one reference-system to another.[2] We here turn a bright new page and

---

1 Kollerstrom, "The Star-Zodiac of Antiquity," *Culture and Cosmos* (vol.1 no.2, winter/autumn 1997) and Linguaccio Astrale (spring 1999); Kollerstrom, "On the Measurement of Celestial longitude in Antiquity," *Optics and Astronomy, Proc. 20th Int. Cong. Hist. Sci.*, Liege, 2001, pp.145–160.

2 Recently, see Steele and Gray, "A Study of Babylonian Observations involving the Zodiac," *Journal for History of Astronomy*, 2007, 38, pp.

use only a sidereal reference. This should give us some much simpler answers than have been obtained hitherto.

We let the computer do the hard work: it computes the "proper motion" of stars, whereby their longitude changes very slowly with time, and takes account of the slow change in rotation rate of the Earth whereby times in the ancient world may be compared to ours, and will measure longitudes from wherever we tell it to.

The figure opposite shows the Solar Fire computation of key stellar longitudes for 200 BC, using that zodiac. Spica here appears as by definition at the 0°00' boundary between the Balance and the Virgin. Other stellar longitudes here given are:

Aldebaran 15°53' of the Bull;
Antares 15°54' the Scorpion
Regulus 6°6' of the Lion
and Pollux 29°42' of the Twins

It is a recent thing, that an astrology program puts the stars into a chart, or gives one the option to do so, and I hope readers agree that this helps one to picture what is going on more clearly.

Searching for a "Prime Reference"

Different suggestions have been made over the years concerning a stellar "prime reference" (if indeed there was one) for the ancient star-zodiac, e.g., John Britton and Christopher Walker wrote that the star β–Gemini (Pollux) defined zero degrees of Cancer.[3] That definition, we see from this star-zodiac diagram, differs by 18 arcminutes from that whereby Spica is the boundary of the Balance and the Virgin, a difference which may turn out to be insignificant.

Or, if Aldebaran were to define 15° of the Bull, as Cyril Fagan originally proposed, more recently endorsed by Robert Powell,[4] then Pollux would be

28°49'. (In the Solar Fire program, choose "Fagan-Allen" for this zodiac). There is a 54 or so arc-minute difference here. These are the main options that have historically been advocated. There is almost one degree at stake here between the different options. Or, maybe all of these marker-stars were "prime fiducial" references, depending upon which part of the zodiac was visible in the sky.

The earliest Babylonian experience of zodiac measure comes from a tablet surmised to be around 400 BC, with stellar longitudes written as "1–30°." That is our first evidence of the human race dividing a circle into 360°—although, the Babylonians may not have seen it that way.

In 1952 Abraham Sachs published a list of these,[5] from a fragment of pre-Seleucid era star-catalogue (NB, that term "Seleucid" alludes to the first three centuries BC). As shown below, the star Spica was given as 28 degrees of the Virgin. Peter Huber in 1958 ascertained some more,[6] from his analysis of almanacs between -122 and -110—i.e., about three centuries later. He confirmed three of the longitudes found by Sachs and disagreed with none. Thereby we have a list of fourteen ancient Babylonian stellar longitudes. For comparison, sidereal longitudes given by Powell for 100 BC (Aldebaran=15°) are given.

Abe Sachs, 1952		**Aldeb.=15°**
θ Leonis	20°Leo Theta Leonis Chertan/Chort	18° LEO 38'
β Virginis	1°Virgo Zavijava	1°VIR 56'
γ Virginis	16°Virgo Porrima	15° VIR 39'
α Virginis	28°Virgo Spica	29° VIR 07'
α Librae	20°Libra Zubenelgenubi	20° LIB 20'
β Librae	25°Libra Zubeneschamali	24° LIB 38'

These half a dozen stellar longitudes fluctuate around the Antares-Aldebaran 15° axis (their mean deviation is a mere 3' to 51'), so that it does look like a feasible reference-framework. Could this have been the earliest zodiac? (We use the term here as meaning a twelvefold equal-interval division of the

---

443–458. The central question as to where the Zodiac they were investigating was positioned, was unanswered, and merely swathed in obscurity by translating all their data into tropical longitudes.

3   John Britton and Christopher Walker, "Astronomy and Astrology in Mesopotamia," in *Astronomy before the Telescope,* Walker (ed.), 1996, p.49.

4   Powell and Treadgold, *The Sidereal Zodia*; Powell, *History of the Zodiac.*

---

5   Abraham Sachs, "A Late Babylonian Star-Catalogue," *Journal of Cuneiform Studies*, 1952,6, 146–50.

6   Peter Huber, "Uber den Nullpunkt der Babylonichen Ekliptik," *Centaurus*, 1958, pp.192–208.

ecliptic—although its root-meaning is more general, as something like, "circle of animals.")

Huber, 1958

η Tauri	3° Taurus Alcyone	5° TAU 14'
ζ Tauri	0° Gemini Zeta Tauri, Alhecka	0° TAU 01'
α Gemini	25° Gemini, Castor	25° GEM 34'
β Gemini	0° Cancer, Pollux	28° GEM 45'
ε Leonis	25° Cancer Epsilon Leonis Ras Elased	25° LEO 56'
α Leonis	5° Leo Regulus	5° LEO 12'
θ Ophiuchi	27° Scorpius Theta Ophuichi	26° SCO 38'
δ Capricorni	0° Aquarius Deneb	28° CAP 35'

(A letter kindly sent by John Britten Oct. 10, 1997, gave this list of "normal stars" with longitudes "directly from Babylonian sources…of which at least eleven seem secure and the rest more probable than not.")

Again this group of star-longitudes fluctuates closely around the same star-axis (their mean deviation being -6' to 68').

Huber has here given zero degrees longitude for three stars. There was no zero then so the meaning here is not at once evident. Planetary ingresses were being recorded—i.e., dates when planets entered a new zodiac sign—as, too, were star-conjunctions. Thus their star-almanacs recorded various planetary conjunctions with β-Gemini (Pollux) *on the same date* as it reached the zodiac sign Cancer. That is why experts have tended to put Pollux at 30° Gemini (=0° Cancer). That's what Huber meant.

John Britton expressed the view that "Had Spica been placed at the very end (i.e., 29° or 30°) of Virgo, β-Gemini [Pollux] would have fallen into the sign Cancer, ς Taurus [zeta Tauri, Alhecka] into Gemini, and δ Capricorni [Deneb] into Aquarius."[7] Three possible "boundary stars" above-quoted are here alluded to. Let's give two different reference-frameworks for these three stars, which may (or may not) help to clarify this:

	Aldeb. = 15°	Spica - Lahiri
β-Gemini [Pollux]	28° 48'	29° 41'
ς Taurus [zeta Tauri, Alhecka]	00°02'	00° 55'
δ Capricorni [Deneb]	28° 41'	29° 34'

More recently the same view has been expressed (in a vague sort of way) by Steele and Gray, that the Babylonian zodiac was defined "either directly in the case of Gemini, Cancer and Aquarius, whose beginnings coincide with zeta Tauri, β-Geminorum and δ Capricorn respectively, or indirectly through the other signs."[8]

Hellenistic Greek sources have given Aldeban (α-Taurus) as 15° Taurus and Antares (α-Scorpio) as 15° Scorpio. Historian Otto Neugebauer cited Cleomedes as stating around AD 370 that the two bright stars Aldebaran and Antares were "both located at 15 of their respective sign;"[9] he also cited a similar comment as appearing in a Greek treatise by Anonymous of the year 379. These are reconstructions from a time centuries after the Babylonian civilization that had somehow "seen" the zodiac longitudes in the heavens.[10] Others have taken the view that Cleomedes lived earlier, maybe in the first century. No one before them ever says this, no Babylonian tablets list their longitude.

These two first-magnitude stars, both close to the ecliptic and both pale-pink in color, so exactly opposite—remaining within an arcminute of opposition to each other during the historical period we are looking at—stand as obvious candidates for primary reference, stars, but in that case, why have no Babylonian tablets yet discovered ever mentioned them? This fact has greatly impeded experts from accepting that they functioned as such a reference.

Seven Babylonian Horoscopes

There remain seven horoscopes from ancient Babylon that give degree longitudes to planets.

---

7   Britton, personal communication, Dec. 11, 1996.

8   Ref (3), 2007, p. 444.

9   Neugebauer and van Hoesen. *Greek Horoscopes.*

10 For discussion, see Powell, *History of the Zodiac,* p.101–105. Powell also claims (p.102) that Hephaeston of Thebes had given the longitude of Aldebaran as 15 Taurus, citing Neugebauer and Van hosen, *Greek Horoscopes,* p.187, but I couldn't see it there.

		Babylonian horoscope Sidereal longitudes						Differences (Historic–Lahiri)				
		SU	SA	JU	MA	VE		SU	SA	JU	MA	VE
-262	Apr. 4	13:30						-3.5				
-248	Dec. 29	9:30	-	-	-	-		-3.0				
-234	Jun. 3	12	6	18	24	4		-1.8	4.1	-3.3	-2.9	4.3
-199	Jun. 4		10	26	10	5			1.5	-3.4	1.3	0.6
-198	Oct. 31		3	10	10	4			-1.4	3.7	1.9	6.4
-87	Jan. 5			27	20	1				-2.4	-1.1	-1.5
-68	Apr. 15	30	15	24	14	13		2.0	-0.6	0.8	2.7	-0.3

Compiled by Francesca Rochberg in her *Babylonian Horoscopes* of 1998, those ancient charts display the miracle, of newly manifesting zodiac longitudes. Times of day are sometimes given, and here lunar longitudes have been used to fine-tune the time of day, and so are not here cited. Mercury is excluded, as generally subject to greater errors than the other planets. No one knows how these longitudes were found, so we compare them here with respect to the simplest possible celestial reference, namely that of the star Spica at the boundary of Libra/Virgo.

No one is in a hurry to conclude that Spica actually defined the zodiac, as pertaining to the Libra/Virgo boundary, on account of the above alluded-to tablet which cited its longitude as 28° of the Virgin.

The culture of ancient Babylon was not interested in ascertaining where the "Vernal point" was: that would have been an abstraction having little or no meaning for their astronomy, which was mainly experiential—however they could and did ascertain solar zodiac longitude in their charts, even though it could not be "seen."

We here follow the example of Professor Rochberg and quite a few other people in misusing the word *horoscope*—the *Horoscopos,* or hour, of rising (i.e., the ascendant) did not appear in Egyptian–Greek horoscopes until years AD.

The earliest of these is the first known natal chart to give zodiac degrees, while the latest at 68 BC is the last known horoscope to be written in the ancient cuneiform script. How strange, that the very earliest charts should give the Sun's position to degrees and minutes—but not the later ones!

The zodiac thus emerges, and science historians and astrologers have been wondering ever since how it was defined. Readers may not need reminding that no-one in the Babylonian culture is on record as dividing a circle into 360° or indeed as measuring an angle more than thirty degrees, which happens only later on with the Greek astronomer Hipparchus on the island of Rhodes in the second century BC.

In the previous table, subtraction gives the (Historical–Lahiri) differences, in degrees of longitude. They seem to be *fluctuating around the Spica-reference zodiac* (11'–166'). They derive from the charts assembled by Francesca Rochberg,[11] most of which give no degrees but only signs. For the -198 chart, Sun and Moon positions are only given as signs but degrees are given for planets, and this suffices to lock the chart into only one possible time/space coordinate. These twenty-three celestial longitudes span two centuries.

The range given is from 1°to 30°, as *there is no zero.* So would their one degree be what we would call 0° to 0°59' and should our best estimate therefore be ½°? I haven't done that, because a few values are expressed in degrees and arcminutes. To rephrase this dilemma, if some of their degree longitudes have arcminutes, then they should not be quoting any at 30°, should they? This could burden our work with a half- degree error.

Rochberg has drawn—like most academics investigating this subject—no conclusion as to the star-zodiac's reference. In a footnote she quotes the late John Britton (p. 19) for a "correction factor" based on Peter Huber's determination in 1958 (!)

---

11 Rochberg, *Babylonian Horoscopes*, pp. 21–22.

		Horoscope Longitudes						Deviation from Spica zodiac					
		SU	MO	SA	JU	MA	VE	SU	MO	SA	JU	MA	VE
40	Apr. 5	19	15	20	6	15	5h	2.0	0.6	-0.1	3.7	3.6	2.8
46	Jan. 3	11:30	11	30	19	14:30	19	-4.2	0.6	4.8	-7.1	7.4	2.9
75	Jul. 19	29:30	12	27	8	7:23	28:18	2.6	-1.3	6.4	0	-5.0	3.8
76	Jan. 24	8	1	5	1	22	12	2.5	5.7	2.1	0.6	-0.1	-4.8
81	Mar. 31	14:6	13:0	5:59	6	16:3	16:4	2.1	-0.6	2.2	2.8	0.2	5.7
110	Mar. 15	25:8	16:53	1:25	25:18	21	8	-0.8	-0.2	4.3	1.4	5.6	-2.6
137	Dec. 4	13:23	3:6	3:38	12:44	30	9:54	-0.5	-0.6	4.3	0.4	4.2	-3.7
218	Nov. 27	7:55	6:51	11:3*	(Me 25 Sco)			1.3		-2.7	0.1		
260	Sep. 29	8	8:32	11:32	3		8:16	0.4	1.5	1.3	0.1	-0.1	0.4
338	Dec. 24			9:1	22	14:16	29			-0.2	1.1	-0.1	0.7

of 4°28' as the "ayanamsa" for -100[12] (i.e., she has presupposed Huber's conclusion). That was based mainly upon the above list of fixed-star positions and planetary ingresses. It was reached well before what is called "Δt" had been ascertained. Caused by a slowing down of Earth's rotation, it is a shift in time by around six hours in our re-computation of the ancient planetary positions and could have interfered with Huber's calculations.

That is one reason why we favor use of a modern program like *Solar Fire,* which will automatically make such an adjustment, so one no longer has to bother about it. As to why Rochberg does not seem able to focus on this matter, the simple answer would be that no sidereal-zodiac program is available to her, assuming that as an academic she does not want to use an astrology program.

Diaries and Alamancs

Ancient Babylonian tablets record the dates of planetary "ingresses"—i.e., when they entered a new zodiac sign, from about 200 BC onward. A thorough analysis of hundreds of these has been published by Steele and Gray, who alas only expressed their conclusions in terms of the tropical zodiac. The best we can do here, is to express their conclusions in terms of the best-fit "ayanamsa" they found, at 100 BC:[13]

Ayanamsa Estimates for 100 BC

Empirical:	Astronomical diaries	4°41'
	Almanacs	4°21'
Theoretical:	Spica zodiac	5°21'
	Aldebaran=15°	4°26'

As regards the last two terms: if one takes a chart for 100 BC, then switching between a tropical zodiac reference and that of the Lahiri (Indian-Spica) zodiac, the planetary positions then shift by about 5°21'—that was then the difference or "ayanamsa" between the two zodiacs. Ditto for a star-zodiac having Aldebaran at 15°, one would see all the longitudes shift by 4°26', from the tropical zodiac reference. No-one was then using the latter, indeed it would be centuries before anyone's solar theory was good enough to use it, but we are here applying it retrospectively as it were. Again, this does look very much as if the Antares-Aldebaran star-axis reference was here being used.

Egyptian Horoscopes

Continuing to check out planetary longitudes, we turn next to Otto Neugebauer's classic text *Greek Horoscopes.*[14] The early "horoscopes" from Babylon were written in cuneiform etched onto clay tablets, then later Egyptian horoscopes were written in Greek on Papyrus, starting 40 AD. These have a *Horoscopus*—i.e., an Ascendant,

---

12 Huber, op. cit.

13 Steele and Grey ref (3), pp.448–449.

14 Neugebauer and van Hoesen, *Greek Horoscopes.* Actually, they were not Greek. I feel the word was just put in the title to help sell the book. They were Egyptian mainly around Alexandria, but Greek was the written language.

		SU	MO	SA	JU	MA					
AD 508	Feb. 1	13°11′	26°4′	14°19′	3°2′	7°9′	+1.7°	-3.1°	-0.2°	+2.0°	+ 0.3°

and these charts we might expect to be more accurate. Mercury is generally excluded because it is too unreliable; its errors tend to be much greater than other planets. The Moon's position is generally used for fine-tuning the time of day so it can't really be included either: unless the chart has a *Horoscopus* which gives the time of day.

Ten of the earliest Egyptian horoscopes that gave planetary degree longitudes plus an Asc/MC position have here been listed (mainly from Neugebauer's *Greek Horoscopes*): giving their longitude degrees for all planets except Mercury, then differences in degrees after subtracting from them the modern-computed Lahiri longitude.

The zodiac used here (see opposite) is some forty-seven arcminutes away from the Spica-reference zodiac, on average. Bearing in mind here that (see figure on page 110) the Antares-Aldebaran is fifty-three arcminutes from this reference, it is considerably nearer to that star-axis measure than were the original Babylonian longitudes.

Alexander Jones has described a few ancient horoscopes unknown to Neugebauer.[15] That from the year 508 (p. 281) cites eight longitudes to both degrees and minutes, including the *Horoscopus*— i.e., the degree of the zodiac rising. For five of these we give longitudes in degrees and minutes, and measure the deviations just as previously (see above)—indicating that this is a sidereal chart (which Jones did not state). However, the latest horoscope given in *Greek Horoscopes*, that of AD 516, is clearly tropical. Thus, we have a shockingly clear delineation, of the last star-zodiac chart and the first tropical zodiac chart.

We thereby conclude that *the same star-zodiac was in use for eight centuries*, from the charts we have examined. It may well have been in use for two centuries earlier, where we maybe only have the less accurate star-longitudes—i.e., for a thousand years.

If we look at the scatter of the longitudes around the Lahiri zodiac for this 508 chart, on average

they deviate by 8 to 106 arcminutes. Going back to the very first horoscope to give a set of longitude values, for the year -234 (see above) this has a scatter on average 5-200 arcminutes from that same reference! Between different cultures, over centuries, the exact *same* zodiac reference has endured. And there is not a single academic in the world who is, apparently, interested in the fact.[16] Earlier in the twentieth century, Otto Neugebauer was sufficiently distinguished that he could publish "astrological" material and have his reputation survive, but I guess that does not apply to academics today.

A Spica-defined star-zodiac would have synchronized with the tropical zodiac around 290 AD, so by the time of the above two charts they would have moved three degrees apart, and could be readily distinguished. Around the time of Ptolemy the two were more or less together so no-one could tell which one was being used, no doubt convenient for Ptolemy writing his immortal opus: which gained its "divine" power partly by having it both ways, defining his zodiac both as seasonal—i.e., tropical and star-based, or sidereal. For an Antares-Aldebaran star-zodiac that synchronizing event happened rather earlier, around AD 220.

Egypt did not have base-sixty mathematics as did Babylon, nor did it have any measure of angles (only of gradient), at which many have been surprised. The researches of Alexander Jones have brought out how in the early centuries AD the techniques of Babylonian mathematics spread around the Mediterranean, being generally superior to those of Greek math, which greatly helps us to appreciate how the Babylonian zodiac continued to be used around the Mediterranean, even after Ptolemy in his *Tetrabiblos* (c. 140 AD) had effectively defined a tropical zodiac reference.

---

15 Jones, *Astronomical Papyri from Oxyrhyncus*, 1999.

16 This author made the claim in 1997 at the Liege History of Science Conference (published in 2001: ref.1); since then, Robert Powell, and probably no one else, has taken an interest in it.

The Incarnation

The charts give readings of astral fate. The very earliest above-cited from -262 (263 BC) reads: "He will be lacking property.... His food will not suffice for his hunger.... His days will be long.... His wife, whom people will seduce in his presence, will" (Rochberg, p.69). Flattery was no aim of this early soothsayer!

Strictly, Francesca Rochberg's title, *Babylonian Horoscopes,* was mistaken, because these charts have no ascendant or MC, they are only for moments in time and apply universally to all the Earth. One may think of these Babylonian charts as applying to the centre of the Earth. The first horoscope proper was in 4 BC, i.e., it had an ascendant. This was the first horoscope for a real person, in that it defined a unique time/space co-ordinate for a birth. The *cross* of an ascendant/MC first appears in a map of personal destiny. Babylonian charts may have been for an aristocratic elite (Rochberg, p.6); to them belonged the destiny written in the stars, and ordinary folk only came to acquire that after the Incarnation.

Rudolf Steiner used to talk about the Incarnation in terms of the coming or development of a personal self-awareness...

> At the turning point of Time
> Entered the World-Spirit Light
> Into the stream of Earthly Being.
> Light that warms the hearts of simple
> shepherds.
> Light that enlightens the wise heads of kings

...and would describe it in terms of the dawning "I am" principle of "I"-consciousness: "I am, the Light of the World."

To check this claim, we need to look at ancient psychology, which was astrology. Here we see how horoscopes do exactly synchronize with that Event. At that moment, astrology moved west, from Babylon to Alexandria, and started to be written in Greek on papyrus. Like it or not, the whole birth of astrology is centered in time around this Event.

A Note from the Editor of the *Journal For Star Wisdom:*

It is with great appreciation that Nicholas Kollerstrom's valuable research article is presented here, an article that seeks to pinpoint the original scientific definition of the Babylonian sidereal zodiac, which was subsequently transmitted to India and continues to be used in astronomy and astrology there to the present day—although knowledge of exactly how the original Babylonian zodiac was scientifically defined in relation to the stars is no longer extant in India. As some readers will know, the theme addressed in Nicholas Kollerstrom's article is the same one that forms the essence of my PhD thesis that was published in book form as *History of the Zodiac* in 2007. Related to this theme: In my article "Zodiacal Ages and Cultural Epochs" published in the previous issue of the *Journal for Star Wisdom* (2015), some indications are given which, I believe, offer support for the conclusion reached in *History of the Zodiac* that the **prime reference** for the original scientific definition of the zodiac in relation to the fixed stars was the Aldebaran (Bull's Eye)—Antares (Scorpion's Heart) axis from the middle of the sign/constellation of Taurus (Aldebaran at 15° Taurus) to the middle of the sign/constellation of Scorpio (Antares at 15° Scorpio). Without going into the extensive material presented in the article "Zodiacal Ages and Cultural Epochs," it suffices to point out that, as indicated in the article, the dates for the cultural epochs found by Rudolf Steiner agree *exactly* with the dates of the zodiacal ages arising from studying the precession of the equinoxes through the signs/constellations of the Babylonian zodiac. This *exact concordance* over a period of some 2,400 years between the ancient Babylonian astronomers who first scientifically defined the zodiac around 500 BC and Rudolf Steiner who shortly after AD 1900 was occupied with precisely dating the cultural epochs, offers definite confirmation of the original Babylonian zodiac as having the Aldebaran (15° Taurus)—Antares (15° Scorpio) axis as the **prime reference** in their scientific definition of the zodiac. As astronomer

The sidereal zodiac
Dates of the Sun´s ingresses into the twelve signs of the zodiac

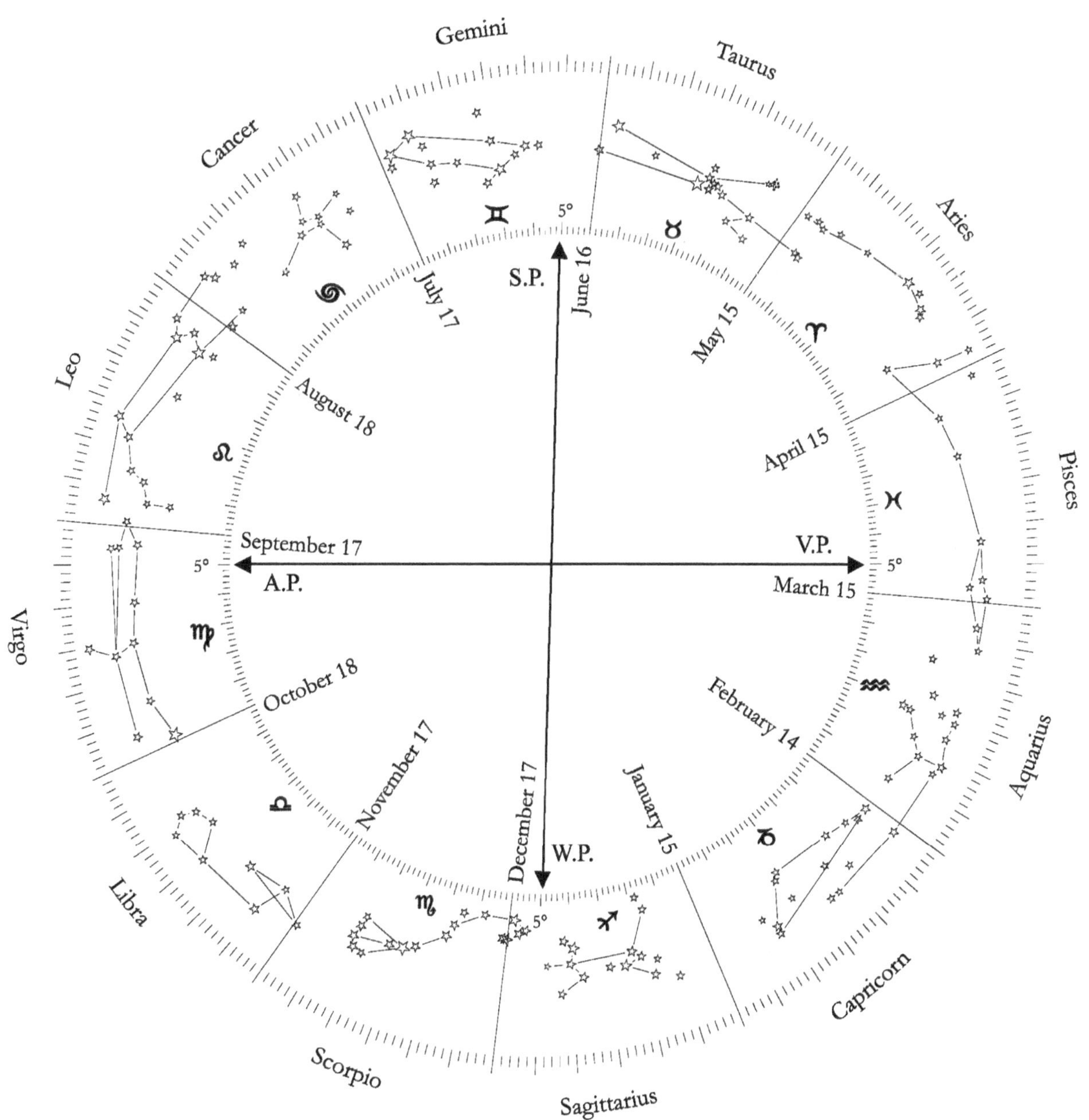

Joachim Schultz, who was a keen observer of the starry heavens, pointed out:

> It is a remarkable fact that the twelve [zodiacal] constellations show on the whole a strikingly symmetrical distribution. The approximate centers of the constellational figures are distributed at roughly equal distances from one another, about thirty degrees apart. Proceeding from Aldebaran, the primary star in the Bull, in taking equal [30°] steps around, there arises a twelvefold division which falls centrally everywhere in [each of the twelve zodiacal] constellations. In terms of [calendar] dates, at the present time the Sun is located at these positions [the central positions, i.e., 15° of the twelve zodiacal constellations] always around the beginning of each [calendar] month.... Rudolf Steiner gave the valuable indication that the seeking out [looking up to] the central

positions of the zodiacal constellations—to the "light centers" of the individual constellations— is significant and can lead to consideration of the arrangement of the zodiacal constellations divided regularly according to the twelve primary divisions of space.[17]

Thus, from the standpoint of observational astronomy—in this case represented by the astronomer Joachim Schultz—the zodiacal constellations appear to be thirty degrees long, as they did also to the Babylonians, who defined them accordingly as the twelve 30° zodiacal signs with the same names as the twelve constellations, since the signs are embedded in their respective zodiacal constellations. In other words, for the Babylonians from around 500 BC onward, there was essentially no difference between the signs and the constellations of the zodiac. However, for their definition of the signs of the zodiac, the Babylonians had to have a prime reference as their starting point in defining the twelve 30° signs (defining each sign by way of the degree positions of the main stars in that sign), and evidently they chose Aldebaran, appearing in the middle of the constellation of Taurus, as their prime reference—Aldebaran being thus located at 15° Taurus. Similarly, they found that Antares, located exactly opposite Aldebaran in the zodiac,

was located at 15° Scorpio. The natural position of Aldebaran, the Bull's Eye, at the exact center of the sign of Taurus, is confirmed observationally by Joachim Schultz, who in the above description of the division of the zodiacal constellations into twelve equal divisions takes Aldebaran as the natural point of departure.

Lastly, taking a look at the Babylonian sidereal zodiac in relation to our modern calendar dates, we see from the figure *The sidereal zodiac: Dates of the Sun's ingresses into the twelve signs of the zodiac* that, on average, each year the Sun is at 15° in the middle of each sign on these dates: 15° Sagittarius on January 1; 15° Capricorn on January 31; 15° Aquarius on March 1; 15° Pisces on March 30; 15° Aries on April 30; 15° Taurus on May 31; 15° Gemini on July 1; 15° Cancer on August 1; 15° Leo on September 1; 15° Virgo on October 3; 15° Libra on November 1; 15° Scorpio on December 2—note that according to the occurrence of leap years, and considering also other astronomical factors (including the time zone of the place where one lives), these dates can change by one day or so from year to year. Nevertheless, we see that the statement made by Joachim Schultz: "In terms of [calendar] dates, at the present time the Sun is located at these positions [the central positions, i.e., 15° of the twelve zodiacal constellations] always around the beginning of each [calendar] month" is more or less valid.

---

17 Schultz, *Rhythmen der Sterne*, p. 44 (tr. RP, also notes in brackets [ ] added by RP). This excellent book by Joachim Schultz has been published in English: *Movement and Rhythms of the Stars: A Guide to Naked-Eye Observation of Sun, Moon, and Planets* (Edinburgh: Floris, 1986). [Note from RP: I have not had an opportunity to compare my translation (above) with the one given in the English edition of Joachim Schultz's book.]

"It became clearer and clearer to me—as the outcome of many years of research— that in our epoch there is really something like a resurrection of the Astrology of the third epoch [the Egyptian–Babylonian period], but permeated now with the Christ Impulse. Today, we must search among the stars in a way different from the old ways. The stellar script must once more become something that speaks to us."
—Rudolf Steiner (*Christ and the Spiritual World and the Search for the Holy Grail*, p. 106)

THE FALL OF THE SPIRITS OF DARKNESS
A SPECTRAL REFLECTION

Kevin Dann

The mental features discoursed of as the analytical, are, in themselves, but little susceptible of analysis. We appreciate them only in their effects. We know of them, among other things, that they are always to their possessor, when inordinately possessed, a source of the liveliest enjoyment. As the strong man exults in his physical ability, delighting in such exercises as call his muscles into action, so glories the analyst in that moral activity which disentangles. He derives pleasure from even the most trivial occupations bringing his talent into play. He is fond of enigmas, of conundrums, of hieroglyphics; exhibiting in his solutions of each a degree of acumen which appears to the ordinary apprehension preternatural. His results, brought about by the very soul and essence of method, have, in truth, the whole air of intuition.

—EDGAR ALLEN POE,
"The Murders in the Rue Morgue," 1841

Why, man, a diamond, and such a one as there isn't a monarch in Europe but would envy Tom Donahue the possession of. Up with your crowbar, and we'll soon exorcise the demon of Sasassa Valley!

—ARTHUR CONAN DOYLE,
"The Mystery of Sasassa Valley," 1879

Literary historians consider Edgar Allen Poe's 1841 story, "The Murders in the Rue Morgue," to be the world's first detective fiction tale, and its hero, C. Auguste Dupin, the world's first "detective" before the word was even coined. Poe's story was a great sensation, leading many to call Poe a genius; Poe himself felt his tale was mere semblance, though a year later he republished it with another, "The Man that Was Used Up." Poe was not yet thirty, but both of his short stories were extraordinarily prescient. Dupin's facility for "ratiocination," bordering on clairvoyance, presaged not just Arthur Conan Doyle's Sherlock Holmes, but also the entire spectrum of perspicacity (the word had only the year before come in to general use) in the natural sciences when surveying the physical realm. Dupin's sharp eye and intellect extended even into the murky terrain of the human brain, allowing him essentially to read the mind of others.

Poe's other tale—about a former military commander whose war injuries necessitate that he be reconstituted each day from mechanical prostheses—suggests that even as the modern, rational, technologically proficient human being was reaching new heights, he was "used up," disappearing, becoming, in the midst of a century of overwhelming materiality, a specter. The appearance of an actual specter, the illusionary Sasassa demon, in Conan Doyle's 1879 tale both points to the popularity of ghost tales in the mid-nineteenth century, and, eight years before the first appearance of Sherlock Holmes, hints at the role that careful deduction will play in Conan Doyle's Holmes tales. Dupin and Holmes are the era's archetypal "sleuths," employing cold reason to solve lesser mysteries (most often violent murders), all the while oblivious, as were their devoted readers, to a much more deadly and decisive mystery—the disappearance of the human being.

As markers of the "abyss" of Materialism, those bookend dates (1841 and 1879) come to us most immediately from Rudolf Steiner, who, though publicly identifying them as early as 1905 (November 3, "The Archangel Michael and the Hosts of Mammon" for 1879) and 1907 (May 8 "Reading the Pictures of the Apocalypse: Remembering Madame Blavatsky" for 1841), did not elucidate their full significance until 1917, in the fourteen-lecture series *The Fall of the Spirits of Darkness:*

> The year 1841 saw the low point of humanity's spiritual life. The opponents of spiritual life had, in that year, the strongest point of attack in the evolution of humankind.[1]

As is so often the case with Rudolf Steiner's teachings, the timing of this lecture series is itself a lesson. Beginning on Michaelmas (September 29) in 1917, and concluding a month later on October 28, the lectures affirm one of the series' central revelations—the "law of spiritual reflection" of historical/esoteric events. Clearly Steiner had a karmic obligation to unveil this law; that he chose to do so in the fall of 1917, thirty-eight years after the end of the nineteenth century "War in Heaven"—as well as the consequent advent of Michael's simultaneous ascent to the regency as Time Spirit (1879–2233) and advancement to the rank of the Archai—underscored the spiritual significance of that date (1879) within human history. At a more immediate level, Rudolf Steiner seized upon the 1841 to 1879 battle because it afforded him an opportunity to illuminate the esoteric background to World War I, and perhaps also served to forewarn of the next wave of the Ahrimanic/Sorathic attack, in the form of the impending Bolshevik Revolution. Indeed, the October Revolution (which occurred on November 7, 1917) took place just over a week after Steiner's last lecture in the series.

Although these 1917 lectures are widely known in anthroposophical circles, at least to the degree that the 1841/1879 dates are canonical truths for understanding both the spiritual history of the nineteenth century and the metahistory of the Fifth post-Atlantean Epoch/Consciousness Soul, they demand close inspection for the light they shed on certain phenomena of our time.

---

1 Steiner, *Reading the Pictures of the Apocalypse.*

1841–1879: "The Abyss of Materialism"

From an exoteric cultural historical perspective, one can find abundant evidence to affirm Rudolf Steiner's characterization of the mid-nineteenth century as the "abyss of Materialism." Rudolf Steiner himself often alluded to the advent of the telegraph (1837) and railroad (steam locomotive, 1840) as significant markers of the Zeitgeist. Other inventions include inexpensive photographic equipment (1840s); the transoceanic cablegram (1844); anesthesia (1846); telephone (1876); and phonograph (1878). An unprecedented outpouring of discoveries in the natural sciences paralleled these technological innovations. In chemistry: Lord Kelvin established the concept of absolute zero in 1848; a year later Louis Pasteur clarified the nature of optical rotation, opening up advances in stereochemistry; in 1855, Benjamin Silliman pioneered petroleum cracking, the foundation of the modern petrochemical industry (four years later Edwin Drake's 1859 strike precipitated the Pennsylvania Oil Rush); in 1856, William Henry Perkins synthesized mauve, the first synthetic dye; 1857 saw August Kekulé's proposal that carbon is tetravalent; in 1859 Gustav Kirchhoff and Robert Bunsen established spectroscopy as the foundation of chemical analysis; from 1860 to 1869, numerous chemists made discoveries which led to Dmitri Mendeleev's 1869 publication of the first modern periodic table of the elements; in 1876, Josiah Willard Gibbs' *On the Equilibrium of Heterogeneous Substances* merged thermodynamics and physical chemistry to explain the basis of chemical equilibria; Ludwig Boltzmann in 1877 established statistical derivations of many important physical and chemical concepts, including entropy.

In London and Edinburgh, physicists William Thomson (Lord Kelvin) and Robert Clerk Maxwell made fundamental discoveries—the conservation of energy (Kelvin, 1842); Doppler effect (Kelvin, 1843); second law of thermodynamics (Kelvin, 1850); kinetic theory (Maxwell, 1857); dynamical theory of the electromagnetic field (Maxwell, 1864); dynamical theory of gases (Maxwell, 1867); vortex model of the atom (Kelvin, 1867). European geologists confirmed Sir Charles Lyell's 1830 (in *Principles of Geology*) claim that the Earth was several 100 million years old, and in 1862, Lord Kelvin brought thermodynamic theory to bear on the question, estimating the Earth's age at between twenty to 400 million years old. After Charles Darwin's and Alfred Russell Wallace's papers on "descent through modification" were read together at the Linnaean Society in London in 1858, every biological science—embryology, taxonomy, physiology, anatomy, and the new science of ecology (coined in 1866 by Rudolf Steiner's friend Ernst Haeckel)—was radically reoriented to express evolutionary principles, according to the theory of natural selection proposed by Darwin. German amateur astronomer Heinrich Schwabe in 1843 announced his discovery of a regular cycle in sunspots, the first clue to the Sun's "anatomy"; in 1845, William Parsons used his 180 cm telescope to study and draw the structure of nebulas (galaxies), and discovered the spiral structure of the Whirlpool Galaxy. The same year, French physicists took the first photograph of the Sun's surface through a telescope; photos of the Moon followed in the next five years. In 1846, Neptune was discovered through the application of mathematical calculations of the planet's gravitational pull on the orbit of Uranus. In 1868, Norman Lockyer gave the name helium to the bright emission line in the spectrum of the Sun's atmosphere during the August 18, 1868 eclipse. American astronomer Henry Draper in 1872 took the first photograph of a star (Vega) showing absorption lines that revealed its chemical makeup, and William Huggins used absorption lines to measure the redshift of stars, giving the first indication of how fast stars were moving. Astronomers began to employ spectroscopy as a tool for understanding stellar evolution.

If one theme emerges from all of these developments in nineteenth-century natural science, it is the *extension of vision.* Optical instrumentation, spectroscopy, and new imaging techniques all vastly extended the range of the human eye into Nature at every scale of perception. Concomitant with this visual enhancement came an acute sharpening of analytical capacity, reflected

in innumerable new patterns of "breaking up" or fragmentation. Nature was inevitably reduced into smaller and smaller parts: cells became mere epiphenomena of their nuclei; nuclei dissolved into "genes"; animal and plant species shattered into populations; molecules were rendered into stochastic probabilities; stars dissolved into constituent gases, which became mere spectral lines. All formerly fleshy phenomena hovered precariously, threatened by the prospect of being reconstituted as mere statistics. In but three short decades, the groundwork had been completely laid for what René Guenon termed "The Reign of Quantity."

SPECTERS I: A (FORE)TELLING TRIPTYCH

Sometime after the fall of 1879 (in 1882), not long after he met the herb gatherer Felix Koguzki on a train to Vienna, Rudolf Steiner met the first of his two Masters—Christian Rosenkreutz, who, in telling the twenty-one-year-old Steiner of his life's mission, placed it within the context of a foundational principle for the unfolding of Rosicrucianism as an exoteric cultural impulse. Saying that the spiritual stream of Rosicrucianism had first entered the world in 1250, Christian Rosenkreutz also told Rudolf Steiner that it would prepare for its task at the turn of the twentieth century by remaining "strictly secret," until three very specific developments in the natural sciences had taken place:

1) the invention of spectroscopy, which revealed the material composition of the cosmos;
2) the introduction of material evolution into organic science;
3) the acknowledgment of the fact of multiple states of consciousness, as revealed by hypnosis.[2]

To the radically empirical nineteenth century mind, Christian Rosenkreutz's ability to peer ahead four centuries (from 1459, when he achieved

---

2 These developments are given by Rudolf Steiner in the "Barr Manuscript" written in 1907 for Eduard Schuré; in *Correspondence and Documents, 1901–1925,* pp. 9–19.

the rank of Knight of the Rose Cross, pledging himself to the secrecy of the body of occult knowledge that Rudolf Steiner would, almost singlehandedly and in service to Michael and Christ, reveal) was impossible. With no concept—foundational to Rudolf Steiner's 1917 lectures—of the reverse astral stream of Time, such exact and far-reaching clairvoyance could never be countenanced.

Christian Rosenkreutz's threefold criteria for the exoteric unveiling of Rosicrucian wisdom is astonishing for its elegance of expression, and absolutely intriguing, given the prodigious range of scientific developments outlined above. Kirchhoff and Bunsen's publication in 1859 of their very simple device for divining the emission spectra of heated elements seems an altogether "innocent" step in scientific knowledge, until, from a century-and-a-half's hindsight, it resolves into the foundation of an entirely materialist astrophysics, capable as it was of revealing the *material* basis of the cosmos, while simultaneously obscuring the spiritual dimension of the heavenly bodies. The year 1859 brought the publication of Darwin's *On the Origin of Species by Means of Natural Selection, or the Preservation of Favoured Races in the Struggle for Life,* with its shattering effect on the human sciences (anthropology, history, psychology, etc.) and the human being. As to Christian Rosenkreutz's third panel of the triptych, the "nightside" of human consciousness as revealed by hypnosis, the associated occult secrets were potentially apocalyptic, and Rudolf Steiner would always tread cautiously when elaborating upon them.

SPECTERS II: APOCALYPTIC FOUNDATIONS

For Rudolf Steiner's audience in Munich during 1907 on White Lotus Day, it must have seemed extreme for him to say that the beings who in 1841 attacked Michael were preparing what John in *Revelation* spoke of as taking place in the distant future, through the agency of "the beast with the horns of the ram and the number 666." In pointing out that the Rosicrucian powers found in Mme. Blavatsky an instrument for laying the groundwork for the upward stream of human evolution

in the far future, Rudolf Steiner also very directly spoke of the adversarial powers—"Those elemental beings who,…[in 1841] found suitable soil, those powers have taken possession of a large part of humanity and, from that position, are exerting their influence."[3]

This quotation, standing as it does a decade before Rudolf Steiner's full elaboration of the 1841-to-1879 period in his 1917 lecture series, yet raises two fundamental questions that will recur later on: 1) *Who* are the beings that take possession of humanity? 2) What is the exact *timing* of this possession? These questions are preliminary to this article's central concern: In which contemporary cultural developments can we discern the continuing effects of the *Geister der Finsternis*—"Spirits of Darkness"—cast down by Michael in 1879?

In the very first lecture of the 1917 series, before he has said a word about 1841 or 1879, Rudolf Steiner goes right to what I see as the central implication of the "War in Heaven"—the possibility of possession by Ahrimanic beings. Hearkening back to the outbreak of World War I, he speaks of statements made by the Russian Minister of War, Vladimir Alexandrovitch Suchomlinov, describing his state of mind on July 29, 1914. Although under orders from the Tsar to refrain from mobilizing, Suchomlinov instead commanded the army to mobilize in support of Serbia; three days later Germany declared war on Russia. Rudolf Steiner paraphrased Suchomlinov's words when questioned in court about his decision—"On that day I almost went out of my mind"—and explains that Suchomlinov had indeed lost his mind momentarily, allowing Ahriman direct access to his thoughts and deeds. "When we speak of the origins of this catastrophe in time to come," Rudolf Steiner concluded, "we must not do so on the basis of written records; instead we shall have to point to real facts through which ahrimanic spirits gained access to the stage of human events."[4]

---

3 Steiner, "Remembering Madame Blavatsky," Lecture 1, May 8, 1907, in *Spiritualism, Madame Blavatsky & Theosophy: An Eyewitness View of Occult History* (Steiner Books: 2002), 109.

4 Steiner, *The Fall of the Spirits of Darkness*, p. 23.

SPECTERS III:
THE MAGIC LANTERN SHOW
OF THE NINETEENTH-CENTURY WEST

One hardly needs to be a Dupin or Holmes to detect in Western culture in the mid-nineteenth century a phantasmagoria of images and events suggesting that something "spectral" was afoot. As materialist science scrutinized ever more deeply into matter, new and often macabre cultural productions were thrown up. In medicine, it was the great age of the medical theater, where new surgical techniques were openly demonstrated before a public eager to witness the new knowledge in action. In London, Paris, New York, and other world capitals, showmen and women like Madame Tussaud and P. T. Barnum paraded a seemingly never ending processional of effigies, mannequins, automatons, wax models, talking dolls, and Feejee mermaids, all calculated to simultaneously shock and seduce spectators into the liminal arena of the not-quite-dead. Dissections and dismemberment proliferated to the point where bodies became a kind of shop window. The very title of Poe's 1841 tale reminds us that in Paris, the spectacle of medical manipulation of the dead had progressed to the point at which morgues had become the scene of salons and like social gatherings; in America, cemeteries were becoming favored venues for summer dinners.

Ghosts were everywhere, stars—thanks to new thaumaturgical theatrical technologies—of the finest opera house stages and bawdy vaudevillian houses alike, as well as in literature. After 1850, when the Fox sisters brought their spirit-rapping spectacle to Barnum's Hotel on Broadway in Manhattan, a host of imitators rose up like ghosts in a cemetery on Halloween. There was perhaps no more dramatic indication of the depths of antebellum Materialism than "Spiritualism," the name given to a worldwide movement that began with two teenage sisters using a stripped down Morse code to communicate with elemental beings. Both skeptical scientists and gullible spirit seekers ignored the rural girls' original moniker for their conjured "spirit"—"Mr. Splitfoot." At mid-century, rural wisdom about the dangers of trafficking with Old Scratch (another folk name whose euphemistic indirection showed the superstitious dread of Satan) and his minions seemed to vanish overnight, as country folk and urban dandies alike crowded into parlors and lecture halls to ogle specters, poltergeists, zombies, and doppelgangers. That the entire affair was instigated by occult brotherhoods, as an earnest and much contested initiative to *counter* Materialism, only adds to the sense that its stranglehold on Western consciousness was complete, even before any cascade of Ahrimanic beings from the Moon Sphere after 1879.[5]

The shadow-like quality of the nineteenth century was profoundly affected by its most popular technological innovations—photography, film, and the phonograph, all of which offered simulacra in the place of the real. The first daguerreotypes were hailed as just the opposite, as such faithful reproductions of the world that painting would soon be obsolete. After Edison, the Lumière brothers, and George Mélies brought motion to photography, boosters were soon declaring that there would no longer be need for history textbooks, as the world's great events could all be captured in moving pictures.

The invention and popularization of an unprecedented apothecary of artificial psychotropic substances—from nitrous oxide and chloroform in the 1840s to cocaine (1855) and heroin (1874)—added to the era's spectral, "Neptunian" quality. Each and every drug was greeted as a boon to humanity; both Sherlock Holmes and Sigmund Freud enthusiastically embraced cocaine as tools for intellectual clarity. Kit Carson and Wild Bill Hickok used it to sharpen their Wild West show shooting and roping skills. But the century is littered with lives hollowed out by drug addiction; Charles Darwin's beloved brother Erasmus, named after their opium-recommending physician grandfather, spent his last years in various states of opiate intoxication, and many of his London

---

5   See Steiner, *The Occult Movement in the Nineteenth Century and Its Relation to Modern Culture;* and Harrison, *The Transcendental Universe.*

neighbors were similarly haunted by the demon drug that made millions for both English aristocrats and Boston Brahmins, while turning China into a nation of addicts.

Erasmus Darwin helped his brother with his earthworm research and orchid studies; so did their cousin Francis Galton, whose unparalleled empiricist obsessions fledged such legacies as eugenics and forensic finger printing. Galton's rage for classification, for number, statistics, order at all costs, was emblematic of the age. His *Hereditary Genius* (1869) of course took as its exemplars of intellect the Wedgwoods, Darwins, and other high Victorian aristocratic families, while consigning non-white peoples to close cousinship with the Ourang-Outang—the creature that held Charles Darwin spellbound all summer of 1838, as he incubated his theory of evolution, helped along considerably by his observations of the captive creatures at the London Zoo.

All of these keynotes, keywords, and telltale gestures of mid-nineteenth century life strongly suggest that Ahriman had a comfortably feathered nest before 1879. Thanks to Rudolf Steiner's spiritual investigations, we have at least the tentative outline of the intersection of the karmic and metahistorical dimensions of this cusp of the Gabriel/Michael regency. When, in 1924, he finally was able to unfold his karmic research, he began with Charles Darwin, Francis Bacon, and F. T. Vischer—all of whom had had previous incarnations in the Arabic world of the eighth and ninth centuries, where they had fallen prey to Ahriman's efforts to prematurely introduce modern scientific knowledge, to derail the Consciousness Soul from its proper path of development. Though he never took up discussions of the other figures associated with Christian Rosenkreutz's diagnostic triptych—Kirchhoff and Bunsen, nor James Braid (who pioneered the "disenchantment" of animal magnetism into "hypnotism" in the 1840s)—Charles Darwin's previous incarnation (according to Rudolf Steiner's indication in his lecture of March 16, 1924) as Tariq Ibn Ziyad (AD 670–720) placed him squarely in the stream of "Arabism," to which

Steiner attributed a sustained assault on any potential Rosicrucian/Goethean scientific pathway as a bridge out of the Kali Yuga. Up until 1859 at least, the development of Materialism in the West seems largely to have been a consequence of individual thinkers bringing back into the social realm in the nineteenth century, the impulses that they had wed themselves to in their earlier "Moorish" incarnations.

LOCATING THE DRAGON

In the fourth lecture of the 1917 series, Rudolf Steiner called attention to the role of elemental beings in human technological innovation: "In laboratories, workshops, really everywhere where the spirit of invention is active, elemental spirits are providing the inspiration." He explained that these guiding elementals were under the influence of Ahriman, whom they originally served as executors of processes of birth and death, but since the eighteenth century, had assumed this new role, under the influence now of the human being. In the next lecture, following remarks about the 1912 Eugenics Congress in London, Rudolf Steiner again speaks of Ahrimanic beings, now pointedly calling them "demons," and says that as humanity crosses the threshold, and the etheric body loosens from the physical body, "their bodies will be empty to such an extent that a powerful ahrimanic spirit can live in them. One will be meeting ahrimanic demons. Human beings will not be what they appear to be."[6]

In lecture six, "The New Spirituality," he continues this theme, calling attention to a new "intimacy" between human thoughts and "the gods." Rudolf Steiner also uses the term "hierarchies" here, without explicitly identifying one or another rank of the Hierarchies. He also speaks of the elemental world, and although he is not explicit, one gets the sense that *both* the Hierarchies—most probably, the Angeloi—and messenger elemental beings under their guidance are the agents of these thoughts/inspirations. Although the language of this lecture is "neutral," his one

---

6   Steiner, *The Fall of the Spirits of Darkness*, pp. 84, 61–62.

example is of Woodrow Wilson, inspired by a nymph, in the manner of Roman ruler Numa Pompilius's relationship with the nymph Egeria. This only further complicates matters, as Rudolf Steiner considered Wilson to be under the influence of demonic/Ahrimanic beings, while Numa Pompilius's Egeria was a benevolent influence upon the Roman king.[7]

In lecture 9, "The Battle Between Michael and 'the Dragon,'" Steiner brings this theme further, saying that since the fall of 1879, the Ahrimanic impulses (and the beings standing behind them) become the "personal property" of humans, and due to this, "personal ambitions and inclinations to interpret the world in materialistic terms came to exist in the human realm. You only have to trace some of the events which have arisen because of personal inclinations since then, to understand that they resulted when the Archangel Michael drove the dragon, that is the crowd of ahrimanic spirits, from the realms of the spirit, from the heavens, down to earth."

There has long existed a tendency among anthroposophists to use "Ahrimanic" in a rather casual, sloppy, manner. For the purposes of this discussion, this issue becomes critical, since there is a world of difference between "Ahrimanic" employed as an adjective, versus its use as a very specific diagnostic of an identifiable source of a discrete thought. A century ago, in this particular lecture series, given at a true "turning point in time" in terms of the history of Western civilization, Rudolf Steiner repeatedly and emphatically underscored the danger humanity faced from *actual possession by Ahrimanic beings*. There was nothing adjectival or metaphorical about the warnings he gave. In a very real sense, we already stand within the future he prognosticated when he said, "There will be situations in the future when it will be difficult to know who one is dealing with."

Rudolf Steiner did humanity a great service in 1917 by elucidating the degree to which the battle with "the Dragon" was no mere figure of speech, but a very real and present danger. In declaring that Ahrimanic beings were invading human thinking, he gave an indication beyond the immediacy of the occult machinations of World War I. He laid at our doorstep an awesome challenge, to fill ourselves with spiritual knowledge, lest those demons take up residence within *us*.

A Specter Hiding in Plain Sight

While researching for my article in the *Journal for Star Wisdom* 2014 on the nature of the vortex within modern natural science, I came upon the work of astronomer George Ellery Hale, and was struck by the final paragraph of his Wikipedia biographical sketch: "Hale suffered from neurological and psychological problems, including insomnia, frequent headaches, and depression. The often-repeated myth of schizophrenia, alleging he claimed to have regular visits from an elf who acted as his advisor, arose from a misunderstanding by one of his biographers. He used to take time off to spend a few months at a sanatorium in Maine. These problems forced him to resign as director of Mount Wilson." My hunch was that indeed, Hale *had* been harassed and harangued by an elemental being, and that this being was the cause of his difficulties. I wondered to what degree this same elemental being may have been responsible for any of Hale's scientific intuitions, and was keen to know if Hale, who was a gifted writer, an enthusiastic poet and composer of children's stories, and indefatigable diarist and letter writer, might have left a record of his relationship with this "elf."

In February 2015, I spent two days in the Hale Papers at the Caltech Archives hunting for answers to these questions. Despite the irresponsible and unscientific dismissal in a Wikipedia entry of Hale's own heartfelt statement, George Ellery Hale was clearly plagued by an elemental being, at least from 1908 until his death in 1938, and the most conspicuous characteristic of this being was its insistence on dominating the thoughts of one

---

7   The mention of Wilson may simply be a droll aside by Rudolf Steiner—understandable given the historical circumstances of 1917, but I feel it is worthy of contemplation within the context of the entire series, given its pointed emphasis on the theme of Ahrimanic possession.

of the twentieth century's most gifted, intellectually generous, convivial, humanitarian natural scientists.[8]

In a manuscript autobiography he composed in 1933, Hale says, "Immediately after the discovery of the magnetic fields in sunspots I had the first intimation of my first severe nervous breakdown, which followed in 1909...forced me to give up all work, was followed by similar breaks in 1913 and 1922."

This dates the onset of Hale's "troubles" to June 1908; his discovery of magnetic fields in sunspots dates to the very first week of that month.[9] At this time, in the wake of having for the second time founded the world's largest observatory, Hale was also taking steps to transform a small technical school in Pasadena—Throop Polytechnic Institute—into the West Coast rival to his alma mater MIT. Hale had a gift for collegiality, and was also making plans to revive and expand the National Academy of Sciences and laying foundations for the Solar Union, an international astronomical society. Famous for his manic energy, his colleagues (and he himself) attributed his psychological disturbances to overwork. Hale complained of chronic insomnia wracked by "terribly hard dreams"; once he found himself attempting to climb the picture frames on his bedroom wall. Severe headaches and indigestion also plagued him.

In August 1910, as the first international gathering of astrophysicists convened at the Mount Wilson Observatory, Hale was too ill ("bad case of brain congestion and exhaustion") to attend; he put in a single brief appearance. Hopeful for a rest cure, he fled with his family to England, and then to the French Riviera; he stayed at Mentone from January 10 to 21. One night in Mentone, Hale awoke to find a "little demon" sitting at the foot of his bed. In March he wrote a letter to his closest friend, his former MIT roommate, and now Dean of the Graduate School at Harvard, Harold M. Goodwin, describing the demon:

> Now I can't keep my mind on the subject, as a little demon stands by my side, and every few minutes prods me with the suggestion, that, after all, the book is not interesting, and that all of my attention belongs to him. How to escape this new form of torture, which is incessant, I do not know. If I could only do a little of my regular work, there would be no difficulty. But work excites me and sets the back of my head to aching, and so appears to be out of the question.

Hale told one of his doctors that the demon's visitation was always preceded by a painful ringing in his ears (a common symptom of possession), and that after this first appearance in Mentone, "he came often, in widely scattered places, until he became almost a mascot."[10]

For his entire adult life, Hale kept a pocket diary, devoted largely to brief entries describing the weather, travel, meetings with colleagues and friends, and often a running list of books he was reading. By 1910 he had taken to making episodic reports of his health. In the wake of the visitation at Mentone, amidst his daily diary entries, no mention is made either of the "demon" or any head troubles. The Hales traveled to Egypt via Genoa, arriving at Alexandria on January 29th. At Karnak, on February twenty-first, his diary notes "All symptoms have grown worse since Genoa." The celebrated Canadian physician William Osler, who was touring in Egypt at the time, gave Hale a thorough examination and recommended rest, diagnosing Hale's condition as fatigue due to overwork. At the rear of the 1911 diary, Hale compiled a list of his symptoms for Osler:

> Soreness of head—top, back
> Effects of letters, slight excitement
>   (photographing, etc.)

---

8 The Wikipedia entry quotes as its source for this dismissal a scholarly article by psychiatrist William Sheehan and historian of astronomy Donald Osterbrock, Sheehan: W. and Osterbrock, D. E., "Hale's 'Little Elf': The Mental Breakdowns of George Ellery Hale," *Journal for the History of Astronomy*, 31 (2000): 93–114.

9 George Ellery Hale, "On the probable existence of a magnetic field in sun-spots," *Astrophysical Journal* 28 (1908): 315–343.

10 George Ellery Hale to HM Goodwin, 25 March 1911, GEH Papers, California Institute of Technology Archives; Wright, *Explorer of the Universe: George Ellery Hale*, p. 264.

Quieting effect of reading. Effects of travel,
    discussion, heat.
Pyramids. Depression. Is solid reading
    objectionable? Nature of
change produced by rest. Is congestion main
    trouble? Effects of
ennui. Time required for improvement in
    similar cases. June plans –
can I work before head trouble entirely
    disappears? Left foot.

Hale and his wife Evelina (daughter of biologist William G. Conklin) had enjoyed travel in Europe since their honeymoon, and returned to Europe—this time to England—that summer. On June 7, while staying in London, he made an uncharacteristically long entry, describing the experience of a Dr. Jessup, Rector of Coving, who had written about his experience of seeing sitting in a chair in his library the specter of a man whom he later recognized from a portrait as a Jesuit priest from the days of Charles I. In November, amidst a string of entries noting "bad head," Hale made notes about other ghost tales told to him by English friends. His interest was clearly to compare these spectral experiences to his own.[11]

Hale spent three months during the summer of 1911 under the care of Dr. John George Gehring, who operated a sanatorium in Bethel Maine, where he put patients through a regime of strenuous outdoor exercise, carefully monitored diet, and a course of "self-suggestion." From Hale's letters to his wife and friends, it is clear that Gehring's methods never achieved any relief for Hale, who returned to Bethel—and a series of other sanatoriums—in future years. The most striking aspect of Hale's biography, as reflected in many dozens of letters to his most intimate correspondents over a period of thirty years, is that he remained completely reticent about the nature of his relationship with the possessing elemental being. Writing to Goodwin in 1936 from his home solar laboratory (which bore a bas relief above the fireplace of the

Egyptian pharaoh Akhenaten driving his chariot toward the sun god Aten, and above the front door a copy of another Aten image—the sun's rays ending in grasping hands—from a Theban tomb), Hale told him that a week before, as soon as he had begun a letter to Goodwin, "the whirligus got me, and I spent some time on my back."[12]

In this same letter, Hale described the progress on the construction of the new observatory on Palomar Mountain; a few months later Hale's health had declined so much that he entered the Las Encinas Sanatorium, only a mile away from the now thriving Caltech. He died there on February 21, 1938, just as the first parts of the new 200-inch telescope were being delivered to the top of Palomar.

All mental illness is tragic, but there is a particular poignancy to Hale's illness, given his dedication to natural science and to the study of our "typical star," the Sun. The *New York Times* called Hale "Priest of the Sun, Zoroaster of Our Time," and indeed, Hale had an unparalleled reverence for, and personal identification with, the Sun. Like Akhenaten, however, his devotion to the *physical* Sun ignored, in fact expurgated, the *spiritual Sun, the Christ*. His scientific career was significantly curtailed, and his personal life painfully injured, by a "little demon," an Ahrimanic elemental being hiding in plain sight from the finest physicians and scientists of the early twentieth century, none of whom could help Hale because they had no room for the reality of such a spectral being in the prevailing materialistic world conception.

"Out of the Blue"

The question remains as to whether this elemental being, about whom we know very little other than its relentless intention to "advise" George Ellery Hale on everything from his plans for civic development in Pasadena to the layout of the observatory on Palomar Mountain, was a source of inspiration for any of Hale's earliest scientific ideas. Outside of his achievements in scientific institution building, Hale is most celebrated for his invention of the spectroheliograph, the instrument that essentially

---

11 Hale Diary, June 7, 1911, Hale Papers. I cannot resist noting that Hale's entry for the following day notes that he received a visit from Charles Darwin's son, astronomer George Darwin; Hale Diary Nov. 16–17, 1911, Hale Papers.

12 GEH—HM Goodwin, April 14, 1936, Hale Papers.

made possible his subsequent solar research, and which revolutionized the natural scientific study of the Sun. In August 1889, just a week or two after his twenty-first birthday—and entry into his Sun period—Hale was on a trolley car in Chicago, when "out of the blue," the idea for the spectroheliograph came to him.

Anecdotal tales of scientific inspiration go back to Archimedes' bathtub "Eureka!" and Isaac Newton's apple-induced gravity epiphany, but the systematic study of the source of scientific ideas is a Michael era practice, dating almost exclusively *after 1879*. Though the approach and the conclusions of the authors vary widely, all of them share a faith in Darwinian evolution; indeed, the post-1879 advent of these studies can be seen as a strictly exoteric result of the extension of Darwinian theory from its initial province—morphology—to consciousness. Darwin's cousin Francis Galton's 1883 work, *Inquiries into Human Faculty and Its Development*, despite its crude materialism and naïve faith in statistics as a revealer of truth, is incredibly valuable for its descriptions—elicited from questionnaires circulated by Galton to his wide and illustrious circle of scientific friends—of mental imagery. Galton himself was an adept imager, as was his grandfather Erasmus Darwin, whose curious feats of imagination were celebrated within the family for generations.

In Galton's work and those that followed,[13] a fantastic array of case studies of scientific invention and inspiration—from August Kekulé's daydream-inspired discovery of the structure of the benzene ring to Henri Poincaré's intuitive flashes into the nether regions of mathematics and physics—has been given to us, *all of it of course in a spirit of celebration of the sublime accomplishments of these individuals*. Living since 1879 in a

world completely permeated by Ahrimanic inspirations, we continue to celebrate as heroic, benign, admirable, and perhaps inevitable not just the invention (and inventors) of spectroscopy, evolution by natural selection, and hypnotherapy, but the countless other Ahrimanic thought-forms that constitute the landscape of the modern world.

Few of these scientists suffered Hale's fate; if their "illuminations" (mathematician Jacques Hadamard's favorite term for his own flashes of insight) were at all the product of Ahrimanic elemental beings, they managed a much more harmonious coexistence with the "demons" who haunted them. Yet, we have such celebrated contemporary cases as mathematician John Nash, whose "beautiful mind" was a Janus-faced monster that crippled him for significant stretches of his life. In the wake of one of his psychotic episodes, Nash's Harvard mathematical colleague George Mackey paid him a visit during his hospitalization, and asked Nash how he could possibly believe, given his devotion to reason and logical proof, that extraterrestrials were sending him messages. Nash replied, "Because the ideas about supernatural beings came to me the same way that my mathematical ideas did. So I took them seriously."[14]

Srinivasa Ramanujan, whose mathematical genius took him from his tiny Madras town to Trinity College, Cambridge, never relented from his explanation that it was the "goddess" (read *elemental*) Namagiri who inscribed the mind-boggling formulae upon his tongue. Ramanujan, educated in a British colony, still benefited from a cultural and spiritual heritage which afforded him a way to make sense of his own inspirer; Nash, Hale, and any other modern whose destiny was intertwined with a brilliant but amoral "whirligus" or "extraterrestrial," had no alternative but to see his blessing turn into a curse, since there was no protocol for even the most cursory conversation with these entities. Rudolf Steiner repeatedly warned that these beings would fall sway en masse to the influence of Ahriman if we did not soon elaborate a full and faithful knowledge of them.

---

13 See for example Nisbet, *The Insanity of Genius and the General Inequality of Human Faculty Physiologically Considered*; Hadamard, *An Essay on the Psychology of Invention in the Mathematical Field*; Gruber and Bödeker, *Creativity, Psychology and the History of Science*. It is actually quite stunning to see how many of the principle names from my provisional 1841 to 1879 list above show up in these studies, as exemplars of "illumination."

14 Sylvia Nasar, "A Beautiful Mind," *Vanity Fair* June 1998.

George Ellery Hale and John Nash are bellwethers, canaries in the mine; their biographies at least can serve as chilling exemplars of the perils of an asymmetric relationship with elemental beings in our time. One must pause to consider how many of our contemporary scientific and technological celebrities, especially in this era of mindless genuflection before technical prowess, are comfortably co-habiting with Ahrimanic elemental beings.

POE, CONAN DOYLE, AND THE HAZARDS OF RATIOCINATION

Edgar Allen Poe, the creator of nineteenth century literature's first rationalist superhero, came to a tragic end that is often itself cast as a Gothic mystery. In October 1849, a delirious Poe wandered about the streets of Baltimore, incoherent, hallucinating, wearing clothes that were not his own. A few days later, he was dead; he was only forty years old. *Delirium tremens*, the nineteenth century's Latin designation for the terrible condition to which so many alcohol-addicted men and women succumbed, was for Poe familiar territory. In the months and years leading up to his death, he had frequently descended into this hellish state, populated with the visions and voices of the addict's idiosyncratic psychic physiology. Poe, having sent forth via his nightmare tales into American and world culture a whole host of ghouls and specters, reaped in spades what he had sown. In his own biography, whatever in him embodied C. August Dupin, the cold and calculating Jekyll, threw up a deadly shadow of a Luciferic Hyde.

So did Western culture, the specters of Spiritualism and the spectatorship of cinema expressing the Hyde half of its clinical, statistic-loving Jekyll public face.[15] Arthur Conan Doyle, our *Zeitgeist* book-

end, had his own dangerous dalliances with the elemental world, immersed as he was for his entire adult life in the Luciferic thrill of the Spiritualist séance room. The Cottingley fairies episode, seen from a century away, is easily understood as the Luciferic answer to Sherlock Holmes's heartlessly infallible gift for detection. The Victorian stability of Baker Street proved a saving grace for Conan Doyle's imagination, if considered alongside the fate of his talented father, Charles Altamont Doyle, whose descent into alcoholism and madness came while he was the British Empire's most celebrated fairy painter. Every time that you see the leering, lecherous face of the *punchinello* in the *Punch* masthead, you are looking at a Charles Altamont Doyle creation. While an inmate for decades in various Scottish insane asylums, Sir Arthur's father produced reams and reams of drawings of altogether real ghouls and goblins.

There are no doubt as intricate karmic aspects to the peculiar hauntings of Edgar Allen Poe and Charles Altamont Doyle as there are to the "little demon" of George Ellery Hale, and it would be exceedingly unwise to generalize from just these destinies to our collective destiny. If nothing else, their biographies illustrate the truism that we *become* what we think. Given the impaired quality of our contemporary thinking, that truism demands renewed contemplation. George Ellery Hale was, for all his altruistic impulses to put science in the service of humanity, more Akhenaten than Zoroaster, his gargantuan telescopes and his National Research Council (dreamed up by him in 1916) today continuing to serve altogether Ahrimanic aims. May we do all we can to give aspiring youth who stare into mud puddles or into the night sky and wonder at Creation, Michaelic and Sophianic gospels along with the microscopes and telescopes and spectroheliographs.

---

15 Jekyll and Hyde's creator, Robert Louis Stevenson, was admirably transparent about the "brownies" who wrote his stories for him.

HOW THE GRAIL SITES WERE FOUND
WOLFRAM VON ESCHENBACH AS A HISTORIAN

BY WERNER GREUB

A Book Review by Robert Kelder
with additional comments by Robert Powell

The thirteenth century German poet-knight Wolfram von Eschenbach assures us that his famous Grail romance *Parzival* contains descriptions of historical events that took place eleven generations before his time (i.e., in the ninth century) exactly in the way he narrates them. The source for his material he describes as a certain "well-known master Kyot the Provençal," thus not, as is still generally assumed, *Perceval* by the French poet Chrétien de Troyes that appeared some twenty years earlier. But because this enigmatic figure Kyot could not, until now, be historically identified, his existence has long been cast in doubt. And so it is widely assumed that Wolfram based his *Parzival* on a poetically created source named Kyot. With respect to his *Willehalm*, an unfinished epic poem on the heroic exploits of the French Count William of Orange, it is still generally believed that Wolfram's source was the semi-historical folklore of the epic poem *Aliscans*, one of the many so-called *Chansons de geste* ("epic songs") of the roving troubadours of the south of France. *Aliscans* extolled the rather pious and fantastic deeds of this paladin of Emperor Charlemagne. He was one of the twelve paladins in Charlemagne's entourage. (Paladin signifies "warrior knight," usually of high-standing nobility.) In the case of William of Orange, he was the "right-hand man" of the emperor, who was entrusted by Charlemagne with the creation of the Spanish March (*Marca Hispanica*) as a buffer zone on the south side of the Pyrenees—between the Pyrenees and the Ebro River—to protect France from invasion by the Saracens coming up from the south. Moreover, he was one of the last protectors of Celtic or Grail Christianity, who in the year 1066 was declared the "patron saint of knights" by Pope Alexander II.

In one of his lectures from the series published under the title *Christ and the Spiritual World: The Search for the Holy Grail*, Rudolf Steiner stated on January 1, 1914, that Kyot is no mere figment of a poet's vivid imagination, but definitely a historical figure who lived not in the twelfth, as is still generally believed, but in the ninth century. In private conversations, moreover, he described the Arlesheim Hermitage—an old Celtic sacred landscape near the site of the Goetheanum in Dornach, Switzerland—as the actual Grail area where Parzival had his eventful meetings with Trevrizent and Sigune, both of whom lived in seclusion as hermits not far from Wolfram's Grail Castle *Munsalvaesche*, often mistakenly thought to be Montségur on the French side of the Pyrenees, or sometimes identified with the mountain monastery San Juan de la Peña, on the Spanish side of the Pyrenees.

The above indications by Wolfram von Eschenbach and Rudolf Steiner motivated the Swiss-born anthroposophist and Grail researcher Werner Greub (1909–1997) to take Wolfram von Eschenbach's words seriously, thereby succeeding, as it were, in bringing the Grail down to earth. Carefully following all of Wolfram's manifold indications from the original Middle High German texts to the letter, and reading the landscape as a largely unspoiled script, he not only found Kyot to be none other than the medieval William of Orange, but also discovered, or rather decoded, most of the historic scenes of actions where—in the first half of the ninth century—most of the actual events in *Parzival* as well as in *Willehalm* must have taken place in an area of what now is now called Alsace, bordering on Switzerland, Germany, and France. This led Werner Greub to formulate his novel and controversial theory that Wolfram von Eschenbach is not only to be regarded as a great poet, but also as an exact chronicler of Parzival's revolutionary inauguration as Grail king. Furthermore, Greub employed astronomy to identify the point in time when Parzival became Grail king as Whitsun Saturday, May 12, 848. Werner Greub also found the Grail castle Munsalvaesche to have been located half-way up a hill on an ancient Roman quarry in the Arlesheim Hermitage. Wolfram's references to various planetary constellations also turned out to be so exact that by means of extensive astronomical calculations the whole chronology of *Parzival* and, indirectly, that of *Willehalm* could be established.[1]

As the title of this voluminous research report suggests, the emphasis lies not so much on the *where* but on the *how*. Werner Greub managed to depict his discovery of the Grail sites on various maps and in the geographical reality itself in such a manner that every scene of action can be represented and experienced step by step within the mind of the attentive reader, inviting him or her to make the next step of visiting the *Parzival* and *Willehalm* geography on the spot in person in order to be able to make an experiential assessment oneself on the merits of this unique book that purports to put the hitherto considered legendary Grail tradition in a completely new light.

How The Grail Sites Were Found was first published under the title *Wolfram von Eschenbach und die Wirklichkeit des Grals* in 1974 by the *Goetheanum, School for Spiritual Science* founded by Rudolf Steiner in 1923 as the research and development center of the *General Anthroposophical Society.* It elicited such controversy that the second and third volumes of this projected Grail trilogy were never officially published. Due to these and other extenuating circumstances, it took twenty-seven years for this book to be translated and first published as a ring-bound manuscript in English in 2001 and another 12 years before this first book edition could finally see the light of day. (A French edition was published as *La Quête du Grala* in 2002, and a Dutch translation, *Willem van Oranje, Parzival en de Graal,* was published by the Willehalm Institute Press, Amsterdam, in 2009.)

The reader interested in the background to this controversy can consult the introduction "How This Publication Came About," while in Appendix V a rebuttal of this scathing criticism can be read as an alternative introduction to this volume. The translator Robert J. Kelder is a graduate of McGill University in Montreal, Canada, and worked as a publicist and guide with Werner Greub during an exhibition in 1985 commemorating the 200th anniversary of the Arlesheim Hermitage as an English Garden famous at that time throughout Europe. This exhibition marked the first time after the publication of this book in 1974 that results of Werner Greub's Grail research were brought out into the open, discussed and mentioned (mostly favorable) in the Swiss national press. The text for this exhibition can be read in Appendix III.

For the third North American edition of the manuscript version a foreword with a postscript was written dealing with the books *Holy Grail across the Atlantic: The Secret History of Canadian Discovery and Exploration,* and its sequels, *The Columbus Conspiracy* and *Grail Knights of North America* by Michael Bradley, in which the views expressed there concerning King Arthur and the Holy Grail, Camelot and

---

1 See comments by Robert Powell at the end of this review.

the Grail Castle Munsalvaesche and Wolfram's source Kyot are contrasted with the views put forward in this book.

For the fourth British edition that was presented at the Rudolf Steiner House in London on October 26, 2001, a special foreword *Willehalm: King of the Jews?* was also written.

This first book edition was presented on May 3, 2013, by the publisher as part of the festivities connected with the international book and art exhibition in Amsterdam City Hall entitled *The Virtues: Towards a New Courtesy,* organized by the Willehalm Foundation. It is dedicated to the recently inaugurated Dutch King William-Alexander of Orange and the Dutch Council of High Nobility as part of a petition that was officially announced on May 28, 2014, to the said king and council. This entailed a formal request to establish a *Willehalm Order of Knights of the Word, as a supplement to the existing Military Willems-Order of the Sword named after Willehalm,* based on the findings of Greub's work, the exhibited book *The Virtues: Seasons of the Soul* by Herbert Witzenmann, his studies *The Just Price-World Economy as Social Organics,* and *Charter of Humanity,* and other forthcoming Grail-related publications as study material for the spiritualization of the principle of civilization.

❧

Contents: Dedication and Petition to King William-Alexander and the Council of High Nobility • Introduction to the Exhibition *The Virtues–Towards a New Courtesy* • How This Publication Came About–Introduction to the First English (American) Edition by Robert J. Kelder • The Holy Grail Across The Atlantic–Foreword to the Third North American Edition • Post Script: Grail Knights of North America? • Foreword to the Fourth British Edition • Introduction to the German edition, Rudolf Grosse • Foreword by the Author.

Part I: Willehalm: Oransch • The Battlefield of Alischanz • Willehalm as the Historical William of Orange • The "Tenth" Book of *Willehalm* • Saint-Guilhelm-le-Désert • Willehalm and Arabel • Willehalm-Kyot of Catalonia • Kyot the Provençal.

Part II: Parzival: Wolfram's Astronomy • The Grail Tradition as Oral History • Bertane–The Land of King Arthur • Terre de salvaesche: Land of the Grail • Klingsor's Schastel Marveil • Trevrizent's Cave and Sigune's Cell • Wolfram the Historian I • The Great Conjunction • Astronomical Excursion • Wolfram the Historian II • Prologue to *Willehalm* • Epilogue.

Appendices: I. The Grail Symbol • II. The Grail Symbol as the Basic Form of the Grail Temple Munsalvaesche • III. The Arlesheim Hermitage as Grail Landscape • IV. Letter from Adalbert Count Keyserlingk on Geub's Work • V. Christoph Lindenberg: Beyond Truth and Reality with Comments by R. J. Kelder • VI. Short Biography of Werner Grueb • VII. The Willehalm Institute and Its Publications • VII. A Letter by Dr. Slobodan R. Mitric on 9/11.

First book edition: Amsterdam, May 2013 / 421 pages, including 111 plates, 32 in color, and including 15 maps/English translation © by Robert J. Kelder / ISBN 9073932272

Willehalm Institute Press, Kerkstraat 386A, 1017 JB Amsterdam, Netherlands/www.willehalm .nl; info@willehalm.nl/Information: Robert Kelder, Tel. +31-20-6944572.

How The Grail Sites Were Found can be ordered through your favorite bookshop or from www.BoekenRoute.nl by sending a check for 40 euros plus shipping charges (NL, 8 euros; Europe, 10 euros; worldwide, 16 euros) made out to "Willehalm Institute" at the address listed above or by depositing the right amount (40 euros pls. shipping) in the Institute's bank account (IBAN: NL28ABNA0571181937; BIC: ABNANL2A). For PayPal an order can be sent by the Institute to the interested party.

COMMENTS BY ROBERT POWELL

Like Robert Kelder, I knew Werner Greub personally and went with him many times to the Arlesheim Hermitage and to the sites he identified there, including the site of the Grail castle. In the course of time, I became aware of Werner Greub's geographical clairvoyance. He was truly able to see beyond the sense-perceptible realm, and making use of this higher faculty of perception, he was called to identify the Grail sites described in the book *Parzival* by Wolfram von Eschenbach.

Whereas I do not question the overall accuracy of Werner Greub's geographical identification of the Grail sites described in *Parzival*, as set forth in this book *How the Grail Sites were Found*, I do question Werner Greub's dating of the Grail events as he sets this forth in the chapter "Wolfram's Astronomy" in the book under review. Whereas his spatial location of the Grail sites is, by and large, very accurate, his temporal specification of the Grail events is questionable because his dating clearly contradicts an indication by Rudolf Steiner in the Grail cycle of lectures *Christ and the Spiritual World: The Search for the Holy Grail*. Rudolf Steiner's indication is explored in William Bento's article "Saturn in the Crab and the Mysteries of the Holy Grail" in the 2005 issue of the *Christian Star Calendar*, the predecessor of the *Journal for Star Wisdom*. In that article, using Rudolf Steiner's indication about the Sun and Saturn being in conjunction in the constellation of Cancer at the time of Parzival's first visit to the Grail castle, William Bento identifies the New Moon in Cancer, with Saturn close by, which took place on July 15 in the year 828, as being the heavenly configuration that Rudolf Steiner was referring to. Six planets were in Cancer on that day of the New Moon in the year 828, and the conjunction of the Sun and Moon was at exactly the same location in the zodiac where Saturn had been at Christ's crucifixion.

According to the account of Wolfram von Eschenbach in *Parzival*, it was not until some five years later *(Parzival 799, 3)* that Parzival returned to the Grail castle and became Grail king. Symbolically, it could be that Parzival became Grail king at Pentecost (Sunday, June 1) in the year 833, some five years after his first visit to the Grail castle. Here, however, is not the place to go into the details of this complex theme of the timing of the Grail events. Perhaps, though, it is important to point out the following: According to Walter Johannes Stein in his book *The Ninth Century: World History in the Light of the Holy Grail*, the historical personage who is called Trevrizent in the Grail story was the French Count Hugo de Tours, who was also one of Charlemagne's twelve paladins. It is known that Hugo de Tours died on October 20 in the year 837, which provides an upper limit for the dating of the Grail events. Whereas June 1, 833, lies within this limit, and is thus a possible date for when Parzival became Grail king, the date offered by Werner Greub on May 13, 848, falls after the death date of Hugo de Tours ("Trevrizent"). This date is simply too late, historically, to be the date when Parzival became Grail king, if we accept that Trevrizent was Hugo de Tours.

It is wonderful that Werner Greub's great work *How the Grail Sites Were Found* is now available in English translation—in such a splendid form, with many photos, maps, and colored plates. With great gratitude to Robert J. Kelder for translating this work and shepherding it into print.[2]

✒

---

2 For further information on the petition to the Dutch king, see www.willehalm-order-of-knights .blogspot.nl (in English).

WORKING WITH THE STAR CALENDAR

Robert Powell, PhD

In taking note of the astronomical events listed in the Star Calendar of the *Journal for Star Wisdom* (*JSW*), it is important to distinguish between long- and short-term astronomical events. Long-term astronomical events—for example, Pluto transiting a particular degree of the zodiac—will have a longer period of meditation than would the five days advocated for short-term astronomical events such as the New and Full Moon. The following describes, in relation to meditating on the Full Moon, a meditative process extending over a five-day period.

Sanctification of the Full Moon

As a preliminary remark, let us remind ourselves that the great sacrifice of Christ on the Cross—the Mystery of Golgotha—took place at Full Moon. As Christ's sacrifice took place when the Moon was full in the middle of the sidereal sign of Libra, the Libra Full Moon assumes special significance in the sequence of twelve (or thirteen) Full Moons taking place during the cycle of the year. In following this sequence, the Mystery of Golgotha serves as an archetype for *every* Full Moon, since each Full Moon imparts a particular spiritual blessing. Hence the practice described here of *Sanctification of the Full Moon* applies to every Full Moon. Similarly, there is also the practice of *Sanctification of the New Moon*, as described in *Hermetic Astrology, Volume 2: Astrological Biography*, chapter 10.

During the two days prior to the Full Moon, we can consider the focus of one's meditation to extend over these two days as *preparatory days* immediately preceding the day of the Full Moon. These two days can be dedicated to spiritual reflection and detachment from everyday concerns, as one prepares to become a vessel for the in-streaming light and love one will receive at the Full Moon, something that one can then impart further—for example, to help people in need, or to support Mother Earth in times of catastrophe. During these two days, it is helpful to hold an attitude of dedication and service and try to assume an attitude of receptivity that opens to what one's soul will receive and subsequently impart—an attitude conducive to making one a true *servant of the spirit.*

The day of the Full Moon is itself a day of *holding the sacred space.* In doing so, one endeavors to cultivate inner peace and silence, during which one attempts to contact and consciously hold the in-streaming blessing of the Full Moon for the rest of humanity. One can heighten this silent meditation by visualizing the zodiacal constellation/sidereal sign in which the Moon becomes full, since the Moon serves to reflect the starry background against which it appears.

If the Moon is full in Virgo, for example, it reminds us of the night of the birth of the Jesus child visited by the three magi, as described in the Gospel of St. Matthew. That birth occurred at the Full Moon in the middle of the sidereal sign of Virgo, and the three magi, who gazed up that evening to behold the Full Moon against the background of the stars of the Virgin, witnessed the soul of Jesus emerge from the disk of the Full Moon and descend toward Earth. They participated from afar, via the starry heavens, in the Grail Mystery of the holy birth.

In meditating upon the Full Moon and opening oneself to receive the in-streaming blessing from the starry heavens, we can exercise restraint by avoiding the formulation of what will happen or what one might receive from the Full Moon. Moreover, we can also refrain from seeking tangible results or effects connected with our attunement to the Full Moon. Even if we observe only the date but not the exact moment when the Moon is full, it is helpful to find quiet time to reflect alone or to use the opportunity for deep meditation on the day of the Full Moon.

We can think of the two days following the Full Moon as a *time of imparting* what we have received from the in-streaming of the full disk of the Moon against the background of the stars. It is now possible to turn our attention toward humanity and the world and endeavor to pass on any spiritual blessing we have received from the starry heavens. Thereby we can assist in the work of the spiritual world by transforming what we have received into goodwill and allowing it to flow wherever the greatest need exists.

It is a matter of *holding a sacred space* throughout the day of the Full Moon. This is an important time to still the mind and maintain inner peace.

It is a time of spiritual retreat and contact with the spiritual world, of holding in one's consciousness the archetype of the Mystery of Golgotha as a great outpouring of Divine Love that bridges Heaven and Earth. Prior to the day of the Full Moon, the two preceding days prepare the sacred space as a vessel to receive the heavenly blessing. The two days following the day of the Full Moon are a time to assimilate and distribute the spiritual transmission received into the sacred space we have prepared.

One can apply the process described here as a meditative practice in relation to the Full Moon to any of the astronomical events listed in the *JSW*, especially as most of these *remember* significant Christ Events. Take note, however, whether an event is long-term or short-term and adjust the period of meditative practice accordingly.

*"The shadow intellect that is characteristic of all modern culture has fettered human beings to the Earth. They have eyes only for earthly things, particularly when they allow themselves to be influenced by the claims of modern science. In our age it never occurs to someone that their being belongs not to the Earth alone but to the cosmos beyond the Earth. Knowledge of our connection with the cosmos beyond the Earth—that is what we need above all to make our own.... When someone says 'I' to themselves, they experience a force that is working within, and the [ancient] Greek, in feeling the working of this inner force, related it to the Sun; ...the Sun and the 'I' are the outer and inner aspects of one being. The Sun out there in space is the cosmic 'I.' What lives within me is the human 'I.'.... Human beings are not primarily a creation of Earth. Human beings receive their shape and form from the cosmos. The human being is an offspring of the world of stars, above all of the Sun and Moon.... The Moon forces stream out from a center in the metabolic system....[The] Moon stimulates reproduction.... Saturn works chiefly in the upper part of the astral body....Jupiter has to do with thinking...Mars [has] to do with speech.... The Mercury forces work in the part of the human organism that lies below the region of the heart...in the breathing and circulatory functions.... Venus works preeminently in the etheric body of the human being."—*RUDOLF STEINER, Offspring of the World of Stars*, May 5, 1921*

SYMBOLS USED IN CHARTS

PLANETS		ZODIACAL SIGNS		ASPECTS	
⊕	Earth	♈	Aries (Ram)	☌	Conjunction 0°
☉	Sun	♉	Taurus (Bull)	✳	Sextile 60°
☽	Moon	♊	Gemini (Twins)	□	Square 90°
☿	Mercury	♋	Cancer (Crab)	△	Trine 120°
♀	Venus	♌	Leo (Lion)	☍	Opposition 180°
♂	Mars	♍	Virgo (Virgin)		
♃	Jupiter	♎	Libra (Scales)		
♄	Saturn	♏	Scorpio (Scorpion)		
♅	Uranus	♐	Sagittarius (Archer)		
♆	Neptune	♑	Capricorn (Goat)		
♇	Pluto	♒	Aquarius (Water Carrier)		
		♓	Pisces (Fishes)		

OTHER

☊	Ascending (North) Node	☌	Sun Eclipse
☋	Descending (South) Node	☌	Moon Eclipse
P	Perihelion/Perigee	☌	Inferior Conjunction
A	Aphelion/Apogee	☌	Superior Conjunction
	Maximum Latitude	⚷	Chiron
	Minimum Latitude		

TIME

The information relating to daily geocentric and heliocentric planetary positions in the sidereal zodiac is tabulated in the form of an ephemeris for each month, in which the planetary positions are given at 0 hours Universal Time (UT) each day.

Beneath the geocentric and heliocentric ephemeris for each month, the information relating to planetary aspects is given in the form of an aspectarian, which lists the most important aspects—geocentric and heliocentric/hermetic—between the planets for the month in question. The day and the time of occurrence of the aspect on that day are indicated, all times being given in Universal Time (UT), which is identical to Greenwich Mean Time (GMT). For example, zero hours Universal Time is midnight GMT. This time system applies in Britain; however, when summer time is in effect, one hour must be added to all times.

** In other time zones, the time has to be adjusted according to whether it is ahead of or behind Britain. For example, in Germany, where the time is one hour ahead of British time, an hour must be added; when summer time is in effect in Germany, two hours have to be added to all times.

Using the calendar in the United States, do the following subtraction from all time indications according to time zone:

- Pacific Time subtract 8 hours
  (7 hours for daylight saving time);
- Mountain Time subtract 7 hours
  (6 hours for daylight saving time);
- Central Time subtract 6 hours
  (5 hours for daylight saving time);
- Eastern Time subtract 5 hours
  (4 hours for daylight saving time).

This subtraction will often change the date of an astronomical occurrence, shifting it back one day. Consequently, since most of the readers of this calendar live on the American Continent, astronomical occurrences during the early hours of day x are sometimes listed in the Commentaries as occurring on days x–1/x. For example, an eclipse occurring at 03:00 UT on the 12th is listed as occurring on the 11/12th since in America it takes place on the 11th.[1]

SIMPLIFYING THE PROCEDURE

The preceding procedure can be greatly simplified. Here is an example for someone wishing to know the zodiacal locations of the planets on Christmas Day, December 25, 2016. Looking at the December ephemeris, it can be seen that Christmas Day falls on a Sunday. In the upper tabulation, the geocentric planetary positions are given, with that of the Sun indicated in the first column, that of the Moon in the second column, and so on. The position of the Sun is listed as 8°39' Sagittarius.

For someone living in London, 8°39' Sagittarius is the Sun's position at midnight, December 24/25, 2016—noting that in London and all of the United Kingdom, the Time Zone applying there is that of Universal Time/Greenwich Mean Time—UT/GMT.

For someone living in Sydney, Australia, which on Christmas Day is eleven hours ahead of UT/GMT, 8°39' Sagittarius is the Sun's position at 11 a.m. on December 25.

For someone living in California, which is eight hours behind UT/GMT on Christmas Day, 8°39' Sagittarius is the Sun's position at 4 p.m. on **December 24.**

For the person living in California, therefore, in order to know the positions of the planets on

---

1 See *General Introduction to the Christian Star Calendar: A Key to Understanding* for an in-depth clarification of the features of the calendar in the *Journal for Star Wisdom,* including indications as to how to work with it.

December 25, it is necessary to look at the entries for **December 26**. The result is:

For someone living in California, which is eight hours behind UT/GMT on Christmas Day, the Sun's position at 4 p.m. on December 25 is 9°40' Sagittarius and, by the same token, the Moon's position on Christmas Day at 4 p.m. on December 25 is 3°23' Scorpio—these are the positions alongside December 26 at midnight UT/GMT—and eight hours earlier equates with 4 p.m. on December 25 in California.

From these examples it emerges that the **planetary positions as given in the ephemeris** can be utilized, but that according to the Time Zone one is in, **the time of day is different** and also for locations West of the United Kingdom **the date changes** (look at the date following the actual date).

Here is a tabulation in relation to the foregoing example of December 25 (Christmas Day).

UNITED KINGDOM, EUROPE, AND ALL LOCATIONS WITH TIME ZONES EAST OF GREENWICH

Look at what is given alongside December 25— these entries indicate the planetary positions at these times:

- 12:00 a.m. (midnight December 24/25) in London (UT/GMT)
- 01:00 a.m. in Berlin (CENTRAL EURO- PEAN TIME, which is one hour ahead of UT/GMT)
- 11:00 a.m. in Sydney (AUSTRALIAN EASTERN DAYLIGHT TIME, which is eleven hours ahead of UT/GMT)

CANADA, USA, CENTRAL AMERICA, SOUTH AMERICA, AND ALL LOCATIONS WITH TIME ZONES WEST OF GREENWICH

Look at what is given alongside December 26— these entries indicate the planetary positions at these times:

- 7:00 p.m. in New York (EASTERN STANDARD TIME, which is five hours behind UT/GMT)
- 6:00 p.m. in Chicago (CENTRAL STAN- DARD TIME, which is six hours behind UT/GMT)
- 5:00 p.m. in Denver (MOUNTAIN STANDARD TIME, which is seven hours behind UT/GMT)
- 4:00 p.m. in San Francisco (PACIFIC STANDARD TIME, which is eight hours behind UT/GMT)
- **IF SUMMER TIME IS IN USE, ADD ONE HOUR—FOR EXAMPLE:**
- 8:00 p.m. in New York (EASTERN DAYLIGHT TIME, which is four hours behind UT/GMT)
- 7:00 p.m. in Chicago (CENTRAL DAY- LIGHT TIME, which is five hours behind UT/GMT)
- 6:00 p.m. in Denver (MOUNTAIN DAY- LIGHT TIME, which is six hours behind UT/GMT)
- 5:00 p.m. in San Francisco (PACIFIC DAYLIGHT TIME, which is seven hours behind UT/GMT)

Note that in the preceding tabulation, the time given in Sydney on Christmas Day, December 25, is in terms of Daylight Time. Six months earlier, on June 25, for someone in Sydney they would look alongside the entry in the ephemeris for June 25 and would know that this applies (for them) to…

- 10:00 a.m. in Sydney (AUSTRALIAN EASTERN TIME, which is ten hours ahead of UT/GMT).

In these examples, it is not just the position of the Sun that is referred to. The same applies to the zodiacal locations given in the ephemeris for *all* the planets, whether geocentric (upper tabulation) or heliocentric (lower tabulation). *All that is necessary to apply this method of reading the ephemeris is to know the Time Zone in which one is and to apply the number of hours difference from UT/GMT.*

The advantage of using the method described here is that it greatly simplifies reference to the ephemeris when studying the **zodiacal positions of the planets**. However, for applying the time indications listed under "Ingresses" or "Aspects" it is still necessary to add or subtract the time difference from UT/GMT as described in the above paragraph denoted.**

"Why does a feeling of grandeur, of reverent awe, come over us when we look up into the starry heavens? It is because without our knowing it the feeling of our soul's home awakens in us. The feeling awakens: Before you came down to earth to a new incarnation, you yourself were in those stars, and out of the stars have come the highest forces that are within you. Your moral law was imparted to you when you were dwelling in the world of stars. When you practice self-knowledge, you can behold what the starry heaven bestowed upon you between death and a new birth—the best and finest powers of your soul. What we behold in the starry heavens is the moral law that is given to us from the spiritual worlds, for between death and a new birth we live in these starry heavens. One should contemplate the starry heavens with feelings such as these.… If we then raise our eyes to the starry heavens, we will be filled with a feeling of reverence and will know that this is the memory of the human being's eternal home."

—RUDOLF STEINER (*Life Between Death and Rebirth*, Nov. 18, 1912)

COMMENTARIES AND EPHEMERIDES
JANUARY–DECEMBER 2016

Monthly Stargazing Preview by Sally Nurney
Commentaries by Claudia McLaren Lainson

JANUARY 2016

We begin the year with the Sun in the middle of Sagittarius, the Archer. The Moon is a waning crescent, visible in the wee hours of the morning, on its way to being New Moon in eight days' time—on the 9th. Between New Year's Day and the coming New Moon, the Moon will join with Mars on the 3rd, and Venus and Saturn on the 6th. You can witness these events by looking to the east in the deep night sky—before sunrise; Mars will rise about six hours before the Sun and Venus, and Saturn will rise four hours before the Sun and Venus.

Mercury stations Retrograde on the 6th (and stations Direct again on the 26th.) Venus and Saturn will come together on the 8th; Venus is the brightest planet in our sky and will therefore obscure Saturn, which will be hidden from view behind Venus. Saturn will be to the right of Venus in the following days, as she moves on through Scorpio.

Jupiter stations Retrograde in Leo on the 9th, appearing to go backward against the stars until the middle of May.

The Sun and Mercury conjunct in Sagittarius on the 14th. The Sun moves into the constellation of the SeaGoat (Capricorn) the following day. Venus enters Sagittarius on the 19th, continuing her role as the "Morning Star" until disappearing into the Sun's light around April as she heads into a superior conjunction with the Sun in June.

The Moon is Full on the 23rd, which is always formed by the Moon being exactly opposite the Sun in the Zodiac. In this case, the Moon is in Cancer across from the Sun in Capricorn. The waning Moon joins up with Jupiter on the 27th in the constellation of Leo, perhaps obscuring Jupiter by its still generous light.

For this entire month Pluto will be within 2° of opposition with Sirius, and Jupiter will be in close conjunction with the North Node (exact on the 23rd and 29th). The waning square between Pluto and Uranus will be within 2°.

Jan. 1: Sun 16° Sagittarius: Birth of the Nathan Jesus (Saturday, Dec/6/2 BC). It was the pure and chaste Nathan Jesus (called the *sister soul* of Adam) who became Jesus Christ and walked among us. This is the Jesus whose genealogy, as written in the Gospel of St. Luke, is traced back to Adam. It is this birth Uranus is remembering this year.[1] (Geocentrically Uranus returns to its position at the birth of the Nathan Jesus: 24°59' Pisces on April 1, and heliocentrically Uranus returns to its position at the birth of the Nathan Jesus on November 6.) Since the event of the Mystery of Golgotha, Jesus Christ is the spirit of the Earth; his sheaths are woven into the very fabric of our living, breathing Mother Earth. The entire future of humanity depends on human beings uniting with the unfathomable love and mercy of this first-born Son of the Father. Through this union, human beings will find their relationship with the "moral ether" now forming as a consequence of yet another sacrifice the Archangel Jesus being is undergoing on behalf of the Etheric Christ. The force of this sacrifice is carried by the angelic presence of the Nathan Jesus in the etheric realm surrounding the Earth; from there the sustaining power of the moral ether is sent to waiting human hearts below. A new school is forming through the emanations raying forth from the activity of the Angel Jesus. What qualities can we anticipate as signatures of this new stream of influence? Robert Powell depicts the nature of the Nathan Jesus:

---

1 See "The Towers We Build," page 47 in this issue.

[The] Solomon Jesus was the leading representative of the stream of wisdom, while the Nathan Jesus represented a spiritual stream that is characterized rather by "peace and goodwill." In fact, according to the spiritual research of Rudolf Steiner, the Nathan Jesus was a representative of the Indian spiritual stream—in contrast to the Persian spiritual stream of Zarathustra. In Buddhism—regarded by many as the highest flowering of India's spirituality—the central impulse is not so much the acquisition of wisdom (such as that of the Magi), but rather the development of inward, heart qualities such as compassion. Just as the Solomon Jesus, the reincarnated Zarathustra, was the leader of the "wisdom stream" stemming back to the Persian culture of the Magi, so the Nathan Jesus was the leader of the Hindu spiritual stream exemplified by Krishna in the Bhagavad Gita, the stream that later brought forth the great teacher of compassion, Gautama Buddha. According to Rudolf Steiner, however, whereas the individuality of the Solomon Jesus had incarnated repeatedly, the individuality of the Nathan Jesus had never incarnated before, apart from an "embodiment" in Krishna. In the Nathan Jesus, the "sister soul" of Adam, a soul that (unlike Adam) had not passed through the Fall, was present. This soul, having never been fully incarnated, was untainted by the consequences of the Fall. It was free of "sin," including the "original sin" incurred through the Fall:

> In the Luke Jesus boy lived a part of humankind's being that had never before entered human evolution on Earth.... It was held back in the soul world, apart from the stream of incarnation. Only those initiated in the mysteries could have any connection with this sister soul.... This sister soul remained in the soul world. It was also the one incarnated in the Luke Jesus boy. But this was not the first time, strictly speaking, that this soul was embodied as physical human being.... The only time this sister soul of Adam became physically visible before its embodiment in the Luke Jesus boy was in Krishna.[2]

The sister soul of Adam, incarnated as the Nathan Jesus, was endowed with childlike innocence, strength of compassion, and a remarkable capacity for self-sacrifice. But this Jesus was not endowed with the remarkable intelligence and wisdom of the other Jesus and did not possess the same ability to learn. The two Jesus children came into contact with each other, however, when, after their return from Egypt, the Solomon Jesus and his family settled in Nazareth.[3]

Considering the Buddhistic nature of the Nathan Jesus, and the influence streaming from this being at this time of the Second Coming, we are wise to notice the soul tendencies carried by children now incarnating. Educational approaches may have to re-envision current practices in order to align with the interests of these children. The rapid rise of educational programs devoted to nature arts seems to reflect a turn toward a "shepherd's schooling"—one directed to an immediate experience with nature's life forces.

The moral ether now forming is depicted by Valentin Tomberg as a renewal of the wisdom revelation of the Rishis of ancient India. This is yet another sign of a future moving toward us with an inherent sympathy for the Indian spiritual stream:

> What once existed as revealed wisdom will be the concrete life of future human beings. "To him that overcometh will I give to eat of the tree of life, which is in the midst of the paradise of God" (Rev. 2:1). This expresses the positive future of the endeavor that moves courageously forward into the future from a reminiscent longing for the comprehensive wisdom of the past. "Overcoming" here means to overcome the desire for the past. True, it means living by a longing that arises from the past, although it must seek satisfaction not in the past but in the future. The drift of the soul's desire toward the past must be overcome permanently, and yet the *essence* of that longing must not only be nurtured but even be strengthened to an energetic striving toward the future. It will then be possible for wisdom to become life and for the wisdom originally revealed from Heaven to live in human beings.

---

2 A newer translation was used here: Steiner, *The Bhagavad Gita and the West*, pp. 86–90.

3 Powell, *Chronicle of the Living Christ*, pp. 61–63.

This transformation indicates the future evolution of the "moral ether" in human nature, and this "moral ether" will be just as full of light as was the original revelation of the wisdom of the Rishis. Moreover, it will not only give light, but also function as does the life force. "Eating of the tree of life" means that the human system will absorb the power to give life.[4]

The Second Coming marks a profound change in the relationship between humanity and the spiritual worlds as well as between humanity and Nature. The moral ether, like all things in our world, has its inversion. Robert Powell long ago named the counterpoint to the "fifth ether" (moral ether) as the "fifth kingdom"—the kingdom of technology. This kingdom of electrified brilliance can successfully abort the spiritual light that bears new capacities. In fact, this is very likely the sole intention of the beings working behind the surging waves of the technological revolution.

The Nathan Jesus was born on a Saturday, a day Valentin Tomberg calls the day of the Holy Virgin. At his death on the cross, Jesus descended into Hell; all of Saturday was spent in the underworld. Who kept watch during this fateful time? The Holy Virgin! Estelle Isaacson (in volume 2 of her trilogy, *Through the Eyes of Mary Magdalene*) writes of the Holy Mother's vision, during which Christ asks her: "Will you accept my sacrifice?" She replies that she will, though her pain in doing so will be immeasurable; for she understands it is the only way.

Every mother knows of the suffering that accompanies the suffering of her children. It is unfathomable to comprehend enduring what the Holy Mother suffered, and continues to suffer. As we enter into another new year, we can pray for our hearts' willingness to suffer with Christ as he bears witness to the suffering of humanity. We can also heighten our awareness of signs pointing toward a shift occurring through the influences streaming into time from the Angel Jesus—leading into a deeper understanding of the mysteries of the Tree of Life ennobling all of Natura.

Jan. 5: ASPECT (1): Mercury 6° Capricorn square Mars 6° Libra: Mercury remembers Jesus as he spoke of the light that should not be hidden under a bushel (Dec/23/29). Mars marks its position at the midpoint of the 40 days in the wilderness. The healer/teacher Mercury is square the power of Michael (Mars)—indicating that through our courage to shine light into the darkness, tempters will be overcome. Today Mercury in Capricorn asks us to find stillness of thought in order that Mars (in Libra) may enact deeds that are directed from a balanced soul. Thus is peace assured.

ASPECT (2): Venus 12° Scorpio square Neptune 12° Aquarius: Venus was at this degree as Jesus spoke of the nearness of the Messiah. Those around him denounced Herod's unlawful (adulterous) union with his brother's wife. Jesus concurred but warned that whoever judges others would himself be judged also (Sep/20/29). We are wise to be merciful, inspired with compassion toward the karma our brothers and sisters must bear. Thus does the Messiah draw near to us.

Jan. 6: Sun 20° Sagittarius conjunct Pluto: The Sun remembers the commissioning of the twelve disciples (Sunday, Dec/10/30). The commissioning occurred on a Sunday—a day forever representing the Resurrection of Christ. As Jesus commissioned the twelve, on a high mountain, we can imagine him raising them above ordinary consciousness:

Today there occurred—for the first time—the sending out of the disciples. At about ten o'clock in the morning, with the twelve and about thirty other disciples, Jesus left Capernaum and went north in the direction of Saphet and Hanathon, accompanied by a large crowd. Around three in the afternoon, they approached Hanathon. Here Jesus and the disciples climbed a mountain used in former times by the prophets. Jesus had taught there less than one year ago, on Tebeth 12. This time, however, the crowd did not go up the mountain. On the mountain, Jesus addressed the disciples, giving them instructions and sending them out into the world with the words found in Matthew 9:36–10:16. Each of the twelve had a small flask of oil, and Jesus taught them how to use it for anointing and also for healing. Afterward, the disciples knelt in a circle around Jesus, and he prayed and laid his hands upon the head of each of the twelve. Then he

---

4 Tomberg, *Christ and Sophia,* p. 320.

SIDEREAL GEOCENTRIC LONGITUDES : JANUARY 2016 Gregorian at 0 hours UT

DAY	☉	☽	☊	☿	♀	♂	♃	♄	⛢	♆	♇
1 FR	15 ♐ 1	1 ♍ 45	29 ♌ 54R	4 ♑ 19	7 ♏ 6	3 ♎ 36	28 ♌ 12	16 ♏ 11	21 ♓ 37	12 ♒ 35	20 ♐ 5
2 SA	16 2	13 34	29 55	4 59	8 19	4 9	28 13	16 17	21 37	12 37	20 7
3 SU	17 3	25 22	29 54	5 30	9 31	4 42	28 14	16 24	21 37	12 38	20 9
4 MO	18 5	7 ♎ 14	29 53	5 52	10 44	5 15	28 15	16 30	21 38	12 40	20 11
5 TU	19 6	19 14	29 48	6 3	11 57	5 48	28 16	16 37	21 38	12 41	20 13
6 WE	20 7	1 ♏ 28	29 42	6 4R	13 11	6 21	28 16	16 43	21 39	12 43	20 15
7 TH	21 8	13 58	29 33	5 53	14 24	6 54	28 16	16 49	21 39	12 44	20 17
8 FR	22 9	26 48	29 21	5 30	15 37	7 27	28 16	16 56	21 40	12 46	20 19
9 SA	23 10	9 ♐ 57	29 10	4 55	16 50	8 0	28 16R	17 2	21 41	12 47	20 22
10 SU	24 12	23 25	28 58	4 9	18 3	8 32	28 16	17 8	21 41	12 49	20 24
11 MO	25 13	7 ♑ 8	28 47	3 13	19 17	9 5	28 16	17 14	21 42	12 51	20 26
12 TU	26 14	21 3	28 40	2 7	20 30	9 37	28 15	17 20	21 43	12 52	20 28
13 WE	27 15	5 ♒ 7	28 34	0 55	21 43	10 9	28 14	17 26	21 44	12 54	20 30
14 TH	28 16	19 14	28 32	29 ♐ 38	22 57	10 41	28 13	17 32	21 45	12 56	20 32
15 FR	29 17	3 ♓ 23	28 32D	28 19	24 10	11 13	28 12	17 38	21 46	12 58	20 34
16 SA	0 ♑ 19	17 32	28 32	27 0	25 24	11 45	28 11	17 44	21 47	12 59	20 36
17 SU	1 20	1 ♈ 38	28 33R	25 44	26 37	12 17	28 9	17 50	21 48	13 1	20 38
18 MO	2 21	15 42	28 32	24 33	27 51	12 49	28 7	17 55	21 49	13 3	20 40
19 TU	3 22	29 42	28 29	23 28	29 4	13 21	28 5	18 1	21 50	13 5	20 42
20 WE	4 23	13 ♉ 36	28 24	22 31	0 ♐ 18	13 52	28 3	18 7	21 52	13 7	20 44
21 TH	5 24	27 23	28 16	21 42	1 32	14 23	28 1	18 12	21 53	13 9	20 46
22 FR	6 25	11 ♊ 0	28 7	21 3	2 45	14 55	27 58	18 18	21 54	13 10	20 48
23 SA	7 26	24 25	27 58	20 33	3 59	15 26	27 55	18 23	21 56	13 12	20 50
24 SU	8 27	7 ♋ 35	27 49	20 12	5 13	15 57	27 52	18 29	21 57	13 14	20 52
25 MO	9 28	20 28	27 42	20 0	6 27	16 28	27 49	18 34	21 58	13 16	20 54
26 TU	10 29	3 ♌ 5	27 36	19 57D	7 40	16 58	27 46	18 39	22 0	13 18	20 56
27 WE	11 30	15 27	27 33	20 2	8 54	17 29	27 43	18 45	22 2	13 20	20 58
28 TH	12 31	27 34	27 33	20 14	10 8	17 59	27 39	18 50	22 3	13 22	21 0
29 FR	13 32	9 ♍ 31	27 33D	20 32	11 22	18 30	27 35	18 55	22 5	13 24	21 2
30 SA	14 33	21 21	27 35	20 58	12 36	19 0	27 31	19 0	22 7	13 26	21 4
31 SU	15 34	3 ♎ 9	27 36	21 28	13 50	19 30	27 27	19 5	22 8	13 28	21 6

INGRESSES :

3	☽→♎ 9:23	21	☽→♊ 4:35
5	☽→♏ 21: 9	23	☽→♋ 10: 7
8	☽→♐ 5:53	25	☽→♌ 18: 4
10	☽→♑ 11:34	28	☽→♍ 4:51
12	☽→♒ 15:17	30	☽→♎ 17:35
13	☿→♐ 17:21		
14	☽→♓ 18:14		
15	☉→♑ 16:43		
16	☽→♈ 21:12		
19	☽→♉ 0:31		
	♀→♐ 18: 6		

ASPECTS & ECLIPSES :

2	☉□☽ 5:29	8	☽ᴺ☊ 4:38		☉□☽ 23:25	23	♃☌☊ 9:46
	☽☌A 12: 3	9	♀☌♄ 4:10	17	☽☍♂ 18:52	24	☉☍☽ 1:44
	☽☍⛢ 16:22		☽☍♃ 18:38	18	♀□♃ 5: 9	26	☽☍♆ 19:51
3	☉□♃ 18:12	10	☉☌♂ 18:12		☉☌☽ 23:57		
	☽☍♂ 19:49		☽☌☿ 17:38	20	☽☍♄ 7:53	28	☽☌♃ 0: 9
5	☿□♂ 12: 0	13	☽☌♆ 13:16		☿□⛢ 18:27	29	♃☌☊ 8:17
	♀□♆ 14:39	14	☉ᴺ♆ 14: 3	21	☽ᴺ☊ 1:32	30	☽☍⛢ 1:33
6	☉☌♆ 3:22		☽☍♃ 15:12		☽☍♀ 7:59		☿☍♆ 5:47
7	☽☌♀ 0:53		☽☌☿ 15:45	22	☿☌♆ 10: 6		☽☌A 9:24
	☽☌♄ 5:25	15	☽☌P 2:24		☽☌♆ 17:16		
	☉☍⛢ 12:19		☽☌⛢ 7:13		☽☌♆ 17:32		

SIDEREAL HELIOCENTRIC LONGITUDES : JANUARY 2016 Gregorian at 0 hours UT

DAY	Sid. Time	☿	♀	⊕	♂	♃	♄	⛢	♆	♇	Vernal Point
1 FR	6:40:22	5 ♈ 37	9 ♍ 56	15 ♊ 2	29 ♌ 22	18 ♌ 11	13 ♏ 28	24 ♓ 25	14 ♒ 11	20 ♐ 14	5 ♓ 2'12"
2 SA	6:44:18	11 20	11 33	16 3	29 49	18 15	13 30	24 25	14 11	20 15	5 ♓ 2'12"
3 SU	6:48:15	17 10	13 10	17 4	0 ♍ 15	18 20	13 32	24 26	14 11	20 15	5 ♓ 2'12"
4 MO	6:52:12	23 8	14 47	18 5	0 41	18 25	13 34	24 27	14 12	20 15	5 ♓ 2'12"
5 TU	6:56: 8	29 13	16 23	19 6	1 8	18 29	13 35	24 27	14 12	20 16	5 ♓ 2'12"
6 WE	7: 0: 5	5 ♉ 23	18 0	20 7	1 34	18 34	13 37	24 28	14 13	20 16	5 ♓ 2'12"
7 TH	7: 4: 1	11 37	19 37	21 9	2 1	18 38	13 39	24 29	14 13	20 16	5 ♓ 2'12"
8 FR	7: 7:58	17 55	21 14	22 10	2 28	18 43	13 41	24 29	14 13	20 17	5 ♓ 2'11"
9 SA	7:11:54	24 14	22 51	23 11	2 54	18 48	13 43	24 30	14 14	20 17	5 ♓ 2'11"
10 SU	7:15:51	0 ♊ 33	24 27	24 12	3 21	18 52	13 44	24 31	14 14	20 17	5 ♓ 2'11"
11 MO	7:19:47	6 51	26 4	25 13	3 47	18 57	13 46	24 31	14 14	20 17	5 ♓ 2'11"
12 TU	7:23:44	13 6	27 41	26 14	4 14	19 1	13 48	24 32	14 15	20 18	5 ♓ 2'11"
13 WE	7:27:41	19 17	29 17	27 15	4 41	19 6	13 50	24 32	14 15	20 18	5 ♓ 2'11"
14 TH	7:31:37	25 22	0 ♎ 54	28 17	5 7	19 11	13 52	24 33	14 15	20 18	5 ♓ 2'11"
15 FR	7:35:34	1 ♋ 20	2 30	29 18	5 34	19 15	13 54	24 34	14 16	20 19	5 ♓ 2'10"
16 SA	7:39:30	7 11	4 7	0 ♋ 19	6 0	19 20	13 55	24 34	14 16	20 19	5 ♓ 2'10"
17 SU	7:43:27	12 53	5 43	1 20	6 27	19 24	13 57	24 35	14 17	20 19	5 ♓ 2'10"
18 MO	7:47:23	18 26	7 20	2 21	6 54	19 29	13 59	24 35	14 17	20 20	5 ♓ 2'10"
19 TU	7:51:20	23 50	8 56	3 22	7 21	19 34	14 1	24 36	14 17	20 20	5 ♓ 2'10"
20 WE	7:55:16	29 4	10 32	4 23	7 47	19 38	14 3	24 37	14 18	20 20	5 ♓ 2'10"
21 TH	7:59:13	4 ♌ 9	12 9	5 24	8 14	19 43	14 5	24 38	14 18	20 21	5 ♓ 2'10"
22 FR	8: 3:10	9 3	13 45	6 25	8 41	19 47	14 6	24 38	14 19	20 21	5 ♓ 2'10"
23 SA	8: 7: 6	13 49	15 21	7 26	9 8	19 52	14 8	24 39	14 19	20 21	5 ♓ 2' 9"
24 SU	8:11: 3	18 25	16 57	8 27	9 35	19 56	14 10	24 40	14 19	20 22	5 ♓ 2' 9"
25 MO	8:14:59	22 53	18 33	9 28	10 1	20 1	14 12	24 40	14 20	20 22	5 ♓ 2' 9"
26 TU	8:18:56	27 11	20 9	10 29	10 28	20 6	14 14	24 41	14 20	20 22	5 ♓ 2' 9"
27 WE	8:22:52	1 ♍ 22	21 45	11 30	10 55	20 10	14 15	24 42	14 20	20 23	5 ♓ 2' 9"
28 TH	8:26:49	5 25	23 21	12 31	11 22	20 15	14 17	24 42	14 20	20 23	5 ♓ 2' 9"
29 FR	8:30:45	9 21	24 57	13 32	11 49	20 19	14 19	24 43	14 21	20 23	5 ♓ 2' 9"
30 SA	8:34:42	13 10	26 33	14 33	12 16	20 24	14 21	24 43	14 21	20 23	5 ♓ 2' 8"
31 SU	8:38:39	16 53	28 8	15 34	12 43	20 29	14 23	24 44	14 22	20 24	5 ♓ 2' 8"

INGRESSES :

2	♂→♍ 10:24
5	☿→♉ 3: 4
9	☿→♊ 21:54
13	♀→♎ 10:35
14	☿→♋ 18:36
15	⊕→♋ 16:34
20	☿→♌ 4:21
26	☿→♍ 16: 2

ASPECTS (HELIOCENTRIC +MOON(TYCHONIC)) :

1	☽☌♀ 19:12		♀□♆ 9:42		☿□♆ 11:26	17	☽☍♀ 7:51
2	☽□♆ 13:34		☿□♀ 9:55	13	☿☌♆ 4: 1		☽□☿ 7:39
	☽☌⛢ 22: 5	8	☿☌♃ 3: 5		☽□♄ 14:51		☿ᴺ☊ 22:45
4	☿☌☊ 1:40		☽□♂ 10:45		☽☌♆ 15:32	18	☽☍♄ 0:46
	⊕☌♇ 3:54		☿☌P 18:21		☿□⛢ 20:46		☽□♆ 1:12
6	⊕☍♇ 3:22	9	♀☌⊕ 13:34	14	☿☌⛢ 14: 3	20	☽□♃ 10:32
	☽☌♇ 15: 6		☽☌♃ 23:53	15	☽☌♂ 3:48		☽□♂ 19:45
	☽☌♄ 23:23	10	♀☌⛢ 0:45		☿□♀ 6:34	22	☽☍♇ 16:41
7	☽□♆ 0:27		☽□⛢ 1:56	16	☽□♆ 4:44	23	☽□⛢ 0:25
	☿☌♄ 7:47		☽□♀ 2: 5		☿□♄ 1:39		☿□♄ 1:39
	☽□♃ 8:51		⊕☌⛢ 7:19		☽☌⛢ 11:58		☿☍♆ 2:33
24	☿☌♃ 8:14	26	☽□♄ 21:40	27	☽☌♃ 9:21	31	☿□♇ 23:23
	☽□♀ 19:52		☽☍♆ 21:49	28	☽☌☿ 23:31		
29	☽☌♂ 4:50		☿☌♂ 17:27		☽□♇ 22: 3		
30	♄□♆ 5: 6		☽☍⛢ 6:52				

blessed the remaining disciples. After embracing one another, the disciples set off, having received indications from Jesus as to where they should go and when they should return to him. Peter, James the Less, John, Philip, Thomas, Judas, and twelve other disciples remained with him. They all came down the mountain together. At the bottom, they met up with a crowd of people returning home from Capernaum. That night Jesus stayed in Bethanat (Matt. 11:1).[5]

Powerful images resound from this event. Whenever we read that Jesus and the disciples went up to a high mountain, we are being told that Jesus was giving initiatory teachings to his chosen disciples. Such was the case at the commissioning of the twelve. They were instructed on what they must do while in a state of heightened consciousness. They were to baptize, bestow hands-on healing, and expel demons. These are capacities that are reemerging as the kingdom of the Mother begins awakening her human children. Jesus taught his disciples how to discriminate between true and false friends and what to do when confronted by the latter. Such discerning is ever more necessary in our time, as evil has many disguises. He also told them not to seek advantage one over another, but reminded them that they were a circle wherein none were greater than the others. He taught them many other things and sent them out with little flasks of oil for effecting cures. All these teachings are resurrecting within spiritually striving individuals who are able to receive the emanations now flowing into time—from both the inner realms of the Earth and the cosmic realms surrounding us. *Disciples of the Etheric Christ are invited to climb high mountains, above the fray of ubiquitous distraction, in order to remember capacities which have long been forgotten.*

Today is Epiphany. The door to the Holy days and Nights closes for another year. We are leaving the "high mountain" of this sacred time in the cycle of the year when the Christ draws so near to us. This is also the time of year when the Archangels draw very close. It is as if their wings touch each other; and through this touch it is as if they encircle the Earth, bestowing the gift of healing. If we choose to become chosen disciples of the Etheric Christ, we can venture out into the world as healers and teachers, asking the question: "What is missing?" What cures can we bring about, and how may we share the oil that we've been given—this consecrated substance born of the fire of love? How will we stand before those we recognize as false friends? How will we find our love for them, while at the same time maintaining our truth?

So many questions can be pondered now, as the cosmic memory of the commissioning of the twelve disciples is intensified by Pluto. We can pray for those who will invert this opportunity, and instead of serving Christ will serve another. Their hearts are cold. They will have no concern for harm done against humanity and nature. They are the possessed, and the remnant of their selfhood is merely a loose garment for Ahriman.

Jan. 7: Sun 21° Sagittarius square Uranus 21° Pisces: Jesus healed many in Hukok (Dec/12/30). Two days after Jesus commissioned the twelve, he arrived in Hukok with the Sun at today's degree. This was a beautiful city that must have once been a strong fortress, as Anne Catherine Emmerich saw it, surrounded by moats now run dry. It was a Tuesday, ruled by the planet Mars. Valentin Tomberg calls Tuesday the day of the Archangel Michael.

Jesus healed many sick people in Hukok. In the synagogue, he spoke of the Messiah and of the significance of prayer. He said that the Messiah was already here; indeed, that they were living at the time of the Messiah, and that he, Jesus, was proclaiming the Messiah's teachings. He taught them devotion to God in spirit and in truth. The doctors of the synagogue asked Jesus, in a friendly way, whether he himself were the Messiah, the Son of God. Jesus did not answer directly. He said that they should not inquire into his origin but consider his teachings and actions. He spoke of the will of the Father (Matthew 12:50; John 5:30). That night, Jesus and the disciples stayed again at the house of the chief elder of the synagogue.[6]

---

5 *ACE Complete*, p. 560.

6 *ACE Complete*, pp. 561–562.

How applicable the statement "that they should not inquire into his origin but consider his teachings and actions." To discern a person's character through their actions reveals a great deal. As we move deeper into this Abraham millennium (AD 2000–3000) new teachers and teachings will approach. The heart perceives the truth, and the deeds and actions of others will lead the heart to recognize if the one they are observing is one in whom they can place their trust. One can only imagine what a different course may have been taken, after the death of Steiner, if his students had held to the advice of Christ.

ASPECT: Venus today is conjunct the heart of the Scorpion—Antares—and tomorrow comes into conjunction with Saturn.

Jan. 8: Venus conjunct Saturn 16° Scorpio: Venus at 15° Scorpio (conjunct Antares) remembers the Baptism in the Jordan River (Friday, Sep/23/29). Anne Catherine Emmerich describes Jesus during the Baptism as appearing perfectly transparent, entirely penetrated by light; she sees how one could scarcely look at him. She saw angels all around him, and other beings lurking nearby:

> But off at some distance on the waters of the Jordan, I saw Satan, a dark, black figure, as if in a cloud, and myriads of horrible black reptiles and vermin swarming around him. It was as if all the wickedness, all the sins, all the poison of the whole region took a visible form at the outpouring of the Holy Spirit, and fled into that dark figure as into their original source. The sight was abominable, but it served to heighten the effect of the indescribable splendor and joy and brilliancy spread over the Lord and the whole island.[7]

With Venus conjunct Antares (the death/resurrection star), we recall the events occurring just prior to the baptism of Jesus. It was a Friday—Venus day—when the individuality (the "I") of the Zarathustra Jesus (the Solomon Jesus) departed the earthly sheaths of the Nathan Jesus to make way for the incarnation of Christ. This year of 2016 marks the beginning of a new 12-year rhythm wherein the "I" of Christ

will penetrate into the eighth subearthly sphere. New subearthly depths are penetrated every twelve years.[8] The antidote to the adversarial forces that will be released from the eighth sphere is: *Blessed are the persecuted for theirs is the kingdom of heaven.* As we read Anne Catherine's account of the evil "things" that fled from the light of Christ, and the black figure around whom they circled, we can imagine that these beings will be fleeing the eighth sphere as Christ enters. Where will they find refuge? Simultaneously, as these beings flee, the Mother will send forces upward from her golden realm of Shambhala for our protection. It is propitious to hold in mind these occult mysteries as we witness developments in the outer world. It is very Promethean to understand the time in which one lives as it is developing.

Saturn today is where it was at the conception of the Nathan Mary (Oct/24/18 BC). Her immaculate grace is ever-present. In renewing our understanding of astrology, we can imagine a conjunction between Saturn and Venus as a conjunction between the Holy Virgin (Saturn) and those seeking to walk their *individual* paths of redemption as did Christ walk the path of the collective redemption of humanity during his Passion (Venus). With Venus so close to Antares, we can contemplate what in us needs to die in order that we may receive the Mother's love from the depths and the Virgin's love from the heights.

Jan. 9: New Moon 24° Sagittarius: Five days after the commissioning of the twelve disciples, on Friday, December 15th, AD 30, Jesus is in Saphet teaching in a synagogue about the second Beatitude. It was during a New Moon Festival:

> This morning Jesus spoke in the synagogue about the second Beatitude. In the afternoon he taught again, and some Pharisees from Saphet came to hear him. They invited him to Saphet for the Sabbath, and Jesus accepted their invitation. He was received with much ceremony, and went straightaway to the synagogue, where a great crowd had assembled. It was not only the start of the Sabbath but also the close of the Feast of Lights; at the same time, it was the New Moon Festival denoting the beginning of the month of Tebeth.[9]

---

7 Ibid., p. 232.

8 Powell, *The Christ Mystery.*

9 *ACE Complete*, p. 565.

A New Moon in Sagittarius calls forth the teachings of the ninth Arcanum of the Tarot, The Hermit—the solitary one with lamp, mantle, and staff:

> For he possesses the gift of letting light shine in the darkness—this is his "lamp"; he has the faculty of separating himself from the collective moods, prejudices and desires of race, nation, class and family—the faculty of reducing to silence the cacophony of collectivism vociferating around him, in order to listen to and understand the hierarchical harmony of the spheres—this is his "mantle"; at the same time he possesses a sense of realism which is so developed that he stands in the domain of reality not on two feet, but rather on three, i.e., he advances only after having *touched* the ground through immediate experience and at first-hand contact without intermediaries—this is his "staff." He creates light, he creates silence and he creates certainty—conforming to the criterion of the *Emerald Table,* namely the triple concordance of what is *clear,* of what *is in harmony with the totality of* revealed truths, and of what is the object of *immediate* experience....

> The Hermit therefore represents not only a wise and good father who is a reflection of the Father in heaven, but also the method and essence of Hermeticism. For Hermeticism is founded on the concordance of three methods of knowledge: the a priori knowledge of intelligence (the "lamp"); the harmony of all by analogy (the "mantle"); and authentic immediate experience (the "staff").[10]

This Moon asks us to make the distinction between the world created by the Word and the evolutionary world of the serpent. The light of the Word and the "ruse" of the serpent's world are separated by a featherweight of difference, dividing the World from the world, as well as Cosmic Intelligence from the human intellect's shadowy illusion. We are to open our eyes, knowing both good and evil. We are to balance the eye that sees into the horizontal world of *maya,* with the eye that sees into the vertical world of virginal creation. Thus does the will-to-power become the will-to-serve.

Our lamp must find the transcendental synthesis between the above and the below; our staff must prudently acknowledge that we stand between two realms of darkness—that of material scientific ignorance and that of unmanifest spiritual potency; our mantle must enfold us in the certainty of absolute faith in regards to the power of the primal truth over all things of temporal existence. Thus will conscience become an organ of cognition that spares us the deluge of deception now threatening our global community.

The second Beatitude (*Blessed are they that mourn, for they will be comforted*) leads us into our willingness to behold what in us has been led astray (mourning), as we simultaneously behold what stands *outside* of us as our guiding star (comforter). Thus will we find clarity, harmony, and immediate experience of the Tri-unity of the hermetic axiom—i.e., concordance between the above and the below in three directions: vertical (thinking), horizontal (feeling), and diagonal (willing).

Jan. 13: Mercury enters Sagittarius. "Attainment concludes joyful striving." Mercury was in Sagittarius at Christ's temptations and during many of his miracles.

Jan. 14: Inferior conjunction Sun and Mercury 29° Sagittarius (square Spica 29° Virgo). The Sun at this degree recalls the Summons of Peter (Monday, Dec/19/29). Less than three months after his baptism in the Jordan River, Jesus is introduced to Simon, the son of Jonas. John 1:42: "Thou art Simon, the son of Jonas; thou shalt be called Cephas" (which means Peter—the rock). Peter was one of three very close disciples whose consciousness could quicken in order to receive the higher mystery teachings of Christ. Yet it was Peter who would later deny him three times. Estelle Isaacson witnessed the shame of Peter and also his healing bestowed upon him by the Risen Christ: "Christ asked Peter three times if he loved him, in order to heal his three denials during the Passion. For Peter's heart could not take in fully Christ's love until he was free of his shame."[11]

---

10 Anon. *Meditations on the Tarot,* pp. 200–201.

11 Isaacson, *Through the Eyes of Mary Magdalene,* vol. 3, p. 262.

Sun/Mercury in Sagittarius asks us—in search of ever deeper truths—to control our speech, to aim toward the ennoblement of our character, and to part the veil obscuring higher worlds. In square to Spica intuitive forces are highlighted. Like Peter, we are encouraged to awaken our conscience; and the proof of this occurrence is oft accompanied by the blush of shame. Shame moves egoism to the surface of the body in the heat of its blush, whereby it is expunged from our being, thus freeing us to receive Christ's love. When, on the other hand, judgment comes from the outer world as contempt, shame is toxic. But when conscience inwardly awakens, it is our willingness to experience our error that bestows the cleansing blush of shame.

Mercury was at this degree when the Solomon Mary entered the temple (Dec/8/19 BC). We can imagine the baleful need of human intelligence (Mercury) to raise itself from the grave danger of materialism in order to recognize the etheric temple now forming as a consequence of Christ's nearness to us. A region is forming that all are invited to enter as the counterforce that keeps the dragon underfoot, lest the gates of Hell break open—loosing beasts that will further degrade human souls.

Jan. 15: Sun enters Capricorn: "May the future rest upon the past" (Steiner, *Twelve Cosmic Moods*). William Bento illumines Steiner's mantra:

> Although this can be said to be a common sense statement, it touches on deeper mysteries within the stream of time. Implicit to this mood is how we all must bear the consequences and deeds of the past as seeds for the future. By being aware of this in the present, we can affect the stream of time with conscious intent and not relegate ourselves to the past. Instead, we step into and through the darkness of the unknown future.

Capricorn, the Goat, is the symbol of sacrificial death and the sign of atonement. Aquila the Eagle extends above the first decan of Capricorn, the main star of Aquila (Altair) being located at 7° Capricorn. The first decan of Capricorn is ruled by Jupiter (Zeus), to whom the Eagle was sacred. Capricorn signifies a special opportunity: Courage becomes the power to redeem, the power to

develop conscience, and the insight to know what is right.

Jan. 16–31: Retrograde Mercury (26°–20° Sagittarius) is in close square to Uranus 21° Pisces, and transiting Pluto (21° Sagittarius): Mercury will be transiting its position during the stilling of the storm on the Sea of Galilee, as well as during the temptations of Christ (Nov/21–30/29). Introspection is a gift of retrograde Mercury. Stilling mental storms, centering, and turning the mind toward spiritual truths, assists us in inwardly calming restlessness that breeds nervous energy.

Jan. 18: Venus 28° Scorpio square Jupiter 28° Leo: Venus was at this degree at the raising of the Youth of Nain (Nov/13/30). It was Monday when Jesus walked by the funeral procession outside the gates of Nain—the day *of* the Holy Trinity. We can imagine the One who is of the Trinity stopping the procession and raising the twelve-year-old child from the dead. Anne Catherine writes:

> It was in consideration of the righteousness of the patriarchs that almighty God, down to the present day, had protected and spared Israel; but now, enchained in sin and covered with the veil of mental blindness, they had become like unto this youth. They were standing on the brink of the grave, and for the last time was mercy extended to them. John had prepared the way and with a powerful voice had called upon their hearts to arise from the slumber of death. The heavenly Father had now, for the last time, pity upon them. He would open to life the eyes of those that did not obstinately keep them closed. Jesus compared the people in their blindness to the youth shut up in his coffin who, though near the tomb, though outside the gate of the city, had been met by salvation. "If," he said, "the bearers had not heeded my voice, if they had not set down the coffin, had not opened it, had not freed the body from its winding sheet, if they had obstinately hurried forward with their burden, the boy would have been buried— and how terrible that would have been!" Then Jesus likened to this picture he had drawn the false teachers, the Pharisees. They kept the poor people from the life of penance, they fettered

them with the bonds of their arbitrary laws, they enclosed them in the coffin of their vain observances, and cast them thus into an eternal tomb. Jesus finished by imploring and conjuring his hearers to accept the proffered mercy of his heavenly Father, and hasten to life, to penance, to baptism![12]

The planet Venus marks the sphere wherein dwell the mighty *archai*—spirits responsible for overseeing great epochs of time. The raising of the Youth of Nain (who later joined the circle of disciples) as well as Christ's words at this event are resonant for our time. We can take lessons from these teachings. We *will* have to live in the world of the Pharisees' arbitrary laws, yet we can also find our way lit justly by the revelation now sounding from both the Mother in the depths and the Father in the heights. This is not a given—one must first cognize and counteract the oppressive apathy caused by blindness, the insanity of false teachers, and the entombment of souls that so prolifically mark our times. In Tomberg's re-envisioning of the planets (*Meditations on the Tarot*, p. 458), today's aspect is a square between the power of the Passion (Venus) and the power of the Holy Spirit (Jupiter). Thus love (Venus) and wisdom (Jupiter) create a dynamic relationship, revealing any excess in our character that may disturb our soul's harmony. A harmonious soul perceives the presence of the Holy Spirit.

Jan. 19: Venus enters Sagittarius: "In existence, growth's power dies." With Venus in the Archer, the soul seeks to overcome instinctual feelings to stand freely vertically with cosmic truth. Venus was in Sagittarius during the start of the 40 days in the wilderness, the raising of Jairus' daughter, the stilling of the storm, and the miraculous draught.

Jan. 23: Full Moon 8° Cancer opposite Sun 8° Capricorn: The Moon at this degree is within 2° of the Moon's position at the visitation to Joseph whereupon an angel announced the forthcoming birth of his son, who was the Solomon Jesus. This is the Jesus of the St. Matthew Gospel, whose genealogy is traced back to Abraham. The Solomon Jesus was the reincarnation of the great Zarathustra.

This wisest of souls represents the Magi stream of kingly wisdom.

Zarathustra was the teacher of teachers, [the teacher] of those who helped and schooled the bearers of culture.

Then Zarathustra returned [in the sixth century BC] under the name Zaratas or Nazaratos [known to the Greeks as Zoroaster]. In this incarnation, which ran its course largely unknown, hidden in the dark, his task was the saving of the mysteries in Babylon from decadence. Again he had disciples. Pythagoras was one of his disciples in Babylon.

In Pythagoras there lived the renewed wisdom of space known to Zarathustra. Pythagoras spoke of the wisdom of the planets, of numbers, of the harmonies of the spheres—all wisdom of space. The entire Greek culture essentially proceeded [in seed form] from Pythagoras.

Daniel and Ezekiel—the "spiritual twins"—were also disciples of Zaratas or Nazaratos. An element of the Apocalypse lived in both of them—[this was a] living into the future [in the stream] of time. So there was a renewal of the hermetic wisdom of space in Pythagoras and of the wisdom of time with Daniel–Ezekiel. All of this derived from Zarathustra.[13]

This Moon calls us to free ourselves from the ordinary intellect's encapsulation within the boundaries of its own skull. Mysteries abound, and Wisdom is calling Her disciples in order that the pall of *maya's* ignorance may be lifted, and the veil to the future be pierced by those so daring to follow in the footsteps of the mighty individualities who once were Zarathustra, Pythagoras, Daniel, and Ezekiel. These four dynamic personalities were together in Babylon, in the 6th century BC. How far could they be from us now? We are collectively crossing the threshold into apocalyptic realms, and preparation is necessary. Those unprepared will be overwhelmed. The rising use of medication for "mood disorders" is telling. Zarathustra's mission in Babylon went largely unknown and even hidden, yet he had his disciples. When the secrets of space

---

12 *ACE Complete*, p. 527.

13 *Starlight*, vol. 6, spring 2006: "The Zarathustra Line of Jesus of Nazareth Part II: Zarathustra–Zoroaster–Jesus," by Valentin Tomberg (brackets [ ] added by Robert Powell).

and time are opening new streams of revelation, the masses tend to become ill due to their separation from cosmic thoughts; yet, out of the masses a few rise to help carry the truths which are continually being born into time.

The Sun at this degree recalls the first miracle of Christ after his baptism in the Jordan River: the turning of water into wine (Wednesday, Dec/28/29). We can practice selflessness (Cancer), which prepares a fertile ground for catharsis. Thus are we spared the retrograde movement which further encapsulates one in the morass of materialism, engendering dis-ease of soul.

Jan. 23–27: Mars will be transiting its position during the time from the three temptations in the wilderness until the end of the 40 days: 15° Libra to 17° Libra (Nov/27–30/29). Mercury is also transiting its position during the three temptations in the wilderness. Mars, the planet representative of Michael, beholds the great temptation of Christ. Balance within our soul, creates right action in the will.

Jan. 26–28: Heliocentric Venus 21° Libra remembers the entire Passion of Christ. With Venus remembering the Passion, we are prudent to contemplate our willingness to suffer that in us which disturbs our peace—in order to find the comforter that attends all who mourn. This was the teaching the stars offered at the New Moon of this month (January 9th).

Jan. 29: Sun 14° Capricorn: Death of John the Baptist (Jan/4/31). The higher waters of virginal nature were the substance from which John drew his revelation.

Jan. 30: Mercury exactly conjunct Pluto 21° Sagittarius. Pluto at this degree recalls the full fervor of persecutions of the first Christians in the year AD 36. This was less than two years after Paul's awakening outside the gates of Damascus. Jesus Christ became the spirit of the Earth at the Mystery of Golgotha; persecutions against the Earth and her beings are thus tantamount to persecutions of Christians. Our minds (Mercury) must awaken if we are to take up the work of protecting our Mother and all her kingdoms. Pluto standing with Mercury offers penetrating depth to our thinking.

Jan. 31: Mercury 22° Sagittarius exact square to Uranus 22° Pisces: Mercury was at this degree during the first temptation in the wilderness (Sunday, Nov/27/29). Now in close conjunction with Pluto, and square Uranus, Mercury can summon clarity of thought and insightful receptivity to cosmic imaginations. Inversely, the dark underworldly nature of Pluto and the scintillating brilliance of Uranian illusory thought can unknowingly lead one to perpetuate evil agendas. The lightning bolt of Uranus destroys all that has been built from self-will. As Mercury is remembering the first temptation, where Christ is tempted to bow to the prince of this world, the will-to-power edges toward us today. Will we be servants of light, or propagators of egoistic compulsion? A featherweight balance separates these two states; yet, as one chooses light, the force of "conscience" aligns one with higher worlds, decidedly tipping the scales in favor of the good. An awakened consciousness (Mercury) births conscience; and it is conscience that directs the gaze of the initiate:

> The initiate is not someone who knows everything. He is a person who bears the truth within a deeper level of his consciousness, not as an intellectual system, but rather as a level in his being, as a "mantle" which envelops him. This truth-imprint manifests itself as unshakeable certainty, i.e., as *faith* in the sense of the *voice of the presence of truth*.[14]

With Pluto standing within a degree of this square, intensity increases. Pluto covers a spectrum that reaches into the heights of heaven, as well as into the depths of the inner Earth. The latter breeds destruction and hatred; the former love's ability to penetrate darkness with light. May the voice of truth be our constant companion, that we may rightly follow the light of revelation (Uranus) ever guiding us forward.

---

14 Anon. *Meditations on the Tarot,* p. 221.

FEBRUARY 2016

The waning Moon in Libra is near Mars in the wee hours of February 1st. Look to the South before sunrise to see red Mars slightly below and to the right of the Moon. As the Moon gradually loses its reflective light it will rise about an hour later each day. The Moon conjuncts with Saturn on the 3rd and with Venus and Mercury on the 6th. These events can be seen before dawn as the Moon continues to wane, heading toward a New Moon with the Sun on the 8th.

The Sun moves into the constellation of Aquarius on the 14th. The Moon is opposite the Sun on the 22nd, forming a Full Moon (Moon in the constellation of Leo.) That same day, Mars will move into the constellation of Scorpio. The Full Moon (still appearing Full) will pass by Jupiter on the 23rd—you will see bright Jupiter slightly above and to the left of the Moon on the days leading up to this conjunction, and then to the right as the swift Moon continues her journey.

This year is a "leap" year and we gain a 29th day in February; the Moon passes through Mars' territory in early Scorpio today. Red Mars will be beneath the waning Moon, rising in the east about five hours before sunrise.

During the first five days of the month, Mercury remembers where it was throughout the temptations of Christ (Nov./27–29/29), and heliocentric Uranus recalls its degree at the conception of the Nathan Jesus (Mar/6/2 BC).

Feb. 2: Candlemas: The seed for our future spiritual potential, which we brought out of the Holy Nights, now quickens with new life.

Feb. 5: Venus conjunct Pluto 21° Sagittarius: Venus at this degree finds Jesus in the synagogue teaching (Dec/2/30). Pharisees there present had laid a snare for him. In a corner cowered a man with a withered hand who, intimidated by the Pharisees, had not made himself known to Jesus. When Jesus claimed to the Pharisees that he came to console and convert sinners, they mockingly presented the man with the withered hand. Jesus healed him, causing wrath in the souls of the Pharisees. It was the Sabbath, and the Pharisees were incensed that he dared to heal on this day. Plans were made to lie in wait for Jesus on the following feast day in Jerusalem. His enemies were growing.

With Pluto conjunct Venus, passions intensify. The karmic group surrounding Jesus was diametrically opposed by the karmic group surrounding the Pharisees. Commitment was tested, loyalty challenged.

Pluto continues to stand close to its position during the full storm of Christian persecutions, therefore, artistry (Venus) may be called for in the face of our enemies.

Feb. 6: Venus/Pluto 22° Sagittarius square Uranus 22° Pisces: With Venus at this degree, Jesus was teaching the sixth Beatutide—*Blessed are the pure in heart* (Dec/3/30). One day after healing the man with the withered hand, Jesus is again teaching in Capernaum. Roman soldiers were sent to observe Jesus—the prophet from Judea, rabble rousing in a province under Roman sway.

Practicing the sixth Beatitude opens the way for human souls to see the natural world in a new light. The Beatitude states: *Blessed are the pure in heart for they shall see God.* This does not mean seeing the cosmic Father God; but instead, it means seeing in nature "the divine archetype of humanity, which is visible in the elemental world as the hope of nature's resurrection in the age of the consciousness soul."[1] Conscientiously taking up our responsibility toward the natural realm results in a deeper knowledge of nature. Just as we have discovered the law of gravity, so also will we discover the law of the fall of nature. The collective body of nature is an indivisible body that reveals the totality of the Fall of humanity. Nature seeks to again become the image and likeness of God, just as the striving human soul seeks to again become the image and likeness of God. With Pluto recalling the persecutions of the Christians, and this year marking the entrance of Christ into the eighth subearthly sphere (*Blessed are the persecuted*), the time for humanity to become caretakers of nature looms as an absolute necessity. The failure to heed the call of the

---

1 Tomberg, *Christ and Sophia,* p. 219.

elemental beings will result in their becoming ahrimanized. Ahrimanized elementals then become predators of the human soul. In this age of the consciousness soul, we must awaken to the task before us and turn our hearts outward toward the suffering of nature. Thus does the heart become pure. Uranus lends a helping hand as a realm from which cosmic imaginations stream into time.

Feb. 7: Sun 23° Capricorn square Mars 23° Libra: The Sun remembers Jesus teaching about Abraham and the fate of the prophets. During his discourse relatives and friends of John the Baptist received an interior revelation of John's death, which had not yet been publically revealed (Jan/12/31). As Anne Catherine Emmerich was witnessing this event, she had a vision of Mary coming to present Jesus in the temple. Besides the usual offering of doves, Mary had brought gifts received from the Three Kings. With the Sun recalling this discourse as well as Emmerich's vision, an interior revelation stirs, bringing the prophets into our sight. They are not behind us, but rather are they with us now. They are beckoning us toward John the Baptist, who sends his messages from the stream of time moving toward us from the future. *The prophets are forming the community of Eternal Israel as a counterforce against the torrent of propagandizing currently spinning webs around the globe.*

Mars at this degree recalls the healing of a possessed man in Gergesa, who was slave to the sorcerers and soothsayers of the land (Dec/8/30). They had seized this man and dragged him around with them by a cord, exhibiting his strength in all kinds of skillful feats accomplished due to the demons who worked within him. It was Friday—the day of Christ's Passion—when Jesus healed this possessed man.

Capricorn is the constellation of kings. Anti-kings are like unto the pagan sorcerers of Gergesa, who enslave the masses, and exhibit extraordinary skills due to the demons that have possessed them. Libra is the constellation holding the scales of Michael. Today Mars speaks the conscience of Michael, asking us to hold fast our crowns lest we be carried away by the words issuing forth from the false kings ruling the world.

Feb. 8: New Moon 24° Capricorn. The Moon at this degree remembers the Transfiguration of Christ on Mt. Tabor (Apr/4/31). Two years after the Transfiguration, Christ would be crucified. A New Moon marks the beginning of a new lunar cycle. At the Transfiguration, Christ embodied the northern mystery initiation stream wherein the aspirant was led into the macrocosm, protected by the hierophants standing watch. This lunar cycle asks us to conscientiously prepare for sleep, praying that morning will bestow upon us some memory of our nightly sojourn into the secrets indwelling the cosmos.

At the Transfiguration, both Moses and Elijah came to greet Jesus—it was a Wednesday, a day Tomberg refers to as that of the pastors and healers of humankind. Indeed, the consummate healer and pastor revealed himself in his full glory to his three disciples as he stood in the presence of Moses and Elijah. As we remember this event, we can—through the activity of spiritual gnosis—recognize Steiner's Michaelic mission as a stream carried forward from Moses, just as we recall John the Baptist's mission as a powerful fulfillment of the work of Elijah, an impassioned call for the purification of the soul. These great guiding spirits stand to the left and right of the Nathan Jesus, the pure sister soul of Adam, transfigured through the radiant light of the new Adam, the spiritualized substance of the new Human Being, the Son of God. It is the Angel Jesus, who then overlighted Jesus of Nazareth who now continues to serve the loving, compassionate stream, referred to as "the shephard's stream" as a guiding presence for the future unfoldment of humankind through the work of the individuality in the process of becoming the Maitreya Buddha. It will be the mission of the Maitreya Buddha to bring to fulfillment the seeds planted through the being of the Old Testament Abraham. As this New Moon is in the constellation of Capricorn, we turn to the seventeenth Arcanum of the Tarot—the Arcanum of growth:

> A tower is built; a tree grows. The two processes have this in common: that they present a gradual increase in volume with a pronounced tendency upward. But there is at the same time the difference that the tower rises by leaps and

bounds, whilst the tree shows a continuous elevation. This is because bricks or hewn stones are put one on top of the other in the process of building the tower, whilst the microscopic "bricks"—the cells—of a tree multiply through division and growth in volume. It is the sap in the tree, rising from the roots into the trunk and branches, which renders growth of the tree possible and which makes it shoot up through the multiplication and growth in volume of its cells. Whilst the tower is dry, the tree is filled with sap in movement, which underlies both the division of its cells and their growth—in a word, it underlies the process of growth. Growth is flowing, whilst construction proceeds by leaps and bounds. And what is true of the artificial and the natural in the physical domain is also true in the psychic and spiritual domain. "The righteous flourish like the palm tree...they are ever full of sap and green ..." (Psalm 92), but "... a downcast spirit dries up the bones..." (Proverbs 27: 22).[2]

The Star of our higher self leads us from within—it is not compelled by outer circumstances. Thus, as we develop our capacity to receive the secrets of the macrocosm, the sap of life will flow into us from the Mother's realm, gently leading us into communities now forming—which will find their full flowering in the future as the explicit realization dawns that there is, in truth, such a thing as the community of Eternal Israel. Moses, Abraham, and Elijah are watering the garden that many will be called to cultivate.

This New Moon calls us to cultivate the intelligence of intuition in order to receive ideas, feelings, and impulses of will relating to the evolution of life and consciousness, concerning their infinite development through the power inherent in growth.

Feb. 9: Mercury enters Capricorn: "To be strong in the present." Mercury was here at the first miracle of Christ, turning water into wine at the wedding in Cana (Dec/28/29).

Feb. 11–14: Heliocentric Mars 17°–19° Virgo remembers the temptations of Christ (Nov/27–30/29).

––––––––––––

2 Anon. *Meditations on the Tarot*, p. 464.

Right action, with our eyes ever turned to the eternal aims of God, is today's teaching.

Feb. 13: Venus enters Capricorn: "May the past feel the future." Venus in Capricorn asks us to courageously stand for spiritual thoughts newly entering time. Timidity breeds fear, through which we seek to expose others rather than expose that in ourselves which is holding us back. Venus was in Capricorn during the last days in the wilderness when the three tempters assaulted him with the last of the temptations.

Feb. 14: Sun enters Aquarius: "May what is bounded yield to the boundless" (Steiner, *Twelve Cosmic Moods*). William Bento illumines this mantra:

All that finds its existence into forms, including all our thoughts, feelings and actions, remains bounded. The bounded are boundaries that too often confine and define who we are. Yielding to the boundless is not a given. It requires a willingness to let go and trust in the boundless, which is full of new possibilities. And the new possibilities, after all, are what allow us to continue our development and become free from the forms and patterns of our lives that tend to be static and inert.

Discretion becomes silence, becomes meditative force, and then becomes power to perceive the imperceptible. The first decan of Aquarius is ruled by Mercury, the planet of movement, and is associated with the Southern Fish, whose main star Fomalhaut is 9° Aquarius.

Sun 0° Aquarius: Healing of the paralyzed man at the pool of Bethesda (Jan/19/31).

Feb. 18/19: Sun 5° Aquarius opposite Regulus 5° Leo. Today potentizes the heart forces, asking us to serve the "Lion of Judah."

Feb. 22: Full Moon 8° Leo opposite Sun 8° Aquarius: The recovery of John the Baptist's head (Apr/19/31). Two weeks ago the New Moon inaugurated this month's lunar cycle with the remembrance of the Transfiguration of Christ. Standing with Christ was Moses and Elijah. Now, as the Full Moon brings this cycle to its blossoming, we again remember Elijah–John (the Baptist). With

SIDEREAL GEOCENTRIC LONGITUDES :   FEBRUARY 2016 Gregorian at 0 hours UT

DAY	☉	☽	☊	☿	♀	♂	♃	♄	♅	♆	♇
1 MO	16 ♑ 35	15 ♎ 1	27 ♌ 37	22 ♐ 5	15 ♐ 4	20 ♎ 0	27 ♌ 23R	19 ♏ 10	22 ♓ 10	13 ♒ 30	21 ♐ 8
2 TU	17 36	27 1	27 36R	22 45	16 18	20 30	27 18	19 15	22 12	13 32	21 10
3 WE	18 37	9 ♏ 14	27 34	23 31	17 32	20 59	27 13	19 19	22 14	13 35	21 12
4 TH	19 37	21 46	27 30	24 20	18 46	21 29	27 9	19 24	22 16	13 37	21 14
5 FR	20 38	4 ♐ 39	27 25	25 12	20 0	21 58	27 4	19 29	22 18	13 39	21 15
6 SA	21 39	17 55	27 19	26 8	21 14	22 27	26 58	19 33	22 20	13 41	21 17
7 SU	22 40	1 ♑ 35	27 13	27 7	22 28	22 56	26 53	19 38	22 22	13 43	21 19
8 MO	23 41	15 36	27 8	28 9	23 42	23 25	26 48	19 42	22 24	13 45	21 21
9 TU	24 42	29 55	27 4	29 13	24 56	23 53	26 42	19 46	22 26	13 47	21 23
10 WE	25 42	14 ♒ 25	27 2	0 ♑ 20	26 10	24 22	26 36	19 50	22 28	13 50	21 25
11 TH	26 43	29 1	27 1D	1 29	27 24	24 50	26 30	19 55	22 31	13 52	21 26
12 FR	27 44	13 ♓ 36	27 2	2 39	28 38	25 18	26 24	19 59	22 33	13 54	21 28
13 SA	28 45	28 6	27 4	3 52	29 52	25 46	26 18	20 3	22 35	13 56	21 30
14 SU	29 45	12 ♈ 26	27 5	5 6	1 ♑ 7	26 13	26 12	20 6	22 37	13 58	21 32
15 MO	0 ♒ 46	26 34	27 6	6 22	2 21	26 41	26 6	20 10	22 40	14 1	21 33
16 TU	1 46	10 ♉ 29	27 6R	7 39	3 35	27 8	25 59	20 14	22 42	14 3	21 35
17 WE	2 47	24 10	27 4	8 58	4 49	27 35	25 53	20 18	22 45	14 5	21 37
18 TH	3 48	7 ♊ 36	27 2	10 18	6 3	28 2	25 46	20 21	22 47	14 7	21 38
19 FR	4 48	20 49	26 58	11 40	7 17	28 28	25 39	20 25	22 50	14 10	21 40
20 SA	5 49	3 ♋ 49	26 55	13 3	8 31	28 55	25 32	20 28	22 52	14 12	21 41
21 SU	6 49	16 35	26 52	14 27	9 46	29 21	25 25	20 31	22 55	14 14	21 43
22 MO	7 50	29 9	26 49	15 52	11 0	29 47	25 18	20 34	22 57	14 16	21 45
23 TU	8 50	11 ♌ 30	26 47	17 18	12 14	0 ♏ 12	25 11	20 37	23 0	14 19	21 46
24 WE	9 50	23 41	26 47	18 46	13 28	0 38	25 3	20 40	23 3	14 21	21 48
25 TH	10 51	5 ♍ 42	26 47D	20 14	14 42	1 3	24 56	20 43	23 5	14 23	21 49
26 FR	11 51	17 36	26 48	21 44	15 56	1 28	24 49	20 46	23 8	14 25	21 51
27 SA	12 51	29 25	26 49	23 15	17 11	1 53	24 41	20 49	23 11	14 28	21 52
28 SU	13 52	11 ♎ 14	26 51	24 46	18 25	2 17	24 34	20 52	23 14	14 30	21 54
29 MO	14 52	23 5	26 52	26 19	19 39	2 41	24 26	20 54	23 17	14 32	21 55

INGRESSES :					ASPECTS & ECLIPSES :			

INGRESSES :

2	☽ → ♏	5:54	19	☽ → ♋	16:54
4	☽ → ♐	15:25	22	☽ → ♌	1:38
6	☽ → ♑	21:15		♂ → ♏	12:18
9	☽ → ♒	0: 8	24	☽ → ♍	12:35
	☿ → ♑	16:51	27	☽ → ♎	1:11
11	☽ → ♓	1:37	29	☽ → ♏	13:52
13	♀ → ♑	2:28			
	☽ → ♈	3:10			
14	☉ → ♒	5:51			
15	☽ → ♉	5:53			
17	☽ → ♊	10:22			

ASPECTS & ECLIPSES :

1	☉ □ ☽	3:26	8	☉ ☌ ☽	14:37	
	☿ □ ♅	3:37	9	☽ ☌ ♆	23: 1	
	☽ ☌ ♂	10:27	10	☽ ☍ ♃	19:54	
3	☽ ☌ ♄	19:29		☽ ☌ ♅	20:43	
4	☽ ᴺ ☊	10:43	11	☽ ☌ P	2:49	
6	♀ ☌ ♇	1:10	12	☽ ☌ ♅	14:49	
	☽ ☌ ♆	5:59	15	☽ ☍ ♂	0:12	
	☽ ☌ ♇	6:27		☉ □ ☽	7:45	
	☽ ☌ ☿	15:38	16	☽ ☍ ♄	17: 8	
	♀ □ ♅	22: 0	17	☽ ⚹ ♅	5: 8	
7	☉ □ ♂	12: 6	19	☽ ☍ ♆	1:32	
20	☽ ☍ ♀	9:44				
	☽ ☍ ☿	19:26				
22	☉ ☍ ☽	18:18				
23	☽ ☍ ♆	5:31				
24	☽ ☌ ♃	2:42				
	☽ ☌ ☊	6:10				
26	☽ ☍ ♅	11:17				
27	☽ ☌ A	3:35				
28	☉ ☍ ♆	15:54				
29	☽ ☌ ♂	19:53				

SIDEREAL HELIOCENTRIC LONGITUDES :   FEBRUARY 2016 Gregorian at 0 hours UT

DAY	Sid. Time	☿	♀	⊕	♂	♃	♄	♅	♆	♇	Vernal Point
1 MO	8:42:35	20 ♍ 30	29 ♎ 44	16 ♋ 35	13 ♍ 10	20 ♌ 33	14 ♏ 25	24 ♓ 45	14 ♒ 22	20 ♐ 24	5 ♓ 2′ 8″
2 TU	8:46:32	24 1	1 ♏ 20	17 36	13 37	20 38	14 26	24 45	14 22	20 24	5 ♓ 2′ 8″
3 WE	8:50:28	27 27	2 56	18 37	14 4	20 42	14 28	24 46	14 23	20 25	5 ♓ 2′ 8″
4 TH	8:54:25	0 ♎ 48	4 31	19 38	14 31	20 47	14 30	24 47	14 23	20 25	5 ♓ 2′ 8″
5 FR	8:58:21	4 5	6 7	20 39	14 58	20 52	14 32	24 47	14 23	20 25	5 ♓ 2′ 8″
6 SA	9: 2:18	7 17	7 42	21 39	15 25	20 56	14 34	24 48	14 24	20 26	5 ♓ 2′ 7″
7 SU	9: 6:14	10 26	9 18	22 40	15 52	21 1	14 35	24 49	14 24	20 26	5 ♓ 2′ 7″
8 MO	9:10:11	13 32	10 53	23 41	16 19	21 5	14 37	24 49	14 24	20 26	5 ♓ 2′ 7″
9 TU	9:14: 8	16 34	12 29	24 42	16 46	21 10	14 39	24 50	14 25	20 27	5 ♓ 2′ 7″
10 WE	9:18: 4	19 34	14 4	25 43	17 14	21 14	14 41	24 51	14 25	20 27	5 ♓ 2′ 7″
11 TH	9:22: 1	22 31	15 39	26 43	17 41	21 19	14 43	24 51	14 26	20 27	5 ♓ 2′ 7″
12 FR	9:25:57	25 25	17 15	27 44	18 8	21 24	14 45	24 52	14 26	20 28	5 ♓ 2′ 7″
13 SA	9:29:54	28 18	18 50	28 45	18 35	21 28	14 46	24 53	14 26	20 28	5 ♓ 2′ 7″
14 SU	9:33:50	1 ♏ 9	20 25	29 46	19 3	21 33	14 48	24 53	14 27	20 28	5 ♓ 2′ 6″
15 MO	9:37:47	3 58	22 1	0 ♌ 46	19 30	21 37	14 50	24 54	14 27	20 29	5 ♓ 2′ 6″
16 TU	9:41:43	6 46	23 36	1 47	19 57	21 42	14 52	24 54	14 27	20 29	5 ♓ 2′ 6″
17 WE	9:45:40	9 33	25 11	2 47	20 25	21 47	14 54	24 55	14 28	20 29	5 ♓ 2′ 6″
18 TH	9:49:37	12 19	26 46	3 48	20 52	21 51	14 55	24 56	14 28	20 30	5 ♓ 2′ 6″
19 FR	9:53:33	15 5	28 21	4 48	21 20	21 56	14 57	24 56	14 28	20 30	5 ♓ 2′ 6″
20 SA	9:57:30	17 50	29 56	5 49	21 47	22 0	14 59	24 57	14 29	20 30	5 ♓ 2′ 6″
21 SU	10: 1:26	20 34	1 ♐ 31	6 49	22 15	22 5	15 1	24 58	14 29	20 30	5 ♓ 2′ 5″
22 MO	10: 5:23	23 6	3 6	7 50	22 42	22 9	15 3	24 58	14 30	20 31	5 ♓ 2′ 5″
23 TU	10: 9:19	26 4	4 42	8 50	23 10	22 14	15 5	24 59	14 30	20 31	5 ♓ 2′ 5″
24 WE	10:13:16	28 50	6 17	9 51	23 37	22 19	15 6	25 0	14 30	20 31	5 ♓ 2′ 5″
25 TH	10:17:12	1 ♐ 35	7 52	10 51	24 5	22 23	15 8	25 0	14 31	20 32	5 ♓ 2′ 5″
26 FR	10:21: 9	4 21	9 26	11 51	24 33	22 28	15 10	25 1	14 31	20 32	5 ♓ 2′ 5″
27 SA	10:25: 5	7 9	11 1	12 52	25 0	22 32	15 12	25 2	14 31	20 32	5 ♓ 2′ 5″
28 SU	10:29: 2	9 57	12 36	13 52	25 28	22 37	15 14	25 2	14 32	20 33	5 ♓ 2′ 4″
29 MO	10:32:59	12 48	14 11	14 52	25 56	22 41	15 16	25 3	14 32	20 33	5 ♓ 2′ 4″

INGRESSES :

1	♀ → ♏	3:58
3	☿ → ♎	18:14
13	☿ → ♏	14:16
14	⊕ → ♌	5:43
20	♀ → ♐	0:55
24	☿ → ♐	10:16

ASPECTS (HELIOCENTRIC +MOON(TYCHONIC)) :

2	☿ ☍ ♅	5:10	15	☽ ☍ ♆	15:56	21	☿ □ ♃	13:32	28	⊕ ☍ ♆	15:54	
	☽ ☌ ♀	9:49	16	☽ ☌ ♆	6:56		☿ ☌ A	18:57	29	⊕ □ ♄	9:33	
3	☽ □ ♄	9:55		☽ ☌ ♃	7:39	23	☽ □ ♆	5:52				
	☽ ☌ ♄	10: 7		☽ □ ♃	19:45		☽ □ ♄	7: 1				
	☽ □ ♃	22: 8	17	☽ ☍ ♀	2: 3	24	☽ ☍ ☿	13:16				
5	☽ □ ♂	19:22		☽ ☌ ♃	21:16	25	☽ ☌ ♀	5: 0				
6	☽ ☌ ♆	4:27	18	☿ □ ♆	18:41	26	☽ ☌ ♆	5:57				
	☽ □ ♅	12:10		☿ ☌ ♄	22:53		☽ ☌ ♂	14:40				
7	☽ □ ⊕	19:30	19	☽ □ ♂	0:57	27	☽ ☍ ♅	15: 4				
9	☽ ☌ ♀	23:21					☿ ☍ ♅	1:14				
10	☽ ☌ ♆	0: 0	11	☿ ☌ ♅	8:34							
12	☽ ☍ ♂	7:43		☽ □ ♆	11:19							
13	☽ ☌ ⊕	5:47	14	♀ ☌ ♃	17:50		♀ ☌ ♅	21:44				

the Moon at today's degree, Jesus was teaching his "Sermon on the Mount." The Pharisees called him a disturber of the peace, claiming they had their own teachings and did not need the innovations of this upstart called Jesus. Later, Lazarus told him of the journey the women had made to Macaerus to recover John's head from Herod's castle.

Jesus would continue his teachings, telling the crowd that they were not to allow themselves to be confounded by oppressors and calumniators. He was most undisturbed by the Pharisees threats to report him to Herod. These are wonderful teachings for us. The presence of the Elijah–John being and the new revelations coming through those who have developed capacities prophesied by Steiner represent the new "upstarts." The discomfort of some anthroposophists should not confound those who have recognized Valentin Tomberg's work as serving toward fulfilling the mission of the Maitreya Bodhisattva individuality—of whom Steiner foretold would incarnate at the beginning of the 20th century. To enclose oneself in the past leads to an inability to be spiritually aware in the present; thus is the future also lost.

Evolution consists of forces of enfoldment (the world of the serpent) and the forces of unfoldment (the created world). God created the world in seven days; yet what he created is continually spoken into time through the creative power of his Son. If a soul completely enfolded itself in itself, it would be in hell, i.e., in complete isolation. Healthy souls strive to become spiritually aware in the present moment, to see, hear, and touch into what is newly coming into time through the Son. Shining light into the darkness releases one from the past, thereby awakening one to the present. When one becomes silent in the present, one beholds the future. As this Full Moon stands before the constellation of Leo, we turn to the tenth Arcanum of the Tarot, The Wheel of Fortune:

> These two tendencies [unfoldment and enfoldment] have their traditional designations. They are "light" and "darkness," i.e., radiation and enfoldment, respectively. This is why the Gospel according to John, in describing the cosmic drama, says: "Light shineth in the darkness, and the darkness apprehendeth it not" (John 1:5)…this expresses that the light was not caught up in the whirlwind of enfoldment and is not obscured by it, but shines in the darkness. This is the quintessence of the Gospel, the "good news."

Thus the Sun and the stars are to the planets (including the Earth) as light is to darkness. And in the microcosm, the system of "lotus flowers" is to the system of endocrine glands as light is to darkness. For the "lotus flowers" are, fundamentally, blossoming glands, whilst the glands are enfolded "lotus flowers." The endocrinal glands are precipitates of the "lotus flowers" in the microcosm, just as the planets are precipitates of the "planetary spheres" in the macrocosm or planetary system.

Now, the world of the serpent is that of enfoldment. The serpent biting his tail and thus forming a closed circle is its symbol. Completely successful enfoldment would be hell or the state of complete isolation.[3]

This Full Moon asks us to ready ourselves for what we do not know, in order that John's new revelation may be recovered from Herod's castle of materialism. The lotus flowers are organs of cognition that see that to which the earthly ego is blind. World Herods have sought to decapitate John—silencing his presence in our time—and these Herods have sought as well to obscure the legacy of Abraham in the 20th century. The two Bodhisattvas of the 20th century, who succeeded the first Bodhisattva of the century (Rudolf Steiner) cannot be dismissed if spiritual guidance is to remain unbroken. As this lunar cycle wanes to the forthcoming New Moon, it may be prudent to revisit our opinions regarding those who have been regarded as "upstarts."

Mars enters Scorpio: "In growth activity persists." Mars was in Scorpio at the birth of the Nathan Jesus.

Feb. 24: Sun conjunct Deneb 10 1/2° Aquarius. The feeding of the five thousand and the walking on water (Jan/29–30/31). In the biblical account of the temptations of Christ, we are being told of the dangers and trials that one encounters when one descends into one's inner nature. In the legends of

---

3 Ibid., p. 247.

the Buddha we hear of similar encounters at the time when he met the demons who came to tempt him as he sat under the Bodhi tree and reached his enlightenment. In the story of the Transfiguration on Mt. Tabor, on the other hand, we are told the story of the radiance that united Christ with his macrocosmic self. There are great dangers on this macrocosmic path as well, for it takes specific preparation to hold the "I" together as it disperses into the vastness of the cosmos. If one goes unprepared, psychosis is the result.

In the fourth and fifth miracles of Jesus Christ, both the macrocosmic initiations (bread) and the microcosmic initiations (fish) were exemplified through the feeding of the five thousand and the walking on water. Herein lay the prophecy of his future descent into Hell (the trial of the fish initiation) and his resurrection (bread initiation). To walk on water, by analogy, is to have a pure and chaste etheric body. All remnants of the Fall create vortices in the etheric body that become infused with a magnetic charge able to pull one down, i.e., suck one in. *From one perspective we can view the walking on water as a seamless reflection of oneness with the radiant qualities of the life body.* Jonah was swallowed by a very large fish, a whale. He spent three days inside this fish, just as Christ spent three days in Hell. Jonah's fish initiation can be regarded as the Earth Trial—wherein we descend into our inner nature in order to encounter all obstacles we have created, and which affect our ability to find our radiant oneness with the Etheric Christ.

As the Sun commemorates these two miracles, we can contemplate where we need to enter into our inner world of egoism with the aim of facing our double. We can also look to where we have obstructed the radiant outpouring of our selfhood, which ever strives toward our truly cosmic nature.

Feb. 28: Sun conjunct Neptune 14° Aquarius: Births of Rudolf Steiner and Valentin Tomberg. Jesus taught on the same theme as the Sermon on the Mount: the Beatitudes and the Lord's Prayer (Matt. 5:3–12; 6:9–13). Both Rudolf Steiner and Valentin Tomberg gave close attention to the Lord's Prayer and the Beatitudes.

[Valentin Tomberg] can be viewed in the line of the great teachers of humanity. He is one such teacher in our time in the post-Christian era, one who is bringing the teaching for the ascending phase of this great movement of Christ on his path of return to the heavenly Father, leading humanity stage by stage on the ascending path leading to the Resurrection. He connected onto the great teacher Rudolf Steiner—this connection shows in their horoscopes, where the Sun's location (14½° Aquarius) at his birth aligned exactly with the position of the Sun (14½° Aquarius) at Rudolf Steiner's birth. Whereas Rudolf Steiner's task was to prepare for the onset of Christ's Second Coming in the etheric aura of the Earth in 1933, the task of the author of *Meditations on the Tarot* was to help humanity align with the Etheric Christ in the period after 1933.

As through antiquity Christ descended from the heights of our galaxy down to the Earth, so now he is uniting with the etheric aura of the Earth all the way down to the golden heart of the Earth (Shambhala), from there to begin his ascending movement from the depths in the spiritualization of the Earth, creating the "New Earth."[4]

As true initiates all work together, coming into incarnation in various cultures at various times in order to continue the work of spiritually guiding humanity, it would follow that one of the tasks of an initiate is to assure his successor is recognized. Rudolf Steiner fulfilled this task, without trespassing upon the freedom of his successor, who was still under the age of thirty-three at the time of Steiner's death. (Before this age an individuality may not as yet have accepted the responsibility of a foreordained mission.) Rudolf Steiner said the individuality in the process of becoming the next Buddha was born in 1900 and would begin teaching in the 1930s.

It was more discreetly, and without putting a particular person in the limelight as candidate, that Dr. Rudolf Steiner, founder of the Anthroposophical Society predicted the manifestation—again in the first half of the 20th century—not of the new Maitreya Buddha or Kalki Avatar, but

---

4   Powell, *Cultivating Inner Radiance and the Body of Immortality*, p. 192.

rather of the Bodhisattva, i.e., the individuality in the process of becoming the next Buddha, whose field of activity he hoped the Anthroposophical Society would serve.[5]

Aquarius is future-oriented and brings something new into the present. Aquarian teachers bear witness to the future. Aquarius is leading us into the next zodiacal age (beginning in 2375)—in which the Slavic cultural epoch will open new possibilities for manas cognition. We are on the doorstep to this Aquarian Age. Both of these great teachers brought change based on the traditions of the past, but not limited by these traditions. For, to be limited is to become rigidified. *The sanctity of humanity's freedom allows each of us to discern for ourselves whom we recognize as bearers of revelation. Error occurs when those in positions of authority misuse their positions by imposing personal opinions as objective truths, thereby transgressing upon the freedom of others.*

The Sun remembers the births of Rudolf Steiner and Valentin Tomberg; and today, with Neptune at this same degree, we can open our hearts to receive inspirations that the guiding Bodhisattvas of humanity may have in store for their loyal disciples.

MARCH 2016

The waning Moon swings past Saturn in Scorpio between the 1st and 2nd hours after midnight. Look for the Moon's rise in the east as early as 3 a.m., and spot Saturn beneath her. Watch over a few days to get a sense of just how quickly the Moon moves through the Stars! By the 7th and 8th, the Moon will have caught up with Venus and Mercury but will be so close to the Sun you must look to the east just before sunrise and the early dawn's light to catch a glimpse. The New Moon is formed (always a Moon and Sun conjunction) on the 8th, also a total lunar eclipse.

The Sun shifts into the constellation of the Fishes (Pisces) on the 15th. The apparently Full Moon will join up with Jupiter in Leo on the 21st; look to the east at sunset on this day and the day before

too, in order to experience the swift movement of the Moon. The Moon will be truly Full (exactly opposite the Sun) on the 23rd, with Moon in Virgo and Sun in Pisces. This will be a penumbral lunar eclipse with Mercury in the mix, conjunct the Sun (and opposite the Moon).

Saturn stations Retrograde on the 26th until mid-August. The waning Moon catches up with Mars in Scorpio on the 28th, visible after midnight rising in the east or look farther to the south closer to sunrise. Saturn will be to the left of these two, with the Moon conjuncting Saturn on the following day.

Deneb is conjunct Mercury on the 8th, and Venus on the 16th. Deneb is a megastar 200,000 times more powerful than our Sun. During this entire month, Jupiter is moving retrograde; Saturn goes retrograde on the 26th.

March 2: Mercury enters Aquarius: "Find bounds within the depths of your soul." Aquarius asks us to find discretion through meditative silence, lest we become enamored by mental gymnastics, foregoing contemplative depth. Mercury was in Aquarius at the birth of the Solomon Jesus, at the healing of the Syrophoenician woman, and when Jesus taught regarding the bread of life, and spoke the prophetic words, "One among you is a devil" (meaning Judas Iscariot).

March 4: Sun 20° Aquarius. The raising of the Essene child from the dead (Tuesday, Feb/7/30). The child lay wrapped in the winding-sheet as Jesus entered the house of Jairus the Essene. Jairus was a pious and charitable man, which had greatly vexed his daughter. He tended the poor and the despised, which resulted in his daughter having little love for him. Jesus roused both her body and her soul from the dead, after which she was reformed and later joined the circle of holy women.

How often do we fail to notice the silent helpers of humankind! Whether of high or low station in life, they serve Christ and yet may go entirely unnoticed. At this healing Jesus warned those present not to speak of what they had witnessed. This was a mere few months after his first miracle of turning water into wine at the wedding of Cana (December of 29). Jesus asked for discretion, as it was not yet time to draw attention to himself.

---

5 Anon., *Meditations on the Tarot*, p. 614.

We can contemplate our readiness to observe our fellow brothers and sisters through the eyes of Angels, and assess whether we have the humility to work without reward. It is also prudent to keep the secret of miracles in our hearts until the proper time for their revelation has dawned. To lack discretion in such matters compromises the selfless work of silently serving Christ.

March 5: Mercury 5° Aquarius square Mars 5° Scorpio. Mercury remembers Jesus's prediction of his impending persecution and death (Feb/3/31); Mars remembers the first of Christ's miracles: turning water into wine at the wedding of Cana (Wednesday, Dec/28/29).

Mercury square Mars—i.e., the pastors of humankind (Mercury)—in dynamic relationship with Michael (Mars). This aspect can cause an argumentative mind if not tempered by conscience. The virtues of discretion and patience lead us to insight regarding the underlying causes (occult) of any given situation. Thus will we find the right action (in word or deed).

Mercury is recalling persecution, and Mars is recalling the reestablishment of the vertical-spiritual union of true marriage. The influences radiating from the heavens today ask us to take measure of any tendency in our soul that compels us to harshly judge others; and they ask us to protect the sanctity of the spirit inherent in all our relationships.

March 6: Sun 21° Aquarius square Saturn 21° Scorpio. Magdalene's first encounter with Jesus (Thursday, Feb/9/30). With the resurrection forces (Sun) in square to the Holy Virgin (Saturn), we may meet fears of rejection. We are not to be distracted. Behind the fear of rejection is our soul's sorrow due to our rejection of some aspect of ourself. Is something in us striving to resurrect from its enchainment to false beliefs? It was on a Thursday that Jesus was teaching in Jezreel with the Sun at today's degree. Lazarus, Martha, Veronica, and Johanna Chusa had collectively persuaded Magdelene to come and hear Jesus speak. The first encounter between Jesus and Magdalene was a mere glance:

Magdalene had yielded to the persuasions of the women and, surrounded by much vain display, accompanied them thither. As she stood at the window of an inn gazing down into the street, Jesus and his disciples came walking by. He looked at her gravely as he passed with a glance that pierced her soul. An unusual feeling of confusion came over her. Violently agitated, she rushed from the inn and, impelled by an overpowering sense of her own misery, hid in a house wherein lepers and women afflicted with the flow of blood found a refuge. It was a kind of hospital under the superintendence of a Pharisee. The people of the inn from which Magdalene had fled, knowing the life she was leading, cried out: "That's the right place for her, among lepers and women tormented with a flow of blood!"

But Magdalene had fled to the house of the leprous through that feeling of intense humiliation roused in her soul by the glance of Jesus, for she had made her way into that respectable position among the other women through a motive of pride, not wishing to stand in the crowd of poor, common people. Accompanied by Lazarus, she returned to Magdalum with Martha and the other women. The next Sabbath was there celebrated by them, for Magdalum could boast a synagogue.[1]

Today's aspect reminds us that when Love bears witness to our naked soul, the first reaction may very possibly be fear. Do we have the patience and humility to await the insight that reveals what is lacking? We can remember that in times of trial the Holy Virgin stands by us, just as she stood with Jesus Christ during his descent into Hell.

ASPECT: Heliocentric Mars is conjunct Spica.

March 8: New Moon Total Solar Eclipse 23° Aquarius. Today four planets (Moon, Neptune, Mercury, and Venus) and the Sun all stand in Aquarius. Surely brother- and sisterhood will prevail during this new lunar cycle. Aquarius sends the Holy Spirit who finds us on the wings of angelic messengers.

The eclipse will be visible from Sumatra, Borneo, Sulawesi, and from locations in the Pacific ocean. A partial eclipse will be visible for people in South and East Asia, as well as in northern Australia. Maximum point of eclipse is 2:00 a.m. (UTC), March 9th. Duration: 4 min. 9 secs.

---

1 *ACE Complete*, p. 290.

We can imagine the Moon (ruler of the brain-bound intellect) eclipsing the Sun as representative of the striving of the adversaries, who seek to entrap us in deeper levels of materialism, thereby attempting to thwart humanity's awakening to new creative levels of consciousness. The occultation of the Sun is a cosmic analogy for the occultation of the future. Through the influence of the solar eclipse, evil will spreads into the cosmos, thus assisting the work of the adversaries:

> The old initiates knew these things. They saw that at such a moment all the unbridled impulses and instincts of humanity surge out into the cosmos. And they gave their pupils [an] explanation. They said: Under normal conditions the evil impulses of will that are sent out into the cosmos by human beings are, as it were, burned up and consumed by the rays of the Sun, so that they can injure only man himself, but can do no universal harm. When, however, there is an eclipse of the Sun, opportunity is given for the evil that is willed on Earth to spread over the cosmos. An eclipse is a physical event behind which there lies a significant spiritual reality.[2]

We can meditate on the spiritual presence of the Sun. The seeds we wish to plant for the coming autumn harvest are the seeds of brotherhood and sisterhood. An Aquarian Moon calls us to serve in communities that are preparing for the coming Age of Philadelphia (Aquarius). We can actively counteract the negative effects of this eclipse by sending love into the cosmos during this period of darkness lasting 4 minutes and 9 seconds. We can imagine a releasing of evil impulses into the wide expanse of the cosmos—into the waiting arms of the Lamb of God, who is now working for the dawning of the Age of Aquarius as the sign of the Son of Man in heaven. He carries our burdens until we are ready to take them upon ourselves. Peace be with us!

The Sun at today's degree remembers Jesus on his way to Dan, a city built of black, shining stone. On the way there, he spoke to his disciples, telling them to be like Jacob—who petitioned God for the dew of heaven and the gift of spiritual illumination. In Numbers 24:17 we read that a star will come out of Jacob. May we find this star as the contemporary light leading us toward the blessings of new capacities!

The Moon was at this degree when Christ received a message, carried by a servant of a high ranking official of Capernaum. The messenger reported that the centurion of Capernaum had a son who was dying. This is the second of the seven healing miracles of Jesus Christ: the healing of the nobleman's son (Thursday, Aug/3/30). Though the messenger spoke of the boy as the son of the centurion of Capernaum, whom he served, the truth was that the boy was actually his own son. The boy had been sick for two weeks (since the time of the previous New Moon in Cancer) and the boy had said to his physicians: "All these medicines do me no good. Jesus, the prophet of Nazareth, alone can help me!" Jesus saw into the father's heart and knew the arrogance there dwelling. He spoke:

> "If you see not signs and wonders, you do not believe. I know your case well. You want to boast of a miracle and glory over the Pharisees, though you have the same need of being humbled as they. My mission is not to work miracles in order to further your designs. I stand in no need of your approbation. I shall reserve my miracles until it is my Father's will that I should perform them, and I shall perform them when my mission calls for it!" And thus Jesus went on for a long time, humbling the man before all the people. He said that man had been waiting long for him to cure his son, that he might boast of it before the Pharisees. But miracles, Jesus continued, should not be desired in order to triumph over others, and he exhorted his hearers to believe and be converted.[3]

After continuing teaching, he finally turned to the chief officer of the centurion, saying:

> "Go, thy son liveth!" The man asked: "Is that really true?" Jesus answered: "Believe me, he has in this very hour been cured." Thereupon the man believed and, no longer importuning Jesus to accompany him, mounted his mule and hastened back to Capernaum. Jesus remarked

---

2 RS, *Human Questions and Cosmic Answers,* lect. 2: "Sunlight and Moonlight, Solar and Lunar Eclipses and Their Relation to Man's Life of Soul."

3 Ibid., p. 386.

SIDEREAL GEOCENTRIC LONGITUDES :   MARCH 2016 Gregorian at 0 hours UT

DAY	☉	☽	Ω	☿	♀	♂	♃	♄	♅	♆	♇
1 TU	15 ♒ 52	5 ♏ 5	26 ♌ 53	27 ♑ 53	20 ♑ 53	3 ♏ 5	24 ♌ 18R	20 ♏ 57	23 ♓ 19	14 ♒ 35	21 ♐ 56
2 WE	16 52	17 16	26 53	29 28	22 8	3 29	24 11	20 59	23 22	14 37	21 58
3 TH	17 52	29 44	26 53R	1 ♒ 4	23 22	3 52	24 3	21 1	23 25	14 39	21 59
4 FR	18 53	12 ♐ 33	26 52	2 41	24 36	4 15	23 55	21 3	23 28	14 41	22 0
5 SA	19 53	25 47	26 51	4 19	25 50	4 37	23 47	21 6	23 31	14 44	22 2
6 SU	20 53	9 ♑ 26	26 51	5 59	27 5	5 0	23 40	21 8	23 34	14 46	22 3
7 MO	21 53	23 31	26 50	7 39	28 19	5 22	23 32	21 9	23 37	14 48	22 4
8 TU	22 53	8 ♒ 0	26 50	9 20	29 33	5 43	23 24	21 11	23 40	14 50	22 5
9 WE	23 53	22 47	26 50	11 3	0 ♒ 47	6 5	23 16	21 13	23 43	14 53	22 7
10 TH	24 53	7 ♓ 45	26 50D	12 46	2 1	6 26	23 8	21 14	23 46	14 55	22 8
11 FR	25 53	22 46	26 50	14 31	3 16	6 46	23 0	21 16	23 50	14 57	22 9
12 SA	26 53	7 ♈ 41	26 50	16 17	4 30	7 7	22 53	21 17	23 53	14 59	22 10
13 SU	27 53	22 23	26 50R	18 4	5 44	7 27	22 45	21 19	23 56	15 2	22 11
14 MO	28 53	6 ♉ 47	26 50	19 52	6 58	7 46	22 37	21 20	23 59	15 4	22 12
15 TU	29 52	20 50	26 50	21 42	8 13	8 5	22 29	21 21	24 2	15 6	22 13
16 WE	0 ♓ 52	4 ♊ 31	26 49D	23 32	9 27	8 24	22 22	21 22	24 5	15 8	22 14
17 TH	1 52	17 50	26 50	25 24	10 41	8 42	22 14	21 23	24 9	15 11	22 15
18 FR	2 52	0 ♋ 50	26 50	27 17	11 55	9 0	22 6	21 24	24 12	15 13	22 16
19 SA	3 51	13 32	26 51	29 11	13 9	9 18	21 59	21 24	24 15	15 15	22 17
20 SU	4 51	26 0	26 51	1 ♓ 7	14 24	9 35	21 51	21 25	24 18	15 17	22 18
21 MO	5 50	8 ♌ 16	26 52	3 3	15 38	9 51	21 44	21 25	24 22	15 19	22 19
22 TU	6 50	20 23	26 52	5 1	16 52	10 8	21 37	21 26	24 25	15 21	22 20
23 WE	7 50	2 ♍ 22	26 53R	6 59	18 6	10 23	21 29	21 26	24 28	15 24	22 20
24 TH	8 49	14 16	26 52	8 59	19 20	10 38	21 22	21 26	24 32	15 26	22 21
25 FR	9 48	26 6	26 51	10 59	20 34	10 53	21 15	21 26	24 35	15 28	22 22
26 SA	10 48	7 ♎ 55	26 49	13 0	21 49	11 8	21 8	21 26R	24 38	15 30	22 23
27 SU	11 47	19 46	26 47	15 2	23 3	11 22	21 1	21 26	24 42	15 32	22 23
28 MO	12 47	1 ♏ 40	26 44	17 4	24 17	11 35	20 54	21 26	24 45	15 34	22 24
29 TU	13 46	13 41	26 42	19 7	25 31	11 48	20 47	21 26	24 48	15 36	22 25
30 WE	14 45	25 53	26 40	21 10	26 45	12 0	20 41	21 25	24 52	15 38	22 25
31 TH	15 44	8 ♐ 18	26 39	23 12	27 59	12 12	20 34	21 25	24 55	15 40	22 26

INGRESSES :

- 2 ☿ → ♒ 8: 0
- 3 ☽ → ♐ 0:30
- 5 ☽ → ♑ 7:30
- 7 ☽ → ♒ 10:48
- 8 ♀ → ♒ 8:43
- 9 ☽ → ♓ 11:35
- 11 ☽ → ♈ 11:36
- 13 ☽ → ♉ 12:36
- 15 ☉ → ♓ 3: 2
- 15 ☽ → ♊ 16: 0
- 17 ☽ → ♋ 22:27
- 19 ☿ → ♓ 10:10
- 20 ☽ → ♌ 7:47
- 22 ☽ → ♍ 19:14
- 25 ☽ → ♎ 7:54
- 27 ☽ → ♏ 20:39
- 30 ☽ → ♐ 8: 1

ASPECTS & ECLIPSES :

- 1 ☉ □ ☽ 23: 9
- 2 ☽ ☌ ♄ 7:14
- 2 ☽ ⚹ Ω 18:33
- 4 ☽ ☌ ♆ 17:15
- 5 ☿ □ ♂ 5:42
- 6 ☉ □ ♄ 6: 2
- 7 ☽ ☌ ♀ 8:45
- 8 ☽ ☌ ☿ 2:28
- 8 ☉ ☌ ♃ 10:56
- 8 ☽ ☌ ♆ 11:10
- 9 ☽ ☍ ♃ 0:46
- ☉ ☌ ☽ 1:53
- ☉ ● T 1:56
- ☽ ☌ ☋ 6:29
- 10 ☽ ☌ P 7: 3
- 11 ☽ ☌ ♅ 1:41
- ☿ ☌ ♆ 6: 4
- ☉ ☍ ♃ 22:46
- 14 ☽ ☍ ♂ 1:41
- ☿ □ ♄ 19:24
- ♀ □ ♂ 20:46
- 15 ☽ ☍ ♄ 0:53
- ☿ ☍ ♃ 9:40
- ☽ ⚹ Ω 10:25
- ☉ □ ☽ 17: 1
- 17 ☽ ☍ ♅ 8: 6
- ☿ ☍ Ω 18:13
- 20 ♀ ☌ ♅ 17:50
- 21 ☽ ☍ ♀ 13:59
- ☽ ☍ ♀ 16:12
- 22 ☽ ☌ ♃ 2:25
- ☽ ☌ Ω 12:59
- 23 ♃ □ ♄ 10:15
- ☽ ☍ ♅ 11:10
- ☽ ⚹ PN 11:45
- ☉ ☍ ♃ 11:59
- ☉ ⚹ ☿ 20: 9
- 24 ☽ ☌ ♅ 20:53
- 25 ♀ ☍ ♃ 11:56
- ☽ ☌ A 14:47
- ♀ □ ♄ 16:47
- 28 ☽ ☌ ♂ 20:10
- 29 ☽ ☌ ♄ 15:16
- ♀ ☍ Ω 22:22
- 30 ☽ ⚹ Ω 1:32
- ☿ □ ♆ 14:50
- 31 ☉ ☌ ☽ 15:15
- ☿ ☌ ♅ 20:47

SIDEREAL HELIOCENTRIC LONGITUDES :   MARCH 2016 Gregorian at 0 hours UT

DAY	Sid. Time	☿	♀	⊕	♂	♃	♄	♅	♆	♇	Vernal Point
1 TU	10:36:55	15 ♐ 39	15 ♐ 46	15 ♌ 52	26 ♍ 23	22 ♌ 46	15 ♏ 17	25 ♓ 4	14 ♒ 32	20 ♐ 33	5 ♓ 2' 4"
2 WE	10:40:52	18 33	17 21	16 53	26 51	22 51	15 19	25 4	14 33	20 34	5 ♓ 2' 4"
3 TH	10:44:48	21 28	18 56	17 53	27 19	22 55	15 21	25 5	14 33	20 34	5 ♓ 2' 4"
4 FR	10:48:45	24 26	20 31	18 53	27 47	23 0	15 23	25 5	14 33	20 34	5 ♓ 2' 4"
5 SA	10:52:41	27 27	22 6	19 53	28 15	23 4	15 25	25 6	14 34	20 35	5 ♓ 2' 4"
6 SU	10:56:38	0 ♑ 30	23 41	20 53	28 43	23 9	15 26	25 7	14 34	20 35	5 ♓ 2' 3"
7 MO	11: 0:34	3 37	25 16	21 53	29 11	23 14	15 28	25 7	14 35	20 35	5 ♓ 2' 3"
8 TU	11: 4:31	6 46	26 50	22 53	29 39	23 18	15 30	25 8	14 35	20 35	5 ♓ 2' 3"
9 WE	11: 8:28	10 0	28 25	23 53	0 ♎ 7	23 23	15 32	25 9	14 35	20 36	5 ♓ 2' 3"
10 TH	11:12:24	13 17	0 ♑ 0	24 53	0 35	23 27	15 34	25 9	14 36	20 36	5 ♓ 2' 3"
11 FR	11:16:21	16 39	1 35	25 53	1 3	23 32	15 36	25 10	14 36	20 36	5 ♓ 2' 3"
12 SA	11:20:17	20 5	3 10	26 53	1 31	23 36	15 37	25 11	14 36	20 37	5 ♓ 2' 3"
13 SU	11:24:14	23 36	4 45	27 53	1 59	23 41	15 39	25 11	14 37	20 37	5 ♓ 2' 3"
14 MO	11:28:10	27 13	6 20	28 53	2 27	23 46	15 41	25 12	14 37	20 37	5 ♓ 2' 2"
15 TU	11:32: 7	0 ♒ 55	7 54	29 53	2 56	23 50	15 43	25 13	14 38	20 38	5 ♓ 2' 2"
16 WE	11:36: 3	4 43	9 29	0 ♍ 53	3 24	23 55	15 45	25 13	14 38	20 38	5 ♓ 2' 2"
17 TH	11:40: 0	8 37	11 4	1 52	3 52	23 59	15 46	25 14	14 38	20 38	5 ♓ 2' 2"
18 FR	11:43:57	12 38	12 39	2 52	4 20	24 4	15 48	25 15	14 39	20 39	5 ♓ 2' 2"
19 SA	11:47:53	16 46	14 14	3 52	4 49	24 8	15 50	25 15	14 39	20 39	5 ♓ 2' 2"
20 SU	11:51:50	21 2	15 49	4 51	5 17	24 13	15 52	25 16	14 39	20 39	5 ♓ 2' 1"
21 MO	11:55:46	25 26	17 24	5 51	5 46	24 18	15 54	25 17	14 40	20 40	5 ♓ 2' 1"
22 TU	11:59:43	29 57	18 59	6 50	6 14	24 22	15 56	25 17	14 40	20 40	5 ♓ 2' 1"
23 WE	12: 3:39	4 ♓ 38	20 34	7 50	6 43	24 27	15 57	25 18	14 40	20 40	5 ♓ 2' 1"
24 TH	12: 7:36	9 27	22 8	8 49	7 11	24 31	15 59	25 18	14 41	20 41	5 ♓ 2' 1"
25 FR	12:11:32	14 25	23 43	9 49	7 40	24 36	16 1	25 19	14 41	20 41	5 ♓ 2' 1"
26 SA	12:15:29	19 32	25 18	10 48	8 9	24 40	16 3	25 20	14 41	20 41	5 ♓ 2' 1"
27 SU	12:19:26	24 48	26 53	11 48	8 37	24 45	16 5	25 21	14 42	20 42	5 ♓ 2' 0"
28 MO	12:23:22	0 ♈ 13	28 28	12 47	9 6	24 50	16 6	25 21	14 42	20 42	5 ♓ 2' 0"
29 TU	12:27:19	5 47	0 ♒ 3	13 46	9 35	24 54	16 8	25 22	14 42	20 42	5 ♓ 2' 0"
30 WE	12:31:15	11 30	1 38	14 46	10 3	24 59	16 10	25 22	14 43	20 42	5 ♓ 2' 0"
31 TH	12:35:12	17 20	3 13	15 45	10 32	25 3	16 12	25 23	14 43	20 43	5 ♓ 2' 0"

INGRESSES :

- 5 ☿ → ♑ 20: 4
- 8 ♂ → ♎ 18:18
- 9 ♀ → ♑ 23:57
- 14 ☿ → ♒ 18: 8
- 15 ⊕ → ♍ 2:53
- 22 ☿ → ♓ 0:13
- 27 ☿ → ♈ 23: 3
- 28 ♀ → ♒ 23:10

ASPECTS (HELIOCENTRIC +MOON(TYCHONIC)) :

- 1 ☿ ☌ ♀ 2:10
- ☽ ☌ ♆ 18:40
- ☽ ☌ ♄ 20:11
- 2 ☽ □ ♃ 10:52
- ☿ ☌ ♄ 16:34
- 4 ♀ ☌ ♇ 0:49
- ☿ □ ♅ 5:15
- ☽ ☌ ♇ 14:38
- ☽ ☌ ♀ 16:30
- ☽ □ ♅ 22:47
- 5 ☽ ☌ ☿ 3:50
- ☽ □ ♂ 4:33
- ☿ □ ♂ 7:27
- 6 ♀ □ ♅ 21:55
- 8 ⊕ ☌ ♃ 10:41
- ☽ ☌ ♆ 10:44
- ☽ ☌ ♄ 12:14
- 9 ☽ ☌ ♃ 0:57
- 10 ♀ □ ♂ 12:25
- ☽ □ ♆ 20:32
- 11 ☽ ☌ ♅ 3:50
- ☽ ☍ ♂ 13:43
- ☽ □ ♀ 15:49
- 12 ☿ ⚹ Ω 23:41
- 13 ☽ □ ♆ 2:39
- 14 ☽ □ ♅ 12:38
- ☽ ☍ ♄ 15: 9
- 15 ☽ ☌ ♃ 5:14
- 17 ☽ ☍ ♆ 5: 8
- ☽ □ ♅ 13:36
- 18 ☽ □ ♆ 6:50
- ☿ ☌ ♆ 11:43
- 19 ☽ ☍ ♀ 1:31
- 20 ♀ ☌ A 15:20
- ♀ ☍ ♃ 17:44
- 21 ☿ ☍ ♆ 12:38
- ☽ □ ♄ 15: 7
- 22 ☽ ☌ ♀ 8: 1
- 23 ☽ ☌ ☿ 7:35
- ☿ ☌ ♅ 20: 9
- 24 ☽ □ ⊕ 12:59
- ☽ ☌ ♅ 22:24
- 26 ☽ ☌ ♂ 0:27
- ☿ □ ♆ 5:21
- 27 ☿ ☌ ♅ 2:27
- ☽ □ ♀ 16:35
- 29 ☽ ☌ ♀ 2: 1
- ☽ ☌ ♂ 4:52
- ☿ ☍ ♀ 17:28
- ☽ □ ♃ 22:13
- 31 ☽ ☌ ♇ 23:23

that he had yielded this time; at another time he would not be so condescending.[4]

The king's servant was a man with a weak ego. The weakness of his ego resulted in his son inheriting a blood organization that could not sustain his "I" as he reached his adolescence. The man indeed served his king well (the centurion); yet by surrendering his "I"—and even giving up his son to appease his king's desire for a child—he weakened his selfhood. In its place was the arrogance that stood as a carricature of his "I." The servant lusted for power over others, for he had lost the certainty of his one true self.

This New Moon reminds us of the strengthening force of the "I" and the humility and compassion that marks one who stands upright under its sovereign influence. Arrogance, boastfulness, and the need to "lord over" others is a sign of one whose ego strength is lacking.

The Moon in Aquarius reminds us of angelic beings and their need to serve. Our guardian Angel protects that in us which had been created in the "image of God," that is forever the form of our perfection. In us also is our "likeness" to God, wherein we are constantly striving to realize our perfection. To be vigilant in our contemplation of our Angel leads us ever forward toward the radiant star our Angel guards on our behalf:

> But—and this is the tragic side of angelic existence—this geniality shows up only when the human being has need of it, when he makes room for the flashing forth of its illumination. The Angel depends on man in his creative activity. If the human being does not ask for it, if he turns away from him, the Angel has no motive for creative activity. He can then fall into a state of consciousness where all his creative geniality remains in potential and does not manifest. It is a state of vegetation or "twilight existence," comparable to sleep from the human point of view. An Angel who has nothing to exist for is a tragedy in the spiritual world.[5]

The miracle of the healing of the nobleman's son occurred on a Thursday (the day of the Holy Spirit). This New Moon asks us to contemplate the angelic presence of spirit and its enduring light. When we meet arrogance in ourselves or in others, we are encountering the fallen likeness, whence the unity between people is forgotten and community life is fractured. There is but one "I" and that is the Christ "I." We are each a spark from this one divine fire.

ASPECT: Sun/Moon 23° Aquarius opposite Jupiter 23° Leo. The Ascension of Solomon Mary (Aug/16/44). The force of resurrection (Sun) stands opposite the Holy Spirit (Jupiter). This aspect bestows the gift of compassion when our soul rests in balance. Compassion for others is a measure of our soul's freedom. The beings in the constellation of Leo ask us to help liberate others from the yoke of slavery—first however, we must liberate ourslves.

Venus enters Aquarius. Venus in Aquarius calls us to practice meditative silence. Venus was in Aquarius at the birth of the Solomon Jesus and at the revealing of John the Baptist's death.

March 9: Sun 24° Aquarius: Healing of the Syrophoenician woman and her daugher (Monday, Feb/12/31). We are reminded that it may be easier to pray for the healing of others (as this woman prayed for the healing of her daughter) than it may be to believe in our own worthiness to be healed.

March 11: Mercury conjunct Neptune 15° Aquarius: In conjuction in the constellation of Aquarius, Mercury—the healer/teacher—can bring about mighty inspirations from angelic realms. Both of these planets stand at the memory of the Sun's location at the births of Steiner and Tomberg (14½° Aquarius). Mercury also remembers the dispute that broke out among the Pharisees, who complained that Jesus and his disciples did not obey the Law when they did not wash their hands before eating. Jesus replied, "There is nothing outside a man which can defile him, but the things that come out of a man are what defile him" (Feb/9/31).

We are reminded that spirit ever triumphs over matter. Acts of "white magic" are stronger than the pesticides, the GMOs, and all other toxicities we must endure in our apocalyptic era. We are encouraged to concentrate our minds so as to align with the Angel Jesus, who nourishes all who turn to him at this time when the Christ has

---

4 Ibid., 386.

5 Anon., *Meditations on the Tarot*, pp. 378–379.

drawn so near to us. Christ is the source of all powers of white magic.

March 14: Venus 8° Aquarius square Mars 8° Scorpio. Mars was at this degree when Jesus healed a man who had fallen from a tower (Saturday, Dec/31/29). This was one month after Jesus' forty days of temptation in the wilderness, and three days after the first of the his seven healing miracles: the changing of water into wine at the wedding in Cana. Reading Anne Catherine Emmerich's account:

> A man had fallen from a high tower. He was taken up dead, all his limbs broken. Jesus went to him, placed the limbs in position, touched the fractures, and then commanded the man to rise and go to his home.[6]

Falling from a high tower symbolically recalls the second temptation in the wilderness, a mere thirty days prior to this healing. When we plunge from the pinnacle of consciousness, we harm the moral-spiritual structure within us that provides the foundation for the moral quality of our deeds (Mars). This miracle occurred on a Saturday—Saturn governs the skeleton and bones.

With the way of the Passion (Venus) square Michaelic courage (Mars), our soul may find a certain angst caused by feelings of oppression. This aspect requires a silent beholding from the pinnacle of consciousness so that we may discover what in us needs to be realigned. Thus, through our courage to face our inner discomfort (Venus), we are able to refine our soul as an instrument for cosmic imaginations.

March 15: Sun enters Pisces: "In what is lost, may the loss find itself" (Steiner, *Twelve Cosmic Moods*). William Bento illumines this mantra:

> Regardless of the nature of what has been released, there is a sense of accompanying loss. With those losses that have been treasured and valued (such as a loved one), there lives the hope that the object or being that is lost will not be forgotten or forlorn, but will find new life in an entirely new realm. The plea that states, "May the loss find itself" is really a statement of hope in the eternal cycle of life.

Above the first decan is the Square of Pegasus, hence the association of this decan with the body of Pegasus, the Winged Horse, also called the Horse of the Fountain. This decan is ruled by Saturn. Pisces bestows Magnanimity born of Love. The challenge is to stay grounded in reality in the inclination toward the mystical.

ASPECT: Mercury 22° Aquarius opposite Jupiter 22° Leo. Jupiter remembers the fall of Jerusalem (Aug/29/70). This was two years after the death of the Emperor Nero. In their victory, the Romans slaughtered thousands, enslaved others to work in the mines of Egypt, and still others were sent to the public arenas throughout the Empire to be butchered for the amusement of the public. Jerusalem is mentioned in the Book of Daniel as well as in the work of Vladimir Solovyov:

> The reference to the prophet Daniel has to do with Daniel's prophecy regarding the city of Jerusalem (the "holy place"). Daniel speaks of "a prince who is to come [who] shall destroy the city and the sanctuary . . . desolations are decreed" (Daniel 9:26). Here Daniel refers to the "prince of this world" (Ahriman/Satan).

In Vladimir Solovyov's inspired work, *A Short Story of the Antichrist* (originally published in Russia at Easter 1900),[7] he describes the false Christ (Antichrist) who, in league with a false prophet (the magician Apollyon), becomes emperor of the world and establishes his residence in Jerusalem. Among Apollyon's magical powers is the ability to make fire come down from heaven. This is a clear allusion to the two-horned beast referred to in the thirteenth chapter of the Book of Revelation. In fact, it is in Revelation that we find an account of the reign of the Antichrist (referred to there simply as "the beast"), who is aided by the two-horned beast:

> The two-horned beast exercises all the authority of the first beast in its presence, and makes the earth and its inhabitants worship the [first beast].... Men worshipped the first beast, saying, "Who is like the beast, and who can fight against it?" And the beast was given a mouth uttering haughty

---

6 *ACE Complete*, p. 278.

7 In Solovyov, *War, Progress, and the End of History: Three Conversations, Including a Short Tale of the Antichrist*.

and blasphemous words, and it was allowed to exercise authority for forty-two months. (Rev. 13: 4–5)[8]

Minds must stay alert as we bear witness to the forces working behind world events. Jupiter represents community life, and there are new communities forming around the increasingly manifest presence of Christ in the etheric. Such communities, and the practices of white magic conducted by the members of these communities, are antidotes to the rising tides of adversarial forces. The constellation of Leo inspires communities to find courage *through* compassion.

March 19: Mercury enters Pisces. "Apprehending [must] seek itself in the comprehended." Mercury in Pisces asks that we separate truth from fantasies despite the prolific intensification of deceptions. Mercury was in Pisces during the Passion of Christ.

March 20: Venus conjunct Neptune 15° Aquarius. This conjunction illumines the Sun's location at the births of both Steiner and Tomberg (14½° Aquarius). Nine days ago Mercury was conjunct Neptune; today Venus stands with the planet (Neptune) that is representative of both divine inspiration and delusions. This aspect sends spiritual tones to earthly humanity. Artistry and music are beautiful expressions in celebration of this influence. When the Sun was at this degree, Jesus spoke of the Beatitudes and the Lord's Prayer, and he referred to himself as the bread of life (Feb/2/31). The people did not understand Jesus's words regarding the bread of life. The Pharisees strongly objected to him:

> The Pharisees again offered the same objections, and when they appealed to their father Abraham and to Moses, asking how he could call God his Father, Jesus put to them the question: "How can ye call Abraham your father and Moses your lawgiver, since ye do not follow the commandments or the example of either Abraham or Moses?" Then he placed clearly before them their perverse actions and their wicked, hypocritical life. They became confused and enraged.[9]

It is striking that the Pharisees invoked both Moses and Abraham when the Sun sojourned at 15° Aquarius. We recall that the Sun at 14½° Aquarius recalls the remembrance of both Rudolf Steiner's (1861) and Valentin Tomberg's birth (1900). Perhaps we can recognize this cosmic connection and influence in reading Valentin Tomberg's lectures on the Old Testament, in which the clarity and depth of understanding are remarkably living and deeply moving. As the spiritual essence of Venus conjunct Neptune sounds into this day, we can imagine Abraham and Moses inspiring their contemporary communities to unite, for divisiveness is the work of the beast. Doubt is a bifurcating beast with two horns.

Spring Equinox: Mother Earth is breathing out her soul. Her breath is half within the Earth and half without. The little seed of our future spiritual potential that we carried out of the Holy Nights last January is also breathing outward. Both microcosmically (in the human being) and macrocosmically (in the body of the Earth) an exhalation is taking place. The Earth Mother is going to sleep, and her dream body engenders the sprouting enlivening of Nature's springtide. *Nature is the soul of the Mother exhaled in sleep.* Just as our soul leaves our body in sleep, so, too, does the great Earth-soul leave her body in sleep, and this manifests as the beauty and majesty of *Natura.* Our Christmas seed is preparing to take flight. It will begin its gradual ascent with the Earth-soul into the heights of summer. Here it will be infused with the creative forces necessary to develop into a full reality. This will come into form later, at Michaelmas. Today marks a sprouting quickening, both within and without. Not until the first Sunday after the first Full Moon following this equinox will the inner spirit of the Earth—Jesus Christ—begin the ascent to meet the warmth of the Sun. This will be on the 27th of March, following the Full Moon of March 23rd:

> While in December the Christ withdrew the Earth-soul element into the interior of the Earth, in order to be insulated from cosmic influences, now with the out-breathing of the Earth he begins to let his forces breathe out, to extend

---

8 *Journal for Star Wisdom* 2010, pp. 19–20.
9 *ACE Complete*, p. 688.

them to receive the forces of the Sun which radiate toward him.[10]

We wait with expectant longing for the Full Moon and the Sunday that follows. The Full Moon is the spatial declaration announcing the triumph of solar forces over lunar forces. The first Sunday, however, marks the union of the spatial event with *time*. This restraint is the meaning behind the Lenten and Easter mystery. The Easter Sun is a benediction that marks the handing of the Earth over into the embrace of cosmic warmth and light.

As we advance in our understanding of the festivals, we will come to realize that while we in the northern hemisphere are celebrating the vernal point at 5° Pisces, in six months' time (around Michaelmas), those who live in the southern hemisphere will celebrate their springtide—with their vernal point occurring at 5° Virgo. With the southern hemisphere holding center, while the northern hemisphere expands to St. John's Tide, there is balance. With the northern hemisphere holding center as the southern peoples celebrate St. John's, the same balance is achieved. This is hygienic for the *one* consciousness of *one* whole Earth in its yearly respiration.

March 23: Full Moon and penumbral lunar eclispe 8° Virgo opposite Sun 8° Pisces. This eclipse will be visible in Asia, Australia, the Pacific, and the western Americas. This is the first Full Moon after the Spring equinox. The Sunday following this Moon is Easter. This Full Moon brings to flowering the inaugurating mystery of this lunar cycle: the healing of the nobleman's son. Two weeks ago we contemplated the necessity of maintaining our vertical-spiritual relationship to our sovereign "I." Now we contemplate the miracles that are possible through the power of the Christ "I."

The mystery of the loaves (Virgo) and the fishes (Pisces) are represented by today's Full Moon. With the Moon at this degree, this very miracle occurred—the feeding of the five thousand with five loaves and two fish (Monday, Jan/29/31). The five loaves, the two fish, and a couple of honeycombs were laid upon a napkin in baskets. As Jesus

divided these foods, they were instantly replenished. After passing the baskets to the hungry multitudes, another basket was passed to gather up the scraps—twelve baskets of bread returned. Of the fish, none was left. The consumption of bread on the Mt. of Beatitudes was a communion with the twelvefold powers of space—the zodiac. Just as only a small piece of bread is necessary in the holy sacrament, so also was the hunger of the masses satisfied with the bread communion of which they partook this day. Christ brought the power of the star beings into the substance of bread, thus filling the souls who hungered and thirsted for righteousness. This occurred on a Monday—the day of the Holy Trinity.

The fish communion is different. It does not depend on the forces descending from the Father; rather, the fish communion involves the inner Earth mysteries in relationship to the Mother in the depths. It was later this night that Christ would walk on water, held up by the powers of spiritual warmth rising upward from the Mother's realm below. Nothing in him caused him to sink, for he was the sinless one.

As the Moon stands witness to this miracle, we choose whether we will be one of the twelve or one of the 5,000. The twelve bore witness to the Christ "I," whereas the 5,000 saw only the earthly power of Jesus and sought to crown him king. The twelve, bearing witness to the spiritual kingliness of Christ, were imprinted with a force that would permeate their being into eternity.

The "force" weaving through the world—represented by the honeycomb—is the force of the divine feminine. Honey is radiantly golden, sweet to both the tongue and the belly. It is woven by hexagonal figures, each forming the "key of David"—signifying the door which opens through our moral development. *Through this door we behold the Omega point of evolution's culmination—the resurrection of both Nature and humanity to the pristine state of original creation.* The hexagram is symbolic of the etheric body, which depends on life forces from the Mother's elemental world in order to maintain its vibrant health. Just as milk and honey wove among the children of ancient Israel, so now is the Mother sending milk and honey to sustain the children

---

10 Steiner, *The Cycle of the Year*, p. 7.

joining her community of Eternal Israel. Her force is the focus of the eleventh Arcanum of the Tarot—Force—"that which overcometh every subtle thing":

There are two principles which one has to understand and distinguish when one wants to go deeply into the Arcanum of Force. The one is the principle of the serpent, and the other is that of the Virgin. The former is opposition from which there proceeds friction which produces energy. The other is concordance from which comes fusion which engenders *force*.

And it is authentic victory that one must hope for and wait for in the conflict that tradition represents as the struggle between the Archistrategist Michael and the dragon. The day when it is achieved will be the day of a new festival—the festival of the coronation of the Virgin on Earth. For then the principle of opposition will be replaced on Earth by that of collaboration. This will be the triumph of life over electricity. And cerebral intellectuality will then bow before Wisdom (Sophia) and will unite with her.

"To overcome every subtle thing" is therefore equivalent to changing opposing forces—mental, psychic and electrical—into friendly and allied forces. The "subtle things" to overcome are the intellectual forces of temptation based on doubt, the psychic forces of temptation based on sterile enjoyment, and the electrical forces of temptation based on power.

In the last analysis, the "subtle things" meant here are therefore equivalent to temptations. However every temptation is similar to a two-way flow of traffic. Because when evil tempts good, it is itself at the same time "tempted" by the latter. Temptation always entails contact, and therefore an exchange of influence. Every beautiful temptress, in attempting to tempt a saint, risks finishing up by "wetting his feet with her tears, wiping them with the hair of her head, kissing them, and annointing them with ointment" (Luke 7:38). Do we not have prefigured here the victory over the "great prostitute Babylon"? Have we not discovered the root and core of the much celebrated and lamented "fall of Babylon," described in chapters 17 and 18 of the Apocalypse?[11]

The Force that the Mother sends from the depths of Shambhala fortifies human beings in preparation for the fish initiation—the Earth trial—that is now upon us. Collectively we are crossing the threshold into our inner world. Herein we will meet the tempters. We can meditate on Force as the eternal presence of the Holy Virgin Mother whose mantle of protection shines from tonight's Moon. A lunar eclipse sends evil thoughts to Earth, the Mother's mantle of force protects us.

March 25: Venus 21° Aquarius opposite Jupiter 21° Leo (square Saturn 21° Scorpio): The healing of the paralyzed man at the pool of Bethesda (Jan/19/31). Venus remembers this third miracle of Christ, which occurred ten days before the feeding of the 5,000 (commemorated two days ago at the Full Moon). With Venus (the Passion) opposite Jupiter (the Holy Spirit) we contemplate any idleness or excess of emotion that hinders our soul's harmonious integration. In square to Saturn in Scorpio, tension mounts as the ego faces mysteries previously concealed. Meditative silence finds the inflowing grace of powers who bestow the quality of compassion (Leo) and the quality of patience (Scorpio).

The healing of the paralyzed man occurred on a Friday—Venus day. The man's egoism in his past life was the cause of his paralysis in his current life. His patience was extraordinary, as he had been waiting 38 years by the side of the healing pool for the One who would help him.

March 26: Saturn stations before moving retrograde 21° Scorpio: Jesus speaks of humankind's indifference before the prophecies (Tuesday, Mar/21/31). Jesus refers to the prophecy of the birth of the Solomon Jesus child, whom the Magi sought:

He drew their attention to man's indifference respecting the completion of the time marked by the prophets. "It was fulfilled thirty years ago, and yet who thinks of it excepting a few devout, simple-minded people? Who now recalls the fact that three kings, like an army from the East, followed a star with childlike faith seeking a newborn king of the Jews, whom they found in a poor child of poor parents? Three days did they spend with these poor

---

11 Anon., *Meditations on the Tarot,* various excerpts from the eleventh Arcanum.

people! Had their coming been to the child of a distinguished prince, it would not have been so easily forgotten!" Jesus, however, did not say that he himself was that child.[12]

Saturn recalls the ancient prophecies relating to the birth of Zarathustra (the Solomon Jesus) and to the kings who noticed this event. The planet of memory asks us also to remember the prophecies. The kings and prophets are not behind us, living only on the pages of history. Scorpio sees into the hidden occult mysteries; and through Saturn's presence in this constellation, we too are encouraged to recognize the prophets of old—prophets, Steiner foretold, who would now be with us yet again.

Today is Holy Saturday, the second of the three days Christ spent in the darkness of the underworld. Holding silence throughout this day, until sunrise tomorrow, allows the burgeoning promise of the Resurrection to build within us. The descent of Christ to the Mother in the heart of the earthly realm was for the redemption of Nature and the entire Earth. In Paradise the kingdom of the Father and the realm of the Mother were interpenetrated. After the Fall, the two kingdoms fell further and further from each other. Christ descended into the depths of the inner Earth and planted his spirit as a seed in the womb of the Earth. As he began his descent, Virgo was rising in the east. This is the constellation connected to the womb, and to the sowing of seeds that will birth new impulses into the womb of all creation. (See CHA, The Mystery of Golgotha.)

It is incumbent upon each of us to render the Antichrist powerless—through recognizing and resisting his presence in the world. For, if left unnamed, this presence causes fear, uncertainty, and denial that such a force even exists. The presence of the Antichrist leads people to seek worldly power and worldly things in a vain attempt to outrun their fear. Avoidance, however, does not work; instead, it divides people and sets each against the other through wars and other atrocities. In "powerlessness" we stand together with Christ, and bring forth the strength of love and courage that pushes fear into the underworld from whence it came.

March 27: Easter Sunday. Today remembers Christ's resurrection. Each human being can partake in resurrection. It is a matter of uniting our individual will with the will of God. We are born from the world of spirit—as vertically descending spiritual human beings—and we are born into horizontal hereditary lines bearing influences of our ancestry. As we mature spiritually, we take less and less from the horizontal stream and become ever closer to the vertical descending force bearing our divine image and likeness. The physical body we are given is an immortal kernel of indestructible will, eternal in its nature. The elemental substance of the physical body may decompose at death, but the spiritual force of the individual will is eternal:

> Death—disincarnation—signifies the separation of the soul and spirit from the physical body, including its indestructible kernel or resurrection body. Whilst the soul and spirit ascend to the spiritual world—accompanied by the forces of vitality (the "etheric" or "vital body") and psychic forces (the "astral body," i.e., psychic habits, desires, character, and psychic dispositions)—the resurrection body descends in the opposite sense, i.e., below, toward the center of the Earth. As it is active will during life, its descent is due to progressive relaxing of the will. The latter withdraws more and more within itself, instead of the effort concentrated previously on the task of rendering and maintaining the physical body in conformity with the soul and spirit of the incarnated individuality. This withdrawal of the resurrection body within itself after death amounts to what one understands by "peace" in speaking of the peace of the dead.[13]

The Resurrection body is a body of perfect freedom, expressive of the manifestation of the eternal individuality itself. It is the fundamental will underlying all matter. It is the fruition of the vertical line of spiritual descent finding both its upper and lower points unified. Freedom is the realization of the individualized will, free of all impediments in the horizontal line of heredity. *This body is born from the heart of the Earth and soars on wings feathered from the heart of the Galaxy.* It can manifest as

---

12 *ACE Complete*, p. 306.

13 Anon., *Meditations on the Tarot*, p. 580.

light (as happened to Paul at the gates of Damascus), or as a current of warmth, or as a breath of vivifying freshness, or even as a luminous human form (like Christ appearing after his resurrection). Tomberg calls it a "synthesis of life and death, i.e., capable of acting here below as a living person and at the same time enjoying freedom from terrestrial links like a deceased person." Yet the descent of Christ, to unite the resurrection force as a possibility for all humanity, was a deed incomprehensible to the spiritual beings who stood witness.

The spiritual worlds held their breath at the descent of Christ into Hell. A world unknown to the higher hierarchies was being penetrated by Jesus Christ:

> The "gardener" who appeared to the woman made clairvoyant by grief was not a "gardener" from only her perspective. In a deeper sense, he was truly a gardener, because he had acquired the power to cause the Earth's soil to produce the fruits of goodness. From that time forward, the highest human initiates have likewise become "gardeners"; they work for the wellbeing of humanity—and not just the direct concerns of humanity, but also those that reach indirectly through nature and Earth's soil.

> What now occurred was the Resurrection of our Savior; and this takes place as a real rhythm of the Earth and as a spiritual power, creating substance every Sunday anew in every single human being. At this moment, the Savior of the world revealed the whole immeasurable grandeur of his love to the world with which he had completely united himself, as well as with the human beings living on it. At this moment, as the Christ Spirit arises from the grave in the first Resurrection body, he merges into the innermost heart of every human soul. It is now up to us in humility, in devotion and in joy, to celebrate daily this inner core of holiness by becoming aware that we ourselves bear him—the highest and most precious—in us.[14]

Today we celebrate the Risen One and the work of his "gardeners."

March 30: Sun 15° Pisces: Birth of the Solomon Jesus (Mar/5/6 BC). The Solomon Jesus was the reincarnation of the great teacher, Zarathustra, who was visited by the Three Kings. The kings brought the wisdom gathered by initiates in the three preceding cultural ages: myrrh from Ancient India, frankincense from Ancient Persia, and gold from Ancient Egypt. The influence of this great teacher, the Master Jesus, is always present on Earth. There is always an initiate who is working with him, even if he himself is not physically incarnated. The ideal of Pisces, the Sun sign at this birth, is "Not I, but Christ in me." To find this alignment is to supplicate oneself to the force of "celestial gravitation" where the personal will follows the dictums of spiritual will:

> The law of terrestrial gravitation, evolution and earthly life in general is *enfoldment,* i.e., the coagulation of mental, psychic and physical stuff around relative centers of gravitation, such as the Earth, the nation, the individual, the organism—whilst the law of celestial gravitation, evolution, and spiritual life in general is *radiation,* i.e., the extension of mental, psychic and physical stuff rising up to an absolute center of gravitation. "Then the righteous will shine like the sun in the kingdom of the Father" (Matt. 13:43)—this is a precise and comprehensive characterization of the law of celestial gravitation.[15]

May our personal will magnanimously serve the aims of higher worlds.

NOTE: Today marks the 91st anniversary of the death and transition of Rudolf Steiner into spiritual worlds—his death Sun conjunct the birth Sun of the Solomon Jesus; his death Moon conjunct the Sun's position at the Ascension of Christ. Also, today remembers the Sun's location at the death and transition of Daniel Andreev (1959), author of the great work *The Rose of the World,* quoted earlier in this volume. This is a special day!

ASPECT: Mercury 22° Pisces square Pluto 22° Sagittarius. The Resurrection. Mercury remembers the day Christ appeared before Mary Magdalene in the Garden of Resurrection. There he spoke to Magdalene: "Touch me not, for I have not ascended to my Father and your Father." The pastors of humankind are those who now feel the touch denied

---

14 Von Halle, *And if He Had not Been Raised,* p. 127.

15 Anon., *Meditations on the Tarot,* p. 314.

Magdalene. For Christ is with us, and he invites us to touch him and thereby to place our faith upon the foundation of his being. Mercury square Pluto produces a clear mental view. May we see into the depths of truth.

March 31: Mercury conjunct Uranus 25° Pisces: The birth of the Nathan Jesus (Saturday, Dec/6/2 BC). Both Uranus and Mercury recall their location at the birth of this pure and chaste being. See the article in this *Journal,* "The Towers We Build." This aspect grants imaginative vision into the apocalyptic realms of being. First we must bring our minds (Mercury) to stillness.

APRIL 2016

The waning Moon catches up with Venus (both hidden in the glare of the Sun) the day before the New Moon on the 7th in Pisces. In the hours following, the Moon conjuncts Mercury but this too is not visible to us as the Sun hides these planets within its brilliant aura.

On the 14th, the Sun shifts into the constellation of Aries, the Ram. On the 17th, Mars stations Retrograde in Scorpio, traveling slowly backward through the constellation (dipping into Libra and stationing Direct again in the end of May.)

On the 18th, the Moon is almost Full when it joins with Jupiter in the sunset sky. The Moon reaches true Fullness on the 22nd, with Moon in Libra. The Moon catches up with Mars in Scorpio on the 24th and Saturn on the 25th. Just like last month, this is a great way to get a felt sense of the movements of the Moon: begin looking for the Moon's rise about three hours after sunset on the 23rd to orient to Mars and Saturn's location against the backdrop of the stars. Continue each successive night, and notice how the Moon rises an hour later each night! Magic!

On the 29th, Mercury begins to travel Retrograde at the last degrees of the constellation of Aries.

April 1: Venus enters Pisces: "In winning may gain be lost." Venus in Pisces reminds us to guard against undue attachments to things of this world; magnanimity of soul draws forth the comfortor as we begin our individual journey into the passion of Christ. Venus was in Pisces during the entire Passion of Christ.

April 3: Mercury enters Aries: "Lay hold of forces weaving." Mercury in the Ram ennobles the mind wherein devotion to ideals opens one to percieve new truths. Ideals devoid of devotion tend to stir zealousness. Mercury was in Aries at the conception of the Nathan Jesus, the Transfiguration, and when Peter received the keys.

April 6: Sun 22° Pisces square Pluto 22° Sagittarius. Jesus is subject to violent attacks by the Pharisees (Mar/12/31). Sun remembers Jesus speaking of his coming Passion, and of the scapegoat:

> Then he spoke of the goat which at the Feast of Atonement was driven from Jerusalem into the desert with the sins of the people laid upon it. He said very significantly (and yet they did not understand him) that the time was drawing near when in the same way they would drive out an innocent man, one that loved them, one that had done everything for them, one that truly bore their sins.[1]

The constellation of the Archer calls us to stand upright, knowing falsehood, seeking truth. Pluto in this sign, in square to the Sun, warns of the destructive spirit of revolution, filled as it may be with ambition for power. The Pharisees saw Jesus as a threat to their lofty positions, and in the end they murdered him. It is *Natura* who is being driven into the desert, with the sins of humanity laid upon her breast. The power of truth must be reclaimed lest the blind altar of science continue to sacrifice the body of the Earth. Who are the contemporary scapegoats?

April 7: New Moon 23° Pisces: Jesus is teaching the seventh and eighth Beatitudes, surrounded by great crowds (Wednesday, Mar/14/31).

> The whole region around, mountains and valleys, was covered with encampments, and everywhere resounded the question: "Where is Jesus?" Jesus taught upon the seventh and the eighth

---

1 *ACE Complete,* p. 706.

Beatitudes, after which, to escape the crowd, he went with the apostles and disciples on board Peter's ship.[2]

This New Moon is conjunct Uranus (25°21 Pisces), very close to Uranus' position at the birth of the Nathan Jesus (24°59 Pisces). Rudolf Steiner spoke of the Nathan Jesus' Buddhistic qualities, depicting that only those initiated in the mysteries could have any connection with him. Love and compassion are the signatures of the Nathan Jesus (now referred to as the Angel Jesus), exemplified by the fact of his birth Sun occurring in the sign of the Archer (Sun 16° Sagittarius), in the region of the shaft of the Archer's arrow, which points directly toward the Galactic Center at 2° Sagittarius, the heart of our Galaxy—the creative source of Love pouring forth from the Divine Heart of the One Whom Jesus called the Father. The Sun today remembers the Beatitude of persecution (eighth) and the Beatitude blessing the peacemakers (seventh). As a descendent of the Hindu tradition, this Jesus, also known as the sister-soul of Adam, potentizes the mystery stream wherein one penetrates into one's inner nature. Like Jonah being swallowed by the whale, all of us are crossing the threshold—whereby we will encounter the anti-etheric forces opposing the new manifestation of Christ in the etheric.

"I am" is the formula of revelation expressing the essence of Jesus Christ. As we cross the threshold, we are to behave like Peter, knowing who it is that comes to us in the stormy seas of etheric disunity:

> Now, the words "I am; do not be afraid" spoken by the one walking on the water amount to the statement: "I am gravitation, and he who holds to me will never sink or be engulfed." Because fear is due to the menace of being engulfed by elemental forces of gravitation of a lower order, i.e., of being carried away by the play of blind forces from the agitated "sea" of the "electrical field" of death. "I am; do not be afraid" is therefore the message of the center, or Master, of celestial gravitation, demonstrated by the action of support with regard to Peter, who was saved from sinking. Thus, there is another field of gravitation than that of death, and he who

unites himself with it can walk on water, i.e., transcend the agitated element of "this world," the electrical gravitational field of the serpent. This message contains not only the invitation to have recourse to the "kingdom of heaven," but also the solemn declaration of the immortality of the soul, in so far as the soul is capable of transcending the engulfing gravitation and "walking on the water."[3]

Peter was elevated above ordinary consciousness, beyond the confines of reason, memory, and sense perception. Therefore was he able to walk on water—he was drawn by Jesus into a state of ecstasy, i.e., raising himself into the attraction of the divine. Jesus on the other hand, was not in a state of ecstasy; rather he walked on water by virtue of *enstasy*—i.e., centering in himself, which is the active virtue of the formula "I am; do not be afraid."

The peacemakers are called children of God; the persecuted gain the kingdom of God. This New Moon calls forth those serving peace and those persecuted for their belief in Christ. *Those initiated into the new mysteries are now receiving revelation from the Angel Jesus, who in turn serves the Archangel Jesus—through whom Christ is able to reach us. The earthly representative of the ministrations of this Archangel is the individuality in the process of becoming the Maitreya Buddha.* Just as Gautama worked from spiritual realms into the Nathan Jesus, so now do the Archangel Jesus and the Angel Jesus work from spiritual realms into Gautama Buddha's successor. There are an increasing number of souls who are perceiving a new kingdom forming within the life forces of *Natura*. Also perceptible to consciousness raised above its ordinary limitations is the lightning bolt of revelation that accompanies the presence of angelic revelation, and with Uranus standing with this New Moon, towers are threatened. The stormy seas of global discord require that we be not afraid; instead we are to lift ourselves into imaginative consciousness. We can pray for understanding and connection to the forces ushering in a critical shift that is changing the world.

April 9: Sun conjuct Uranus 25° Pisces. The feeding of the four thousand (Thursday, Mar/15/31). Two

---

2 Ibid., p. 707.

3 Anon., *Meditations on the Tarot*, p. 310.

SIDEREAL GEOCENTRIC LONGITUDES : APRIL 2016 Gregorian at 0 hours UT

DAY	☉	☽	☊	☿	♀	♂	♃	♄	♅	♆	♇
1 FR	16♓44	21♐3	26♌39	25♓14	29♒14	12♏23	20♌28R	21♏24R	24♓59	15♒42	22♐26
2 SA	17 43	4♑9	26 40	27 16	0♓28	12 33	20 21	21 23	25 2	15 44	22 27
3 SU	18 42	17 40	26 41	29 16	1 42	12 43	20 15	21 23	25 5	15 46	22 27
4 MO	19 41	1♒38	26 42	1♈15	2 56	12 53	20 9	21 22	25 9	15 48	22 28
5 TU	20 40	16 2	26 43	3 11	4 10	13 2	20 3	21 21	25 12	15 50	22 28
6 WE	21 39	0♓49	26 43R	5 6	5 24	13 10	19 57	21 20	25 16	15 52	22 29
7 TH	22 38	15 54	26 42	6 58	6 38	13 17	19 52	21 18	25 19	15 54	22 29
8 FR	23 37	1♈7	26 40	8 47	7 52	13 24	19 46	21 17	25 22	15 56	22 29
9 SA	24 36	16 20	26 37	10 33	9 6	13 30	19 41	21 16	25 26	15 58	22 30
10 SU	25 35	1♉21	26 33	12 15	10 21	13 36	19 36	21 14	25 29	16 0	22 30
11 MO	26 34	16 3	26 29	13 53	11 35	13 41	19 31	21 13	25 33	16 2	22 30
12 TU	27 33	0♊19	26 25	15 27	12 49	13 45	19 26	21 11	25 36	16 3	22 30
13 WE	28 32	14 8	26 23	16 57	14 3	13 49	19 21	21 9	25 40	16 5	22 30
14 TH	29 31	27 30	26 22	18 21	15 17	13 52	19 16	21 7	25 43	16 7	22 31
15 FR	0♈30	10♋27	26 23D	19 41	16 31	13 54	19 12	21 6	25 47	16 9	22 31
16 SA	1 28	23 3	26 24	20 56	17 45	13 55	19 8	21 4	25 50	16 11	22 31
17 SU	2 27	5♌21	26 26	22 5	18 59	13 56	19 3	21 1	25 53	16 12	22 31
18 MO	3 26	17 27	26 27	23 9	20 13	13 56R	18 59	20 59	25 57	16 14	22 31
19 TU	4 24	29 24	26 27R	24 8	21 27	13 55	18 56	20 57	26 0	16 16	22 31R
20 WE	5 23	11♍16	26 26	25 1	22 41	13 54	18 52	20 55	26 4	16 17	22 31
21 TH	6 21	23 5	26 23	25 48	23 55	13 51	18 49	20 52	26 7	16 19	22 31
22 FR	7 20	4♎54	26 18	26 29	25 9	13 49	18 45	20 50	26 10	16 21	22 31
23 SA	8 18	16 45	26 11	27 5	26 23	13 45	18 42	20 47	26 14	16 22	22 31
24 SU	9 17	28 40	26 3	27 35	27 37	13 40	18 39	20 44	26 17	16 24	22 30
25 MO	10 15	10♏40	25 55	27 59	28 51	13 35	18 37	20 41	26 20	16 25	22 30
26 TU	11 14	22 48	25 47	28 17	0♈4	13 29	18 34	20 39	26 24	16 27	22 30
27 WE	12 12	5♐5	25 40	28 30	1 18	13 22	18 32	20 36	26 27	16 28	22 30
28 TH	13 10	17 35	25 35	28 37	2 32	13 15	18 29	20 33	26 30	16 30	22 29
29 FR	14 9	0♑19	25 32	28 38R	3 46	13 7	18 27	20 30	26 34	16 31	22 29
30 SA	15 7	13 21	25 31	28 34	5 0	12 58	18 26	20 27	26 37	16 32	22 29

INGRESSES :

1 ♀ → ♓ 15: 2
   ☽ → ♑ 16:29
3 ☿ → ♈ 8:53
   ☽ → ♒ 21:14
5 ☽ → ♓ 22:41
7 ☽ → ♈ 22:13
9 ☽ → ♉ 21:49
11 ☽ → ♊ 23:27
14 ☽ → ♋ 4:34
   ☉ → ♈ 11:56
16 ☽ → ♌ 13:29
19 ☽ → ♍ 1:12
21 ☽ → ♎ 14: 3
24 ☽ → ♏ 2:40
25 ♀ → ♈ 22:32
26 ☽ → ♐ 14: 6
28 ☽ → ♑ 23:25

ASPECTS & ECLIPSES :

1 ☽ ☌ ♇ 2:35
4 ☽ ☌ ♆ 23:41
5 ☽ ☍ ♃ 6:32
   ☽ ☌ ☋ 17:24
6 ☽ ☌ ♀ 7:59
   ☉ □ ♇ 20: 7
7 ☉ ☌ ☽ 11:22
   ☽ ☌ ♅ 14:55
   ☽ ☌ P 17:42
8 ☽ ☌ ☿ 13:40
9 ☉ ☌ ♅ 21:24

10 ☽ ☍ ♂ 20: 4
11 ☽ ☍ ♄ 8:35
   ☽ ⬚S ☊ 17:23
13 ☽ ☍ ♇ 14:56
14 ☉ □ ☽ 3:58
17 ☽ ☍ ♆ 21:33
18 ☽ ☌ ♃ 3: 3
   ☽ ☌ ☊ 18: 3
19 ♀ □ ♇ 20:46
21 ☽ ☍ ♀ 1:53
   ☽ ☍ ♅ 6:12

   ☽ ☌ A 16:17
22 ☉ ☍ ☽ 5:22
   ♀ ☌ ♅ 20:57
23 ☽ ☍ ☿ 21:44
25 ☽ ☌ ♂ 5:44
   ☽ ☌ ♄ 19:46
26 ☽ ⬚N ☊ 5:47
28 ☽ ☌ ♇ 9:19
30 ☉ □ ☽ 3:27

SIDEREAL HELIOCENTRIC LONGITUDES : APRIL 2016 Gregorian at 0 hours UT

DAY	Sid. Time	☿	♀	⊕	♂	♃	♄	♅	♆	♇	Vernal Point
1 FR	12:39: 8	23♈18	4♒48	16♍44	11♎1	25♌8	16♏14	25♓24	14♒44	20♐43	5♓ 2' 0"
2 SA	12:43: 5	29 23	6 23	17 43	11 30	25 12	16 16	25 24	14 44	20 43	5♓ 2' 0"
3 SU	12:47: 1	5♉33	7 58	18 42	11 59	25 17	16 17	25 25	14 44	20 44	5♓ 2' 0"
4 MO	12:50:58	11 48	9 34	19 42	12 28	25 22	16 19	25 26	14 45	20 44	5♓ 1'59"
5 TU	12:54:55	18 5	11 9	20 41	12 57	25 26	16 21	25 26	14 45	20 44	5♓ 1'59"
6 WE	12:58:51	24 24	12 44	21 40	13 26	25 31	16 23	25 27	14 45	20 45	5♓ 1'59"
7 TH	13: 2:48	0♊44	14 19	22 39	13 55	25 35	16 25	25 28	14 46	20 45	5♓ 1'59"
8 FR	13: 6:44	7 1	15 54	23 38	14 25	25 40	16 26	25 28	14 46	20 45	5♓ 1'59"
9 SA	13:10:41	13 16	17 29	24 37	14 54	25 44	16 28	25 29	14 46	20 46	5♓ 1'59"
10 SU	13:14:37	19 27	19 4	25 36	15 23	25 49	16 30	25 29	14 47	20 46	5♓ 1'59"
11 MO	13:18:34	25 32	20 40	26 35	15 52	25 53	16 32	25 30	14 47	20 46	5♓ 1'59"
12 TU	13:22:30	1♋30	22 15	27 34	16 22	25 58	16 34	25 31	14 48	20 46	5♓ 1'58"
13 WE	13:26:27	7 20	23 50	28 32	16 51	26 2	16 36	25 31	14 48	20 47	5♓ 1'58"
14 TH	13:30:24	13 2	25 25	29 31	17 20	26 7	16 37	25 32	14 48	20 47	5♓ 1'58"
15 FR	13:34:20	18 35	27 1	0♎30	17 50	26 12	16 39	25 33	14 49	20 47	5♓ 1'58"
16 SA	13:38:17	23 59	28 36	1 29	18 20	26 16	16 41	25 33	14 49	20 48	5♓ 1'58"
17 SU	13:42:13	29 13	0♓11	2 27	18 49	26 21	16 43	25 34	14 49	20 48	5♓ 1'58"
18 MO	13:46:10	4♌17	1 47	3 26	19 19	26 25	16 45	25 35	14 50	20 48	5♓ 1'58"
19 TU	13:50: 6	9 12	3 22	4 25	19 48	26 30	16 47	25 35	14 50	20 49	5♓ 1'57"
20 WE	13:54: 3	13 57	4 58	5 23	20 18	26 35	16 48	25 36	14 50	20 49	5♓ 1'57"
21 TH	13:57:59	18 33	6 33	6 22	20 48	26 39	16 50	25 37	14 51	20 49	5♓ 1'57"
22 FR	14: 1:56	23 0	8 8	7 20	21 18	26 44	16 52	25 37	14 51	20 50	5♓ 1'57"
23 SA	14: 5:53	27 19	9 44	8 19	21 48	26 48	16 54	25 38	14 52	20 50	5♓ 1'57"
24 SU	14: 9:49	1♍30	11 19	9 17	22 17	26 53	16 56	25 39	14 52	20 50	5♓ 1'57"
25 MO	14:13:46	5 33	12 55	10 16	22 47	26 57	16 57	25 39	14 52	20 51	5♓ 1'57"
26 TU	14:17:42	9 28	14 30	11 14	23 17	27 2	16 59	25 40	14 53	20 51	5♓ 1'56"
27 WE	14:21:39	13 17	16 6	12 12	23 47	27 7	17 1	25 40	14 53	20 51	5♓ 1'56"
28 TH	14:25:35	17 0	17 42	13 11	24 18	27 11	17 3	25 41	14 53	20 52	5♓ 1'56"
29 FR	14:29:32	20 36	19 17	14 9	24 48	27 16	17 5	25 42	14 54	20 52	5♓ 1'56"
30 SA	14:33:28	24 7	20 53	15 7	25 18	27 20	17 6	25 42	14 54	20 52	5♓ 1'56"

INGRESSES :

2 ☿ → ♉ 2:24
6 ☿ → ♊ 21:14
11 ☿ → ♋ 17:55
14 ⊕ → ♎ 11:46
16 ♀ → ♓ 21: 8
17 ☿ → ♌ 3:39
23 ☿ → ♍ 15:19

ASPECTS (HELIOCENTRIC +MOON(TYCHONIC)) :

1 ☿ ☌ ☊ 1: 0
   ☽ □ ♅ 8: 3
2 ☽ □ ♂ 13:38
3 ☿ □ ♀ 12:31
4 ☿ □ ♆ 11:16
   ☽ ☌ ♀ 14:56
   ☿ ☍ ♄ 17:21
   ☽ ☌ ♆ 21:53
5 ☽ □ ♄ 0:31
   ⊕ □ ♇ 1:27
   ☽ □ ☿ 5:55

   ☽ ☍ ♃ 15:24
   ☿ ☌ P 17:41
6 ☿ □ ♃ 4:14
7 ♀ ☌ ♆ 6:47
   ☽ □ ♇ 7:39
   ☽ ☌ ♅ 15: 5
8 ♀ □ ♄ 8:19
   ☽ ☍ ♂ 21:39
9 ⊕ ☍ ♅ 21:24
10 ☿ ☍ ♇ 5:10
   ☽ □ ♆ 21:55
15 ☽ □ ♂ 14:33

   ☿ □ ♅ 23:53
11 ☽ ☍ ♄ 0:48
   ☿ □ ⊕ 5: 0
   ☽ □ ♀ 8:38
   ☽ □ ♃ 16:33
   ♀ ⬚S ☊ 18: 7
13 ☽ ☍ ♇ 11:49
   ☽ □ ♅ 20:24
14 ♀ ☍ ♃ 11: 3
   ☿ □ ♂ 20:21
16 ☽ ☌ ☿ 3: 9
17 ☽ ☍ ♆ 18:45

   ☿ ⬚N ☊ 22: 4
   ☽ ☌ ♄ 12:29
   ☽ □ ♄ 22:34
18 ☽ ☌ ♃ 18: 6
19 ☽ ☍ ♀ 9:15
20 ☿ ☍ ♆ 4:34
   ☿ □ ♄ 14:52
   ☽ □ ♇ 19:24
21 ☽ ☍ ♅ 5: 8
22 ☿ ☌ ♃ 21: 2

23 ☽ ☌ ♂ 10:37
25 ☽ □ ♆ 8:20
26 ☽ □ ♃ 8:21
27 ☽ □ ☿ 22:26
28 ☽ □ ♀ 0:15
   ☽ ☌ ♇ 6:14
   ☿ ☍ ♀ 8:10
   ☽ □ ♅ 15:21
   ♂ ☌ ♇ 20:17
29 ☿ □ ♆ 1:44

   ♀ □ ♇ 23:49
30 ☿ ☍ ♅ 11: 3
   ☽ □ ♂ 22:17

days after the events recalled in the New Moon (two days ago), Christ performed this miracle. Sun and Uranus are today exactly conjunct the position of Uranus at the birth of the Nathan Jesus. As revealed by Steiner, the stages of evolution describe the unfolding of existence in time. This is depicted in the feeding of the 4,000 with seven loaves of bread and seven fish. Time has torn asunder the "likeness of God" in which we were created. The eternal aspect of our "Image" however, cannot be defiled. Our "likeness" must find faith like unto Abraham:

> Faith is the firm assurance of things hoped for, the conviction of things not seen…. By faith Abraham obeyed when he was called to go out to a place which he was to receive as an inheritance; and he went out, not knowing where he was to go. (Heb. 11, 1:8)

Abraham had therefore had "the firm assurance of things hoped for" after having experienced "the conviction of things not seen," i.e., his will knew, whilst his mind and imagination "did not see" or did not have the kind of assurance proper to them. All the same, he obeyed and left without knowing where he was going, i.e., he acted before his thought and imagination had understood the whole world implied in his action. When he left, therefore, his head followed his feet; his feet were then "above," in so far as they experienced the commandment of heaven, and his head obeyed them and was turned "below," in so far as it saw nothing but the privations, risks and perils of the enterprise. Abraham therefore found himself precisely in the condition of the Hanged Man of our Arcanum.[4]

The feeding of the 4,000 is bound up with the "seven days of existence," the seven days of creation.

> We are now in the fourth day of existence, three preceding days having already elapsed, and three days are to come. Each day of existence has a Christian aspect which solarizes the course of evolution, so that in the course of time each day takes on a solar apsect through Christ.[5]

To obey intuitions as did Abraham, we will find our way into the solar stream of revelation now fructifying during this Abraham millennium (2000–3000 AD). Faith is key when the future is calling us onto unknown ground.

April 15: Sun enters Aries: "Arise, O shining light" (Steiner, *Twelve Cosmic Moods*). William Bento illumines this mantra:

> A call is heard as the Sun enters the sign of Aries. It is a call to not merely arise, but to awaken. The Sun effortlessly does this every morning, bestowing light upon us all. Should we not follow the Sun in this way? In the heart of every human being there lives this light that can be made available to others every day. It is our mandate to make it available to all every day, and in every way that aids an awakening to the many miracles that take place daily.

Aries and "The Lamb and his Bride" reflect the process of spiritualization (Christ) and interiorization (Sophia). The teachings of Hermes in ancient Egypt, in particular the teachings of Isis and Osiris, contained a pre-Christian understanding of the relationship between the Lamb and his Bride. The first decan is ruled by Mars and is associated with the Girdle of Andromeda, symbolizing the power of unity and purity worn by the Mystic Woman who represents the soul of humanity.

April 18: Mars stations 14° Scorpio before moving retrograde. Mars was opposite today's degree at the feeding of the 4,000.

April 19: Venus 22° Pisces square Pluto 22° Sagittarius. Venus remembers Jesus entering a castle where prisoners were held (Jan/25/33). When Jesus made known his intention to enter the castle, his disciples made objections, fearing he would give occasion for scandal. He told them he would enter with or without them. Within were all kinds of people, some prisoners, others sick and infirm. The inmates gathered around him, whereby he separated several from the rest. After giving bail for those he had separated he departed with them and his disciples, traveling up the Jordan throughout the night.[6]

Venus square Pluto can cause storms in the emotional life if passions are not governed by the free

---

4 Anon., *Meditations on the Tarot*, p. 317.
5 *CHA*, p. 93.

6 See *ACE, Complete*, p. 944.

will. This dynamic tension bestows awakenings to instinctual impulses, which may be striving for the light. By analogy we see that in the castle of prisoners Jesus separated two groups: those who were prepared to release themselves from bondage to lower passions and those who may not have been so willing. Three months after this event, Jesus was crucified. The Age of Pisces has taken us fully into the material world and woefully beyond—into subearthly depths of existence. Those who long ago made pacts with anti-forces are now empowered by laws born of instincts spawned from Hades (lower Pluto). Vaccinations and the legal protection of Monsanto's agenda are some examples of such hellish laws. It will take a massive (and peaceful) uprising to separate moral law from immoral oppression.

Pluto stations at 22° Sagittarius before moving retrograde. We recall the persecution of the early Christians and the holy task of protecting our Mother Earth.

April 22: Full Moon 7° Libra opposite Sun 7° Aries: The cleansing of the temple (Thursday, Apr/6/30).

> Vendors had again erected tables to sell their wares, and Jesus demanded that they withdraw. When they refused, he drew a cord of twisted reeds from the folds of his robe. With this in hand, he overturned their tables and drove the vendors back, assisted by the disciples. Jesus said: "Take these things away; you shall not make my Father's house a house of trade."[7]

It was also the day of a Full Moon when Jesus cleansed the temple. The light of the Aries Sun shines on the pious lunar face as it recalls the cleansing of the temple. We can imagine the shame that rightly would accompany our awakening to the enormity of debasing influences we have allowed to enter our culture. *A culture is the expression of the morality of a society—it defines what it means to be human. It is the temple in which the human soul finds its inspiration toward goodness. The totality of all souls forms the social organism which, in memory of our Edenic origins, ever strives to become a chaste reflection of the world soul: Sophia—wisdom—the one virgin body from whence all souls originate.* Moon in Libra calls forth social consciousness:

> Carl Gustav Jung, whilst admitting the partial truth of the doctrines of Freud and Adler, was led by his clinical experience to the discovery of a much deeper layer of the psyche than that studied by Freud and Adler. He had to admit the reality of a religious layer, which lies at a much greater depth than the layers of sex and of the will-to-power. Thus, thanks to the work of Jung, [the human being] is fundamentally *Homo religiosus*, a religious being, though he may also be an economic entity, a sexual entity and an entity aspiring to power.
>
> Now, Carl Gustav Jung reestablished the principle of chastity in the domain of psychology—the other psychological schools mentioned being contrary to chastity, since they break down the unity of the spiritual, psychic and physical elements of the human being. He discovered the divine breath at the core of the human being.
>
> At the same time, the work of Jung constitutes the inauguration of a new method in the domain of psychology. It is the method of exploration of psychic layers in succession—corresponding to the layers of archaeology, paleontology and geology. And just as archaeology, paleontology and geology regard the layers with which they have to do as archives of the past (as time becomes space), so does the depth psychology of the school of Jung treat psychic layers as the living past of the soul, which is as distant as the layer in question is deep. The measure of depth here is at the same time that of the history of the soul's past, going back beyond the threshold of birth. One can well discuss whether the layers are collective or individual, whether their continuance is due to heredity or reincarnation—but one can no longer deny the reality of these layers or their value as a key to the psychic history of [humankind]. More than that: one can no longer deny the fact that in the psychic domain, *nothing dies* and that the whole past *lives*, present in the diverse layers of the depths of consciousness—the "unconscious" or subconsciousness—of the soul. Paleontological and geological layers contain only the imprints and fossils of the now dead past; psychic layers, in

---

7 Ibid., p. 311.

contrast, constitute a living witness to the actual past. They are the past, which continues to live. They are *memory*—not intellectual, but psychically *substantial*—of the actual past. For this reason nothing perishes and nothing is lost in the domain of the psyche; essential history, i.e., real joy and suffering, real religions and revelations of the past, continue to live in us, and it is in we ourselves that the key to the essential history of mankind is to be found.[8]

The increase of animal behavior in human beings reveals the fact that sub-realms are rising from shadowy depths to destroy the organism of culture. Hence does Sophia weep, as did Rachel, for her children notice not the presence of the depraved, nor the influence that seeps from the womb of the anti-Sophia. It is up to each of us to play our part in cleansing the culture in preparation for the coming Age of Sophia. Change can occur more quickly than we may imagine.

ASPECT (2): Venus conjunct Uranus 26° Pisces: Accompanying this Full Moon, we can imagine Venus raising a "pleading cup" in which to receive the revelation now streaming from the Angel Jesus. This pleading cup is related to the reemerging of the pineal gland as a spiritual organ of sight. Venus at this degree remembers Jesus teaching of the inner union (symbolized by milk and water) which represented his eternal union with those who follow him. This aspect increases receptivity to the *manas*-light of revelation. Venus at 26° Pisces reaches her exaltation (27°).

April 24: Sun 10° Aries. The visitation of Mary to Elizabeth (Sunday, Mar/30/2 BC). The Sun remembers the quickening of the Adam soul through the power of the higher "I" overlighting the Jesus child in Mary's womb.

April 25: Venus enters Aries: "Take hold of growth's being." As the Full Moon's influence wanes, we are called to practice loving devotion to ideals that can truly manifest a renewal of culture. Venus was in Aries at the conception of the Nathan Jesus, as well as at the Ascension and at Pentecost.

April 26: Sun 12° Aries: Cosmic memory of the Last Anointing (Wednesday, Apr/1/33). Mary Magdalene's last anointing of Christ set the betrayal by Judas in motion. "Truly, I say to you, wherever this gospel is proclaimed in the whole world, what she has done will also be told in memory of her" (Matt. 26:13). Magdalene's devotional comprehension stands in opposition to Judas's inability to see what was right before him—Christ. It takes courage to represent the new in the face of those muttering against its possibility, as Judas muttered against Magdalene. Now Christ is present in the etheric realms surrounding the Earth; he is with us. Will we know him or those proclaiming him? Are we Judas—or Magdalene?

April 28/29: Sun 13°/14° Aries: Cosmic memory of The Last Supper through the Nailing on the Cross: (Apr/2–3/33). The Sun today remembers the most wretched moments in the life of Christ up to his final victory on the hill of Golgotha. All that Christ then experienced *from* humanity, allows him to *give to* humanity now. The deeds done to him during the Passion created the opening in the laws of karma that allows him to now spiritually *touch* us in this time of the Second Coming. Christ gives all his love to humanity, as humanity once gave all of its hatred to him. Each step of the way must be contemplated as the greatest mystery of Earth evolution. The Passion of Christ is the path of the initiate. *We may pray for the strength to willingly carry the cross of our own burdens, for this lightens the Cross of Christ.* In the words of Judith von Halle:

> There can be no fantasy or even wish on the part of the spiritual pupil of entering upon a path of cognition that would be broad and well-trodden, easy and without effort. The path of cognition that one takes is one's own. Hence no one has entered upon it before. At the beginning of the journey, at the time of one's decision to commit, it actually does not exist at all. It is one's task to direct oneself through the morass of one's soul urgings, and to direct one's I through the "soul emptiness of space," through the "time-destroying stream."[9]

---

8 Anon., *Meditations on the Tarot*, pp. 128–129.

9 Von Halle, *The Descent into the Depths of the Earth*, p. 20.

The sacred freedom that Christ brought to all humanity is a force of guidance directing each of us to find our *own way,* upon *our own untrodden path,* to realize *our own initiation.* This demands sobering sanctification for the preservation of free impulses as intended by Rudolf Steiner, in devotion to his founding of the School for Spiritual Science. He could only have founded this school as an affirmation for the necessity of independent research. This is the sacred ground upon which Anthroposophy has been founded.

Mercury goes retrograde.

April 30: Sun 15° Aries: Cosmic memory of the Descent into Hell and the Resurrection (Apr/5/33). The depth of this mystery holds the promise that each human being may become a Christ Bearer. The words of the Risen Christ to Mary Magdalene sound throughout time: "Touch me not, for I am not yet ascended unto the Father; but go unto my brethren, and say to them, I ascend unto my Father and your Father, and my God and your God" (John 20:17). These words contain the powerful fact that Christ, following his descent to the Mother on Holy Saturday, would then, following the Resurrection, ascend to his Father, thereby restoring the unity between the Mother in the depths and the Father in the heights. The coming Ascension (forty days from this memory) was a deed that would also unite fallen humanity with its divine archetype—an archetype sacrificed at the time of the Fall. From the moment of the Resurrection onward he has been within us. This eternal oneness with Christ interconnects the whole of humanity into brotherhood and sisterhood. The actual awakening of the disciples to the reality of this oneness came only later at the Holy Whitsun Festival. During the forty days between the Resurrection and the Ascension, the disciples were in a kind of sleep. Images from their daily life with Christ during his three and one half years on Earth rose into their consciousness (etheric images). These images helped them understand the cosmic teachings Christ was giving during these forty days after the Resurrection. It is just these cosmic teachings that were culled from mainstream Christianity, and these cosmic teachings are resurrecting in this time of the Second Coming through great teachers now working with us.

Valentin Tomberg, in his summary of the last four stages of the Passion (the carrying of the cross, the crucifixion, the entombment, and the resurrection) brought the image of the Rose Cross:

> This picture is the Rose Cross, which epitomizes not only the higher stages of the Passion but also, in fact, the whole path of Christian initiation. It is the symbol of the narrow way of sacrifice and the forces of resurrection that flower on this path. Death and resurrection are the two fundamental themes of the Christian spiritual path, and the two were united in the symbol of the Rose Cross.
>
> Thus the black cross with the glowing red roses can summarize all we have said here about Christian initiation; it can stand, if only for a moment, before the inner eye of the reader's soul as a token of the solemn spirit world and, at the same time, as the author's Easter greeting to his readers.[10]

The Sun at this degree sends strengthening forces to anyone whose heart opens to receive the unfathomable mercy of Christ in one's devotion to a path of initiation.

MAY 2016

The New Moon is on the 6th, in the constellation of Aries. Both Venus and Mercury (who is still Retrograde in Aries) are very close to the Sun now, with the Mercury Sun conjunction on the 9th and Venus and Mercury coming together on the 13th. (Venus and the Sun, however, will wait until June to conjunct!)

Jupiter stations Direct on the 9th in the constellation of the Lion, and the waxing Moon catches up on the 14th. The Sun shifts into Taurus (the Bull) on the 15th, and by the 21st the Moon is across the Zodiac from the Sun, forming the Full Moon of Scorpio with the Sun in Taurus. Once again Venus and Mercury are in the mix, but cannot be seen because of their close proximity to the Sun.

---

10 Tomberg, *Christ and Sophia,* p. 290.

The next night, the 22nd, Mars will be exactly opposite the Sun and so at its brightest of the year. Mars will rise on the eastern horizon as the Sun sets (as any object will do when it is opposite the Sun) but will show off its brilliance best later in the month once the Full Moon isn't competing with it's light!

Shining Saturn is also in Scorpio with Mars, to the left of the red planet. In between the two lies the star Antares, the "Heart of the Scorpion." It, like Mars, is quite red [hence the name "Ant-Ares," not Aries, the god of war]; enjoy this opportunity to learn the difference between these two! The apparently still Full Moon joins Saturn on the 22nd. Mercury stations Direct on the 23rd.

This month, heliocentric Venus, moving through the whole of Aries and the first decan of Taurus, recalls a wealth of events: the birth (Sep/7/21 BC), death (Aug/15/44), and Ascension (Aug/16/44) of the Blessed Virgin (on the 29th, 13th, and 14th, respectively), as well as the miracles of the feeding of the five thousand and the walking on water (Jan/29–30/31) on the 10th of May.

May 1: Sun 16° Aries: Cleansing of the temple. See commentary for April 22, wherein the Full Moon recalled this event.

May 2: Sun 17° Aries: Appearance in Emmaus (Apr/6/33). It is not through our limited "horizontal perception" that we discern spirits who walk with us; rather, it is the heart that sees what the horizontal occludes. In the days following the Resurrection, Christ walked with his disciples:

The heart perceives diverse presences as impressions and nuances of spiritual warmth. It is thus that the hearts of the two disciples going to Emmaus recognized the One who went on the way with them before their eyes and their understanding did, and who said to one another after their eyes opened and they recognized him: "Did not our hearts burn within us while he talked to us on the road, while he opened to us the scriptures?" (Luke 24:32).

The day after the Resurrection, Luke and Cleophas were traveling to Emmaus when a third person joined them. That evening the three went to a guesthouse, where they were served food. The third person took the bread, blessed it, and broke it into small pieces. Through this act the disciples recognized their traveling companion, who was Christ.

May we open to the warmth of our heart's knowing, so that we too may recognize who now walks with us.

May 5: Today marks the Christian celebration of Ascension Thursday. Ascension marks the 40th day following Easter Sunday, commemorating Christ growing increasingly radiant before disappearing into the clouds. He comes again in the clouds as the Etheric Christ.

May 6: New Moon 21° Aries. The Moon was at this degree shortly after the Ascension of Christ (May/14/33).

The apostles and disciples now felt themselves alone. They were at first restless and like people forsaken. But by the soothing presence of the Blessed Virgin they were comforted, and putting entire confidence in Jesus's words that she would be to them a mediatrix, a mother, and an advocate, they regained peace of soul.[1]

Christ has now returned to the realm from whence he departed from his disciples at the Ascension. The Holy Virgin remains the eternal mediatrix between the human soul and Christ. The Maitreya Bodhisattva individuality serves as a bearer of the Christ and Sophia mystery. (Sophia united with the Blessed Virgin at the event of Pentecost).

Counter to the above reality, we find in the most recent phenomena of our epoch the strong movement toward social and collective state control; however subtle its means, it is ridiculously blatant. Desires are being met by faux measures, and as the eye turns toward insatiable hunger for things of this world, the beast stalks the cities.

Wisdom in the eyes of humankind is folly in the eyes of God; therefore, in certainty of its intellectual knowledge, the human spirit blindly lives in folly. Inversely, Hermeticists sacrifice the intellect to spirituality, lest imaginative consciousness become enfeebled and atrophied. This is the consciousness now needed so desperately. Avatars are beings who

---

1 *ACE Complete*, p. 1362.

SIDEREAL GEOCENTRIC LONGITUDES :   MAY 2016 Gregorian at 0 hours UT

DAY	☉	☽	☊	☿	♀	♂	♃	♄	♅	Ψ	♇
1 SU	16 ♈ 5	26 ♉ 44	25 ♌ 32	28 ♈ 24R	6 ♈ 14	12 ♏ 48R	18 ♌ 24R	20 ♏ 23R	26 ♓ 40	16 ≈ 34	22 ♐ 28R
2 MO	17 3	10 ≈ 31	25 33	28 10	7 28	12 37	18 22	20 20	26 44	16 35	22 28
3 TU	18 1	24 42	25 33R	27 51	8 42	12 26	18 21	20 17	26 47	16 36	22 28
4 WE	19 0	9 ♓ 18	25 32	27 29	9 56	12 14	18 20	20 13	26 50	16 38	22 27
5 TH	19 58	24 13	25 29	27 2	11 10	12 1	18 19	20 10	26 53	16 39	22 27
6 FR	20 56	9 ♈ 22	25 24	26 32	12 24	11 48	18 18	20 6	26 57	16 40	22 26
7 SA	21 54	24 35	25 17	26 0	13 37	11 34	18 18	20 3	27 0	16 41	22 26
8 SU	22 52	9 ♉ 42	25 8	25 26	14 51	11 19	18 17	19 59	27 3	16 43	22 25
9 MO	23 50	24 32	25 0	24 50	16 5	11 3	18 17	19 55	27 6	16 44	22 25
10 TU	24 48	8 ♊ 58	24 52	24 13	17 19	10 47	18 17D	19 51	27 9	16 45	22 24
11 WE	25 46	22 56	24 46	23 37	18 33	10 31	18 17	19 48	27 12	16 46	22 23
12 TH	26 44	6 ♋ 24	24 42	23 1	19 47	10 14	18 18	19 44	27 15	16 47	22 23
13 FR	27 42	19 25	24 40	22 26	21 0	9 56	18 18	19 40	27 19	16 48	22 22
14 SA	28 40	2 ♌ 1	24 39D	21 53	22 14	9 38	18 19	19 36	27 22	16 49	22 21
15 SU	29 38	14 18	24 40	21 22	23 28	9 19	18 20	19 32	27 25	16 50	22 21
16 MO	0 ♉ 36	26 20	24 40R	20 54	24 42	9 0	18 21	19 28	27 28	16 51	22 20
17 TU	1 34	8 ♍ 14	24 39	20 29	25 56	8 41	18 22	19 24	27 31	16 52	22 19
18 WE	2 31	20 2	24 36	20 8	27 9	8 21	18 24	19 20	27 34	16 53	22 18
19 TH	3 29	1 ♎ 51	24 31	19 50	28 23	8 1	18 25	19 15	27 37	16 54	22 17
20 FR	4 27	13 41	24 22	19 37	29 37	7 40	18 27	19 11	27 39	16 55	22 16
21 SA	5 24	25 37	24 12	19 28	0 ♉ 51	7 20	18 29	19 7	27 42	16 55	22 16
22 SU	6 22	7 ♏ 39	24 0	19 23	2 4	6 59	18 31	19 3	27 45	16 56	22 15
23 MO	7 20	19 50	23 47	19 23D	3 18	6 38	18 34	18 58	27 48	16 57	22 14
24 TU	8 17	2 ♐ 10	23 34	19 27	4 32	6 17	18 36	18 54	27 51	16 57	22 13
25 WE	9 15	14 39	23 23	19 36	5 46	5 56	18 39	18 50	27 54	16 58	22 12
26 TH	10 13	27 19	23 15	19 49	6 59	5 35	18 42	18 45	27 56	16 59	22 11
27 FR	11 10	10 ♑ 11	23 9	20 7	8 13	5 14	18 45	18 41	27 59	16 59	22 10
28 SA	12 8	23 18	23 6	20 29	9 27	4 53	18 48	18 37	28 2	17 0	22 9
29 SU	13 5	6 ≈ 40	23 5	20 55	10 41	4 32	18 51	18 32	28 4	17 0	22 8
30 MO	14 3	20 21	23 5	21 26	11 54	4 11	18 55	18 28	28 7	17 1	22 7
31 TU	15 1	4 ♓ 22	23 5	22 1	13 8	3 51	18 58	18 23	28 10	17 1	22 6

INGRESSES :

1	☽ → ≈	5:45	21 ☽ → ♏	8:46
3	☽ → ♓	8:47	23 ☽ → ♐	19:49
5	☽ → ♈	9:11	26 ☽ → ♑	5:2
7	☽ → ♉	8:34	28 ☽ → ≈	12:5
9	☽ → ♊	9:0	30 ☽ → ♓	16:35
11	☽ → ♋	12:29		
13	☽ → ♌	20:7		
15	☉ → ♉	9:10		
16	☽ → ♍	7:21		
18	☽ → ♎	20:15		
20	♀ → ♉	7:29		

ASPECTS & ECLIPSES :

2 ☽ ☌ Ψ 10:22	☉ ☌ ☿ 15:11	☉ ☍ ☽ 21:13	30 ☽ ☌ ☋ 4:43
☽ ☍ ♃ 13:21	10 ☽ ☍ ♇ 23:2	☽ ☌ ♂ 22:42	
3 ☽ ☌ ☋ 1:24	13 ☉ □ ☽ 17:1	22 ☉ ☍ ♂ 11:16	
5 ☽ ☌ ♅ 4:15	☿ ☌ ♀ 19:9	☽ ☌ ♄ 22:19	
6 ☽ ☌ P 4:27	15 ☽ ☍ Ψ 5:2	23 ☽ □N ☊ 7:34	
☽ ☌ ♀ 5:11	☽ ☌ ♃ 8:0	25 ♀ ☍ ♂ 2:37	
☉ ☌ ☽ 19:28	☽ ☌ ☊ 20:39	☽ ☌ ♇ 14:19	
7 ☽ ☌ ☿ 2:9	18 ☽ ☍ ♅ 15:21	26 ♃ □ ♄ 12:26	
8 ☽ ☍ ♂ 2:32	☽ ☌ A 22:12	29 ☉ □ ☽ 12:11	
☽ ☍ ♄ 16:30	20 ☽ ☍ ♇ 11:46	☽ ☌ Ψ 18:11	
9 ☽ □S ☊ 0:44	21 ☽ ☍ ♀ 11:38	☽ ☍ ♃ 21:29	

SIDEREAL HELIOCENTRIC LONGITUDES :   MAY 2016 Gregorian at 0 hours UT

DAY	Sid. Time	☿	♀	⊕	♂	♃	♄	♅	Ψ	♇	Vernal Point
1 SU	14:37:25	27 ♍ 33	22 ♓ 29	16 ♎ 5	25 ♎ 48	27 ♌ 25	17 ♏ 8	25 ♓ 43	14 ≈ 54	20 ♐ 52	5 ♓ 1'56"
2 MO	14:41:22	0 ♎ 54	24 4	17 4	26 18	27 29	17 10	25 44	14 55	20 53	5 ♓ 1'56"
3 TU	14:45:18	4 11	25 40	18 2	26 49	27 34	17 12	25 44	14 55	20 53	5 ♓ 1'55"
4 WE	14:49:15	7 23	27 16	19 0	27 19	27 38	17 14	25 45	14 55	20 53	5 ♓ 1'55"
5 TH	14:53:11	10 32	28 51	19 58	27 50	27 43	17 16	25 46	14 56	20 54	5 ♓ 1'55"
6 FR	14:57: 8	13 38	0 ♈ 27	20 56	28 20	27 48	17 17	25 46	14 56	20 54	5 ♓ 1'55"
7 SA	15: 1: 4	16 40	2 3	21 54	28 51	27 52	17 19	25 47	14 57	20 54	5 ♓ 1'55"
8 SU	15: 5: 1	19 40	3 39	22 53	29 21	27 57	17 21	25 48	14 57	20 55	5 ♓ 1'55"
9 MO	15: 8:57	22 37	5 15	23 51	29 52	28 1	17 23	25 48	14 57	20 55	5 ♓ 1'55"
10 TU	15:12:54	25 31	6 51	24 49	0 ♏ 22	28 6	17 25	25 49	14 58	20 55	5 ♓ 1'55"
11 WE	15:16:51	28 24	8 27	25 47	0 53	28 10	17 26	25 50	14 58	20 56	5 ♓ 1'54"
12 TH	15:20:47	1 ♏ 15	10 2	26 45	1 24	28 15	17 28	25 50	14 58	20 56	5 ♓ 1'54"
13 FR	15:24:44	4 4	11 38	27 43	1 55	28 20	17 30	25 51	14 59	20 56	5 ♓ 1'54"
14 SA	15:28:40	6 52	13 14	28 40	2 26	28 24	17 32	25 52	14 59	20 57	5 ♓ 1'54"
15 SU	15:32:37	9 39	14 50	29 38	2 57	28 29	17 34	25 52	14 59	20 57	5 ♓ 1'54"
16 MO	15:36:33	12 25	16 27	0 ♏ 36	3 28	28 33	17 35	25 53	15 0	20 57	5 ♓ 1'54"
17 TU	15:40:30	15 10	18 3	1 34	3 59	28 38	17 37	25 53	15 0	20 57	5 ♓ 1'54"
18 WE	15:44:26	17 55	19 39	2 32	4 30	28 42	17 39	25 54	15 1	20 58	5 ♓ 1'53"
19 TH	15:48:23	20 40	21 15	3 29	5 1	28 47	17 41	25 55	15 1	20 58	5 ♓ 1'53"
20 FR	15:52:20	23 25	22 51	4 27	5 32	28 51	17 43	25 55	15 1	20 58	5 ♓ 1'53"
21 SA	15:56:16	26 10	24 27	5 25	6 3	28 56	17 45	25 56	15 2	20 59	5 ♓ 1'53"
22 SU	16: 0:13	28 55	26 3	6 23	6 35	29 1	17 46	25 57	15 2	20 59	5 ♓ 1'53"
23 MO	16: 4: 9	1 ♐ 40	27 40	7 20	7 6	29 5	17 48	25 57	15 2	20 59	5 ♓ 1'53"
24 TU	16: 8: 6	4 27	29 16	8 18	7 38	29 10	17 50	25 58	15 3	21 0	5 ♓ 1'52"
25 WE	16:12: 2	7 15	0 ♉ 52	9 16	8 9	29 14	17 52	25 59	15 3	21 0	5 ♓ 1'52"
26 TH	16:15:59	10 3	2 29	10 13	8 41	29 19	17 54	25 59	15 3	21 0	5 ♓ 1'52"
27 FR	16:19:55	12 53	4 5	11 11	9 12	29 23	17 55	26 0	15 4	21 1	5 ♓ 1'52"
28 SA	16:23:52	15 45	5 41	12 8	9 44	29 28	17 57	26 1	15 4	21 1	5 ♓ 1'52"
29 SU	16:27:49	18 39	7 18	13 6	10 15	29 32	17 59	26 1	15 4	21 1	5 ♓ 1'52"
30 MO	16:31:45	21 34	8 54	14 3	10 47	29 37	18 1	26 2	15 5	21 2	5 ♓ 1'52"
31 TU	16:35:42	24 32	10 31	15 1	11 19	29 42	18 3	26 2	15 5	21 2	5 ♓ 1'52"

INGRESSES :

1	☿ → ♎	17:28
5	♀ → ♈	17:11
9	♂ → ♏	6:27
11	☿ → ♏	13:28
15	⊕ → ♏	9: 0
22	☿ → ♐	9:27
24	♀ → ♉	10:59

ASPECTS (HELIOCENTRIC +MOON(TYCHONIC)) :

2 ☽ ☌ ♂ 7:31	9 ☽ ☌ ♀ 5:45	16 ☽ ☍ ♃ 4:28	☽ ☌ ♄ 20: 0	31 ⊕ □ Ψ 1:47
☽ □ ♄ 11:22	☿ ☌ ☋ 7:46	☿ □ Ψ 22:30	23 ☽ □ ♃ 18: 9	☿ □ ♅ 12: 4
3 ♀ ☌ ♅ 1: 7	☿ ☌ ⊕ 15:11	17 ☿ ☌ ♄ 21:36	24 ☽ ☌ ☿ 5:42	♀ ☍ ♂ 17:57
☽ ☍ ♃ 4:46	10 ☽ ☍ Ψ 20:29	18 ☽ □ ♇ 1:52	25 ☽ ☌ Ψ 12: 4	
4 ☽ □ Ψ 18:41	11 ☽ ☍ ♅ 5: 5	☽ ☍ ♅ 11:56	☽ □ ♅ 21:29	
5 ☽ ☌ ♅ 2:27	12 ☿ ☌ ♂ 1:35	19 ☿ ☌ A 18: 8	29 ☽ □ ♀ 1:15	
☽ ☌ ♀ 8:14	☽ ☌ ♀ 7:33	20 ☽ ☌ ♇ 21:18	☽ ☌ Ψ 6:36	
6 ☽ ☍ ☿ 8:24	14 ☽ □ ♂ 0:49	21 ☽ ☌ ♂ 21:45	☽ ☌ Ψ 14:48	
7 ☽ ☍ ♂ 6:58	☽ ☍ ☿ 12:10	22 ☿ □ ♃ 0:51	☽ □ ♄ 19:55	
8 ☽ □ Ψ 8:26	15 ☽ ☍ Ψ 1:22	⊕ ☌ ♂ 11: 4	30 ☽ ☍ ♃ 16: 1	
☽ ☍ ♄ 12:20	☽ ☌ ♄ 6:29	☽ □ Ψ 14:34		

are culminating points of the revelation streaming from above, whilst Buddhas are culminating points for certain epochs of human history (wherein the soul awakens). Avatars represent the descent of the divine; Buddhas represent the ascent of the human through individual striving. Jesus Christ was, and is, the complete union of Avatars and Buddhas. The world awaits the Kalki Avatar and the Maitreya Bodhisattva:

> It was more discreetly, and without putting a particular person in the limelight as candidate, that Dr. Rudolf Steiner, founder of the Anthroposophical Society, predicted the manifestation—again in the first half of the twentieth century—not of the new Maitreya Buddha or Kalki Avatar, but rather of the Bodhisattva. i.e., the individuality in the process of becoming the next Buddha, whose field of activity he hoped the Anthroposophical Society would serve. A new disappointment! This time the disappointment was due not to an error with regard to the awaited individuality, nor even with regard to the time of the beginning of his activity, but rather to an overestimation of the Anthroposophical Society on the part of its founder—thus nothing became of it.[2]

The Kalki Avatar awaited by the Hindus and the Maitreya Buddha awaited by the Buddhists will manifest in a single personality. Cognition of the presence of this great spiritual teacher will be through the mediatrix of the Holy Virgin. After Christ's Ascension, the disciples were bereft, lacking awareness of the fuller meaning of the promise of Christ's future return "in the clouds." The presence of Christ can now be felt by all, and the Etheric Christ will speak through the single personality—the Kalki Avatar / Maitreya Bodhisattva. We must recognize this teacher in our time.

Does it still remain true that Steiner's overestimation of his followers must continue? Without the continual guidance of spiritual teachers, souls on Earth will become ever more restless and forsaken.

The New Moon in Aries asks us to stay awake, to pioneer rather than follow, and to grasp the ideals streaming from the future *as it manifests.* Leaders

see what is not yet evident; thus are they often the heretics of history.

May 7: Sun 22° Aries: Jesus appears to eleven disciples (Saturday, Apr/23/33). Still under the influences of the Full Moon, the Sun recalls the Risen One, who appears when hearts are prepared to receive him.

May 9: Inferior conjunction Sun and Mercury 24° Aries. Mercury remembers Solomon Mary's first communion (Thursday, Apr/23/33). Shortly after midnight the Blessed Virgin Mary received the holy sacrament from Peter (three weeks after the Last Supper). During this communion, Jesus appeared to her. Later she retired to her room to pray, and toward dawn the Lord appeared to her again and gave her power over the Church, a protective force, such that light flowed from him into her. In this we see a stage in the preparation for the event of Pentecost coming in the weeks that follow. The Virgin Mary could listen to the presence of the Christ. In stark contrast to this radiant event, we have in modern life a tragic assault on silence, damaging not only our faculty of hearing but also overriding the sense of inner quietude required for inner listening. Constant noise tends to drown out the inspiration of idealism which the healthy soul is seeking.

One of the attributes of Sophia is the "voice of silence" that enables one to hear the heart of another. We can remember the Virgin Mary's first communion and her ability to hear the presence of Christ, and we can pray for harmlessness toward all the creatures of our Mother's Earth.

May 10: Sun 25° Aries: The appearance of the Risen One to the seven disciples (Wednesday, Apr/15/33). This occurred at the northeast end of the Sea of Galilee (John 21:1–23). Here Peter is bid three times to "Feed my sheep." He is given the task to be the spiritual leader of the Church, to ensure that the sacraments, Holy Communion above all, continue to be celebrated for all time. Peter asks what will become of John, and the Risen One answers: "If it is my will that he remain until I come, what is that to you?" Implicit here is the task of the Church of John to wait until the Second Coming of Christ in

---

2 Anon., *Meditations on the Tarot,* p. 614.

the etheric realm. The Church of Peter has the task to lead human beings to the threshold of the spiritual world, and the Church of John has the task of leading them across the threshold into the spiritual world. John and Peter work together, united in their service to Christ and Sophia. The Church of John is centered in the heart, and those who choose to join this Church are summoned by the call of the Grail. Corresponding to the Mass in the exoteric church is the Grail Mystery in the esoteric church. Grail communion is communion with the Beings of the stars, which requires a crossing of the threshold—which in turn requires a meeting with the fallen nature of the soul in the depths of the underworld. This is why it is the John being that Rudolf Steiner claims will be with us at the end of the century. For it was John who accompanied Lazarus through the underworld after his death, and before he was raised by Christ.

We live now in the time of the Second Coming, a time when the Church of John is opening. This is a time when humanity is both collectively and individually crossing the threshold. Moreover, it is a time when star wisdom is being reborn as communion with heavenly beings. With the Sun in Aries—the constellation of self-sacrifice, spiritual strength and leadership—we may feel inspired to open to the vastness of the mysteries surrounding us in our everyday life. Alternatively we may find we are excessively caught up in the small story of our "little" biography. As our interest in others and in the vastness of other worlds that interact with us increases, new possibilities are revealed. We may ask ourselves: What about John? Where do I stand before the Hermetic mysteries? The John mystery is complex.[3]

May 13: Mercury conjunct Venus 22° Aries. Mercury remembers Jesus visiting the beekeepers (May/6/31).

> They pursued their journey for about an hour to a place which was the principal seat of the bee-raising industry. Far off toward the rising sun stood long rows of white beehives, about the

height of a man and woven, I think, of rushes or bark. They had many openings, and were placed one above another. Every group had in front of it a flowery field, and I noticed that balm grew here in abundance. Each field, or garden, was hedged in, and the whole bore the appearance of a city. [4]

Honey is an elixir for the astral body (Mercury). We die because we fray our nerves. Nervous disorders are increasing. The faster the speed of technology, the more rapidly does time slip through our fingers. Even young children are being deprived of the wonder of endlessly flowing time. The more we hurry them, the greater we tax their nervous system, thus causing forces of death to draw closer to them. With today's conjunction occurring in Aries, we can practice devotion to measured movement through time. Time has a marvelous ability to contract or expand according to our perceptions—it is a living Being: it is Christ indwelling the present moment!

May 15: Sun enters Taurus: Sun in Taurus: "Shine forth, O glory of being" (Steiner, *Twelve Cosmic Moods*): William Bento illumines this mantra:

> The shining light is here defined as a glorious being. It is not a phenomenon dissected as a scientific empirical fact. It is alive with being-ness. And surrounding this being is an aura of glory. Can you now gaze at the Sun with new eyes? Can you now look into another's eyes and see a glimmer of this glorious being? When this indeed occurs in our seeing we can experience the awe, wonder, and reverence of the sacredness of the "I/Thou" consciousness out of which each human being shines forth.

In Taurus, Inner Balance becomes Progress. The work of transforming the will is paramount. The first decan is ruled by Venus and is associated with Perseus, who was helped by Athena to overcome the Medusa.

NOTE: Today is the Christian celebration of Pentecost.

May 20: Venus enters Taurus: "Feel growth's power." Venus in Taurus asks us to take in cosmic

---

3 For deeper clarity and understanding, see Powell, *The Mystery, Biography and Destiny of Mary Magdalene,* ch. 3.

4 *ACE Complete,* p. 755.

thoughts, digest them, and make them our own. Thus will our words bring forth wisdom and healing. Venus was in Taurus at the Transfiguration.

May 21: Full Moon 6° Scorpio opposite Sun 6° Taurus. The Moon was at this degree on the day Jesus commissioned the disciples to go into the world and heal (Sunday, Dec/10/30). The Sun on the Epiphany (January 6th, 2016) recalled this event, thus proclaiming that this memory is to be carried throughout the seasons of this year into the coming time of Michaelmas. At the commissioning, Jesus told the disciples to go forth with what they had learned, proclaiming the advent of the kingdom. The rising of the kingdom now forming, from the forces of the Etheric Christ within the body of *Natura,* is a theme for the entire Abraham millennium (2000–3000 AD). With the Moon in Scorpio the virtue of patience is highlighted, as this is what allows us to gain insight into the work of the adversarial beings. Gautama Buddha gave us the eightfold path as a means of encountering the forces lying within our unconscious soul. He was the great teacher of "wakefulness." In light of the intensification of the presence of the Angel Jesus, working in etheric realms in our surrounding, we are called to awaken to the healing powers he is bestowing on behalf of the Etheric Christ. Yet, forces lying deep within oppose just this. In the thirteenth Arcanum of the Tarot we read:

> The human machine *functions* according to the determined program "maximum pleasure at minimum cost" in such a way as to lend itself to precise prediction in its reactions to given circumstances. In the intellectual domain it rejects every notion and every idea which does not harmonize with the intellectual system established in it; in the psychic domain it rejects all that does not harmonize with the complex of "happiness" established in it; and in the physical domain it automatically follows the orders transmitted by the complex "instinct" established in it.
>
> It is only the *functioning* of the human machine when a rich man declares himself anti-communist and a poor man declares himself pro-communist. But it is a *miracle*—that is to say an act of freedom—when a rich man

abandons his possessions and embraces poverty, as did St. Anthony the Great and also many other saints, and also Carmelites, Franciscans, Dominicans, etc., who took the vow of poverty. The *miracle* of St. Francis is not only the healing of a leper but also the love of St. Francis for "Lady Poverty." Did not the miracles of Jesus Christ, after the resurrection of Lazarus, culminate in the cross on Calvary where, in the full agony of torture, he said: "Father, forgive them, for they know not what they do" (Luke 23:34)?

All that one *does* is miraculous; all intellectual, psychic, and physical *functioning* according to "nature"—i.e., according to human automatism, is mechanical. The *Sermon on the Mount* is the teaching of *doing* and of the triumph over functioning.

> Love your enemies, do good to those who hate you, bless those who curse you…and pray for those who persecute you, so that you may be sons of your Father who is in heaven. (Luke 6:27–28; Matt. 5:44–45)

Is this not a teaching that aims at the liberation of the machine, i.e., of all *functioning,* and which is a school for the miraculous?

> Because to bless those who curse you is a miracle from the point of view of the "normal and natural" functioning of the reactions of the human machine. This does not just happen, it is done (it is created); and I repeat, one only does miracles, and all that is done is a miracle, and nothing is done without it being a miracle. All that is not a miracle is not really done—it happens, as part of automatic functioning. It is only through the miracle that true being expresses itself, that the creative Word is revealed.[5]

The Moon shining in tonight's sky reminds us of miracles, of the power Christ bestows to his disciples in order that miracles may be *done.* We are to recall all that is in us which is dead, in order to resurrect our intuitive capacities from the ghosts within who have swallowed our faith. *To awaken on the path of illumination is to recall the nightside of our being, wherein our "image" constantly beckons us to prodigally return to the One from*

---

5 Anon., *Meditations on the Tarot,* p. 350.

whom we were created. May we find the courage to remember the divine order, so as to gain insight into the usurper's world of deception.

May 22: Sun 7° Taurus opposite Mars 7° Scorpio. Mars, the planet representing Michael, faces the power of resurrection inherent in the Sun. This aspect asks us to shine light into the darkness, choosing the path of Michaelic service, rather than merely entertaining conflict for the love of battle. The mighty Thrones speak from the sphere of Mars, and in Scorpio the call to reveal evil sounds forth. The influence of the Full Moon is still with us. Michael asks us to do what needs to be done! The Sun was at this degree when Jesus spoke of the sacredness of marriage.

May 23: Mercury goes direct.

May 24: Venus 6° Taurus opposite retrograde Mars 6° Scorpio. Venus remembers the healing of Theokeno (Sept/28/32). This aspect calls for the art of compromise and a firm grasp of our emotional nature. The Passion of Christ stands across the heavens from Michael, presenting a wonderful opportunity to transform any aggressive tendencies. Anger is a primary signature of luciferic influences:

> Lucifer's light glitters in the soul, distracting it from the light of Christ. These dazzling flashes of light have a certain delusiveness about them, by which I mean they do not fill the measure of the soul with life-giving light, but instead elicit a feeling of a shallow pleasure in the astral body, which is one aspect only of the soul. But because Lucifer's light is ephemeral, it cannot abide continuously within the soul, and so recedes, leaving the astral body hungering for more such passing pleasure.[6]

Our souls ultimately seek peace, yearning to be raised from their fallen state—just as Theokeno rose from his sickbed with Venus so very near today's degree.

Venus in Taurus imaginatively invokes the gold crown of Isis—she who could read the cosmic script. When Jesus was visiting the remaining two magi, he spent considerable time in conversations with the gold king, who represented the Egyptian mysteries and the solar consciousness of star wisdom. Venus marks the sphere wherein dwell the Archai—Time Spirits overseeing great evolutionary cycles. Indeed, the return to star wisdom dawns anew in our time. This aspect stirs the will to serve Michael's battle against evil.

May 26: Jupiter 19° Leo square Saturn 19° Scorpio. Saturn remembers the birth of the Nathan Mary (Sunday, July/17/17 BC). The Nathan Mary was connected with the spiritual stream of love and compassion that attained its high point in Hinduism and in Buddhism. In the microcosmic mystery initiations originating from these peoples, aspirants learned how to descend into their inner world as did Gautama Buddha. With Saturn remembering the birth of the Nathan Mary who bequeathed her etheric sheath upon the Soloman Mary at the Baptism in the Jordan, we can strive to awaken to our inner (unconscious) desire nature in dynamic relationship with the wise gaze of the Queen of Heaven—Wisdom–Sophia, calling forth our attunement to Jupiter. This aspect offers us the courage to find compassion (Leo) for all beings, and the will to see into the hidden realms (Scorpio) of the underworld.

May 29: A grand square forms today between Saturn (18° Scorpio), Neptune (17° Aquarius), Venus/Sun (15°–17° Taurus), and Jupiter (19° Leo). In the re-envisioning of the planets (see article in this *Journal*, "The Towers We Build"), we see the Holy Virgin (Saturn) in dynamic relationship to the Goddess Night (Neptune) and the Holy Spirit (Jupiter), opposite the Passion and Resurrection forces (Venus/Sun). This grand square occurs in the fixed stars—closely aligned with the Royal Stars of Persia—thus calling forth restraint in the feeling nature. Alternatively, a lack of restraint may result in explosive passions. This square is active through the 6th of June. See *Meditations on the Tarot*, Letter XVI, The Tower of Destruction, p. 458, for a deeper understanding of these hermetic analogies.

May 31: Sun today is conjunct Aldebaran 15° Taurus, one of the four royal stars of Zoroastrian

---

6 Isaacson, *Through the Eyes of Mary Magdalene*, vol. 2, p. 145.

teaching—Aldebaran, together with a second royal star, Antares (15° Scorpio) forming the defining axis of the zodiac. As described in Robert Powell's book *Astrogeographia: Correspondences between the Stars and Earthly Locations* (coauthor: David Bowden), the city of Vienna mirrors the star Aldebaran on earth.

JUNE 2016

The month begins with the Sun very close to the "Eye of the Bull": the Royal Star of Aldebaran, at 15° of Taurus (the Bull). On the 3rd the Sun is opposite Saturn, which makes it an excellent time to observe its rings through a telescope, especially now with the dark skies of a New Moon; see if a local observatory has viewing hours and prepare to be amazed!

The 4th brings the New Moon in Taurus, Venus hidden beneath the Sun's rays and the exact conjunction between these two unfolding about a day later, the only exact conjunction they will share this year.

By the 11th, the waxing Moon catches up with Jupiter in Leo. Retrograde Mars dips back into Libra on the 12th and the Sun moves forward into Gemini on the 15th. The almost Full Moon joins Mars on the 17th, Saturn on the 18th and is truly Full on the 20th (Moon in Sagittarius, Sun in Gemini.)

The month ends with Mars stationing Direct (on the 30th) in Libra.

In the first week of June, the Sun squares Neptune, opposes Saturn, and squares Jupiter; because Venus is only a few hours behind the Sun, Venus follows the Sun to form these same aspects, all of which occur in the fixed signs of Taurus, Leo, Scorpio, and Aquarius.

June 1: Sun 17° Taurus square Neptune 17° Aquarius. Jesus spoke of the prophet Malachi (May/7/31). There was an unbroken line of prophets from Abraham to Malachi. Each prophet prepared his successor. It was in serene tranquility, without commotion, that the schools of the prophets performed their exercises, studying to master a deep silence in the presence of the spiritual world. Once the silence reached a certain stage, the spiritual world began to speak.

Today's aspect can affect our emotional nature, disrupting inner silence, as Neptune tends to dissove egoism, thus revealing that in us which has fallen into illusion. The higher aspect of this transcendental planetary sphere is the Goddess Night—Sophia. Inversely, in its lower octave it represents the antiSophia (referred to in the Bible as the whore of Babyon). In contemplation of Malachi we can enter into silence, and therein we may discover the prophecy of the coming of the beast, whose presence in now near—and likely intensifying. Allowing Neptune/Sophia to dissolve the maya of egoism prepares the way for hearing higher inspirations. May we find this guidance as we face the trial of unmasking the anti-Christ and the anti-Sophia in our time.

June 3: Venus 17° Taurus square Neptune 17° Aquarius (opposite Saturn 18° Scorpio). Now Venus squares Neptune, as did the Sun two days ago. To progress in our inner development we need to cultivate a conscious relationship between our etheric body and the world etheric. Thus do we find a kingdom "not of this world," as protection for the growing menace of adversarial influences. They too inspire. Stalin was inspired by demons sounding from the anti-etheric worlds. Through these heinous beings he was informed of the murders he would execute the following day. *This aspect cautions us to overcome any defensiveness originating from our lack of honesty regarding our shadow nature.* The truth sets us free and in freedom we become instruments for higher hearing—Divine Inspiration—Neptune. It is not insignificant that Neptune in Aquarius stands opposite its position during the mournful years of Stalin's dark rule in the 1930s of the twentieth century.

ASPECT (2): Sun 18° Taurus opposite Saturn 18° Scorpio: Jesus taught regarding the second petition of the Lord's Prayer: Thy kingdom come (May/9/31). Indeed, through developing a healthy etheric body, one is able to perceive the new kingdom now forming, through the instreaming of the moral ether. This is something that will not be fully realized until the far future. Yet, due to the awakening of forces from Shambhala rising upward, and the descending forces of the Angel Jesus (carrying the messages of the Etheric Christ), a virginal goodness is forming around all things. It is critical that we spend our attention carefully. To see evil as well as the good develops *manas* cognition. Sun opposite Saturn is a Full Saturn—meaning Saturn is being fully illumined by the Sun. Saturn, the planet of memory, quickens under the gaze of the Sun, reminding us of the occult forces (Scorpio) battling behind the world of appearances.

June 4: New Moon 19°54' Taurus. A Great Cross appears in the heavens today. This cross has been with us since the end of May and will remain active through the 6th of June—today it is very tight. The two beams of the cross: (1) Moon/Venus/Sun (Taurus) opposite Saturn (Scorpio); (2) Jupiter/North Node (Leo) opposite Neptune/South Node (Aquarius). Dynamic tension abounds! This New Moon is the inaugural event to the cosmic memory of the Ascension of Christ commemorated in four days time. At this exact degree (also during a New Moon) Jesus healed three blind boys (Thursday, May/10/31). "Jesus asked the boys if they would like to see the light, and then—much to their joy—he healed them."[1]

"Would you like to see the light?" This same question is currently being asked by the Angel Jesus, who is now serving the fifth sacrifice of Christ—wherein *manas* cognition is the *new light* bestowing revelation to those willing to see through higher capacities. Taurus is the constellation of rationalism, whereby the idealism of Aries must now become substantive thought. The bull digests (through four stomachs) in order to resurrect cosmic thoughts (from out of one's own self) into creative power on Earth. Thus does the speech of the cosmos become the creative word of individuals. It is through faith in the power of the healing word that we are able to resurrect what is dead. All efforts toward this goal serve the manifestation of the New Heaven and the New Earth—wherein both Nature and humanity will rise from all effects of the Fall. Jesus embodied the New Heaven and the New Earth as representative of our future.

Jesus wept, and used the power of the Word to raise Lazarus from the dead. This same power will resurrect Nature when human will aligns with divine will:

> Now, Jesus weeping manifests the tender love of the mother; Jesus, deeply moved again, coming to the tomb and saying, "Take away the stone," manifests the active love of the father; and Jesus crying with a loud voice, "Lazarus, come forth," sounds the trumpet in serving as the Angel of Resurrection. The loud voice crying, "Lazarus, come forth" is the sound of the trumpet of Resurrection, which changes the love of the mother and the love of the father into a magical call.
>
> The magic of resurrection, aspired to by the twentieth Arcanum of the Tarot, is therefore that of the sound of the voice of love of the mother and that of love of the father united. Just as the earthly father and mother give life to the child at his incarnation, where the Angel of Life sounds the trumpet in order to call his soul into incarnation—and the "trumpet" formed by his outspread wings is then turned above—so do the celestial Father and Mother restore the child to life at his resurrection, where the Angel of resurrection sounds the trumpet in order to call his soul and his body to resurrection—and the "trumpet" formed by his outspread wings is then turned below.[2]

This New Moon can remind us that we too can be raised from our entombment in the serpent's illusory world. An Angel is calling in a loud voice, asking us to awaken. We must awaken! If we do not align our will with the will of creation, the serpent will swallow us whole. Blindness is not an option. There are three Akashic chronicles: the higher chronicle consists solely of *symbolic* facts, the lower chronicle consists precisely of concrete facts. The latter is quantitative, the former qualitative. Yet, there is still a third chronicle of which the Apocalypse speaks:

> Books were opened...also another book was opened, which is the book of life. And the dead

---

1 *ACE* Complete, p. 758.

2 Anon., *Meditations on the Tarot,* p. 560.

were judged by what was written in the books, by what they had done. (Revelation 20:12)

The third chronicle is called the "Book of Life." It contains only what is of eternal value—what is worthy of resurrection:

The "Book of Life" is therefore the moral memory of the world. Therefore it does not contain forgiven and atoned-for sins. All forgiving and atonement entails change in the "book of life" or the third Akashic chronicle. For this reason it is constantly modified—written and rewritten from day to day. For just as within the individual's moral memory the accounts to be adjusted are cancelled for those whom one has pardoned—consciously forgetting them—so forgiven and atoned-for sins are effaced from the "Book of Life." Divine memory forgets forgiven and atoned-for sins.

A cross stands in the fixed signs of the Zodiac as the Full Moon remembers the healing of three blind boys. When we atone for our transgressions and forgive with purity of heart, we efface inscriptions from the Book of Life. Thus do we prepare to receive the *manas* light the Angel of Resurrection now bestows—so we too may see. We can rejoice, knowing that in four days we commemorate the Ascension, when the Angels of the Ascension trumpet the good news of the etheric return of Christ.

NOTE: Today marks the entrance of heliocentric Jupiter into Virgo. In Robert Powell's characterization of the descent of Christ through the nine subearthly spheres, he outlines the twelve-year cycle that indicates this descent. The descent is marked by Jupiter's heliocentric ingress into sidereal Virgo. Each time Jupiter enters sidereal Virgo hermetically (from the perspective of the Sun, i.e., heliocentrically), a new layer of the interior of the Earth begins to be penetrated by the Christ consciousness. The transition from the seventh subearthly sphere to the eighth subearthly realm has commenced!

The "I" of Christ shines its fire into the darkness of the subearthly realms; and the fire's light is illumined by Sophia, who understands the emanations Christ is bringing. Light without understanding only blinds. Understanding without light only betrays. For the past twelve years Christ has been in the seventh subearthly realm known as the "mirror Earth." The antidote to this sphere is contained in the seventh Beatitude: *Blessed are the peacemakers for they shall be called children of God.* Today the "I" of Christ enters the eighth subearthly sphere, which finds its antidote in the eighth Beatitude: *Blessed are those who are persecuted for righteousness sake, for theirs is the kingdom of heaven.* This new twelve-year cycle will be active until 2028.

June 5: Sun superior conjuction with Venus 21° Taurus. Jesus described the Persian King Djemschid as a false type of Melchizedek (Friday, May/11/31). Jesus is teaching among the pagans and answering all kinds of questions. When he was asked about the wise Djemschid, Jesus agreed that Djemschid was wise and intelligent in things of the sense world, but that he was nonetheless a false Melchizedek. Jesus told them to direct their attention to Melchizedek, as well as to Abraham and his descendents. Jesus said many more things concerning the prophets, and he dwelt especially upon the prophet Malachi, the last in the prophetic tradition (marking those carrying the blessing of Melchizedek) of ancient Israel. Each prophet foresaw the coming of the Messiah.

A superior conjunction between Sun and Venus means Venus is behind the Sun, gathering intuitions and streaming them to Earth as impulses of will. We can follow the advice of Jesus and direct our attention to the presence of Abraham. He *speaks the good,* continuing the blessing of Melchizedek, thus quickening the soul's quest to find its communion with Christ.

June 8: Sun 23° Taurus: Cosmic memory of the Ascension of Christ. The vision of the Ascension is wondrous to behold:

To those foregathered there, the heavens appeared to open. They saw veils of light drawing apart like great curtains, and lustrous clouds gathering and swelling. Every level of heaven was beginning to open!

If Jacob had been there to watch the Ascension (and I am certain that in some form he was), he surely would have seen again the "ladder"

SIDEREAL GEOCENTRIC LONGITUDES :   JUNE 2016 Gregorian at 0 hours UT

DAY	☉	☽	☊	☿	♀	♂	♃	♄	♅	♆	♇
1 WE	15 ♉ 58	18 ♓ 42	23 ♌ 3R	22 ♈ 40	14 ♉ 22	3 ♏ 31R	19 ♌ 2	18 ♏ 19R	28 ♓ 12	17 ♒ 2	22 ♐ 4R
2 TH	16 56	3 ♈ 20	22 59	23 22	15 36	3 11	19 6	18 15	28 15	17 2	22 3
3 FR	17 53	18 12	22 52	24 9	16 49	2 51	19 10	18 10	28 17	17 3	22 2
4 SA	18 51	3 ♉ 9	22 43	24 59	18 3	2 32	19 15	18 6	28 20	17 3	22 1
5 SU	19 48	18 5	22 32	25 53	19 17	2 13	19 19	18 1	28 22	17 3	22 0
6 MO	20 45	2 ♊ 48	22 21	26 50	20 31	1 55	19 24	17 57	28 25	17 4	21 59
7 TU	21 43	17 12	22 11	27 51	21 44	1 37	19 29	17 52	28 27	17 4	21 57
8 WE	22 40	1 ♋ 10	22 2	28 55	22 58	1 20	19 34	17 48	28 29	17 4	21 56
9 TH	23 38	14 41	21 56	0 ♉ 2	24 12	1 4	19 39	17 43	28 32	17 4	21 55
10 FR	24 35	27 45	21 53	1 13	25 26	0 48	19 44	17 39	28 34	17 4	21 54
11 SA	25 32	10 ♌ 23	21 51	2 27	26 39	0 32	19 49	17 35	28 36	17 4	21 52
12 SU	26 30	22 42	21 51	3 44	27 53	0 17	19 55	17 30	28 38	17 5	21 51
13 MO	27 27	4 ♍ 46	21 51	5 4	29 7	0 3	20 1	17 26	28 40	17 5	21 50
14 TU	28 24	16 40	21 50	6 27	0 ♊ 20	29 ♎ 50	20 6	17 22	28 42	17 5R	21 48
15 WE	29 22	28 29	21 47	7 53	1 34	29 38	20 12	17 17	28 45	17 5	21 47
16 TH	0 ♊ 19	10 ♎ 19	21 41	9 23	2 48	29 26	20 19	17 13	28 47	17 5	21 46
17 FR	1 16	22 13	21 33	10 55	4 2	29 15	20 25	17 9	28 49	17 4	21 44
18 SA	2 14	4 ♏ 15	21 23	12 30	5 15	29 5	20 31	17 5	28 51	17 4	21 43
19 SU	3 11	16 26	21 11	14 8	6 29	28 55	20 38	17 0	28 52	17 4	21 42
20 MO	4 8	28 49	20 58	15 49	7 43	28 47	20 44	16 56	28 54	17 4	21 40
21 TU	5 5	11 ♐ 24	20 45	17 33	8 56	28 39	20 51	16 52	28 56	17 4	21 39
22 WE	6 2	24 10	20 34	19 20	10 10	28 32	20 58	16 48	28 58	17 4	21 37
23 TH	7 0	7 ♑ 8	20 26	21 10	11 24	28 26	21 5	16 44	29 0	17 3	21 36
24 FR	7 57	20 17	20 20	23 2	12 37	28 20	21 12	16 40	29 1	17 0	21 35
25 SA	8 54	3 ♒ 38	20 17	24 57	13 51	28 16	21 20	16 36	29 3	17 3	21 33
26 SU	9 51	17 10	20 16	26 54	15 5	28 12	21 27	16 32	29 5	17 2	21 32
27 MO	10 49	0 ♓ 55	20 16D	28 54	16 19	28 9	21 35	16 28	29 6	17 2	21 30
28 TU	11 46	14 52	20 16R	0 ♊ 56	17 32	28 7	21 42	16 24	29 8	17 1	21 29
29 WE	12 43	29 3	20 15	2 59	18 46	28 6	21 50	16 21	29 9	17 1	21 27
30 TH	13 40	13 ♈ 24	20 12	5 5	20 0	28 5D	21 58	16 17	29 11	17 0	21 26

INGRESSES :

1	☽ → ♈	18:34		
3	☽ → ♉	18:56		
5	☽ → ♊	19:23		
7	☽ → ♋	21:57		
8	☿ → ♉	23:11		
10	☽ → ♌	4:13		
12	☽ → ♍	14:28		
13	♂ → ♎	6: 7		
	♀ → ♊	17:21		
15	☽ → ♎	3: 4		
	☉ → ♊	16: 2		
17	☽ → ♏	15:33		
20	☽ → ♐	2:16		
22	☽ → ♑	10:50		
24	☽ → ♒	17:29		
26	☽ → ♓	22:24		
27	☿ → ♊	13: 5		
29	☽ → ♈	1:36		

ASPECTS & ECLIPSES :

1	☽ ☌ ♅	15:41		☽ ☌ ♀	2: 7
2	☉ □ ♆	2:50		☉ ☌ ☽	2:58
3	♀ □ ♆	4:20		☽ ⚻ ☊	7: 8
	☉ ☍ ♄	6:36	6	☉ ⚻ ♀	21:48
	☽ ☌ ☿	10: 6	7	♀ □ ☊	7:40
	☽ ☌ P	11:11		☽ ☍ ♇	8: 4
	☽ ☍ ♂	23: 1		☉ □ ☊	10: 6
4	♀ ☍ ♄	0:46	9	☿ ☍ ♂	17: 0
	☉ □ ♃	10:56	11	☽ ☍ ♆	12:57
	☽ ☍ ♄	23:54		☽ ☌ ♃	18:28
5	♀ □ ♃	0:47		☽ ☌ ☊	22:19
12	☉ □ ☽	8: 8		☿ □ ♆	17:15
15	☽ ☍ ♅	0:31		☽ ☍ ♀	18:50
	☽ ☌ A	12: 3	21	☽ ☌ ♇	19:15
17	☽ ☌ ♂	13:51	22	☿ □ ☊	15: 5
18	♄ □ ♆	1:24		☿ □ ♃	22:57
	☽ ☍ ☿	18:47	25	☽ ☌ ♆	23:45
19	☽ ☌ ♄	1: 5	26	☽ ☌ ☋	5:25
	☽ ⚻ ☊	9: 4		☽ ☍ ♃	7:35
20	☉ ☍ ☽	11: 1	27	☉ □ ☽	18:17
	☿ ☍ ♄	14:54	29	☽ ☌ ♅	0:11
	♃ ☌ ☊	16:41			

SIDEREAL HELIOCENTRIC LONGITUDES :   JUNE 2016 Gregorian at 0 hours UT

DAY	Sid. Time	☿	♀	⊕	♂	♃	♄	♅	♆	♇	Vernal Point
1 WE	16:39:38	27 ♐ 33	12 ♉ 7	15 ♏ 58	11 ♏ 51	29 ♌ 46	18 ♏ 5	26 ♓ 3	15 ♒ 6	21 ♐ 2	5 ♓ 1'52"
2 TH	16:43:35	0 ♑ 36	13 44	16 56	12 23	29 51	18 6	26 4	15 6	21 3	5 ♓ 1'51"
3 FR	16:47:31	3 43	15 20	17 53	12 55	29 55	18 8	26 4	15 6	21 3	5 ♓ 1'51"
4 SA	16:51:28	6 53	16 57	18 51	13 27	0 ♍ 0	18 10	26 5	15 7	21 3	5 ♓ 1'51"
5 SU	16:55:24	10 6	18 34	19 48	13 59	0 4	18 12	26 6	15 7	21 3	5 ♓ 1'51"
6 MO	16:59:21	13 24	20 10	20 46	14 31	0 9	18 14	26 6	15 7	21 4	5 ♓ 1'51"
7 TU	17: 3:18	16 46	21 47	21 43	15 3	0 13	18 15	26 7	15 8	21 4	5 ♓ 1'51"
8 WE	17: 7:14	20 12	23 24	22 41	15 35	0 18	18 17	26 8	15 8	21 4	5 ♓ 1'51"
9 TH	17:11:11	23 43	25 0	23 38	16 8	0 23	18 19	26 8	15 8	21 5	5 ♓ 1'50"
10 FR	17:15: 7	27 20	26 37	24 35	16 40	0 27	18 21	26 9	15 9	21 5	5 ♓ 1'50"
11 SA	17:19: 4	1 ♒ 2	28 14	25 33	17 13	0 32	18 23	26 10	15 9	21 5	5 ♓ 1'50"
12 SU	17:23: 0	4 50	29 51	26 30	17 45	0 36	18 25	26 10	15 10	21 6	5 ♓ 1'50"
13 MO	17:26:57	8 45	1 ♊ 28	27 28	18 18	0 41	18 26	26 11	15 10	21 6	5 ♓ 1'50"
14 TU	17:30:53	12 46	3 5	28 25	18 50	0 45	18 28	26 12	15 10	21 6	5 ♓ 1'50"
15 WE	17:34:50	16 55	4 41	29 22	19 23	0 50	18 30	26 12	15 11	21 7	5 ♓ 1'50"
16 TH	17:38:47	21 11	6 18	0 ♐ 19	19 56	0 54	18 32	26 13	15 11	21 7	5 ♓ 1'49"
17 FR	17:42:43	25 34	7 55	1 17	20 28	0 59	18 34	26 14	15 11	21 7	5 ♓ 1'49"
18 SA	17:46:40	0 ♓ 6	9 32	2 14	21 1	1 3	18 35	26 14	15 12	21 8	5 ♓ 1'49"
19 SU	17:50:36	4 47	11 9	3 11	21 34	1 8	18 37	26 15	15 12	21 8	5 ♓ 1'49"
20 MO	17:54:33	9 36	12 47	4 8	22 7	1 13	18 39	26 16	15 12	21 8	5 ♓ 1'49"
21 TU	17:58:29	14 34	14 24	5 6	22 40	1 17	18 41	26 16	15 13	21 8	5 ♓ 1'49"
22 WE	18: 2:26	19 41	16 1	6 3	23 13	1 22	18 43	26 17	15 13	21 9	5 ♓ 1'49"
23 TH	18: 6:22	24 58	17 38	7 0	23 46	1 26	18 44	26 17	15 14	21 9	5 ♓ 1'48"
24 FR	18:10:19	0 ♈ 23	19 15	7 57	24 19	1 31	18 46	26 18	15 14	21 9	5 ♓ 1'48"
25 SA	18:14:16	5 57	20 52	8 55	24 52	1 35	18 48	26 19	15 14	21 10	5 ♓ 1'48"
26 SU	18:18:12	11 40	22 29	9 52	25 26	1 40	18 50	26 19	15 15	21 10	5 ♓ 1'48"
27 MO	18:22: 9	17 31	24 7	10 49	25 59	1 44	18 52	26 20	15 15	21 10	5 ♓ 1'48"
28 TU	18:26: 5	23 29	25 44	11 46	26 32	1 49	18 54	26 21	15 15	21 11	5 ♓ 1'48"
29 WE	18:30: 2	29 34	27 21	12 43	27 6	1 54	18 55	26 21	15 16	21 11	5 ♓ 1'48"
30 TH	18:33:58	5 ♉ 44	28 59	13 41	27 39	1 58	18 57	26 22	15 16	21 11	5 ♓ 1'48"

INGRESSES :

1	☿ → ♑	19:16
4	♃ → ♍	1:17
10	☿ → ♒	17:21
12	♀ → ♊	2:17
15	⊕ → ♐	15:52
17	☿ → ♓	23:26
23	☿ → ♈	22:19
29	☿ → ♉	1:41
30	♀ → ♋	15: 8

ASPECTS (HELIOCENTRIC +MOON(TYCHONIC)) :

1	☽ □ ♇	3:52	6	♀ ☍ ⊕	21:48		☽ ☌ ♃	15:46	
	☽ ☌ ♂	12: 7	7	♀ ☌ ♆	16:21	19	☽ ☌ ♄	20:36	
	☽ □ ☿	18:23		♂ □ ♆	3:24	13	♂ ☌ ♄	6:50	
2	♀ □ ♆	20:30		☽ ☍ ♇	6:34	14	☽ □ ♇	9: 0	
3	⊕ ☌ ♄	6:20		☽ □ ♅	15:14		☿ ☌ ♆	14: 1	
4	☽ ☍ ♂	17: 8	8	♃ ☍ ☊	22:53		☽ ☍ ♅	19:21	
	♀ ☍ ⊕	18:30	9	☽ ☍ ☿	22:55	15	☿ □ ♄	9: 5	
	☽ ☍ ♇	19:13	11	☽ ☌ ♆	19:13	16	⊕ ☌ ♃	15:55	
5	☽ ☍ ♀	0:11		☽ □ ♂	13:49	18	☿ ☍ ♃	5: 2	
	☽ ☌ ♀	0:52		☽ ☌ ♀	15:32		☿ □ ⊕	13:50	
	☽ □ ♃	19:36	12	♀ ☌ ♃	11:48				
	☽ □ ♆	21:34	25	♀ ☍ ♇	4:19				
	☽ ☌ ♂	10:26		☽ ☌ ♄	20:36				
20	☽ □ ♃	4:37	26	☽ □ ♄	2:55				
21	☽ ☍ ♀	6:29		☽ ☌ ♂	15: 4				
	☽ □ ♅	9:57	27	☽ ☍ ♃	1:26				
	☽ ☍ ♇	18:20	28	☿ ☌ ☊	0:16				
22	☽ □ ♄	3:55		♀ □ ♇	9: 6				
	☿ □ ♆	6:42		☽ □ ♆	10:43				
23	☿ ☌ ♅	5:57		☽ ☌ ♂	19:28				
				☽ □ ♀	20:47				

reaching into heaven upon which the Angels ascend and descend.

This ladder is symbolic of the various levels of heaven attained and surpassed as one ascends to Heaven. Christ was to ascend through the Hierarchies now as he went to the Father, and at each stage of his Ascension there was an important work to be done.

And so, there Christ Jesus stood upon the highest point of the Mount of Olives, overlooking the great city of Jerusalem. After speaking briefly to his friends and disciples, he began his ascent, as Angels also descended, passing by him as they drew near to the Earth.[3]

June 9: Mercury 1° Taurus opposite Mars 1° Scorpio. Mars enters the place of the Sun at 1° Scorpio which bears the remembrance of the Sun's location at the summons of Judas and the arrival of Jesus at the Mount of Temptations (Attarus). A Michaelic force stands across from the pastors and healers of humankind (Mercury). Words are to be carefully formed, and righteously spoken in conscientiousness of the eternal truth.

June 13: Retrograde Mars enters Libra: "And being effects being." Mars will stand in the night sky until the middle of next month. In Libra the Word seeks equanimity of purpose, and warns us not to fall asleep before the mighty revelation currently enlightening the new knights of the threshold. There are deeds to be done for the good of the social organism! Mars was in Libra during the forty days of Christ's temptation.

June 14: Neptune 17° Aquarius stations before moving retrograde. Neptune opposite today's degree remembers the death of German President Hindenburg (August 1934). Upon Hindenberg's death, Hitler combined the post of President and Chancellor and called himself thereafter "Führer." This word means "leader" and especially applies to one exercising the power of a tyrant. Neptune has been at this degree all month and will remain so until early July.

June 15: Sun enters Gemini the Twins. "Reveal thyself, Sun life" (Steiner, *Twelve Cosmic Moods*). William Bento characterized this mantra:

> Within this phrase there is a hidden mystery. How does the Sun hide from our view? It is certainly not the physical Sun we see daily that is being referred to here—but the living, etherically permeated Sun, felt and experienced, though rarely perceived. Within this Sun exist the threefold sources of health, life and goodness. How easily we forget to place our trust in this ever-present stream of divinity when we are faced with illness, death and evil! For this reason alone, it is well worth reminding ourselves to see beyond appearances and behold the true revelation of the Sun, which reveals itself to our hearts, where its life resides.

The first decan of Gemini is ruled by Jupiter and associated with Orion, whose bright star Betelgeuse is located at 4 degrees Gemini.

June 17: Saturn 17° Scorpio square Neptune 17° Aquarius. The Holy Virgin (Saturn) holds her mantle over the abyss. She awaits those who can penetrate into the realm of evil and offer to the waiting gods above the knowledge thus gained. Only then can spiritual beings understand the ghouls and specters that prey upon earthly human beings. In square to Neptune, mighty inspirations accompany such daring. Inversely, the square causes demons to shake the tree of fear indwelling subconscious realms; thus do souls quake rather than face what beneath them pulses. When the Sun was 17° Scorpio, Magdalene underwent her first conversion (Nov/8/30). Christ spoke: "Come to me, O sinners…and share the kingdom with me!" We choose which kingdom we shall revere, and afterward the kingdom we have chosen then chooses us. Therefore we are to choose wisely.

June 18: Sun 2 1/2° Gemini: Cosmic Pentecost (May/24/33). The Sun was 2 1/2° Gemini at Pentecost, when Sophia descended, through the Holy Spirit, and entered into the being of the Blessed Virgin Mary. At this degree, the Sun is directly opposite the Galactic Center (2° Sagittarius). The Galactic Center, also known as the Central Sun, is

---

3 Isaacson, *Through the Eyes of Mary Magdalene,* vol. 3, pp. 252–253.

the Divine Heart of the galaxy, which is the source of the Holy Spirit. The Blessed Virgin Mary, who was presented by Jesus Christ (before the Ascension) as the center of the community, served here—at Pentecost—as this heart-center and as the bearer of Divine Sophia.

> Because of extremely complicated influences and experiences coming from the spiritual world, Mary had an astral body that was so purified it could receive the revelations of Sophia and pour them out again as inspirations of the soul. This faculty was the very reason why, at the time of Pentecostal revelation, the Virgin Mary occupied the central position in the circle of the twelve. Without her, the revelation would have been only spiritual; there would have been twelve prophets, united in the Holy Spirit as was ancient prophecy. Through the cooperation of Mary, however, something more could happen; the disciples' hearts beat in harmony with hers while they experienced the Pentecostal revelation as personal human conviction. Through this experience, they became not prophets but specifically apostles.[4]

The difference between prophets and apostles is that prophets proclaim revelations impersonally, whereas apostles reveal the Holy Spirit as it lives *within* their own souls. This was possible only because the Virgin Mary transmitted *ensouled* revelation to the disciples. Through her, revelation became personal and yet maintained its objective spiritual truth.

From the moment of Pentecost onward, the silence imposed on Sophia through Lucifer's intervention in human destiny was released. Sophia became free to reach down into groups of earthly human beings. This was a great event for both the earthly and spiritual worlds.

The sparks of fire that issued from her blessed soul were the ensouled manifestation of Christ's cosmic I Am. This eternal "I" of the world was born into the disciples through the immaculate heart of the divine Mary–Sophia, who was standing at the heart of their community. Since that first Pentecost, the Christ spirit has lived within human souls on Earth. Pentecost was the awakening of Christ's disciples

from a dreamlike state, whereby they united with the principle of Christ's love as an experience within their own being. We also are to awaken from our dreamlike sleep to meet the challenge of our time with hearts attuned in wakeful awareness.

Emanations from the heart of the galaxy are increasing in our time, leading us ever forward. Sun in Gemini asks that we revere the "I" in others, that we follow our star and find our way to the manger of the heart.

June 20: Full Moon 4° Sagittarius opposite Sun 4° Gemini. This Full Moon is the flowering of the New Moon two weeks ago which remembered Jesus healing three blind boys. Now, the Full Moon remembers Jesus's visit to the pagan kings (Sep/28/32). Jesus spent time in long conversations with Mensor (the Gold King). The Gold King had been a student of Zarathustra in a previous life. Mensor remembered much from that incarnation; knowledge came to him as a kind of direct knowing/remembering. The elders who taught him remarked that he could actually *hear* the stars. By the time the young Mensor turned eighteen years of age, all the old astrologers had died, and as so often happens, a schism broke out in the remaining circle of astrologers. None were left who could understand the prophetic genius of Mensor. He became increasingly isolated. Mensor traveled far and wide, striving to uncover the ancient teachings of the stars. He never lost faith in his vision of the descent of the Sun being—therefore he was later one of the three kings who came to adore the kingly Solomon Jesus child.[5]

Where are the modern Magi? They are the ones who hold a lantern at the prow of a ship, navigating by reading the stars, guiding communities into the new mysteries. Within the folds of their mantles they harbor secrets of the Word from whom all was created, and they remain faithful to the Sun Being—above and beyond all ruse of the serpent:

> But the darkness of the world that is not penetrated by the Word is not the source of consciousness, and the human intellect that is not illumined by the Word is not the principle of

---

4 Tomberg, *Christ and Sophia*, p. 306.

5 See Isaacson, *Through the Eyes of Mary Magdalene*, vol. 2, p. 263.

the world. In the phenomenal world there are "objective illusions," i.e., "things which are not real" which have not been made by the Word, but which have arisen for an ephemeral existence from the substrata of darkness. In the domain of subjective consciousness there are illusions, i.e., notions, ideas and ideals which are not real, which have not been engendered by the light of the Word, but which have arisen for an ephemeral existence from the depths of darkness in the subconscious....

Now, the "world" of our experience is the phenomenal manifestation of both the world created by the Word and the evolutionary world of the serpent. The "intellect" of our experience, also, is the manifestation both of the light of the Word and of the "ruse" (to take the Biblical term for the method where darkness imitates light without receiving it) of the serpent. This is why it is still necessary to distinguish, before one professes to realism, between the World and the world. Similarly, before one embraces idealism, one has to distinguish between cosmic Intelligence and the human intellect.[6]

The Full Moon is remembering Jesus's visit to Mensor (six months before his crucifixion). With the Sun within 2° of Pentecost, we can imagine ancient teachings shining from the pages of "The Book" which the elders keep for us in the Moon sphere, in which all past wisdom is recorded. Perhaps these ancient teachings, and teachers, are again resounding the streams of ancient wisdom, now Christianized. *These teachings may now seem unintelligible to many, as were the intuitions of Mensor unintelliglible to his fellow astrologers so long ago.* Under the light of this Full Moon, we can contemplate the light of the Word and, inversely, the "ruse" of the serpent that can only imitate the true light. We are to overcome our blindness.

ASPECT: Mercury 17° Taurus opposite Saturn 17° Scorpio square Neptune 17° Aquarius. Closely holding this Grand Square is Jupiter at 20° Leo. Mercury shines light into the abyss of Scorpio's hidden secrets, as the Goddess Night (Neptune) oversees all things. Mercury opposite Saturn tends toward conservatism of thought, as well as a tendency to see only the dark side. Yet, when mercurial light illumines the darkness, much is revealed. To progress in spiritual strength we need patience, tolerance, and compassion.

June 22: Mercury 21° Taurus square Jupiter 21° Leo. Jupiter remembers the fall of Jerusalem (Aug/29/70). The community of Eternal Israel and her prophets pray for the eternal star of Jerusalem, and for the protection of all peoples. The prophets of ancient Israel are with us at this time when Christ has drawn so near to us:

> It will be of the utmost importance to recognize and understand this event of Christ's appearance, for it will be followed by other events. Just as other occurrences preceded the Christ event in Palestine, so, after the time I have referred to—after he himself has become visible to humanity again in the etheric body—those who foretold his coming will follow his reappearance. Those who prepared his coming will be recognizable in a new form to people who experience the new Christ event. Those who lived on Earth as Moses, Abraham, and the prophets will be recognizable once again.[7]

This aspect can destabilize our rationale, causing us to misjudge the scope of things. It is important to listen and bear witness to the unvarnished truth. Thus do we attain the freedom to follow the light—revealing the prophets who are now forming the community of Eternal Israel.

June 28: Sun 12½° Gemini: Birth of John the Baptist (Jun/4/2 BC). John the Baptist was revealed by Christ to be the reincarnated Elijah, and later came to Earth as the Renaissance painter Raphael, and still later as the German romantic poet, Novalis. John fulfilled his mission when he baptized Jesus in the Jordan River in AD 29, when he bore witness to the incarnation of Christ—the true Light of the World and the Lamb of God. After the fulfillment of this mission, his new mission began, which was in service to Sophia. Just as John was the guide and preparer for those who would recognize the incarnated Christ, so too is he the preparer and guide for those working on behalf of Sophia, in recognition

---

6 Anon., *Meditations on the Tarot,* p. 203.

7 Steiner, *The Second Coming of Christ,* p. 37.

of the etheric return of Christ. This is a day to open our eyes and ears to the truth ringing through the world—a truth enlightened by wisdom and born of love. John works in the apocalyptic realms where the Book of Revelation lives eternally. He needs us to wake up to the presence of adversaries and to face this truth as would the Grail Knights. To know evil, is to bring forth the good. This is true for those following a Christ-centric Grail path. For those who do not know Christ, such knowledge regarding evil is imprudent. John is the bearer of strength, and he works through the power of the Word.

May we find our fullness of voice and proclaim the Light, lest we become swallowed in the shadows of illusion!

June 30: Venus 21° Gemini opposite Pluto 21° Sagittarius. Jesus was questioned by one hundred Pharisees. He replied with such powerful words that they were reduced to silence (Jun/9/32). Dogs bark and bite when they are afraid; so also did the fear of the Pharisees cause them to behave like dogs when Jesus stood before them. Their words were biting, and their logic cunning. Karmic circles (Venus) that turn their backs on the truth lose awareness of spirit. Yet, when truth speaks, even the dogs lay low.

This aspect cautions us to take our passions in hand, to faithfully follow our star and to keep the dragon forces underfoot. When fear gives way to love, all things are possible!

JULY 2016

The New Moon is on the 4th of this month, with both Sun and Moon in Gemini. Mercury is a bit behind the Sun, and Venus is a bit ahead of the Sun; neither can yet be seen by star gazers upon the Earth. The Sun and Mercury are exactly (and invisibly) conjunct on the 6th.

The waxing Moon joins Jupiter in Leo on the 8th; Mars in Libra on the 14th; and Saturn in Scorpio on the 15th. Look to the west after sunset to see them. Quick-stepping Mercury gains ground to catch up with Venus for a conjunction in Cancer on the 16th. This is the 2nd of three conjunctions

they will share this year. They are trailing the Sun in their "evening star" aspects, but will be just a bit too close to the Sun to be visible.

Mars reenters the constellation of the Scorpion on the 16th, while the Sun shifts into Cancer. The Moon enters Capricorn opposite the Sun to form the Full Moon on the 19th.

Uranus at 29° Pisces is squared by Venus, Mercury, and the Sun (all in Gemini) on the 7th, 11th, and 16th, respectively. Uranus at this degree remembers the forming of the Gestapo, the Nazi secret police, known for its terroist methods directed against those suspected of treason or of questionable loyalty.

July 2: Sun 16° Gemini: The conception of the Solomon Jesus (June/7/7 BC). The Solomon Jesus is depicted in the Gospel of St. Matthew. This Jesus descended from the kingly line of David, and at his birth he was visited by the three wise men (kings) from the east, who followed his radiant star shining from the heavens, proclaiming his birth. As disciples of Zarathustrian star wisdom, the kings understood when the time of the incarnation of their great teacher had arrived—for in the Persian mystery initiations the aspirant prepared for the macrocosmic path of initiation, wherein one journeyed consciously into the vastness of starry worlds. Gemini is the constellation that asks us to follow our star, as did the wise men follow their star—the Star of the Magi.

July 4: New Moon 18° Gemini. The Moon remembers Peter receiving the keys to the kingdom of heaven (Monday, Mar/19/31). During this event, Peter recognized Jesus as "the Son of the living God." Thus did he prove himself worthy to receive the keys to the kingdom of heaven. Jesus responded to Peter's recognition with the words: "Thou art a rock, and upon this rock I will build my church, and the gates of hell shall not prevail against it. And I will give to thee the keys of the kingdom of heaven. And whatsoever thou shalt bind upon Earth, it shall be bound also in heaven; and whatsoever thou shalt loose upon Earth, it shall be loosed also in heaven!" Peter's intelligence united with spontaneous wisdom; thus did he intuit the mighty spiritual being who stood before him as Christ. In like manner, we are all encouraged to unite our intellect with intuition—so as to be born into worlds wherein we are woven into communion with the divine.

With Sun and Moon shining from this constellation, we are to persevere in faithfulness to our star, and to no other. We are not to consult with Herods, nor are we to compromise our light. Just as the three kings sought the manger, so too does this Moon ask us to find the manger that rests in our heart's center—wherein we unite with our divine "I."

Just as the mages from the East made a long journey and brought presents to the Child, in following the "star," so also Hermeticism is on the way from century to century to arrive at the manger—not to arrive there with empty hands, but to place there the presents which are the fruit of the millennial-old effort of human intelligence which follows the "star."

The "star" which Hermeticists follow leads them to the manger—to the center of history, to the center of the psychic life (individuation), to the center of universal evolution or the "supreme focus of the personalizing personality," to the Alpha and Omega of revelations, to the Heart which is at the center of all hearts. For there is a center of gravitation of hearts, just as there is a center of gravitation of the planets. Like the latter, it causes the "seasons" of the life of the soul. This is why it is not without reason that the manger is venerated by the Church each year and that a unique light is lit in the world each Christmas. What I want to say is that Christmas is not only the festival dedicated to the memory of the historical nativity of Christ, but that it is in addition the event of the nativity which is repeated each year, where Christ becomes Child anew and where the history of mankind becomes the manger. Then all that is in us of the nature of the shepherds of Bethlehem and all that is in us of the nature of the mages from the East responds as in the past. What is in us of the nature of the mages from the East is enamoured of the "star" and sets out en route with the little incense, myrrh and gold gathered during the year which is drawing to an end; and what is in us of the shepherds of Bethlehem kneels down before

the Child whose reality and presence is revealed from above.[1]

The Church is the eternal "place" wherein the heart of Christ rests. It was the Church that was inaugurated when Peter received the keys. Whatever is bound to the promise of Christ's heart is bound also in heaven; and whatsoever is loosed from this heart shall also be loosed in heaven. Too many have loosed themselves from the Christ heart, and have therefore loosed the dragon—and the open gates of Hell are prevailing upon us. Our star calls us to recognize the original sanctity of the sacred heart, so that the gates of Hell may be sealed, and adversaries revealed.

Faithfulness to our star, which is a spark from the divine "I," can lead us into the majesty radiating from tonight's Full Moon. Tomorrow marks the Sun's conjunction with Sirius—known as the star of the Master Jesus, who has been the subject of our meditations the past few days.

July 5: Sun 19½° Gemini conjunct Sirius: Sirius shines as the leading star of the Greater Dog, Canis Major. This megastar is 24 times more luminous than our Sun, and is the most radiant star in our heavens. At the conception of the Solomon Jesus, the Sun was 16° Gemini; and at his death the Sun was 14° Gemini. The Solomon Jesus was called "radiant star." This aspect encourages us to meet opposition as a teaching and to deepen our commitment toward realization of our higher intentions.

July 6: Superior conjunction of Sun and Mercury 20° Gemini: The Sun remembers Jesus as he visitied a madhouse, where many raged uncontrollably. As Jesus spoke to them they became quiet (June/15/29). The little town of Dothaim was sparsely settled, but its soil was good.

Abraham had once owned fields there [Dothaim] for his cattle, intended for offerings. Joseph and his brethren used to guard their flocks in this same region, and it was here that the former was sold.[2]

---

1 Anon., *Meditations on the Tarot*, pp. 530–531.
2 *ACE Complete*, p. 185.

SIDEREAL GEOCENTRIC LONGITUDES :   JULY 2016 Gregorian at 0 hours UT

DAY	☉	☽	☊	☿	♀	♂	♃	♄	♅	♆	♇
1 FR	14 ♊ 37	27 ♈ 55	20 ♌ 7R	7 ♊ 12	21 ♊ 14	28 ♎ 6	22 ♌ 6	16 ♏ 13R	29 ♓ 12	17 ♒ 0R	21 ♐ 24R
2 SA	15 35	12 ♉ 29	19 59	9 20	22 27	28 7	22 14	16 10	29 13	16 59	21 23
3 SU	16 32	27 1	19 50	11 30	23 41	28 9	22 23	16 6	29 15	16 59	21 21
4 MO	17 29	11 ♊ 24	19 41	13 40	24 55	28 12	22 31	16 3	29 16	16 58	21 20
5 TU	18 26	25 32	19 32	15 50	26 8	28 16	22 40	15 59	29 17	16 57	21 18
6 WE	19 24	9 ♋ 20	19 25	18 0	27 22	28 20	22 48	15 56	29 18	16 57	21 17
7 TH	20 21	22 44	19 20	20 10	28 36	28 25	22 57	15 53	29 19	16 56	21 15
8 FR	21 18	5 ♌ 45	19 17	22 20	29 50	28 31	23 6	15 49	29 21	16 55	21 14
9 SA	22 15	18 23	19 16	24 29	1 ♋ 3	28 38	23 15	15 46	29 22	16 55	21 12
10 SU	23 12	0 ♍ 43	19 16D	26 38	2 17	28 46	23 24	15 43	29 23	16 54	21 11
11 MO	24 10	12 48	19 17	28 45	3 31	28 54	23 33	15 40	29 24	16 53	21 9
12 TU	25 7	24 44	19 17R	0 ♋ 50	4 45	29 3	23 42	15 37	29 24	16 52	21 8
13 WE	26 4	6 ♎ 35	19 16	2 55	5 58	29 13	23 52	15 34	29 25	16 51	21 7
14 TH	27 1	18 27	19 14	4 58	7 12	29 24	24 1	15 32	29 26	16 50	21 5
15 FR	27 58	0 ♏ 24	19 9	6 59	8 26	29 35	24 11	15 29	29 26	16 49	21 4
16 SA	28 56	12 31	19 3	8 59	9 40	29 47	24 20	15 26	29 27	16 49	21 2
17 SU	29 53	24 50	18 55	10 57	10 53	0 ♏ 0	24 30	15 24	29 28	16 48	21 1
18 MO	0 ♋ 50	7 ♐ 23	18 47	12 53	12 7	0 13	24 40	15 21	29 29	16 47	20 59
19 TU	1 47	20 13	18 39	14 48	13 21	0 27	24 50	15 19	29 29	16 46	20 58
20 WE	2 45	3 ♑ 17	18 32	16 41	14 35	0 42	25 0	15 17	29 30	16 44	20 56
21 TH	3 42	16 37	18 26	18 32	15 48	0 57	25 10	15 15	29 30	16 43	20 55
22 FR	4 39	0 ♒ 9	18 23	20 21	17 2	1 13	25 20	15 12	29 31	16 42	20 53
23 SA	5 36	13 52	18 21	22 8	18 16	1 29	25 30	15 10	29 31	16 41	20 52
24 SU	6 34	27 44	18 21D	23 54	19 29	1 46	25 40	15 8	29 31	16 40	20 51
25 MO	7 31	11 ♓ 44	18 22	25 38	20 43	2 4	25 51	15 7	29 32	16 39	20 49
26 TU	8 28	25 49	18 24	27 20	21 57	2 22	26 1	15 5	29 32	16 38	20 48
27 WE	9 26	9 ♈ 59	18 24R	29 0	23 11	2 41	26 12	15 3	29 32	16 36	20 46
28 TH	10 23	24 12	18 23	0 ♌ 39	24 24	3 0	26 23	15 1	29 32	16 35	20 45
29 FR	11 20	8 ♉ 26	18 21	2 15	25 38	3 20	26 33	15 0	29 32	16 34	20 44
30 SA	12 18	22 37	18 17	3 50	26 52	3 41	26 44	14 58	29 32R	16 33	20 42
31 SU	13 15	6 ♊ 43	18 12	5 24	28 6	4 2	26 55	14 57	29 32	16 31	20 41

INGRESSES :

1	☽→♉ 3:26		☽→♐ 9:56
3	☽→♊ 4:56	19	☽→♑ 18:0
5	☽→♋ 7:41	21	☽→♒ 23:44
7	☽→♌ 13:19	24	☽→♓ 3:53
8	♀→♋ 3:20	26	☽→♈ 7:5
9	☽→♍ 22:35	27	☿→♌ 14:32
11	☿→♋ 14:21	28	☽→♉ 9:46
12	☽→♎ 10:39	30	☽→♊ 12:32
14	☽→♏ 23:12		
17	♂→♏ 0:21		
	☉→♋ 2:58		

ASPECTS & ECLIPSES :

```
 1  ☽ ☍ ♂   0:17      ♀ □ ♅  14:22      ☽ ∥ ☊  12:40      ☽ ☍ ♃  20:24
    ♀ ☍ ♇   3:27      ☉ ☍ ♇  22:21      ☉ ☍ ♅  13:29   26 ☽ ☌ ♅   6:17
    ☽ ☌ P   6:37    8 ☽ ☍ ♆  21:10      ☿ ☌ ♀  21:58      ☉ □ ☽  22:58
 2  ☽ ☍ ♄   6: 1    9 ☽ ☌ ☊   1:41   18 ☽ □ ♅   2:54   27 ☽ ☌ P  11:50
    ☽ ∥ ☊  12:14      ☽ ☌ ♃   9:30   19 ☽ ☌ ♆   1:23   28 ☽ ☍ ♂  15:12
 4  ☽ ☌ ☿   4:28   11 ☿ □ ♅   7:26      ☉ ☍ ♂  22:55   29 ☽ ☍ ♄  11: 4
    ☉ ☌ ☽  11: 0   12 ☉ □ ☽   0:50   20 ☽ ☍ ♀  22:24      ☽ ∥ ☊  16:42
    ☽ ☍ ♆  16:46      ☽ ☍ ♂   9:28   21 ☽ ☍ ☿   3:57      ☿ □ ♂  20:48
 5  ☽ ☌ ♀   1: 8   13 ☽ ☌ A   5:36   23 ☽ ☍ ♆   4:53
 7  ☉ ∥ ☿   3:22   14 ☽ ☌ ♂  22:20      ☽ ☌ ♅   7:47
    ☿ ☍ ♆  11:51   16 ☽ ☌ ♄   5:43      ☉ □ ♅  18:58
```

SIDEREAL HELIOCENTRIC LONGITUDES :   JULY 2016 Gregorian at 0 hours UT

DAY	Sid. Time	☿	♀	⊕	♂	♃	♄	♅	♆	♇	Vernal Point
1 FR	18:37:55	11 ♉ 59	0 ♋ 36	14 ♐ 38	28 ♏ 13	2 ♍ 3	18 ♏ 59	26 ♓ 23	15 ♒ 16	21 ♐ 12	5 ♓ 1'47"
2 SA	18:41:51	18 16	2 13	15 35	28 47	2 7	19 1	26 23	15 17	21 12	5 ♓ 1'47"
3 SU	18:45:48	24 36	3 51	16 32	29 20	2 12	19 3	26 24	15 17	21 12	5 ♓ 1'47"
4 MO	18:49:45	0 ♊ 55	5 28	17 29	29 54	2 16	19 4	26 25	15 17	21 13	5 ♓ 1'47"
5 TU	18:53:41	7 12	7 5	18 27	0 ♐ 28	2 21	19 6	26 25	15 18	21 13	5 ♓ 1'47"
6 WE	18:57:38	13 27	8 43	19 24	1 2	2 25	19 8	26 26	15 18	21 13	5 ♓ 1'47"
7 TH	19: 1:34	19 37	10 20	20 21	1 36	2 30	19 10	26 27	15 19	21 13	5 ♓ 1'47"
8 FR	19: 5:31	25 42	11 58	21 18	2 10	2 34	19 12	26 27	15 19	21 14	5 ♓ 1'46"
9 SA	19: 9:27	1 ♋ 40	13 35	22 16	2 44	2 39	19 14	26 27	15 19	21 14	5 ♓ 1'46"
10 SU	19:13:24	7 30	15 13	23 13	3 18	2 44	19 15	26 28	15 20	21 14	5 ♓ 1'46"
11 MO	19:17:20	13 12	16 50	24 10	3 52	2 48	19 17	26 29	15 20	21 15	5 ♓ 1'46"
12 TU	19:21:17	18 45	18 28	25 7	4 26	2 53	19 19	26 30	15 20	21 15	5 ♓ 1'46"
13 WE	19:25:14	24 8	20 5	26 4	5 0	2 57	19 21	26 30	15 21	21 15	5 ♓ 1'46"
14 TH	19:29:10	29 22	21 43	27 2	5 35	3 2	19 23	26 31	15 21	21 16	5 ♓ 1'46"
15 FR	19:33: 7	4 ♌ 26	23 20	27 59	6 9	3 6	19 24	26 32	15 21	21 16	5 ♓ 1'45"
16 SA	19:37: 3	9 20	24 58	28 56	6 43	3 11	19 26	26 32	15 22	21 16	5 ♓ 1'45"
17 SU	19:41: 0	14 5	26 35	29 53	7 18	3 15	19 28	26 33	15 23	21 17	5 ♓ 1'45"
18 MO	19:44:56	18 41	28 13	0 ♉ 51	7 52	3 20	19 30	26 34	15 23	21 17	5 ♓ 1'45"
19 TU	19:48:53	23 8	29 50	1 48	8 27	3 25	19 32	26 34	15 23	21 17	5 ♓ 1'45"
20 WE	19:52:49	27 26	1 ♌ 28	2 45	9 2	3 29	19 33	26 35	15 24	21 18	5 ♓ 1'45"
21 TH	19:56:46	1 ♍ 37	3 5	3 42	9 36	3 34	19 35	26 36	15 24	21 18	5 ♓ 1'45"
22 FR	20: 0:43	5 39	4 43	4 39	10 11	3 38	19 37	26 36	15 24	21 18	5 ♓ 1'44"
23 SA	20: 4:39	9 35	6 20	5 37	10 46	3 43	19 39	26 37	15 24	21 19	5 ♓ 1'44"
24 SU	20: 8:36	13 23	7 58	6 34	11 21	3 47	19 41	26 38	15 25	21 19	5 ♓ 1'44"
25 MO	20:12:32	17 6	9 35	7 31	11 56	3 52	19 43	26 38	15 25	21 19	5 ♓ 1'44"
26 TU	20:16:29	20 42	11 13	8 29	12 31	3 56	19 44	26 39	15 25	21 19	5 ♓ 1'44"
27 WE	20:20:25	24 13	12 50	9 26	13 6	4 1	19 46	26 40	15 26	21 20	5 ♓ 1'44"
28 TH	20:24:22	27 39	14 28	10 23	13 41	4 5	19 48	26 40	15 26	21 20	5 ♓ 1'44"
29 FR	20:28:18	1 ♎ 0	16 5	11 21	14 16	4 10	19 50	26 41	15 27	21 20	5 ♓ 1'44"
30 SA	20:32:15	4 16	17 43	12 18	14 51	4 14	19 52	26 41	15 27	21 21	5 ♓ 1'43"
31 SU	20:36:12	7 29	19 20	13 15	15 26	4 19	19 53	26 42	15 27	21 21	5 ♓ 1'43"

INGRESSES :

3	☿→♊ 20:31
4	♂→♐ 4:15
8	☿→♋ 17:14
14	☿→♌ 2:58
17	⊕→♑ 2:48
19	♀→♌ 2:22
20	☿→♍ 14:39
28	☿→♎ 16:48

ASPECTS (HELIOCENTRIC +MOON(TYCHONIC)) :

```
 1  ☿ □ ♆  12:34      ⊕ ☌ A  19: 6      ☽ □ ♂   5:20   17 ☿ ☍ ♆   6:38   24 ☽ ☍ ♃  10:27   30 ☽ □ ♃  19:53
 2  ☿ ☍ ♄   2:49    5 ☽ □ ♅   1:31      ♀ ☌ P  23:48      ☽ □ ♃  16:15   25 ☽ □ ♂   0:21   31 ♀ □ ♄   8:20
    ☽ □ ♆   4:36      ☽ ☌ ♀  22:46   11 ☽ □ ♇  16:58   18 ☽ ☌ ♂   0:57      ☽ ☍ ☿  12:20      ☽ ☍ ♂  15:39
    ☽ ☍ ♄  10:46    7 ☿ ☍ ⊕   3:22      ☿ ☌ ♀  22:13      ☿ □ ♄   4:22      ☽ □ ♇  16:21
    ☽ ☌ ☿  16:52      ☿ ☍ ♇   6:17   12 ☽ ☍ ♅   3:34   19 ☽ ☌ ♇   1:59   26 ☽ ☌ ♅   1:24
    ☿ ☌ P  16:58      ⊕ ☌ ♇  22: 4      ☿ ∥ ☊  21:23      ☽ □ ♅  11:44      ☿ □ ♇   4:12
 3  ☽ ☍ ♂   3:59    8 ☿ □ ♅   2:59   13 ⊕ □ ♅  11: 1   21 ☿ ☌ ♃  11:41   27 ☿ ☍ ♅  17: 4
    ☽ □ ♃   8:38      ☽ ☍ ♆  18: 7   14 ☽ □ ♀   7:37   22 ☽ ☍ ♀   9: 6   28 ♀ ☍ ♆  14:23
    ☿ ☍ ♂  19:46      ♂ □ ♃  20:19   15 ☽ □ ☿  13:33   23 ☽ ☌ ♆   2:40   29 ☽ □ ♆  11:51
 4  ☿ □ ♃   5:14    9 ☽ □ ♄   1:37   16 ☽ □ ♆   5:36      ☿ □ ♂   8:42      ☽ □ ♀  14:37
    ☽ ☍ ♇  16:35   10 ☽ ☌ ♃   3:59      ☽ ☌ ♄  13:35      ☽ □ ♄  10: 3      ☽ ☍ ♄  19:19
```

When Jesus entered the large buidings where lived the possessed, they became perfectly furious and dashed themselves almost to death. The mind that has lost its star becomes frenzied, dashing about as autonomous intelligences *think them*. The astonishing increase in individuals taking psychotropic drugs is testimony to a rising global madness. Just as the star of the Christ Sun quieted the insane, so also will our star steady us in times of trial. Possession is rampant. Yet, we have brought destiny forces of strength with us into birth. These forces lie in our inner world as potential, and in persevering faithfulness to our own star—through which the voice of Christ can be heard—we find them.

The fact that Jesus was in the place where Jacob's son was sold into slavery, reminds us of the "star that will come forth from Jacob," as prophesied in Numbers 24:17. Joseph's coat of many colors represents, by analogy, the seven planetary spheres of influences that enfold each of us as we journey into incarnation. Joseph could see into these realms and therefore he could interpret the Pharaoh's dreams. Without a star to follow, madness will render many to the lot of those Christ encountered in Dothaim. Intuition intensifies with today's aspect.

July 7: Late this evening Venus enters Cancer: "Create life warmth." Venus in Cancer asks us to practice selflessness in order to find the catharsis that awaits the soul when selfishness is relinquished. Venus was in Cancer at the death of the Solomon Mary and at the conception of the Solomon Jesus. Today Mercury and Sun come into opposition with Pluto; Venus squares Uranus:

ASPECT (1): Mercury 21° Gemini opposite Pluto 21° Sagittarius. Mercury at this degree remembers when Jesus said to the apostles and disciples, "Now you cling to me, because you fare well. In the time of need, you will act otherwise" (May/28/32). This aspect can cause abruptness in our interpersonal communication as well as mental intensity. Intellectual arrogance may rise if patience does not temper the lower aspect of Pluto—power. In times of trial we reveal who we really are. Where were the disciples when Christ really needed them? Following the Christ Sun leads us to discover ever deeper layers of truth.

ASPECT (2): Sun 21° Gemini opposite Pluto 21° Sagittarius: The healing of ten lepers (Jun/12/32). Truth is a force that reveals that in us which errantly longs for personal power, and in the content of our speech is revealed what truly lives in our heart. When defiance and resentment give way to love, we are able to face our greatest fears—thus do the skies clear, and our star again becomes visible.

ASPECT (3): Venus 29° Gemini square Uranus 29° Pisces: Venus recalls Jesus as he taught before hundreds near Chytroi, and spoke of the prophet Malachi (May/7/31). Again the heavens recall Malachi, the last of Israel's prophets. The prophetic tradition inaugurated by Abraham is again rising through the current work of the Maitreya Bodhisattva. Now, however, this tradition is carried out in full consciousness, under the direction of the sovereign "I." Many are awakening to new revelation and these numbers will increase as the current Abraham millennium unfolds. In square to Uranus, Venus yearns to soar in free-spirited celebration of the Hermetic mysteries.

July 11: Mercury 29° Gemini square Uranus 29° Pisces (Mercury enters Cancer today): The brith of John the Baptist (Jun/4/2 BC). John the Baptist could see into apocalyptic realms, wherein the future revelation stream illumined him, granting certainty to him of the one he perceived as the Lamb of God. Mercury in Cancer seeks to ensoul matter with the life-bestowing power of spirit, thus ennobling all things with the force of original creation.

Jul 16: Sun 29° Gemini square Uranus 29° Pisces: The Sun remembers Jesus, the apostles, and disciples, walking to a hill two hours from Cana (Thursday, Jun/21/31). They talked of their missionary journeys; and then, raising his eyes to heaven, Jesus said: "I saw Satan fall like lightning from heaven" (Luke 10:18–20). Anne Catherine Emmerich saw in this same moment, a lurid light whirling and shooting through the air. This aspect can cause one to feel as if some unpredictable event is pending—as if the future is whispering, yet not quite heard. What was the lurid lightning that whirled about? Was this the ghastly presence of Satan, disturbing the atmosphere around the One who was seeing him?

Uranus brings the promise of revelation; however, when Uranus's forces are inverted by sub-forces, the subverted influences can engender the manic confusion that overtakes one who has stumbled into Lucifer's "belt of lies."

Mercury conjunct Venus 10° Cancer: The conversation with Dina of Samaria at Jacob's Well. Venus recalls when Jesus said, "[But] whoever drinks of the water that I shall give him will never thirst," (Jul/26/30). Jacob had dug this well. The well led into the earthly depths—toward the Mother's realm of Shambhala. By analogy, we can see this well as representing the etheric forces of the Mother, rising to grace all who turn to her now; for just as Jacob fathered the twelve tribes of ancient Israel, so too can we imagine Jacob currently forming twelve tribes devoted to the community of Eternal Israel. The water from Jacob's Well quenches the parched thirst of all souls whose hearts are longing for the new mysteries as revelation from the Mother in the depths. This aspect bestows the living waters of grace through the catharsis (Cancer) that meets one who has gained selflessness.

Sun enters Cancer: "You resting, luminous glow" (Steiner, *Twelve Cosmic Moods*). William Bento illumines this mantra:

> As the Sun reaches its zenith in the summer sky, it appears to rest and emit a luminous glow of warmth and light. This high point of the yearly cycle offers us the opportunity to express our gratitude for all the life we see around us, knowing that its existence is due to the Sun's luminosity. This phase opens the breast and allows our heart to enter into dialogue with the mighty orb of warmth and light that bestows life to all.

In Cancer "Selflessness becomes Catharsis." The instinct to purify oneself is amplified. The Cathars were the "pure ones." The first decan is ruled by Mercury and is associated with the constellation of Argo the Ship—in which, according to Greek mythology, Jason and the Argonauts recovered the Golden Fleece.

Mars enters Scorpio: "In growth activity persists." Mars in Scorpio seeks to unveil the hidden mysteries. If the desires in one's astral body are not governed through the "I," patience is reduced to impetuosity, which is easily antisocial.

July 19: Full Moon 3° Capricorn opposite Sun 3° Cancer. The Moon at this degree remembers Jesus in Capernaum, teaching the baptism by fire (Jun/23/31). The flowering of the event of Peter opening the Church (last New Moon) resounds today in the promise of the new baptism—by fire—which is exemplified in the raising of Lazarus from the dead. Christ proclaimed that no one could enter the kingdom of God unless they were born of *water* and the *spirit* (John 3:5). Nicodemus reflects the new "water" initiation; Lazarus the new "spirit/fire (air)" initiation.

> And just as Christ brought the old mystery initiation out of the darkness of the night into daylight, he also led the Israelite initiation out of the daylight into night consciousness. Abraham and Nicodemus are the names that mark the limits of Israelite initiation. But Nicodemus is also an initiate of the new night initiation that grew out of the old day initiation, just as the Lazarus–John event was also an initiation of the new day initiation that grew out of the old night initiation.[3]

During this discourse remembered by today's Full Moon, Jesus also cautioned his disciples to be awake to the coming of the Son of Man. Such wakefulness is granted to those who are able to transcend the ordinary intellect's entombment:

> Our intelligence, as it leaves the hands of Nature, has for its chief object the unorganized solid…. Of the discontinuous alone does the intellect form a clear idea…. Of immobility alone does the intellect form a clear idea…. The intellect lets what is *new* in each moment of history escape. It does not admit the unforeseeable. It rejects all creation…. The intellect is characterized by a natural inability to comprehend life…. But it is to the very inwardness of life that intuition leads us—by intuition I mean instinct that has become disinterested, self-conscious, capable of reflecting upon its object and of enlarging it indefinitely. [Henri Bergson][4]

---

3   Tomberg, *Christ and Sophia,* p. 35.
4   Anon., *Meditations on the Tarot,* p. 492.

When we achieve disinterest toward the life of instincts—and the life of instincts become capable of pure reflection upon its object—gnosis is attained. *Gnosis is the direct knowing (intuition) of things that lie at the depths of our being, where eternity has inscribed its memory into the elemental substance of our being.* Intuition lives in these primal depths, and we are to unite with this force. The inward path of descent leads us into these realms, and there we meet our fallen likeness; these aspects appear like corpses hanging from the gallows tree—aspects we have buried in subconscious layers of our psyche. Thus have aspects of our intuition been swallowed by death. To become conscious of the signs of the coming of the Son of Man—and to journey into the worlds where the fire of the spirit baptizes us with the naked truth—we must overcome the limitations of the intellect that "lets what is new in each moment of history escape." Tomes have been written regarding the errant intellect's inability to perceive history as it is being written. In hindsight, the biographies of heretics unfold before us, revealing the daring of those who have advanced by surpassing the dogmas of their time. They did not retreat; rather they aligned themselves with the principle of "continuity"—ever promising the precipice, over which the intellect must propel itself, in order to reach into gnostic realms reclaiming the power of intuition.

This Full Moon asks us to unbind our bound mind—in order to find our baptism by fire and stand witness to the signs of the Coming of the Son of Man. To safely remain in our shells is easier by far; yet, the world will pass us by, rendering us forever hungry and thirsting for what we cannot touch.

July 20: Saturn 15° Scorpio: The conception of the Nathan Mary (Oct/24/18 BC). Saturn at this holy birth stood at the death/ resurrection star— Antares. The orbit of Saturn marks the sphere in which the mighty Seraphim hold sway—the spirits of Love. In this planetary sphere we are given our destiny tasks on our path to rebirth. It is poignant beyond measure that Mary's destiny was to bear witness to the Earth's greatest death mystery, as prophesied by Saturn at the moment she was conceived into the earthly world.

July 29: ASPECT: Mercury 3° Leo square Mars 3° Scorpio: The birth of the Nathan Jesus (Saturday, Dec/6/2 BC) is recalled by Mars at this degree. The pastors and healers are to see into the hidden mysteries so as to align their will with the Archangel Michael, who is calling those prepared to fight against the evil that is holding sway. The orbit of the planet Mars marks the sphere in which the Thrones directly serve the Father spirit in the heights, as well as the Mother in the depths. They work through the Kyriotetes in the Sun sphere, and from there they send their impulses of will to the Archai in the third Hierarchy. These are the beings who govern great epochs of Time. We live in the time of the Second Coming, and are called to receive the teachings issuing forth from the Archangel Jesus into the Angel Jesus—who now seeks to resurrect in the *manas* body of the new disciples.

July 30: Uranus stations 29° Pisces before moving retrograde. The Sun at this degree holds the memory of the triumphant entry into Jerusalem (Thursday, Mar/19/33).

As we meditate upon his triumphant entry into Jerusalem, we may picture ourselves standing along that same road, with eyes that see and ears that hear, receiving him into our hearts also with the burning certainty that he is the Messiah! This testimony will support us in the times to come. It will carry us through the difficult turnings along our journeys—just as the colt carried Christ on the road leading into the City of Peace![5]

AUGUST 2016

The New Moon is on the 2nd this month in Cancer. The still-not-visible crescent Moon conjuncts Venus on the 3rd, and Mercury on the 4th, all within the glow of our Sun. By the 5th, the new crescent Moon might be visible with Jupiter in Leo in the west at sunset.

By the 11th, the Moon will have made her way over into Scorpio, where Mars and Saturn await,

---

5 Isaacson, *Through the Eyes of Mary Magdalene,* vol. 2, p. 71.

joining with them each in turn. On the 17th, the Sun enters Leo, the Lion while Jupiter exits the same constellation and moves into Virgo on the 15th! The Moon lines up in Aquarius opposite to the Sun forming the Full Moon on the 18th.

Mercury joins Jupiter in Virgo on the 22nd, Venus meets up with Jupiter on the 27th, and with Mercury on the 29th, the last of their three exact meetings this year and the only one that is visible—look to the west at/after sunset for this whole series of planetary beauty!

Mars joins Saturn on the 24th in Scorpio—very close to one of the four Royal Stars of Persia. This one is Antares, the "Heart of the Scorpion" at 15° of Scorpio. It shines with a reddish glow and can be mistaken for Mars! Reread May's stargazing tips to orient to what is what here; what a chance to learn this powerful star's location and light!

To end the month, Mercury stations Retrograde in Virgo on the 31st.

Aug. 1: Venus enters Leo: "Existing ground of worlds." The mantra for the constellation of Leo is "courage becomes compassion." Wherever we are unconsciously bound to our lower instincts, we have little tolerance for the imperfections of others. The planet of love today enters the constellation of Sun-born compassion, guiding us to draw forth the higher "I" within both our friends and our enemies. Venus will be in Leo until the 26th of this month. Venus was in Leo at the births of both the Nathan Mary and the Solomon Mary, as well as at the raising of Lazarus.

Aug. 2: New Moon 16° Cancer: The Adoration of the Solomon Jesus (Dec/26/6 BC). The Moon bore witness at this zodiacal position as the three wise men offered their precious gifts to the newborn child, who was to become the Master Jesus. This constellation asks us to touch into the glory of manifest creation. Thus do we experience our adoration for the work of the divine Father/Mother. Zarathustra—who reincarnated as the Soloman Jesus—became the Master Jesus at the event of the Baptism, when he withdrew his "I" from the sheaths of the Nathan Jesus in order to make room for the incarnation of Christ into the bodily vessel of the

pure Nathan Jesus being. In his earlier incarnation as Zarathustra, he had perceived Christ supersensably in the Sun sphere and called him Ahura Mazda. Master Jesus worked under the principle of the "intuition of faith," the principle belonging to springtime. This is the principle of the living Word, through whom all things were made. For the Word belongs to spring—to the act of "sowing" the seeds that, over long eons of time, gradually bring into time what the Father created at the beginning of existence. Inverse to the "intuition of faith" is the brain-bound intellect, which is predominately trained upon the autumn: the harvest. It devotes itself to what can be produced, gained, increased through quantity. The New Moon in Cancer asks us to follow the beginning of John's Gospel and to participate in all that is in the process of becoming. If the intellect does not raise itself to the living revelation of the Word, our heart is threatened by the shadowed forces notable in an eclipse. Intelligence is falling ever deeper into the serpent's world, and its revival depends on beholding what is in the process of becoming. For at the heart of life is the Word, and in this life is the light of humanity that shines into the darkness of materialism:

> Now, the Gospel of St. John appeals to the human soul to transpose its intelligence from autumn into full springtime—to rejuvenate it by placing it in the domain of creativity instead of that of the created, i.e., to accomplish a "conjunction" of the Sun and Moon, expressing it in astrological terms....
>
> And all this it will do not in order to understand—i.e., in order to reap what is—but rather in order to effect an act of becoming, in order to accomplish the birth of the new, i.e., of what is not. Because "to all who received him, who believed in his name, he gave power to become children of God, who were born, not of blood nor of the will of the flesh nor of the will of man, but of God" (John 1:12–13).[1]

The nature of ordinary intelligence differs widely from what Tomberg calls the "intuition of faith"; the former is autumn-like, the latter carries the renewing forces of spring. Autumn understands

---

1 Anon., *Meditations on the Tarot,* p. 502.

what is—*what has become* as the harvest of thinking. Spring, on the other hand, participates in the becoming of *what is to be*. If we cannot participate in the sprouting possibilities that are now striving to awaken us into a new genius of culture, we will harvest things ever more mechanized, and thus absent of life. Today's aspect asks us to say "yes" to something virginally beginning, and to serve possibilities barely comprehensible. Master Jesus served the triumph of new beginnings; he indwelled the vessel through whom the Father and the Mother were reunited when Christ incarnated in the flesh. He therefore gave us the possibility to revere *Natura* as the manifestation of the unity of love between the Father and the Mother. Under the influences of this new lunar cycle, we can contemplate our willingness to selflessly serve all of creation as protectors and redeemers, turning our hearts to the new Christ-imbued forces working powerfully in Nature. Just as the wise men came to adore the Jesus child, so too can we adore the "sowing" of the Word as it will sound through the influences of Christ that manifest through his earthly spokesperson, the Maitreya Bodhisattva.

Aug. 6: Mercury 15° Leo square Saturn 15° Scorpio. The Sun was where Saturn is today when, shortly after the raising of Lazarus, Jesus departed from Judea with three young shepherds (Aug/7/32). Due to the upheaval caused by his having raised Lazarus from the dead, he needed to be forgotten…for a time. This aspect can cause mental restraint, as the planet Saturn leans heavily on tradition. Jesus told his disciples that nine weeks would pass before they should join him again. There is no written account of this journey, for no apostles accompanied him.

Mercury can be seen as representative of the healers and pastors of humankind; and Saturn signifies the holy Virgin. The higher influences of this square of Mercury and Saturn (in their respective constellations) undergo a transformation, revealing the fruits that can be acheived by our higher intelligence when the compassionate heart sees into hidden realms of being. Thus does the mantle of the Virgin open before us, revealing unconscious layers of our soul that we are to encounter. As we face

our inner darkness, we settle upheavals originating from deeper layers of our psyche.

Aug. 7: Mercury 16° Leo opposite Neptune 16° Aquarius. The Moon was where Mercury is today at the Baptism of Jesus (Sep/23/29). This aspect influences communication, bestowing creativity and imagination. However, one must master susceptibility to the deception of the sense nature, and instead penetrate into the motivations of others with clarity of consciousness. When John baptized Jesus, and witnessed thereby the descent of the Holy Spirit, he was a man of extreme clarity, unwavering in his faith. As this aspect streams revelatory imaginations from the future-oriented constellation of Aquarius, we are called to encounter and overcome doubt. *Doubt is the mask that often shields consciousness from the soul's fear when it is faced with the unknown.*

Aug. 12: Sun 25° Cancer: Birth of the Nathan Mary (Jul/17/17 BC). The Nathan Mary was connected with the spiritual stream of love and compassion that attained its high point in Hinduism as well as in Buddhism. She bore the vessel for the Logos. Purity and gentleness are remembered today. At this birth, Venus, Mars, and Moon were all conjunct the star Regulus, 5° in the heart of the Lion, providing a beautiful contemplation for the purity of heart we are all striving to attain—the purity of the Nathan Mary.

Aug. 13: Venus 15° Leo square Saturn 15° Scorpio. Jesus was near Hanathon, where he taught the disciples regarding the petitions of the Lord's Prayer and the eighth Beatitude (Jun/24/31). Venus now squares Saturn, as did Mercury one week ago. The planet of love, representing the Passion of Christ, in square to the forces emanating from the Holy Virgin (Saturn), asks us to discern those who are our true karmic brothers and sisters. The spirits of Time, working from the planetary sphere marked by the orbit of Venus, know where and with whom we are to serve. This encourages us to transform all fears of rejection into a courageous willingness to fight for the sake of righteousness—in acceptance of our karmic trials.

SIDEREAL GEOCENTRIC LONGITUDES :   AUGUST 2016 Gregorian at 0 hours UT

DAY	☉	☽	☊	☿	♀	♂	♃	♄	♅	♆	♇
1 MO	14 ♋ 12	20 ♊ 39	18 ♌ 7R	6 ♌ 55	29 ♋ 19	4 ♏ 23	27 ♌ 6	14 ♏ 56R	29 ♓ 32R	16 ♒ 30R	20 ♐ 40R
2 TU	15 10	4 ♋ 22	18 2	8 25	0 ♌ 33	4 45	27 17	14 55	29 32	16 29	20 38
3 WE	16 7	17 49	17 59	9 53	1 47	5 8	27 28	14 54	29 32	16 27	20 37
4 TH	17 5	0 ♌ 57	17 56	11 19	3 1	5 31	27 39	14 53	29 31	16 26	20 36
5 FR	18 2	13 48	17 55	12 43	4 14	5 54	27 51	14 52	29 31	16 25	20 34
6 SA	19 0	26 20	17 55D	14 6	5 28	6 18	28 2	14 51	29 31	16 23	20 33
7 SU	19 57	8 ♍ 37	17 57	15 27	6 42	6 42	28 13	14 50	29 30	16 22	20 32
8 MO	20 55	20 42	17 58	16 45	7 55	7 7	28 25	14 50	29 30	16 20	20 31
9 TU	21 52	2 ♎ 38	18 0	18 2	9 9	7 33	28 36	14 49	29 30	16 19	20 29
10 WE	22 50	14 30	18 1	19 16	10 23	7 58	28 48	14 49	29 29	16 17	20 28
11 TH	23 47	26 22	18 1R	20 29	11 37	8 25	28 59	14 49	29 28	16 16	20 27
12 FR	24 45	8 ♏ 20	18 0	21 39	12 50	8 51	29 11	14 49	29 28	16 14	20 26
13 SA	25 43	20 29	17 58	22 47	14 4	9 18	29 23	14 48	29 27	16 13	20 25
14 SU	26 40	2 ♐ 51	17 56	23 53	15 18	9 46	29 34	14 48D	29 27	16 11	20 23
15 MO	27 38	15 30	17 53	24 56	16 31	10 13	29 46	14 49	29 26	16 10	20 22
16 TU	28 35	28 29	17 50	25 57	17 45	10 41	29 58	14 49	29 25	16 8	20 21
17 WE	29 33	11 ♑ 49	17 48	26 55	18 59	11 10	0 ♍ 10	14 49	29 24	16 7	20 20
18 TH	0 ♌ 31	25 27	17 46	27 50	20 12	11 39	0 22	14 49	29 23	16 5	20 19
19 FR	1 28	9 ♒ 23	17 45	28 43	21 26	12 8	0 34	14 50	29 22	16 4	20 18
20 SA	2 26	23 32	17 45D	29 32	22 39	12 38	0 46	14 51	29 21	16 2	20 17
21 SU	3 24	7 ♓ 51	17 45	0 ♍ 18	23 53	13 8	0 58	14 51	29 20	16 0	20 16
22 MO	4 22	22 14	17 46	1 0	25 7	13 38	1 10	14 52	29 19	15 59	20 15
23 TU	5 19	6 ♈ 39	17 47	1 39	26 20	14 9	1 23	14 53	29 18	15 57	20 14
24 WE	6 17	21 0	17 48	2 13	27 34	14 40	1 35	14 54	29 17	15 56	20 13
25 TH	7 15	5 ♉ 14	17 48	2 44	28 47	15 11	1 47	14 55	29 16	15 54	20 12
26 FR	8 13	19 20	17 48R	3 10	0 ♍ 1	15 42	1 59	14 56	29 15	15 52	20 11
27 SA	9 11	3 ♊ 15	17 47	3 32	1 15	16 14	2 12	14 57	29 13	15 51	20 11
28 SU	10 9	16 58	17 46	3 48	2 28	16 46	2 24	14 59	29 12	15 49	20 10
29 MO	11 7	0 ♋ 29	17 46	4 0	3 42	17 19	2 37	15 0	29 11	15 47	20 9
30 TU	12 5	13 46	17 45	4 5	4 55	17 52	2 49	15 2	29 9	15 46	20 8
31 WE	13 3	26 48	17 44	4 6R	6 9	18 25	3 2	15 3	29 8	15 44	20 7

INGRESSES :

1	♀ → ♌	13:13	
	☽ → ♋	16:19	
3	☽ → ♌	22:13	
6	☽ → ♍	7: 5	
8	☽ → ♎	18:41	
11	☽ → ♏	7:17	
13	☽ → ♐	18:31	
16	☽ → ♑	2:44	
	♃ → ♍	3:50	
17	☉ → ♌	11:13	
18	☽ → ♒	7:53	
20	☽ → ♓	10:52	
	☿ → ♍	14:34	
22	☽ → ♈	12:55	
24	☽ → ♉	15: 9	
25	♀ → ♍	23:40	
26	☽ → ♊	18:21	
28	☽ → ♋	23: 8	
31	☽ → ♌	5:56	

ASPECTS & ECLIPSES :

```
 1 ☽☍♆   0: 1      8 ☽☍♅ 17:40     18 ☉☍☽  9:25          ☽☍♄ 16:28
 2 ☉☌☽  20:43        ☿☌☊ 23:18     19 ☽☌♆ 11:20          ☽☍♂ 17:33
 4 ☽☌♀   4:11     10 ☽☌A  0:11         ☽☌☋ 14:13          ☽⚷☊ 21:22
   ☽☌☿  21:43         ☉☌♅ 22:23     26 ♂□♆  7:10
 5 ☽☍♆   4:56     12 ☽☌♂  1: 3     20 ☽☍☿ 10:39       27 ♀☌♃ 22:27
   ☽☌☊   7:49         ☽☌♄ 12:50         ☽☍♃ 12:19       28 ☽☍♆  5:37
 6 ☽☌♃   3:19     13 ☽⚼☊ 19: 5     22 ☽☌P  1:23       29 ☿☌♀  6:31
   ☿□♄  13:16         ♀□♅ 14:30         ☿☌♃  9: 4          ♂□☊ 19: 8
   ☉□♅  19:51     14 ♀☍♇ 17: 9         ☽☌♅ 11:46
 7 ♀□☿   0:19     15 ☽☍♄  9: 3     24 ♂☍☊ 11:24
   ☿☍♆  16:29     16 ♀☌☊  1:38     25 ☉☍☽  3:39
```

SIDEREAL HELIOCENTRIC LONGITUDES :   AUGUST 2016 Gregorian at 0 hours UT

DAY	Sid. Time	☿	♀	⊕	♂	♃	♄	♅	♆	♇	Vernal Point
1 MO	20:40: 8	10 ♎ 37	20 ♌ 58	14 ♑ 13	16 ♐ 2	4 ♍ 24	19 ♏ 55	26 ♓ 43	15 ♒ 28	21 ♐ 21	5 ♓ 1'43"
2 TU	20:44: 5	13 43	22 35	15 10	16 37	4 28	19 57	26 43	15 28	21 22	5 ♓ 1'43"
3 WE	20:48: 1	16 45	24 12	16 8	17 12	4 33	19 59	26 44	15 28	21 22	5 ♓ 1'43"
4 TH	20:51:58	19 45	25 50	17 5	17 48	4 37	20 1	26 45	15 29	21 22	5 ♓ 1'43"
5 FR	20:55:54	22 41	27 27	18 3	18 23	4 42	20 2	26 45	15 29	21 23	5 ♓ 1'43"
6 SA	20:59:51	25 36	29 4	19 0	18 59	4 46	20 4	26 46	15 29	21 23	5 ♓ 1'42"
7 SU	21: 3:47	28 29	0 ♍ 41	19 58	19 35	4 51	20 6	26 47	15 30	21 23	5 ♓ 1'42"
8 MO	21: 7:44	1 ♏ 20	2 19	20 55	20 10	4 55	20 8	26 47	15 30	21 24	5 ♓ 1'42"
9 TU	21:11:41	4 9	3 56	21 53	20 46	5 0	20 10	26 48	15 30	21 24	5 ♓ 1'42"
10 WE	21:15:37	6 57	5 33	22 50	21 22	5 4	20 12	26 49	15 31	21 24	5 ♓ 1'42"
11 TH	21:19:34	9 44	7 10	23 48	21 58	5 9	20 13	26 49	15 31	21 24	5 ♓ 1'42"
12 FR	21:23:30	12 30	8 47	24 45	22 34	5 14	20 15	26 50	15 32	21 25	5 ♓ 1'42"
13 SA	21:27:27	15 15	10 24	25 43	23 9	5 18	20 17	26 51	15 32	21 25	5 ♓ 1'41"
14 SU	21:31:23	18 0	12 1	26 41	23 45	5 23	20 19	26 51	15 32	21 25	5 ♓ 1'41"
15 MO	21:35:20	20 45	13 38	27 38	24 21	5 27	20 21	26 52	15 33	21 26	5 ♓ 1'41"
16 TU	21:39:16	23 29	15 15	28 36	24 58	5 32	20 22	26 52	15 33	21 26	5 ♓ 1'41"
17 WE	21:43:13	26 14	16 52	29 33	25 34	5 36	20 24	26 53	15 33	21 26	5 ♓ 1'41"
18 TH	21:47:10	29 0	18 29	0 ♒ 31	26 10	5 41	20 26	26 54	15 34	21 27	5 ♓ 1'41"
19 FR	21:51: 6	1 ♐ 45	20 6	1 29	26 46	5 45	20 28	26 54	15 34	21 27	5 ♓ 1'41"
20 SA	21:55: 3	4 32	21 43	2 27	27 22	5 50	20 30	26 55	15 34	21 27	5 ♓ 1'40"
21 SU	21:58:59	7 19	23 20	3 24	27 59	5 54	20 31	26 56	15 35	21 28	5 ♓ 1'40"
22 MO	22: 2:56	10 8	24 56	4 22	28 35	5 59	20 33	26 56	15 35	21 28	5 ♓ 1'40"
23 TU	22: 6:52	12 58	26 33	5 20	29 11	6 4	20 35	26 57	15 36	21 28	5 ♓ 1'40"
24 WE	22:10:49	15 50	28 10	6 18	29 48	6 8	20 37	26 58	15 36	21 29	5 ♓ 1'40"
25 TH	22:14:45	18 44	29 46	7 16	0 ♑ 24	6 13	20 39	26 58	15 36	21 29	5 ♓ 1'40"
26 FR	22:18:42	21 40	1 ♎ 23	8 13	1 1	6 17	20 41	26 59	15 37	21 29	5 ♓ 1'40"
27 SA	22:22:39	24 38	2 59	9 11	1 37	6 22	20 42	27 0	15 37	21 29	5 ♓ 1'40"
28 SU	22:26:35	27 39	4 36	10 9	2 14	6 26	20 44	27 0	15 37	21 30	5 ♓ 1'39"
29 MO	22:30:32	0 ♑ 42	6 12	11 7	2 51	6 31	20 46	27 1	15 38	21 30	5 ♓ 1'39"
30 TU	22:34:28	3 49	7 48	12 5	3 28	6 35	20 48	27 2	15 38	21 30	5 ♓ 1'39"
31 WE	22:38:25	6 59	9 25	13 3	4 4	6 40	20 50	27 2	15 38	21 31	5 ♓ 1'39"

INGRESSES :

6	♀ → ♍	13:45	
7	☿ → ♏	12:48	
17	⊕ → ♒	11: 3	
18	☿ → ♐	8:45	
24	♂ → ♑	7:59	
25	♀ → ♎	3:26	
28	☿ → ♑	18:32	

ASPECTS (HELIOCENTRIC +MOON(TYCHONIC)) :

```
 1 ☽☍♇   1:14      8 ☽□♇  1:23     15 ☽☌♇ 11: 1      21 ☽□♇ 22:42      28 ☽☍♇  7:59
   ☽□♅  10:34         ☽☍♅ 12:13         ☽☌♂ 17:13      22 ☽☍♀  5: 3          ☽□♅ 17:48
   ♀⚼☊  13:17      9 ♀☌♃ 16:35         ☿☌A 17:27          ☽☌♅  7:49      29 ☽☍♀  0:31
 2 ☿□⊕  16:44     10 ♂☌♇  1:35         ☽☌♆ 10:32          ☽□♂ 11: 1          ☽☍♂  4:27
   ☽□☿  21:32         ☽□♅ 21: 2     19 ♂□♅  5:39      23 ♀☍♅  6: 1          ☽□♀ 11:42
 5 ☽☍♆   3:11     12 ☽☌☿ 10:41         ☽☍♄ 20:44      25 ♀□♂ 15:17          ☿☌♂ 20:38
   ☿☌☋   7: 6         ☽□♆ 14:15     20 ☿□♃ 11:30          ☽□♆ 17:37
   ☽☌♄  11:54         ☽☌♄ 23:37         ☽☌♆ 10:32      26 ☽☍♇  2:18          ☿☌♅ 18:55
 6 ☽☌♀   6: 5     13 ☿□♀  2:26         ☽□♄ 18:51      27 ☽□♃  5:26          ♀□♆ 20: 8
   ☽☌♃  16:31     14 ☽□♃  4:52                                                 ☿□♀ 22:34
 7 ☽☌♂  22:53         ☽□♀ 19:59                                                 ☽□☿ 22:55
                      ☿☌♄ 20:26
```

When Jesus was instructing his disciples near Hanathon, he tirelessly and patiently reiterated the petitions of the Lord's Prayer, enabling the disciples to repeat exactly the same thing throughout their various and widespread missions. The eighth Beatitude blesses the persecuted; the anti-forces to this Beatitude (i.e., the forces of persecution) are intensifying. This is signified by the entrance of heliocentric Jupiter into Virgo this past June, which marked the entrance of Christ into a new sphere within the Earth's interior. Geocentric Jupiter enters Virgo in two days. New demons are being released from the eighth subearthly sphere. This aspect challenges us to face any anxiety head-on, with a faithfulness to the power of prayer. Patiently praying these petitions gives way to peace—and we can hope that our practice of prayer has forged a mighty force that we can use in the face of persecution.

Aug. 14: Venus 16° Leo opposite Neptune 16° Aquarius. Venus was at this degree as Pharisees were agitating and Mary Salome was requesting her sons (James and John) to become disciples of Jesus (Jul/24/32). This was two days before the raising of Lazarus, which occurred that year on the New Moon of July 26th. On this day Mary Salome was sternly rebuked by Christ for again asking favors for her two sons, John and James of Zebedee (see Chron., p. 316). Intensity was mounting. The Pharisees were aggressively reporting on the activity of Jesus, Lazarus lay dying, Jesus's disciples were questioning his delay in going to Bethany, and the time of his impending sacrifice was drawing ever nearer. St. Matthew records this rebuke:

> She [Mary Salome] said: "Grant that one of these two sons of mine may sit at your right and the other at your left in your kingdom." "You don't know what you are asking," Jesus said to them. "Can you drink the cup I am going to drink?" "We can," they answered.
>
> Jesus said to them, "You will indeed drink from my cup, but to sit at my right or left is not for me to grant. These places belong to those for whom they have been prepared by my Father."

Jesus goes on to teach of officiousness exercised by authorities in this world vs. the humility that marks one who serves with no expectation of reward: "Just as the Son of Man did not come to be served, but to serve, and to give his life as a ransom for many." Today's aspect warns of delusion born of unconscious forces.

James and John had no idea that the cup to which Christ referred was the bitter cup of sacrifice he would accept in nine months' time, in the Garden of Gethsemane. How could they have known? They were urged by their mother, Mary Salome, to attain position, and foolishly she petitioned the servant of all humanity to grant this to them. This event can remind us of the true nature of service, and the dangers of attaining "position"; for once one has this thing, one must defend it.

Officious "position" vs. humility can be our contemplation. We are urged to find our willingness to drink the bitter cup that is the portion of Christ's Passion which we are to take upon ourselves. Elijah–John goes before us as one preparing the way for our Aquarian future.

Today Saturn (14° Scorpio) goes direct.

Aug. 15: Jupiter enters Virgo: "Build upon experiences undergone": On June 4th, during the New Moon in Taurus, heliocentric Jupiter entered Virgo, marking Christ's descent into a new realm of the subearthly worlds. Today geocentric Jupiter ingresses into Virgo. The constellation of Virgo bestows the protective quality of "Force" as an antidote to the most cunning persecutions the beast can spawn, using his hosts released from the eighth subearthly sphere. As new demons are released into terrestrial regions, they will seek to attain even more heinous power. Communities will need to be on guard against divisive forces posing as caricatures of divine impulses. Ahriman's aim is to create a machine-like human being. Just as there are nine cosmic–spiritual realms in which the hierarchies dwell ("above"), so, too, are there nine subearthly planes in which demonic beings dwell ("below"). Christ bears the archetype of the spiritualized human being of the future, reflecting the nine ranks of the spiritual hierarchies above. His archenemy, Ahriman, is in the process of using modern technology to create another kind of human being— indeed, a subhuman being—out of the forces of the nine subearthly planes. Jupiter in Virgo asks that we awaken to the phenomenon of our Mother and seek, at all costs, to protect her from the debasement she suffers due to the heinous acts of ahrimanically directed human beings. Jupiter was in Virgo at the death of the Solomon Jesus and at the death of the Nathan Mary.

Aug. 17: Sun enters Leo: "Irradiate with senses' might." William Bento illumines this mantra:

One of the most primal gifts we received from the Cosmos was the possibility to be endowed with senses, to have the capacity to witness the creation of all things upon the Earth. It is a gift we can too easily take for granted. Yet, when we ponder how the Sun being has gathered the forces of the entire Zodiac and poured them down upon our uprightness in such a way as to create portals into the external world, we can sensitize ourselves to feel how this streaming of forces has never ceased. It is there, in the infusion and invigoration of our senses' activity in grasping the world with all its beauty.

The first decan, ruled by Saturn, is associated with the faint constellation of Leo Minor, the Lesser Lion, above Leo and below the Great Bear. The virtue: Compassion becomes Freedom. This freedom is the foundation of the spiritualized "I."

Aug. 18: Full Moon 1° Aquarius opposite Sun 1° Leo: The Moon in tonight's sky stands at its position when the resurrected One appeared to eleven disciples (Saturday, Apr/11/33). Jesus's first words to those assembled were "Peace be to you." Thomas was among the apostles, and this was when Jesus showed him his wounds. Anne Catherine Emmerich saw the wounds as radiant Suns. Afterward, Jesus gave communion to Peter, gracing him with strength and vigor as Jesus breathed upon him. Emmerich witnessed this:

Jesus put his mouth to Peter's mouth, then to his ears, and poured that strength into each of the three. It was not the Holy Spirit himself, but something that the Holy Spirit was to quicken and vivify in Peter at Pentecost. Jesus laid his hands on him, gave him a special kind of strength, and invested him with chief power over the others.[2]

The sense of hearing is precious beyond measure. We can imagine the Eustachian tubes rising from the larynx, forming the sense of hearing—which in its highest manifestation is able to listen into the silence of inaudible regions from whence comes inspiration. Thus does one hear the heart of God. Now that we are living in the time when the Maitreya Bodhisattva is *speaking the good,* our sense of hearing needs to be protected from the onslaught of noise the adversaries create. In quietude we perceive messages from angelic realms. Jesus Christ seemed to bless Peter with the ability to hear higher worlds, from whence messages of the Holy Spirit descend to meet the one silently listening. *The Maitreya will speak a new language, and he must wait for human beings to learn how to hear him. It is not the human being who awaits the Maitreya, rather it is the Maitreya who waits for human beings to comprehend him.* When Jesus Christ breathed into Peter's ears and into his mouth, it was as if Peter was joined to a larger community—overseen by an Archangel—representing the community of Christians being formed at that time. Since the founding of Peter's Church, the apostolic succession has been representative of something larger than the priests themselves:

There is what is called in Christian Hermeticism the "freeing of the guardian Angel." The guardian Angel is freed—often in order to be able to acquit new missions—when the soul has acquired the disposition of its part of "likeness" in order to experience the Divine more intimately and more immediately, which corresponds to another hierarchical degree. Then it is an *Archangel* who replaces the freed guardian angel. Human beings whose guardian is an Archangel have not only new experiences of the Divine in their inner life, but also, through this very fact, receive a new and objective vocation. They become *representative* of a human group—a nation or a human karmic community—which means to say that from this time onward their actions will no longer be purely personal but will at the same time have significance and value for those of the human community that they represent.[3]

---

2 *ACE Complete,* p. 1350.

3 Anon., *Meditations on the Tarot,* p. 379.

The anti-forces would rather fill all space with noisy discord, confounding humankind's ability to truly hear. The serpent has formed a closed circle, in which increasing decibels of ubiquitous noise sentence a deaf humanity to a *spiritually silent* world. The Maitreya comes to lead us out of the serpent's hellish isolation on behalf of Christ. Turning to goodness raises us into realms of inspiration where the cacophony of the serpent's clawing greed cannot reach:

> For "the Fall" is a cosmic event, a whirlwind set in motion by the closed circle of the serpent "biting" his tail and "sweeping down part of the created world" (Rev. 12:4). And "redemption," to say it directly, is the cosmic act of the Reintegration of the fallen world, first in creating an opening in its closed circle (religion, initiation, prophecy), then in instituting a path of exit (Buddhas) and entrance (Avatars) through this door, and lastly in transforming the fallen world from within by the radiation of the incarnated Word (Jesus Christ).[4]

In silence we too may hear the greeting of the Risen One: "Peace be to you."

Aug. 20: Sun 3° Leo: The raising of Lazarus from the dead (July/26/32). With the forces of the New Moon still in effect, we recall the seventh miracle of Christ. At Lazarus's death, his Angel placed him in the custody of John the Baptist, who was then to quide him from the spiritual world. A contemporary Christian mystic beheld the mystery of the descent of Lazarus into the subearthly spheres, wherein she experienced the pain of fallen Nature:

> Here we paused. We were at the threshold of hell. John the Baptist held his hands over Lazarus's head, whereupon a radiant garment of light spilled from his hands. It was like water pouring out. The light completely enveloped Lazarus, and the garment of his being grew ever more luminous. Then John told him that he was going to escort him on a further descent, a descent into the Earth, and that he was to experience a "burial" in the Heart of the Mother. The garment of light he was being provided was to
>
> protect him as they passed further through the subearthly spheres—the realms of darkness.
>
> And so the descent began. As we proceeded through the subearthly spheres, Lazarus heard the cries of souls that had become trapped in the bowels of hell. They cried out to him for release. John, however, was not moved by these cries. When Lazarus looked to John for solace, John said, "One who is mightier than both of us shall come to save these souls. Turn your ears away; heed not their cries, lest you lose yourself in the darkness!"
>
> A golden sphere came into view. Peace and warmth emanated from this sphere. We were enveloped in its golden light, light of a different quality than that of the sunlight at the surface of the Earth. This light seemed to have more substance to it. I felt pulled more and more deeply into the light, as if the light wished to receive us into its midst.
>
> Whereas the light of the sun is expansive, offering itself magnanimously to all, touching us wherever we may be, the light at the center of the Earth has a quality of "drawing in," of enfolding. I felt the golden light all through my being as we journeyed into it, drawn toward its center. Lazarus and John appeared completely golden, as though turned to gold.
>
> Then I heard a whispering voice saying, O My son Lazarus! O My Son!
>
> Beings in service to the Mother encircled us. They made a sound like delicate chimes and the soft unfolding of wings. They were winged creatures, each with many wings. Upon their faces was the smile of eternity. We were as though enveloped in the sweet smile of the Mother, who smiles into your soul![5]

Each of us will at some time be called to experience what may be called the *Earth trial:* inwardly beholding our fallen nature and having to endure all that we must suffer. What is fallen in us contributes to the entire paradigm of fallen Nature. The forces in the inner Earth—which *draw inward* toward the Earth's center—represent what we call "gravity." Seen in this light, Gravity is the binding power of love emanating from the womb of the

---

4 Ibid., 244.

5 Isaacson, *Through the Eyes of Mary Magdalene,* vol., 1, p. 188.

Earth, wherein dwells the Earth–Sun. We can contemplate our ability to face that in us which, until we transform ourselves, contributes to the enchainment of our Mother.

Aug 22: Mercury conjunct Jupiter 1° Virgo. Jesus was in Shechem with Mercury at today's degree, teaching the whole day regarding the persecution of the prophets (Matt. 21:33–43). This was the day after the conversation between Jesus and Dina at Jacob's Well. Now he speaks of the persecution of prophets with Dina in attendance, for she had resolved to dedicate herself to his work (Thursday, July/27/30). Standing on the same ground that was walked by Abraham, Jacob, and their offspring must have inspired Jesus's teachings regarding the persecutions of prophets. The parable of the vineyard and the slaying of the messenger is as applicable today as it was in the time Christ spoke these words. With heliocentric Jupiter in Virgo we stand witness to global developments wherein persecutions may be increasing—against both individuals and the Earth herself.

This aspect bestows confidence in our imaginative capacities. The Mother's forces flow upward from the mystery site centered at Jacob's Well, streaming forces of strength to those open to receive her grace. Mercury rules Virgo, enhancing mental capacities. Healers and pastors today stand together with the Holy Spirit (Jupiter)—a blessing for those disposed to receive cosmic imaginations.

Sun conjunct Regulus 5° Leo: The Pharisees asked Jesus the meaning of Jonah's three days and nights in the belly of the whale (Saturday, July/29/30). Leo is the only constellation ruled by the Sun. We most need the Christ–Sun when we enter into the Earth trial that is exemplified by Jonah. Christ's descent into Hell can also be seen as an Earth trial. It is no coincidence that this event occurred on a Saturday (the day of the Holy Virgin). The Pharisees were rebuked by Jesus for claiming knowledge of the Ten Commandments while following them not. Jesus's words fell upon deafened hearts, long-hardened by the rigidifying forces operative in their souls. Jonah's trial is a theme for our time, as we encounter the mysteries of descent into our inner world. It

represents a crossing of the threshold on a global scale. We will need the courage of the Lion.

Aug. 24: Mars conjunct Saturn 15° Scorpio (Antares). Saturn remembers the conception of the Nathan Mary (Oct/24/18 BC). Mars brings the power of the Archangel Michael to the Holy Virgin (Saturn). This aspect calls forth the sanctity of Holy Saturday, when Christ descended into Hell. It was the Holy Virgin who held vigil for him through the dark hours he would spend in the inner realms of the Earth. The Holy Virgin Mary, united inwardly with the blessed Nathan Mary, was experiencing a twofold sorrow as Jesus Christ—the Son of God—encountered the full forces of evil.

The conjunction between these two planets lends energetic discipline to our activities, tempering impulsive anger and negative thoughts that could otherwise overcome us. We can contemplate the Nathan Mary's equanimity of soul as the archetype of soul harmony—through which each of us will be able to face the darkness of our personal inner realms. To bear witness to the hidden realms of evil, both personally and collectively, is the work of our time. Antares today arms us with restraint born of courage, and asks us to develop the patience that brings forth powerful insights into hidden realms of existence.

Aug. 25: Venus enters Virgo: "May the soul fathom worlds." Venus in Virgo urges the soul to read the phenomena of nature and comprehend the story the Mother is telling. Her elemental beings are in need of our protection, and she is sending a "force" of protection for all who receive her now. Through practicing the virtue of Courtesy we find tactfulness of heart; this leads us to knowledge of what the heart of the other longs to hear. Venus was in Virgo at the conception of the Nathan Mary.

Aug. 26: Mars 16° Scorpio square Neptune 16° Aquarius: The Sun at Mars' location recalls Jesus as he prepared for the Sermon on the Mount, which he would deliver on the following day. Over sixty friends, relatives, and disciples gathered in expectation; among them was Mary Magdalene, who would experience her first conversion the next day (Nov/7/30):

There was in Magdalene a mixture of true and false shame. She was partly ashamed of her simple, pious, and plainly dressed sister who went around with Jesus's followers so despised by her visitors and associates, and she was partly ashamed of herself before Martha. It was this feeling that prevented her taking the latter into the apartments that were the scenes of her follies and vices. Magdalene was somewhat broken in spirits, but she lacked the courage to disengage herself from her surroundings.[6]

Michael (Mars) in square to Neptune creates a dynamic tension, for the desire nature of our personal will here meets the gaze of the Goddess Night (Neptune)—who works in tandem with the Archangel Michael. Magdalene's shame is an example of this tension; she will become inwardly confused and thrown into an interior struggle with the words Jesus Christ will speak tomorrow. Like Magdalene, our desire nature seeks resonance with spiritual inspiration (Neptune). We are to wakefully penetrate all possible entanglement in delusions born of egoism. Hidden realms are being revealed (Scorpio), motives may be questioned. Do we have the courage to name our various follies and vices despite the cleansing blush of shame this may call forth?

Aug. 27: Venus conjunct Jupiter 2° Virgo: Venus remembers Jesus as he taught on the subject of Jacob and Joseph. He said: "One day another also shall be sold by one of his brethren. But he will pardon his penitent brethren and in the time of famine feed them with the Bread of Eternal Life."[7] Venus in conjunction with Jupiter sees beauty in all things, blessing communities with the refined and noble aspects of life. The earth sign Virgo bestows courtesy and openhearted mindfulness. When jealousies rage in the soul, dark motives gain control. Thus did Judas sell Jesus to the Pharisees, and thus also did Joseph's brothers sell him into slavery. This aspect reminds us of the Bread of Life that eternally feeds those whose hearts are directed toward peace. We are now living in the time of famine; yet, materialism cannot suffocate one who has learned how to breathe spiritual air,

which literally can inbreathe the seed forces of life's eternal Bread.

Aug. 29: Mercury conjunct Venus 4° Virgo: Venus recalls the conception of John the Baptist (Sept/9/3 BC).

Aug. 31: Mercury goes retrograde 4° Virgo.

SEPTEMBER 2016

The month begins with retrograde Mercury in Virgo, which will drop back into Leo on the 9th and station Direct on the 23rd of this month.

We are also met with the New Moon on the 1st, in Leo; an annular solar eclipse. The 2nd brings Mercury and Jupiter together again in Virgo (and they will meet once more in October this year). The Sun and Moon are just close enough that we may not see this, but if we do it will be in the moments of sunset and right after, directly to the west. Venus is here, too, just a wee bit farther to the south and visible.

The waxing crescent Moon will join Saturn on the 8th and Mars on the 9th, all in Scorpio. Look to the south to see this dance beginning as the Sun sets. Saturn will be right above the Royal Star of Antares, so here's your chance to "learn" this star if you missed the opportunity last month.

The next Mercury Sun conjunction unfolds on the 12th, unseen due to the Sun's light. By the 16th, the Moon aligns opposite both of these beings in Aquarius for the Full Moon, which is also a penumbral lunar eclipse. The next day, the 17th, the Sun shifts into the constellation of Virgo.

On the 19th, Mars moves back into Sagittarius (the Archer). On the 23rd, Mercury stations Direct in Leo. On the 25th, the Sun is far enough into Virgo to meet up with Jupiter, and the Moon does the same by the 30th in the hours before the New Moon in Virgo.

The month starts and ends with a New Moon, occurring at 14° Leo on the 1st, and at 13° Virgo on the 30th.

Sept. 1: New Moon 14° Leo and Total Solar Eclipse: The total eclipse will be visible from Sumatra,

---

6 *ACE Complete*, p. 490.
7 Ibid., p. 431.

Borneo, Sulawesi, and from locations in the Pacific Ocean. The eclipse will be partial for people in South and East Asia and northern and eastern Australia. The eclipse will begin at 11:20 p.m. (UTC), on March 8 with the maximum point of the eclipse occuring at 2 a.m. (UTC) on March 9: duration 4 min. 9 secs.

The conversation between the Soloman Mary and the Nathan Jesus before the Baptism in the Jordan River (Sept/23/29). From the perspective of the Sun (heliocentric), this Moon stands in the constellation of Aquarius, remembering the births of Rudolf Steiner and Valentin Tomberg. A Leo New Moon calls us to find our lion-hearted courage, to irradiate our senses with the power of existence streaming from the very grounds of the world. We are not to submit to the yoke of slavery, but to compassionately find our freedom and serve the sanctity of freedom in others. Our sovereign "I" must face trials that encapsulate us in the sense world's falsehoods. There is a truth that is ours to realize—regardless of the opinions of others. Truth creates a vibration and it is this vibration that establishes the "field" inspiring our actions.

The Nathan Jesus was unwavering in his obedience to truth. He had a spiritually profound conversation with his stepmother, the Soloman Mary before leaving for the Baptism. In the words he spoke, he poured out the truth he had witnessed, of humanity's condition of utter decadence. Like a flash of lightning the truth came that the Soloman Jesus hitherto living within the sheaths of the Nathan Jesus, was to sacrifice himself to make way for the descent of Christ. This foretold the second sacrifice of the Soloman Jesus, who was the reincarnated Zarathustra. His first sacrifice had come at the age of seventeen when he relinquished his astral, etheric, and physical bodies in order to unite on the level of the "I" with the twelve year old Nathan Jesus child in the temple, when the Nathan Jesus began teaching the Elders.. For seventeen years the Soloman Jesus had lived within the sheaths of the Nathan Jesus; now, during this conversation, through the heart of the Soloman Mary (the stepmother of the Nathan Jesus), the Soloman Jesus met Christ and knew what he was to do. He obeyed.

The Solomon Jesus left the sheaths of the Nathan Jesus. Thus, the Nathan Jesus walked as a pure vessel to meet John the Baptist. The Moon at 14° Leo remembers this event. The Nathan Jesus remained completely free of the forces originating from the conditions of the Earth's evolution; in him dwelt the virginal forces of paradise—ennabling him to be the perfect vessel for Christ, whose every moment was in connection to the virgin purity of the beings indwelling all the stars:

> In the case of Christ Jesus, the cosmic–spiritual powers alone remained active in him after the Baptism. The laws of the Earth's evolution did not influence him at all.
>
> During the time that Jesus of Nazareth pursued his ministry and journeys as Jesus Christ in Palestine in the last three years of his life—from the age of thirty to thirty-three—the entire cosmic Christ-being continued to work in him. In other words, Christ always stood under the influence of the entire cosmos; he did not take a single step without cosmic forces working in him. The events of these three years in Jesus' life were a continuous realization of his horoscope, for in every moment during those years there occurred what usually happens only at birth.[1]

The "I" of Jesus Christ lives in all hearts, and when two or more are gathered together in his name, Christ can be found in our midst.

With Moon and Sun in Leo the matter before us is to avoid being locked in an endless circle by restricting ourselves to perceptions born of the physical sensory nature alone. Higher worlds are eternally real, and influences from these worlds are continuously informing us through our higher capacities (imagination, inspiration, intuition). Our earthly sensory nature alone, for example, will not inform us of when we stand in the presence of an initiate. It was not the earthly sensory nature of John that recognized Christ at the Baptism; it was intuition arising into consciousness, revealing the miracle before which he stood. *Every moment in Christ's life was a new birth, a new horoscope, from which he wove together the world of the senses and the worlds of the cosmos.* He lived the truth of every

---

1 Steiner, *The Spiritual Guidance of the Individual and Humanity*, p. 65.

moment. The duality of the world of the senses and the higher worlds is resolved when we both weep and sing praise for creation:

> This is the origin of the problem of the Fall: that the world is worthy of being sung for and wept for at the same time.

The world is not what it should be. There is a contradiction between the totality and the details. For whilst the starry heavens represent a harmony of equilibrium and perfect cooperation, animals and insects devour one another and innumerable legions of infectious microbes bear sickness and death to human beings, animals and plants.

It is this contradiction which the term "the Fall" alludes to. In the first place, it designates a state of affairs in the world which gives the impression that the world is composed of two independent, if not opposed, worlds, as if in the organism of the great world of the "harmony of the spheres" there is interpolated another world with its own laws and evolution—as if a cancerous outgrowth has taken place in the otherwise healthy organism of the great world.[2]

The Hermeticist regards the sense-bound nature of scientific inquiry as separate from the Nature created by God. The former is the *field* where the created world meets with the world of the serpent. Discerning between the two worlds is the message of this new lunar cycle. In our hearts we know the truth that is ours to carry, no matter the opinion of others. Out of integrity, one must choose a direction born of the collaboration between the self and the cosmos. At the borderline between the sense world and the starry worlds is an encircling round in which the touch of Christ can be felt by all seeking him. From this periphery, in constant relationship with the center point of the "I," each of us can experience Christ and the great truths revealed in each and every moment.

ASPECT: Sun 14° Leo square Saturn 14° Scorpio. The Sun remembers Jesus and three shepherd youths as they parted company with the disciples. Andrew, Peter, and Philip returned to their homes. Jesus and his companions journeyed on into the land of the three holy kings (Aug/6/32). The Sun

remembers Jesus leaving for pagan lands, searching for the kings, two of whom had remained alive. The king in us is our "I." Promises were made as we journeyed through the planetary spheres on our path to birth. This aspect creates a dynamic tension between our divine "I" (Sun) and the spiritual resolves (Saturn) we carry in the depths of our hearts. Is there resonance?

Sept. 2: Sun 15° Leo opposite Neptune 15° Aquarius. The Sun in the center of Leo recalls Jesus teaching in the synagogue at Bethsaida. Afterward, he went with Saturnin to a home for lepers and simpletons, where he consoled and healed them (Aug/7/30). The lonely hospital in which Jesus found the sick and needy was filled with miserable and forlorn creatures, who had been quite forgotten by the rest of the world. This aspect suggests that we reevaluate challenges in our lives (or in the world) that may not be clearly defined. Inspiration streams from the higher Neptunian realms into our heart, calling us to encounter all in us that is sick and needy, as well as to serve others so afflicted. Compassion is the gift bestowed when we have the courage to name—and therefore release ourselves—from what tethers us to endless circles of egoism and illusion. Still under the influence of yesterday's New Moon, we remember the Master Jesus, who sacrificed himself so that Christ could be born into earthly existence. We are called to arise with the might of our senses permeated with the presence of firmly willed existence.

Rudolf Steiner depicted the rising again of the sybilline stream, now Christianized. Leo imbues the senses with both the Earth mysteries and the Sun mysteries. We are each to find a relationship to revelation and play our part in the shift now upon us.

ASPECT (2): Mercury conjunct Jupiter 4° Virgo. Mercury remembers Jesus setting off with three disciples to Atharot, where some Sadducees tried to trick him into raising from the dead someone who had already been dead for eight days. Jesus exposed their plot (Jul/30/30). This aspect bestows a love of higher learning as imaginations quicken, enlightening us to all forms of trickery now being used against us.

---

2 Anon, *Meditations on the Tarot,* p. 245.

SIDEREAL GEOCENTRIC LONGITUDES :   SEPTEMBER 2016 Gregorian at 0 hours UT

DAY	☉	☽	☊	☿	♀	♂	♃	♄	♅	♆	♇
1 TH	14 ♌ 1	9 ♌ 37	17 ♌ 44R	4 ♍ 0R	7 ♍ 22	18 ♏ 58	3 ♍ 14	15 ♏ 5	29 ♓ 6R	15 ♒ 42R	20 ♐ 7R
2 FR	14 59	22 12	17 44D	3 48	8 36	19 32	3 27	15 7	29 5	15 41	20 6
3 SA	15 57	4 ♍ 34	17 44	3 30	9 49	20 6	3 39	15 9	29 3	15 39	20 5
4 SU	16 55	16 44	17 45	3 6	11 3	20 40	3 52	15 11	29 2	15 37	20 5
5 MO	17 53	28 45	17 45R	2 35	12 16	21 14	4 5	15 13	29 0	15 36	20 4
6 TU	18 52	10 ♎ 40	17 44	1 59	13 30	21 49	4 17	15 15	28 58	15 34	20 3
7 WE	19 50	22 31	17 44	1 16	14 43	22 24	4 30	15 17	28 56	15 33	20 3
8 TH	20 48	4 ♏ 23	17 44	0 28	15 57	22 59	4 43	15 20	28 55	15 31	20 2
9 FR	21 46	16 19	17 44	29 ♌ 36	17 10	23 34	4 56	15 22	28 53	15 29	20 2
10 SA	22 45	28 26	17 44D	28 39	18 24	24 10	5 8	15 25	28 51	15 28	20 1
11 SU	23 43	10 ♐ 46	17 44	27 40	19 37	24 46	5 21	15 28	28 49	15 26	20 1
12 MO	24 41	23 25	17 44	26 39	20 50	25 22	5 34	15 30	28 47	15 24	20 0
13 TU	25 40	6 ♑ 25	17 45	25 38	22 4	25 59	5 47	15 33	28 46	15 23	20 0
14 WE	26 38	19 50	17 46	24 38	23 17	26 35	6 0	15 36	28 44	15 21	19 59
15 TH	27 37	3 ♒ 39	17 47	23 40	24 30	27 12	6 13	15 39	28 42	15 19	19 59
16 FR	28 35	17 51	17 47	22 46	25 44	27 49	6 26	15 42	28 40	15 18	19 59
17 SA	29 34	2 ♓ 22	17 47R	21 58	26 57	28 26	6 38	15 45	28 38	15 16	19 58
18 SU	0 ♍ 32	17 7	17 46	21 16	28 10	29 3	6 51	15 49	28 36	15 15	19 58
19 MO	1 31	1 ♈ 58	17 44	20 41	29 23	29 41	7 4	15 52	28 33	15 13	19 58
20 TU	2 29	16 47	17 43	20 15	0 ♎ 37	0 ♐ 19	7 17	15 55	28 31	15 12	19 58
21 WE	3 28	1 ♉ 28	17 41	19 58	1 50	0 57	7 30	15 59	28 29	15 10	19 58
22 TH	4 27	15 55	17 40	19 51	3 3	1 35	7 43	16 3	28 27	15 8	19 57
23 FR	5 25	0 ♊ 4	17 39	19 54D	4 16	2 13	7 56	16 6	28 25	15 7	19 57
24 SA	6 24	13 54	17 39D	20 6	5 30	2 52	8 9	16 10	28 23	15 5	19 57
25 SU	7 23	27 24	17 40	20 29	6 43	3 30	8 22	16 14	28 20	15 4	19 57
26 MO	8 22	10 ♋ 37	17 41	21 1	7 56	4 9	8 35	16 18	28 18	15 2	19 57
27 TU	9 20	23 33	17 43	21 41	9 9	4 48	8 48	16 22	28 16	15 1	19 57D
28 WE	10 19	6 ♌ 14	17 44	22 31	10 22	5 28	9 1	16 26	28 14	14 59	19 57
29 TH	11 18	18 43	17 44R	23 28	11 35	6 7	9 14	16 30	28 11	14 58	19 57
30 FR	12 17	1 ♍ 2	17 44	24 33	12 48	6 47	9 27	16 34	28 8	14 57	19 57

INGRESSES :

2	☽→♍ 15: 5	♂→♐	12: 2
5	☽→♎ 2:30	20 ☽→♉	21:34
7	☽→♏ 15: 9	22 ☽→♊	23:52
8	☿→♌ 13:11	25 ☽→♋	4:40
10	☽→♐ 3: 4	27 ☽→♌	12: 9
12	☽→♑ 12:14	29 ☽→♍	21:58
14	☽→♒ 17:44		
16	☽→♓ 20: 7		
17	☉→♍ 10:50		
18	☽→♈ 20:49		
19	♀→♎ 11:57		

ASPECTS & ECLIPSES :

1 ☉ ☌ ☽ 9: 2	5 ☽ ☍ ô 0:29	13 ☉ □ ♂ 20:39	22 ☽ ☍ ♄ 0:12
☉ ● A 9: 6	6 ☽ ☌ A 18:57	15 ☽ ☌ ♆ 19:44	☽ ☌ ☊ 2:55
☽ ☍ ♆ 11:32	8 ☽ ☌ ♄ 22: 5	☽ ☌ ♅ 23:53	23 ☽ ☍ ♂ 3:52
☽ ☌ ☊ 15:26	9 ☽ ♅ ☊ 2:48	16 ☽ ☍ ☿ 7:44	☉ □ ☽ 9:55
2 ☉ □ ♄ 3:21	☉ □ ☽ 11:47	☽ ⚹ PN18:56	24 ☽ ☍ ♇ 10:41
☉ ☍ ♆ 16:45	☽ ☌ ♂ 15: 9	☉ ☍ ☽ 19: 4	26 ☉ ☌ ♃ 6:59
☿ ☌ ♃ 17:16	10 ♄ □ ♆ 15: 3	17 ☽ ☍ ♃ 7: 5	28 ☽ ☍ ♆ 16:45
☽ ☌ ☿ 21:58	11 ♀ □ ♇ 7:42	18 ♀ ☍ ô 8: 3	☽ ☌ ☊ 22: 5
☽ ☌ ♃ 22:11	☽ ☌ ♇ 17:35	☽ ☌ P 17: 4	29 ☽ ☌ ☿ 10: 4
3 ☽ ☌ ♀ 11:28	12 ☿ □ ♂ 18:56	☽ ☌ ô 18:30	30 ☽ ☌ ♃ 16:53
4 ☉ ☌ ☊ 20:19	☉ ☌ ♅ 23:39	☽ ☍ ♀ 19:28	

SIDEREAL HELIOCENTRIC LONGITUDES :   SEPTEMBER 2016 Gregorian at 0 hours UT

DAY	Sid. Time	☿	♀	⊕	♂	♃	♄	ô	♆	♇	Vernal Point
1 TH	22:42:21	10 ♉ 12	11 ♎ 1	14 ♒ 1	4 ♑ 41	6 ♍ 44	20 ♏ 51	27 ♓ 3	15 ♒ 39	21 ♐ 31	5 ♓ 1'39"
2 FR	22:46:18	13 30	12 37	14 59	5 18	6 49	20 53	27 4	15 39	21 31	5 ♓ 1'39"
3 SA	22:50:14	16 52	14 13	15 58	5 55	6 53	20 55	27 4	15 39	21 32	5 ♓ 1'39"
4 SU	22:54:11	20 19	15 50	16 56	6 32	6 58	20 57	27 5	15 40	21 32	5 ♓ 1'38"
5 MO	22:58: 8	23 50	17 26	17 54	7 9	7 3	20 59	27 5	15 40	21 32	5 ♓ 1'38"
6 TU	23: 2: 4	27 27	19 2	18 52	7 46	7 7	21 0	27 6	15 41	21 33	5 ♓ 1'38"
7 WE	23: 6: 1	1 ♒ 9	20 38	19 50	8 23	7 12	21 2	27 7	15 41	21 33	5 ♓ 1'38"
8 TH	23: 9:57	4 58	22 14	20 49	9 0	7 16	21 4	27 7	15 41	21 33	5 ♓ 1'38"
9 FR	23:13:54	8 53	23 50	21 47	9 37	7 21	21 6	27 8	15 42	21 34	5 ♓ 1'38"
10 SA	23:17:50	12 54	25 25	22 45	10 14	7 25	21 7	27 9	15 42	21 34	5 ♓ 1'38"
11 SU	23:21:47	17 3	27 1	23 43	10 51	7 30	21 10	27 9	15 43	21 34	5 ♓ 1'37"
12 MO	23:25:43	21 19	28 37	24 42	11 29	7 34	21 11	27 10	15 43	21 34	5 ♓ 1'37"
13 TU	23:29:40	25 43	0 ♏ 13	25 40	12 6	7 39	21 13	27 11	15 43	21 35	5 ♓ 1'37"
14 WE	23:33:37	0 ♓ 16	1 48	26 39	12 43	7 43	21 15	27 11	15 44	21 35	5 ♓ 1'37"
15 TH	23:37:33	4 56	3 24	27 37	13 20	7 48	21 17	27 12	15 44	21 36	5 ♓ 1'37"
16 FR	23:41:30	9 46	5 0	28 36	13 58	7 52	21 19	27 13	15 44	21 36	5 ♓ 1'37"
17 SA	23:45:26	14 44	6 35	29 34	14 35	7 57	21 20	27 13	15 45	21 36	5 ♓ 1'37"
18 SU	23:49:23	19 52	8 11	0 ♓ 33	15 13	8 2	21 22	27 14	15 45	21 36	5 ♓ 1'36"
19 MO	23:53:19	25 8	9 46	1 31	15 50	8 6	21 24	27 15	15 45	21 37	5 ♓ 1'36"
20 TU	23:57:16	0 ♈ 34	11 22	2 30	16 28	8 11	21 26	27 15	15 46	21 37	5 ♓ 1'36"
21 WE	0: 1:12	6 9	12 57	3 28	17 5	8 15	21 28	27 16	15 46	21 37	5 ♓ 1'36"
22 TH	0: 5: 9	11 52	14 33	4 27	17 43	8 20	21 29	27 17	15 46	21 38	5 ♓ 1'36"
23 FR	0: 9: 6	17 43	16 8	5 26	18 20	8 24	21 31	27 17	15 47	21 38	5 ♓ 1'36"
24 SA	0:13: 2	23 41	17 43	6 24	18 58	8 29	21 33	27 18	15 47	21 38	5 ♓ 1'36"
25 SU	0:16:59	29 46	19 19	7 23	19 35	8 33	21 35	27 19	15 47	21 39	5 ♓ 1'36"
26 MO	0:20:55	5 ♉ 57	20 54	8 22	20 13	8 38	21 37	27 19	15 48	21 39	5 ♓ 1'35"
27 TU	0:24:52	12 11	22 29	9 21	20 51	8 42	21 39	27 20	15 48	21 39	5 ♓ 1'35"
28 WE	0:28:48	18 29	24 4	10 20	21 28	8 47	21 40	27 20	15 49	21 39	5 ♓ 1'35"
29 TH	0:32:45	24 48	25 39	11 19	22 6	8 51	21 42	27 21	15 49	21 40	5 ♓ 1'35"
30 FR	0:36:41	1 ♊ 7	27 15	12 18	22 44	8 56	21 44	27 22	15 49	21 40	5 ♓ 1'35"

INGRESSES :

6 ☿ → ♒ 16:34	
12 ♀ → ♏ 20:48	
13 ☿ → ♓ 22:39	
17 ⊕ → ♓ 10:39	
19 ☿ → ♈ 21:30	
25 ☿ → ♉ 0:53	
29 ☿ → ♊ 19:44	

ASPECTS (HELIOCENTRIC +MOON(TYCHONIC)) :

1 ☽ ☍ ♆ 11:27	⊕ □ ♄ 6:36	15 ☿ ☌ ♃ 14:32	☽ ☌ ♆ 23:45	☽ ☍ ♂ 18:41
☿ □ ♆ 11:36	☽ □ ♆ 22:44	☽ ☍ ♄ 20:28	22 ☽ ☌ ♄ 9:24	27 ☿ □ ♆ 13:48
☽ □ ♄ 21:28	9 ☽ ☌ ♄ 9:32	16 ☽ □ ♄ 5:47	♀ □ ♆ 18:37	28 ☿ ☍ ♄ 12:10
2 ⊕ ☌ ♆ 16:29	10 ☿ ☌ ♂ 16:17	17 ☽ ☍ ♃ 9:10	23 ☿ □ ♂ 2:48	☿ ☌ P 16:11
3 ☽ ☌ ♃ 4:35	☽ □ ♃ 17:38	18 ☽ ☌ ♅ 6:52	☽ □ ♃ 14:28	☽ ☍ ♂ 18:22
4 ☽ □ ♇ 9:32	11 ☽ ☌ ♆ 20:32	☽ □ ♆ 7:16	♀ ☌ ☊ 23:27	29 ☿ ☍ ♀ 4:20
☽ ☍ ô 20:39	☿ ☌ ♄ 23:16	♀ □ ♇ 8: 0	24 ☽ ☍ ♅ 13:41	☽ □ ♄ 5:47
☿ ☌ ☊ 22: 6	12 ☽ ☌ ô 16:22	☽ ☌ ô 23:49		☽ □ ♀ 15:29
5 ☽ □ ♂ 17:49	☿ ☌ ⊕ 23:39	19 ☿ ☌ ô 9:23	26 ⊕ ☍ ♃ 6:59	30 ☽ □ ♀ 0:21
6 ☽ ☌ ♀ 19:35	13 ☽ ☌ ♂ 10:44	☽ ☌ ♂ 23:26	♀ ☌ ♄ 11: 0	☽ ☌ ♃ 15:39
8 ☽ □ ☿ 1:45	14 ☽ □ ♀ 23:31	21 ☽ ☍ ♀ 21:24	♀ ☌ ♅ 14:30	

Sept. 10: Saturn conjunct Antares 15° Scorpio square Neptune 15° Aquarius: Saturn remembers the conception of the Nathan Mary (Oct/24/18 BC). Hidden worlds taunt us with their shadowy dreams, perhaps confusing us due to a lack of discrimination between our own thoughts and the thoughts of others. We must discern the difference that exists between illusory specters and angelic messengers. Void of clarity, the soul may fall into fear and anxiety. Lower Neptune rules mass media and the torrential rivers of mass thought constantly circling the globe. These thoughts can too easily worm their way into our inner world. Thus does it become ever more difficult to differentiate what is truly our own thinking from what has been seeded from the thoughts of the masses. The Nathan Mary drew her light from virginal streams of wisdom, preserving her soul from the polluting influences of the antiSophia—who preys upon all that is pure. With Saturn conjunct Antares, the death/resurrection star, the Holy Virgin is our guide into the mysteries of underworld agendas. Fear stalks us until we turn to face it—then does its illusion dissolve, revealing its nothingness.

Sept. 11: Venus 20° Virgo square Pluto 20° Sagittarius. Venus remembers when Jesus was in Abila and Gadara, where he commanded the possessed and spoke of Elijah whose cave was located nearby (Sep/21/31). After healing many, a throng of possessed souls pressed toward Jesus, raging through the crowd as if to tear him to pieces. He cast upon them a single glance, and they fell like whining dogs at his feet. With a word of command, he drove the devils out, and a dark vapor then escaped from them (Sep/20/30). With Venus square Pluto, passions are aroused. Karmic groups stand in dynamic relationship with forces of the personal as well as of the collective unconscious.

In union with Christ, our "I" can settle agitated storms as did the Christ "I" settle the storm of demons in the possessed. Soul impulses are to be governed, for Hades works through the slumbering unconscious, possessing those who lack self-will. Our Venus chakra remembers those with whom we have Sun karma (positive karma), and those with whom we have Moon karma (something to be redeemed). The latter can cause impulsivity. The

power of Love expels the senseless activity of dark vaporous ghosts that wish to inhabit us. Venus in Virgo streams a "force" that works with us when we cooperate with Divine Love, through which the heart is able to reconcile all karmic discord.

This day reverberates with the memory of 9/11. Love did not triumph over our enemies following this event; rather, it was the power of hatred, stirred from the abyss, that drove nations into never-ending conflict.

Sept. 12: Inferior conjunction Mercury and Sun 25° Leo. The Sun at this degree remembers Jesus as he spoke at a synagogue next to a madhouse. The inmates, along with their custodians, came to hear him. One of them said, "This is Jesus of Nazareth…visited by wise men from the east." When Jesus spoke the words, "The spirit that speaks [through you] is from below and should return there," the inmates became quiet and were healed (Aug/18/29). The healing power of the Christ–Sun is remembered today, as it was yesterday. Today's conjunction stimulates the heart forces of courage, strengthening us to receive apocalyptic revelation.

ASPECT: Sun/Mercury 25° Leo square Mars 25° Scorpio. Sun/Mercury recalls Jesus at Lazarus's castle the day after he had prayed to his heavenly Father for the strength to fulfill his mission (Jul/22/30). Anne Catherine witnessed Jesus praying on the Mt. of Olives:

> It was also shown to me that Jesus (chiefly on the Mount of Olives) prayed and sorrowed, because Adam and Eve, when driven from Paradise, had here first trodden the inhospitable Earth. I saw them in that cave sorrowing and praying; and it was on this mountain, which Cain was cultivating for the first time, that he became so enraged as to resolve to kill Abel. I thought of Judas. I saw Cain murdering his brother in the vicinity of Mount Calvary; and on the Mount of Olives he was called by God to account for the same.[3]

Our Mother weeps for the spilling of blood perpetuated by her children. One can only imagine her suffering in our times of such painful global strife. Sun/Mercury square to Mars, calls us to petition

---

3 *ACE Complete*, p. 371.

the Archangel Michael to help us forge the sword of hatred into the Word of truth. Thus will revelatory imaginations reach us from the higher worlds, rather than stealing our souls through deceptions born of subearthy inversions of truth.

Sept. 16: Full Moon 29° Aquarius opposite Sun 29° Leo and Penumbral Lunar Eclipse. This eclipse will be visible from Europe, most parts of Asia and Australia and from eastern Africa. The eclipse begins at 4:45 p.m. (UTC) and ends at 8:53 p.m. (UTC).

The summons of Judas Iscariot (Oct/24/30). At the summons of Judas, Mars (15° Aquarius) was opposite Uranus (15° Leo). The betrayer was invited to join the circle with Mars very close to where the Sun was at the births of both Rudolf Steiner and Valentin Tomberg. They too met betrayers. The lower influence of this aspect propels one to competition, argumentativeness, and revolution. Its higher aspect is the Michaelic courage to forge the word in harmony with the will of the Logos, continually inspired by the light of the Holy Spirit. Judas fell into the trap of the anti-Logos, through whom the word is used in service to revolution (as indicated by the opposition between Mars and Uranus that day).

The New Moon (and total solar eclipse) of this month reminded us of the sanctity of truth as it then occurred; it remembered the sacrifice of the Master Jesus (Solomon Jesus). The Full Moon now shines with the inspirations born of the constellation representing the Angel Human (Aquarius), remembering when Judas asked to become a disciple. It is interesting that the Earth will occult the Moon in this constellation, giving us the imagination of the occultation of the truly human being, by ahrimanic interventions.

When Judas was presented for discipleship, Jesus Christ gave Judas the inspired response: "Thou mayst have a place among my disciples, unless thou dost prefer to leave it to another." His betrayal was already written in the Book of Life that is guarded by the Angels.

What is inspiration? It is the source from which the Gospels were written, and the source as well of all great religious teachings. *It is also the source from whence spiritual beings and human beings speak together chorally.* When Rudolf Steiner was inspired to speak of the Maitreya Bodisattva during his lectures on the Gospel of St. Matthew, he said, "We live only for the truth, which we express in terms learned from the inspiration of the bodhisattva himself and from his revelation of the future appearance of the Christ and the form he will assume."[4] It was then assumed by many that the mission of the Maitreya Bodhisattva was thus fulfilled, creating a fateful error that drastically hindered the spiritual guidance of the twentieth century. The marriage of opposites is an influence shining from this Full Moon, where two vases pour different waters from the same source—the Angel.

The Angel and the Lion constitute the other pair of opposites on the cross of humankind's instinctivity. Here it is a matter of the transformation of combative courage into moral courage—into the courage of conscience. For the instinct that we call "moral conscience" is the effect of inspiration on the part of the Angel; and it is by elevating instinctual courage—i.e., the desire for heroism, adventure and struggle, that the latter is united with conscience and becomes the moral courage that we admire in martyrs and saints.

Steiner spoke of the incarnation of the individuality who would be the "actual proclaimer" of the Etheric Christ, for he understood that this Bodhisattva (already then incarnated) works with the Archangel Jesus—from the Christ School—in his various incarnations. As such, he is united with the living Word and therefore he *speaks the good.* We are to hear the voice of inspiration—to dare to know the whisper of the inner Word:

> *Inspiration,* truth to tell, is what constitutes the Hermetic community. It is inspiration which is the link between its members and within which *all* its members meet one another. The community of inspiration—this is what in reality the community of Hermeticists is.
>
> It is inspiration in common which underlies the mental and symbolic language common to Hermeticists—the language of analogy, the marriage of opposites, synthesis, moral logic, the dimension of depth added to those of clarity and breadth of knowledge, and above all the

---

4 Steiner, *According to Matthew,* p.179

ardent belief that all is knowable and revealable, that the mystery is infinite knowability and revealability....

This common inspiration, this language that we have in common, is the inner *Word* which guides and impels us—inwardly and outwardly at the same time—in all our aspirations.[5]

When we think in unity with the anonymous "choir" of thinkers above, below, yesterday and tomorrow, then "I think" becomes "It thinks." *We celebrate the marriage of opposites through understanding the efforts of both prayer and labor as the method through which the voice of inspiration becomes one with our voice—thus does a choir sing within us.* The more we think in the isolation of our astral bodies, the more separate we become, increasing the division that will eventually lead us to the war of all against all. Judas showed us the tragedy of betrayal (by necessity). The path he walked led to his death. Death is the final resting place of truth when it is ignored, misunderstood, divided, or entombed. Two waters pouring from one source is a signature for the collaborative actions of the Bodhisattva circle. This we are to remember, as we participate in our various communities.

Sept. 17: Sun enters Virgo: "Behold worlds, O soul!" (Steiner, *Twelve Cosmic Moods*). William Bento illumines this mantra:

> The more engaged we are with the phenomena of *Natura,* the accompanying rhythms of social life, and the planetary and starry celestial dances above us, the more awe and wonder arise in our soul. This beholding is more than a seeing; it is an immersion into a conscious participation mystique. The mystery of worlds is precisely what the longing of the soul seeks to know; and so this beholding is indeed not a static event, but the movement of the soul into worlds known and unknown.

The first decan is ruled by the Sun, and is associated with the constellation of the Cup (Crater): here we can think of the Grail chalice held by the Queen of Peace, represented by the Virgin. The virtue of Virgo is here invoked: Courtesy becomes

tactfulness of heart. The inner work of descent (Persephone) brings the awareness of self-knowledge. Hydra ("the Serpent") stretches its undulating life force throughout the entire region beneath Virgo. To become self-aware, we must confront the serpent.

Sept. 18: Mars conjunct Lesath 29° Scorpio, the tail of the scorpion (the Greek word for sting is lesos). Under the influence of the Scorpion's tail, Jesus spoke to shepherds, telling them the parable of the lost sheep (Apr/8/31). The good shepherd delights in finding his lost sheep; inversely, shepherds of another kind lead their sheep into pastures, wherein they will eternally hunger and thirst for the One they have lost. With the planet of war conjunct Lesath, we are called to see into realms of apocalyptic revelation, as does the eagle—this being the higher aspect of the sociopathic underbelly of the scorpion. The Word is a vessel that can be crafted both as a chalice or as a cauldron.

ASPECT (2): Venus 28° Virgo opposite Uranus 28° Pisces. Venus at this degree recalls Jesus and the disciples journeying to Jogbeha, where members of the Karaites sect lived; they were descendants of Jethro, the father-in-law of Moses, and lived a very simple life in expectation of the coming Messiah. They received Jesus with great reverence, and Jesus commended them for their charitable way of life (Sept/27/30). The passions of Venus may become destabilized by the sudden and unexpected nature of Uranus. When the soul can fathom world movement (Virgo) it dances with contant change that is the signature of Nature. If movement is arrested, we fail to adapt to outer circumstances; thus are we rendered paralyzed, unable to participate in Sophia's moving sermon of wisdom.

Moses had to journey into the land of the dead (across the threshold) in order to ask forgiveness from the Egyptian he had killed. In like manner this aspect asks us to shed light on where our unconscious memories and passions may need to awaken into compassion. Virgo is the constellation of continuous movement, change, and metamorphosis—the seasons are her expression of wonder. We are called to face the light and unite our soul with the penetrating presence of spirit that indwells

---

5 Anon., *Meditations on the Tarot,* p. 397.

all that surrounds us, freeing us to dance in celebration of the world's becoming.

Venus will be conjunct Spica (29° Virgo) late this day.

Sept. 19: Venus enters Libra: "In being experience being." The planet of love enters the constellation of the Scales, wherein the balance point between all things rests at the fulcrum, held by Michael, who from this point of absolute stillness reveals the truth living in each and every moment. The constellation of the Scales asks us to constantly adjust to a state of equilibrium that brings harmony to the soul. Venus was in Libra when Jesus healed the blind youth Manahem.

Mars enters Sagittarius: "In life's active force of will." The planet of the word enters the constellation of the Centaur, asking us to speak truth, remaining independent of automatic speech that rises from the animal within. Mars was in Sagittarius when Jesus healed the woman bent double.

Sept. 23: Mercury goes direct 20° Leo.

Sept. 26: ASPECT: Sun conjunct Jupiter 8° Virgo: The union in the temple (Apr/3/12). Jupiter was at this degree at this event, which marked the first death of the Solomon Jesus (his second death would come as he left the sheaths of the Nathan Jesus just prior to the Baptism in the Jordan River). This aspect bestows great determination and penetrating insight. At the union in the temple not only were two individualities united, but also did two streams of initiation come together in a single soul. These were the Solomon Jesus's Persian initiations (during his life as Zarathustra) and the Nathan Jesus's ancient Indian initiations. The former represents more the path of the magi; the latter more the path of the shepherds. Wisdom Sophia (Jupiter), Queen of Heaven, bore witness to this union from her throne in Virgo. She calls us to know ourselves from within, to create proper boundaries, and to ever seek harmonious resonance between our inner nature and the phenomena of Nature. The heart yearns to speak with tenderness toward all beings. We are called to build upon life's experiences, for thus do we acquire wisdom.

After the union in the temple, seventeen years would pass before Christ would enter into the sheaths this union prepared for him. By analogy, we are called to know when something greater than us is striving to become one with us. The initiatory streams of both magi and shepherds are informing us every moment; we are to collaborate in the symphony of revelation moving toward us from above as well as rising within us from below—from the realm of our Mother.

Sept. 27: Pluto stations 20° Sagittarius before going direct. The Sun at this degree remembers the commissioning of the disciples (Dec/10/30). Pluto at this degree remembers the intensification of persecutions. We are commissioned to speak the truth that brings healing to all who receive its resonant tones.

Sept. 30: New Moon 13° Virgo. The Moon remembers Jesus presenting a child, and saying to his enemies: "Ye must become like unto these" (Tuesday, 1/30/31). The day after the feeding of the five thousand and the walking on water, Jesus was teaching in a hamlet between Magdala and Dalmanutha. Many women were present with their children. At some distance Pharisees and Sadducees were standing around Jesus; among them were some Herodians. The same accusations were again hurled at him; that he frequented the society of publicans and sinners as well as traveling with women of ill repute. The following day he gave instruction on the eucharistic bread of life.

Miracles, magic, and purity of heart are evoked with this New Moon. What is the source of this profundity? It is the primal revelation streaming from the presence of God. It is the prodigious conviction of hope and faith which vibrates both in the whole world and within each individual. The Virgin protects the sacred space that surrounds us. She asks that we listen to the womb of silence she provides for our protection. She is the voice singing throughout the natural world, as well as the voice that sings to us from the beating of our heart.

The sea of glass surrounding the throne of God is to be reflected below in a sea of glass we create as a mantle embracing our physical being. If we cannot find resonance with her purity, we lose connection with the force she generates as the primal vibration of our soul's origin. *Without her mantle interpenetrating our earthly mantle, we are in danger of being swept away on the fanatical and agitated currents of the serpent's river of misery:*

> In so far as my heart beats, that I breathe, that my blood circulates—in so far, in other words, that faith and hope work in me—in so far do I take part, thereby, in the great cosmic ritual in which all beings participate, all the hierarchies from the Seraphim down to butterflies…namely, in natural religion's "sacrament of baptism," which is immersion in the waters of the "sea of glass," and natural religion's "sacrament of confirmation," which takes place day and night through the chorus of choirs of animated Nature: "Holy, holy, holy …" All beings are baptized and confirmed in natural religion. Because, in so far as they live, they have faith and hope. But the baptism and confirmation with "fire and Spirit," the sacraments of love, surpass those of natural religion. They bear forgiveness and healing to fallen nature.

Fallen Nature also has its unconscious mystery, i.e., its collective instinctivity of perception (its "waters") and its collective instinctivity of reaction (its "creatures"). Again, it is the Apocalypse of St. John which reveals this. The following is the origin of the "sea" of fallen Nature according to the Apocalypse:

The serpent poured water like a river out of his mouth after the woman, to sweep her away with the flood. But the earth came to the help of the woman, and the earth opened its mouth and swallowed the river which the dragon had poured from his mouth. (Rev. 12:15–16)

The difference between the waters of the "sea of glass" before the throne and the waters poured forth by the serpent is that the former are the calm, peace and stability of contemplation, or pure perception—they are "as glass," "like crystal"—whilst the latter are in movement, "poured forth," "like a river," in the pursuit of an aim, namely that of sweeping away the woman.[6]

Our enemies surround us, yet our hearts seek to become like that of a child. For the child accepts all things as they are, ever seeking the unceasing

wonder of the world. Thus does the Holy Virgin draw near to us, enfolding us in her mantle of love. When the heart speaks, courtesy flows from one heart to the other, healing discord through contemplative calm.

OCTOBER 2016

The month opens with the Moon emerging as a new crescent; begin by looking to the west at sunset on the 3rd to see it meet up with Venus in Libra. Then observe the Moon joining with Saturn on the 5th in Scorpio, and Mars on the 8th in Sagittarius. This kind of lineup is perfect for learning about the sky: by watching on successive nights you deepen a sense of the speed of the Moon, both in distance across the stars each day, and in the changing shape of the Moon because of changes in the light of the Sun reflecting off it's face. Additionally you can gain a sense of the different qualities of Venus, Saturn, and Mars. By spending time with their light, shape, and color you will be able to identify them simply by their "character" in the coming star gazing times!

On the 11th, Mercury and Jupiter are conjunct in Virgo; this is the 3rd time they are together this year, and the first time in the morning hours. It will be tight, but you just might see them in the east as the horizon brightens with the dawning of the Sun's light.

By the 16th, the Moon is in Pisces and exactly across from the Sun in the last degrees of Virgo: the Full Moon! The Sun moves on into Libra on the 17th. The waning Moon joins Jupiter in Virgo on the 28th, and Venus and Saturn conjunct in Scorpio on the 29th, with the New Moon formed in Libra the following day.

As Mercury nears a superior conjunction with the Sun (10/27), it follows the Sun's square to Pluto (Sun on the 7th; Mercury on the 15th) and then the two oppose Uranus (Sun on the 15th; Mercury on the 20th).

Oct. 3: Mercury enters Virgo: "May the spirit penetrate being."

---

6 Anon., *Meditations on the Tarot*, p. 271.

Oct. 5: Mars 11° Sagittarius square Jupiter 11° Virgo. Jupiter recalls Jesus instructing from the restored teacher's chair formerly used by the prophets Elijah and Elisha (Feb/3/30). These chairs had been restored due to the fact that John baptized near this place. John, who was once Elijah, was again being revered. We are living in a time when the John being is with us anew; he serves Sophia (Jupiter), who bestows revelation from the stream of time moving toward us from the future. We can imagine that our divine self approaches also from the future's revelatory currents, ever seeking our attention. Our eternal "I" is one with the image of God in which we were created—it cannot be harmed. As time moves from the past toward the future, so, too, does it move from the future to meet the present. All efforts we exert toward the realization of our true self invite our higher "I" to draw nearer to us.

This aspect increases whatever passions and desires may dominate our astral body. We are called to seek Jupiterian cosmic thoughts, sculpting our words in such a way that they become vessels for the Logos and Sophia. On our path into incarnation we visited the Kyriotetes, who indwell the sphere marked by the orbit of Jupiter. From this realm we gathered the wisdom necessary to carry our spiritual resolves. In the Mars sphere we gathered the will to manifest this wisdom as gifts of the Thrones. We are not to shrink back from what we have thus been given; rather, we are to serve in our communities as participants of the world's becoming. Communities that are now forming around the presence of John ask each of us to take the teacher's chair as wise and benevolent collaborators, using our words consciously for the benefit of all. If our "I" relinquishes its throne, passions can erupt, resulting in carelessly spent words that may even border on fanaticism. We must constructively build upon the experience we have gained in both this world and higher worlds, so as to aim the archer's arrow toward the living Word, who helps us tame ungoverned desires born of self-will. Our "I" carries eternity into time, thus bestowing the potential for ever-expanding consciousness of the planetary influences, which, in turn can then grace us with their highest octaves of conscience.

Oct. 7: Sun 20° Virgo square Pluto 20° Sagittarius. The Sun at this degree remembers learned men from Nazareth sent by the Pharisees to test Jesus's wisdom. Jesus displayed such extraordinary knowledge that all present were excited about his teaching. The parents of three wealthy youths had sent their sons to seek to become Jesus's pupils. When they were rejected, the parents were incensed (Tuesday, Sep/13/29). This event occurred on Mars day, ten days before the Baptism in the Jordan River. Jesus rejected the youths, for they sought to buy their way into his circle, promising him money from their parents. He spoke most severely to them, confusing the nine disciples Jesus had called to bear witness to his response. Among the learned men who came to test Jesus was an astrologer:

> There was an astrologer present who spoke of the course of the stars. He (Jesus) explained how one constellation ruled another, how different stars possess different influences, and he discoursed upon comets and the signs of the Zodiac.[1]

If only Anne Catherine Emmerich could have told us in detail what Jesus said to the astrologer! We can trust that Rudolf Steiner's *Twelve Cosmic Moods* were directly inspired from realms wherein the substance of Jesus's words are revealed. Sun in Virgo calls us to behold worlds—all worlds. And in square to Pluto we are to temper all personal ambition, lest we be excused from entering the circle of disciples gathering around the Etheric Christ. It is often challenging to separate our latent desire for power from our longing to selflessly serve the higher authority we are to follow.

Oct. 11: Mercury conjunct Jupiter 12° Virgo. Mercury remembers the day before the Baptism of Jesus in the River Jordan, when Jesus visited Silent Mary (Thursday, Sep/22/29). It was the day of the Holy Spirit when Martha took Jesus to visit her sister, who lived like a hermit in part of the castle owned by Lazarus. Normally silent before strangers, Mary began to speak, telling Jesus of the mysteries of his incarnation, passion, and death.

---

1   *ACE Complete*, p. 208.

This aspect blesses us with the penetrating power of spirit that seeks to illumine our thinking; thus are we filled with imaginations imbued with Sophianic wisdom. Silent Mary came into incarnation to experience Christ. She died before his death, as what lay in store for him was much too painful for her gentle soul to bear. The Holy Spirit needs many more vessels through which cosmic imaginations may become earthly reality. Taking up this task will be a path of suffering; for, when our eyes open, we can no longer deny the dire consequences that have resulted due to the barrenness of arbitrary and spiritless human thinking. Jupiter was at this degree when the Nathan Jesus was born. Thus are we reminded of the community now forming.

Oct. 13: Venus enters Scorpio: "Yet in being existence endures." Venus rules the second chakra, representing the etheric body of life forces; and the manner in which we live determines the state of our inner soul harmony. Impulses are to be governed by our "I." Venus was in Scorpio during Jesus's visit to silent Mary and at the Baptism in the Jordan River.

ASPECT: Mercury 16° Virgo square Mars 16° Sagittarius. The birth of the Nathan Jesus (Saturday, Dec/6/2 BC). Mars is at the zodiacal location of the Sun at the birth of the Nathan Jesus (Dec/6/2 BC). Born on the day of the Holy Virgin, Jesus bequeaths to all the comfort of the Virgin's loving mantle. Words are to be carefully chosen, for the mind is to seek the penetrating light of spirit, and we are to overcome all impulsive speech. Mercury's location marks the location of the Sun 16° Virgo at the birth of the Solomon Mary.

Oct. 15: Sun 27° Virgo opposite Uranus 27° Pisces: The Sun recalls those who believed Jesus to be an envoy of the King of the Jews, awaited by the kings Mensor and Theokeno in their tent city. A message was sent to Mensor, informing him of Jesus's imminent arrival (Friday, Sep/19/32). When Mensor received Jesus, he offered him splendid garments. Jesus accepted these gifts, though he would not consent to wear them. The independence of Jesus was born not of self-will, but of obedience to his Father's will. He had no need to set himself apart from others, rather he sought to be the most humble in all situations. When the "I" stands vertically, it is independent—and humility results. The lower ego, however, is relegated more to the horizontal world, seeking embellishments that prove one's status above others. This aspect calls us to find our vertical relationship with our higher "I" so as to overcome all pride, which renders behaviors eratic (Uranus). Constancy, in contrast, is a distinquishing feature of one who stands in uprightness under the guidance of the Light of the World.

ASPECT (2): Mercury 20° Virgo square Pluto 20° Sagittarius: The raising of a pagan child (Sep/23/30). Many of the children in this pagan quarter of the town suffered due to their parents worship of Moloch. Those ensnared in the dark occult forces of these false idols needed exorcisms by Jesus. Such was the fate of the pagan child healed with Mercury at today's degree. **Mental clarity is the mark of one who has overcome luciferic anger and aggression.** Jesus raised this child on a Saturday, a day influenced by the forces of the Holy Virgin. With clear minds we bear witness to the tragedy of our collective worship of the false idols of our culture, and especially the false idol of technology—which deadens our capacity to reveal the Molochs standing right in front of us.

Oct. 16: Full Moon 28° Pisces opposite Sun 28° Virgo. The Moon remembers the steward of an inn begging Jesus for a decision regarding a dispute over a well that provided water for two tribes' cattle. Jesus replied that each side should set free an equal number of cattle; and from whichever side the greater number went to the well of their own accord, this side should have the greater use of the well. Jesus then used this as an analogy for the living water that the Son of Man would give— that it would belong to those who most earnestly desired it (Wednesday, Dec/20/30). Jesus's teaching reminds us that all are free to drink from the well of their own choosing, and no one should interfere, or seek to dominate, the choices made by anyone else. For, the well that is ours is where we will find the living water seeking to quench our soul's thirst. This teaching begs the question: How do we decide which well is ours, especially when others speak against its holy waters? Eventually each of us will

SIDEREAL GEOCENTRIC LONGITUDES :   OCTOBER 2016 Gregorian at 0 hours UT

DAY	☉	☽	☊	☿	♀	♂	♃	♄	♅	♆	♇
1 SA	13 ♍ 16	13 ♍ 11	17 ♌ 42R	25 ♌ 44	14 ♎ 1	7 ♐ 26	9 ♍ 40	16 ♏ 39	28 ♓ 7R	14 ♒ 55R	19 ♐ 57
2 SU	14 15	25 13	17 38	27 1	15 15	8 6	9 53	16 43	28 4	14 54	19 57
3 MO	15 14	7 ♎ 10	17 34	28 23	16 28	8 46	10 6	16 47	28 2	14 52	19 58
4 TU	16 13	19 2	17 28	29 49	17 41	9 26	10 19	16 52	28 0	14 51	19 58
5 WE	17 13	0 ♏ 52	17 23	1 ♍ 19	18 54	10 7	10 32	16 57	27 57	14 50	19 58
6 TH	18 12	12 44	17 18	2 53	20 7	10 47	10 45	17 1	27 55	14 48	19 58
7 FR	19 11	24 39	17 14	4 29	21 20	11 28	10 57	17 6	27 52	14 47	19 59
8 SA	20 10	6 ♐ 43	17 12	6 8	22 32	12 9	11 10	17 11	27 50	14 46	19 59
9 SU	21 9	19 0	17 11	7 48	23 45	12 49	11 23	17 16	27 48	14 45	19 59
10 MO	22 9	1 ♑ 33	17 11D	9 30	24 58	13 30	11 36	17 21	27 45	14 43	20 0
11 TU	23 8	14 28	17 12	11 12	26 11	14 12	11 49	17 26	27 43	14 42	20 0
12 WE	24 7	27 47	17 14	12 56	27 24	14 53	12 2	17 31	27 40	14 41	20 1
13 TH	25 7	11 ♒ 35	17 15	14 40	28 37	15 34	12 15	17 36	27 38	14 40	20 1
14 FR	26 6	25 50	17 15R	16 24	29 50	16 16	12 27	17 41	27 35	14 39	20 2
15 SA	27 5	10 ♓ 30	17 13	18 8	1 ♏ 2	16 57	12 40	17 46	27 33	14 37	20 2
16 SU	28 5	25 30	17 9	19 52	2 15	17 39	12 53	17 52	27 31	14 36	20 3
17 MO	29 4	10 ♈ 42	17 4	21 36	3 28	18 21	13 6	17 57	27 28	14 35	20 3
18 TU	0 ♎ 4	25 55	16 58	23 20	4 40	19 3	13 18	18 3	27 26	14 34	20 4
19 WE	1 4	10 ♉ 58	16 51	25 4	5 53	19 45	13 31	18 8	27 23	14 33	20 5
20 TH	2 3	25 44	16 45	26 47	7 6	20 27	13 44	18 14	27 21	14 32	20 5
21 FR	3 3	10 ♊ 5	16 41	28 29	8 18	21 10	13 56	18 19	27 18	14 31	20 6
22 SA	4 2	24 1	16 39	0 ♎ 12	9 31	21 52	14 9	18 25	27 16	14 30	20 7
23 SU	5 2	7 ♋ 30	16 38D	1 53	10 43	22 35	14 22	18 31	27 14	14 29	20 8
24 MO	6 2	20 35	16 39	3 34	11 56	23 17	14 34	18 36	27 11	14 29	20 8
25 TU	7 2	3 ♌ 19	16 40	5 15	13 8	24 0	14 47	18 42	27 9	14 28	20 9
26 WE	8 2	15 47	16 41	6 55	14 21	24 43	14 59	18 48	27 6	14 27	20 10
27 TH	9 1	28 2	16 40R	8 35	15 33	25 25	15 11	18 54	27 4	14 26	20 11
28 FR	10 1	10 ♍ 8	16 37	10 14	16 46	26 8	15 24	19 0	27 2	14 25	20 12
29 SA	11 1	22 7	16 32	11 52	17 58	26 52	15 36	19 6	26 59	14 25	20 13
30 SU	12 1	4 ♎ 2	16 24	13 30	19 10	27 35	15 48	19 12	26 57	14 24	20 14
31 MO	13 1	15 54	16 14	15 8	20 23	28 18	16 1	19 18	26 55	14 23	20 15

INGRESSES :

2 ☽ → ♎ 9:34		20 ☽ → ♊ 7: 3
4 ☿ → ♍ 2:56		21 ☿ → ♎ 21:16
☽ → ♏ 22:14		22 ☽ → ♋ 10:34
7 ☽ → ♐ 10:40		24 ☽ → ♌ 17:41
9 ☽ → ♑ 21: 4		27 ☽ → ♍ 3:52
12 ☽ → ♒ 3:54		29 ☽ → ♎ 15:51
14 ♀ → ♏ 3:27		
☽ → ♓ 6:53		
16 ☽ → ♈ 7: 7		
17 ☉ → ♎ 22:24		
18 ☽ → ♉ 6:28		

ASPECTS & ECLIPSES :

1 ☉ ☌ ☽ 0:10	☉ □ ☽ 4:32	☽ ☌ P 23:37	♀ □ ♆ 2: 0
2 ☽ ☍ ♅ 5:41	11 ☿ ☌ ♃ 9:44	18 ☽ ☍ ♀ 15: 8	27 ☉ ☍ ☿ 16:15
3 ☽ ☌ ♀ 20:56	13 ☽ ☌ ♆ 5:15	19 ☽ ⚻ ☊ 9:25	♀ □ ☊ 21:26
4 ☽ ☌ A 11: 9	☽ ☌ ☋ 9:39	♂ ☌ ♇ 11:14	28 ☽ ☌ ♃ 10:41
5 ♂ □ ♃ 21:42	☿ □ ♂ 20:59	☽ ☍ ♄ 11:39	29 ♂ □ ♅ 4: 1
6 ☽ ☌ ♄ 8:43	15 ☽ ☍ ♃ 3:32	20 ☿ ☍ ♅ 7:46	☽ ☍ ♅ 9:45
☽ ⚼ ☊ 9:10	☉ ☍ ♅ 10:40	21 ☽ ☍ ♇ 17:11	30 ♀ ☌ ♄ 0:44
7 ☉ □ ♆ 19:27	☽ ☍ ☿ 13:51	☽ ☍ ♂ 20: 3	☉ ☌ ☽ 17:37
8 ♄ □ ☊ 4:14	16 ☿ □ ♇ 2:25	22 ☉ □ ☽ 19:12	☽ ☌ ☿ 22:11
☽ ☌ ♂ 11:17	☽ ☌ ♅ 3:10	25 ☽ ☍ ♆ 21:24	31 ☽ ☌ A 19:46
9 ☽ ☌ ♇ 1:55	☉ ☍ ☽ 4:22	26 ☽ ☌ ☊ 1:44	

SIDEREAL HELIOCENTRIC LONGITUDES :   OCTOBER 2016 Gregorian at 0 hours UT

DAY	Sid. Time	☿	♀	⊕	♂	♃	♄	♅	♆	♇	Vernal Point
1 SA	0:40:38	7 ♊ 25	28 ♏ 50	13 ♓ 17	23 ♑ 22	9 ♍ 1	21 ♏ 46	27 ♓ 22	15 ♒ 50	21 ♐ 40	5 ♓ 1'35"
2 SU	0:44:35	13 39	0 ♐ 25	14 16	24 0	9 5	21 48	27 23	15 50	21 41	5 ♓ 1'35"
3 MO	0:48:31	19 49	2 0	15 15	24 37	9 10	21 49	27 24	15 50	21 41	5 ♓ 1'34"
4 TU	0:52:28	25 54	3 35	16 14	25 15	9 14	21 51	27 24	15 51	21 41	5 ♓ 1'34"
5 WE	0:56:24	1 ♋ 51	5 10	17 13	25 53	9 19	21 53	27 25	15 51	21 42	5 ♓ 1'34"
6 TH	1: 0:21	7 41	6 45	18 12	26 31	9 23	21 55	27 26	15 51	21 42	5 ♓ 1'34"
7 FR	1: 4:17	13 23	8 20	19 11	27 9	9 28	21 57	27 26	15 52	21 42	5 ♓ 1'34"
8 SA	1: 8:14	18 55	9 55	20 11	27 47	9 32	21 58	27 27	15 52	21 43	5 ♓ 1'34"
9 SU	1:12:10	24 18	11 30	21 10	28 25	9 37	22 0	27 28	15 52	21 43	5 ♓ 1'34"
10 MO	1:16: 7	29 31	13 5	22 9	29 3	9 41	22 2	27 28	15 53	21 43	5 ♓ 1'33"
11 TU	1:20: 4	4 ♌ 35	14 40	23 8	29 41	9 46	22 4	27 29	15 53	21 44	5 ♓ 1'33"
12 WE	1:24: 0	9 29	16 15	24 8	0 ♒ 19	9 50	22 6	27 29	15 54	21 44	5 ♓ 1'33"
13 TH	1:27:57	14 14	17 50	25 7	0 57	9 55	22 8	27 30	15 54	21 44	5 ♓ 1'33"
14 FR	1:31:53	18 49	19 25	26 6	1 35	9 59	22 9	27 31	15 54	21 44	5 ♓ 1'33"
15 SA	1:35:50	23 16	20 59	27 6	2 13	10 4	22 11	27 31	15 55	21 45	5 ♓ 1'33"
16 SU	1:39:46	27 34	22 34	28 5	2 51	10 9	22 13	27 32	15 55	21 45	5 ♓ 1'33"
17 MO	1:43:43	1 ♍ 44	24 9	29 5	3 29	10 13	22 15	27 33	15 55	21 45	5 ♓ 1'33"
18 TU	1:47:39	5 47	25 44	0 ♈ 4	4 7	10 18	22 17	27 33	15 56	21 46	5 ♓ 1'32"
19 WE	1:51:36	9 42	27 19	1 4	4 45	10 22	22 18	27 34	15 56	21 46	5 ♓ 1'32"
20 TH	1:55:33	13 30	28 54	2 4	5 23	10 27	22 20	27 35	15 56	21 46	5 ♓ 1'32"
21 FR	1:59:29	17 12	0 ♑ 29	3 3	6 1	10 31	22 22	27 35	15 57	21 47	5 ♓ 1'32"
22 SA	2: 3:26	20 49	2 4	4 3	6 39	10 36	22 24	27 36	15 57	21 47	5 ♓ 1'32"
23 SU	2: 7:22	24 19	3 38	5 3	7 17	10 40	22 26	27 37	15 58	21 47	5 ♓ 1'32"
24 MO	2:11:19	27 45	5 13	6 2	7 55	10 45	22 27	27 37	15 58	21 48	5 ♓ 1'32"
25 TU	2:15:15	1 ♎ 6	6 48	7 2	8 33	10 49	22 29	27 38	15 58	21 48	5 ♓ 1'31"
26 WE	2:19:12	4 22	8 23	8 2	9 11	10 54	22 31	27 39	15 59	21 48	5 ♓ 1'31"
27 TH	2:23: 8	7 34	9 58	9 2	9 50	10 58	22 33	27 39	15 59	21 49	5 ♓ 1'31"
28 FR	2:27: 5	10 43	11 33	10 2	10 28	11 2	22 35	27 40	15 59	21 49	5 ♓ 1'31"
29 SA	2:31: 2	13 48	13 8	11 2	11 6	11 7	22 36	27 41	16 0	21 49	5 ♓ 1'31"
30 SU	2:34:58	16 50	14 43	12 2	11 44	11 12	22 38	27 41	16 0	21 50	5 ♓ 1'31"
31 MO	2:38:55	19 50	16 17	13 2	12 22	11 17	22 40	27 42	16 0	21 50	5 ♓ 1'31"

INGRESSES :

1 ♀ → ♐ 17:43	
4 ☿ → ♋ 16:27	
10 ☿ → ♌ 2:13	
11 ♂ → ♒ 12:13	
16 ☿ → ♍ 13:55	
17 ⊕ → ♈ 22:13	
20 ♀ → ♑ 16:43	
24 ☿ → ♎ 16: 6	

ASPECTS (HELIOCENTRIC +MOON(TYCHONIC)) :

1 ☿ □ ♃ 6:11	8 ☽ □ ♃ 5:34	☽ □ ♄ 17:52	☽ □ ♆ 8: 0	26 ☽ ☍ ♆ 0:22
☽ □ ♆ 16:54	☽ ☌ ♀ 7:13	14 ☿ □ ♄ 18: 4	☽ ☍ ♄ 18:25	☽ □ ♄ 13:10
2 ☿ □ ⊕ 2:47	☿ ⚼ ☊ 20:37	☽ ☍ ♃ 23:17	21 ☽ □ ♃ 0:44	27 ☿ ☍ ⊕ 16:15
☽ ☍ ♅ 4:19	9 ☽ ☌ ♆ 5:15	15 ⊕ ☌ ♅ 10:24	☽ □ ☿ 16:27	28 ☽ ☌ ♃ 1:50
3 ♂ ⚻ ☊ 3:26	⊕ □ ♆ 13:28	♀ ☌ ♆ 11:29	☽ ☍ ♆ 20: 6	☿ □ ♀ 13: 8
☿ ☍ ♆ 7:18	☽ □ ♅ 16:15	☽ □ ♆ 18: 1	22 ☽ □ ♅ 6:19	☽ □ ♆ 23:23
4 ☿ □ ♅ 6: 2	☿ ☍ ♂ 21:27	☽ □ ♀ 18:47	☿ □ ♆ 6:36	29 ☽ ☍ ♅ 11:11
☽ □ ♂ 13:19	12 ☽ ☌ ♂ 4:40	16 ☽ ☌ ♅ 3:13	☽ ☍ ♀ 16: 8	♂ ☌ P 11:16
6 ☽ □ ♆ 6:18	13 ☽ ☍ ☿ 6:44	18 ☽ □ ♂ 13:35	23 ☿ ☍ ♅ 23: 6	31 ☽ □ ♀ 0:53
☽ ☌ ♄ 18:32	☽ ☌ ♆ 7:21	19 ♀ □ ♅ 3:49	25 ♀ □ ⊕ 9:35	♀ ☌ A 8: 5
7 ♀ □ ♃ 17:57	☿ ☍ ♆ 8:39	☿ ☌ ♃ 4:16	☽ ☍ ♂ 10:33	☽ ☌ ☿ 10:34

orient our will toward the spiritual powers dwelling at the Sun's center. Herein lies the field of celestial gravitation as opposed to the gravitational field of the serpent's world:

> The domain of our freedom itself, our spiritual life, shows the real and active presence of gravitation of a spiritual order. For what is the phenomenon of religion if not the manifestation of spiritual gravitation toward God, i.e., toward the center of spiritual gravitation of the world? It is significant that the term "the Fall"—chosen for the primordial event which brought about the change of [humankind's] state from that named "paradise" to the terrestrial state of toil, suffering and death—is borrowed from the domain of gravitation. In fact, there is nothing against the conception of the Fall of Adam as the passage from a spiritual gravitational system, whose center is God, to a terrestrial gravitational system, whose center is the serpent (that we have characterized in the preceding Letter as the "principle of electricity"). The Fall, as a phenomenon, can certainly be understood as the passage from the one gravitational field to the other.[2]

The human being is placed between two gravitational systems, with two different centers: the kingdom of God and the kingdom represented by the cunning prince of this world. Through enticing human beings into his field, the serpent captures souls. When Peter came out of the boat to meet Christ as he walked on water, it was the "I Am" of Christ, exemplifying celestial gravitation, that drew Peter forward. Christ was centered entirely in himself: he was the center of celestial forces of gravitation—he was the Son of the Father God. Christ is not isolated from us as we navigate the stormy seas of life. Rather he calls each of us to remember the source from whence we were created, ever representing the eternal truth of the one center of all life, all religions, and all souls:

> The boat with his disciples is, therefore, and will be until the end of the world, the aim of the I am walking on the water. His enstasy, his profound centering in himself, does not distance him from the navigators on the agitated sea of history and evolution, and does not make him disappear into the other sea—the calm sea of nirvana—but rather, on the contrary, it entails that he walks, until the end of the world, after the boat with his disciples.[3]

We are the disciples in the destiny community of our choosing and we are all free to drink from the well our "I" calls us to visit. This Full Moon calls forth the loaves (Virgo) and the fishes (Pisces) that fed the 5,000 so they could awaken to the source of grace that stills all hunger and quenches all thirst.

NOTE: The Sun will be conjunct Spica later this day.

Oct. 17: Sun enters Libra: "Worlds are sustaining worlds" (Steiner, *Twelve Cosmic Moods*). William Bento illumines this mantra:

> Everything is connected to everything, and so it is with any attempt to grasp how the Cosmos has given birth to worlds that sustain worlds. Nothing can be truly understood when it is taken out of the context of relatedness. Modern scientific thinking has unfortunately lost this understanding and continues to attempt to explain the complexity of nature, man and the heavens by abstracting it from its natural habitat. The result is a kind of lifelessness. The antidote to this edifice of abstractions is to apply the principles of a spiritual scientific thinking, which is based on the premise that "worlds sustain worlds."

The first decan is ruled by the Moon and is associated with the constellation of Bootes the Ploughman. The deeper meaning of Bootes has to do with the Hebrew Bo, which means coming; hence Bootes is the Coming One. How appropriate that the baptism of the Coming One, the Messiah, took place when the Sun entered this decan! Libra calls for balanced thought, which becomes balanced action, as well as a certain standard of uprightness that requires an alignment with higher consciousness. In Libra contentment becomes equanimity, whereby we enter the connectivity of all creation.

Oct. 19: Mars conjunct Pluto 20° Sagittarius. Pluto and Mars rest near Pluto's position when the full storm of persecutions against the Christians began

---

2 Anon., *Meditations on the Tarot*, p. 306.

3 Ibid., 311.

in 36 AD. When the "I" indwells the forces of aggression that stem from the planetary sphere of war and unrest (Mars), such tendencies then transform into Michaelic forces of will that battle not one against the other—rather do they serve the battle against the dragon on behalf of all.

The Sun was 20° Sagittarius when the disciples were commissioned to go out and heal. We are all called to go forth and work in the name of Christ and Michael as warriors serving the spiritual triumph of good over evil. We must speak the truth to reveal the danger we are facing on a global scale. The animal in human nature, which represents the lower forces of the Centaur, is blind to the destructive course we are setting. May we aim our will and our words toward alignment with the mighty beings of the Thrones, who indwell the sphere marked by the orbit of Mars, streaming powers of strength to all who will to take up the fight with evil.

Oct. 20: Mercury 27° Virgo opposite Uranus 27° Pisces. The Sun at Uranus's degree recalls the scribes and Pharisees, disturbed by Jesus teaching regarding his forthcoming triumphant entry into Jerusalem, as they proclaimed that henceforth it was forbidden for anyone to harbor Jesus and the disciples (Mar/17/33). Still under the influence of yesterday's exact conjunction between Mars and Pluto, we today remember the march into Jerusalem by the greatest (peaceful) rebel in the history of the world. Uranus quickens our receptivity to enlightening new revelations. The stream of time moving toward us carries the future, which so often tends to overturn the norm so vehemently protected by our current Pharisees and scribes. Hopefully it will prove to be true that a time will come when humanity will arise together and say: "Enough! We must change our ways." For, many are choosing the path leading toward heavenly Jerusalem as the metamorphosis of the Jerusalem Christ entered; those who resist this turn will eventually separate from those who choose this path: resistance to the Christed path leads toward becoming a different race, and ultimately into dwelling on a different planet. This choice does not lead one to the New Jerusalem we have been promised.

Oct. 21: Mercury enters Libra: "In existing embrace existence."

Oct. 23: Sun 6° Libra: The healing of Theokeno (Sep/28/32). When Christ was visiting Mensor and Theokeno, he healed the latter, who had long been bedridden. After this, Mensor showed Jesus what was written in the stars as the prophecy of Jesus' ultimate sacrifice—including the how and when of it. It was of utmost importance that Jesus and Mensor conversed in preparation for his return to Jacob's Well, where he would meet up with his disciples again, and walk toward the fulfillment of his destiny. Jesus was drawing ever closer to his sacrifice. Estelle Isaacson bears witness to the culmination of the incarnation of Christ and its effect in the being of Jesus:

> This aspect of his incarnation is a very challenging and sensitive thing to explain. I gained the understanding that while entering more and more into the physical body of Jesus, Christ encountered limitations he had never before experienced.
>
> At this important juncture in the ministry of Jesus, the Magus was there to recall to his awareness what was written in the stars regarding his ultimate sacrifice, and when it would take place. Jesus of course knew of this sacrifice, but it was brought to the forefront during his visit with this grandfatherly sage who revered Jesus, recognizing in him the bearer of Christ. The Magus had known that Jesus would come to him.[4]

Estelle goes on to describe the agony and the ecstasy of Jesus as the Christ descended ever deeper into his being. Christ had to become fully human, for it was not a God that was hung on the cross, but rather was it a human being.

Oct. 25: Venus 14° Scorpio square Neptune 14° Aquarius. Venus remembers Jesus in Atom. After having left the tent city where he had visited with Mensor (the one known as the Gold King), he entered into this city, where idols were worshiped. Jesus healed a wife of a man called Azaria, who was afflicted with an issue of blood, and she was one

---

4 Isaacson, *Through the Eyes of Mary Magdalene,* vol. 2, ch. 1.

of the idolaters who bowed before a beautiful pedestal upon which sat a dog with a thick, flat head (Oct/3/32):

> Flames shot forth from it, and in the dense black smoke issued horrible dog-like figures that disappeared in the air. The sick woman became perfectly miserable. She sank down faint and exhausted like one in a dying state, saying "These idols cannot help me! They are wicked spirits! They cannot longer remain here, they are fleeing from the prophet, the king of the Jews, who is amongst us. We have seen his star and have followed him! The prophet alone can help me!" After uttering these words, she fell back immovable and, to all appearances, lifeless.[5]

When Venus aspects Neptune, a harp sounds from the heights of heaven and, inversely, from the depths of Hell. When it is the Goddess Night who plucks the strings, healing forces stream into the listening soul. In contrast, the instrument played by the one who rules Babylon, depicted in the Bible as a fallen woman, strums notes that lure hapless souls into a fallen realm of decadence—a caricature of the heavenly Goddess. The decisive factor in a square between Venus and Neptune is the origin of the sound that calls the soul. Venus marks the sphere wherein the Archai hold sway. *These are the beings guarding mega-currents in the continuous waves of evolution.*

What is the task of our time? What idols dominate our culture? Time is fractured by the adversaries and restored to wholeness through the spiritual guardians of Time. Truly, it is the prophet alone who can help us, and he is one with the Bride who is the Goddess Night. When Jesus healed this wife of Azaria, he called out in earnest vehement words, inveighing against idols and their worship, calling them the servants of Satan.

This aspect calls us to rethink the idols we place on beautiful pedestals, in the vain hope that such ornamentation makes us master of the being that shines out from such things.

Delusions wrap an illustrious reality around us, and gradually we may find that we have become pawns in a game we did not even know we were playing.

____

5   *ACE Complete*, p. 895.

Oct. 27: Sun superior conjunction Mercury 10° Libra. Mercury at this degree remembers Jesus as he taught in Shiloh from the teacher's chair made of stone. He spoke of God's mercy to the people of Israel, the destruction of the temple, and the present time of grace, whereby he made it clear that it was he who was to bring salvation (Thursday, Oct/5/30). During his discourse, Jesus told the Jews that if they rejected his last grace, never to the end of time would they, as a nation, receive another. In superior conjunction with the Sun, Mercury is behind the Sun, serving as a chalice into which intuitions from the cosmos flow. These intuitions may later arise in our soul as a kind of direct knowing. We are called to participate in the grace that today fills the pleading cup of Mercurial illumination with messages born of the true light of the world.

Oct. 29: Mars 27° Sagittarius square Uranus 27° Pisces. Mars recalls Jesus in Jerusalem. He visited Obed, son of Simeon, and afterward walked the streets of the city. That evening when he returned to Bethany, Saturnin and some of John the Baptist's disciples came to him, as did Nicodemus (Monday, Mar/20/30). Herod was harassing John the Baptist, so that few came to him anymore. Herod's luciferic nature filled him with a light that was in direct contrast to the light Jesus shone. Uranus in square to Mars asks us to act without hesitation in response to the true light that shines through one's soul when words are offered as vessels for spirit illumination.

ASPECT (2): Venus conjunct Saturn 19° Scorpio: The birth of the Nathan Mary (Jul/17/17 BC). Venus at this degree recalls the healing of the son of Achias (Monday, Nov/6/30). The Roman officer Achias lived in the house where St. Paul had been born. Jephthah, the son of Achias, later became a very zealous disciple of St. Thomas. In conjunction with Saturn (remembering Saturn's location at the birth of the Nathan Mary), Venus may exert a feeling of tension between the illusion of restriction and the forming power of destiny. These restrictions may foreshadow adjustments that are necessary in the hidden realms of our soul. Nothing outside ourselves can restrict us if we are aligned with higher will. Nathan Mary's birth reminds us of our direct connection to suprasensory worlds and beings, from whence we experience the pierced heart through which we may suffer with the Earth and all her beings. The Virgin can raise us from all limitations born of the lower self.

Oct. 30: New Moon 13° Libra: The death of the Nathan Jesus (Apr/3/33). The Moon remembers the crucifixion of our Lord, and the Sun stands opposite its position during this fateful event. With Sun and Moon in relationship to the Crucifixion of Christ, we visit the eighth Arcanum of the Tarot, Justice:

> One of the meanings of the first commandment—"Thou shalt have no other gods before me" (Exodus 20:3)—is that one should not substitute an intellectual abstraction of God for the spiritual reality of God. One therefore sins against the first commandment when one substitutes for the fiery, luminous and vibrant Being of life the abstractions of a "principle" or "idea"—be it the "First Cause," or the "Absolute"—which are, truth to tell, only mentally "graven images" or mental idols created by the human intellect.[6]

Estelle Isaacson writes of her vision of Lucifer during the Crucifixion:

> Then I saw Lucifer at the cross. He was an imposing being of intense light. But his light was nothing like that of Christ. If we liken Christ's light to the Sun—its holy rays all warm and full of life—we can only say that Lucifer's is the most artificial of lights, so much so that it is disturbing to the soul. I was able to trace the effects of Lucifer's light upon the human soul, and will try to describe its working.
>
> I saw a pure soul incarnated in an earthly body and understood that the light of Christ surrounds and gently imbues all souls. Then I saw the light of Lucifer approach the soul in the form of a temptation—the temptation of false light. Such a temptation can find its foothold in the guise of information conveyed to us by another person, or by a book, or by other means. Regardless how it comes, it remains a temptation because it leads us—even if ever so slightly—from our true path, and away from Christ.
>
> The effect of Lucifer's light upon our souls is addictive, titillating, captivating. We want more of it. And although its effects seem subtle, from a higher perspective they are quite pronounced. Lucifer's light flares up in the soul, distracting it from the light of Christ. These flashes of light have a certain veneer about them, by which I mean they do not fill the measure of the soul with life-giving light, but instead elicit a feeling of shallow pleasure in the astral body, which is one aspect of the soul. But because Lucifer's light is ephemeral, it cannot emanate continuously within the soul, and so it recedes, leaving the astral body hungering for more such pleasure.
>
> Although we are surrounded at all times by both streams of light—that of Christ and that of Lucifer—they cannot cohabit in the soul's vessel. And because the light of Lucifer gives pleasure, the soul is all too prone to seek more of it, turning a blind eye to the light of Christ.[7]

We are called, during this season of Michaelmas 2016, to strive against the idols of shallow pleasure. The titillating is captivating and therefore dangerous. At this new beginning in the lunar cycle, we are called to stand at the fulcrum point of balance between the two pans of Libra's scale, always seeking equilibrium. When the two sides of the scale adjust to the still point of the fulcrum, we are in the dynamic process of ever reestablishing a new perspective. If, however, the fulcrum itself sways, our "I" is vacillating between the idolatrous light and the Christ light. We are to find our conscience as the center point and proceed with care as the autumnal light grows into the shadow of winter.

NOVEMBER 2016

We'll be greeted with beautiful views of Saturn and Venus shining from Scorpio in the west at sunsets at the beginning of November, with the newly waxing Moon joining them on the 2nd. By the 6th, the growing Moon reaches Mars in the first degrees of Capricorn.

---

6 Anon., *Meditations on the Tarot*, pp. 174–175.

7 Isaacson, *Through the Eyes of Mary Magdalene*, vol 2, pp. 144–145.

The Full Moon is on the 14th, with Moon in Aries and Sun in Libra. On the 16th, the Sun shifts into the constellation of Scorpio. Mercury, always near to the Sun, is a bit ahead of it and conjuncts Saturn on the 23rd, while Venus stays farther out of reach, visible in the southwest at sunset. Mercury and Saturn might be difficult to see at sunset, unless you have a good unobstructed western view: they will be following just behind the Sun, as it sinks in the west.

The waning Moon joins Jupiter in Virgo on its way to New Moon on the 29th. To see them, you will need to look upon the sky before sunrise (or in the late, late night) to see them rising in the east and climbing toward the south. By the New Moon, Saturn and Venus will disappear into the brightness of the Sun.

Nov. 2: Mars enters Capricorn: "In face of life's inner resistance" (Steiner, *Twelve Cosmic Moods*). To manifest the future we must find our strength in the present and overcome all resistance that cleaves to the past. Thus, through the power of the mighty Thrones (Mars), does the past become the pillar upon which the future find's its rest in each moment of time. Mars was in Capricorn when Jesus cleansed the temple, at the conception of John the Baptist, and at the attempted murder of Jesus.

Nov. 7: Venus enters Sagittarius, "In existence growth's power dies" (Steiner, *Twelve Cosmic Moods*). The spirits of Time (Venus) ask us to rejoice in the wonder of creation and take heed of growth's power of life that ever reforms itself anew. Venus was in Sagittarius during the stilling of the storm, the miraculous draught, and the start of the forty days of temptation.

Nov. 9: Mercury enters Scorpio, "In activity growth disappears" (Steiner, *Twelve Cosmic Moods*). The planet representing healers and teachers enters into the consuming existence that eternally sustains all beings through enduring activity. Mercury was in Sagittarius during the same events remembered by Venus two days ago: the stilling of the storm, the miraculous draught, and the last temptations of Christ (until the fortieth day).

Jupiter 18° Virgo: The death of the Nathan Mary (Aug/5/12).

Nov. 11: Mars 7° Capricorn: The cleansing of the temple (Apr/6/30). A day to remember the original chastity of our bodies as well as the chastity of our Mother Earth's body. These are the temples we are to set about perpetually cleansing.

Nov. 14: Full Moon 28° Aries opposite Sun 28° Libra. The Sun at this degree recalls Jesus and his disciples arriving at a hostel near Bethany. Jesus spoke of the dangers facing those who follow him, and urged each to consider carefully the role of disciple (Thursday, Oct/20/29). Shortly after his baptism in the Jordan River, Christ was gathering those who had the strength to follow him. On the day of the Holy Spirit he asked if they would be able to stand by him in his future sufferings. It would have been foolish for any to assume this strength before the true test would face them; nonetheless, many assumed the task.

The New Moon inaugurating this lunar cycle remembered the Crucifixion. Holding this in our inner gaze, we direct our view to the opponent of Christ who has given the human being unlimited magic—through which he strives to tear us away from the more difficult task of evolving toward God:

Oswald Spengler, the author of *The Decline of the West,* calls modern man "Faustian man" (*der faustische Mensch*)—and he was right to call him so. For Faust is indeed the dominant archetype of the epoch following the Middle Ages, which is characterized by the enormous growth of humankind's power over Nature and of the facilities for satisfying his desires—comprising those of the boldest of magicians of the past: flying through the air, seeing and hearing at a great distance, travelling without horses (e.g., by car), the evocation of living images and sounds of past events or events at a great distance, etc. It is just as if the prince of this world has obtained full power to satisfy, one after the other, all the desires of contemporary humankind, so as to demonstrate for himself that the power and enjoyment of the relative and transitory world here below can make man forget the absolute and eternal, can make him forget God.

SIDEREAL GEOCENTRIC LONGITUDES :   NOVEMBER 2016 Gregorian at 0 hours UT

DAY	☉	☽	☊	☿	♀	♂	♃	♄	♅	♆	♇
1 TU	14♎1	27♎46	16♌2R	16♎45	21♏35	29♐1	16♍13	19♏25	26♓52R	14♒22R	20♐16
2 WE	15 1	9♏37	15 50	18 22	22 47	29 45	16 25	19 31	26 50	14 22	20 17
3 TH	16 1	21 31	15 39	19 58	23 59	0♑28	16 37	19 37	26 48	14 21	20 18
4 FR	17 2	3♐29	15 29	21 33	25 11	1 12	16 49	19 43	26 45	14 21	20 19
5 SA	18 2	15 34	15 22	23 9	26 23	1 55	17 1	19 50	26 43	14 20	20 20
6 SU	19 2	27 49	15 17	24 44	27 36	2 39	17 13	19 56	26 41	14 20	20 21
7 MO	20 2	10♑19	15 15	26 18	28 48	3 23	17 25	20 3	26 39	14 19	20 23
8 TU	21 2	23 7	15 15D	27 52	0♐0	4 7	17 37	20 9	26 37	14 19	20 24
9 WE	22 3	6♒17	15 15	29 26	1 11	4 51	17 49	20 16	26 34	14 18	20 25
10 TH	23 3	19 54	15 15R	0♏59	2 23	5 35	18 1	20 22	26 32	14 18	20 26
11 FR	24 3	4♓0	15 14	2 32	3 35	6 19	18 12	20 29	26 30	14 18	20 28
12 SA	25 3	18 33	15 10	4 4	4 47	7 3	18 24	20 35	26 28	14 17	20 29
13 SU	26 4	3♈31	15 3	5 37	5 59	7 47	18 35	20 42	26 26	14 17	20 30
14 MO	27 4	18 47	14 54	7 10	7 10	8 31	18 47	20 49	26 24	14 17	20 32
15 TU	28 5	4♉9	14 44	8 41	8 22	9 16	18 58	20 55	26 22	14 17	20 33
16 WE	29 5	19 26	14 33	10 13	9 33	10 0	19 10	21 2	26 20	14 17	20 34
17 TH	0♏5	4♊27	14 23	11 44	10 45	10 44	19 21	21 9	26 18	14 16	20 36
18 FR	1 6	19 3	14 14	13 15	11 56	11 29	19 32	21 16	26 16	14 16	20 37
19 SA	2 6	3♋10	14 9	14 46	13 8	12 13	19 43	21 22	26 14	14 16	20 39
20 SU	3 7	16 47	14 6	16 16	14 19	12 58	19 54	21 29	26 13	14 16	20 40
21 MO	4 8	29 55	14 5	17 47	15 30	13 42	20 5	21 36	26 11	14 16D	20 42
22 TU	5 8	12♌39	14 5	19 16	16 41	14 27	20 16	21 43	26 9	14 16	20 43
23 WE	6 9	25 3	14 5	20 46	17 52	15 12	20 27	21 50	26 7	14 16	20 45
24 TH	7 9	7♍12	14 3	22 15	19 3	15 56	20 38	21 57	26 6	14 17	20 46
25 FR	8 10	19 11	13 59	23 44	20 14	16 41	20 49	22 4	26 4	14 17	20 48
26 SA	9 11	1♎4	13 52	25 12	21 25	17 26	20 59	22 11	26 2	14 17	20 50
27 SU	10 12	12 55	13 42	26 40	22 36	18 11	21 10	22 18	26 1	14 17	20 51
28 MO	11 12	24 46	13 29	28 7	23 46	18 56	21 20	22 25	25 59	14 17	20 53
29 TU	12 13	6♏38	13 14	29 33	24 57	19 41	21 30	22 32	25 58	14 18	20 55
30 WE	13 14	18 34	12 59	0♐59	26 8	20 25	21 41	22 39	25 56	14 18	20 56

INGRESSES :			
1 ☽→♏ 4:31	☉→♏ 21:51		
2 ♂→♑ 8:26	18 ☽→♋ 18:32		
3 ☽→♐ 17:1	21 ☽→♌ 0:9		
6 ☽→♑ 4:13	23 ☽→♍ 9:44		
8 ♀→♐ 0:9	25 ☽→♎ 21:50		
☽→♒ 12:38	28 ☽→♏ 10:36		
9 ☿→♏ 8:45	29 ☿→♐ 7:28		
10 ☽→♓ 17:16	30 ☽→♐ 22:51		
12 ☽→♈ 18:24			
14 ☽→♉ 17:31			
16 ☽→♊ 16:49			

ASPECTS & ECLIPSES :

2 ☽☌☊ 12:20	☉☍☽ 13:51	22 ☽☌☊ 2:45	☉□☊ 19:16		
☽☌♄ 20:8	15 ☽☍♅ 7:53	☽☍♆ 3:7	♀□♅ 20:17		
3 ☽☌♆ 5:31	☽⊡☿ 16:22	23 ☿☌♄ 18:42	30 ☽☌♄ 8:15		
5 ☽☌♅ 9:23	☽☌♄ 2:33	24 ♃□♇ 22:28			
6 ☽☌♂ 9:55	17 ☽☍♅ 11:9	25 ☽☌♃ 3:19			
7 ☉□☽ 19:50	♆☍☊ 17:14	♀☌♇ 11:45			
9 ☽☌♆ 14:13	18 ☽☍♆ 2:37	♀□♃ 13:44			
☽☌♅ 15:54	☿□♅ 14:37	☽☍♅ 13:51			
11 ☽☍♃ 23:44	☿□♆ 16:8	27 ☽☌A 20:12			
12 ☽☌♅ 12:43	19 ☽☍♂ 16:47	29 ☉☌☽ 12:17			
14 ☽☌P 11:15	21 ☉□☽ 8:32	☽⊡☊ 13:0			

SIDEREAL HELIOCENTRIC LONGITUDES :   NOVEMBER 2016 Gregorian at 0 hours UT

DAY	Sid. Time	☿	♀	⊕	♂	♃	♄	♅	♆	♇	Vernal Point
1 TU	2:42:51	22♎46	17♑52	14♈2	13♒0	11♍21	22♏42	27♓42	16♒1	21♐50	5♓ 1'30"
2 WE	2:46:48	25 41	19 27	15 2	13 38	11 26	22 44	27 43	16 1	21 50	5♓ 1'30"
3 TH	2:50:44	28 34	21 2	16 2	14 16	11 30	22 46	27 44	16 2	21 51	5♓ 1'30"
4 FR	2:54:41	1♏24	22 37	17 2	14 54	11 35	22 47	27 44	16 2	21 51	5♓ 1'30"
5 SA	2:58:37	4 14	24 12	18 2	15 33	11 39	22 49	27 45	16 2	21 51	5♓ 1'30"
6 SU	3: 2:34	7 2	25 47	19 2	16 11	11 44	22 51	27 46	16 3	21 52	5♓ 1'30"
7 MO	3: 6:31	9 48	27 22	20 3	16 49	11 48	22 53	27 46	16 3	21 52	5♓ 1'30"
8 TU	3:10:27	12 34	28 57	21 3	17 27	11 53	22 55	27 47	16 3	21 52	5♓ 1'29"
9 WE	3:14:24	15 20	0♒32	22 3	18 5	11 57	22 56	27 48	16 4	21 53	5♓ 1'29"
10 TH	3:18:20	18 5	2 7	23 3	18 43	12 2	22 58	27 48	16 4	21 53	5♓ 1'29"
11 FR	3:22:17	20 49	3 42	24 4	19 21	12 6	23 0	27 49	16 4	21 53	5♓ 1'29"
12 SA	3:26:13	23 34	5 17	25 4	19 59	12 11	23 2	27 50	16 5	21 54	5♓ 1'29"
13 SU	3:30:10	26 19	6 52	26 4	20 37	12 15	23 4	27 50	16 5	21 54	5♓ 1'29"
14 MO	3:34: 6	29 4	8 27	27 5	21 15	12 20	23 5	27 51	16 5	21 54	5♓ 1'29"
15 TU	3:38: 3	1♐50	10 2	28 5	21 53	12 25	23 7	27 52	16 6	21 54	5♓ 1'29"
16 WE	3:42: 0	4 37	11 37	29 5	22 31	12 29	23 9	27 52	16 6	21 55	5♓ 1'28"
17 TH	3:45:56	7 24	13 13	0♉6	23 9	12 34	23 11	27 53	16 7	21 55	5♓ 1'28"
18 FR	3:49:53	10 13	14 48	1 6	23 47	12 38	23 13	27 54	16 7	21 55	5♓ 1'28"
19 SA	3:53:49	13 3	16 23	2 7	24 25	12 43	23 14	27 54	16 7	21 56	5♓ 1'28"
20 SU	3:57:46	15 55	17 58	3 7	25 3	12 47	23 16	27 55	16 8	21 56	5♓ 1'28"
21 MO	4: 1:42	18 49	19 33	4 8	25 41	12 52	23 18	27 55	16 8	21 56	5♓ 1'28"
22 TU	4: 5:39	21 45	21 9	5 9	26 19	12 56	23 20	27 56	16 8	21 57	5♓ 1'28"
23 WE	4: 9:35	24 43	22 44	6 9	26 57	13 1	23 22	27 57	16 9	21 57	5♓ 1'27"
24 TH	4:13:32	27 44	24 19	7 10	27 34	13 5	23 24	27 57	16 9	21 57	5♓ 1'27"
25 FR	4:17:29	0♑47	25 54	8 11	28 12	13 10	23 25	27 58	16 9	21 58	5♓ 1'27"
26 SA	4:21:25	3 54	27 30	9 11	28 50	13 14	23 27	27 59	16 10	21 58	5♓ 1'27"
27 SU	4:25:22	7 4	29 5	10 12	29 28	13 19	23 29	27 59	16 10	21 58	5♓ 1'27"
28 MO	4:29:18	10 18	0♓40	11 13	0♓6	13 23	23 31	28 0	16 11	21 59	5♓ 1'27"
29 TU	4:33:15	13 36	2 16	12 14	0 43	13 28	23 33	28 1	16 11	21 59	5♓ 1'27"
30 WE	4:37:11	16 58	3 51	13 14	1 21	13 32	23 34	28 1	16 11	21 59	5♓ 1'26"

INGRESSES :	
3 ☿→♏ 12:7	
8 ♀→♒ 15:54	
14 ☿→♐ 8:5	
16 ⊕→♉ 21:39	
24 ☿→♑ 17:52	
27 ♀→♓ 13:51	
♂→♓ 20:26	

ASPECTS (HELIOCENTRIC +MOON(TYCHONIC)) :

1 ☿☌☋ 6:25	☽□☿ 20:2	16 ☽□♂ 5:5	♀⊡☊ 10:48	29 ☽□♆ 19:13	
2 ☽□♂ 8:34	☽☌♂ 21:50	☽☍♄ 5:54	☽☍♀ 18:48	30 ☽☌♄ 10:3	
☽□♆ 12:55	10 ☽□♄ 5:18	17 ♂□♄ 1:14	☽□♄ 20:42		
3 ☽☌♄ 2:29	☿□♂ 7:14	☽☍☿ 5:55	23 ☽☍♂ 3:55		
4 ☽□♃ 16:12	11 ☽☍♃ 13:32	☽□♃ 13:18	♀□♄ 9:45		
5 ☽☌♇ 12:22	☿☌A 16:47	18 ☽☍♇ 4:48	24 ☿□♅ 1:50		
♂☌♆ 18:52	☿☌♄ 19:15	☽□♅ 14:56	☽☌♃ 11:50		
☽□♅ 23:52	12 ☽□♇ 5:24	♀☌♆ 20:3	25 ☽□♇ 5:35		
8 ☽☌♀ 12:11	☽☌♅ 14:56	☿□♃ 21:2	☽☍♅ 17:44		
9 ☿□♆ 6:23	15 ☽□♀ 10:16	22 ☿☌♇ 1:38	26 ☽□☿ 7:47		
☽☌♆ 17:19	☽□♆ 18:44	☽☍♆ 6:42	27 ♀☌♂ 9:32		

And with respect to God, it is so as to demonstrate to the hierarchies of evil that man is of another caliber than the relative and the transitory, that whatever the power and enjoyment is here below it can never satisfy him. The trial of our epoch is that of Faust. It is the trial of satisfied desires.[1]

In becoming a disciple of the Etheric Christ the danger exists that one becomes "seen" by his vengeful opponent. Ever does this dark figure circle around spiritual groups, seeking to gain entrance through the weakest link. Thus can devotion be destroyed. It is the manas consciousness that now bestows a protection against the dangers of the Antichrist. It calls us to awaken where only fools dare tread:

The Arcanum "The Fool" teaches the "know-how" of passing from intellectuality, moved by the desire for knowledge, to the higher knowledge due to love. It is thus a matter of transition from the consciousness that theosophical literature calls "lesser manas" to the consciousness that it calls "greater manas" (= "manas-buddhi")—which corresponds to the transition from ego consciousness to the consciousness of the spiritual self in anthroposophic literature. In other words, the Tarot Arcanum "The Fool" is related to the transformation of personal consciousness into cosmic consciousness, where the self (ego) is no longer the author of the act of consciousness but is its receiver—obedient to the law of poverty, obedience and chastity.

These can be our contemplations under this Full Moon in Aries. The wisdom in the eyes of God is so often seen as foolishness in the eyes of human beings; yet, when the author is no longer only the individual, something great can be born.

Nov. 16: Sun enters Scorpio, "Existence consumes being" (Steiner, *Twelve Cosmic Moods*). William Bento illumines this mantra:

What a riddle this phrase proposes to us! Existence as a term expressing the state of life, and the experience of living has a primary activity that cannot be denied. It does not preserve, as much as it consumes. It is a force of changing all things. As the force empowering life, it is always aiming at the inevitable end—death. And so it is: life begets death and in death new existence springs forth. This is a riddle that is equally valid in understanding the passage of human life on Earth and in understanding the forces playing out through the course of nature.

The first decan is ruled by Mars and is associated with the constellation of Lupus the Wolf. Sun entering Scorpio began the forty days in the wilderness. With Sun in Scorpio, we are asked to be patient in order to gain insight.

Nov. 18: Mercury 14° Scorpio square Neptune 14° Aquarius. Mercury at this degree marks the beginning of the Age of Michael (Nov/10/1879). This date has been indicated from statements made by Rudolf Steiner. (See the article in this Journal.) Mercury square Neptune calls us to be awake to the inspirational qualities Neptune bestows when the mind has mastered stillness. The Archangel Michael has sent cosmic thought to Earth; he waits for us to become the recipients of these great thoughts of the spirit by developing powers of keen awareness. The danger exists that we get swept away by the mass thoughts that are broadcasting across our various screens and gadgets. Instead of shallow tidbits, this aspect asks us to venture into a deepening silence in order to become vessels for the cosmic thoughts seeking quiet minds.

Sun 2° Scorpio: The summons of Judas Iscariot (Oct/24/30).

Nov. 23: Mercury conjunct Saturn 22° Scorpio. The Sun at this degree remembers the raising of the Youth of Nain (Nov/13/30). This aspect deepens mental capacities. The Youth of Nain was an incarnation of Mani/Parsifal. Concerning this individuality, Rudolf Steiner said:

Mani will not incarnate during this century [20th] but intends to do so in the next century, if he can find a suitable body. The ordinary kind of education does not provide any possibility for Mani to develop: only Waldorf education would do so. If the right conditions are provided he will appear as a teacher of humankind and take up leadership in matters of art and religion.

---

1 Anon., *Meditations on the Tarot,* p. 597.

He will act from the power of the Grail Mysteries, and he will instruct humankind so that they may decide even about good and evil.[2]

Mani teaches his disciples how to *love evil good.* When the skeletal fingers of fear release the soul from their stony grasp, love grows stronger. And love is the powerless presence before which evil trembles.

Nov. 24: Jupiter 21° Virgo square Pluto 21° Sagittarius. When the Sun reached 21° Virgo in the year 32, Jesus informed some shepherds that it was he who was the King of the Jews whom the kings of the east had traveled to Judea to meet, and that he now wanted to visit these men again (Saturday, Sep/13/32). The shepherds exhibited a childlike joy and love for Jesus. Now that the Maitreya Bodhisattva serves as a vessel for the inspiring presence of the Archangel Jesus, it will most likely be the shepherd-like heart who will recognize him.

Jupiter at today's degree remembers that the kings—those who so long ago saw Jesus coming to them—may yet be here again with us. Rudolf Steiner told us the prophets of old must be recognized in their new form. The gold king was one of the prophets of old. Perhaps he is leading us to adore the Christ in his Second Coming and to recognize the one who speaks as the messenger of the Etheric Christ. Herods are everywhere—they remind us of the peril that accompanies the new disciples of Christ. Is it possible that the Boddhisattva—whom Steiner foretold would begin his work in the 1930s—was ignored and ultimately scorned when his work served as the proclaimer of Christ in the twentieth century? Will he be heard in the twenty-first century, as he continues to inspire through the future Matraiya's mantle, now bearing the Angel Jesus' presence?

The Spirits of Wisdom (Kyriotetes/Jupiter) call communities together in the name of love (Phanes). When Wisdom and Love stand square to each other, the "lawless one" may create the inverse of this aspect—tyrannical hatred against all who oppose him. Yet, behind the mask of certainty worn by the ahrimanic hordes, lurks their fear, and even their

boredom, for, they know their time is short, and that their ultimate defeat has already been written.

This aspect encourages communities to deepen their commitment to truth by aiming their arrows to the seed and source of all revelation, Christ, whose messengers are carried on the wings of the Holy Spirit.

Nov. 25: ASPECT: Venus 21° Sagittarius conjunct Pluto and square Jupiter 21° Virgo. Venus remembers Jesus as he went to the house of Jairus and cautioned Jairus's daughter Salome, whom he had raised from the dead, to follow the word of God. Later, the Pharisees came to Jesus, asking him to heal the man with a withered hand (Saturday, Dec/2/30). When Venus and Pluto are conjunct, passions intensify and specters can rise from the grottos of unconsiousness. Alternatively, those who strive may find the trials their destinies have prepared for them. The latter is the higher manifestation of this aspect. The Pharisees set a trap for Jesus by bringing him the man with the withered hand on the Sabbath. When Jesus healed the man, the Pharisees were filled with wrath, for healings were forbidden on the Sabbath.

This healing occurred on the day of the Holy Virgin (Saturday). The Holy Virgin knows the work of the Herodians, the Pharisees, and all those who uphold rigid laws at the expense of bearing witness to new revelation. With Venus/Pluto square Jupiter, we must ask if our communities are prepared to hear the Living Word as it now expresses itself through the continual unfolding of Time. For the Time spirits themselves reign from the sphere marked by the orbit of Venus, and they direct spiritual guidance in obedience to evolution's necessities. As we are in the early beginnings of a new 600-year cultural rhythm, it is wise to listen to apocalyptic revelation, for these dispensations will fill us with the intensity of truth at a time when deception would instead distract us to death.

Nov. 29: Mercury enters Sagittarius, "Attainment concludes joyful striving" (Steiner, *Twelve Cosmic Moods).*

New Moon 13° Scorpio: The raising of the Youth of Nain (Monday, Nov/13/30). At the exact time of

---

2   Steiner, *From the History and Contents of the First Section of the Esoteric School , 1904–1914,* p. 227.

the raising of the Youth of Nain, the Moon was 11° Scorpio. Shortly after this miracle, with the Moon approaching today's degree was when Anne Catherine Emmerich beheld Jesus teaching of the precipitious abyss before which the children of Israel stood:

It was in consideration of the righteousness of the patriarchs that almighty God, down to the present day, had protected and spared Israel; but now, enchained in sin and covered with the veil of mental blindness, they had become like unto this youth. They were standing on the brink of the grave, and for the last time was mercy extended to them. John had prepared the way and with a powerful voice had called upon their hearts to arise from the slumber of death. The heavenly Father [had] now, for the last time, pity upon them.

He would open to life the eyes of those that did not obstinately keep them closed. Jesus compared the people in their blindness to the youth shut up in his coffin who, though near the tomb, though outside the gate of the city, had been met by salvation. "If," he said, "the bearers had not heeded my voice, if they had not set down the coffin, had not opened it, had not freed the body from its winding sheet, if they had obstinately hurried forward with their burden, the boy would have been buried—and how terrible that would have been!" Then Jesus likened to this picture he had drawn the false teachers, the Pharisees.[3]

The community of Eternal Israel represents the community of humanity. We collectively stand on the brink of death—the second death, wherein our star falls from heaven and we remember not that we have been born of spirit. With the New Moon in Scorpio, we turn to the thirteenth Arcanum of the Tarot—Death:

Similarly, beyond clinical death there is a psychic death and a moral death. During our seventy or eighty years of life we bear within us layers of death in our psychic being. There are things which are missing from our psychic and moral being. The *absence* of faith, hope and love cannot be remedied either by arguments or by exhortations or even by a living example. An act of divine magic—or grace—is necessary to accomplish the *infusion* of life into what is dead. And if Christ is worshipped as the Risen One it is because those who bear death within them know that it is only divine magic which can raise what is dead within them and that the risen Christ is the guarantor of this.[4]

The anonymous author goes on to note the eternal truth of vertical memory. This is the memory that lies at our soul's depths, ever remembering our birth from the Divine:

Vertical memory is the more effective to the extent that the three sacred vows—obedience, poverty and chastity—render the lower man capable of listening to, perceiving and receiving things from above without distortion. Vertical memory is fundamentally only moral memory carried in its development to a still higher degree. This is why it is only moral purification, which the practice of the three sacred vows entails, that counts in the case of vertical memory. Intellectual interests, as such, do not count here.[5]

During this entire year, Uranus remembers the immaculate conception of the Nathan Jesus. Thus a quickening is occurring in the vertical stream of eternity through which each of us has descended into birth. This memory lies in the innermost kernel of our hearts, continuously seeking the light and warmth of God. This New Moon asks that we turn to this immaculate source of sustenance and experience the world beyond this world, where something greater than us is seeking to unite with us—and is already us. Union with this truth raises us from the grave into which we have been led by the cunning of the serpent. Can we choose the light? Will we see the lies that tether us to untruth? This miracle occurred on a Monday—the day of the Holy Trinity. With Venus square Uranus, the trinity of our thinking, feeling, and willing is seeking harmony with our body, soul, and spirit. Quietude in patient silence will bring forth the highest in today's aspects.

ASPECT: Venus 26° Sagittarius square Uranus 26° Pisces: The healing of the two demoniacs (Wednesday, Dec/6/30). Venus recalls the healing of two possessed by demons. A few weeks after raising the

---

3 *ACE Complete*, p. 527.

4 Anon., *Meditations on the Tarot*, p. 343.

5 Ibid., 347.

Youth of Nain, Jesus was in Gergeza, casting out demons. In square to Uranus, Venus can excite the soul to agitative distraction; conversely, it can assist one in freeing oneself from constrictions born of ghosts from the past. The freed spirit, like a dove, rises toward the Sun. We are invited to soar on spirit wings through the powers of this New Moon, and of this Venus aspect to Uranus. The Nathan Jesus (now the Angel Jesus) can be contemplated as the one through whom we find the light of the World as the source for healing the oppressive asphyxiation of materialism.

Nov. 30: ASPECT: Sun 14° Scorpio square Neptune 14°Aquarius. The Sun at Neptune's degree remembers Jesus as he taught on the theme of the "Sermon on the Mount," as described in Matthew 5:3–12, 6:9–13. Having called himself the bread of life, there was an uproar. Jesus replied to the Pharisees that he would give them the food of which he spoke "in its own time" (Feb/2/31).

In the Egyptian mysteries there were four sacred substances: wine, honey, milk, and bread. In our epoch we are to become the Christianized metamorphosis of ancient Egypt. John is calling from the wilderness, and the Maitreya is inspiring the living speaking of the good. Slithering through cracks and crannies, the shadow-walkers of deception seek to subvert the blessings of the holy sacraments. The Devil seeks to co-opt the honey; Satan seeks to co-opt the milk; the Asuras seek to co-opt the bread; and the Sun Demon seeks to co-opt the wine. With Neptune square the Sun, reality can quicken into the elixir of divine inspiration—or dissolve into mere fantasy.

Each of us must stay awake. We must remember the power of the Word that streamed to all humanity through the Beatitudes spoken upon the Sermon on the Mount. We must reclaim the sacredness of the bread, the milk, the honey, and the wine, and see these substances as the true sources of nourishment—for this is the time of the Second Coming, wherein the holy mysteries are being restored. The four substances represent (respectively) our physical, etheric, and astral bodies, as well as our "I." Receptivity to the divine origin of nourishment quickens our earthly bodies as vessels for higher nourishment.

This aspect brings a sensitivity toward suffering. Suffering brings us to the "I" enthroned in our heart, and through this we are able to feel the hearts of others.

DECEMBER 2016

The new crescent Moon joins Mars in the last degrees of Capricorn on the 5th, and Mars shifts into Aquarius on the 12th. The Full Moon (Sun in Scorpio and Moon in Taurus) occurs on the 13th, and the Sun shifts into Sagittarius on the 16th. Mercury stations Retrograde on the 20th in Sagittarius and remains so for the rest of this year.

The waning Moon reaches Jupiter in Virgo by the 22nd, visible in the pre-dawn hours. By the 27th, the Moon begins to dip into invisibility passing by Saturn and Mercury and becomes "officially" New Moon on the 29th. Venus shifts from the constellation of Capricorn into Aquarius the 29th.

From Dec 23–26, the Sun recalls the three temptations in the wilderness that lasted until the end of the forty-day fast (Nov/27–30/29). With the single exception of the day after Christmas, when Mars is opposite the North Node and Jupiter is opposite Uranus, all of the major aspects this month involve the Sun.

Dec. 1: Sun conjunct Antares 15° Scorpio. Antares the star associated with death/resurrection stands with the Sun today. The mysteries of the underworld are illumined for those who have the patience to hold judgment until bestowed with insight. May we find awareness of occult mysteries through presence of mind.

Dec. 3: Venus enters Capricorn: "May the past feel the future" (Steiner, *Twelve Cosmic Moods*). When past and future meet in the present moment, illumined thinking shines forth. Venus was in Capricorn during the temptations of Christ—he whose courage brought the power of redemption to all humanity.

Dec. 8: Sun 22° Scorpio: The raising of the Youth of Nain (Monday, Nov/13/30). As Jesus raised the

Youth of Nain, Anne Catherine Emmerich saw numbers of small, dark figures like insects, beetles, toads, snakes, and little black birds issuing from many of the bystanders. She witnessed that the crowd became purer and brighter as the consequence of the death-like creatures that were lifted from them. As we turn to the presence of the Etheric Christ, we too may find ourselves healed from death-like creatures which adversaries have loosed in the realm of our Mother.

Dec. 9: Mars 28° Capricorn reaches its degree of classical exaltation.

Dec. 10: Sun conjunct Saturn 24° Scorpio. The Sun remembers Jesus wandering in the fields east of Megiddo, teaching in parables to the workers who were busy sowing. Disciples of John the Baptist accompanied him. Jesus healed the many sick people who were gathered there, and spoke to John's disciples the words seen in Matthew 11:2–6 and Luke 7:18–23. He also said, "[A]mong those born of women, none is greater than John; yet he who is least in the kingdom of God is greater than he" (Nov/15/30). These words spoken by Jesus remind us that our births from heredity lineages, from male/female generation, are incomparable to even the smallest portion of the element that is not "born of woman" but enters the human being directly from the kingdom of heaven. It is this virginal element—of vertical generation—that is greater by far. In this year, with Uranus remembering the birth of the Nathan Jesus, this vertical generation is quickening for all who turn to the power of the Holy Spirit. The fields of Megiddo have been war-torn throughout history. Yet, we can attune ourselves even in fields of battle to the voice of truth. We are not to be distracted. This aspect enhances self-control and concentration.

Dec. 12: Mars enters Aquarius: "And should arise in life's stream" (Steiner, *Twelve Cosmic Moods*). Mars in Aquarius asks us to manifest the power that lives in the depths of our being, to rise with this power in remembrance of the boundless spheres from which we have descended.

Dec. 13: Full Moon 28° Taurus opposite Sun 28° Scorpio: The Moon was at today's degree when Jesus began his Sermon on the Mount (Tuesday, Nov/28/30). What began on this day would last another fourteen days, but its conclusion would not be reached for another three months. Jesus began with the first Beatitude: *Blessed are the poor in spirit, for theirs is the kingdom of heaven:*

> Only in the physical body can we awaken the force of courage and the humility needed to go through the "needle's eye" of initiation. Only those who are conscious of the range of human guilt and the human need arising from it can develop the necessary humility in the presence of the spiritual world—a necessary condition of acceptance by that world and security against rejection by the spiriutal world as a moral alien.[1]

The consciousness soul is to penetrate fully into the physical body, wherein intuition is achieved. Often we may find that we flee from this process due to the fact that it entails meeting with the Lesser Guardian of the Threshold. Nonetheless, facing judgment is not to be avoided, for ultimately the source of judgment is not God, but rather the soul itself. Our courage will be overshadowed by reluctance if we do not resurrect the dead ego-forms we have dragged with us from past incarnation. *Gnosis is the direct knowing of past wisdom, illumining the kingdom that ever stands behind the illusions of sense existence. To reintegrate into wholeness, we are called to remember heaven so that heaven can remember us:*

> It is the same with the "awaking and resurrection of the dead." Here it is not cosmic indifference (that we call "matter") which will effect anything, but rather it is cosmic love (that we call "spirit") which will accomplish the magical act of resurrection, i.e., the reintegration of an inseparable unity—the unity of spirit, soul and body—not by way of birth (reincarnation) but by way of the magical act of divine memory.[2]

Today's Full Moon brings to fruition the memory of the raising of the Youth of Nain at the past New Moon. Again the Moon asks us to contemplate

---

1 Tomberg, *Christ and Sophia*, p. 197.
2 Anon., *Meditations on the Tarot*, p. 562.

SIDEREAL GEOCENTRIC LONGITUDES :   DECEMBER 2016 Gregorian at 0 hours UT

DAY	☉	☽	☊	☿	♀	♂	♃	♄	♅	♆	♇
1 TH	14 ♏ 15	0 ♐ 34	12 ♌ 44R	2 ♐ 24	27 ♐ 18	21 ♑ 10	21 ♍ 51	22 ♏ 46	25 ♓ 55R	14 ♒ 18	20 ♐ 58
2 FR	15 16	12 40	12 32	3 48	28 28	21 55	22 1	22 53	25 54	14 19	21 0
3 SA	16 16	24 53	12 22	5 11	29 39	22 40	22 11	23 0	25 52	14 19	21 2
4 SU	17 17	7 ♉ 15	12 15	6 32	0 ♑ 49	23 26	22 21	23 7	25 51	14 20	21 3
5 MO	18 18	19 48	12 11	7 52	1 59	24 11	22 31	23 14	25 50	14 20	21 5
6 TU	19 19	2 ♒ 36	12 10	9 11	3 9	24 56	22 40	23 21	25 49	14 21	21 7
7 WE	20 20	15 42	12 10	10 27	4 18	25 41	22 50	23 28	25 48	14 21	21 9
8 TH	21 21	29 9	12 10	11 41	5 28	26 26	22 59	23 35	25 46	14 22	21 11
9 FR	22 22	13 ♓ 2	12 8	12 52	6 38	27 11	23 9	23 42	25 45	14 22	21 12
10 SA	23 23	27 19	12 5	14 0	7 47	27 56	23 18	23 49	25 44	14 23	21 14
11 SU	24 24	12 ♈ 0	11 58	15 4	8 56	28 42	23 27	23 57	25 43	14 24	21 16
12 MO	25 25	27 1	11 49	16 4	10 5	29 27	23 36	24 4	25 43	14 24	21 18
13 TU	26 26	12 ♉ 12	11 38	17 0	11 14	0 ♒ 12	23 45	24 11	25 42	14 25	21 20
14 WE	27 27	27 24	11 27	17 50	12 23	0 57	23 54	24 18	25 41	14 26	21 22
15 TH	28 28	12 ♊ 25	11 16	18 33	13 32	1 43	24 2	24 25	25 40	14 27	21 24
16 FR	29 29	27 7	11 8	19 10	14 40	2 28	24 11	24 32	25 39	14 28	21 26
17 SA	0 ♐ 30	11 ♋ 21	11 1	19 38	15 49	3 13	24 19	24 39	25 39	14 29	21 28
18 SU	1 31	25 7	10 58	19 58	16 57	3 58	24 28	24 46	25 38	14 30	21 30
19 MO	2 32	8 ♌ 23	10 57	20 8	18 5	4 44	24 36	24 53	25 38	14 30	21 32
20 TU	3 33	21 13	10 57D	20 8R	19 13	5 29	24 44	25 0	25 37	14 31	21 33
21 WE	4 34	3 ♍ 40	10 57R	19 56	20 20	6 14	24 52	25 7	25 37	14 32	21 35
22 TH	5 35	15 51	10 57	19 33	21 28	7 0	25 0	25 14	25 36	14 34	21 37
23 FR	6 36	27 50	10 55	18 57	22 35	7 45	25 7	25 21	25 36	14 35	21 39
24 SA	7 37	9 ♎ 42	10 50	18 11	23 42	8 30	25 15	25 28	25 36	14 36	21 41
25 SU	8 39	21 32	10 42	17 14	24 49	9 16	25 22	25 35	25 35	14 37	21 43
26 MO	9 40	3 ♏ 23	10 33	16 7	25 56	10 1	25 29	25 42	25 35	14 38	21 45
27 TU	10 41	15 19	10 21	14 53	27 2	10 46	25 37	25 49	25 35	14 39	21 48
28 WE	11 42	27 21	10 9	13 34	28 8	11 32	25 44	25 56	25 35	14 41	21 50
29 TH	12 43	9 ♐ 30	9 58	12 12	29 14	12 17	25 50	26 3	25 35	14 42	21 52
30 FR	13 44	21 48	9 48	10 50	0 ♒ 20	13 2	25 57	26 10	25 35D	14 43	21 54
31 SA	14 46	4 ♑ 16	9 40	9 32	1 26	13 48	26 4	26 17	25 35	14 44	21 56

INGRESSES :

3 ♀ → ♑ 7:20 ; 20 ☽ → ♍ 16:52
  ☽ → ♑ 9:58 ; 23 ☽ → ♎ 4:22
5 ☽ → ♒ 19:10 ; 25 ☽ → ♏ 17:8
8 ☽ → ♓ 1:28 ; 28 ☽ → ♐ 5:15
10 ☽ → ♈ 4:25 ; 29 ♀ → ♒ 16:37
12 ☽ → ♉ 4:43 ; 30 ☽ → ♑ 15:49
  ♂ → ♒ 17:34
14 ☽ → ♊ 4:7
16 ☽ → ♋ 4:48
  ☉ → ♐ 12:16
18 ☽ → ♌ 8:44

ASPECTS & ECLIPSES :

1 ☉ □ ♆ 1:24
  ☽ ☌ ☿ 4:7
2 ☽ ☌ ♆ 16:25
3 ☽ ☌ ♀ 10:15
5 ☽ ☌ ♂ 8:47
6 ☽ ☌ ♅ 17:35
  ☽ ☌ ♆ 21:34
7 ☉ □ ☽ 9:2
9 ☽ ☍ ♃ 17:14
  ☽ ☌ ♅ 21:23
10 ☉ ☌ ♄ 11:50
12 ☽ ⚼ ☊ 23:7
   ☽ ☌ P 23:20
13 ☽ ☍ ♄ 19:2
14 ☉ ☍ ☽ 0:4
   ☽ ☍ ☿ 10:23
15 ☽ ☍ ♆ 14:36
17 ☽ ☍ ♀ 8:22
18 ☽ ☍ ♂ 16:54
19 ☽ ☌ ☊ 4:44
   ☽ ☍ ♆ 11:22
21 ☉ □ ☽ 1:54
22 ☽ ☌ ♃ 18:29
   ☽ ☍ ♅ 19:30
25 ☽ ☌ A 6:14
26 ♅ ☌ ♄ 0:31
   ☽ ⚼ ☊ 14:12
   ♃ ☍ ♅ 18:16
27 ☽ ☌ ♄ 21:10
28 ☉ ⚻ ☿ 18:46
29 ☽ ☌ ♇ 4:45
   ☉ ☌ ☽ 6:52
30 ☽ ☌ ♇ 0:10

SIDEREAL HELIOCENTRIC LONGITUDES :   DECEMBER 2016 Gregorian at 0 hours UT

DAY	Sid. Time	☿	♀	⊕	♂	♃	♄	♅	♆	♇	Vernal Point
1 TH	4:41: 8	20 ♑ 24	5 ♓ 26	14 ♉ 15	1 ♓ 59	13 ♍ 37	23 ♏ 36	28 ♓ 2	16 ♒ 12	21 ♐ 59	5 ♓ 1'26"
2 FR	4:45: 4	23 56	7 2	15 16	2 36	13 42	23 38	28 3	16 12	22 0	5 ♓ 1'26"
3 SA	4:49: 1	27 33	8 37	16 17	3 14	13 46	23 40	28 3	16 12	22 0	5 ♓ 1'26"
4 SU	4:52:58	1 ♒ 16	10 13	17 18	3 52	13 51	23 42	28 4	16 13	22 0	5 ♓ 1'26"
5 MO	4:56:54	5 4	11 48	18 19	4 29	13 55	23 43	28 5	16 13	22 1	5 ♓ 1'26"
6 TU	5: 0:51	8 59	13 24	19 20	5 7	14 0	23 45	28 5	16 14	22 1	5 ♓ 1'26"
7 WE	5: 4:47	13 1	14 59	20 21	5 44	14 4	23 47	28 6	16 14	22 1	5 ♓ 1'25"
8 TH	5: 8:44	17 10	16 35	21 21	6 22	14 9	23 49	28 7	16 14	22 2	5 ♓ 1'25"
9 FR	5:12:40	21 27	18 11	22 22	6 59	14 13	23 51	28 7	16 14	22 2	5 ♓ 1'25"
10 SA	5:16:37	25 51	19 46	23 23	7 37	14 18	23 53	28 8	16 15	22 2	5 ♓ 1'25"
11 SU	5:20:33	0 ♓ 23	21 22	24 24	8 14	14 22	23 54	28 8	16 15	22 3	5 ♓ 1'25"
12 MO	5:24:30	5 5	22 58	25 25	8 52	14 27	23 56	28 9	16 16	22 3	5 ♓ 1'25"
13 TU	5:28:27	9 54	24 33	26 26	9 29	14 31	23 58	28 10	16 16	22 3	5 ♓ 1'25"
14 WE	5:32:23	14 53	26 9	27 27	10 6	14 36	24 0	28 10	16 16	22 4	5 ♓ 1'25"
15 TH	5:36:20	20 1	27 45	28 28	10 44	14 40	24 2	28 11	16 17	22 4	5 ♓ 1'24"
16 FR	5:40:16	25 18	29 21	29 29	11 21	14 45	24 3	28 12	16 17	22 4	5 ♓ 1'24"
17 SA	5:44:13	0 ♈ 44	0 ♈ 56	0 ♊ 30	11 58	14 50	24 5	28 12	16 17	22 4	5 ♓ 1'24"
18 SU	5:48: 9	6 19	2 32	1 31	12 35	14 54	24 7	28 13	16 18	22 5	5 ♓ 1'24"
19 MO	5:52: 6	12 3	4 8	2 32	13 12	14 59	24 9	28 14	16 18	22 5	5 ♓ 1'24"
20 TU	5:56: 2	17 54	5 44	3 33	13 49	15 3	24 11	28 14	16 18	22 5	5 ♓ 1'24"
21 WE	5:59:59	23 53	7 20	4 35	14 27	15 8	24 12	28 15	16 19	22 6	5 ♓ 1'24"
22 TH	6: 3:56	29 58	8 56	5 36	15 4	15 12	24 14	28 16	16 19	22 6	5 ♓ 1'23"
23 FR	6: 7:52	6 ♉ 9	10 32	6 37	15 41	15 17	24 16	28 16	16 20	22 6	5 ♓ 1'23"
24 SA	6:11:49	12 23	12 8	7 38	16 18	15 21	24 18	28 17	16 20	22 7	5 ♓ 1'23"
25 SU	6:15:45	18 41	13 44	8 39	16 54	15 26	24 20	28 18	16 20	22 7	5 ♓ 1'23"
26 MO	6:19:42	25 0	15 20	9 40	17 31	15 30	24 21	28 18	16 21	22 7	5 ♓ 1'23"
27 TU	6:23:38	1 ♊ 20	16 56	10 41	18 8	15 35	24 23	28 19	16 21	22 8	5 ♓ 1'23"
28 WE	6:27:35	7 37	18 32	11 43	18 45	15 39	24 25	28 19	16 21	22 8	5 ♓ 1'23"
29 TH	6:31:31	13 52	20 8	12 44	19 22	15 44	24 27	28 20	16 22	22 8	5 ♓ 1'22"
30 FR	6:35:28	20 2	21 44	13 45	19 58	15 48	24 29	28 20	16 22	22 9	5 ♓ 1'22"
31 SA	6:39:25	26 6	23 20	14 46	20 35	15 53	24 30	28 21	16 22	22 9	5 ♓ 1'22"

INGRESSES :

3 ☿ → ♒ 15:54
10 ☿ → ♓ 21:57
16 ♀ → ♈ 9:52
   ⊕ → ♊ 12:5
   ☿ → ♈ 20:47
22 ☿ → ♉ 0:7
26 ☿ → ♊ 18:57
31 ☿ → ♋ 15:39

ASPECTS (HELIOCENTRIC +MOON(TYCHONIC)) :

1 ☽ □ ♂ 2:57
  ☽ □ ♀ 11:9
  ☿ ⚻ ☊ 21:27
2 ☽ □ ♃ 2:2
  ☽ ☌ ♆ 18:21
  ⊕ □ ♆ 22:10
3 ☽ □ ♅ 6:11
6 ♀ ☍ ♃ 9:25
  ☽ ☌ ☿ 16:59
7 ☽ ☌ ♆ 0:58
  ☽ □ ♄ 14:32
  ☿ ☌ ♆ 18:39
8 ☽ ☌ ♂ 13:9
9 ☽ ☍ ♃ 2:2
  ☿ □ ⊕ 6:40
  ☽ ☌ ♀ 9:50
  ☿ □ ♄ 13:16
  ☽ □ ♆ 15:12
10 ☽ ☌ ♅ 1:20
   ⊕ ☍ ♄ 11:50
11 ♀ □ ♇ 10:13
12 ☿ ☌ ♂ 21:37
13 ☽ □ ♆ 6:24
   ☽ ☍ ♄ 18:35
   ☿ ☍ ♃ 22:37
14 ☽ □ ♂ 21:8
15 ☽ □ ♃ 3:39
   ♀ ☌ ♅ 6:36
   ☿ □ ♇ 9:23
   ☽ ☍ ♇ 15:41
   ☽ □ ☿ 19:16
16 ☽ □ ♅ 1:48
   ☽ □ ♀ 4:10
   ☿ ☌ ♅ 12:53
17 ☿ ☌ ♀ 1:15
19 ☽ ☍ ♆ 14:44
20 ☽ □ ♄ 5:40
   ☿ ☌ ☊ 22:42
21 ☽ ☍ ♂ 22:20
   ☽ ☌ ♃ 22:42
22 ♂ ☍ ♃ 6:21
   ☽ □ ♇ 12:29
23 ☽ ☍ ♅ 0:53
24 ☽ ☍ ♀ 5:41
   ☿ □ ♆ 15:3
25 ☿ ☌ P 15:24
   ☿ ☍ ♄ 21:31
27 ☽ □ ♆ 2:4
   ☽ ☌ ♄ 18:9
28 ♃ ⚼ ☊ 1:38
   ☿ ☌ ⊕ 18:46
29 ☿ □ ♃ 7:20
   ☽ □ ♃ 12:15
   ☽ ☍ ☿ 17:7
   ☽ □ ♂ 20:15
   ☿ □ ♂ 23:45
30 ☽ ☌ ♇ 0:39
   ☿ ☍ ♆ 8:19
   ☽ □ ♅ 12:39
31 ☿ □ ♅ 9:3

the inner path of descent, through the "eye of the needle" of initiation, so as to recall to memory our divinity.

Tomberg references three Akashic chronicles. Regarding the first two, he writes of a separation between memories that are spiritualized (rising into records above) from memories that are concretized (sinking into records below). He speaks of yet another chronicle, the Book of Life. Here is inscribed all that has eternal value, all that is worthy of resurrection. The past is recorded only in so far as it is of significance for the future, and the future is recorded only in so far as it is of significance for eternity. The Book of Life is the moral memory of the world:

> The third Akasha chronicle [the Book of Life] is the source of strength for hierarchies of the right; it contains the supporting reasons for their faith in justice for the sake of world evolution and humanity, as well as for ultimate universal salvation. The third chronicle aspires to resurrection—to the reintegration of beings—whilst the second is the history of equilibrium, i.e., the karma of the world, the equilibrium between good and evil. The first chronicle—that of facts, pure and simple—supplies the points of support for the arguments of the hierarchies of the left, who do not believe in humankind and accuse humankind at all reproachable points.[3]

Forgiven and atoned-for errors are not recorded in the Book of Life. It is constantly being modified due to human forgiveness (of self and others). This Moon calls us to find hidden places that cleave to judgments we now need to reevaluate. Thus will we find the courage to forgive, in self-accountability, so as to realize the kingdom we yearn to enter. Moon in Taurus asks us to listen to the thoughts of the gods, and align our will with the power of righteousness.

Dec. 16: Sun enters Sagittarius, "Growth attains power of existence" (Steiner, *Twelve Cosmic Moods*). William Bento illumines this mantra:

> When existence is regarded not merely as a noun, but also as a verb, we enter the realm of

becoming. It is being, in dynamic movement. Such movement is purposeful, for being seeks a state in which it can be a power of "presence," a reality of the here and now. This achievement "to be" is the drama of human potential. Each human being seeks "to be" what he or she has resolved to become. The arrival of that becoming is both a joyful and empowering experience—where there is nothing to do but be.

Control of Speech becomes Feeling for Truth. Blessed are the self-disciplined, for they shall know the truth.

Dec. 18: Sun 2° Sagittarius conjunct the Galactic Center. The healing of the man born blind (Friday, Nov/23/31). See Robert Powell's article in this Journal, wherein he describes his new research regarding this sixth miracle of our Lord—who is the Light of the World.

Dec. 20: Mercury goes retrograde 20° Sagittarius. Mercury remembers the stilling of the storm on the Sea of Galilee (Tuesday, Nov/21/30). After the final call of the disciples Peter, Andrew, James, and John, the future twelve apostles boarded Peter's boat to cross the water. Though the weather was calm as the disciples set sail, they had scarcely reached the middle of the lake when a violent tempest arose. Anne Catherine Emmerich found it very strange that "although the sky was shrouded in darkness, the stars were to be seen. The wind blew in a hurricane and the waves dashed over the boat, the sails of which had been furled."

In great anxiety the disciples woke Jesus with the words: "Master! Hast thou no care for us? We are sinking!" Jesus quietly arose, and spoke as if to the elements themselves saying: "Peace! Be still!"

As Mercury stations before moving retrograde, we can imagine the tempests rising around all humanity and Nature herself, asking ourselves what measure of calm can we bring through the certainty of our "I." Our "I" is the star that shines in us no matter how ominous the wind and waves of storms. When retrograde, Mercury strengthens our power of introspection.

Winter Solstice: The yearly rhythm through the seasons now comes to rest. Seeds from the past year

---

3 Ibid., 566.

burrow into the earthly depths. In a few days we enter the holy days and nights of 2016, after which a new cycle will begin. As we gather with friends and families, we remember the past and look toward the future. Gautama Buddha spoke of the sacredness of the present moment: "The secret of health for both body and mind is not to mourn for the past, nor to worry about the future, but to live the present moment wisely and earnestly." May we heed this wisdom in the quietude of winter's longest hour.

Dec. 23: Sun 7° Sagittarius: The first temptation in the wilderness (Nov/27/29). In his studies on the New Testament, Valentin Tomberg writes the following:

> [I]t was not God who was tempted there, but the divine submerged in the human. The point of attack for the temptation was the human in him, not the divine.

The three temptations of Jesus Christ exemplify the path into one's inner nature—the microcosmic path of the southern mystery stream. Through the eightfold path, Gautama Buddha showed us the way to successfully descend into the wilderness of our personal temptations. The spiritual world was not present with Jesus until after the temptations. His resistance was not due to spiritual support, but rather through the human forces of waking consciousness. When Jesus Christ spoke "It is written," in response to the tempters, he was remembering the truth despite the isolation he was then experiencing. We can remember this in times of trial, for deep within us a truth has been written which illumines our way through the labyrinth of our biographies.

The first temptation was the temptation to bow to the prince of this world. Satan hung a globe from his hand in which all the marvels of the world were contained. Jesus would not look into the globe, but instead spoke the words: "My kingdom is not of this world." Thus, the will-to-power was overcome. The globe of Satan sounds so very much like the globe of virtual reality.

If we cannot imagine spiritual reality, we are sentenced to life in unspiritual time: days running endlessly until we take our last breath. Communion and the sacraments wither in the eveningtide of persevering faith. As the inner spiritual light fades, we hold neither karmic concerns nor the necessity for righteousness of action. Thus do we become vulnerable to the possibility of possession. We forget the Father, and are left with inner dullness.

The Rosicrucian mantra *Ex Deo Nascimur* aligns us with the truth that we have been born from the Divine. We must not sleep before the necessities of developing moral consciousness. We are to live into the eternal vastness that holds the beings of Time themselves—the mighty Archai who reveal to us our place in the great evolutionary wave to which we belong. Thus does the past become the foundation stone for the revelation of Time's future.

As Christmas approaches, we gather with friends and family. In answer to the first temptation, Christ replied: *My kingdom is not of this world.* At this time of the fifth sacrifice of Christ a new kingdom is forming, born of the moral ether. May we find the holiness of His etheric embrace as we celebrate the miracle that is born into winter's darkest nights.

Dec. 24: Christmas Eve. Sundown marks the opening to the wonder of the twelve holy days and nights. This is the time when Christ and his chorus of Archangels gather together around the Earth, blessing all of goodwill with peace. The Archangels mediate between the mighty spheres of the Archai, and the Angels. Their wings hold the memory of creation; from this realm the Cosmic Christ emanates through the Archangel Jesus. At his Ascension, Christ rose into this realm. For the next twelve days and nights, this realm draws near to us:

> In the Archangels' wings are contained the records and histories of the peoples for whom they have stewardship. They bear this in their wings; and their wings are emanations of what is in their hearts. I beheld Christ bearing the entire history of all peoples in his own being, emanating out from his heart throughout his whole being, just as the Archangels were bearing the histories of their peoples.
>
> He was the ultimate archangelic being when he entered into their realm. He became one of them; and indeed in every realm that he entered during his Ascension he became the ultimate

ideal of whatever beings he encountered. When in the human realm, he was the ultimate human. When he rose into the angelic realm he became the ultimate Angel. Thus he showed the Angels the way of their own evolution, what they were to ultimately achieve. And he bore in his being the experience of being an Angel in its totality, to its greatest fulfillment; and all Angels witnessed this great being who would bend to meet them at their present level of being and then uplift them to the higher level. He did this by becoming one with them—just as he had become one with humanity by meeting humanity at its level. He descended below all things and then ascended to the angelic realm, and then to the archangelic realm, and on.

In his Ascension, he brought to the Archangels full account of his deeds on the Earth—what he had done for humankind. And symbolically he laid this great gift at the feet of the Archangels who were spiraling around him.[4]

We are called to contemplate the nearness of holy beings and the eternal oneness that weaves between all peoples of the Earth.

Sun 8° Sagittarius: The second temptation in the wilderness (Nov/28/29). Throughout the period of temptations, Christ was the representative of human freedom. In times of temptation we must make our decisions not from the spiritual world, but from within ourselves. After finding our pure, divine conviction, born of freedom and human discretion, the Angels will come and minister to us—the spiritual world will again open before us. We must all make decisions out of our sovereign freedom as we pass through this bleak period of global temptation; a time when true human freedom hangs in the balance.

The second temptation asked Jesus Christ to plunge from the pinnacle of the temple. Instead, he rejected the onslaught of the adversaries and spoke the words: "Thou shall not tempt the Lord thy God." When this temptation succeeds, the abyss into which we thus plunge is made up of the instinctive urges that are hidden from consciousness. This creates a desire for miracles without any conscious effort. We then surrender to something unknown

and unseen. Moreover, the temptation to plunge from the pinnacle of our highest consciousness is increasing, as is witnessed in addiction and other forms of substance abuse. When we fall into the instinctual forces of the unconscious, the Angels who will catch us are not the good ones.

Insanity approaches the mind when time loses its connection to the great rhythms of the cosmic year. The seasons, celebrations, and festival life all contribute to our feeling of belonging to something greater than ourselves. The Rosicrucian mantra: *In Christo Morimur* (In Christ we die) strengthens us to stay awake in each moment, to feel the presence of the Etheric Christ in the encircling round, and to await his touch in moments of silent devotion.

Dec. 25: Christmas Day. The Christian celebration of the birth of Jesus.

Sun 9° Sagittarius: The third temptation in the wilderness (Nov/29/29). The third temptation was not overcome, for Ahriman held something back that Christ could not encounter. Only later, when he sweated blood in the Garden of Gethsemane, would Ahriman approach again to thrust his last blows against the incarnated Son of God. The temptation to turn stones into bread is an ominous threat through money, through seed manipulation, and through a perpetual need to be continuously "hooked up" in technological realities. Religious life is dying, and in its place the quantitative has triumphed over the qualitative. Materialism causes humankind to see a world pathetically void of spiritual guidance, absent of direction. Behind this lurks a fear of karma and—ultimately—a fear of judgment. Without deference to karmic consequences, we are freed from feelings of responsibility; we can instead rest in self-justified contentment. Yet, this can cause us to fall into the hallucination that life can be mechanized, abstracted from its living reality. Lower beings can thus find their way into our consciousness, feigning importance and giving false direction. Finally, the bread of life and the stones of Ahriman become equal—and then the latter ominously begins to supercede the former.

The Rosicrucian mantra *Per Spiritum Sanctum Reviviscimus* (In the world thoughts of the spirit the soul awakens) is the antidote to this temptation.

---

4 Isaacson (unpublished manuscript).

When we receive the impulses streaming from the future, we serve what is in the *process of becoming*. Space becomes an open field of possibilities, weaving light, bestowing revelation. In the kingdom forming through Christ's etheric presence, a Grail nourishment can be found; and it will be found as we develop new capacities now in their infancy. This kingdom is part of the new miracle that accompanies Christ's fifth sacrifice: *the forming of the moral ether.*

As we gather to celebrate the sacred birth of Jesus, we can imagine that the foods we share are not only filled with the blessings of the Mother, but also bear the living word of God. When time reaches its end, we will come to know the eternal truth—that we live not by bread alone, but by every word that is issued from the mouth of God.

Dec. 26: Sun 10° Sagittarius: The end of the forty-day fast (Nov/30/29). Today we celebrate the end of the forty days of temptation, when Angels came to minister to Jesus. Christ emerged from the isolation of his human nature, wherein he encountered the collective temptations of all humanity, into the embrace of angelic beings. The Holy Nights mark a time when the Archangels surround the Earth, so close that it is as if their wings touch. They proclaim peace among all beings and all nations. As these mighty beings witnessed Christ's temptations, they may have shed tears—and in their tears dwelled the Angels of those who would soon become the twelve disciples. These Angels gathered around Jesus Christ as he emerged from the inner torment of demons.

The Holy Nights sanctify the mystery of Christ's nearness to us. Also do these holy days and nights call us to reach into angelic realms, so that in the tears of Archangels we too may find the Angel who ministers to us.

ASPECT: Jupiter 26° Virgo opposite Uranus 26° Pisces. The Sun at Jupiter's degree recalls Jesus teaching about Isaac's sacrifice (Genesis 22). Jesus and his disciples then proceeded to Abila, where there was a pillar erected in memory of Elijah. There he taught in an open place (Monday, Sep/18/30). When speaking of Isaac, who was placed on the altar of sacrifice by his father Abraham, a new age was prophesied; for instead of his son, Abraham sacrificed a ram. Thus was the coming Age of Aries proclaimed—an astrological Age in which yet another was placed on the altar of sacrifice—Christ. Christ had gathered around himself the fishers of men, announcing the coming Age of Pisces.

We now stand on the doorsteps to the Age of Aquarius. The vernal point has not been in this zodiacal constellation since the time of ancient Atlantis. In every passing of the torch from one stage of consciousness to another, the altar of sacrifice runs red with the blood of those proclaiming the new. Elijah–John now appeals to all whose hearts are open, calling us to gather with him at the gates of the threshold—from whence the new revelation is sounding, shining light on the path forward.

Jupiter opposite Uranus is a mighty call for communities to become "organs of cognition" for spiritual worlds and spiritual beings. May we heed the call, lest the altar of sacrifice again be used against our contemporary prophets, mystics, and harbingers of change.

Dec. 28: ASPECT: Sun inferior conjunction Mercury 28° Sagittarius: Behold the Lamb of God! (Thursday, Dec/1/29).

After suffering his forty days of continual temptation, Jesus Christ returns to the east bank of the River Jordan, where John sees him. Some of John's disciples ran after Jesus, and he bid them to follow him. Jesus spoke of his teaching mission and his intention to choose his disciples. Those who would be in the circle of twelve were gathering. As we come to the end of 2016 we can contemplate the circle of disciples gathering around the Maitreya Bodhisattva in service to the Etheric Christ. And we can ask ourselves if we are to join this group.

Dec. 29: Venus enters Aquarius, "What lacks bounds, finds bounds" (Steiner, *Twelve Cosmic Moods*). Venus in Aquarius calls us to penetrate into the depths of being; to realize the Time in which we live, and to remember the harmony we promised to create. Venus was in Aquarius at the birth of the Solomon Jesus, at the adoration of the magi, and at the death of John the Baptist.

New Moon 13° Sagittarius. The Sun remembers Jesus as he continued the Sermon on the Mount

(**Monday, Dec/4/30**). He spoke of the fourth Beatitude: *Blessed are those who hunger and thirst for righteousness, for they shall be filled.* The Moon was at this degree on the day that Jesus spoke of King David, who had fallen into sin on account of the superabundance of forces within him (Monday, Sep/1/32).

Moon and Sun stream forth the healing nourishment that fills us when our attention "grails" (opens longingly) for heavenly manna. This King David did, yet still he fell. Jesus spoke of how this fall was on account of the superabundance of forces within him—forces he should have consumed within himself, but instead wasted. David communed with the Elohim through manas cognition, yet he could not bring this cognition into relationship with Nature. Thus were his forces squandered until another five hundred years would pass, when through Pythagoras, manas cognition could be brought all the way from Above into Below, bringing the mysteries of the archetypal form of things right into numbers and figures. Ordinary cognition ascends from cognition of the phenomenal to the beings behind it. In constrast, David's cognition met the being of the Elohim (Spirits of Form—Exusiai in Greek) first, and he was unable to apply his revelation to Nature:

> Thus the kindgoms of nature must be studied first to find definite archetypal forms expressed in them. Once the archetypal forms are found, it becomes possible to ascend from there to cognizing the spirits of form, or Elohim. In manas cognition, however, the beings of the Elohim will be recognized first, and only later (sometimes after a long time) their revelations in natural processes. King David's cognition was of this kind. He consciously interacted with the Elohim being, but his knowledge of nature was meager. This type of knowledge could reach his soul forces only in the areas of human history and human morality; he lacked the forces needed by the rational and consciousess souls for a comprehensive knowledge of nature.[5]

David experienced the manas cognition in ways that revealed to him his own imperfection and his own guilt. Thus did he become the penitent one who developed the faculty called the "key of David"—the door that opens and no other may shut:

> The faculty of penitence, properly understood, is the very force that in the future (beginning in the twentieth century and continuing into the sixth cultural epoch) will open, for an ever increasing number of people, the gates that close out the spirit world. For this faculty is none other than "the key of David…that openeth, and no man shutteth," about which John speaks in the Apocalypse in relation to the Philadelphic cultural community (Revelation 3:7).[6]

I can think of no better note to end the commentaries for this year. The Maitreya gives his guidance, informing us that manas cognition will continue to quicken in many more souls. The immaculate stream of revelation that this year has remembered as Uranus returned to its position at the birth of the Nathan Jesus—son of David—has served to potentize humankind's awakening to Lazarus–John. The revelation John protects is the trumpeting force of apocalyptic new beginnings. It signals also the end of the old. The inspiration of the Abraham individuality, since, according to Rudolf Steiner, humanity together with the Earth entered the Age of Abraham in the year 2000, speaks through the books we have oft quoted in these commentaries and is ever present with us. He listens to the immaculate heart, while holding the "key of David," and he will be ever by our side as we enter into the year 2017.

---

5 Tomberg, *Christ and Sophia,* p. 111.

6 Ibid., p. 113.

GLOSSARY

This glossary of entries relating to Esoteric Christianity lists only some of the specialized terms used in the articles and commentaries of the *Journal for Star Wisdom*. For reasons of space, the entries are very brief, and the reader is encouraged to read the works of Rudolf Steiner for a more complete understanding of these terms.

Ahriman: An adversarial being identified by the great prophet Zarathustra during the ancient Persian cultural epoch (5067–2907 BC) as an opponent to the Sun God, *Ahura Mazda,* or *Ahura Mazda* (obs.; "Aura of the Sun"). Also called Satan, Ahriman represents one aspect of the Dragon. Ahriman's influence leads to materialistic thinking devoid of feeling, empathy, and moral conscience. Ahriman helps inspire science and technology, and works through forces of sub-nature such as gravity, electricity, magnetism, radioactivity—forces that are antithetical to life. The influence of Ahriman's activity upon the human being limits human cognition to what is derived from sense perception, hardens thinking (materialistic thoughts), attacks the etheric body by way of modern technology (electromagnetic radiation, etc.), and hardens hearts (cold and calculating).

ahrimanic beings: Spiritual beings who have become agents of Ahriman's influences.

Angel Jesus: A pure immaculate Angelic being who sacrifices himself so that the Christ may work through him. This Angelic being is actually of the status of an Archangel, who has descended to work on the Angelic level in order to be closer to human beings and to assist them on the path of confrontation with evil.

Ascension: An unfathomable process at the start of which, on May 14, AD 33, Christ united with the etheric realm that surrounds and permeates the earth with Cosmic Life. Thus began his cosmic ascent to the realm of the heavenly Father, with the goal of elevating the Earth spiritually and opening pathways between the Earth and the spiritual world for the future.

astral body: Part of the human being that is the bearer of consciousness, passion, and desires, as well as idealism and the longing for perfection.

Asuras: Fallen Archai (Time Spirits) from the time of Old Saturn, whose opposition to human evolution comes to expression through promoting debauched sexuality and senseless violence among human beings. So low is the regard that the Asuras have for the sacredness of human life, that as well as promoting extreme violence and debauchery (for example, through the film industry), they do not hold back from the destruction of the physical body of human beings. In particular, the activity of the Asuras retards the development of the consciousness soul.

bodhisattva: On the human level a bodhisattva is a human being far advanced on the spiritual path, a human being belonging to the circle of twelve great teachers surrounding the Cosmic Christ. One who incarnates periodically to further the evolution of the Earth and humanity, working on the level of an angelic, archangelic, or higher being in relation to the rest of humanity. Every 5,000 years, one of these great teachers from the circle of bodhisattvas takes on a special mission, incarnating repeatedly to awaken a new human faculty and capacity. Once that capacity has been imparted through its human bearer, this bodhisattva then incarnates upon the earth for the last time, ascending to the level of a Buddha in order to serve humankind from spirit realms. See also Maitreya Bodhisattva.

Central Sun: Heart of the Milky Way, also called the Galactic Center. Our Sun orbits this Central Sun over a period of approximately 225 million years.

chakra: One of seven astral organs of perception through which human beings develop higher levels of cognition such as clairvoyance, telepathy, and so on.

Christ: The eternal being who is the second member of the Trinity. Also called the "Divine 'I AM,'" the Son of God, the Cosmic Christ, and the Logos/Word. Christ began to fully unite with the human vessel (Jesus) at the Baptism in the Jordan, and for 3½ years penetrated as the *Divine I AM* successively into the astral body, etheric body, and physical body of Jesus, spiritualizing each member. Through the Mystery of Golgotha Christ united with the Earth, kindling the spark of Christ consciousness (*Not I, but Christ in me*) in all human beings.

consciousness soul: The portion of the human soul in which "I" consciousness is awakening not only to its own sense of individuality and to the individualities of others, but also to its higher self—spirit self (Sanskrit: *manas*). Within the consciousness soul, the "I" perceives truth, beauty, and goodness; within the spirit self, the "I" becomes truth, beauty, and goodness.

crossing the threshold: a term applicable to our time, as human beings are increasingly encountering the spiritual world—in so doing, crossing the threshold between the sense-perceptible realm and non-physical realms of existence. To the extent that spiritual capacities have not been cultivated, this encounter with non-physical realms beyond the sense world signifies a descent into the subconscious (for example, through drugs) rather than an ascent to knowledge of higher worlds through the awakening of higher levels of consciousness.

Decan: The zodiac of 360° is divided into twelve signs, each of 30°. A decan is 10°, thus one third of one sign or $1/36$ of the zodiac.

Devil: Another name for Lucifer.

Dragon: As used in the Apocalypse of John, there are different appearances of the dragon, each one representing an adversarial being opposed to Michael, Christ, and Sophia. For example, the great red dragon of chapter 12 opposes Sophia, the woman clothed with the Sun (Sophia is the pure Divine-Cosmic Feminine Soul of the World). The imagery from chapter 12 of Revelations depicts the woman clothed with the Sun as pregnant and that the great red dragon attempts to devour her child as soon as it is born. The child coming to birth from the woman clothed with the Sun represents the Divine-Cosmic "I AM" born through the assistance of the pure Divine Feminine Soul of the World. The dragon is cast down from the heavenly realm by the mighty Archangel Michael. Cast down to the Earth, the dragon continues with attempts to devour the cosmic child (the Divine-Cosmic "I AM") coming to birth among humankind.

ego: The soul sheath through which the "I" begins to incarnate and to experience life on Earth (to be distinguished from the term *ego* used in Freudian and Jungian psychology—hence written capitalized "Ego" to make this distinction). The terms *ego, "I,"* and *soul* are often used interchangeably in Spiritual Science. The ego maintains threads of integrity and continuity through memory, while experiencing new sensations and perceptions through observation and thinking, feeling, and willing. The ego is capable of moral discernment and also experiences temptation. Thus, it is often stated that the "I" comprises both a higher nature ("Ego") and a lower nature ("ego").

Emmerich, Anne Catherine (also "Sister Emmerich"): A Catholic stigmatist (1774–1824) whose visions depicted the daily life of Jesus, beginning some weeks before the event of the descent of Christ into the body of Jesus at the Baptism in the River Jordan and extending for a period of several weeks after the Crucifixion.

Ephesus: The area in Asia Minor (now Turkey) to which the Apostle John (also called John Zebedee, the brother of James the Greater) accompanied the Virgin Mary approximately three years after the death of Jesus Christ. Ephesus was a very significant ancient mystery center where cosmic mysteries of the East found their way into the West. Initiates at Ephesus were devoted to the goddess Artemis, known as "Artemis of Ephesus," whose qualities are more those of a Mother goddess than is the case with the Greek goddess Artemis, although there is a certain degree of overlap between Artemis and Artemis of Ephesus with regard to many of their respective characteristics. A magnificent Ionic mystery temple was built in honor of Artemis of Ephesus at a location close to the Aegean Sea. Mary's house, built by John, was located high up above, on the nearby hill known as Mount

Nightingale, about six miles from the temple of Artemis at Ephesus.

etheric body: The body of life forces permeating and animating the physical body. The etheric body was formed during Ancient Sun evolution. The etheric body's activity is expressed in the seven life processes permeating the seven vital organs. The etheric body is related to the movements of the seven visible planets.

Fall, The: A fall from oneness with spiritual worlds. The Fall, which took place during the Lemurian period of Earth evolution, was a time of dramatic transition in human evolution when the soul descended from "Paradise" into earthly existence. Through the Fall the human soul began to incarnate into a physical body upon the earth and experience the world from "within" the body, perceiving through the senses.

Fifth Gospel: The writings and lectures of Rudolf Steiner based on new spiritual perceptions and insights into the mysteries of Christ's life on earth, including the Second Coming of Christ—his appearance in the etheric realm in our time, beginning in the twentieth century.

Golgotha, Mystery of: Rudolf Steiner's designation for the entire mystery of the coming of Christ to the Earth. Sometimes this term is used more specifically to refer to the events surrounding the Crucifixion and Resurrection. In particular, the Crucifixion—the sacrifice on the cross—marked the birth of Christ's union with the Earth. Also referred to as the "Turning Point of Time," whereby at the Crucifixion Christ descended from the sphere of the Sun and became the "Spirit of the Earth."

Grail: An etheric chalice into which Christ can work to transform earthly substance into spiritual substance. The term *Grail* has many deep levels of meaning and refers on the one hand to a spiritual stream in service of Christ, and on the other hand to the means by which the human "I" penetrates and transforms evil into good. The power of transubstantiation expresses something of this process of transformation of evil into good.

Grail Knights: Those trained to confront evil and transform it into something good, in service of Christ. Members of a spiritual stream that existed in the past and continues to exist—albeit in metamorphosed form—in the present.

Every human being striving for the good can potentially become a Grail Knight.

I AM: One's true individuality, that—with few exceptions—never fully incarnates but works into the developing "I" and its lower bodies (astral, etheric, and physical). The **Cosmic I AM** is the "I AM" of Christ, through which—on account of the Mystery of Golgotha—we are all graced with the possibility of receiving a divine spark therefrom.

Jesus (see Nathan Jesus and Solomon Jesus): The pure human being who received the Christ at the Baptism in the River Jordan.

Jesus Christ: The Divine-Human being; the God-Man; the union of the Divine with the Human. The presence of the Cosmic Christ in the physical body of the human being called the Nathan Jesus during the 3½ years of the ministry.

Jesus of Nazareth: The name of the human being whose birth is celebrated in the Gospel of Luke, also referred to as the Nathan Jesus. When Jesus of Nazareth reached the age of twelve, the spirit of the Solomon Jesus (Gospel of Matthew) united with the body and sheaths of the pure Nathan Jesus. This union lasted for about 18 years, until the Baptism in the River Jordan. During these eighteen years, Jesus of Nazareth was a composite being comprising the Nathan Jesus and the spirit ("I") of the Solomon Jesus. Just before the Baptism, the spirit of the Solomon Jesus withdrew, and at the Baptism Jesus became known as "Jesus Christ" through the union of Christ with the sheaths of Jesus.

Jezebel: Wife of King Ahab, approximately 900 BC, who worked through the powers of black magic against the prophet Elijah.

Kali Yuga: Yugas are ages of influence referred to in Hindu cosmography, each yuga lasting a certain numbers of years in length (always a multiple of 2,500). The Kali Yuga is also known as the Dark Age, which began with the death of Krishna in 3102 BC (-3101). Kali Yuga lasted 5,000 years and ended in AD 1899.

Kingly Stream: Biblically, the line of heredity from King David into which the Solomon Jesus (Gospel of Matthew) was born. The kings (the three magi) were initiates who sought to bring the cosmic will of the heavenly Father to expression on the Earth through spiritual forces working from spiritual beings dwelling in the stars. The minds of the wise kings were enlightened by the coming of Jesus Christ.

Krishna: A cosmic-human being, the sister soul of Adam that overlighted Arjuna as described in the Bhagavad Gita. The overlighting by Krishna of Arjuna could be described as an incorporation of Krishna into Arjuna. An incorporation is a partial incarnation. The cosmic-human being known as Krishna later fully incarnated as Jesus of Nazareth (Nathan Jesus—Gospel of Luke).

Lazarus: The elder brother of Mary Magdalene, Martha, and Silent Mary. At his raising from the dead, Lazarus became the first human being to be fully initiated by Christ (see Lazarus–John).

Lazarus–John: At the raising of Lazarus from the dead by Christ, the spiritual being of John the Baptist united with Lazarus. The higher spiritual members of John (Spirit Body, Life Spirit, Spirit Self) entered into the members of Lazarus, which were developed to the level of the consciousness soul.

Lucifer: The name of a fallen spiritual being, also called the Light-Bearer, who acts as a retarding force within the human astral body and also in the sentient soul. Lucifer inflames egoism and pride within the human being, often inspiring genius and supreme artistry. Arrogance and self-importance are stimulated, without humility or sacrificial love. Lucifer stirs up forces of rebellion, but cannot deliver true freedom—just its illusion.

luciferic beings: Spiritual beings who have become agents of Lucifer's influences.

magi: Initiates in the mystery school of Zarathustra, the Bodhisattva who incarnated as Zoroaster (Zaratas, Nazaratos) in the sixth century BC and who, after he came to Babylon, became a teacher of the Chaldean priesthood. At the time of Jesus, the magi were still continuing the stargazing tradition of the school of Zoroaster. The task of the magi was to recognize when their master would reincarnate. With their visit to the newborn Jesus child in Bethlehem (Gospel of Matthew), to this child who was the reincarnated Zarathustra/Zoroaster, they fulfilled their mission. The three magi are the "priest kings from the East" referred to in the Gospel of Matthew.

Maitreya Bodhisattva: The bodhisattva individuality that is preparing to become the successor of Gautama Buddha and will be known as the Bringer of the Good. This bodhisattva was incarnated in the second century BC as Jeshu ben Pandira, the teacher of the Essenes, who died about 100 BC. Rudolf Steiner indicated that Jeshu ben Pandira reincarnated at the beginning of the twentieth century as a great bodhisattva individuality in order to fulfill the lofty mission of proclaiming Christ's coming in the etheric realm, beginning around 1933: "He will be the actual herald of Christ in his etheric form" (lecture about Jeshu ben Pandira held in Leipzig on November 4, 1911). There are differing points of view as to who this individuality actually was in his twentieth century incarnation.

manas: Also called the Spirit Self; the purified astral body, lifted into full communion with truth and goodness by becoming the true and the good within the essence of the higher self of the human being. Manas is the spiritual source of the "I," and as it is the eternal part of the human being that goes from life to life, Manas bears the human being's true "eternal name" through its union with the Holy Spirit. The "eternal name" expresses the human being's true mission from life to life.

Mani: The name of a lofty initiate who lived in Babylon in the third century AD. The founder of the Manichean stream, whose mission is the transformation of evil into goodness through compassion and love. Mani reincarnated as Parzival in the ninth century AD. Mani/Parzival is one of the leading initiates of our present age—the age of the consciousness soul (AD 1414–3574). One of the highest beings ever to incarnate upon the earth, he will become the future Manu beginning in the astrological age of Sagittarius. This future Manu will oversee the spiritual evolution of a sequence of seven ages, comprising the seven cultural epochs of the Sixth Great Age of Earth evolution from the Age of Sagittarius to the Age of Gemini—lasting a total of 7 x 2,160 years (15,120 years), since each zodiacal age lasts 2,160 years.

Manu: Like the word Buddha, the word Manu is a title. A Manu has the task of spiritually overseeing one Great Age of Earth evolution, comprising seven astrological ages (seven cultural epochs)—lasting a total of 7 x 2,160 years (15,120 years), since each zodiacal age lasts 2,160 years. The present Age of Pisces (AD 215–2375)—with its corresponding cultural epoch (AD 1414–3574)—is the fifth epoch during the Fifth Great Age of Earth evolution. (Lemuria was the Third Great Age, Atlantis the Fourth Great Age, and since the great flood that destroyed Atlantis, we are now in the Fifth Great Age.) The present Manu is the exalted Sun-initiate who guided humanity out of Atlantis during the ancient flooding that destroyed the continent of Atlantis formerly in the region of the Atlantic Ocean—the Flood referred to in the Bible in connection with Noah. He is the overseer of the seven cultural epochs corresponding to the seven astrological ages from the Age of Cancer to the Age of Capricorn, following the sequence: Cancer, Gemini, Taurus, Aries, Pisces, Aquarius, Capricorn. The present Manu was the teacher of the Seven Holy Rishis who were the founders of the ancient Indian cultural epoch (7227–5067 BC) during the Age of Cancer. He is known in the Bible as Noah, and in the Flood story belonging to the Gilgamesh epic he is called Utnapishtim. Subsequently this Manu appeared to Abraham as Melchizedek and offered Abraham an agape ("love feast") of bread and wine. Jesus "was designated by God to be high priest in the order of Melchizedek" (Heb. 5:10).

Mary: Rudolf Steiner distinguishes between the Nathan Mary and the Solomon Mary (see corresponding entries). The expression "Virgin Mary" refers to the Solomon Mary, the mother of the child Jesus whose birth is described in the Gospel of Matthew.

Mary Magdalene: Sister of Lazarus, whose soul was transformed and purified as Christ cast out seven demons who had taken possession of her. Christ thus initiated Mary Magdalene. Later, she anointed Jesus Christ. And she was the first to behold the Risen Christ in the Garden of the Holy Sepulcher on the morning of his resurrection.

megastar: Stars with a luminosity greater than 10,000 times that of our Sun.

Nain, Youth of: Referred to in the Gospel of Luke as the son of the widow of Nain. The Youth of Nain—at the time he was twelve years old—was raised from the dead by Jesus. The Youth of Nain later reincarnated as the Prophet Mani (third century AD) and subsequently as the Grail King Parzival (ninth century AD).

Nathan Jesus: From the priestly line of David, as described in the Gospel of Luke. An immaculate and pure soul whose one and only physical incarnation was as Jesus of Nazareth (Nathan Jesus).

Nathan Mary: A pure being who was the mother of the Nathan Jesus. The Nathan Mary died in AD 12, but her spirit united with the Solomon Mary at the time of the Baptism of Jesus in the River Jordan. From this time on, the Solomon Mary—spiritually united with the Nathan Mary—was known as the Virgin Mary.

New Jerusalem: A spiritual condition denoting humanity's future existence that will come into being as human beings free themselves from the *maya* of the material world and work together to bring about a spiritualized Earth.

Osiris: Osiris and Isis are names given by the Egyptians to the preincarnatory forms of the spiritual beings who are now known as Christ and Sophia.

Parzival: Son of Gahmuret and Herzeloyde in the epic *Parzival* by Wolfram von Eschenbach. Although written in the thirteenth century, this work refers to actual people and events in the ninth century AD, one of whom (the central figure) bore the name Parzival. After living a life of dullness and doubt, Parzival's mission was to seek the Castle of the Grail and to ask the question "What ails thee?" of the Grail King, Anfortas—moreover, to ask the question without being bidden to do so. Parzival eventually became the new Grail King, the successor of Anfortas. Parzival was the reincarnated prophet Mani. In the incarnation preceding that of Mani, he was incarnated as the Youth of Nain (Luke 7:11–15). Parzival is a great initiate responsible for guiding humanity during the Age of Pisces, which has given birth to the cultural epoch of the development of the consciousness soul (AD 1414–3574).

Pentecost: Descent of the Holy Spirit fifty days after Easter, whereby the cosmic "I AM" was birthed among the disciples and those individuals close to Christ. They received the capacity to develop Manas or Spirit Self within the community of striving human individuals, whereby the birth of the Spirit Self is facilitated through the soul of the Virgin Mary. See also World Pentecost.

phantom body: The pure spiritual form of the human physical body, unhindered by matter. The far-distant future state of the human physical body when it has become purified and spiritualized into a body of transformed divine will.

Presbyter John: Refers to Lazarus-John who moved to Ephesus about twenty years after the Virgin Mary had died there. In Ephesus he became a bishop. He is the author of the Book of Revelations, the Gospel of St. John, and the Letters of John.

Risen One: The initial appearance of Christ in his phantom body (resurrection body), beginning with his appearance to Mary Magdalene on Easter Sunday morning. Christ frequently appeared to the disciples in his phantom body during the forty days leading from Easter to Ascension.

Satan: The traditional Christian name for Ahriman.

Serpent: Another name for Lucifer, but sometimes naming a combination of Lucifer and Ahriman: "The great dragon was hurled down—that ancient serpent called the devil, or Satan, who leads the whole world astray" (Rev. 12:9).

Shepherd Stream: Biblically, the genealogical line from David the shepherd through his son Nathan. It was into this line that the Nathan Jesus was born, whose birth is described in the Gospel of Luke. Rudolf Steiner describes the shepherds, who—according to Luke—came to pay homage to the newborn child, as those servants of pure heart who perceive the goodwill streaming up from Mother Earth. The hearts of the shepherd were kindled with the fire of Divine Love by the coming of the Christ. The shepherds can be regarded as precursors of the heart stream of humanity that now intuits the being of Christ as the spirit of the Earth.

Solomon Jesus: Descended from the genealogical line from David through his son Solomon. This line of descent is described in the Gospel of Matthew. The Solomon Jesus was a reincarnation of Zoroaster (sixth century BC). In turn, Zoroaster was a reincarnation of Zarathustra (6000 BC), the great prophet and founder of the ancient Persian religion of Zoroastrianism. He was a bodhisattva, who as the founder of this new religion that was focused upon the Sun Spirit Ahura Mazda, helped prepare humanity for the subsequent descent into incarnation of Ahura Mazda, the cosmic Sun Spirit, as Christ.

Solomon Mary: The wise mother of the Solomon Jesus, who adopted the Nathan Jesus after the death of the Nathan Mary. At the time of the Baptism of Jesus in the River Jordan, the spirit of the Nathan Mary united with the Solomon Mary. Usually referred to as the Virgin Mary or Mother Mary, the Solomon Mary bore witness at the foot of the cross to the Mystery of Golgotha. She died in Ephesus eleven years after Christ's Ascension.

Sophia: Part of the Divine Feminine Trinity comprising the Mother (counterpart of the Father), the Daughter (counterpart of the Son), and the Holy Soul (counterpart of the Holy Spirit). Sophia, also known as the Bride of the Lamb, is the Daughter aspect of the threefold Divine Feminine Trinity. To the Egyptians Sophia was known as Isis, who was seen to belong to the starry realm surrounding the earth. In the Book of Proverbs, attributed to King Solomon, Sophia's temple has seven pillars (Proverbs 9:1). The seven pillars in Sophia's temple represent the seven great stages of Earth evolution (from Ancient Saturn to Future Vulcan).

Sorath: The great enemy of Christ who works against the "I" in the human being. Sorath is identified with the two-horned beast that rises up from the depths of earth, as described in the Apocalypse of St. John. Sorath is the Sun Demon, and is identified by Rudolf Steiner as the Antichrist. According to the Book of Revelations his number is 666.

Sun Demon: Another name for Sorath.

Transfiguration: The event on Mt. Tabor where Jesus Christ was illumined with Divine Light raying forth from the purified etheric body of Jesus, which the Divine "I AM" of Christ had penetrated. The Gospels of Matthew and Luke describe the Transfiguration. The sunlike radiance that shone forth from Jesus Christ on Mt. Tabor was an expression of the purified etheric body that had its origin during the Old Sun period of Earth evolution.

Transubstantiation: Sacramental transformation of physical substance—for example, the transubstantiation of bread and wine during the Mass to become the body and blood of Christ. During the Holy Eucharist the bread and wine are transformed in such a way that the substances of bread and wine are infused with the life force (body) and light (blood) of Christ. Thereby the bread and wine are reunited with their divine archetypes and are no longer "merely" physical substances, but are bearers on the physical level of a spiritual reality.

Turning Point of Time: Transition between involution and evolution, as marked by the Mystery of Golgotha. The descending stream of involution culminated with the Mystery of Golgotha. With the descent of the Cosmic Christ into earthly evolution, through his sacrifice on Golgotha an ascending stream of evolution began. This sacrifice of Christ was followed by the events of his Resurrection and Ascension, which were followed in turn by Whitsun (Pentecost)—all expressing the ascending stream of evolution. This path of ascent was also opened up to all human beings by way of the power of the divine "I AM" bestowed—at least, potentially—on all humanity by Christ through his sacrifice on the cross.

Union in the Temple: The event of the union of the spirit of the Solomon Jesus with the twelve-year-old Nathan Jesus. This union of the two Jesus children signified the uniting of the priestly (Nathan) line and the kingly (Solomon) line—both lines descended from King David.

Whitsun: "White Sunday"; Pentecost.

World Pentecost is the gradual event of cosmic revelation becoming human revelation as a signature of the end of the Dark Age (Kali Yuga). Anthroposophy (Spiritual Science) is a language of spiritual truth that could awaken a community of striving human beings to the presence of the Holy Spirit and the founding of the New Jerusalem.

Zarathustra: The great teacher of the ancient Persians in the sixth millennium BC (around 6000 BC). In the sixth century BC, Zarathustra reincarnated as Zoroaster. He then reincarnated as the Solomon Jesus (6 BC–AD 12), whose birth is described in the Gospel of Matthew.

Zoroaster: An incarnation of Zarathustra. Zarathustra–Zoroaster was a Bodhisattva. Zoroaster lived in the sixth century BC. He was a master of wisdom. Among his communications as a teacher of wisdom was his specification as to how the zodiac of living beings in the heavens comes to expression in relation to the stars comprising the twelve zodiacal constellations. Zoroaster subsequently incarnated as the Solomon Jesus, whose birth is described in the Gospel of Matthew, to whom the three magi came from the East bearing gifts of gold, frankincense, and myrrh.

"The stars are the expression of love in the cosmic ether.... To see a star means to feel a caress that has been prompted by love.... To gaze at the stars is to become aware of the love proceeding from divine spiritual beings.... The stars are signs and tokens of the presence of gods in the universe." (*Karmic Relationships,* vol. 7, June 8, 1924)

"We must see in the shining stars the outer signs of colonies of spirits in the cosmos. Wherever a star is seen in the heavens, there—in that direction—is a colony of spirits." (*Karmic Relationships,* vol. 6, June 1, 1924)

"They looked up above all to what is represented by the zodiac. And they regarded what the human being bears within as the spirit in connection with the constellations, the glory of the fixed stars, the spiritual powers whom they knew to be there in the stars." (*Karmic Relationships,* vol. 4, Sept. 12, 1924)

BIBLIOGRAPHY AND REFERENCES

See "Literature" on page 10 for an annotated list of books on Astrosophy.

Andreev, Daniel. *Rosa Mira: Die Weltrose.* Frankeneck, Germany: Vega, 2009.

———. *The Rose of the World.* Gr. Barrington, MA: Lindisfarne Books, 1997.

Anonymous. *Meditations on the Tarot.* New York: Tarcher/Putman, 2002.

Bento, William, Robert Schiappacase, and David Tresemer. *Signs in the Heavens: A Message for Our Time.* www.StarWisdom.org, 2001.

Bock, Emil. *The Childhood of Jesus.* Edinburgh: Floris Books, 2008.

———. *The Life and Times of Rudolf Steiner* (vol. 1): *People and Places.* Edinburgh: Floris Books, 2008.

Childs, Gilbert. *Secrets of Esoteric Christianity.* London: Temple Lodge, 2005.

Gruber, Howard, and Katja Bödeker (eds)., *Creativity, Psychology and the History of Science.* New York: Springer, 2005.

Dorsan, Jacques. *The Clockwise House System: A True Foundation for Sidereal and Tropical Astrology.* Gr. Barrington, MA: Lindisfarne Books, 2011.

Douglass, William. *JFK and the Unthinkable: Why He Died and Why It Matters.* New York: Simon & Schuster, 2012.

Emmerich, Anne Catherine. *Visions of the Life of Christ* (3 vols.). Taos, NM: LogoSophia, 2014.

Gsanger, Hans. "Zaratas," *Mercury Star Journal,* Michaelmas 1979. London: Temple Lodge, 1979.

Hadamard, Jacques. *An Essay on the Psychology of Invention in the Mathematical Field.* New York: Dover, 1945.

Harrison, C. G. *The Transcendental Universe: Six Lectures on Occult Science, Theosophy, and the Catholic Faith.* Hudson, NY: Lindisfarne Press, 1993.

Hillman, James. *The Soul's Code: In Search of Character and Calling.* New York, Warner, 1996.

Isaacson, Estelle. *Through the Eyes of Mary Magdalene,* 3 vols. Taos, NM: LogoSophia, 2012–2015.

Keyserlingk, Adalbert Graf von, ed. *The Birth of a New Agriculture: Koberwitz 1924.* London: Temple Lodge, 1999.

Madsen, Jon (ed.). *The New Testament: A Rendering.* Edinburgh: Floris Books, 1994.

Malthus, Thomas Robert, and Geoffrey Gilbert. *An Essay on the Principle of Population.* London: Oxford University, 2008.

Meyer, Michael. *Ibsen.* Harmondsworth: Penguin, 1967.

Michelsen, Neil F. *American Sidereal Ephemeris 1976–2000* (2nd ed.). San Diego, CA: ACS Publications, 1996.

Nesfield-Cookson, Bernard. *The Mystery of the Two Jesus Children: And the Descent of the Spirit of the Sun.* London: Temple Lodge, 2005.

Neugebauer, Otto, and H. B. van Hoesen. *Greek Horoscopes.* Philadelphia: American Philosophical Society, 1959.

Nisbet, John F. *The Insanity of Genius and the General Inequality of Human Faculty Physiologically Considered.* New York: Scribners, 1891.

O'Leary, P. V. (ed.) *The Inner Life of the Earth: Exploring the Mysteries of Nature, Subnature, and Supranature.* Gr. Barrington, MA: SteinerBooks, 2008.

Ovason, David. *The Two Children: A Study of the Two Jesus Children in Literature and Art.* Gr. Barrington, MA: Lindisfarne Books, 2010.

Powell, Robert. *The Christ Mystery.* Fair Oaks, CA: Rudolf Steiner College, 1999.

———. *Christian Hermetic Astrology: The Star of the Magi and the Life of Christ.* Gr. Barrington, MA: Lindisfarne Books, 2009.

———. *Chronicle of the Living Christ: The Life and Ministry of Jesus Christ: Foundations of Cosmic Christianity.* Hudson, NY: Anthroposophic Press, 1996.

———. *Cultivating Inner Radiance and the Body of Immortality: Awakening the Soul through Modern Etheric Movement.* Gr. Barrington, MA: Lindisfarne Books, 2012.

———. *Elijah Come Again: A Prophet for Our Time: A Scientific Approach to Reincarnation.* Gr. Barrington, MA: Lindisfarne Books, 2009.

———. *Hermetic Astrology,* vols. 1 and 2. San Rafael, CA: Sophia Foundation Press, 2006.

———. *History of the Zodiac.* San Rafael, CA: Sophia Academic Press, 2007.

———. *The Most Holy Trinosophia: The New Revelation of the Divine Feminine.* Gr. Barrington, MA: SteinerBooks, 2000.

———. *The Mystery, Biography, and Destiny of Mary Magdalene: Sister of Lazarus John & Spiritual Sister of Jesus.* Gr. Barrington, MA: Lindisfarne Books, 2008.

———. *Prophecy-Phenomena-Hope: The Real Meaning of the year 2012*. Gr. Barrington, MA: SteinerBooks, 2011.

———. *The Sophia Teachings: The Emergence of the Divine Feminine in Our Time*. Gr. Barrington, MA: Lindisfarne Books, 2007.

Powell, Robert, and David Bowden. *Astrogeographia: Correspondences between the Stars and Earthly Locations: Earth Chakras and the Bible of Astrology*. Gr. Barrington, MA: SteinerBooks, 2012.

Powell, Robert, and Kevin Dann. *The Astrological Revolution: Unveiling the Science of the Stars as a Science of Reincarnation and Karma*. Gr. Barrington, MA: SteinerBooks, 2010.

———. *Christ and the Maya Calendar: 2012 & the Coming of the Antichrist*. Gr. Barrington, MA: SteinerBooks, 2009.

Powell, Robert, and Estelle Isaacson. *Gautama Buddha's Successor: A Force for Good in our Time*. Gr. Barrington, MA: SteinerBooks, 2013.

———. *The Mystery of Sophia: Bearer of the New Culture: The Rose of the World*. Gr. Barrington, MA: SteinerBooks, 2014.

Powell, Robert, and Lacquanna Paul. *Cosmic Dances of the Planets*. San Rafael, CA: Sophia Foundation Press, 2006.

Powell, Robert, and Peter Treadgold. *The Sidereal Zodiac*. Tempe, AZ: AFA, 1985.

Proclus, "Commentary on Timaeus," in: *The Chaldean Oracles*. Fintry, UK: Shrine of Wisdom, 1979.

Rochberg, Francesca, *Babylonian Horoscopes*. Philadelphia: American Philosophical Society, 1998.

Schipflinger, Thomas. *Sophia–Maria: A Holistic Vision of Creation*. York Beach, ME: Samuel Weiser, 1998.

Schultz, Joachim. *Rhythmen der Sterne*. Dornach: Verlag am Goetheanum, 1977.

Selg, Peter. *Rudolf Steiner and Christian Rosenkreutz*. Gr. Barrington, MA: SteinerBooks, 2012.

———. *Rudolf Steiner: Life and Work: 1861–1890, Childhood, Youth, and Study Years*. Gr. Barrington, MA: SteinerBooks, 2014.

Sheldrake, Rupert, and Matthew Fox. *The Physics of Angels: Exploring the Realm Where Science and Spirit Meet*. Rhinebeck, NY: Monkfish, 2014.

Smith, Edward Raugh. *The Burning Bush: Rudolf Steiner, Anthroposophy, and the Holy Scriptures: Terms & Phrases*. Hudson, NY: Anthroposophic Press, 1998.

———. *The Incredible Births of Jesus*. Hudson, NY: Anthroposophic Press, 1998.

Solovyov, Valdimir. *War, Progress, and the End of History: Three Conversations, Including a Short Tale of the Antichrist*. Hudson, NY: Lindisfarne Press, 1990.

Steiner, Rudolf. *According to Luke: The Gospel of Compassion and Love Revealed*. Gr. Barrington, MA: SteinerBooks, 2006.

———. *According to Matthew: The Gospel of Christ's Humanity*. Gr. Barrington, MA: Anthroposophic Press, 2003.

———. *The Apocalypse of St. John: Lectures on the Book of Revelation*. Hudson, NY: Anthroposophic Press, 1993.

———. *Astronomy and Astrology: Finding a Relationship to the Cosmos*. London: Rudolf Steiner Press, 2009.

———. *Background to the Gospel of St. Mark*. London: Rudolf Steiner Press, 1968.

———. *The Bhagavad Gita and the West: The Esoteric Significance of the Bhagavad Gita and Its Relation to the Epistles of Paul*. Gr. Barrington, MA: SteinerBooks, 2006.

———. *The Book of Revelation: And the Work of the Priest*. London: Rudolf Steiner Press, 2008.

———. *Building Stones for an Understanding of the Mystery of Golgotha: Human Life in a Cosmic Context*. London: Rudolf Steiner Press, 2015.

———. *Christ in the Spiritual World and the Search for the Holy Grail*. London: Rudolf Steiner Press, 2008.

———. *Christianity as Mystical Fact: And the Mysteries of Antiquity*. Gr. Barrington, MA: SteinerBooks, 2006.

———. *The Concepts of Original Sin and Grace*. London: Rudolf Steiner Press, 1973.

———. *Correspondence and Documents, 1901–1925*. Hudson, NY: Anthroposophic Press: 1988.

———. *The Cycle of the Year: As Breathing Process of the Earth*. Gr. Barrington, MA: SteinerBooks, 1984.

———. *Death as Metamorphosis of Life: Including "What Does the Angel Do in our Astral Body?" & "How Do I Find Christ?"* Gr. Barrington, MA: SteinerBooks, 2008.

———. "The Deed of Christ and the Opposing Spiritual Powers: Lucifer, Ahriman, Asuras" (single lecture). London: Rudolf Steiner Press, 1976.

———. *Deeper Secrets of Human History in the Light of the Gospel of St. Matthew*. Hudson, NY: Anthroposophic Press, 1985.

———. *Esoteric Christianity and the Mission of Christian Rosenkreutz*. London: Rudolf Steiner Press, 2005.

———. *The Fall of the Spirits of Darkness*. London: Rudolf Steiner Press, 1993.

———. *The Festivals and Their Meaning*. London: Rudolf Steiner Press, 1996.

———. "The Four Sacrifices of Christ." in *Approaching the Mystery of Golgotha*. Gr. Barrington, MA: SteinerBooks, 2006.

——. *From Buddha to Christ.* Great Spring Valley, NY: Anthroposophic Press, 1978.

——. *From the History and Contents of the First Section of the Esoteric School, Letters, Documents, and Lectures, 1904–1914.* Gr. Barrington, MA: SteinerBooks, 2010.

——. *From Jesus to Christ.* London: Rudolf Steiner Press, 2005.

——. *The Gospel of St. John.* New York: Anthroposophic Press, 1962.

——. *Guidance in Esoteric Training.* London: Rudolf Steiner Press, 1999.

——. *How to Know Higher Worlds: A Modern Path of Initiation.* Hudson, NY: Anthroposophic Press, 1995.

——. *Inner Development.* Gr. Barrington, MA: SteinerBooks, 1992.

——. *Intuitive Thinking as a Spiritual Path: A Philosophy of Freedom.* Hudson, NY: Anthroposophic Press, 1995.

——. *Isis–Mary–Sophia: Her Mission and Ours.* Gr. Barrington, MA: Steiner Books, 2003.

——. *Karmic Relationships: Esoteric Studies,* vol. 7. London: Rudolf Steiner Press, 2009.

——. *Macrocosm and Microcosm.* Hudson, NY: Anthroposophic Press, 1986.

——. *Man: Hieroglyph of the Universe.* London: Rudolf Steiner Press, 1972 (current edition: *Mystery of the Universe: The Human Being, Model of Creation.* Rudolf Steiner Press, 2001).

——. *The Mysteries of the Holy Grail: From Arthur and Parzival to Modern Initiation.* London: Rudolf Steiner Press, 2010.

——. *The Occult Movement in the Nineteenth Century and its Relation to Modern Culture.* London: Rudolf Steiner Press, 1973.

——. *An Outline of Esoteric Science.* Hudson, NY: Anthroposophic Press, 1997.

——. "The Pre-earthly Deeds of Christ." in *Approaching the Mystery of Golgotha.* Gr. Barrington, MA: SteinerBooks, 2006.

——. *Reading the Pictures of the Apocalypse: Notes from Sixteen Lectures.* Hudson, NY: Anthroposophic Press, 1993.

——. *The Second Coming of Christ.* London: Rudolf Steiner Press, 2008.

——. *Soul Exercises: Word and Symbol Meditations, 1903–1924.* Gr. Barrington, MA: SteinerBooks, 2014.

——. *Spiritual Guidance of the Individual and Humanity.* Gr. Barrington, MA: Anthroposophic Press, 1992.

——. *Theosophy: An Introduction to the Spiritual Processes in Human Life and in the Cosmos.* Hudson, NY: Anthroposophic Press, 1994.

——. *Universal Spirituality: And Human Physicality—Bridging the Divide: The Search for the New Isis and the Divine Sophia.* London: Rudolf Steiner Publishing, 2014.

Sucher, Willi. *Isis Sophia I: Introducing Astrosophy.* Meadow Vista, CA: Astrosophy Research Center, 1999.

——. *Isis Sophia II: An Outline of a New Star Wisdom.* Meadow Vista, CA: Astrosophy Research Center, 1985.

Tarnas, Richard. *Cosmos and Psyche.* New York: Viking, 2006.

Tomberg, Valentin. *Christ and Sophia: Anthroposophic Meditations on the Old Testament, New Testament, and Apocalypse.* Gr. Barrington, MA: SteinerBooks, 2006.

——. *Inner Development.* Hudson, NY: Anthroposophic Press, 1992.

von Halle, Judith. *And If He Had Not Been Raised…: The Stations of Christ's Path to Spirit Man.* London: Temple Lodge Press, 2007.

——. *Descent into the Depths of the Earth on the Anthroposophic Path of Schooling.* London: Temple Lodge Press, 2011.

Tresemer, David (ed.). *The Counselor…As If Soul and Spirit Matter: Inspirations from Anthroposophy.* Gr. Barrington, MA: SteinerBooks, 2015.

Tresemer, David, and Robert Schiappacasse. *Star Wisdom & Rudolf Steiner: A Life Seen through the Oracle of the Solar Cross.* Gr. Barrington, MA: SteinerBooks, 2007.

Welburn, Andrew. *The Book with Fourteen Seals: The Prophet Zarathustra and the Christ-Revelation.* London: Rudolf Steiner Press, 1991.

Wilber, Ken. *Integral Psychology: Consciousness, Spirit, Psychology, Therapy.* Boston: Shambhala, 2000.

Wright, Helen. *Explorer of the Universe: George Ellery Hale.* New York: Dutton, 1966.

ABOUT THE CONTRIBUTORS

DANIEL ANDREEV (1906–1959) was born in Berlin. His father was the well-known Russian writer Leonid Andreev. His mother, Alexandra Veligorsky, died during childbirth. Daniel's father, overcome with grief, gave up Andreev to Alexandra's sister Elizabeth Dobrov, who lived in Moscow. It was a critical event in Daniel Andreev's life, for in contrast to many of the Russian intelligentsia at the time, the family maintained its Russian Orthodox faith. Daniel's childhood included contact with persons such as his godfather Maxim Gorky. Daniel was conscripted as a noncombatant in the Soviet Army in 1942, and after the war he returned to writing fiction and poetry. He was arrested in 1947, along with his wife and many of his relatives and friends, and sentenced to twenty-five years in prison, while his wife received twenty-five years of labor camp. All of his previous writings were destroyed. With the rise of Khrushchev, Andreev's case was reviewed and his sentence reduced to ten years. He was released to his wife in 1957, his health ruined following a heart attack in prison. While in prison, he had written the first drafts of *The Rose of the World* and *Russian Gods* (a collection of poetry), as well as *The Iron Mystery,* a play in verse. Andreev spent the last two years of his life finishing these works. Andreev's wife Alla, realizing the negative reception the books would get from the Soviet authorities, hid them until the mid-1970s and did not publish them until Gorbachev and glasnost. The first edition of *The Rose of the World* (100,000 copies) quickly sold out, and since then several editions have been equally popular in Russia.

WILLIAM BENTO, PhD, worked in the field of human development for more than thirty years. He was a recognized pioneer and a published author in psychosophy and astrosophy and travels extensively as a speaker, teacher, and consultant. Dr. Bento was the Associate Dean of Academic Affairs at Rudolf Steiner College, Fair Oaks, California, and worked as a transpersonal clinical psychologist at the Center for Living Health in Gold River, California, and was a clinical psychologist at Folsom State Prison Crisis Treatment Center. His involvement in guiding social therapy seminars for Camphill Communities was well received for more than two decades. He was coauthor of *Signs in the Heavens: A Message for Our Time* and author of *Lifting the Veil of Mental Illness: An Approach to Anthroposophical Psychology.* William Bento passed away on June 5, 2015.

ESTELLE ISAACSON is a contemporary mystic and seer whose first books were published by LogoSophia in 2012: *Through the Eyes of Mary Magdalene: Early Years and Soul Awakening.* In volume 1 in her trilogy on the life of Mary Magdalene, Estelle Isaacson presents her visions of the life of Christ as seen through Magdalene's own eyes. Volume 2, *Through the Eyes of Mary Magdalene: From Initiation to the Passion,* enters the profound mysteries of Christ's Passion, culminating in the Resurrection. Estelle is coauthor with Robert Powell of *Gautama Buddha's Successor: A Force for Good in Our Time* (2013) and *The Mystery of Sophia: Bearer of the New Culture: The Rose of the World* (2014).

KEVIN DANN, PhD, has taught history at SUNY Plattsburgh, the University of Vermont, and Rutgers University. His books include *Bright Colors Falsely Seen* (1998); *Across the Great Border Fault* (2000); *Lewis Creek Lost and Found* (2001); *A Short Story of American Destiny, 1909–2009* (2008); and (with Robert Powell) *Christ & the Maya Calendar: 2012 & the Coming of the Antichrist* (2009) and *The Astrological Revolution: Unveiling the Science of the Stars as a Science of Reincarnation and Karma* (2010).

BRIAN GRAY trained as an architect and environmental planner and has deep interests in astrology, art, music, and Anthroposophy. Since 1981, he has taught at Rudolf Steiner College in Fair Oaks, California. His research topics include cosmology, sacred architecture, the constitution of the human being, biography, life cycles, karma and reincarnation, esoteric Christianity, and Astro-Gaiasophy. A student of astrology since 1967, Brian has interpreted astrological charts for thousands of people and offers classes in star wisdom and observation of the stars. He has discovered hidden astrological keys in Wolfram von Eschenbach's *Parzival* and in the Bible, particularly Genesis, the Gospel of St. John, and the Book of Revelation. Brian's lecture on compassion and forgiveness can be viewed on YouTube at "Compassion and Forgiveness by Brian Gray.mov."

ROBERT J. KELDER was born in The Hague, Netherlands, in 1939 and is the founding director of the Amsterdam-based Willehalm Institute Press Foundation. During a 1985 exhibition in Arlesheim, Switzerland, commemorating the bicentennial anniversary of the Arlesheim Hermitage, he worked as a publicist and guide with Werner Greub in making known Greub's Grail research, which located Wolfram von Eschenbach's Terre de salvaesche and the Grail castle Munsalvaesche.

NICK KOLLERSTROM is the director of New Alchemy Press, and has long been interested in Hermetic matters. For thirty years he has produced Britain's lunar gardening calendar *Planting by the Moon*. He has also been a Fellow of the Royal Astronomical Society for more than two decades and has published academic articles on the history of astronomy. For eleven years he was a Fellow of University College London in its Science and Technology Studies Department, though his somewhat unorthodox views made it difficult for him to continue in that capacity. His articles for *Mercury Star Journal* (edited by Robert Powell) consider evidence for lunar-sidereal rhythms in vegetable growth. His latest book, *Metal-Planet Affinities: The Alchemical Bridge between Heaven and Earth,* reviews work

he has been involved with since the 1970s, based on the pioneering work of Lily Kolisko.

CLAUDIA MCLAREN LAINSON is a teacher and Therapeutic Educator. She has been working in the field of Anthroposophy since 1982, when she founded her first Waldorf program in Boulder, Colorado. She lectures nationally on various topics related to Spiritual Science, human development, the evolution of consciousness and the emerging Christ and Sophia mysteries of the twenty-first century. Claudia is the founder of Windrose Farm and Academy near Boulder. Windrose is a biodynamic farm and academy for collaborative work in anthroposophic courses, therapeutic education, cosmic and sacred dance, and nature-based educational programs. Claudia most recently founded the School for the Sophia Mysteries at Windrose.

SALLY NURNEY has been interested in astrology all her life, beginning her research with her "Sun sign" in elementary school. After several years of travel and exploration, she arrived at The StarHouse in Boulder, Colorado, in 1997 and quickly transitioned to the Sidereal perspective of reading the stars. Along with her studies in the Path of the Ceremonial Arts, she has deepened her direct understanding of the stars through research with David Tresemer at The StarHouse and study with Brian Gray at the Rudolf Steiner College in Fair Oaks, California. She currently lives in the Rocky Mountain foothills near the StarHouse of Boulder.

ROBERT POWELL, PhD, is an internationally known lecturer, author, eurythmist, and movement therapist. He is founder of the Choreocosmos School of Cosmic and Sacred Dance, and cofounder of the Sophia Foundation of North America. He received his doctorate for his thesis *The History of the Zodiac,* available as a book from Sophia Academic Press. His published works include *The Sophia Teachings,* a six-tape series (Sounds True Recordings), as well as *Elijah Come Again: A Prophet for Our Time; The Mystery, Biography, and Destiny of Mary Madgalene; Divine Sophia— Holy Wisdom; The Most Holy Trinosophia and the New Revelation of the Divine Feminine; Chronicle of the Living Christ; Christian Hermetic Astrology; The Christ Mystery; The Sign of the*

Son of Man in the Heavens; Cultivating Inner Radiance and the Body of Immortality; and the yearly *Journal for Star Wisdom* (previously *Christian Star Calendar*). He translated the spiritual classic *Meditations on the Tarot* and co-translated Valentin Tomberg's *Lazarus, Come Forth!* Robert is coauthor with David Bowden of *Astrogeographia: Correspondences between the Stars and Earthly Locations* and coauthor with Estelle Isaacson of *Gautama Buddha's Successor* and *The Mystery of Sophia.* Robert is also coauthor with Kevin Dann of *The Astrological Revolution: Unveiling the Science of the Stars as a Science of Reincarnation and Karma* and *Christ and the Maya Calendar: 2012 & the Coming of the Antichrist;* and coauthor with Lacquanna Paul of *Cosmic Dances of the Zodiac* and *Cosmic Dances of the Planets.* He teaches a gentle form of healing movement: the sacred dance of eurythmy, as well as the Cosmic Dances of the Planets and signs of the zodiac. Through the Sophia Grail Circle, Robert facilitates sacred celebrations dedicated to the Divine Feminine. He offers workshops in Europe and Australia, and with Karen Rivers, cofounder of the Sophia Foundation, leads pilgrimages to the world's sacred sites: Turkey, 1996; the Holy Land, 1997; France, 1998; Britain, 2000; Italy, 2002; Greece, 2004; Egypt, 2006; India, 2008; Turkey, 2009; the Grand Canyon, 2010; South Africa, 2012; and Peru, 2014. Visit www.sophiafoundation.org and www. astrogeographia.org.

ROBERT SCHIAPPACASSE has been a student of Rudolf Steiner's Anthroposophy for more than thirty years. He developed a deep interest in humanity's relationship to the world of the stars and, in 1977, began studies with Willi Sucher, a pioneer researcher in the field of Astrosophy, or star wisdom. He presents at conferences and workshops on star wisdom themes and other anthroposophic topics. He is coauthor with David Tresemer and William Bento of the book *Signs in the Heavens: A Message for our Time,* about the comets Hyakutake and Hale-Bopp and their crossing of the mysterious and ominous star Algol at the end of the twentieth century. Robert most recently worked with David Tresemer on the book *Star Wisdom and Rudolf Steiner: A life Seen through the Oracle of the Solar Cross.* He also coauthored with David Tresemer the articles "The Chain Reaction Experiment"; "The Signature of Saturn in Jesus Christ' Life"; and "The Signature of Pluto in the Events of Jesus Christ' Life."

DAVID TRESEMER, Ph.D., has a doctorate in psychology. In 1990, he cofounded the StarHouse in Boulder, Colorado, for community gatherings and workshops (www. TheStarHouse.org) and cofounded, with his wife Lila, the Healing Dreams Retreat Centre in Australia (www.MountainSeas.com.au). He has also founded the Star Wisdom website (www.StarWisdom.org), which offers readings from the Oracle of the Solar Crosses, an oracle relating to the heavenly imprint received on one's day of birth. Dr. Tresemer has written in many areas, including *The Scythe Book: Mowing Hay, Cutting Weeds, and Harvesting Small Grains with Hand Tools* and a book on mythic theater, *War in Heaven: Accessing Myth Through Drama.* With his wife, he also coauthored several plays produced in the U.S., including *My Magdalene* (winner of Moondance 2004, Best Script). With William Bento and Robert Schiappacasse, he wrote *Signs in the Heavens: A Message for Our Time.* He is also the author, with Robert Schiappacasse, of *Star Wisdom & Rudolf Steiner: A Life Seen through the Oracle of the Solar Cross,* and with his wife, the recent book, *One-Two-ONE: A Guidebook for Conscious Partnerships, Weddings, and Rededication Ceremonies.* He celebrated 2012 with his book *The Venus Eclipse of the Sun 2012.*

THE MYSTERY OF SOPHIA

BEARER OF THE NEW CULTURE
THE ROSE OF THE WORLD

Robert Powell and Estelle Isaacson

Estelle Isaacson is a contemporary seer who is gifted with a remarkable ability to perceive new streams of revelation. Dr. Robert Powell is a spiritual researcher who, in this concise work—and in many other books—brings the results of his own research investigations. Both have been blessed  in an extraordinary way by virtue of accessing the realm wherein Sophia is presently found.

In Part 1 of *The Mystery of Sophia,* a series of fourteen visions with which Estelle Isaacson was graced lead the reader into a direct and immediate connection with the mystery of Sophia in our time. In the four chapters of Part 2, Robert Powell opens up the cosmic dimension of Sophia and her path of descent toward humanity and the Earth as the bearer of a new spiritual culture: the Rose of the World, a culture founded on love and wisdom. Karen Rivers, cofounder with Robert Powell of the Sophia Foundation, has contributed a foreword to the book. And in the appendix, "Sources of Sophia," Robert Powell and Estelle Isaacson offer an overview of inspired literature for all those who wish to deepen their study of Sophia.

ISBN: 9781584201755 | 182 pages | pbk | $18.00

The books on these pages are also available as e-books from Amazon, iTunes, Barnes & Noble, and other online booksellers.

GAUTAMA BUDDHA'S SUCCESSOR
A FORCE FOR GOOD IN OUR TIME

Robert Powell and Estelle Isaacson

The significance of 2014 is addressed in this book by Robert Powell and Estelle Isaacson. Dr. Powell makes the critical point that 2014 not only denotes the beginning of a new 600-year cultural wave in history, but also that there is an ancient prophecy applying to 2014, which can be  interpreted as pointing to the onset of the 21st-century incarnation of the Bodhisattva who will become the future Maitreya Buddha, the successor to Gautama Buddha. Powell also makes the crucial point that the Maitreya Buddha awaited in Buddhism is the same as the Kalki Avatar expected in Hinduism.

Powell's contribution serves as an introduction to Isaacson's offering, comprising a series of six visions relating to the future Maitreya Buddha. The visions are highly inspirational, communicating something of the profound spirituality, peace, radiance, and, above all, goodness of this bodhisattva, who is Gautama Buddha's successor. His title, *Maitreya,* means "bearer of the good," and in Isaacson's visions he emerges as a remarkable force for good in our time.

Also included in this book are two appendices: "A Survey of Rudolf Steiner's Indications Concerning the Maitreya Buddha and the Kalki Avatar" and "Valentin Tomberg's Indications Concerning the Coming Buddha-Avatar, Maitreya-Kalki." A third appendix discusses the significance of Rudolf Steiner's Foundation Stone of Love meditation as a herald of Christ's Second Coming.

ISBN: 9781584201618 | 158 pages | pbk | $18.00

ASTROGEOGRAPHIA

Correspondences between the Stars and Earthly Locations
A Bible of Astrology and Earth Chakras

Robert Powell and David Bowden

"As above, so below" is the foundation of all star wisdom. It was known in ancient times that there are correspondences between the macrocosm (heavenly realm) and the microcosm (human being) and the Earth. Astrogeographia is a modern form of that ancient star wisdom.

According to the astronomer Johannes Kepler:

"There radiates into the Earth soul an image of the sense-perceptible zodiac and the whole firmament as a bond of sympathy between Heaven and Earth.... This imprint into the Earth soul through the sense-perceptible zodiac and the entire sphere of fixed stars is also confirmed through observation."

Moreover, Rudolf Steiner said in his course on astronomy, "We can conceive of the active heavenly sphere mirrored in the Earth." The authors of *Astrogeographia* set out to determine the correspondences between the starry heavens and the earthly globe: *As above, so below.*

There are numerous books on the sacredness and the spirituality of our Earth. However, few books deal with the relationship between the Earth and the cosmos, which is the central theme for the research presented in *Astrogeographia*. Its point of departure is the one-to-one correspondence between the encircling starry heavens—the celestial sphere—and the sphere of the earthly globe. David Bowden has not only worked out the mathematics of this one-to-one correspondence, but has also written a computer program that applies it in practice. Thus, a new science has been born—Astrogeographia—concerning the one-to-one correspondence between the earthly sphere and the celestial sphere.

ISBN: 9781584201335 | 360 pages | pbk | $25.00

THE CLOCKWISE HOUSE SYSTEM

A True Foundation
for Sidereal and Tropical Astrology

Jacques Dorsan
Wain Farrants and Robert Powell, editors

Jacques Dorsan, a leading pioneer of sidereal astrology in France, uses more than eighty sidereal horoscopes to illustrate his clockwise house system. With charts from the original French edition and many added, this book embodies one of the most important astrological discoveries of twentieth and twenty-first centuries. Astrology normally views the twelve houses in astrology in a counterclockwise direction, the direction of the zodiac signs. According to Dorsan, however, we should view them in a clockwise direction.

By using this clockwise house system along with the sidereal zodiac, everything falls into place in a horoscope, unlocking the mystery of the horoscope. We are given access to a true form of astrology, enabling a giant leap forward in the practice of astrology. It allows us to recover the original astrology. Moreover, Rudolf Steiner's indications, as well as the research of the French statistician Michel Gauquelin, confirm that the astrological houses run in a clockwise direction.

This English translation includes more than eighty charts, both those in Dorsan's original work in French and more added by the editor of this edition.

JACQUES DORSAN was born December 22, 1912, in Orléans, France. In 1936, he moved to the Ivory Coast, where he drew his first horoscope. It was more than seven years before he began to do consultations. Fourteen years later, after intense practice in Brazil and before returning to France, he had become convinced that the houses actually move in the direction opposite the zodiacal signs. He put his idea to the test for more than twenty years before publishing the original version of this book, *Le véritable sens des maisons astrologiques* (1984). Jacques Dorsan lived in Morocco, New York City, Monaco, Luxembourg, Belgium, Zaire, and New Caledonia. He died September 8, 2005, in Nice.

ISBN: 9781584200956 | 330 pages | pbk | $30.00

PROPHECY · PHENOMENA · HOPE
THE REAL MEANING OF 2012
CHRIST AND THE MAYA CALENDAR—AN UPDATE

Robert Powell

Robert Powell, explores what 2012 really means, updating the research presented in the ground-breaking book, *Christ and the Maya Calendar: 2012 and the Coming of the Antichrist* (coauthored with Kevin Dann). Here, Powell focuses on two significant prophecies by Rudolf Steiner. The first (from 1909) concerns the Second Coming of Christ, his appearance to humanity as the Etheric Christ. The second (from 1919) represents the shadow side of Christ's Second Coming—the incarnation in human form of Ahriman.

Powell points to the steady, multifaceted encroachment of ahrimanic forces today, especially as the harmful effects of modern technology on the etheric body. After looking into Steiner's prophetic remarks on the Book of Revelation, Powell looks into the prophecies of the Russian poet/mystic Daniel Andreev and examines the prophecy of the American clairvoyant Jeane Dixon concerning the human birth of the Antichrist. He also includes spiritual research by Judith von Halle regarding an earlier incarnation of Jospeh Stalin, as well as Andreev's indications relating to Stalin's earlier incarnations, which may be seen as preparation of this individuality for his role as "Mr. X," the human vessel for the incarnation of Ahriman.

Applying the astrological rules of reincarnation, Powell's research supports Jeane Dixon's prophecy, that Mr. X was born in 1962, a finding whose accuracy was also confirmed by Willi Sucher, Powell's mentor in Astrosophy. This finding, seen in relation to various contemporary phenomena, confirms Rudolf Steiner's prophetic statement that the incarnation of Ahriman into his human vessel would take place shortly after the year 2000.

Nonetheless, great hope for humankind is offered by the return of Christ in the etheric realm, an event to which human beings can connect, as humanity and the Earth pass through the great trials associated with 2012.

ISBN: 9781584201113 | 138 pages | pbk | $16.00

THE ASTROLOGICAL REVOLUTION
UNVEILING THE SCIENCE OF THE STARS AS A SCIENCE OF REINCARNATION AND KARMA

Robert Powell & Kevin Dann

The reader is invited to question the basis of modern astrology—the tropical zodiac, which emerged through Greek astronomers from what was originally a calendar dividing the year into twelve solar months. Ninety-eight percent of Western astrologers use the tropical zodiac, meaning that it is based on a calendar system that no longer embodies the reality of the stars.

Astrology needs to be brought back into alignment with the stars in the heavens. The first step in this astrological revolution is to recognize the sidereal zodiac. In antiquity, the Babylonians, Egyptians, Greeks, Romans, and Hindus used the sidereal zodiac, and today Hindu (Vedic) astrologers still use the sidereal zodiac. Based on recognition—through the newly discovered rules of astrological reincarnation, that the sidereal zodiac presents an authentic astrological zodiac—a new practice of astrology is possible that offers tools to reestablish a wisdom-filled astrology in the modern world. This new astrology, based on the sidereal zodiac, is similar to the classic sidereal form but in a modern form, as that practiced by the three magi, who—prompted by the stars—journeyed to Bethlehem two thousand years ago.

Drawing on specific biographical examples, *The Astrological Revolution* reveals new understandings of how the starry heavens work into human destiny. The book points to the astrological significance of the entire celestial sphere, including all the stars and constellations beyond the twelve zodiacal signs. This discovery is revealed by studying the megastars, the most luminous stars of our galaxy, illustrating how megastars show up in an extraordinary way in Christ's healing miracles by aligning with the Sun at the time of those miraculous events.

KEVIN DANN, PhD, has taught history at SUNY Plattsburgh, the University of Vermont, and Rutgers University. He is also the coauthor of *Christ and the Maya Calendar* with Robert Powell.

ISBN: 9781584200833 | 254 pages | pbk | $25.00

THROUGH THE EYES OF MARY MAGDALENE

A Trilogy

Estelle Isaacson

In the first book of the trilogy—*Early Years & Soul Awakening*—Estelle Isaacson presents her visions of the life of "the Apostle to the Apostles" as seen through Magdalene's own eyes. Following a Prologue "in the starry heavens," Part One encompasses Magdalene's childhood, her journeys and education in  Egypt, her struggle with temptations, and her conversion. Part Two takes the reader through some of Magdalene's experiences as she lays down her former life and follows Jesus as his disciple. Part Three visits the Lazarus mysteries and includes revelations concerning his initiation, death, and resurrection. Part Four comprises five appendices. The book is graced with many illustrations by James J. Tissot (1836–1902), whose work resonates also with Estelle in a very special way, the artist's depictions being so very close to what she herself witnesses in vision.

Estelle Isaacson presents further visions of the life of Mary Magdalene in the second book of the trilogy—*From Initiation to the Passion.* As in volume 1, this text is graced with many illustrations by James J. Tissot. Part One opens two months after the raising of Lazarus, as Jesus returns from his journeys in pagan lands. In  Part Two we learn of plots against Jesus and witness the Triumphant Entry, the Cleansing of the Temple, the Address to the Greeks, and another anointing by Magdalene. Part Three encompasses the Passion and Resurrection. New light is shone upon many mysteries of the Passion, including the great mystery of Magdalene's role in the Passion.

The crowning event of this book is of course the glorious Resurrection—the most important event of all time!—which we witness through Magdalene's eyes, gaining new insight into its profound mystery. Part Four comprises seven appendices.

In the third volume of the trilogy—*From the Ascension to Journeys in Gaul*—Estelle Isaacson presents further visions of the life of Mary Magdalene— spanning more than three decades. Once again, the text is illustrated by the paintings of James J. Tissot. Part One opens on the morning after the Resur-  rection and takes us through the forty days leading up to the Ascension, which we witness, receiving new revelations regarding this mysterious event. In Part Two we follow Magdalene as she lives in hiding for approximately three years, teaching and healing in secret, until captured and then sent to sea in a boat without tiller—along with her siblings Lazarus and Martha—together also with Celidonius (the healed man who had been born blind), Maximin (one of the seventy-two disciples), and Sarah and Marcella (handmaids to Magdalene and Martha). Part Three opens as the seven in their little boat arrive in Gaul. Many exciting events take place in that new land. Magdalene spends time in the wilderness contemplating Christ Jesus's sacrifice and resurrection, while doing her great work of expiation. She retreats to a cave to live out her final years. During that time she is blessed with divine visions, especially of the Virgin Mother. Her glorious death is portrayed in vivid detail. The Epilogue brings us forward to the time of the Grail. Part Four offers eight appendices.

Early Years & Soul Awakening
ISBN: 9781597315043 | 300 pages | pbk | $16.95

From Initiation to the Passion
ISBN: 9781597315050 | 344 pages | pbk | $17.95

From the Ascension to Journeys in Gaul
ISBN: 9781597315067 | 320 pages | pbk | $17.95